THE DARK PATH

THE
DARK
PATH

The Structure of War and
the Rise of the West

WILLIAMSON MURRAY

Yale
UNIVERSITY PRESS
New Haven and London

Published with assistance from the Kingsley Trust Association
Publication Fund established by the Scroll and Key Society of
Yale College.
Published with assistance from the foundation established in
memory of Calvin Chapin of the Class of 1788, Yale College.

Yale University Press books may be purchased in quantity
for educational, business, or promotional use. For
information, please e-mail sales.press@yale.edu
(U.S. office) or sales@yaleup.co.uk (U.K. office).

Set in Janson type by IDS Infotech Ltd.
Printed in the United States of America.

Library of Congress Control Number: 2024935191
ISBN 978-0-300-27068-6 (hardcover : alk. paper)

A catalogue record for this book is available from the British
Library.

This paper meets the requirements of ANSI/NISO Z39.48-1992
(Permanence of Paper).

10 9 8 7 6 5 4 3 2 1

To
Richard Hart Sinnreich
Soldier, Thinker, and Teacher
and
Frank G. Hoffman
Marine, Scholar, and Teacher

Contents

THE DARK PATH

PART I

The First Military-Social Revolution: The Emergence of the Modern State and Military

CHAPTER ONE

The Dark Path of War in the Western World

For after all allowances have been made for historical
differences, wars still resemble each other more than they
resemble any other human activity. All are fought, as Clausewitz
insisted, in a special element of danger and fear and confusion.
In all, large bodies of men are trying to impose their will on one
another by violence; and in all, events occur which are
inconceivable in any other field of experience.

—MICHAEL HOWARD, *The Causes of War and Other Essays*

DESPITE WHAT MODERN HISTORIANS like to believe, war has formed much
of the world in which we live. As the ancient Greek philosopher Heracli-
tus noted, "War is the father of all things," a depiction certainly true of
the world of *poleis* in which he lived and wrote. Wars determined the rise
and collapse of city-states. The Greeks' replacement as the dominant
power in the Mediterranean by the Macedonians and then the Romans
did not end conflict in Europe but rather expanded it—at least until
Augustus forced the Mediterranean basin into a single political entity.
The stability and survival of the Roman Empire depended on the discipline and training of the Roman legions, a model that would play
a major role in the tactical innovations of European armies in the

I

seventeenth century.[1] But in the end, climate, disease, and geography conspired to bring about Rome's replacement by barbarian tribes whose power rested on the naked sword and spear.[2]

The collapse of the Western Roman Empire in the fifth century AD initiated a dark age. What ensued was not war but rather the meanderings of powerful tribes bent on loot, rapine, slaughter, and land. By the eleventh century, fragmentation and recombination had brought some order to what was left of the Roman world in Western Europe, but it was a fractured, violent system of small polities in perpetual conflict. In many ways, the medieval entities' constant warring resembled that of the Greek *poleis*, except that it was more murderous and destructive to the inhabitants.[3]

The Europeans of 1500, divided by language, geography, and soon religion, hardly appeared positioned to dominate the world.[4] They enjoyed no superiority over other centers of civilization in mathematics, science, or engineering. In many ways they were borrowers of those disciplines from the Arab world and China.[5] It was their warlike, competitive framework which led them to explode on the global scene in a fashion that had never before occurred in history. As William H. McNeill has noted, "Only when one remembers the all but incredible courage, daring, and brutality of Cortés and Pizarro in the Americas and reflects upon the ruthlessness of [the Portuguese explorers] Almeida and Albuquerque in the Indian Ocean . . . does the full force of European warlikeness, when compared with the attitudes and aptitudes of other major civilizations of the earth, become apparent."[6]

This book offers an examination of the military changes that led to the West's position of dominance over the globe. It is about the Western way of war and the path that has taken it from 1500 to the present. Its focus is on the competition among the ruthless and at times murderous states that made up the Western world—a competition that forced constant change, innovation, and adaptation on its participants. It is not a history of the (often quite interesting) military organizations of other civilizations. In the end, their armies and navies failed in the contests with the West, and while Japan, China, India, and others have entered the global military competition in the twentieth century, they have done so by accepting the military framework that the West took four centuries to create.

How Europe exploded across the global commons, the scale and extent of its long-term results, and the underlying factors that accounted for the West's military superiority are at the heart of this study. One can record Europe's course in the history of battles, as military history generally does, or tell it in terms of technological development.[7] I do not do that here. The development of technologies in the Western way of war were, of course, important; so too were the outcomes of battles and campaigns. But both reflected larger trends and developments that undergirded the conduct of war. Factors such as logistics, finance, innovation, and the culture of military organizations are what drove the West's expansion and domination over the globe.[8] Above all, the explosive growth of European power was driven by fierce competition among aggressive, greedy states, which forced them to innovate and develop new approaches.

Yet all too often, military historians focus on the great clashes of arms. In the five hundred years since 1500, however, few battles have proven decisive.[9] Certainly there were none in the sixteenth century, when sieges dominated war and finances determined the ability of political regimes and their military organizations to carry out major wars. In the seventeenth century, Gustavus Adolphus's supposedly decisive victory at the Battle of Breitenfeld in 1631 did prevent the Hapsburg emperor from creating a united Catholic Germany, but the Thirty Years' War continued for another eighteen years. Seventy-five years later, the Duke of Marlborough's victories in the War of the Spanish Succession represented a break with past campaigns, which had largely involved sieges.[10] But while Marlborough's allied armies humiliated those of Louis XIV, they did not prevent a settlement that placed the Sun King's grandson on the Spanish throne.

Waterloo aside, Napoleon has been the demigod for generals since his death. Most historians and students of war regard his campaign of 1805, which culminated in the Battle of Austerlitz, as the most impressive piece of military campaigning in history. Yet Austerlitz hardly ended the Napoleonic Wars. Only eight years later, in the aftermath of the catastrophic Russian campaign, Napoleon had to utilize a far weaker military instrument than the "Grand Army" of 1805. In 1813, he would win a series of impressive victories—Bautzen, Lützen, and Dresden—that did little more than delay his defeat.[11]

In October 1813, allied armies cornered the emperor at Leipzig and engaged in a massive battle of attrition, which saw the allies suffer over 54,000 casualties while the outnumbered French lost only 38,000 before their retreat. Leipzig's outcome had little to do with generalship; more crucial were the numbers of infantry and cavalry battalions and artillery batteries, and the supplies of ammunition the combatants brought to the field. As Napoleon reportedly said, "God favors the side with the biggest battalions." One might expand the point to note that God favors not only those with the most battalions but those with the greatest resources. Even in Napoleonic warfare, there was no such thing as decisive victory. Military history also suggests that this was true for the wars before Napoleon and for the great wars of the mid-nineteenth and twentieth centuries.

Yet the ghost of Napoleon, as the British pundit B. H. Liddell Hart called it, has haunted generalship into the twenty-first century. Robert E. Lee sought decisive battles throughout his three years in command of the Army of Northern Virginia.[12] Yet in his greatest victory, Chancellorsville, his army lost a higher percentage of soldiers than the Army of the Potomac.[13] In his search for decisive victory, Lee invaded the North twice and suffered casualties at Antietam and Gettysburg that the South, with its smaller population base, could not afford.[14] In virtually every one of Lee's battles, the Army of Northern Virginia suffered a higher percentage of casualties than did its opponents. The Union won the Civil War not through victories on the battlefield but through attrition, which the Confederacy, weaker in manpower and resources, suffered in both defeat and victory.

While there were no decisive battles in the First World War, Germans began the war by trying to defeat the French in just weeks so they could turn against the Russians. The Schlieffen Plan represented an effort to replicate the victories of 1866 and 1870, but the Germans failed to recognize that Prussia's success in the wars of German unification had been possible only through Otto von Bismarck's strategic wizardry. The French victory on the Marne in 1914 halted the Germans and then forced them to retreat.[15] The battle saved the French from disastrous defeat but ensured the war would continue for four dismal years. In March 1918, General Erich Ludendorff attempted to win a decisive victory against the Allies with a series of blows, starting with the Michael offensive. These efforts achieved impressive tactical and territorial gains, but without either a strategic framework or operational goals, they cost the Germans nearly 1 million casualties and exhausted the army, which collapsed in fall 1918 before the Allied onslaught.[16] The determining factors in Allied victory were not tactical excellence but superior manpower and resources.[17]

The next war, barely twenty years later, taught the same lesson even more clearly, namely that manpower and resources dominate even supe-

rior generalship. In its June 1941 invasion of the Soviet Union, the Wehrmacht won a series of astonishing victories. At Minsk, the Germans
captured approximately 300,000 Soviet troops; at Smolensk another
300,000; at Kyiv over 600,000; and in the double Battle of Bryansk and
Vyazma another 600,000. But as historians look at the campaign today,
it is clear that even as early as October 1941—perhaps earlier—the Germans had lost the campaign and the war.[18]

The reason lies in the difference between operational victories and
strategic defeat. The Soviet Union, with superiority in manpower, raw
materials, and industrial production, could absorb heavy losses while the
Wehrmacht could not. Moreover, the Germans' logistical and intelligence systems fundamentally undermined whatever tactical and operational superiority they enjoyed. Only appalling Soviet incompetence in
the war's early months enabled the Wehrmacht to drag its undersupplied
and underequipped troops to the gates of Moscow in December 1941.
The defeat that month owed more to the attrition suffered in the campaign than to the atrocious winter weather. From that point, German
tactical expertise only prolonged the conflict and inflicted even greater
suffering on Europe.

The specter of attrition has hung over war since 1500. It has dominated both the conduct and strategic outcomes of great campaigns and
has forced statesmen and commanders to make unpalatable choices. It
has soaked up finances as well as resources, and it has transformed decisive victory into a mirage. In the First World War, the German Army
never fully recovered from the terrible bloodlettings at Verdun and the
Somme in 1916. In the Second World War, the Wehrmacht never recovered from the manpower and material losses it suffered in the Russian
campaign of 1941; from 1942 on it suffered continuous de-mechaniza-
tion of its forces as its divisions possessed fewer and fewer motorized vehicles and had to turn to horse-drawn transport because Germany lacked
the industrial strength and raw materials to match its opponents.

The processes of attrition have always affected opposing forces differently. During the first years of the French Revolutionary Wars, the
armies of the republic sustained heavier casualties but controlled the
pace of operations, because the *levée en masse* allowed for swifter replacement of casualties, while the armies of the *ancien régime* found it difficult
to replace losses because they relied on longer and more costly training
of recruits. Yet whatever history suggests, the search for decisive victories
continues. As late as the last years of the twentieth century, the American

military engaged its staffs and thinktanks in a search for "rapid decisive operations." The invasion of Iraq in February 2003 was meant to follow such a path. And certainly, if we think only of the destruction of Saddam Hussein's army, it achieved its purpose. But without a political or strategic framework, the occupation turned into a morass.[19]

The American debacle in Iraq is only the latest (for now) in a long list of failures by military and political leaders to develop strategic frameworks that reflect a realistic appraisal of their war aims. As the German theorist Carl von Clausewitz dismally noted, "No one starts a war—or rather no one in his senses ought to do so—without first being clear in his mind what he intends to achieve and how he intends to conduct it."[20] But few of those who have started wars have bothered to connect the means available to the goals that war was supposed to achieve.

One of the few cases in history where a political leader did balance military means with political ends to achieve a decisive strategic result was Otto von Bismarck's masterful handling of the wars that brought about German unification, in 1864 against the Danes, 1866 against the Austrians, and 1870 against the French. But although Bismarck created a strategic framework that allowed Prussia to realize its goals on the battlefield, his successors disastrously misunderstood his emphasis that political concerns must always outweigh military considerations.[21] In the end, effective strategy, whatever its military weaknesses, will almost always defeat a flawed strategic approach, no matter how impressive a nation's military capabilities.

By its nature, the political and military competition of the European states prevented the appearance of a superpower capable of crushing its competitors, as the Romans had done to the Carthaginians and Greeks in the third and second centuries BC. The strategic difference between winners and losers remained constrained by resources, finances, friction, chance, and will.

Adding to the cost and the reality of wars of attrition was the fact that armies continued to grow from 1500 AD, partly because of the strategic challenges and partly because the tactical framework changed. With the appearance of the *trace italienne*, the revolutionary system of fortification developed in the fifteenth century, campaigns came to be dominated by sieges.[22] That very increase in expenses placed additional pressure on the ability of states to maintain their militaries and conduct wars. In the case of the Spaniards in the mid-sixteenth century, Philip II confronted multifaceted challenges in the Low Countries, Italy, and the Mediterranean, all demanding the commitment of major military forces. He proved incapable of making hard choices since he placed religious hopes over strategic reality in determining Spanish strategy.[23] Moreover, in the Low Countries, the proliferation of fortified towns presented a nightmare both in garrisoning them and in attacking those in possession of the Dutch. Overstretch, then, affected not only military capabilities but the financial and economic regime's stability. Incapable of paying his creditors, Philip found himself forced to declare bankruptcy while at the same time unable to pay his soldiers. The mutinies that resulted then undermined Spanish efforts to defeat the Dutch Republic.[24]

By the time of the full emergence of the modern state and its military institutions at the end of the seventeenth century, wars were won or lost on the ability of financial and economic systems to sustain and support armies in the field and navies at sea. Victory often went to the last one standing.[25] These conditions proved particularly difficult for the French in their eighteenth-century wars against the British. Given France's major commitments to the war on land, it found itself forced to reduce support for the navy in both the Nine Years' War and the Seven Years' War. In the latter case, reduced funding for the French Navy guaranteed both the loss of Quebec and Britain's overwhelming victory in India.

The Ever-Changing Character of War

For Western military leaders, the allure of technology lies in the promise that it may break the iron grip of attrition in deciding wars' outcomes, but this is a bit like hoping to evade the Second Law of Thermodynamics. In the aftermath of the first Gulf War in 1991, for instance, the American defense establishment became enthralled with what it initially called a military-technical revolution. Defense pundits argued that this revolution had allowed American military forces to defeat Saddam Hussein's military in just weeks, and that this development had changed not just the visible characteristics but the very nature of war.[26] Admiral William Owens, vice chair of the Joint Chiefs of Staff, claimed to an interviewer: "Technology could enable US military forces to lift the 'fog of war.' . . . Battlefield dominant awareness—the ability to see and understand everything on the battlefield—might be possible."[27] He also commented that "the emerging system of systems promises the capacity to use military force without the same risks as before."[28] But American experiences in Iraq just a decade later put paid to such claims. Iraqi insurgents armed with little more than car bombs and AK-47s caused no end of difficulty for the American military.

The response to the American success in 1991 reflected a misunderstanding of the difference between war's fundamental nature, which has never changed, and its character, which in the West has been changing continuously since 1500. The former involves the dominance of nonlinear factors, from the sharp end to the strategic. Friction, uncertainty, chance, and above all the horror of combat combine to create unpredictable outcomes: "Uncertainty pervades battle in the form of unknowns about the enemy, about the environment, and even about the friendly situation. . . . The very nature of war makes certainty impossible; all actions in war will be based on incomplete, inaccurate, or even contradictory information."[29] Above all, the interplay of nonlinear factors remains unpredictable.

Friction lies at the heart of war's fundamental nature. No amount of technology can eliminate it. The twin sister of friction is chance, a dominant theme in both Thucydides and Clausewitz, the two greatest theorists of war.[30] Thucydides's word for chance, *tychē,* contains the understanding that nearly all events are contingent: on personalities, on the relationships among statesmen and military leaders, on the impact of unforeseen events, and on the ability of a single individual, even at the lowest level, to retard or thwart the best-laid plans. Chance has always dominated war and will continue to do.

If the fundamental nature of war never changes, the opposite is true of war's character. Since the fifteenth century, radical and evolutionary changes have become integral to war in the West. Because it remains a human endeavor, a conflict between two learning and adapting military forces, changes in the political and strategic framework, innovation and adaptation, and the march of technology have formed and altered war's character.[31]

The most important frameworks for change have come in two forms: the great military-social revolutions, which have warped the playing field in a fundamental fashion, and the more numerous revolutions in military affairs, which have immediately affected how wars are fought. Military-social revolutions have altered not only the character of war but the economic, financial, and political frameworks of first the West and then the world.[32] As prequels or spinoffs, the revolutions in military affairs have directly or indirectly improved the ability to wage war and have helped build the foundations for broader change. In the financial and economic spheres, they have extended the support structure necessary for military organizations to conduct sustained wars and project power over greater and greater distances.

The Patterns of Military-Social Revolutions and Revolutions in Military Affairs

First Military-Social Revolution: The creation of the modern state and its disciplined military organizations (1500 to the present)

Revolutions in Military Affairs: The gunpowder revolution; development of ocean-going navies; *trace italienne* fortifications; the seventeenth-century tactical revolution

Second Military-Social Revolution: The Industrial Revolution

Revolutions in Military Affairs: Beginning of fundamental changes in modes of production; the coal revolution; steam engines (1750 to the present)

Third Military-Social Revolution: The French Revolution (1789 to the present)

Revolutions in Military Affairs: Ideological mobilization of society and its resources; beginnings of "total war"

Fourth Military-Social Revolution: Combination of Industrial and French Revolutions (1861 to the present)

Revolutions in Military Affairs: The transportation revolution; communications revolution; internal combustion engine; aircraft; combined arms; over-the-hill artillery firing; strategic bombardment; agricultural revolution; steel ships driven by steam turbines

Fifth Military-Social Revolution: The scientific-computing revolution (1944 to the present)

Revolutions in Military Affairs: Nuclear weapons; computers; precision strike; artificial intelligence

Change has sometimes been rapid; at other times, it has occurred over considerable lengths of time. Clifford Rogers has noted that "the rise of the West did not occur in a single revolution, but rather through a process of 'punctuated equilibrium evolution'—that is through a series of intense revolutionary episodes, each built on a more extended base of slow evolutionary change. ... The length of time [for such revolutions] can range from a year to a century, depending on the scope of the revolution—depending on whether it is a government, a social structure, an idea, or an economy that is overturned."[33]

Thus, change at times can come with great suddenness, such as it did during the French Revolution, or, like the Industrial Revolution, evolve over a sustained period. But in both cases, these changes have continued to affect the character of war. The punctuated equilibrium simile catches the fact that during much of the period before the mid-nineteenth century, change came at a relatively slow pace. Innovations were important, such as that of the ring bayonet in the late seventeenth century, but they did not alter the fundamental structure of military operations. Nevertheless, inherent in the heart of the Western way of war has been the willingness to innovate and adapt. Change, since the onset of the Industrial Revolution, has been exponential in the acceleration of technology as well as tactics. That in turn has meant ever more rapid changes in the character of war. This has been particularly true in the twentieth century with the interplay of science, technology, and innovation, which have combined to make the battlefield increasingly lethal.

The first and most important of these military-social revolutions, the creation of the modern state and its disciplined military organizations, took up much of the period from 1500 to 1700 before coming to fruition at the beginning of the eighteenth century. Was that process revolutionary? I submit that it was because it involved systemic changes that altered Europe's political frameworks as well as its military institutions. It also served as an enabler of the French and Industrial Revolutions at the end of the eighteenth century.

These great revolutions did not replace the earlier military-social revolution, which had seen the creation of the modern state and its military organizations, or the revolutions in military affairs as they appeared. Rather they built on and molded those earlier developments. In some cases, they combined to alter the character of war in terrible ways. Moreover, military-social revolutions at times have folded into each other. The establishment of the modern state in the late seventeenth century formed the basis of the French Revolution, which then molded the state into a more effective form to mobilize the population and its resources. In turn, the combination of the French and Industrial Revolutions, which created the fourth military-social revolution, helps us understand why the American Civil War lasted so long and cost so much. The merging of those two revolutions then also explains the length and cost of the World Wars.

Revolutions in military affairs have occurred as prequels, alongside, or following great military-social revolutions. One might think of them as the initial shocks or aftershocks that accompany the great earthquakes that have altered war's landscape.[34] What then set off these revolutions that so affected the Western way of war? The essential precipitator was the arrival in Europe of gunpowder in the 1200s, barely a century after hand-held gunpowder weapons appeared in China.[35]

That bizarre concoction of saltpeter, sulfur, and charcoal represented a major break in the character of war in comparison to previous millennia. It opened the way for advances in weapons, tactics, and logistics, and it made war more expensive and complex. Because it offered so many new approaches to killing and destroying the landscape, it demanded innovation and adaptation in the intense competition among Europe's political entities. In that sense, gunpowder was the first and most important revolution in military affairs. Even though the Chinese invented it, the absence of intense competition in their sphere of interest meant they had little incentive to innovate with it. In Europe, where political and military competition was intense, the gunpowder revolution drove ceaseless innovation and improvement in all aspects of warmaking.

On the other side of that divide before gunpowder's arrival, the killing processes and weapons of war had remained constant for thousands of years. Killing was done with the sharp ends of spears, swords, arrows, and assorted other cutting, bashing, and thrusting weapons. The shapes and metals forming these weapons differed with time and place, but their similarities were greater than their differences. Battles were person against person. The distance a soldier could throw a spear or shoot an arrow defined the playing field of combat, and most killing occurred directly through weapons that sliced, pierced, or crushed.

From the Stone Age to the Middle Ages, tactical formations remained largely the same. Innovations in peacetime and adaptations in war hardly occurred. Swiss fighting formations in the fourteenth century resembled the phalanxes of Greek city-states. The armored Parthian cavalry of the third century AD was not all that different from armored knights of the Middle Ages. The main Greek warship in the fifth and fourth centuries BC was the trireme. Similar vessels remained the backbone of Mediterranean navies into the sixteenth century AD. Only the introduction of cannons into galley warfare altered ship design and the conduct of naval battles in the Mediterranean.[36]

Once gunpowder arrived amid Europe's fractious, warlike, and ambitious states and semi-states, it spurred vast changes in the character of war. Competition created a climate of innovation among a governing class that was almost fanatically preoccupied with war and the ruthless search for power. In his monumental history of the Peloponnesian War, Thucydides spelled out the Athenians' rationale for their pursuit of empire: "Our opinion of the gods and our knowledge of men lead us to conclude that it is a general and necessary rule of nature to rule whatever one can. This is not a law that we made ourselves, nor were we the first to act upon it when it was made. We found it already in existence, and we shall leave it to exist for ever among those who come after us."[37] This view, a product of intense competition among small polities, fit the European approach to the world as well.

Not all innovations were a direct result of war. The financial revolution, introduced initially by the Dutch and brought to the British Isles by the "Glorious Revolution" of 1688, allowed the British to solidify their financial power and play a major role in the War of the Spanish Succession.[38] By creating a system whereby the government, rather than the king, could borrow against itself by selling annuities on which it guaranteed the return, the British punched well above their weight given their relatively small population and economy. They emerged as the winners in the Wars of Spanish and Austrian Succession, and the Seven Years' War. Financial stability proved even more important in supporting their military and their allies during the wars against Revolutionary and Napoleonic France.[39]

Between 1500 and 1815, innovations came slowly, particularly in weapons. The musket with its bayonet emerged at the end of the seventeenth century—the bayonet removing the need for the pike to protect the infantry from cavalry—and remained in use until the 1840s. The Brown Bess musket, the main weapon of Wellington's army in the early 1800s, was much the same as the weapon Marlborough's redcoats used one century earlier. One reason for the slow development was cost; introducing a new infantry weapon required major financial outlays. That would not change until the American Eli Whitney invented the concept of interchangeable parts in the early nineteenth century, which lowered the cost of producing new weapons considerably.

The last decades of the eighteenth century saw the second and third great military-social revolutions, which drastically changed the character of war. The beginning of the Industrial Revolution in Britain reached critical mass sometime after the mid-eighteenth century. Much like the gunpowder revolution (but more peacefully), it led to great changes in how human beings interacted. It altered the processes of manufacture, which for the first time in history were powered by something other than animal muscle, water, or wind.

Initially, the impact on the great conflicts of 1792 to 1815 was indirect. At that point, the Industrial Revolution had not yet altered weapons technology. It did, however, alter the speed, cost, and products of the British economy, and it created surpluses that enabled Britain to provide financial support and weapons in quantities sufficient to sustain the armies of the Central and Eastern European powers. In the end, Napoleon found himself defeated not only by the overwhelming manpower marshaled by his enemies but also by the financial and economic power the British provided their allies.

The third of these great military-social revolutions was the French Revolution, which had a direct impact on the character of war. First, it strengthened the state's ability to call on manpower and resources. Faced with the collapse of its armies on the frontiers and rebellions within France from counterrevolutionaries, the French Assembly called for the *levée en masse*, which mobilized the nation's manpower and resources. In its ruthless purge of internal enemies, it set an example for revolutionary regimes in the twentieth and twenty-first centuries.

Built from a horde of ill-trained volunteers and an officer corps decimated by the flight of nobles, the French revolutionary armies of 1792 confronted the well-trained forces of the *ancien régime*. But the republic's soldiers learned on the fly, and their greater numbers eventually counted. Lazare Hoche, one of the emerging generals in the Republican Army, known for both competence and ruthlessness, commented on the army's tactics: "no maneuvers, no skill, steel, firepower and patriotism."[40] Hoche was exaggerating, because it was not just patriotism and enthusiasm that enabled France's revolutionary soldiers to fight successfully but their increasing tactical and operational skills. Napoleon took advantage of the precedents established by the republic and its leaders, especially the Jourdan Conscription Law of 1798, to build an administrative state that had many modern attributes. Ironically, having benefited from the revolution's superior manpower and resources, the Napoleonic Empire fell in 1814 and 1815 before a similarly empowered Europe supported by British money and resources.

In some ways, the American Civil War echoed the Napoleonic Wars.[41] Both sides tried to replicate Napoleon's supposedly decisive victories. Robert E. Lee would achieve great fame as a general, but his successes ultimately contributed to the Confederacy's collapse because his "victories" came with such high casualty totals. However, the struggle also marked the emergence of the fourth military-social revolution, a combination of the French and Industrial Revolutions. The latter was indirectly crucial: steam-powered locomotives and ships provided the means to project Union military power over continental distances.[42] The beginnings of the transportation revolution provided the logistical underpinnings for the great Union campaigns of 1864 and 1865 that broke the Confederacy's back. That revolution in military affairs would expand military capabilities throughout succeeding decades. The transportation revolution also, of course, profoundly affected the economy and society at large.

But the reflection of the French Revolution likewise played its part. Ulysses S. Grant wrote in his memoirs about the revolution's influence on Confederate mobilization: "Up to the Battle of Shiloh I, as well as thousands of other citizens, believed that the rebellion against the government would collapse suddenly and soon, if a decisive victory could be gained over any of its armies. Donelson and Henry were such victories. . . . But when Confederate armies were collected which . . . assumed the offensive and made such a gallant effort to regain what had been lost, then, indeed, I gave up all idea of saving the Union except by complete conquest."[43] With a media of newspapers and journals, both North and South mobilized popular opinion to fight the war to its bitter end. Tragically, the Europeans failed to see the warning the American Civil War represented. America was far off, and European interpretations of the war tended strongly toward false narratives, particularly in Britain, where analyses of the conflict were dominated by stories of the Army of Northern Virginia's noble cavaliers going down to heroic defeat before overwhelming Union numbers.

Exacerbating World War I's cost and complexities were a plethora of new technologies and capabilities. Before 1914, most of these advances had come in the civilian world. The invention of nitroglycerine and its derivatives to improve construction of highways and tunnels altered artillery's capabilities. Barbed wire, invented to contain cattle in the American West, played a major role in the stalemate on the Western Front.[44] Improvements in naval capabilities before 1914 underlined the rapidity of technological change. Admirals who as youths had gone to sea in sailing ships now commanded twenty-thousand-ton battleships that could move at speeds exceeding twenty knots. Changes in land warfare were equally immense. The internal combustion engine altered the logistical equation significantly, while the appearance of the airplane brought a new dimension to the character of war.

The horrific death toll of the war's first months reflected the arguments of prewar civilian pundits that the modern world was inherently fragile and would collapse economically or through revolution should a major war occur. Generals therefore sought quick, decisive victories without regard to the casualties.[45] Moreover, increased populations and industrial capabilities provided the major powers with the staying power both to maintain the necessary industrial production and to supply the battlefront with seemingly inexhaustible manpower. The fourth military-social revolution, combining the French Revolution's example with the Industrial Revolution, provided the political support and productive capabilities to keep the war going until four years of attrition led to the collapse of Russia in 1917 and of Turkey, Austria-Hungary, and Germany in 1918.

The tactical problems in 1914 were not a result of generals' being too stupid to understand the significance of peacetime technological changes. The problem, rather, was that these changes had complex implications and offered no obvious or easy solutions. The four dark years of war thus brought a number of revolutions in military affairs. For land war, the most important was creation of combined operations—the complex combination of infantry with artillery support, tanks, and aircraft to suppress enemy defenses.

Innovations drove other innovations. The most obvious of these, the use of aircraft, forced adaptations on the ground. Once the stalemate ensued, there was a need for reconnaissance aircraft, particularly over the enemy's trench systems. That led to an effort to shoot down the enemy's reconnaissance aircraft and protect one's own. Fighters soon emerged, followed by bombers. Despite its newness, war in the air evolved around two essentials: the need for air superiority to accomplish missions without suffering unacceptable losses, and the fact that the conduct of air operations demanded unprecedented levels of industrial production and logistical support. By 1918, except for airborne operations, every major air mission that would come to fruition in the next world war had appeared. Ironically, given how history has judged its generals, the First World War involved more imaginative and complex technological and tactical developments than the next war did.[46]

In the end, however, this war, like all others, was about attrition. There were no decisive battles. The Allies won because they reduced the German Army's manpower and materiel until it broke. Without a strategy, the Germans lost. With at least a glimmering of strategy that utilized their superior resources, the Allies won. Not surprisingly, those who had conducted or suffered in the Great War fled from its grim lessons. Britain's leaders concluded that the war had been a terrible mistake and that no other European power should ever again consider it as a serious option.[47] As a result, Britain's military, with little financial support, prepared for the next war in desultory fashion. By 1939, it had forgotten most of the last war's tactical lessons.

The Germans followed a different path. The lesson they drew from the war was that on the brink of victory, Jews and Communists had stabbed their unbeaten army in the back.[48] Their army carefully studied the tactical lessons, leading to the Wehrmacht's impressive performance in the first years of the next war.[49] What the Germans failed to examine were the strategic lessons of war, and in the next conflict they repeated every strategic mistake they had made in the last one. They also ignored the logistic and intelligence errors that had marked their performance in World War I.

Much of the contemporary military analysis after World War I emphasized the elixir of the decisive battle. The most reckless were the air power enthusiasts, particularly in America and Britain, who argued that the bomber was a decisive weapon that would make armies and navies obsolete and end the attrition of the trenches. The irony of such arguments was that the strategic bombing campaigns waged by the Royal Air Force (RAF) and the American Eighth and Fifteenth Air Forces against Germany in the Second World War involved a ferocious attrition of aircraft and crews flying those missions.[50] Air war also came at a great cost in industrial resources, but it eventually paid significant dividends.[51]

The Second World War saw fewer major new weapons than the first. For the most part, its revolutions in military affairs continued paths laid out in the previous conflict. It was not the further development of technology that drove major improvements but rather conceptual thinking. Thus, the Germans' marriage of combined-arms exploitation tactics with armored fighting vehicles accounted for the Wehrmacht's astonishing success against the French in spring 1940.[52] In the same year, Britain's Fighter Command combined existing air defenses with radar to create a systemic approach that significantly improved the air defense of the British Isles.

Technological add-ons significantly improved the performance of weapons systems. Compared to World War I, which had been a chemists' war, World War II was a physicists' war. The most impressive contribution from that discipline was the invention of the cavity magnetron by two British physicists, John Randall and Harry Boot, in early 1940. That invention made possible development of microwave radar, which gave the Anglo-Americans an advantage in the air war by allowing aircraft to identify both airborne and ground targets. At sea, radar was invaluable against the German U-boats once it came into widespread use.

From the beginning of the war, the Western Powers enjoyed an advantage in the intellectual war of applying science and analysis to the various environments, particularly in the air and naval wars.[53] Here the German leaders' arrogance, which caused them to overestimate their capabilities and underestimate the sophistication of their opponents, aided the Allies. Moreover, the Germans seem never to have recognized how far behind they were in such crucial areas as radar technology and systems analysis. No arena shows this more clearly than the intelligence war.

The war's last years saw the emergence of the fifth military-social revolution—an accelerating feedback loop combining technological adaptation and innovation with scientific developments. The Cold War added to the steady improvement of weapons systems and their capabilities, and the existence of nuclear weapons all but demanded the inclusion of science and technology in military preparations. Ironically, the destructive potential of these weapons probably played a crucial role in preventing the United States and Soviet Union from stepping over the boundary between peace into a Third World War, which might have ended civilization.

Throughout the Cold War, military competition drove technological change in the West's civilian societies. The efforts to miniaturize computers to support America's missile force played a major role in developing the chip technology that began the civilian explosion of computers in the early 1980s. But since the Cold War ended, the opposite has been happening. For the first time since before the outbreak of the First World War, civilian technological developments have been driving military technology. The implications are not entirely clear, but they are profound and worrisome.

The Past as Prologue

The dark path that led the West to create ever-new weapons and approaches to war since the early fifteenth century has now spread to much of the rest of the world. It was a path that lured contenders to seek the magic elixir of decisive battle—a search that never succeeded—and that made wars ever-more costly. Battles do not decide wars; they are won by attrition and political support. Over the past five centuries, great military-social revolutions have further altered the landscape of war and spawned the revolutions in military affairs that have so directly affected war's character.

This book, then, addresses two great themes. The first is that the brutal competition among the European states created an atmosphere in which the second theme emerges: the great military-social revolutions and the accompanying revolutions in military affairs have forced a continuing evolution of the fundamental character of war. Driving these revolutions has been a restless willingness to innovate and adapt. This restlessness was in turn motivated by the search for decisive victory, which ironically the revolutions and institutional changes turned into an increasingly distant mirage. But it was also driven by the intense competition that existed among the European states. The more the character of war evolved, the more strongly attrition emerged as the decisive factor.

The fifth military-social revolution, as it bores more deeply into the twenty-first century, is likely to make non-nuclear war ever more lethal. It will also make nuclear war ever more possible. Whether human beings will unleash Armageddon is a question only the future can answer. The evidence of the past suggests the odds are against wisdom.

CHAPTER TWO

The Rise of the Modern State and
Its Military Institutions

In the best modern spirit, the successors of the Greeks sought
ever more ingenious ways to lengthen, to expand, to glorify, and
to continue the fighting until their very social structure was
brought out onto the battlefield itself.

—VICTOR DAVIS HANSON, *The Western Way of War*

THE MODERN STATE AND the military institutions that were under its direct control began to emerge in Europe in the sixteenth century, but
their maturation required the administrative and organizational developments of the seventeenth century. The bureaucratization of the modern
state and its military from the sixteenth century to the eighteenth laid
the foundation for the West's dominance of the world.[1]

The ferocity of political, economic, and military competition among
these nascent states is best captured in Machiavelli's writings. This intense rivalry forced technological and tactical innovations in military organizations, and entities that failed to adapt fell by the wayside, with the
decline of Spain being a good example.[2] The increasing lethality and cost
of armies, and to a lesser extent navies, also forced change and adaptation, including political and financial changes in civilian societies.
By 1700, European fleets were capable of dominating the world's oceans.

Significantly, new technologies and methods of war rapidly passed from competitor to competitor within the contested European framework.

A major factor in the contest was the Dutch and English approach to politics, which eventually created a competitive oligarchy that proved more efficient politically than a traditional monarchy and created more effective means to raise the money and resources required to support wars. The political form that European states developed in the seventeenth century thus shaped the outcome of the great wars of the eighteenth, and those wars determined control of the global commons.

Revolutions in Military Affairs and Their Influence on Change

In the fourteenth century a number of factors altered the millennia-old framework within which war and society had interacted. It was not that Europeans became less warlike; if anything, they became more so. The arrival of the bubonic plague in 1346 and a period of global cooling beginning in 1315 had major impacts on the continuities of the medieval *Weltanschauungen*.[3] The plague exterminated one-third of Europe's population, and its long-term psychological and cultural impacts led many to question the sureties on which medieval religion, politics, and economics rested.

The fourteenth century also saw the first challenge to the dominance of the armored knight. The victory of infantry-based armies over feudal armies underlined that a new age of warfare had begun—what one historian has termed the infantry revolution.[4] At the Battle of Courtrai in 1302, Flemish rebels defeated the French. Twelve years later, at Bannockburn, a Scots army under Robert the Bruce decisively drove back the army of King Edward II of England to secure Scottish independence, while in 1315 the Swiss routed the Austrian Army at Morgarten. But the real threat to the dominance of the armored knight came with the appearance of the longbow.[5] In every respect it was an extraordinary weapon: "A 150-pound bow could drive a heavy sixty-gram arrow 320 yards and a light arrow 350 yards. The broadhead arrow would break through mail with ease, while a narrow-pointed bodkin shaft could be lethal even through plate armor."[6] The longbow, with its drawstring pull, was the most effective human-launched killer the world had ever seen. It possessed range, rapidity of fire, and punch.[7]

The longbow allowed the English to win a series of great victories over the French. In 1346, Edward III led a *chevauchée* through Normandy and then on to Paris. Retreating from there, he led his army up the Seine and then crossed that river and then the Somme. Just short of Calais, the French king and his army caught up, and the English long-bows dealt the attacking cavalry a devastating defeat. Ten years later, a French army chased down another English army, this one led by Ed-ward's son, Edward the Black Prince. The French attacked on foot, but the results were the same. The longbows decimated the French knights, while English foot soldiers captured the French king. Barely fifty years later, the English king Henry V replicated English successes at Agin-court. Within a decade he was close to uniting the crowns of England and France.

Yet the longbow was a dead end. Innovations were simply not possi-ble with a weapon that could be used only by those who had trained on it from an early age. It represented what we might call a cultural weapon, use of which could only emerge from a particular society. And by the late fifteenth century the societies of the Welsh highlands and northern Eng-land were no longer conducive to training young men in the longbow. It represented an impressive improvement on an ancient weapon system, but it was not replicable by other societies nor was it a weapon that of-fered future possibilities.

Until the sixteenth century, killing in war had been a matter of hu-man-on-human actions with swords, spears, and arrows: to put it in Monty Python terms, hacking and hewing in massive abattoirs. From century to century, neither the weapons nor the tactical formations in which soldiers fought looked all that different. Rome's five hundred years of military superiority depended on discipline and training, and when that collapsed in the third century AD, Roman soldiers proved no more capable than their barbarian opponents. Simply put, there was little tech-nological innovation in the methods of killing in the several millennia that preceded the fifteenth century, although obviously tactics did change.

The French monarchy's eventual triumph over the English invaders was made possible by a new factor: the arrival of gunpowder cannons. Gunpowder had appeared in China, originally as a medicine, in the tenth century. Its ability to burn quickly led the Chinese to use it in fire arrows and eventually in primitive firearms.[8] But their approach to war was largely defensive. When barbarian armies descended from the north, the Chinese holed up in their cities and tried to exhaust the attackers. Without internal competition, they had little reason to innovate with gunpowder. But when the knowledge of how to make gunpowder spread from China through the Islamic world and eventually to Europe, the intensely competitive European states seized on it as a means to gain an advantage over their neighbors.

A depiction of a primitive cannon exists in a manuscript dating from 1326.⁹ Edward III's army supposedly used such cannons against the French at Crécy, but they were so inaccurate that the damage they inflicted hardly compared to what English and Welsh arrows could do. In the intensely competitive European political environment, however, many saw the potential of gunpowder weapons and expended great efforts to increase their lethality.¹⁰ Ironically, one of the Europeans' best assets in the effort to develop more effective cannons was their considerable experience in casting bronze to make church bells.

By the middle of the fifteenth century, the French possessed sufficiently strong artillery to bring down castle walls in days rather than months.¹¹ In a series of swift campaigns, they drove the English out of Normandy and their other holdings in southwestern France. In the East, the Ottoman Turks cracked open the walls of Constantinople in 1453 by using enormous cannons transported from their foundries to the Byzantine capital, while others were cast within their siege works. The impact of French artillery on the fortresses of the Italian city-states at the turn of the fifteenth century led Machiavelli to note, "No wall exists, however thick, that artillery cannot destroy in a few days."¹²

The gunpowder revolution was the first revolution in military affairs, and it has echoed through succeeding centuries. European armies, working ever harder to figure out how to kill their opponents, quickly invented much better cannons and small arms.¹³ Such weapons caused a major break with the character of war in the millennia that preceded their arrival. Not only were gunpowder weapons more powerful, increasing killing distances by an order of magnitude, but their obvious, if untapped, power inspired continuous innovation in the design of cannons and composition of gunpowder. From 1325 to 1425, "gunpowder artillery developed rapidly, so that gunners of each new generation worked with weapons quite different from those their fathers employed."¹⁴ The character of war underwent steady changes as efforts at innovating to increase these weapons' lethality continued ceaselessly across Europe. That competition set in motion the creation of the nation with its effective bureaucracy and disciplined military organization.

As important as the gunpowder revolution was, the invention of the printing press by Johannes Gutenberg in the mid-fifteenth century, at about the same time as the fall of Constantinople, altered Europe's political and religious framework. It helped Gutenberg's revolution that vellum was replaced by paper, a much cheaper material, in the printing of books. With Constantinople's fall, a large number of Greek and Roman manuscripts arrived in the West, where the printing press made learning available to an increasingly sophisticated public. The ancient texts influenced not only Renaissance political and religious thought but military thinking as well. A short quote from Flavius Josephus, the first-century AD historian of the Roman Jewish War, suggests what these military texts brought: "[The Roman] battle drills are no different from the real thing; every man works as hard at his daily training as if he were on active service. . . . It would not be far from the truth to call their drills bloodless battles, their battles bloody drills."[15]

If Machiavelli believed artillery would be forever invincible, he was wrong.[16] Once the castles began crumbling under the onslaught of cannons, revolutionary changes in fortification design began within decades. The first efforts to counteract artillery involved great towers built with vast amounts of masonry, but these had serious defects and were too expensive. The answer lay in fortifications that were lower and extended by stone or earth works so that their extensive depth could absorb artillery shots. A cheaper response was simply to pile up masonry, dirt, and other detritus in front of the older walls. Such improvisations initially occurred in fortresses under siege when large amounts of masonry had fallen to make a breach.[17] Here we also see that innovations by one military rapidly led opponents to copy and, if possible, improve on them. The quadrilateral, angled bastion fortress built in 1515 at the papal port of Civitavecchia provided the model for an increasing number of fortresses. Its major contribution was that it made it more difficult for attackers to breach the walls of defending fortresses or cities. By providing depth in its walls and flanking fire at virtually all points, it reversed the advantage artillery had enjoyed. This, in effect, represented a second revolution in military affairs. The threat of increasingly powerful artillery had forced a major innovation in fortress design. The *trace italienne*, as such fortifications became known, gave defenders a significant advantage against gunpowder weapons that lasted for two centuries.

These two revolutions in military affairs added to the costs of war. In the long run, they demanded reforms in administration, financial support, tactics, and the nature of European armies.[18] By countering gunpowder artillery, the *trace italienne* introduced a wholly new element into the character of war. The only method of seizing a major fortress now lay in a total blockade by "armies of unprecedented size."[19] Sieges also required sustained logistical support over many months, which obviously increased the costs involved in war. Adding to the military problem, as well as expense, was the rapid spread of the new form of fortifications to important cities and towns and their growth in size.

To meet the altered tactical environment, states assembled armies of a size never before seen. The cost of deploying and supporting military forces doubled between the 1530s and the 1540s.[20] Before 1530, the largest armies numbered in the neighborhood of 30,000 soldiers. In 1537, Charles V, emperor of the Holy Roman Empire, mobilized an army of 60,000 in Italy. Sixteen years later, threatened by enemies in the Netherlands, Germany, and the Mediterranean, he mobilized nearly 150,000 soldiers. By 1574, the Spanish Army of Flanders numbered 86,000 men.[21] The result was a concomitant expansion of financial and logistical support needed to fuel wars. Not surprisingly, paying for such armies brought difficulties, which in turn led unpaid soldiers to mutiny. In 1527, the emperor's inability to pay his soldiers caused the Duke of Bourbon, commander of the Hapsburg army—many of whom were Lutherans—to march on Rome instead. The result was a ten-day sack of the eternal city with eight thousand slaughtered, including large numbers of nuns and priests. One eyewitness wrote that the atrocities "were so numerous that there would not be enough paper or ink—or memory—to record them all."[22]

Matters hardly improved under Charles V's successor in Spain, Philip II. Although gold and silver bullion flooded into Spain from the Americas over the sixteenth century, the Spanish king declared bankruptcy on five different occasions (1557, 1560, 1569, 1575, and 1587). With bankruptcies came a failure to pay the soldiers. Between 1572 and 1607, there were no fewer than forty-five mutinies in the Spanish Army of Flanders. Some Spaniards even argued that mutinies played a greater role in Spain's failure in the Netherlands than Dutch resistance.[23] The sack of Antwerp in 1576 occurred because the Duke of Alva reneged on a promise to give back pay to mutineers at Haarlem. The resulting rampage ended with a thousand houses destroyed and eight thousand burghers dead, causing such outrage throughout Holland that it ended Spain's best chance to bring the Netherlands under control.[24]

The *trace italienne* spread across the Alps in the 1530s. In the Low Countries, between 1529 and 1572, as Geoffrey Parker points out, "some forty-three kilometers of modern defenses had been built . . .: four citadels, twelve entirely new circuits of walls, and eighteen substantially new circuits"[25] This building came at great expense. Such structures drove the price of war steadily upward, in terms of cost and the number of soldiers required. By the 1580s, the building of *trace italienne* had spread to the New World; threatened by English privateers, the Spanish built such fortresses throughout the Caribbean, beginning at Havana. The Spanish attempt to protect Havana underlined the explosive expansion of Europeans on the world's oceans after Columbus's discovery of the islands of the Caribbean in the 1490s.

Two essential developments opened the dark oceans to the west of Europe. In the early fifteenth century, sturdier construction allowed European ships to survive the pounding of the Atlantic Ocean. Over the past decade, historians have made much about Chinese exploration efforts that pushed into waters surrounding Southeast Asia. But for the Confucian bureaucrats who ran the empire, such capabilities held little importance. On the other hand, Europeans, always hard-pressed to feed their populations, viewed efforts to push deeper into the Atlantic to harvest its great fisheries as essential. New-model ships, married up to improved rigging and rudders, enabled European vessels to sail into the wind.[26] Equally critical was the improvement in astronomical knowledge, which allowed more precise determination of a ship's location at sea, along with a divining of the repetitive nature of currents and winds over the year. At the end of the fifteenth century, for the second time in history, sailors rounded the Cape of Good Hope on the way from Gibraltar to the Indian Ocean.[27]

Significantly, the new ships also could carry gunpowder cannons without suffering structural damage from the recoil. Yet it took time and innovation before the Atlantic sailing ships could become effective weapons of naval power. Again, competition among the Europeans drove innovation and change. The steady improvement of sailing vessels from the fifteenth century to the seventeenth century must count as a significant revolution in military affairs. Moreover, it affected not just naval power but European economies as well. In the long term, it allowed the Europeans to project their military, economic, and political power farther into the darkness that enshrouded the world's oceans.

This capability decisively changed the global balance of power. Four years before Columbus entered American waters, Portuguese explorers had reached the Cape of Good Hope. In 1498, Vasco da Gama led the first Portuguese fleet into the Indian Ocean.[28] In 1517, a Portuguese fleet even threatened Jiddah, within a stone's throw of Mecca, but was repulsed. By 1542, the Portuguese had reached Japan. The appearance of their fleets in South Asia and eventually Southeast Asia undermined the Middle Eastern monopoly on the profitable spice trade and prompted a shift of Europe's focus from the Mediterranean outward to the world's oceans. Meanwhile, the Spanish had conquered the Aztec Empire in Mexico by 1521 and destroyed the last Inca stronghold in 1572 through a combination of ruthless military action, technological superiority, and disease.[29] The conquest of Mexico and Peru brought unheard of wealth to Spain and the Hapsburg Empire, allowing them to fund the great wars they waged in the sixteenth and seventeenth centuries. It also began a cycle of inflation throughout Europe that further raised the cost of waging war.

For most of the sixteenth century, the improved sailing vessels of the Atlantic had little effect on naval warfare in the Mediterranean, where galleys dominated both fighting at sea and onshore raids. This difference in naval warfare had to do with several factors: the geography of the Mediterranean, the fact that it has virtually no tides, differences in the weather between the Mediterranean and the Atlantic, and the cost of cannons in the 1500s.[30] Mediterranean ships did not need to survive the winter storms of the Atlantic and Pacific. Outside that sea, the ships of Europe's Atlantic powers now had the potential to reach out on a global scale.[31]

The Great Strategic Struggles of the Sixteenth Century

Competition among the European powers in the sixteenth century largely revolved around the Hapsburgs. On one side of a three-way struggle was the immense territory and power the Hapsburg family had accumulated, largely by marriage. The inheritor of this vast territory was Charles V. Born in 1500, Charles became the Duke of Burgundy in 1508 and thus the ruler of the Netherlands, King of Spain in 1516, and Holy Roman Emperor and Duke of Austria in 1519. He was still a teenager at the time. Throughout his reign he would also control much of Italy.[32] The extent of Hapsburg domains had the consequence of expanding the theaters of war into a number of areas, which added to expenditures. Undergirding Charles's wars was the windfall he gained from the conquest of the Aztec and Inca Empires and the resulting flow of gold and silver into Spain, first from the conquest and then from the massive mining operations the Spanish undertook.

Political subdivisions in Europe, 1580. Cartography by Bill Nelson.

In the center of the Hapsburg lands lay France, a populous and martial nation whose rulers had no intention of allowing the Hapsburgs to extend their territory. Much of the sixteenth century was thus taken up with a struggle between Hapsburg and French kings. The third great power fighting for dominance was the Ottoman Empire, which, from its newly acquired center at Constantinople, pressed on Europe from two directions: to the northwest through the Balkans toward Austria and Vienna, and through the Mediterranean with the help of piratical Islamic city-states on the North African coast. The Ottomans also confronted the Iranians to the east, and their battles against Shi'a Islam often distracted them from their struggles against the Europeans.

Religion was a wild card. Christianity and Islam had been enemies since Arabic tribes burst onto the Mediterranean in the seventh century.

But Christianity's tensions between the Orthodox and Catholic churches would be complicated by the Protestant Reformation, which began when Martin Luther nailed his ninety-five theses to the door of his church in 1517. Ironically, Charles V's wars in Italy prevented him from stamping out the seeds of religious rebellion in the Germanies until it was too late, as Lutheranism had gained a significant following. Charles depended on the Germanies for a significant portion of the soldiers who formed his armies. Consequently, he had to appease the Protestant princes from whose domains those soldiers came.

The contest between the Hapsburgs and their European enemies had begun at the end of the fifteenth century. For most of that century, the Italian city-states had waged an endless series of conflicts among themselves. In 1494, Charles VIII of France invaded Italy after laying claim to Naples, and after that, outside powers came to dominate wars on the Italian peninsula.[33] The French king seems to have had aims beyond southern Italy. His invasion set off a series of wars between the Valois kings of France and the Hapsburgs. By 1497, defeats and the attrition of his forces led Charles VIII to retreat from Italy, while Spanish troops mopped up what the French left behind. Three years later, the French returned with a larger army to avenge their defeat and suffered an even greater humiliation.

Equally important in this struggle for supremacy was the sea war in the Mediterranean among the Spanish, Venetians, and Ottomans. All three based their naval power on galleys, but there were significant strategic and tactical differences in how they used their navies.[34] The entrance of gunpowder artillery into the equation at the beginning of the sixteenth century greatly changed Mediterranean galley battles. From 1510, bronze cannons, mounted on the bow, began to dominate the fleets' weapons as well as tactics.

Why precisely these changes occurred is difficult to calculate. As John Francis Guilmartin Jr. wrote in *Gunpowder and Galleys*, "The increase in tactical power was the product of a slight increase in the size of galleys, a sharp increase in the size of their complements, and an increase in the size of the galley fleets." Thus, the fleets that fought at Lepanto in 1571 were approximately twice the size of those that fought at Prevesa in 1538.[35] But a second major factor occurred outside of the Mediterranean. In 1543, the English discovered how to make cast-iron cannons. While no more effective than bronze cannons, and more dangerous because of a propensity to explode, cast-iron cannons were easier to make and one-third cheaper.

Less than four decades later, virtually everyone in northern Europe was mass-producing the cheaper iron cannons. The lower cost and thus the larger number of available cannons provided sailing vessels with sufficient weapons for broadsides, which made them more effective weapons of war than galleys. The impact of the increasing cost of galley fleets and their decreasing effectiveness against cannon-armed sailing ships spelled the doom of galley warfare and a new era of sailing power in the Mediterranean. But the era of galley warfare lasted long enough for Spanish and Venetian fleets to halt the Ottoman tide in the western Mediterranean at the Battle of Lepanto.[36]

The other challenge Charles V confronted was French ambition. That struggle revolved around Italy. For the most part he succeeded in thwarting his French opponents, but troubles in Italy distracted him from the other strategic threats to Hapsburg lands. Spanish efforts to eliminate the Ottoman-allied North African pirates consistently failed at great cost. And the Turkish advance in the Balkans, coming at the same time as French efforts in Italy, kept Charles constantly having to draw on Spain and the Germanies for troops. His armies usually defeated his French and Italian opponents, but he could not eliminate them. Monarchs who felt threatened by the ascendency of the Hapsburgs joined forces against him. In every respect, Charles's reign was one of war: a series of wars against the French, 1521–1529, 1536–1537, 1542–1544, and 1551–1558; wars with the Turks, 1521–1538 and 1541–1547; and a war with the German Protestants, 1546–1547.

Between October 1555 and July 1556, Charles abdicated every position he occupied. He had been a hands-on ruler in peace as well as war, but Philip II, his successor to his Spanish, Italian, and Low Country domains, spent almost his entire career ensconced in his palaces in Spain. Not surprisingly, he displayed little understanding of the currents swirling throughout the lands he ostensibly ruled, while holding firm to his belief that God would overcome whatever difficulties confronted him.[37] Nevertheless, Philip was the ruler of the greatest power in Europe, his wealth magnified by the gold and silver of the New World, while his Spanish troops with their *tercios*, the basic tactical formation of Spanish troops, were Europe's most effective military force.

Philip's grand strategic problem, much like his father's, was overstretch.[38] The Ottomans were increasingly aggressive in the Mediterranean. Their attempt to overthrow the Knights Hospitaliers' rule over Malta in 1565 and their support of pirate states in North Africa were clear signs of their ambitions in the western Mediterranean. Equally worrisome was the possibility the Protestants might gain control of France, which would make Philip's control of the Netherlands impossible. Moreover, the French were making continual incursions into northern Italy, which was crucial for the movement of Spanish reinforcements to the Netherlands.

The Netherlands were the site of Philip's greatest difficulties. By the time Charles V abdicated, his decrees had broken most centers of heresy in Holland; the only problem he left to his heir was a serious financial situation, which caused Philip to declare bankruptcy in 1557. Two years later, Philip left the Netherlands for Spain, never to return. From then on, he dealt with the deteriorating situation in the Low Countries from the safe distance of Madrid. The period after his departure saw a rise in heresy throughout the Netherlands, coupled with a refusal by local authorities to prosecute the heretics. Not surprisingly, given his fanatical adherence to Catholicism, Philip refused to tolerate Protestantism. That led to political crisis and then rebellion, and by summer 1566, the authorities in the Netherlands had lost control.[39] There was a breakdown of public order; widespread riots destroyed Catholic shrines and images. Philip's response was to send the Duke of Alba with a large army from Italy to stamp out heresy.

But while the king debated whether to divert troops from northern Italy, Margaret of Parma, Philip's representative in the Netherlands, had brought the Calvinists under control. The first revolt, such as it was, was over. The king decided to send Alba and the Spanish troops anyway. On arriving in Brussels, Alba informed Margaret that he would billet his troops in the towns that had remained loyal. The Spaniards made a terrible impression right away: "The nineteen companies of the *tercio* of Naples . . . entered Ghent on 30 August, marching into the city in ranks of five followed by a large number of prostitutes decked in flounced Spanish dresses and perched on small nags. A horde of camp-followers brought up the rear, with bare feet and bare heads, escorting the regiment's horses, carts, and baggage."[40] This was not a modern army in the form that would emerge in the next century. Possessing neither uniform appearance nor civil discipline, the companies hardly represented a force to impress the staid burghers of the Low Countries. However, whatever their appearance, the Spanish were ferocious soldiers.

Alba proceeded to take over the government from Margaret of Parma, paid no attention to the political and religious complexities, and imposed Spanish military rule. The new regime put twelve thousand heretics on trial, fined nearly nine thousand, and executed over a thousand. A 1568 attempt to overthrow Alba's rule failed dismally. But the duke finally overreached when he tried to impose a permanent tax to support his troops.

The second Dutch revolt began on 1 April 1572. Dutch pirates, operating in the English Channel from ports controlled by French Huguenots, seized the small port of Brill in southern Holland and used it as a base from which to ravage shipping from the Scheldt and Rhine estuaries. The "Sea Beggars" soon controlled the English Channel as well as ports up and down the coast of Holland. To deploy reinforcements to the Netherlands, the Spanish had to move them by sea to Italy and along a tortuous route through the Alpine passes and along the Rhine, the famous "Spanish Road." William of Orange, the leader of the rebels, and his followers quickly achieved some striking successes; all of Holland came over to their side. Nevertheless, Alba was a hard-bitten general commanding a formidable military force. By the end of the year, he had brought 90 percent of the rebel areas back under Spanish control.

Yet three stumbling blocks remained. Because of his many other commitments, Philip had no money to pay the troops, bringing them to the brink of mutiny. Second, the towns that had been brought back under Spanish control had to be garrisoned to maintain order but doing so siphoned off much of Alba's field army. Finally, the two provinces that remained in rebellion possessed no fewer than twenty-four fortified towns, and Alba lacked sufficient soldiers to complete the conquest.[41] To assuage his soldiers' annoyance at being unpaid for nine months, he allowed them to sack the town of Mechelen, even though the town had surrendered without resistance. Thus, the greatest block to a successful end to the war remained the Spanish government's consistent inability to pay its soldiers and their resulting mutinous behavior. Between 1573 and 1576, the Army of Flanders mutinied three times. They had good cause to be angry. In the mutiny at Mook in 1574, the soldiers were due over three years' back pay; those who mutinied in 1576 had gone unpaid for almost two years.[42]

It was not just a lack of military effectiveness but political and religious pigheadedness that eventually defeated the Spanish. Constant mutinies hobbled their efforts on the brink of success. In fall 1576, after Philip had agreed to concessions to the Dutch, Spanish troops attacked and then sacked Antwerp in one of the worst atrocities of the sixteenth century. When the "Spanish fury" subsided, eight thousand citizens had been murdered and much of the city was in ruins.[43] In effect, the military's actions, motivated by arrears in pay, had undermined Spanish policy in the Netherlands. The difficulties the Spanish confronted were not unique; other European armies had similar problems.

Like most political leaders who have run into difficulty, Philip blamed outside interference for his army's failure, in this case the French and English. He was right on both counts. The French had given substantial financial aid to the Dutch at the start of the revolt. The English were more careful. Elizabeth of England, always cautious in making major strategic decisions, was aware of her military weaknesses compared to the Spanish monarchy. But in 1568 she had authorized seizure of 400,000 florins off Spanish ships that had taken refuge from pirates in Southampton and Plymouth, setting off a trade war as well as a rebellion of Catholics in northern England, who aimed to replace Elizabeth with Mary Stuart. Continued plotting led Elizabeth to aid the Dutch rebels, which Alba believed was a major factor in the revolt.[44]

What tipped Elizabeth's hand into courting a major war with Spain? First, the new Spanish commander in the Netherlands, the Duke of Parma, was having considerable success against the Dutch state, which had declared its independence from Spain, raising the danger that if the Spaniards regained control of the Low Countries, they would turn on England. Elizabeth and the Dutch allied themselves in 1585 in the Treaty of Nonsuch, a move that Elizabeth and her counselors understood meant war with Spain. They unleashed Sir Francis Drake, already well known to the Spanish for his piratical exploits, with twenty ships to attack Spanish trade in the Caribbean. Nothing underlined the impact of improved European technology better than that barely ninety years after Columbus's three-ship expedition in 1492, the English were able to put together a twenty-ship raiding party and launch it across the Atlantic.

Adding to Elizabeth's willingness to confront Spain was her awareness that Philip had supported several plots to assassinate or overthrow her. The assassination of William of Orange in 1584 by a fanatical Catholic alerted Elizabeth to the dangers of such plots. In 1587, after Mary Queen of Scots was beheaded for participating in efforts to assassinate Elizabeth, Philip responded by launching an invasion of England. His complex plan involved a great fleet, the Armada, to sortie from Spain, work its way up the English Channel, defeat the English fleet, meet up with the Spanish Army of the Netherlands, and then escort the Duke of

Parma's troops across the Channel to remove Elizabeth.[45] The English fleet, however, proved more adept at sailing and carried more modern armaments. With heavier cannons, the English kept their distance from the Spaniards and bombarded them from long range. Although they sank only one ship, they damaged others so heavily that several sank in heavy seas on the return journey around the British Isles.

From that point, the major European powers focused on building up their navies. There would be a steady development of ships of the line, the battleships of the period. By the last decades of the seventeenth century, the Dutch and French appeared in the lead, but once the English had removed the Stuarts, they became a major player in the wars at sea. The sea dogs who had beaten off the Spanish Armada in 1588 had set the course.

Tactics and Technology

Throughout the fifteenth and sixteenth centuries, military competition among the Europeans occasioned steady and impressive innovations, particularly in cannons. Hand-held gunpowder weapons played a relatively small role in the few battles that took place. In 1571, Spanish infantry in the Netherlands possessed two gunpowder soldiers for every five pikemen. Three decades later, however, the ratio had shifted to three armed with firearms to one pikeman. The premier military unit of the sixteenth century was the Spanish *tercio*, not because of its tactical effectiveness but because of the toughness of its troops.

The formations of every major European army resembled those of the *tercios*: approximately 1,600 soldiers deployed in a square, with a combination of pikemen and arquebusiers (later musketeers), either interspersed or on the corners. These pike formations were not much different from ancient Greek phalanxes. By its denseness, the *tercio* provided its soldiers with a feeling of protection against the horrors of combat. In danger, human beings tend to bunch together for support, and that psychological support is precisely what the *tercio* provided. It also had the advantages of requiring relatively few officers and sergeants to keep troops aligned and not requiring a complex set of commands to maneuver.

The disadvantage of the *tercio* was that once deployed, it had little maneuverability. Much like the Greek phalanxes, it depended on positioning. Moreover, as the number of arquebusiers and musketeers increased over the 1500s, the *tercio* had the disadvantage of minimizing its

firepower, since these weapons could be deployed only on the formation's edges. The basic tactical and psychological problem was that thin-
ning formations to maximize firepower would diminish the psychological
strength *tercios* provided individual soldiers. The way to maximize infantry firepower was clear—spread soldiers out into more linear formations.
Such a change, however, required imagination and careful experiments,
not to mention money. It also required more officers, greater discipline
among the soldiers, and consistent training.

The breakthrough came at the end of the sixteenth century. In the
late 1500s, Maurice of Orange, stadtholder of the Dutch Republic, along
with his cousin John VII, Count of Nassau-Siegen, addressed the problem of how to thin out units to increase firepower. As with serious students of military matters in the sixteenth century, they were students of
Greek and Roman military texts. One aspect of these works that caught
their attention was the set of commands the Romans used to maneuver
legions in battle. The German historian Hans Delbrück notes that "it is
precisely here that we can speak of the renaissance of a lost art."[46] Initially, the Dutch innovators ran into the problem that they could not
make the commands work. After experimentation they discovered that
Roman military commands were two steps, a preparatory command and
an execution command: "Atten ... shun," rather than "Attenshun," or
"Right ... face" rather than "right-face."

A number of results flowed from this insight. Soldiers had to be silent
on the drill field to hear commands. With drill and training Maurice's soldiers could now form up in slightly more than one-third the time it took
to form up similar-sized units of other armies.[47] Drill with its emphasis on
marching in time furthered the bonding of units and may well, in its psychological import, have carried soldiers back to prehistoric times and the
use of dance to celebrate triumphs.[48] The Romans also influenced the
Dutch in another fashion. Maurice decreased the size of his regiments
from approximately 1,600 soldiers to 580, close to the size of a Roman co-
hort. This decreased size made the regiments more maneuverable.[49]

Finally, the Dutch innovators significantly increased the number of
officers, doubling the number per soldier. "The Netherlandish captains,"
writes Delbrück, "with the other higher-ranking soldiers supporting
them, became officers in the modern concept. They did not simply lead,
but they created; they first formed the soldiers they later led. Maurice of
Orange, by becoming the renovator of the art of drill and the father of
true military discipline, also became the creator of the officer status."[50]

The introduction of rigorous discipline and training required two essential elements. First, soldiers had to be soldiers full time, committed to the state or monarch; second, the state had to pay them regularly, which the Dutch, with their wealth, could afford to do. By the time these changes reached fruition, they amounted to another revolution in military affairs that would change the character of war and the way armies fought.

Maurice and his captains never worked out the full implications of their reforms. Nor did these reforms necessarily provide a major advantage against the Spanish, since the war in the Netherlands remained one of sieges and positions. By the time the Dutch gained uncontested independence in the mid-seventeenth century, they had so worn down the Spanish forces that Spain never regained its position as a major European power. The Dutch innovations spread rapidly throughout Europe, helped considerably by the establishment of an academy at Siegen in Germany in 1616 by Count John of Nassau. This school not only educated officers in the art of war; it also provided a series of manuals based on the Dutch system.[51] Nevertheless, innovation in infantry tactics came slowly, and for every two steps forward there was a step back.

The Killing Time

If the sixteenth century had seen a steady increase in the size, violence, and length of European wars, it was barely a hint of what the next century would bring. In the first half of the seventeenth century, exactly one year passed without a major war; in the second half there were two.[52] Exacerbated by the coldest period of the Little Ice Age, war cast its grim visage over smoking villages, slaughtered soldiers and civilians, and starving and disease-ridden populations. Added to the unending wars among European states were any number of civil wars and revolts, both usually exacerbated by religious conflict. With the repetition of storms, drought, and persistent cold, the impact of ravaging armies, especially in the Germanies, was catastrophic.

Armies continued to grow. In 1626, Philip IV of Spain claimed to have 300,000 men under pay, although he may have been stretching the concept of payment. The construction of fortifications added more to the costs of war. Between 1572 and 1648, opposing sides in the Netherlands built fifty fortresses and modernized the fortifications of sixty towns.[53] That construction required larger armies and greater logistical support while also turning military operations into a series of sieges. It was the

Swedes who first worked out the full implications of Maurice of Orange's reforms. The occasion would be the Thirty Years' War, which exploded after nearly a century of rising tensions between Catholics and Protestants in Germany. It was sparked by the election of Ferdinand II, a fanatical Catholic, to replace Rudolf II as Holy Roman Emperor. Ferdinand, who was also King of Bohemia, announced his intent to impose the Catholic faith on those who had fallen away from the true faith in the Czech lands.

In May 1618, the response in Prague was to toss Ferdinand's deputies out of a second-story window and declare Frederick, elector of the Palatinate and a Calvinist, as the King of Bohemia. That was unacceptable to both the Austrian and Spanish branches of the Hapsburg family. In May 1619, seven thousand Spanish soldiers from the Army of Flanders were on the march to Vienna. John A. Lynn has described these armies of the early seventeenth century as "aggregate contract armies" consisting of "a small nucleus of the king's own troops, local traditional forces, hired mercenaries, and private armies raised by powerful nobles."[54] By 1620, forty thousand of Philip III's soldiers and substantial funds were supporting Ferdinand in Germany. With their help, on 8 November, the new emperor crushed the Czechs at the Battle of the White Mountain. In 1621, war resumed between the Dutch and Spanish, while the Swedes and Poles also fought each other.

Following his victory over the Czechs, Ferdinand proceeded to execute many of the Czech nobles and turn their lands over to German Catholic nobles.[55] Had he stopped at that point, the Thirty Years' War would probably have ended after just three years. Instead, Ferdinand moved his armies against Frederick with the aim of dispossessing him as elector of the Palatinate and replacing him with a Catholic, Duke Maximilian of Bavaria. The emperor's most effective military force, led by Count Johann von Tilly, did not take long to chase Frederick out of the Palatinate. By 1625, the Catholic League was in a dominant position while the Protestants were in serious disarray. The next phase of the war began in 1625 with the intervention of the Danes, led by their king, Christian IV, on the side of the Protestants. The Catholic armies were led by Tilly and a Czech noble, Albrecht von Wallenstein, who was distinguished by his ability to recruit colonels with the resources and credit to borrow large sums of money.[56] Born a Protestant, he converted to Catholicism in his early twenties, married well, and used his wife's money to build up his army of mercenaries to support the Hapsburgs. Having impressed his employers, he came into his own against the Danes.

Between 1625 and 1629, Wallenstein grew his mercenary army from 45,300 infantry and 16,600 cavalry to 111,000 and 17,900, respectively. There was nothing innovative about his approach. His forces consisted of regiments recruited by freebooters like himself. The logistical systems of the time rested on foraging over whatever territory an army occupied, whether friendly or enemy. A plague of locusts could not have done better in stripping Germany clean.[57] Wallenstein's solution to winning the war was to urge the emperor to keep growing the army and occupy all of Germany. By the end of 1629, Ferdinand's forces had thoroughly defeated the Danes, with Wallenstein's army occupying all of Jutland. Only the Danish islands remained out of his hands.[58]

It was at this point that victory slipped out of the imperialists' grasp. Like the Spanish kings, Ferdinand valued religious orthodoxy above political expedience. His Edict of Restitution, issued in 1629, restored to the Catholic Church all of its lands that the Protestant princes had seized since 1552. It was an exceedingly dangerous move, because it pushed the Protestant princes toward opposition and opened the way for Swedish intervention. Ferdinand's Jesuit confessor explained the decision to the Bavarian elector: "The Edict must stand firm, whatever evil might come from it. It matters little that the emperor, because of it, lose not only Austria but all of his kingdoms . . . provided he save his soul, which he cannot do without the implementation of the Edict."[59] The second major mistake was to remove Wallenstein, whose army disbanded with its leader's departure.[60]

And so the wild card of the Thirty Years' War arrived. Gustavus Adolphus and his Swedish army landed in Germany in July 1630.[61] By that time, he had fought several major campaigns in the Baltic against the Poles and Russians, during which he carried out a series of reforms of the Swedish government as well as the army's tactics. He drew heavily on Maurice of Nassau's reforms but carried them further. When the Swedish Army landed in Germany, its basic tactical formation was the battalion, consisting of approximately five hundred men. Significantly, the soldiers' oath of allegiance was to their sovereign, not their captains. The King's "Articles of War" clarified the soldiers' duties, including the demand they dig trenches when ordered, something soldiers had rarely done since Roman times. All battalions possessed standardized artillery ammunition and weapons, with cartridges prepared ahead for rapid firing. Finally, Gustavus trained the Swedish cavalry to charge with swords drawn.[62] The Swedish state conscripted its soldiers, who formed a more homogenous group that prepared for war under a rigorous training regime.

The organized training included volley firing. This tactic was not new; what was new was the disciplined way the Swedes went about it. Light artillery, accompanying the infantry, allowed a battalion to fire devastating volleys to smash enemy formations before the pikemen could charge. The Swedes used a six-deep linear formation, which allowed for sustained fire. Particularly important in Gustavus's tactics was the emphasis on combining arms—infantry, artillery, and cavalry. In the end, it was the combination of training and discipline that made the army so deadly.

The German Protestants had little enthusiasm for Swedish support. The Saxon elector in particular thought Ferdinand would allow the Protestants their own religion. Even the sack of Magdeburg by Count Tilly's army in May 1631 following a two-month siege failed to move him. Imperialist soldiers, enraged by the costly siege, destroyed the entire town and slaughtered approximately 20,000 out of Magdeburg's 25,000 inhabitants, a shocking atrocity even by the standards of the time. In August, short of supplies, Tilly moved into Saxony, and the elector found himself forced to join the Swedes. The allies met Tilly's army at Breitenfeld on 17 September. Tilly commanded 35,000 soldiers, while the Swedes possessed 24,000 and the Saxons 18,000. The latter, however, had little experience, a factor that both Tilly and Gustavus took into account.[63] Besides a slight advantage in numbers, the Swedes and their allies enjoyed artillery superiority.

With the Saxons on the left of the Allied line, Tilly launched the bulk of his *tercios* against them. The Saxons fled. Meanwhile, the Swedish cavalry made quick work of Tilly's cavalry on the right, while Swedish artillery battered the imperialists in the center. Having chased Tilly's cavalry off the field, Gustavus's horsemen returned to capture the largely immobile imperialist artillery. Tilly's *tercios* advanced slowly onto the flank abandoned by fleeing Saxons, the imperialists cheering as they advanced to what they thought was victory. But at that point the nemesis appeared. With his troops redeploying more swiftly than their opponents, Gustavus swung his well-trained regiments to the left and caught the imperialists on their flank. Supported by cavalry, the Swedes battered and then smashed the *tercios* with volley fire. By the time it was over, eight thousand of Tilly's soldiers had been killed and another nine thousand taken prisoner.

Breitenfeld was a devastating defeat for Ferdinand, who briefly considered fleeing to Graz, and it ended whatever chance the imperialists had to create a united, Catholic Germany. In that sense, Breitenfeld was a decisive battle. The Swedish system of war represented a new approach to tactics and must be counted as one of the more important revolutions in military affairs. By the end of the century, virtually every major power had copied and expanded the Swedish example of a disciplined, highly trained, state-controlled army.

In April 1632, at the Battle of the River Lech, the Swedes mortally wounded Tilly and destroyed his army. Desperate, the emperor found himself forced to recall Wallenstein. In 1632, the greatest generals of the war met on the cold, fog-enshrouded battlefield of Lützen. By now the imperialists had improved their artillery, while fog reduced the Swedes' maneuverability. Wallenstein had thinned out his *tercios* ten soldiers deep to increase firepower.[64] In the battle, both sides lost heavily: the Swedes lost Gustavus, their most valuable asset, but Wallenstein found himself forced to retreat. Believing that some of his officers had betrayed him, he carried out a savage purge.[65] Slightly more than a year later, feared, thoroughly disliked, and distrusted by all, he was assassinated.

For all of Gustavus's success at Breitenfeld, the unique army he brought to Germany was too small to balance the Swedes' strategic aims with their means. Sweden lacked the population and resources to wage war in Germany on its own. Even before Gustavus landed in Pomerania, his agents had hired 43,000 German mercenaries. Swedish soldiers won Breitenfeld, and Swedish generalship remained impressive throughout the war, but Gustavus was irreplaceable. Moreover, the armies his successors led were no longer Swedish. By 1633, the Protestant army of 85,000 numbered only 3,000 of Swedish extraction.[66]

By the time the Thirty Years' War ended in 1648, as much from exhaustion as for any other reason, armies had ravaged the Germanies from the Baltic to the Tyrol. The war lasted so long because those immediately affected, the German citizens, were incapable of controlling events. The Swedes and French pursued their own objectives, which had little to do with those living in the Germanies. As for the conduct of the war, Geoffrey Parker notes, "On the local level, the war never seemed to stop. Large armies starved and small ones were beaten, but nothing could check marauding garrisons and freebooters."[67] Short-term enlistments through mercenary captains meant that soldiers lacked training, discipline, and much incentive to focus on military objectives. Armies roamed the countryside looking for plunder or simply something to eat.

If the end of the Thirty Years' War failed to bring peace, it did lead to major changes in international relations and the nature of the European states. By the terms of the Peace of Westphalia in 1648, religion could no longer be a cause of disputes between major powers. Equally important was the emergence of the modern state and military organizations. States might still recruit mercenaries, but they were recruited into regiments, which swore allegiance to the monarch. Even in peacetime, they served all year under the sustained discipline demanded by the new tactical systems of Maurice of Orange and Gustavus Adolphus. In thin lines, carefully watched by their officers and sergeants, troops could endure ferocious bombardments and volleys. In effect, the armies of late seventeenth-century Europe reinvented the disciplined formations of Rome's legions.

The decisive developments in creating modern military organizations came in France during the reign of Louis XIV.[68] The Battle of Rocroi in 1643, won by the French, left no doubt that the day of the Spanish *tercio* was over. A French army under the Duc d'Enghien, utilizing a tactical system similar to that of Gustavus Adolphus, defeated the Spanish Army of Flanders. France now emerged as the premier power in Europe. Under the Sun King's military and administrative reforms, it dominated European wars for over a half-century. Armies continued to grow. In their war against Spain in the 1650s, the French possessed 80,000 to 90,000 soldiers; by the 1690s, Louis XIV's marshals were deploying 362,000 in fortress garrisons and field armies.[69]

The growth of armies, especially in peacetime, required major improvements in the administrative support structure. Whereas in the 1630s the French Army's administrative paperwork averaged around one thousand letters per year, by the late 1680s it had reached ten thousand.[70] The bureaucrats who made the essential administrative reforms possible were Louis's two secretaries of state for war: Michel Le Tellier and his son, the Marquis de Louvois. Under them, civilian intendants ensured that supplies arrived in the right places in the necessary quantities.[71]

The weakness in the French efforts was that Louis was neither willing nor able to reform France's fiscal system.[72] Its most debilitating weakness was that the nobility and clergy paid minimal taxes, meaning that the richest elements of French society did little to support the wars financially. Admittedly, noblemen had to pay considerable sums to serve in the army. They not only had to purchase commissions but make up shortfalls in the government's provisions of equipment, rations, and pay to the regiments.[73]

Just as importantly, the French failed to develop a system for mobilizing credit in the way the Dutch and British were establishing. Instead of financing his wars by long-term borrowing, Louis followed traditional methods of borrowing through expensive, short-term credit or by mortgaging future revenues. In his early wars, he escaped the consequences by having his armies fight on foreign territory and extracting their costs from the enemy. But the War of the Spanish Succession (1701–1714) largely occurred on French territory, which added enormously to Louis's expenses.

We might ask which came first, the chicken or the egg: the modern state or the modern military? The most plausible answer is that the modern state and its military institutions emerged symbiotically over the last half of the seventeenth century. If the innovations in the French Army were incremental, there were still key moments, such as in 1662, when Louis created the Régiment du Roi as a test bed for formalizing doctrine and training. Its commander was Lieutenant Colonel Jean Martinet—the king was the regiment's colonel. Five years later Martinet, who gave his name to nitpicking discipline, became the inspector of infantry, a position from which he placed his imprint on the whole army and eventually on history. In the 1670s, he developed the tactic of firing by ranks.[74] As Paul Kennedy has written, the "monopolization and bureaucratization of military power by the state [was] clearly a central part of the story of 'nation building'; and the process was a reciprocal one, since the enhanced authority and resources of the state gave to the armed forces a degree of *permanence* which had often not existed a century earlier."[75]

The development of more sophisticated designs for the *trace italienne* gave rise to improved methods of conducting sieges. The master of both sieges and fortification design was Sébastien de Vauban, who created a network of forts across France's major frontiers. These were not just individually brilliant fortifications but an interlocking system. The logistical requirements for sieges were extraordinary. One general noted that a major siege would require 3.3 million rations for the troops as well as 730,000 horse rations, 40,000 24-pound shot, and 472 tons of gunpowder.[76] In addition, to prevent the enemy from relieving the besieged, the attackers would probably require a covering army. The need to feed armies in the field to prevent the marauding of the Thirty Years' War gave added importance to fortresses, since they served as supply dumps. The increasing size of the armies and newly imposed constraints on foraging—particularly given the penchant of soldiers to desert—increased the importance of the dismal military science of logistics. As European states professionalized their militaries into year-round armies, it became as important to feed the soldiers in garrison as in the field.

At the beginning of Louis's reign, the French followed Gustavus's pattern of lining infantry formations six deep. Later, they modified their tactical approach to four deep and then three deep. These changes had to do with two factors: first, increased training time, and second, the need to tighten the discipline of formations to ensure units would not collapse. In other words, soldiers needed to fear their sergeants and officers more than the enemy and combat.

Incremental improvements in gunpowder weapons continued as well. But because each weapon had to be manufactured separately, major changes in infantry firearms were expensive. The flintlock musket, which did not require a slow-burning match to fire, did not completely replace the matchlock in the French Army until 1699.[77] The invention of the plug bayonet and then the socket bayonet gradually did away with the pike. Muskets with bayonets allowed infantry formations to ward off cavalry.

In retrospect, the musket was not an impressive weapon. In the late eighteenth century, a Prussian unit firing at a target the size of a barn from eighty yards away achieved only fifty hits out of every hundred fired.[78] The problem was that muskets had no rifling, and with a ball smaller than the barrel, accuracy was not possible. Yet it was a generally reliable weapon, and peasants who were dragooned into service could be easily trained on its use.

The French approach became the model for other European armies. Having a professional standing army, rather than relying on mercenary captains and their soldiers, gave German princes a more coherent justification for independence from the emperor.[79] A standing army was also a more reliable instrument with which to play in international politics. Significantly, two of the emerging German states, Bavaria and Prussia, played roles in the War of the Spanish Succession. Despite its small population and size, Prussia became a major power by the middle of the eighteenth century, something it could not have done without the ability to absorb the new system of war and field an army beyond its resource base.

By the end of the seventeenth century, there had been major changes in the overall framework of the great powers. In 1678, the Ottomans launched a major effort to overthrow the Austrian Hapsburgs, and in 1683 their army began a siege of Vienna itself. But just when the Hapsburg capital seemed on the brink of falling, a Polish relief force under King Jan Sobieski arrived and destroyed the Ottoman Army. The campaign represented the last gasp of Turkish efforts to dominate the unbelievers to their west. From that point they were on the defensive.

While the Turks faded, a new power was rising in the east. In 1682, Peter I, later Peter the Great, became the Tsar of Russia. The framework was now set for two competitive systems to contest for power in Europe: in the east, Russia, Sweden, Prussia, and Austria; in the west, England (soon to be Britain), France, and Holland.[80] The interplay of these systems added to the complexity of European strategy and politics. But it was war that would determine the outcomes. The rise of organized, bureaucratic states with disciplined, responsive military organizations represented the first and most important of the military-social revolutions, because it set in motion all the others.

Conclusion: Two Steps Forward, One Back

The history of war after 1500 is a series of revolutions in how soldiers fought. After the Chinese invented gunpowder sometime during the twelfth century, it quickly found its way across the trade routes to Europe. Yet neither the Chinese nor the Ottomans developed gunpowder to its full potential. Simply put, they were not in the business of innovation and adaptation. The walls of Constantinople collapsed in 1453 with cannons designed, built, and fired by experts from Europe. The Ottomans continued to draw on European technology and experts until the late seventeenth century, when they fell out of the competition. They lost their position because they failed to innovate, in the military sphere as well as politically and economically.

The unceasing conflicts among the European states led to changes and adaptations in weapons, tactics, and the underlying structures of logistics and finance that supported war. Those changes occurred not only on land but on the world's seas and oceans. The Europeans adapted quickly and effectively, while those unwilling to adapt, or incapable of adapting, lost their position. Technological changes, such as new means of ship construction and designs in the fifteenth century, flowed seamlessly into military applications.

This murderous environment made few, if any, decisive victories. Gustavus Adolphus's victory at Breitenfeld was decisive only in that it prevented the Hapsburgs from creating a united, Catholic Germany.

What mattered in war was not the battles waged but rather the materiel, manpower, and finances that each side brought to the struggle. Attrition of these determined the outcomes. Even victory on the battlefield usually resulted in unacceptable casualties. For the most part, hope rather than strategic thinking governed the decision to go to war. Rarely was there any effort to connect ends with means. That alone ensured that attrition of men and finances would result in nothing resembling a decisive victory.

Wars in the sixteenth and seventeenth centuries steadily increased in cost, as well as in the size of the armies and navies that fought them. That process began early in the sixteenth century and has continued. Philip II possessed enormous amounts of gold and silver robbed from the Indian civilizations of the Americas, but those riches were never sufficient to pay the costs of his wars. As important as military forces was the logistical and financial support that the emerging states deployed. The disaster of the Thirty Years' War was the result of the fact that the contestants could neither pay their troops nor provide them with sufficient sustenance. The Treaty of Westphalia is commonly credited with bringing a modicum of order to relations among the European states. But as important as that was, the horrors of an unpaid and undisciplined soldiery were more important in forcing the European states to create military organizations, disciplined both in battle and in their permanent garrisons. Undergirding the significant changes was a willingness to adapt and innovate.

CHAPTER THREE

The Arrival of the Modern State

Our opinion of the gods and our knowledge of men leads us to conclude that it is a general and necessary law of nature to rule whatever one can. This is not a law that we have made ourselves, nor were we the first to act upon it when it was made. We found it already in existence, and we shall leave it to exist forever among those who come after us.

—THUCYDIDES, *History of the Peloponnesian War*

THE LAST HALF OF the seventeenth century saw drastic changes in two essential elements for creating the modern state. On one hand, these nascent states created steadily improving bureaucracies that were effectively able to handle their business including the collection of taxes, the systematic organization of their militaries, and the day-to-day execution of law courts and governance. What was crucial to conflicts in the eighteenth century was that armies and navies were organized and deployed by states and under their control. This period saw the rise of both England (Britain) and Russia as great powers.[1]

Moreover, naval capabilities meant that the Europeans could project military and economic power over oceanic distances, involving themselves directly or indirectly in the contest for control of the world's oceans. Three emerging powers competed in this new environment: first Spain, and then France and England. The smallest and seemingly least

powerful proved the winner. One of its major advantages was that continental strategists had to devote substantial resources to defending against
threats on land, whereas Britain did not.[2]

Spain's leaders, particularly Philip II, exacerbated their strategic
problems by having too many enemies: the French, the Dutch, the
Turks, and eventually the English.[3] This overstretch contributed to
Spain's eventual collapse. France's position was in many ways worse geo-
graphically than Spain's. As it rose under Louis XIV to become the para-
mount European power, France confronted an often-hostile Spain as
well as threats from Hapsburg and Dutch military power on France's
northern border with the Austrian Netherlands (modern-day Belgium).
Thus, nearly always the French focused on the Continent before turning
to the sea. Moreover, with two widely separated coasts, the French had
to split their navy between the Mediterranean at Toulon and the Atlantic
at Brest.

For the British, the strategic necessities were reversed. Their priority
had to be naval power to protect the British Isles. Their strategy concentrated first on control of the English Channel, followed by the North
Sea, the Mediterranean, and finally the Atlantic. Then came continental
support, but Britain's sophisticated financial system allowed for monetary
aid to allies as well as the resources required by the Royal Navy. Britain
nearly always supported a balance of power on the Continent.[4] In the
great contests with France, Britain's most important geographic advantage was the first-rate harbors on the coasts of southern England. The
other side of the Channel had few equivalents. Between Brest and the
Scheldt Estuary, there are no deep-water harbors able to shelter battle-
fleets. Even Brest presented a difficult anchorage, adverse prevailing
winds, and an inconvenient location for deploying fleets of ships of the
line.

From 1672 to 1690, Louis XIV's naval minister, Jean-Baptiste Colbert, built an impressive battlefleet of over eighty ships of the line. Yet
that effort had a major weakness: Colbert spent less than half the amount
on the navy's support structure than he spent on new ships.[5] He constructed virtually no major dry docks. The English, on the other hand,
paid serious attention to the logistics and maintenance of sea power. In
1691, the Royal Navy began construction of a great stone dry dock that
eventually cost over £67,000. By 1698, the Chatham dockyards were valued at nearly £45,000 and those at Portsmouth £35,000. Thirteen years
later those two facilities employed a total of 6,488 officers and staff. One

naval historian, N. A. M. Rodger, notes that "the dockyards had entered the industrial age a hundred years before the rest of the country."[6]

The "Glorious Revolution," which saw James II replaced by his daughter Mary and her husband, William of Orange, represented a major turning point in English and British history.[7] In November 1688, while Louis XIV was distracted by events in Germany, William led an army of 20,000 Dutch troops and a fleet of 463 ships across the Channel on a "Protestant wind," and landed to find the way prepared by his supporters.[8] James fled the country. Ironically, this peaceful revolution in England proved the most serious strategic defeat Louis suffered during his reign. The revolution of 1688 ended England's contentious quarrel between monarchs and parliament in favor of the latter. Parliament now met on a regular basis, with elections every three years (later seven), and had charge of the nation's taxes and finances. The settlement authorized a standing army but placed it firmly under parliament's control rather than the king's.[9] Crucially, William brought over the Dutch financial system, having the government finance a portion of its wars through long-term loans, which it guaranteed when it sold them.[10] Because the propertied classes bought these loans, they had a major reason to support the regime politically as well as financially, eliminating the possibility of a Stuart return.

The new regime also carried out a wholesale reform of taxation, which was extended to all segments of society, including the nobility, while Henry VIII had solved the church problem by confiscating its lands a century and a half earlier. In 1694, the new regime established the Bank of England, "while customs and excise officers, the foot soldiers of the 'fiscal-military state,' fanned out across the nation." The result was that the British government, which under the Stuarts had found it difficult to finance its wars, raised £49,320,145 to support the Nine Years' War (1688–1697)—£16 million from loans.[11] The financial reforms were also important for the navy; the Bank of England paid off the navy's debts, restored its credit, and established its long-term financial stability.[12] These political and financial reforms represented a revolution in military affairs because they revolutionized the monetary support necessary to support English and then British military forces. Even while bearing the great expense of maintaining a world-class navy, Britain was able to deploy ground forces to the Continent and provide substantial subsidies to its allies.

As the wars of the eighteenth century grew increasingly expensive, the British were able to bear increases in their average military expenditure from £5,355,583 a year during the War of the Spanish Succession to £12,154,200 during the American War of Independence, while the national debt rose from £36,200,000 to £242,900,000.[13] Yet despite these costs, the British never had to declare bankruptcy. In 1715, they completed their financial revolution by selling perpetual annuities with a 5 percent return. Holders could not demand principal repayment, but the treasury could redeem annuities if interest rates fell below 5 percent. Owners of annuities could, however, sell them to other investors on a growing stock market.[14]

The Nine Years' War, between Louis XIV's France and an alliance of the Dutch, English, Austrian Hapsburgs, and smaller German states, was the first of the great wars after the arrival of modern states. Most operations were sieges, although at Neerwinden in late July 1693, a French Army of eighty thousand defeated William III's allied army of fifty thousand. The French suffered eight thousand casualties while the allies lost twelve thousand and most of their artillery. The French held the ground, but the allies could replace their losses.[15]

On the naval side, a conventional struggle between the French and the allies resolved little. But the pressures of the war on land and a bad harvest in 1693–1694 forced the French to turn to a *guerre de course*, an effort to destroy Britain's commerce by raiders. That year the navy's budget fell by 52.7 percent, establishing a pattern that would continue in subsequent wars.[16] French privateers captured four thousand English merchant vessels during the war, but this was not enough to break British trade.[17] By 1697, both sides were exhausted. At the Peace of Rijswijk, the French gained territory in Alsace but little else. In the largest sense, the war was a French defeat because it solidified the Glorious Revolution and established England as a major power inimical to French interests.

Astonishingly, an even greater war broke out within four years.[18] The overt cause was the death of the Spanish king without an heir. Carlos II left all his lands to Louis XIV's grandson, yet Louis's acceptance of that bequest was a less important cause of the War of the Spanish Succession than his other decisions. First, he sent French troops to occupy the barrier fortresses in the Spanish Netherlands, essential to Dutch defense. Second, he had his grandson grant French merchants the sole right to supply enslaved people to the Spanish colonies, cutting the Dutch and English out of that reprehensible but lucrative trade. Third, after James II's death in September 1701, Louis recognized James's son as the legitimate King of England, directly threatening the 1688 settlement. Thus, in

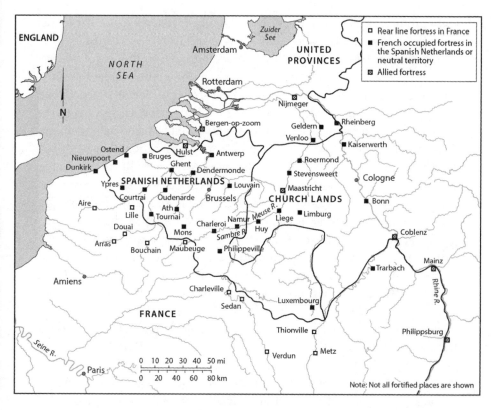

□	Rear line fortress in France
■	French occupied fortress in the Spanish Netherlands or neutral territory
⊠	Allied fortress

The War of Spanish Succession: Vauban's defensive system, 1701. Cartography by Bill Nelson.

a few months, Louis had attacked England's and Scotland's strategic, commercial, political, and religious interests.[19]

Almost immediately after the war started, William III died, to be succeeded by Anne, daughter of James II. She was also a confirmed Protestant, and there was little difficulty over the succession. Anne was close to John Churchill, the eventual Duke of Marlborough, and his wife, Sarah. Churchill, with Anne's blessings, became the leader of the coalition against France.[20] By 1707, the French would have 255,000 troops in the field and Spanish troops fighting at their side. Against them, the English promised to put 40,000 soldiers in the field, the Dutch 60,000, and the Austrians 90,000.[21]

The Dutch thought the campaigns of 1702 and 1703 were successful. Allied armies captured a number of fortresses. But in Marlborough's view, these campaigns had failed because the Dutch, thinking a major battle was too risky, had refused to allow him to fight in favorable circumstances. If they had been less cautious, he felt he could have won a major victory over the French Army. In 1704, worried about the French threat in southern Germany, Marlborough changed allied strategy. Having prepared the way logistically with supply dumps along the Rhine, the English Army, reinforced by contingents from smaller German states, made its way up the Rhine to join Prince Eugene of Savoy. On 12 August 1704, they surprised Marshal Tallard's combined Franco-Bavarian Army near Blenheim. As the battle unfolded, Marlborough and Eugene fixed the French and Bavarians on their left flank and center.²² In the late afternoon, led by Marlborough, allied cavalry smashed the French right wing and trapped eighteen infantry battalions in Blenheim. Only about a third of the Franco-Bavarian Army escaped. The allies captured 40 generals, 1,150 other officers, and 13,000 soldiers. French casualties were approximately 20,000 killed and wounded, while a further 7,000 deserted. Allied casualties were 13,000.²³ Blenheim was the worst defeat Louis's army had ever suffered.

In 1705, Marlborough returned to the Low Countries, where, to his frustration, he found the Dutch unwilling to fight. But the next year proved different. Louis and his armchair generals in Versailles concluded that Blenheim had resulted from bad French leadership and not Marlborough's generalship. Worried by France's financial situation, Louis instructed his marshals to seek battle. Marlborough obliged. At Ramillies on 23 May 1706, the allies again caught the French by surprise. When it was over, the French had suffered 13,000 casualties with many more deserting. Allied casualties were slightly over 2,500. The rout that followed was disastrous for the French.

The great column at Blenheim Palace records the pursuit: "The vigour and conduct with which he pursued his successes were equal to those with which he gained it. Louvaine, Brussels, Malines, Liege, Ghent, Oudenarde, Antwerp, Damme, Bruges, Courtray, surrendered. Ostende, Menin, Dendermonde, Ath, were taken. Brabant and Flanders were recovered."²⁴ Yet there was no French collapse. Louis hurried reinforcements and the competent Marshal Vendôme to Flanders to restore the situation, and the rot halted. All in all, 1706 was a terrible year for the French. Besides the disasters in Flanders, Prince Eugene dealt a devastating defeat to French forces besieging Turin.

The year 1708 was another disastrous one for Louis. In July 1708, Eugene and Marlborough forced an engagement by a rapid movement of fifty miles in two and a half days. The allies pushed their forces as fast as they could over the bridges at Oudenarde while the French commander, Vendôme, became involved in the tactical fight. As evening approached, the allies were close to encircling and destroying the French right wing, but night allowed most of the French to escape. Casualty totals again underlined allied success: close to three thousand allied soldiers killed and wounded; French, including prisoners, thirteen thousand. But that was Marlborough's last triumph. In 1709, facing political troubles at home, he again joined with Eugene to attack a heavily fortified French position at Malplaquet. But he had sought decisive victory once too often. When it was over, the allies held the ground, but their casualties hardly suggested even a pyrrhic victory: 25,000 allied killed and wounded, the French half that.[25]

While Marlborough was gaining his victories, the allies were putting pressure on the French and Spanish elsewhere. In 1703, the Treaty of Methuen tied Portugal to England; the following year an allied force captured Gibraltar.[26] The British were now a power in the Mediterranean.[27] But in January 1712, Marlborough's political position in Britain collapsed, and he found himself removed from office by the queen. In 1715, the queen died, succeeded by George I of Hanover, who restored Marlborough's positions in the government. But the war was over. The Peace of Utrecht changed little. France lost no important territory, and Louis XIV's grandson remained on the Spanish throne.

But appearances deceive. France had financed the war on short-term loans; its debt from Louis XIV's wars had reached 2.6 billion livres.[28] The British, meanwhile, were now a major member of Europe's strategic club, economically as well as militarily. The war had not only harmed France's overall strategic position but had also weakened the Dutch, Britain's great trade rival. The British held Minorca and Gibraltar, giving them a strategic position in the Mediterranean. In North America they held a stranglehold over New France with control of Acadia, Newfoundland, and Hudson Bay.

The importance of the War of the Spanish Succession is that it was the first global war fought by modern states with disciplined, organized, logistically supported military institutions. While both sides encountered difficulties, they still found the means to pay for wartime expenditures. There were no great bankruptcies. The opposing sides mounted military operations on the Indian subcontinent, the Caribbean, and North America. Like the Roman Empire's legions, Europe's new model armies wore uniforms. They deployed and fought in highly trained formations. They were disciplined not only in a military sense but in a civil sense, responsive and obedient to the state that recruited, organized, and paid them. The War of the Spanish Succession represented the final stage of the first military-social revolution: the creation of the modern state and its military. Yet improvements in military organizations from those of the early seventeenth century failed to make wars more decisive. Conflicts still revolved around lengthy campaigns of sieges and possession of key terrain. No matter how impressive Marlborough's and Eugene's battles were, they failed to end the conflict. In the end, the cost in soldiers, finances, and resources exhausted both opponents. A recent estimate of battle deaths in the war places the total of those wounded and killed at approximately 1.25 million, and that does not include deaths due to disease.[29] As always, attrition determined the outcome.

As the War of the Spanish Succession fought itself to its eventual stalemate, another major war was occurring in northern and Eastern Europe, where the Swedish imperium created by the Thirty Years' War was attempting to maintain its position against the other Baltic states. The challenger to the Swedes would be an emergent Russia under Peter the Great, undoubtedly one of Russia's greatest leaders. Besides the difficulties involved in dragging Russia out of the sixteenth century, Peter's strategic problem was Sweden, led by a warrior king, Charles XII, in possession of a first-class military system.[30] The Tsar's initial effort at conquest, against the Crimean Tatars, led him to conclude he needed to modernize Russian society and military. After a trip to Holland and England in 1697 and 1698, in which he absorbed much technological and military information and left behind a trail of smashed furniture and glassware, he returned to Russia determined to westernize his realm. That vision included expansion of Russia's territory to the eastern shores of the Baltic.

When the fourteen-year-old Charles XII assumed the Swedish throne in 1697, Denmark, Poland, and Russia formed a coalition, intending to take advantage of his youth. The Danes aimed at grabbing the province of Holstein, the Poles and the Russians Swedish control of Livonia and Estonia. Almost immediately they regretted their decision. Charles proved to be a superb combat commander, but like Napoleon he lacked the strategic and political sense to know when to stop. With a relatively small army Charles struck first at Copenhagen in summer 1700, and with the support of the English and Dutch fleets forced the Danes out of the Great Northern War five months after they had entered.

Meanwhile, the Poles and Russians had moved into what are now the northern Baltic states, the former besieging Riga and the latter Narva. Charles went after the besiegers of Narva and on 20 November 1700 launched his army of eight thousand against some forty thousand Russians. In the middle of a blinding snowstorm, the Swedes destroyed Peter's army. Swedish casualties were approximately two thousand; the Russian army virtually destroyed. Then, instead of advancing on Russia, Charles turned against Augustus the Strong, elector of Saxony and King of Poland. There then followed a series of campaigns across Poland during which Charles consistently crushed the Poles, but his efforts in Poland kept Charles from focusing on Russia. Eventually Charles chased Augustus into his German province, Saxony, and in 1706, at the Battle of Fraustadt, destroyed the Saxons and only then turned back to deal with the Russians, who had caused considerable trouble in the Baltic provinces.

Peter, however, had continued reforming the Russian state and military institutions, and as has often occurred throughout history, his opponent underestimated the Russians. Charles and his Swedish Army crossed the Vistula into Russia on 1 January 1708 during what was one of the coldest winters in European history, perhaps the strangest start date for an invasion in history. After defeating a Russian Army at Holowczyn despite being outnumbered three to one, Charles decided to march on Moscow instead of against Peter's unfinished capital of St. Petersburg. But the combination of the Russian winter and the scorched-earth efforts of the Russians forced the Swedes to turn south to Ukraine.

With relieving armies defeated by the Russians and his army reduced to twenty thousand soldiers, Charles attempted to besiege Poltava, but wounded, he had to leave the battle largely to his generals. Peter's refurbished and retrained army of 45,000 moved to relieve the Poltava garrison. The Swedes attacked and came close to breaking the Russian line. But numbers told, and eventually the Swedes collapsed. Charles fled to Constantinople.[31] He continued fighting until his assassination in 1718 but Poltava represented the peak of Sweden's position as a great power. As a result of Charles's defeat, Russia emerged as its replacement. The resulting peace found Peter with control of Livonia and Estonia, with Russia now a Baltic power and a major political player on the European scene. Peter was also to imprint on the Russian state a drive to expand outward—a disease that a number of his successors from Catherine the Great to Vladimir Putin embraced with enthusiasm.

The Wars for Global Supremacy

After the War of the Spanish Succession left the European powers exhausted, it took them another quarter-century before they again embarked on a major conflict. The War of Austrian Succession brought the rise of another major power, Prussia. Under the Great Elector, Frederick William (1640–1688), who tied his scattered domains into a tight web while building up its army, Prussia emerged as the strongest of German polities after Austria. Frederick William's immediate successor played intelligent politics and allied Prussia with the allies in the War of the Spanish Succession. By the time Frederick the Great came to the throne in 1740, Prussia's highly trained and disciplined army was the best in Europe.[32] But the Prussian state had little else to recommend it: insignificant industry, not much trade, and unimpressive agriculture. It was either a misshapen version of an overmilitarized state or the epitome of the European marriage of state and military.

The next great war began when the newly crowned Frederick the Great threw a grenade into the pond of European politics. Having just written a pamphlet titled *The Anti-Machiavelli*, he announced he intended to protect the inheritance of Maria Teresa, who had just inherited the Hapsburg lands. To do so, he sent Prussian troops to occupy the province of Silesia—an act of naked aggression even by the standards of the time. The move gave the French an opportunity to strike at their old Hapsburg enemies. Frederick's performance in his first battle, at Mollwitz, was hardly impressive: he abandoned the field in the belief that the Prussians had lost. In fact, under Field Marshal Kurt von Schwerin, they had won. Frederick then displayed how dishonest his diatribe against Machiavelli had been by dropping out of the war and then rejoining it. By the time the powers agreed to peace, in 1748, little had changed. But Frederick retained Silesia, nearly doubling Prussia's population.

The most significant war of the eighteenth and nineteenth centuries, the Seven Years' War, began just eight years after the War of Austrian Succession. Most importantly, it secured Britain's control of the world's oceans. Given its wealth and population, France should have been able to fight a continental war while matching the British at sea. But an inefficient revenue system ensured that it could not. The war underlined the extraordinary power European nations had achieved through the military-social revolution which turned them into bureaucratized states that could organize, discipline, and support armies over continental distances.

The Seven Years' War broke out in two places, thousands of miles apart. In late May in 1754, not far from present-day Pittsburgh, a group of Virginian land speculators led by the young George Washington caused a major incident involving the murder of a French officer after he had surrendered.[33] With war still not having broken out in Europe, the British sent two regiments of foot soldiers under General Edward Braddock to settle matters. In 1755, unprepared for either the political or military conditions in North America, Braddock's redcoats met disaster against a French and Indian army near the Monongahela River.[34]

Meanwhile, in Europe a diplomatic revolution occurred: Austria broke its long alliance with Britain and joined France and Russia. Women effectively ruled all three nations: Empress Maria-Teresa in Austria and Empress Elizabeth in Russia, while in France, Louis XV's mistress, Madam Pompadour, exercised great influence over the king. Frederick had managed to anger all three, and they determined to bring him down. The Prussians and the British formed a counter-alliance. The French seem to have gone into the war with considerable overconfidence, some minimizing Britain's ability to finance its wars through borrowing. As one French commentator noted at the time: "Everything here [in France] is real fertile land, precious goods, clinking cash; a lack of credit would not influence any of this."[35]

It was a disastrous miscalculation. In the great contest between the French and the British for control of the global commons, Britain found the financial resources to keep the French busy on the Continent while the Royal Navy dominated the seas. The French had found themselves pushed toward war by the impressive growth of Britain's North American colonies, which were increasing steadily in population and economic strength. The problem was not so much the threat the colonies represented to New France but the strength they added to Britain's global power. But if the French found that worrisome, it did not prevent them from embroiling themselves in Central Europe.[36]

With no clear strategic priorities and a leadership epitomized by Louis XV's comment *"après moi, le deluge"* (after me the deluge), the French floundered. Their leadership at almost every level was incompetent, ignorant, and obtuse. They not only lost the war but came close to bankrupting the nation and economy. On the other hand, if the British

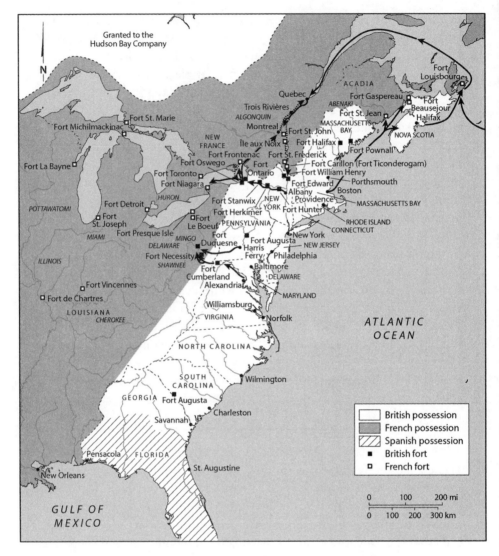

Principal campaigns of the French and Indian War. Cartography by Bill Nelson.

had begun the war on the wrong foot, William Pitt righted the strategic ship. He provided extraordinary vision and leadership, such that one must count him alongside Bismarck and Churchill as one of history's great strategists.

Like his successors in 1914, Frederick responded aggressively to the threat posed by Austria, Russia, and France: in August 1756, he launched his army into Saxony to eliminate the Saxons.[37] The Prussians then moved into Bohemia, where they achieved little. Matters were not much better on the British side. In the Mediterranean, a British fleet fought a drawn battle to protect Minorca, but after an inconclusive battle, instead of resuming the struggle Admiral John Byng retreated to Gibraltar. For that, a court martial sentenced him to death, which Voltaire characterized with the immortal phrase: *"pour encourage les autres"*—to encourage the others. A firing squad executed Byng in March 1757.[38] Interestingly, the court martial did not convict him of cowardice but rather for "failing to do his utmost to take or destroy the enemy's ships."[39] It is not clear whether Byng's execution had an impact; the navy's leadership certainly improved under the First Lord of the Admiralty, Admiral George Anson, who chose hard, first-rate admirals to command the fleets.

Most of 1757 brought bad news for the Anglo-Prussian side. Frederick had begun by besieging Prague, but the Austrians forced him to abandon the siege and then defeated him at Kolín. Matters went no better to the east and west. A Russian army arrived on the borders of East Prussia, besieged Memel, and followed that success by defeating the Prussian Army in East Prussia in late August. In the west, the Duke of Cumberland, used to hanging poorly armed Scots, led an army of allied British and German regiments into a trap. Ensnared, he agreed to the Convention of Kloster-Zeven, infuriating his father, King George II, who saw it as a humiliation. It was. Cumberland's removal from the political scene established Pitt in control of Britain's strategy.[40]

But if the British were having difficulties, the French were making disastrous choices. Over the winter of 1756–1757, they assembled an army on the lower Rhine to march into Germany, aiming to seize the Electorate of Hanover, George II's principality. The army represented the worst sort of corruption of which the French monarchy was capable. No fewer than forty-six lieutenant generals and sixty-five senior officers and princes of the blood accompanied the expedition.[41]

Pitt proceeded to turn Britain's strategy around by focusing on the war against France's colonies, particularly New France in North America. But he did not ignore what was happening on the Continent, where Britain supplied its German allies with enough financial support to keep the French occupied in western Germany and protect Hanover. Britain also subsidized Frederick on a scale never before seen in British history. For Pitt's strategy to work, it was crucial to keep the French sufficiently engaged on the Continent to weaken support for their navy.

Nothing displayed that strategy more than the action he took to support the British colonists in North America. The campaign of 1757 had been a general failure. The theater commander, Lord Loudon, had nothing but disdain for the colonists, who returned the sentiment. In late winter 1758, before a recalcitrant Massachusetts Assembly, he demanded 2,128 provincial soldiers; the colonists refused to provide any. At a moment of total impasse, Pitt's new instructions arrived. Loudon was relieved of his command, and equally important, parliament "would grant Compensation" for all the expenses the colonists incurred in raising regiments. Instead of 2,128 soldiers, the Massachusetts Assembly agreed to raise 7,000. Other colonial assemblies were equally enthusiastic.[42] Importantly, Pitt's new instructions recognized the social and political realities in the colonies, put them on a war footing, and provided support for a great campaign against "new France."[43] Yet Pitt was not following a "blue-water" strategy. In the crucial years of 1758 and 1759, Britain devoted as many soldiers to the European war as to the war across the Atlantic.

While these events were in train, the strategic position on the Continent had altered. In November 1757, Frederick caught a French army on the march, and after his cavalry smashed its columns, his infantry and artillery finished the job. French casualties at the Battle of Rossbach were over 10,000; Prussian barely 500. One month later, Frederick caught the Austrians at Leuthen, and advancing his infantry in oblique formation, destroyed his opponent's left wing. Austrian casualties were over 22,000; Prussian slightly over 6,000.[44] The two victories reversed the strategic situation in Central Europe. While he still confronted considerable odds, Frederick had breathing space. With Prussia's position improved, Pitt approved an annual subsidy of £670,000 and committed 12,000 British troops to defend the western Germanies.

The war in Europe continued in 1758 with battles that were costly but not decisive. But at sea and in the global struggle, matters tilted in Britain's favor. For the amphibious operation to take Louisbourg in Nova Scotia, the British assembled an overwhelming force of twenty-one ships of the line protecting a landing force of twelve thousand troops. On 26 July 1758, the fortress surrendered; along with the capture of Louisbourg, the British destroyed five French ships of the line trapped in the bay.[45] The way was now open for a direct attack up the St. Lawrence to Quebec City.

The British would call 1759 the *annus mirabilis*, the year of miracles. In North America, two major drives achieved the conquest of New

France. French defenses had depended on the peculiarities of the Native American way of war, which certainly looked barbaric to the British.[46] It also looked savage to the new French commander, Louis-Joseph Marquis de Montcalm, who found it appalling.[47] The Native American leaders found the European approach to war equally bizarre. As a result, Montcalm held France's Indian allies at arms-length and thus made the defense of French Canada impossible. Still, the British drive from Albany up Lake George toward Montreal made little progress because its commander, General Jeffery Amherst, refused to take any risks in spite of his overwhelming superiority in numbers.

Initially, the assault on Quebec City, led by Major General James Wolfe, failed to make better progress. Wolfe hoped to force Montcalm to come out from behind his defenses at Quebec City and fight, but the French refused. Nor did ravaging of the farmlands lying along the lower St. Lawrence budge Montcalm. Wolfe bemoaned that "war is an option of difficulties."[48] Finally, in desperation, with summer almost over, he took the risk of moving his redcoats up the St. Lawrence and scaling the cliffs behind Quebec City to the Plains of Abraham. The French sentinels failed to alert the garrison until the British troops had deployed across the plains. Montcalm, who had sent a contingent of troops up the St. Lawrence, might have waited for them to return, trapping the redcoats between two forces with greater strength. Instead, he brought out his regulars and Canadian militia from the protection of the fortifications of the city. The highly trained British troops waited until the French were at point-blank range and then blew them away. Wolfe died on the field; Montcalm succumbed that night. Yet with a Canadian winter coming, the victors were in a desperate position: they had hardly any supplies, and their depredations over the summer had left little in the farms along the lower St. Lawrence.[49] French forces along the upper river, however, lacked artillery to attack the city's walls. The first fleet to arrive with reinforcements and supplies in spring 1760 would thus determine Canada's fate.

A naval battle off the French coast in November 1759 decided matters. The previous summer, the Royal Navy had established a stranglehold over the French fleet in Brest. In 1758, it had mounted a distant blockade of the port for six weeks, but scurvy forced the fleet to return home. The next year, Admiral Edward Hawke, commander of the Western Squadron, solved the problem of maintaining a continuous, close blockade without the nightmare of scurvy. By August 1759, he had enough ships of the line (thirty-two) to return a number to port for re-supply and maintenance. Equally important, he created a system of re-supply at sea that solved the scurvy problem.

Their financial problems increasingly serious, the French prepared a transport fleet and army to invade the British Isles; they used Quiberon Bay because the logistical structure at Brest could not support an army as well as a fleet. The plan was for the fleet to leave Brest, sail to Quiberon, and then escort the transports and the united fleet to Britain. On 7 November, a gale blew Hawke from his station off Brest to the southwest coast of England. On 16 November, the French fleet under Admiral Hubert de Conflans sailed from Brest with twenty-one ships of the line. Difficult winds kept them on an erratic course.

As the French approached Quiberon with another gale building, they spied Hawke and his fleet in pursuit. Despite worsening weather and the fact that the British possessed no charts for the dangerous reefs surrounding Quiberon Bay, Hawke flew the pennant "general chase." His ships crowded on full sail. As the ships reached the bay, darkness arrived along with a full storm. By morning it was over: two French ships of the line had escaped, two had sunk, one was captured, one ran aground, and another was damaged and soon sank. Conflans's flag ship was burned. Helped by a storm tide, twelve French ships fled up the Vilane River, where they remained, because once the tide ran out a sandbar blocked them from returning downriver. Hawke lost two ships. It was an extraordinary performance, the most impressive naval battle ever won by a British admiral.[50]

Because of Quiberon Bay there could be no serious French effort to supply Quebec; Hawke had crushed the French battlefleet, and there was no money to resurrect it. The battle "was the decisive military event of 1759."[51] In addition to closing the Canadian campaign, Britain's success at sea ensured it a stranglehold over India. The French could no longer compete for control of the subcontinent.

In the larger sense, the French Navy was out of the contest even before Quiberon Bay. It had gone into the war with a debt of 14.5 million livres; by June 1758, its debt had ballooned to 42 million, a substantial portion in unsecured notes, all at high rates of interest. News of the fall of Quebec brought bankruptcy and a near halt to naval activity.[52] In 1761, the government cut the navy's budget by 50 percent.

British superiority was also reflected in their ability to maintain their ships. The French did not construct their first fully functioning dry dock until 1756, and that one could not take three-deckers until 1780.[53] The British also had a massive logistical system that enabled the Royal Navy to establish a close blockade over the main French ports as well as project its power over the globe. Between 1750 and 1757, that system supplied 27,321 tons of bread, 2,249 tons of beef, 3,367 tons of pork, 3,132 tons of flour, 110,047 tons of beer, and 351,692 gallons of brandy to the fleet, along with other items.[54] By the middle of the eighteenth century, naval power rested on the sustainability of ships, dockyard maintenance, logistics, and finances. Here lay the Royal Navy's superiority, one buttressed by admirals like Hawke. In many ways the Royal Navy's support structure represented the first stirrings of the Industrial Revolution.

Pitt's brilliant strategy had won Britain a global empire. One historian has aptly explained his success in the following terms: "Pitt had co-opted and refined a strategic tradition which went back to the Glorious Revolution. He created—for the time being at least—the perfect strategic virtuous circle, in which Germany was defended in America, and America was won in Germany. He turned Hanover from a liability into a geographic asset. He created a Protestant heir to replace the 'old system.' He rallied a motley collection of radicals, planters, Tories, and orthodox Whigs. He made lions lie down with lambs. He . . . persuaded many to bite their lips."[55]

But Pitt's political position in Britain collapsed when George II died in November 1760. His throne went to his grandson, George III, who would do much to destroy the first British Empire. The new king saw little sense in spending money to defend Hanover and even less in supporting Prussia. The death of Frederick's mortal enemy, Empress Elizabeth of Russia, saved him with the accession to the throne by Peter III, a great admirer of the Prussian king. The new Tsar lasted barely six months before his wife, Empress Catherine the Great, overthrew him, but that short period saved Frederick. In 1763, with the British having withdrawn from the war, France almost bankrupt, and Austria exhausted, the powers agreed to the Treaty of Paris. The only winners were the British, who gained Quebec and the French possessions in India. Above all, the Seven Years' War established the Royal Navy and its supporting infrastructure as the dominant power on the global commons.

But success had an adverse impact on Britain's leadership. George III, not the brightest of kings, showed little understanding of the factors that had led to Pitt's successes. Within a few years, the British had created the potential for a major rebellion in their North American colonists.[56] Still, stupidity and incompetence represent only a partial explanation for the British leaders' errors. None of those making policy toward the colonies had ever visited them; George III and his advisors possessed not the slightest inkling of the conditions on the other side of the Atlantic. A few senior officers had fought against the French in North America, but nearly all analyzed how a war against the colonists might unfold through a lens of upper-class snobbery. Perhaps the greatest difficulty lay in developing an understanding of the distances such a war involved. One British commentator on the war later noted, "The small scale of our maps deceived us, and as the word 'America' takes up no more room than the word 'Yorkshire,' we seemed to think the territories as they are represented are much the same bigness, though Charleston is as far away from Boston as London from Venice."[57] In the ensuing war, the British faced many problems of which the most important was logistics. They could occupy only small portions of territory, never large enough to feed their army; thus, everything except hay had to come from Britain.[58]

The French and Indian War had also transformed the forces the colonists brought to the fight. The experiences of a multitude of Americans serving in militia regiments against the French created a pool of officers and noncommissioned officers (NCOs) who would figure prominently in the colonists' victory. They formed the backbone of militia units that could make deadly opponents for British forces in the field.[59] As one of the few British officers to view the colonists dispassionately warned after the Lexington-Concord fiasco, "They have men among them who know very well what they are about, having been employed by the Rangers against the Indians and Canadians, and this country being very much covered with wood and hill is very advantageous for their method of fighting."[60]

On the other hand, the colonists confronted the basic problem of keeping the colonial economy functioning while supporting an army in the field. Since they lacked excess labor to allow farmers to leave their farms for substantial periods of time, they had to fight a hybrid war.[61] As long as the colonists could keep a small regular army in the field, the British had to concentrate their forces. With colonial farms spread over considerable distances, foraging required dispersing forces over expanses of territory. Deploying small units to forage carried the risk that the militia would gobble them up, as happened at the Battle of Bennington in 1777, which set the stage for the Battle of Saratoga. Furthermore, except in the coastal cities, there was nowhere the British could remain long enough to support creation of sufficient indigenous armed and trained Tories to overcome the local rebel militia.

The support of major military forces over oceanic distances underlines the enormous advances of the eighteenth century. From the perspective of global history, the ability to project military power and support distant forces represented one of the most impressive of all the revolutions in military affairs that followed from the creation of the nation-state. Yet for the British, it could not overcome the American rebellion. The distances were too great. Whatever hope the British might have had disappeared with the failure of the invasion of New York and its environs in 1776. The inability of William Howe's army to destroy George Washington's nascent military force in these early battles allowed the Americans to husband sufficient force to strike back at the Battles of Trenton and Princeton in the winter of 1776–1777. In military terms, those battles were mere skirmishes, but that is not how the Americans saw them. After 1777, once the British faced the French again, the war against the colonists grew increasingly unpopular at home, and defeat in North America became inevitable.

Conclusion: The Arrival of the State

As that wonderful French phrase comments on the human condition, *plus ça change, plus c'est la même chose.* That saying characterizes the explosive arrival of the modern nation and its military organizations at the end of the seventeenth century. War now became a disciplined reflection of the nation-state and its society, utilized and controlled in a fashion that was not typical of war in previous centuries. Carl von Clausewitz's famous comment that "war is the continuation of politics with other means" represents a truism that hardly fits the centuries before 1700. That famous aphorism certainly does not describe the looting expeditions that Edward III, the Black Prince, or Henry V embarked on in their invasions of France in the fourteenth and fifteenth centuries. Nor does it reflect what occurred in the Germanies during the Thirty Years' War.

Yet in the eighteenth century, the new nation-states at least brought some order to what thus far in European history had resembled a murderous free-for-all, in which peace rarely, if ever, occurred. Thus, in the eighteenth century, the major powers engaged in war over lesser periods of time. The irony lay in the fact that these wars were more violent, with greater casualties, because of the very organizational abilities of the state. Moreover, if the battles appeared more impressive in a tactical sense, they proved no more decisive in their strategic effect than the conflicts occurring in earlier centuries. And as in the past, attrition and financial exhaustion proved as important as battlefield victories. But at the turn of the century, the very stability of the state, not to mention the international system, was about to be called into question.

PART II

Drivers of Change:
The Second and Third
Military-Social Revolutions

CHAPTER FOUR

The French Revolution and the Industrial Revolution

Later Westerners sought a greater complexity and "science" to
warfare as if the introduction of such skills could somehow make
battle more controllable or predictable and perhaps thereby
more humane; instead all they really accomplished was to allow
the killing to intrude into the very lives of the citizens or subjects
they hoped to protect, as they created a cult of youthful heroism
out of something so mundanely simple and brutal.

—VICTOR DAVIS HANSON, *The Western Way of War*

As THE EIGHTEENTH CENTURY approached its last decade, it appeared the
great powers were entering a period of relative peace and gradual political change.[1] Yet as so often happens in human affairs, seismic changes
thrust their heads into the political landscape on which war and humanity interacted. In less than three years, starting in 1789, the French people overthrew the Bourbon monarchy and created a revolutionary
situation that altered the character of war. The French Revolution was
one of the two military-social revolutions that exploded in the last decades of the eighteenth century.

Those political and social changes precipitated a quarter-century of
great-power conflicts whose extent, scope, and casualties had no precedent

in human history. The French Revolution also altered the nature of the state and the relationship between state and citizen. Significantly, by representing the government as an expression of the popular will, it increased the willingness of the *populus* to contribute to war efforts. Moreover, these changes set the stage for the administrative and political frameworks that would exercise greater control over the state's citizenry in both war and peace. In effect, the French Revolution created the base on which the bureaucratic and institutional frameworks of the twentieth-century state would rest.

The revolution in France was also the cause of the great wars that broke over Europe in 1792. It was the revolutionaries in Paris who declared war on the *ancien régime*. The threat that the Prussian and Austrian monarchies intended to rescue their fellow monarch Louis XVI provided the revolutionaries with the excuse for war. The revolutionaries' eventual success, particularly in gaining control of the Low Countries, then presented the British with what they regarded as an existential threat to their security. So, Britain, with its growing economic strength, distrusted not only by the French but by its own allies on the Continent, would bring the great revolutionary experiment to a temporary end in 1815.

Although the regime it spawned was ultimately not democratic, the French Revolution was inspired by the democratic movement of the late eighteenth century.[2] The spirit of revolutionary France, with its emphasis on mobilizing popular will as well as the resources of the state, mutated in various forms to reemerge during the American Civil War, the Franco-Prussian War, and in the World Wars of the twentieth century. Moreover, the Jacobins' creation of effective bureaucratic institutions, further refined by Napoleon and responsive to direction from above, allowed the state to maximize popular enthusiasm. When enthusiasm was lacking, the modern state's mechanisms of control provided the *force majeure* required to regiment the citizenry.

While the French were in the midst of one military-social revolution, another was underway across the English Channel: the Industrial Revolution. The economic and productive transformations it initiated had an equally long-term impact on war. While it had little direct influence on the weaponry used on Europe's battlefields over the next quarter-century, the Industrial Revolution had an indirect impact. The economic and financial power it created, as well as its hardware, gave Britain the means to support the *anciens régimes* of Central and Eastern

Europe and to sustain their armies in the field. That economic power allowed the Royal Navy to blockade French coasts throughout the wars and control a growing global trade driven by the Industrial Revolution. Finally, it supported an impressive army on the Iberian Peninsula, which, with the help of Spanish guerrillas through a long and exhausting war, drove the French out of Spain.[3]

The French Revolution

There were a number of causes for the political explosions that resulted in the French Revolution.[4] The most obvious was the growth of France's population, which led to an increase in the number of rootless young men with few prospects.[5] It was not that economic growth had failed to keep pace; rather, it created rising expectations, which the *ancien régime* exacerbated, particularly with the privileges of the nobility. Finally, the ineffectual policies of Louis XVI and his failure to follow a consistent political line contributed to the revolution.

In the 1780s, the political landscape of France was ripe for revolution.[6] French leaders had gained a measure of revenge over the British for the humiliating outcome of the Seven Years' War by helping the Americans gain their independence. Yet France itself had gained little from that conflict except to add to the mountain of debt it had accumulated over the eighteenth century. Louis XIV's wars had cost 2 billion livres; the Seven Years' War, 1.2 billion livres; and supporting the American Revolution, another 1 billion.[7] By the late 1780s, France's finances were in desperate shape. Exacerbating financial difficulties was a taxation system that placed little burden on the nobility. To make matters worse, the nobility possessed rights and privileges that infuriated those who worked the land. It was not that France's population was badly off, at least compared to the serfs in Central and Eastern Europe. But the population's increasing literacy made the nobility's privileges hard to swallow and allowed revolutionary ideas to spread throughout society, particularly in the army.[8]

Economic factors and intellectual currents soon exacerbated an explosive situation. After a period of improving performance, the economy suffered a significant downturn immediately before the revolution. A disastrous harvest in 1788 reverberated in the cities with skyrocketing food prices. (Ironically, the price of bread reached its highest point on 14 July 1789, the day Parisian mobs stormed the Bastille.)[9] The failed harvest also caused a collapse of industry. Bread riots were already occurring in the cities, while the peasants carried out wholesale assaults on the castles and country homes of the nobles and burned the records of traditional obligations.

In 1789, Louis XVI convened the Estates General for the first time since 1614 in an effort to address both the unrest and the underlying financial crisis. It was a serious mistake. The Estates General—France's intermittent deliberative body, initially divided into three estates (the nobility, the clergy, and the commoners)—opened in early May 1789. Almost immediately, some in the assembly pushed forward a revolutionary agenda. The king and his ministers soon lost control of what was becoming a revolutionary situation. On 14 July, an urban mob in Paris, supported by soldiers, assaulted, seized, and then destroyed the Bastille, a symbol of royal authority. The rioters stabbed the fortress's commander to death and paraded his head on a pike.[10] The willingness of soldiers to participate was a clear sign the king could no longer rely on the army. In October, a crowd of over six thousand *sans-culottes* (the poor of Paris) marched to Versailles, overwhelmed the Royal Guards, and escorted Louis XVI, the queen, and the dauphin back to Paris to reside in the palace of the Tuileries. There, they were hostages to ever wilder political currents. In June 1791, the king sought to flee to the Austrian Netherlands to escape an increasingly dangerous situation. But militia caught the royal family and trundled them back to Paris. The result was twofold: the effort to escape showed that the king was no friend of the revolution, while it encouraged the further radicalization of French politics.

Equally important, it encouraged a half-hearted foreign intervention to restore Louis XVI's position. The three intervening powers—Austria, Prussia, and Russia—were not really focused on what was happening in France. At the time, they were busy dividing and eventually exterminating the kingdom of Poland.[11] Each deeply mistrusted their partners in crime and feared it would fail to gain its share of the Polish carcass. Only the Austrians seriously concerned themselves with the revolution, because the Austrian Netherlands shared a border with France. A quarter-century later, Clausewitz noted that "at the outbreak of the French Revolution . . . Austria and Prussia expected to find a seriously weakened French Army."[12] They thought they could restore the French monarchy with minimal force.

As for the danger the revolution represented to European peace, even the British had little sense of how explosive it was. Just weeks before Britain found itself again at war with France, William Pitt the Younger remarked that "there was never a time in the history of this country when, from the situation in Europe, we might more reasonably expect fifteen years of peace, than we may at the present moment."[13] Seven years later, justifying war to his critics, he would say, "We are not in arms against the opinions of the closet, nor the speculations of the school. We are at war with *armed* opinions."[14]

In April 1792, in response to threats from the continental powers, the French Assembly declared war on Austria and Prussia. Particularly enraging the revolutionaries in Paris was the promulgation of the Declaration of Pillnitz by the Austrian emperor and Prussian king, which demanded restoration of Louis XVI. Led by the Girondists, the radicals in the assembly, the French launched into a war with no clear strategic objectives except to protect the revolution from internal as well as external enemies. Undoubtedly, turmoil inside France fueled a desire for war. A leading Girondist declared, war was "indispensable for consummating the revolution."[15] Politically, such assumptions proved correct, but militarily they were disastrous. At the war's outset, revolutionary enthusiasm did not translate into military effectiveness.

But the Girondists did believe they were waging a new form of conflict. One of its leaders noted, "This is a war of Frenchman against Frenchman, brother against brother, combined with the war of prince against nation; it is a civil war combined with a foreign war. This is a war of the nobility against equality, a war of privileges against the common good, a war of the vices against public and private morality; of all tyrannies against liberties and against personal security."[16] For many, revolutionary France's victory over the *ancien régime* was a given: "With 400,000 slaves Louis XIV could defy all the powers of Europe: should we, with our millions of armed men, fear them?"[17]

With the flight of senior and midlevel officers, the army was in disarray. The first battles were a disaster. In their first encounter with the Austrians in April 1792, the troops ran away, shouting as they fled, "We are betrayed! Every man for himself!" They murdered their general on their way back into France.[18] Later engagements hardly indicated an improvement in the army. The appearance of Prussians on the frontier increased insecurities in Paris, particularly in the assembly, leading to the famous slogan "*Citoyens, la Patrie est en danger.*"[19] But revolutionary enthusiasm did little to repair weaknesses in weapons, tactics, or discipline. The revolutionaries had real cause for worry, because in late July the Duke of

Brunswick, leading the invading Prussian Army, underlined his intention to save the king and queen and, if they were harmed, to destroy Paris.

The movement of Prussian and Austrian troops into France only increased the panic. When news of Verdun's fall reached Paris in late July 1792, the "second revolution" began. As mobs stormed the Tuileries, the king fled to the assembly for protection while the revolutionaries, including national guardsmen, slaughtered his Swiss Guards. In early September, shortly after news reached the capital that the Prussians were advancing on Paris, the madness reached new heights. Mobs attacked the prisons and murdered nobles, recalcitrant priests, and common criminals as well as women and children, some tortured hideously. When the slaughter ended, over a thousand had died.[20] But the Prussian Army lacked the means to restore Louis and overthrow the revolution. On 20 September, Brunswick's forces turned away from French artillery at Valmy, ending the prospect of allied forces reaching Paris.[21] The allied army retreated into Belgium. Goethe, accompanying the Prussians, had the foresight to comment to his officer acquaintances: "At this place, on this day there has begun a new era in the history of the world; and all can claim to have been present at its birth."[22]

But in the fall, the French Army's initial military successes changed into defeats, largely because the government lacked the administrative capability to supply the troops. This only exacerbated revolutionary feelings. A formerly obscure lawyer named Maximilien Robespierre proved a master at manipulating the political situation to eliminate those he regarded as France's enemies, particularly in the assembly. He and his supporters exhibited a high degree of paranoia: as Thucydides wrote of an earlier revolution, "Any idea of moderation was just an attempt to disguise one's unmanly character; an ability to understand a question from all sides meant that one was totally unfit for action. Fanatical enthusiasm was the mark of a real man."[23] Robespierre summed up his cold-blooded political philosophy by noting, "If the mainspring of popular government in peacetime is virtue, amid revolution it is at once *virtue* and *terror*: virtue, without which terror is fatal; terror, without which virtue is impotent. ... It has been said that terror was the mainspring of despotic government. . . . Subdue liberty's enemies by terror, and you will be right, as founders of the Republic."[24]

Robespierre and his followers led the cry for the king to be executed for corresponding with the émigrés; Louis XVI was guillotined on 21 January 1793. Under great pressure from the deteriorating military situation and with the flow of volunteers drying up, the assembly introduced conscription in March 1793. That act, along with changes that minimized the position of the Catholic Church, which the revolutionaries had instituted, sparked an uprising in the Vendée on the western coast of France, threatening the republic's internal stability. The internal threat to the revolutionaries was now as dangerous as that posed by their external enemies. The reaction of those in Paris was savage. The town of Lyon received the revolution's full fury. Its representatives stood several hundred rebels before cannons and mowed them down with grapeshot. Over the carnage, they erected a placard that simply said, "Lyon made war against liberty; Lyon no longer exists."[25]

Events on the frontier failed to improve the army's performance. In March 1793, General Charles Dumouriez's army suffered two major defeats, first at Neerwinden and then at Louvain, which pushed the French out of Belgium. The penalty for generals who lost battles was the guillotine. After attempting and failing to persuade his army to march on Paris, Dumouriez fled to the Austrians, an action adding to paranoia in Paris.[26] Dumouriez had made an intelligent decision. In 1793, revolutionary tribunals ordered the execution of seventeen generals; the following year the number executed ballooned to sixty-seven.[27]

For the most part, those surrounding Robespierre were ferocious revolutionaries and nationalists. Louis de Saint-Just, one of Robespierre's most enthusiastic supporters, expressed Jacobin feelings best in demanding the heads of Georges Danton and other Girondists: "There is something terrifying in the sacred love of one's country. It is so all-exclusive that it sacrifices everything, without pity, without fear, without regard for humanity, to the public interest."[28] Another Jacobin urged "a call to the people to rise up *en masse*; only the people can annihilate so many enemies; only the people can secure the triumph of freedom. . . . It is necessary that in our hands the aristocracy become the instrument of its own destruction."[29]

Defeats on the frontier found their echo in uprisings at home—a clear warning of the regime's weakening political and social control. There were particularly virulent rebellions in the south throughout the Loire Valley. In early summer, royalists seized Toulon and turned the French naval base and its ships over to the Royal Navy. With the republic teetering on collapse, those in charge took more extreme measures. In April 1793, the National Convention, now under the control of the Jacobins, established the Committee of Public Safety. Dumouriez's flight provided ammunition for the Jacobins to attack and then guillotine the Girondists. Increasing terror brought the internal situation under control, while the Committee of Public Safety possessed sufficiently ruthless and competent individuals to mobilize the nation's resources.

On the military side, the key figure was Lazare Carnot, who had served with distinction in the prewar army and possessed extensive administrative skills. For his efforts, he eventually received the soubriquet "Organizer of Victory." Given the difficulties in supplying the front, Carnot pushed for the armies to live off the territories they conquered. As he commented, "War must pay for war."[30] In the end, these efforts created the armies Napoleon used. There was, however, a political downside to Carnot's logistics. The revolution's motto, "liberty, fraternity, equality," hardly resonated in foreign countries as French foragers ravaged the landscape.

In August 1793, with the foreign threat looming, the Committee of Public Safety drew up and the assembly issued the decree for the *levée en masse*, a universal draft. "From this moment until the enemy has been chased from the territory of the Republic," the order read, "all the French are in permanent requisition for the services of the armies. Young men will go to battle; married men will forge arms and transport supplies; women will make tents, uniforms and serve in the hospitals; children will pick rags; old men will have themselves carried to public squares, to inspire the courage of warriors, and preach hatred of kings and the unity of the Republic."[31] The Committee of Public Safety took measures to discipline civil society as well. It decreed that "coalitions or meetings of any kind are forbidden. . . . In no case are workers allowed to meet in order to express their complaints; meetings are to be dispersed, instigators and ringleaders will be arrested and punished according to the law."[32]

The revolution was already in the process of creating the first modern authoritarian state. One historian writes that "the new politics abolished, along with the society of orders, all theoretical limits on the state's actions. Individual lives and property were now unconditionally at the nation's service. Pervasive police surveillance, persecution, and extermination of real and imagined enemies on a scale and with a brutality unseen again in Europe until 1917–45, and quasi-universal military service became the order of the day."[33] As Marshal Jean-Baptiste Jourdan's conscription law of 1798 proclaimed, "Any Frenchman is a soldier and owes himself to the defense of the nation."[34]

The crucial point is that the revolution influenced history in two important ways. On one side would be the revolutionary tradition that inspired movements as disparate as Hitler's Third Reich and the Russian and Chinese revolutionaries. But equally important was the bureaucratic state control that increasingly characterized national entities. For all the eloquence of the *levée en masse*, it was its bureaucratic infrastructure that imposed the nation's will. That process began under the Committee of Public Safety, and Napoleon's empire would further solidify the system. From there it would migrate across Europe over the course of the nineteenth century.

The *levée* was only a reflection of attitudes throughout the threatened areas of France. Even before Paris promulgated it, authorities in the north declared a levy of their own: "A war of tactics will not suffice to drive off our enemies; it is necessary for all citizens capable of bearing arms . . . to rise in mass to crush them."[35] Driven by a combination of fanaticism and administrative competence, the results were extraordinary. Initially, the *levée en masse* provided approximately 300,000 men to reinforce the army. Within a year, the French had a million soldiers on army rolls, of whom some 750,000 were in the field.[36] The army's unprecedented expansion triggered a restructuring of the officer corps. Rapid promotion of junior officers and NCOs now became the order of the day; the only criteria were ruthlessness and competence on the battlefield. By 1794, 49 percent of the officer corps had not even been in the army in 1789. There was no choice but to promote those who could handle the challenges of war.[37]

The *levée* also had a major influence on the production of French armaments. The economy now served the state, and the state demanded that the armories of France extend themselves as never before. The factories at St. Etienne, which had produced between 10,000 and 26,000 muskets per year before the revolution, raised their numbers to 56,600 per year from 1794 to 1796.[38] Production of cannons and pistols was equally impressive. In 1789, the army had possessed 1,300 field pieces. Six years later that number had risen to 2,550.[39] One member of the committee to increase arms production later commented that "to get men, we called out everyone who, no matter what his trade, knew how to work iron, and we gave them models of the Charleville musket to work with. There were no pattern makers so we drafted sculptors and cabinet makers. . . . We needed guns, and we got them, finally, almost 750 a day."[40]

Most impressive was the dramatic increase in the field armies. In his classic *On War*, Clausewitz summed up the results: "In 1793 a force appeared that beggared all imagination. Suddenly war again became the business of the people—a people of thirty millions, all of whom considered themselves citizens. . . . The people became a participant in war; instead of governments and armies as heretofore, the full weight of the nation was thrown into the balance. The resources and efforts now available for use surpassed all conventional limits; nothing now impeded the vigor with which war could be waged, and consequently the opponents of France faced the utmost peril."[41] To ensure competence as well as political reliability, the Committee of Public Safety sent political operatives as "Representatives on Mission," the eighteenth century's equivalent of commissars, to ensure the generals' loyalty.

In this unprecedented mobilization, one sees the willingness of a Western state to adapt and innovate. The French established a particularly effective method of integrating volunteers and conscripts into the army: they combined two battalions of volunteers with one line battalion to create demi-brigades.[42] The army did not separate volunteers from line soldiers but rather integrated them. By so doing, it ensured the transfer of battlefield experience to the volunteers and conscripts flowing into the army. At first these new units were not particularly well-trained by the standards of the *ancien régime*, but they made up for deficiencies through numbers and responsiveness to innovative tactics that took advantage of the soldiers' enthusiasm and commitment. Unburdened by the traditions of the *ancien régime*, the French experimented. They began to win victories, but sometimes victory was not enough. In September 1793, General Jean-Nicolas Houchard defeated the Austrians at the Battle of Hondschoote and broke the siege of Dunkirk. Yet two months later he found himself condemned to the guillotine because he had failed to pursue the defeated enemy with sufficient vigor.[43] By fall 1793, the influx of new soldiers had reversed the war's course.[44]

By summer 1794, the French had driven the Austrians out of modern Belgium. In early 1795, Holland fell, and French cavalry actually captured fourteen Dutch ships of the line, frozen in place by a harsh winter.[45] It was not Republican enthusiasm or tactical brilliance that provided French armies with their success. It was the fact that the new armies, although relatively untrained, could absorb casualties the armies of the *ancien régime* could not. Attrition had less impact on the French than on their opponents because the French had a vast pool of willing volunteers to replace those who fell. The combination of idealism, innovative operational and tactical concepts, and a willingness to take losses rendered French armies deadly on the battlefield.

They also learned on the fly. The large numbers of inexperienced soldiers required tactical innovations. French generals were able to utilize clouds of skirmishers in front of their main units to cover maneuvers and disrupt the enemy. The soldiers in the new model army ensured that few skirmishers deserted, while the looser control their officers exercised provided opportunities for even the enlisted to display initiative. The new armies possessed the manpower to accept the heavier casualties that skirmishing formations caused. Moreover, greater manpower allowed French generals to launch troops in column formations, which, while they took heavy losses, often broke enemy linear formations, particularly if artillery furnished sufficient softening up.[46] Column formations provided inexperienced soldiers with the psychological support of group dynamics not available in linear formations. Throughout the revolution's early years, French tactics proved a work in progress, an adaptation to war's ever-changing character.

In terms of weapons technology, the eighteenth century had seen considerable improvement in the manufacture of artillery. In midcentury the Dutch began drilling out the bores of their cannons. The results were guns with improved tolerances, weighing less, and possessing greater accuracy, an important advantage for Bonaparte, a master of artillery. Equally important were the reforms occurring immediately before the revolution. In the 1760s, influenced by the French Army's wretched performance in the Seven Years' War, General Count Jean Baptiste de Gribeauval took the changes in technology and married them to a reformation of French artillery. First, he standardized the caliber of artillery pieces, which simplified the provision of ammunition on campaign and thus improved logistics. Second, he had the traces, carriages, and caissons lightened by approximately 50 percent and also had them standardized, which made replacement and repair easier. Finally, the French introduced prepackaged rounds, wrapped in serge bags along with shot and powder, thus increasing speed of firing.[47] By the 1770s, the army had institutionalized these reforms.

The second major reform after the Seven Years' War was to create all-arms divisions of approximately eight to ten thousand men. By training these independent branches together, the French created a more mobile and effective force—one, moreover, that was able to act independently. It added to French commanders' flexibility on the battlefield, both in speed of deployment and rapidity of fire. Napoleon would combine these divisions into corps of two to four divisions, creating mini armies capable of acting even more autonomously, which could combine rapidly into the main army when necessary. These new formations enabled the French to spread their armies over greater territory, useful in foraging, and also allowed them to gain a sense of the enemy's deployments while shielding their own movements. These organizational reforms represented a revolution in military affairs because they permitted the control and deployment of larger armies.

Armed with the *levée en masse* and conscription, French armies defeated the armies of the *ancien régime* by their numbers as well as by their tactics. The revolution had endowed the new French state with powers far exceeding those of the *ancien régime*, allowing it to survive and then provide the future emperor with the means to conquer much of Europe. From 1800 to 1815, conscription provided Napoleon with 2 million new soldiers to replace those lost in his murderous battles.[48] Yet even the number provided by conscription was insufficient to make up for the army's steady attrition. By summer 1795, the number of soldiers on the rolls had declined from 750,000 to 480,000; a year later it had dropped to 400,000. But even 400,000 soldiers represented a greater total than Louis XIV's army at its height.[49]

The French also enjoyed another advantage: the enemies of the republic, still believing the division of Poland was more important than the rising danger of France, failed to focus on the real threat. Each power jealously watched to ensure it received its fair share while suppressing the desperate efforts of Polish nationalists to rebel. Prussia, moreover, had little interest in cooperating with Austria against the French because it was more interested in intra-German squabbles.[50] After 1795, the Prussians dropped out of the wars against France.

Meanwhile, Robespierre and his Jacobin supporters had taken the revolution to bloodier heights. Approximately 20,000 French citizens died during the Great Terror of 1793 and 1794. At its height, in summer 1794, some 1,300 Parisians found themselves trundled off to the guillotine. By that point, military efforts at home and abroad had achieved considerable success. The key French victory came on 26 June, when General Jean-Baptiste Jourdan crushed a coalition army of British, Dutch, and Austrians at Fleurus. In effect, this victory meant that the rationale for the Terror had disappeared. One month later came the reaction against the Jacobins. By this point, Robespierre had lost all caution. On 26 July (8 Thermidor), the former lawyer gave a long and rambling speech, stressing that *he* was "a slave of freedom, a living martyr to the Republic," and making clear who his enemies were.[51] However, instead of moving against them, he threatened them without mobilizing his supporters. Those threatened got the message that Robespierre and his followers were a direct threat to their lives.

Lazare Carnot had been a friend of Robespierre before the war, and while the republic was in danger, the two worked closely together. But when the danger receded, Carnot rejected Robespierre's radicalism. He and two other key members of the Committee of Public Safety, Paul Barras and Joseph Fouché, knew Robespierre was ready to send them to the guillotine.[52] They were ruthless men, less murderous than Robespierre and Saint-Just, but more willing to act.[53] They struck first. On 29 July, Robespierre and his fellow Jacobins went to the guillotine. Some seventy of those implicated as Robespierre's associates joined him.

The survivors, in what became known as the Thermidorian Reaction, found themselves in a highly uncomfortable position. Beside Robespierre's surviving supporters, there were the *sans-culottes* and other dispossessed. Those who seized power following Robespierre's fall, taking the title of the Directory, seem to have been motivated solely by the desire to remain in power. They tried to ensure that goal by promulgating the Constitution of the Year III, which maintained their control, but found themselves threatened by twenty thousand National Guardsmen and the *communes*. They appointed Paul Barras, one of the Directory, to protect the assembly.

Only five thousand loyal troops stood between the Directory and either slaughter or the guillotine. Barras, having no military background, turned to an obscure brigadier general named Napoleon Bonaparte, temporarily unemployed in Paris. Bonaparte responded with the ruthlessness of the revolutionaries. He sent a certain Captain Joachim Murat, soon his cavalry commander, to bring an artillery park to the Tuileries, where the assembly was meeting. Bonaparte deployed the guns, armed with grapeshot, to meet the crowds. His artillery fired on the mob at point-blank range in what he later described as "a whiff of grapeshot." In fact, it involved an hour-long battle. When the smoke cleared, two hundred were dead and more than four hundred wounded. Bonaparte's own losses were not light: thirty dead and sixty wounded.[54] Nevertheless, the young general's ruthlessness saved the Directory, and his way to the top was clear through his actions in suppressing the mob. With his political connections, and helped by his lover, Barras's former mistress Josephine de Beauharnais, Bonaparte received command of the broken-down Army of Italy, which to that point had done little to distinguish itself.

Napoleon Bonaparte proved to be one of the wild cards of history. He was a man of genius who jettisoned contemporary preconceptions and turned history in a fundamentally different direction. Unlike the dictators of the twentieth century—Lenin, Stalin, Hitler, and Mao—he left behind positive contributions to his country and the world. His foremost military biographer puts his persona in perspective: "We must enumerate the almost unbelievable range and sheer power of Napoleon's intellectual capabilities. . . . Here was no narrow-minded professional soldier—his interests were legion. His mind was rarely at a loss for a new idea no matter what the subject, and he possessed to a very marked degree the ability of seeing every aspect of a problem without slipping into the danger of failing to 'see the wood for the trees.' "[55] Yet one ingredient of that genius was a willingness to do the morally unthinkable.

The Army of Italy was not only the weakest of the French armies but the least important strategically. The Directory did not expect much. Bonaparte, however, saw the possibilities, and taking command in March 1796, he began one of the great campaigns of military history. The overall plan was for the main French armies to advance on Vienna: those of Jean Victor Marie Moreau and Jourdan across the Rhine and down the Danube, while Bonaparte kept the Austrians occupied in Italy. In early April, after crossing the Alps into Italy from southern France, Bonaparte won a series of sharp victories over the Austrians and Piedmontese.[56] More importantly, he separated the enemy armies and then crushed the Piedmontese, who agreed to a peace ceding Nice and Savoy to France. Bonaparte then pursued the Austrians and besieged them in Mantua. Before the city fell, he faced a relieving army whose commander cooperated by dividing his forces. To defeat the relieving force in detail, Bonaparte had to break off the siege. The Austrians resupplied Mantua's garrison, which he proceeded to besiege again.

Meanwhile, French generals north of the Alps had defeated the Austrians at Neresheim and Friedberg but soon found themselves driven back to the west bank of the Rhine. Only in Italy had the French made progress. Faced with another large relieving force, Napoleon displayed his extraordinary qualities. He outmaneuvered his Austrian opponents and broke them with the speed and ruthlessness of his moves. As Austria's position in Italy deteriorated, Napoleon exploited his victories. In March 1797, the Army of Italy defeated Archduke Charles at the Battle of Tarvis and advanced to within sixty miles of Vienna, forcing the Austrians to sue for peace. After protracted negotiations they signed the Treaty of Campo Formio, which ended William Pitt's First Coalition, the initial alliance to contain the French.[57] Bonaparte returned to Paris a hero.

But the peace applied only on the Continent. As long as the British remained at war, their money and resistance to French expansion threatened to encourage the major continental powers to resume the struggle. The Directory initially ordered Bonaparte to explore invading the British Isles, but he concluded such an attempt would fail until France possessed a navy to contest the English Channel. He suggested a strike at Egypt instead, a venture inspired both by romantic dreams of replicating the campaigns of Alexander the Great and the hope of disrupting British trade with the Orient. In mid-May, Bonaparte's force sailed from Toulon and other ports along France's southern coast. The army numbered some 35,000 men and 1,200 horses. But following in the fleet's wake was Horatio Nelson.

Instead of sailing directly to Alexandria, the French stopped at Malta and then Crete. The diversion to Crete distracted Nelson: the British sailed for Alexandria but finding no French ships, returned to the central Mediterranean. Within two hours after the last British ship departed Alexandria, Bonaparte, his transports, and the French fleet arrived. The French Army quickly destroyed the Mameluke forces, which had controlled Egypt for centuries. Nelson, however, proved himself a master of the sea; he returned to Alexandria on 1 August 1798. The Battle of Aboukir Bay wiped out the French fleet, the British sinking or capturing eleven ships of the line and two frigates.[58] Bonaparte and his army found themselves isolated in Egypt.

While Bonaparte was attempting to solidify French control of Egypt and invading Syria, France's strategic position in Europe collapsed. The Directory's high-handed diplomacy had allowed the British to form another anti-French alliance, this one including Russia and Austria. French generals proved no more competent than the Directory's diplomats. By June 1799, the French had lost most of Italy, while matters went little better in Germany. General Jourdan received the nickname of "the anvil because he was always being hammered."[59] Nevertheless, Jourdan would play a crucial role in Napoleon's success. In September 1798, he

persuaded the Directory to pass a law introducing "universal and obliga-
tory conscription" for all men between the ages of twenty and twenty-
five. This gave the Directory the manpower it needed to keep the war
going.[60]

Bonaparte, having abandoned his troops in Egypt, arrived back in
Paris in October 1799 to find the city seething with discontent. In the
maelstrom of plots, he and his allies seized power in the *coup d'ètat de
Brumaire* on 9 and 10 November 1799. The most significant factor in
Napoleon's seizure of power was the army's dissatisfaction with the Directory. Most soldiers believed in the ideals of the republic, and the Directory's corruption hardly inspired their loyalty. Ironically, Napoleon's
pretext for overthrowing the Directory was his claim that he could bring
peace.

The Industrial Revolution

During the great war against France of 1792–1815, Britain supported an
extraordinary effort to bring its opponent down. The Royal Navy's
blockade bottled the French up on the Continent, controlled the world's
oceans, and protected British commerce from raiders. Britain also committed its armies to the Continent, where they were largely unsuccessful
until the Duke of Wellington took control of the war on the Iberian
Peninsula, beginning in Portugal and eventually reaching into Spain. Finally, the British provided major financial support in subsidies and military equipment to sustain their allies, who confronted Napoleon on the
Continent.[61]

The reasons for British animosity toward the French, and vice versa,
are not hard to fathom: the two powers had a fundamental clash of strategic interests. Since the time of Queen Elizabeth, English and then
British security had rested on a strategy of preventing any major power
from controlling the Low Countries; Elizabeth had risked the fury of
Philip II of Spain to aid the Dutch rebellion against Spanish rule in the
Netherlands, while supporting pirating raids against Spanish commerce
in the Caribbean. In both the Nine Years' War and the War of the Spanish Succession, Britain had involved itself financially and militarily in exhausting the power of Louis XIV so as to prevent French expansion in
the Low Countries. For France, meanwhile, the greatest threats to its
territory had always come through the Low Countries, and it had long
sought to improve its security by controlling this region at least to the

Rhine. Each side's efforts inevitably threatened the other's security. What bears explaining is why Britain, after fighting the French to a standoff for centuries, was ultimately able to prevail.

The factor allowing the British to play a crucial role in the wars that eventually defeated France was the immense financial and material support Britain provided to its allies. Admittedly financial and direct military aid had played a role in previous conflicts in the eighteenth century, but the period 1793 to 1815 was qualitatively different, because Britain was undergoing an economic transformation, now termed the first Industrial Revolution. In effect it was undergoing a military-social revolution as significant as the French Revolution. And that revolution provided Britain with the money to fund all the coalitions that tried to, and eventually did, end the French experiment. One historian calculates the British contribution as "between 1793 and 1815 Britain poured out her treasure in an increasing flow of aid to her allies. By the end of the war, she had given them £65,830,228." Almost half of this was spent over the last five years of the war, and in 1815 more than thirty European powers, great and small, shared Britain's bounty.[62]

But the British supported their allies with more than just financial aid. In November 1813, Viscount Castlereagh informed the House of Commons that over the year, Britain had shipped nearly 1 million muskets to its allies on the peninsula and in northern Europe to support the war against Napoleon.[63] Castlereagh may have exaggerated, but the shipments of muskets and ammunition represented an impressive effort. The number of cannons and mortars Britain provided reached into the hundreds, if not thousands, along with the ammunition and accoutrements such weapons required. The shipments of British weapons and munitions underlined Britain's role in breaking Napoleon's power. The Prussians and Russians each received over 100,000 muskets, while the Russians received an additional 116 artillery pieces, along with 1,200 tons of ammunition. At the same time, the British also shipped 40,000 muskets to the Swedes to support their participation in the war.

One shipment to Straslund, a major depot for moving British arms to the Continent, in August 1813 contained 2,000 barrels of powder, 5 million cartridges, and 20,000 muskets along with other supporting items meant for the Prussian Army.[64] Significantly, the British provided these goods at the same time they were supporting Wellington's Peninsula Army and its allies, the Portuguese. The size of the Prussian Army suggests the shipment's importance: at the time it consisted of 228,000 infantry, 31,100 cavalry, and 13,000 gunners.[65] The material aid was necessary because, following the Battle of Jena-Auerstedt in October 1806, Napoleon had absorbed Prussia into the French Empire and stripped its army of virtually all its armaments. The resupply helped restore the nation's independence as part of the Sixth Coalition. The quantity of small arms the British produced between 1795 and 1815, 3,212,000, underlined their importance as an arms supplier. In 1814, there were almost three-quarters of a million muskets in British warehouses.[66]

Napoleon reputedly called the English "a nation of shopkeepers." At the time, however, Britain was a nation of entrepreneurs busy creating the Industrial Revolution. While the French were attempting to bring Europe under their control, the British economy was beginning an economic expansion never before seen. The upsurge in that economy, beginning in the 1770s, supplied the financial and economic power that eventually broke France.[67]

While expansion of British trade and manufacturing was obviously crucial to Napoleon's defeat, the ability of the Bank of England to finance the allied coalitions was just as important. Pitt's reformation of the tax system in the 1790s also added to British strength. The income tax ensured that those profiting from the economy supported the war effort. In 1797, 37 percent of the government's income came from taxes and 63 percent from borrowing in one form or another. By remodeling "the whole fiscal system, [Pitt] succeeded in making Britain's economic successes pay for her military trials."[68]

Undergirding British finances was the Industrial Revolution. For the first time, humanity engaged forces other than muscle, water, or wind power to drive its productive processes. In this case, coal drove the machinery that powered the extraordinary changes. An entrepreneurial spirit also provided imagination and support. *The Cambridge Economic History of Europe* notes, "The abundance and variety of these innovations that drove the Industrial Revolution almost defy compilation, but they may be subsumed under [several] principles: the substitution of machines ... for human skill and effort; the substitution of inanimate for animate sources of power, in particular, the introduction of engines for converting heat into work, thereby opening to man a new and almost unlimited supply of energy."[69]

The Industrial Revolution not only provided economic and financial support for the war against the French; it also picked up speed during the quarter-century of the French Wars. The surest indication of its impact lies in the increase in British per capita income. Between 1700 and 1750, per capita income in Britain increased at a rate of 0.3 percent per year; from 1750 to 1800, it increased almost four times faster, and between 1800 and 1831 it reached 1.5 percent per year. Overall, the share of GDP coming from manufacturing rose from 20 percent in 1770 to 25 percent in 1812.[70] The motor that drove this growth was trade. Between 1781 and 1801, total imports into Britain increased by more than 150 percent, domestic imports by 186 percent, and reexports by 244 percent.[71]

The financial system also provided stability. Creation of the Bank of England in 1694 stands in stark contrast to the French failure to establish such a bank until 1804. The British financial system's coherence not only enabled the British to support the war but also provided capital for investments in the first stages of the Industrial Revolution. Inventors and entrepreneurs found it relatively easy to obtain the financing required to set their projects in motion.[72]

A number of factors came together in eighteenth-century Britain to fuel the expansion of the economy. The first—crucial to preventing unrest in an expanding population—was a slow but significant increase in food production.[73] Innovations in farming reached a peak between 1751 and 1814. But equally important were enclosures of agricultural land, converting large tracts from common to private use. Enclosure was never popular with rural populations, who had traditionally grazed their cattle and sheep on common lands, but it increased yields. In 1830, Britain had no more agricultural workers than it had in 1750, but they were feeding a population twice as large. The increase in productivity freed up workers for Britain's factories and mills.[74]

The expansion of the canal network and improvement of roads throughout northern England also aided economic expansion.[75] In 1750, there were approximately a thousand miles of navigable waterways in Britain, but from that point the pace of canal building accelerated.[76] The most significant canals were built in 1757 and 1761 to carry coal, which was so heavy that only water could transport it. Between 1750 and 1850, canal mileage grew from 1,000 miles to 4,250, most concentrated in the Midlands, eventually the industrial heart of England. That British coal production exceeded that of the French by a factor of twenty in 1800 suggests the canals' significance. By that year, coal use in Britain was one ton per person per year, twice as much as in 1700 with a far larger population.[77]

In addition to efficient water transport, the British also enjoyed an advantage in the labor force. There appears to have been greater technical skill among British workers as well as a wider interest in machines than on the Continent. Pushing that interest was the willingness of firms to recruit and train a workforce from outside the location of their factories. Combined with a lack of farm jobs because of increased agricultural productivity, this recruitment made for a more mobile labor force than on the Continent. By the century's turn, industrial concerns in Lancashire were drawing craftsmen as far away as London.[78]

Coal, iron, and cotton drove the first Industrial Revolution. In the early eighteenth century, Abraham Darby developed a new method of smelting iron using coke, but the process was not widely used until the century's midpoint. When combined with "puddling" and rolling processes, it allowed iron mongers to produce iron in shapes useful for constructing bridges. But the war effort also drove increased iron production. In 1788, total pig iron production had been approximately 70,000 tons, 20 percent from obsolete charcoal furnaces. Eighteen years later, in 1806, there were 162 coke furnaces with only 11 remaining charcoal furnaces. The total tonnage of iron produced had risen by 350 percent to over 260,000 tons.[79] In 1750, Britain had imported twice as much pig iron as it produced; by 1814, British exports of pig iron were five times greater than its imports.[80] Rising production of ever-cheaper iron and eventually steel facilitated every sort of industry and eventually allowed the creation of the next transformative technology, railroads.[81]

Superior iron production, along with better boring techniques, created more accurate cylinders. These were important for the steam engine and had military applications as well. They added a new weapon to the Royal Navy, the carronade or short naval cannon, and made traditional cannons more accurate. Increased iron production allowed British arsenals to turn out vast numbers of muskets and cannons. British cotton and wool mills equipped substantial portions of the allied armies with clothing as well.

The development that brought coal, iron, and cotton together was James Watt's improved steam engine in the 1770s. In 1776, James Boswell, the Scottish diarist, visited the factory producing steam engines and was shown around by Watt's partner, Matthew Boulton. "I wished [Samuel] Johnson had been with us," Boswell wrote. "The vastness and contrivance of some of the machinery would have 'matched his mighty mind.' I shall never forget Mr. Bolton's expression to me, 'I sell, Sir, what all the world desires to have—power.' He had about seven hundred people at work."[82] The Boulton-Watt partnership produced a more effective steam engine than its predecessors. Watt claimed in his memoirs that he had aimed "upon making engines *cheap* as well as *good*." Here the creation of successful boring machines by John Wilkinson was a key factor in providing the tolerances for the cylinders and their sleeves that made Watt's engine possible. By the end of the eighteenth century, British entrepreneurs had produced 2,500 engines in Britain, 30 percent of them by Boulton and Watt.[83]

Wilkinson had patented his machine for boring iron blocks, with the aim of making cannons, in 1774. Within two years he had joined Boulton and Watt to produce cylinders of much higher tolerances. This was effectively the first step toward producing machine tools. As economic historian Joel Mokyr has pointed out, "With the production of machines by machines ... it [became] possible to use iron and steel as the material whenever it appeared functional to do so."[84] The first steam engines went where there was an existing market, namely to pump water from mines.[85] Yet it was soon apparent that they had other applications, particularly in the making of cloth. Here the 1780s represented the key decade. By then the breakthroughs in industrialized production of cloth were in place.[86] For making cotton an ever more accessible and productive raw material, all that was needed was Eli Whitney's invention of the cotton gin, in 1793.

The use of steam to supply power to spinning jennies and water frames allowed British industry to produce cotton cloth in unheard-of amounts. The result was a higher quality cloth, cheaper and more durable than that produced by hand-spinning. It drove the price of cloth steadily downward, which in turn drove obsolete competitors out. The violent response of the now unemployed handweavers gave us the term "luddite." The sudden appearance of textile factories inspired William Blake's famous phrase "these dark Satanic Mills." But those mills, by concentrating resources and labor, greatly increased production. Under the old system it took about fifty thousand hours to spin one hundred pounds of cotton. By the 1790s, that amount could be spun in just three hundred hours.[87] The result was the extraordinary expansion of cloth production from less than 1 million pounds in 1730 to 100 million by 1815. Between 1780 and 1850, the price of cloth fell by 85 percent.[88] In 1760, the British had imported 2.5 million pounds of raw cotton; a quarter of a century later that total had grown to 22 million pounds.[89] Yet what was now produced, using steam- and water-driven machinery and far less labor, had a much higher profit margin.

Napoleon's efforts to block British goods from the Continent with the Berlin Decrees had a relatively brief effect on British trade, mainly from 1807 to 1812, when the French forced their conquests to abide by the continental system, which imposed an embargo on British goods. Nevertheless, leakages were too many and varied to shut down British trade entirely. Smuggling increased every year, and French authorities found it impossible to halt the flow. Moreover, Napoleon found himself under considerable pressure to allow the export of foodstuffs to Britain, since his farmers depended on those sales. The totals for British exports from 1805 to 1811 show the futility of Napoleon's attempt to strangle the British economy: 1805, £48.5 million; 1806, £40.8 million; 1808, £35.2 million; 1810, £61 million; and 1811, £39.5 million. Ironically, Napoleon's invasion of Spain in 1808 opened Spain's American colonies to British trade, nearly doubling Britain's exports there.[90] Elsewhere on the Continent, French authorities ruthlessly enforced import regulations by seizing and destroying British goods. But this went on for only three years (from mid-1807 to mid-1808 and mid-1810 to mid-1812), and Napoleon never imposed the same hardships on France that he imposed on those he conquered. The trade war led to economic collapse in the occupied countries, which in turn fueled anti-French feeling. As Metternich noted, "This mass of ordinances and decrees which will ruin the position of the merchants throughout the Continent will help the English more than it harms them."[91]

Undergirding Britain's expanding economy, and an intimate part of it, was the steady growth in merchant shipping. In 1761, Britain's merchant marine had a cargo capacity of 460,000 tons; by 1788, it had grown to nearly 600,000 tons, and by 1800 to 1,656,000 tons.[92] Here the quarter-century of wars between Britain and France played an important role. The British blockade of French ports as well as those of the Low Countries closed off Britain's commercial rivals from an expanding global trade, so the products of the Industrial Revolution ended up being carried in British-flagged ships. Moreover, significant improvements in merchant ship design lowered crew requirements while increasing profits.[93] The port of London, which carried at least half of the ships arriving and leaving British ports, recorded approximately thirteen thousand arrivals and departures every year during the wars with France. Between 1792 and 1800, the value of British commerce rose from £44,500,000 to £73,700,000, an annual increase of 7 percent.[94] This created plenty of targets for French raiders. The Admiralty took a number of measures to meet the threat, the most effective of which was a global system of convoys, in which up to eight hundred merchant vessels all sailed together.[95]

The support structure undergirding the Royal Navy underlined its importance to the economy. After the Seven Years' War, the navy had spent approximately £680,000 on upgrades and improvements on its two greatest dockyards at Plymouth and Portsmouth. The requisitions that the Royal Navy made throughout the war demonstrated the extent of its logistical effort. Over six months in the early 1800s, the 36,000 sailors of the Channel Fleet consumed "2,925 tons of biscuit, 1,671 tons of beef, 835 tons of pork, 626 tons of pease, 313 tons of oatmeal, 156 tons of butter, 313 tons of cheese, and 32 tuns of beer." In 1765, constructing a first-rate ship of the line like the 100-gun *Victory* cost the British taxpayer £63,174, while in 1800 the fixed value of the 243 woolen mills in West Riding was estimated at £402,651. Nelson, with his fleet off Sicily, ordered 30,000 gallons of lemon juice, a purchase that underlined the Royal Navy's recognition of the scurvy problem.[96] By 1795, the Admiralty had finally recognized that issuing lemon juice would cure scurvy.[97] In fact, the healthiest place in early nineteenth-century Europe was on a Royal Navy ship blockading French ports.

The military as a whole was one of the most important contributors to the Industrial Revolution in Britain. The explosion in public expenditures, from £22 million in 1792 to £123 million in 1814, suggests the extent of the war effort.[98] It represented significant deficit spending. Underlining the economic effort was the fact that excise taxes rose from £13.57 million in 1793 to £44.89 million in 1815.[99] For the most part, economic historians have minimized the importance of the wars to the explosive growth of the British economy.[100] Yet the £65.8 million the government dispersed to its allies provided a major boost to the economy: the allies spent those funds on equipment, clothing, and weapons to outfit and support their armies. The acquisition of cannons, muskets, and other weapons were particularly important to the growth of pig iron production. Similarly, the navy and army required a considerable tonnage of iron for weapons. Investments in blast furnaces reflected the fact that the ongoing wars guaranteed a ready market in the military sector. These investments would facilitate the construction of railroads and steamships in the 1820s and 1830s.[101]

The Napoleonic Adventure

Having overthrown the Directory, Napoleon confronted the problem of achieving peace by driving the Austrians and their British supporters out of the war.[102] He made the first step by defeating an Austrian army at Marengo in June 1800. But it took a second victory, at Hohenlinden in December 1800, to force the Austrians to make peace. In March 1802, tired of the war, the British agreed to the Peace of Amiens, which had no chance of surviving. Not only was French control of the Low Countries antithetical to British strategic interests but Napoleon instituted harsh tariffs that undermined the political position of those in Britain who hoped peace would bring economic opportunities. The peace was scuttled by his ambitions. According to historian Felix Markham, "It is impossible to say if the task was beyond his genius; it was certainly beyond the capacity of his character."[103]

Fourteen months after signing the peace, the British withdrew their ambassador from Paris. Two years after resumption of hostilities, Napoleon completed his reformation of France and prepared to launch an invasion of Britain.[104] Peace on the Continent allowed Napoleon to train his troops rigorously into what eventually became the Grand Army, the finest army he ever led. Among Napoleon's military reforms was the amalgamation of divisions into corps, which provided the army with greater flexibility. The Grand Army consisted of seven corps, each with between two and four divisions, a cavalry and artillery reserve, and the imperial guard.[105] This force and an array of barges spent the summer of 1805 concentrated around Boulogne, waiting for the French fleet to arrive. By August it was apparent the fleet would not appear. It was on its way to the Battle of Trafalgar, where it met Napoleon's naval nemesis, Horatio Nelson.[106]

There is an interesting contrast between how the British paid for war—taxes and loans spun off by economic growth from the Industrial Revolution—and how Napoleon did. One of the factors that drove the emperor to seek a quick victory over his opponents in 1805 was France's serious financial difficulties.[107] After his victory at Austerlitz and achievement of French control of Central Europe from 1806 to 1813, the empire was kept afloat by reparations from the defeated, indemnities from nations that had lost a major war and were now occupied, and contributions from allies. From 1804 to 1814, extractions, indemnities, and contributions from the allies and defeated paid half of Napoleon's military expenditures.[108]

The "Third Coalition" of 1805 had emerged over the previous three years among the British and the reluctant Austrians and Russians.[109] The latter two had concluded they had no choice but to oppose the insatiable demands and actions of the newly crowned French emperor. In May 1805, after innumerable arguments, Britain, Austria, and Russia agreed to put nearly half a million troops in the field.[110] Yet throughout the negotiations, the Russians had been unwilling to commit their forces to a campaign in central Europe. As historian Paul W. Schroeder noted, "Only Napoleon could have saved the Anglo-Russian alliance, and he obliged. By his actions, he insured that the young Russian monarch, Alexander I, found himself driven to support the British and Austrians."[111]

Confronting a gathering storm, and with his fleet nowhere in sight, on 24 August Napoleon ordered the Grand Army to march east against his enemies. In its greatest campaign five French corps swept into Germany to catch a forward deployed Austrian Army near Ulm and trap the "unfortunate General Mack" and his troops in mid-October 1805. The French juggernaut then chased a Russian army down the Danube to capture Vienna. It finally caught up with the Austrians and Russians deep in Bohemia near Austerlitz in late November.

On 2 December, the allies attacked an apparently weak French right. Meanwhile, at precisely the right moment Napoleon launched Marshal Soult's corps at the Pratzen Heights in the center, a move that ripped the allied front apart. The result was catastrophe. When he heard the news, William Pitt commented, "Roll up that map; it will not be needed these ten years."[112] Austerlitz represented the epitome of the French military reforms in battle organization emerging during the revolutionary period. It was indeed a revolution in military affairs. Movement and deployment of the Grand Army was extraordinary throughout the campaign.

Napoleon had no illusions as to what had brought about the war; it was British money and encouragement to the *ancien régime* that allowed them to mobilize and fight the campaign of 1805. The emperor's victory bulletin pointed to the British as France's main enemy: "May all the blood shed here, may all these misfortunes fall upon the perfidious islanders who caused them. May the cowardly oligarchs of London support the consequences of so many woes."[113] Yet for all his success on the battlefield, Napoleon displayed little interest in addressing the larger political and strategic issues his victories raised. Instead, his answer for every major strategic and political problem was more war.

It was the turn of Prussia in 1806. Annoyed by Napoleon's actions in the Germanies, the Prussians went to war believing that, as the heirs to Frederick the Great, they possessed the best army in Europe. They were wrong. In a lightning campaign in October 1806 the Grand Army destroyed the Prussian Army in a single day, 14 October, at the Battle of Jena-Auerstedt. In the seven-week campaign that followed, the French pursued the fleeing remnants to the Baltic, killing or wounding 25,000 Prussians, capturing 140,000, and taking more than 2,000 cannons.[114] Then, after the bloody but inconclusive Battle of Eylau in East Prussia in February 1807, Napoleon finished off the Russians at the Battle of Friedland in June. He now bestrode Europe as no ruler had since Roman times. The Peace of Tilsit brought a temporary halt to the fighting in Eastern Europe. Napoleon's military victories had cowed Russia and Austria for the time being. But while they placed him in an almost unchallengeable position, they did not end his efforts to expand his control.

Prussia's collapse would have both immediate and long-term impacts. To begin with, it resulted in a fundamental restructuring and reformation of not only the Prussian Army but the state.[115] In the long term, the creation of a general staff system in response to defeat revolutionized the army's culture, a move eventually copied by the other Western armies.[116] Prussia's reforms introduced the serious study of war and military operations into its officer corps, making the education of officers a major factor in preparing for war. As the Prussian military reformer Gerhard von Scharnhorst noted, "A claim to the position of officer shall from now on be warranted in peacetime by knowledge and education."[117] If the Prussians could not match Napoleon's genius, they aimed to develop a superior command system.

The Peace of Tilsit in 1807 between the French and the Russians represented the high point of Napoleon's career. From this point he made a series of increasingly serious political and strategic errors. The Berlin Decree, issued shortly after Jena-Auerstedt, declared "the British Isles ... to be in a state of blockade." The Milan Decree, issued a year later, tightened the economic war. But the British remained recalcitrant. Shortly after the Peace of Tilsit, the Royal Navy sailed into Copenhagen's harbor and seized fifteen ships of the line from the neutral Danes.[118] That fall, a French army moved through the Iberian Peninsula to chase the Portuguese court and regent out of Lisbon, the latter shepherded to Brazil by the Royal Navy. That operation served as the opening move of Napoleon's most disastrous mistake, an effort to control the

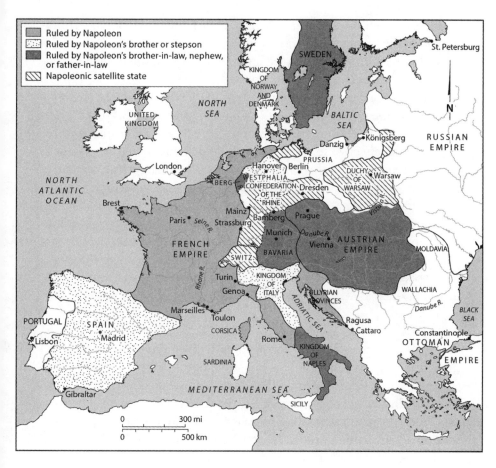

Europe under Napoleon, 1810. Cartography by Bill Nelson.

Iberian Peninsula directly. The emperor proceeded to overthrow the Spanish monarchy with the weak explanation that "the old dynasty is worn out. ... It is necessary for me to refashion the work of Louis XIV."[119]

But the conservative, highly religious Spanish had little interest in having their government reformed by foreigners. The result was an uprising throughout the cities and countryside to protect the status quo rather than overthrow it. The Spanish Army joined the revolt. Although the French soon crushed the troubles in the cities, the Spanish Army remained a threat in outlying areas, while guerrillas harassed French foragers throughout the countryside. The guerilla war soon became a

murderous contest to see who could slaughter the most. In modern terminology the war in Spain was a hybrid war.[120] The existence of regular
Spanish forces, however badly led and trained, forced the French to concentrate their forces, making foraging virtually impossible.

The British were delighted to fish in these troubled waters. In 1809,
Arthur Wellesley, future Duke of Wellington, arrived in Portugal.[121] His
leadership of the ensuing campaign finally provided the British government with an effective strategy to attack French military power. Wellington represented one of three branches of British strategy: first, control of
the world's oceans through a blockade of French ports; second, financial
and military aid for those on the Continent willing to fight Napoleon;
and third, Wellington's army on the Iberian Peninsula. Keeping Wellington there proved expensive. It cost £3 million in 1809, twice that in 1810,
and by 1811 nearly £11 million. Once the Peninsula Army left Portugal
for good in 1813 to invade Spain, the British faced the problem of
providing increased arms and financial aid to the Spanish as well as the
Portuguese.[122]

The French campaign of 1811, led by Marshal André Masséna,
against Wellington's base in Portugal, underlined the weaknesses of the
French logistic system as well as the advantages the British gained from
controlling the sea. In 1810, Wellington had ordered construction of an
extensive line of fortifications, called the Lines of Torres Vedras, from
the Tagus River to the coast. These lines basically protected the peninsula on which Lisbon rested. As the French advanced, Wellington fell
back on the Lines of Torres Vedras.[123] Once there, the French found
themselves facing impregnable fortified positions they dared not attack.

Moreover, the British had stripped everything edible from the Portuguese frontier to the lines. With fragile logistics incapable of providing
either food or ammunition, the French were in a hopeless position. By
mid-November, half starving, with most of their animals dead or suffering heavily from disease, they retreated. The British, meanwhile, had no
difficulty feeding themselves and their allies. During 1810 they imported
over 1 million barrels of American flour to Lisbon.[124] The well-fed British and Portuguese watched Masséna's broken army leave Portugal in the
fall. Wellington refused to pursue them, noting that "I could lick these
fellows any day, but it would cost me 10,000 men, and, as this is the last
army England has got, we must take care of it."[125] In the end, the "Spanish ulcer" cost the French 300,000 soldiers, a level of attrition that
weighed heavily on the battles of 1813 and 1814.[126]

After the Austrian defeat at Wagram in early July 1809, few in Europe believed there was any hope of overthrowing the French while Napoleon possessed his armies. The desperate Austrians virtually allied themselves with the French by marrying one of their princesses to the emperor. Metternich commented that Austria's policy must be "to tack, to efface ourselves, to come to terms with the victor. Only thus may we perhaps preserve our existence till the day of general deliverance."[127] As Napoleon gathered his forces to invade Russia in 1811, virtually every European state supported the French.

In hindsight, it is easy to perceive the fragility of Napoleon's empire, built as it was on one man's military genius. But at the time, contemporaries saw little sign of French weakness. The question then is what led Napoleon to the mistake of invading Russia. The most obvious cause was his megalomania. He could not tolerate that Russia remained an independent entity, and while he obviously felt the same way toward Britain, until France possessed a battle-ready fleet that could defeat the Royal Navy, there was nothing he could do about the British.

By summer 1811, Napoleon's preparations for invasion, including an extensive buildup of logistical support for the invading armies, were well under way. But the logistical challenges of moving and supplying great armies over continental distances lay beyond French capabilities—just as they proved insurmountable to Hitler and his generals some 129 years later.[128] As a disciple of Lazare Carnot, Napoleon believed that in every way, war should pay for war.[129] The problem was that the area between the Polish frontier and Smolensk produced little food. To traverse that area, Napoleon made major efforts to ensure his troops had sufficient supplies. The invading forces possessed provisions for twenty-four days. The 250,000 horses that accompanied the invasion meant that Napoleon had to delay it until June, when sufficient grass was available.

On 24 June 1812, the Grand Army, led by Polish cavalry, began its invasion. As the French and their allies advanced, the Russians slipped away to the east. By the time the Grand Army reached Smolensk, it was steadily losing its strength through Cossack raids, disease, and the need to protect its supply lines.[130] Nevertheless, Napoleon continued the advance while the Russians destroyed foodstuff, forage, and virtually anything of any worth. Logistically, the territory between Smolensk and Moscow should have supported the French, but the Russians had turned the landscape into a desert. The steady drop in the numbers of soldiers available to the main army underlined the impact of attrition. At the start, the Grand Army had numbered 422,000 soldiers; by the time it reached Vitebsk it had dropped to 275,000; Smolensk to 145,000; Moscow to 100,000; thereafter on the retreat from 100,000 to 96,000, to 82,000, to 55,000, to 32,000, to 28,000.[131] Eventually only 8,000 managed to reach Polish territory in December.[132]

On 7 September 1812, at the Battle of Borodino, the Russians fought. With the French Army reduced to approximately 130,000, too few to attempt an outflanking maneuver, the emperor launched a frontal attack with diversionary attacks on the flank. Napoleon's chief aide, Armand de Caulaincourt, recorded the emperor's astonishment at the enemy's performance: "The Russians showed the utmost resistance; their field works, and the ground they were forced to yield, were given up without disorder. Their ranks did not break; pounded by artillery, sabered by the cavalry, forced back at the bayonet-point by our infantry their somewhat immobile masses met death bravely. . . . Several times the Emperor repeated that it was quite inexplicable to him that the redoubts and positions so audaciously captured and so doggedly defended should yield us so few prisoners."[133]

At the end of the day, the Russians retreated, leaving the French to occupy a dismal, gory scene. French casualties numbered over 30,000 killed and wounded, while the Russians lost at least 44,000. Napoleon also lost 14 lieutenant generals and 33 major generals.[134] Nevertheless, Borodino opened the way to Moscow. Yet if Napoleon expected that seizing the ancient Russian capital would lead Tsar Alexander to capitulate, he was sadly mistaken. After waiting thirty-five days in Moscow for Alexander to recognize reality, Napoleon ordered the Grand Army to retreat, a move that cost him virtually the entire army. While Britain devoted its treasure to defeating Napoleon in Spain, Russia sacrificed manpower and territory to the same end. Napoleon had no answer for either.

The shock of Napoleon's defeat exploded throughout Europe. Nevertheless, the great coalition that eventually defeated the emperor proved difficult to assemble. As French survivors struggled back to Poland and Lithuania, many Russians argued against a continuation of the war. The Prussian king, Frederick William, at first refused to consider joining an anti-French coalition, but his generals forced his hand. As the French and their allied troops retreated from Russia, General Ludwig Yorck von Wartenburg, commander of the Prussian detachment, signed the Convention of Tauroggen with the Russians, taking his corps out of the alliance with the French. Strategically the convention meant that Napoleon could not create a defensive position in eastern Prussia but would have to defend in central Germany.[135]

Popular feeling, especially in his eastern provinces, eventually forced Frederick William to join the Russians in the Convention of Kalisch in March 1813. His generals began the desperate process of building a large army out of a small one. Here, as in France in 1792, the revolutionary impulses of nationalism, supported by British weapons, uniforms, and other accoutrements of war, allowed the Prussians to field an army of 228,000 infantry, 31,100 cavalry, and 13,000 gunners.[136]

While his opponents were bickering, trying to cobble a coalition together, Napoleon confronted the difficulty of patching an army together from the survivors of the invasion, new conscripts, those who had not been called to the colors in previous years, and units from Spain.[137] Then this reconstituted army had to be equipped. Here both the administrative structure Napoleon had created and the nationalism of the revolution sprang to the rescue. According to Caulaincourt, "The entire French nation overlooked his reverses and vied with one another in displaying zeal and devotion. It was as glorious an example of the French character as it was a personal triumph for the Emperor, who with amazing energy directed all the resources of which his genius was capable into organizing and guiding the great national endeavor. Things seemed to come into existence as if by magic."[138]

The campaign opened in April 1813 with the Austrians remaining on the sidelines. Metternich apparently feared that Russia might become too powerful and believed the allies could persuade a "reasonable" Napoleon to settle for half a loaf, namely control of the Rhineland, while abandoning his other conquests. But Napoleon was still Napoleon. His patched-together armies won two major victories at Lützen and Bautzen in spring 1813, but with a totally inadequate cavalry, there was no pursuit. The heavy casualties on both sides led the emperor to remark, "These animals have learned something."[139] Both sides were exhausted by June.

That exhaustion forced Napoleon to agree to an armistice, but there was no chance of peace. Hostilities resumed in August with not only Austria but Sweden joining the Russians and Prussians; all were supported by British subsidies of money and equipment. The allied strategy was simple: when Napoleon was present, retreat; when not present, attack. Thus, the emperor won an impressive battle at Dresden, but allied numbers, propped up by British aid, gradually prevailed. Finally, in October 1813, the allies brought him to ground at Leipzig.

Nothing underlined the importance of overwhelming numbers in this new age of war more than that battle. Historians have rightly termed it "the Battle of the Nations." Cold numbers rather than generalship determined the outcome. Covering Leipzig in a great ring from the north to the east and south, Napoleon possessed 177,500 soldiers at the battle's beginning, along with 700 guns; 18,000 reinforcements arrived during the battle. Against this, the Allied armies totaled 257,000 soldiers in two armies, plus 108,000 reinforcements received during the battle. The allies' guns totaled 1,400.

Napoleon had minimal room for maneuver, while the allied generals displayed the qualities that had brought them so little success over the previous quarter-century. By 19 October, French artillery reserves had fallen to 20,000 rounds, and Napoleon had no choice but to retreat. Allied losses in killed and wounded were approximately 54,000, while French losses were 38,000 killed and wounded with 30,000 captured. Moreover, Napoleon lost nearly half of his cannons as well as much of his supply trains and military stores.[140]

The defeat at Leipzig ended French control over central Germany. Almost immediately Allied pursuit led to the loss of the Rhineland. The allies then followed Napoleon into France, where they accomplished what the Prussians had failed to achieve at Valmy: the total defeat of France, leading to the emperor's abdication on 6 April 1814. There followed exile to Elba and a brief interlude of return and final defeat on the field of Waterloo at the hands of Wellington, the only general of the period who came close to being Napoleon's equal.[141]

The Interplay Between the Two Revolutions

The French and Industrial Revolutions—the two great military-social revolutions of the late eighteenth century—were signposts to the future. The impact of the Industrial Revolution was indirect: Britain's industrial and financial power provided the means for allied armies to swamp Napoleon in 1813. The French Revolution's ideological impetus was obvious. Equally important, however, were the administrative and political reforms the revolutionaries instituted in the republic's darkest days of 1793 and 1794, and which the Directory and then Napoleon institutionalized and spread throughout much of Europe. Despite France's defeat in 1813–1815, those reforms continue to influence the modern world.

Unlike those of the American Civil War and the twentieth century's two great World Wars, the weapons and conduct of battles during the Napoleonic Wars were little affected by the Industrial Revolution. Nothing underlined this fact more than Wellington's victory over the French at Waterloo. Except in its organization, his army was little different from the redcoats the Duke of Marlborough led against the French in the War of the Spanish Succession a hundred years earlier. Artillery had hardly changed, except that it was now more accurate and better organized. The introduction of corps and divisions did much to speed up the movement and deployment of armies in the field, but the technology of war was centuries old.

The transformation in the character of war came in the size and organization of armies. The most obvious explanation is the considerable increase in population that had occurred during the eighteenth century, as well as the increasingly effective bureaucratic systems emerging in Europe, particularly in France and Britain. In the case of France, the revolution provided the ideological as well as the administrative means to ensure that the French armies of 1793–1815 possessed sufficient manpower. Beyond that ideological drive, the authors of the *levée en masse* and then Napoleon also created the political and administrative structures to ensure conscription worked effectively. The conscription law passed by Jourdan played a crucial part in keeping the French in these wars by enabling the state to force the population to support them.

The combination of ideological fervor and conscription proved devastating to the French population, which lost some 1.5 million young men on the battlefield between 1792 and 1815.[142] In the case of the British, the national effort did not require full-blown conscription. Much of Britain's surplus manpower found its way voluntarily into the Industrial Revolution. While Britain and France were able to sustain their military efforts, that was not true of the *anciens régimes* of Eastern Europe. From almost the beginning of the war against Revolutionary France, they required financial and material aid from Britain. But even after they became willing to mobilize their populations to match the French, they lacked the economic and motivational strength to support those armies without British assistance.

It was a common French saying that "God is on the side of the biggest battalions." In 1813, the allies, partially motivated by nationalism and supported by the riches of the Industrial Revolution, overthrew armies led by the greatest general in history. The Austrian, Russian, and

Prussian Armies would not have been at Leipzig without the support made possible by the Industrial Revolution and the financial strength it provided to Britain. What is astonishing is that despite the war's massive economic and financial demands, the British economy still grew.

Napoleon stands out as quite simply the greatest operational commander in Western history. Perhaps one might consider Alexander the Great as his equal, but we know far too little about the Macedonian's phalanxes, while the periods are so different that comparison is almost impossible. So, Napoleon has stood as the benchmark for great generalship. Nevertheless, after he won his great victories over the Austrians and Prussians in 1805 and 1806, war began to pass him by. Austerlitz and Jena-Auerstedt appeared decisive to him and his contemporaries, but those victories never extinguished the opposition.[143] Moreover, Napoleon never possessed the strategic and political vision to bring his interminable wars to an end. His answer to every political and strategic problem was to seek another "decisive" victory.

But after his coup in Spain overthrew the Bourbon monarchy, there were no more decisive victories. French armies had little difficulty in defeating Spanish armies but never succeeded in destroying them. Meanwhile, guerrillas throughout the countryside bled the French white. The disaster in Spain was a forerunner to the Russian catastrophe, in which neither victory at Borodino nor the capture of Moscow was sufficient to persuade Alexander to agree to peace. Then came 1813 and a consistent series of Napoleonic victories that made little difference because the allies, supported by Britain's finances and industrial power, kept coming at him until his armies broke at Leipzig.

Throughout the Industrial Revolution, and for the French Revolution's ideological descendants, there would be no more decisive victories. Yet that did not stop Robert E. Lee or Graf von Schlieffen or the Wehrmacht's generals from seeking them. But the victories of the Army of Northern Virginia in the American Civil War only delayed the inevitable. The casualties these victories entailed bled the Confederate population until surrender was the only possibility. The Schlieffen Plan, launched in August 1914, not only failed but ensured that Germany faced a war of attrition it could not win. The German operational victories of 1940 and 1941 created a strategic context in which defeat was that much more horrendous.

The casualty bills of the Napoleonic Wars were a harbinger of those wars to come. Over the fifteen years during which the French emperor ravaged Europe, somewhere between 2 and 3 million died on both sides—as many as died in the Thirty Years' War but in half the time. Such were the advances in the European art of war over two centuries.[144]

The Prussian General August von Gneisenau summed up the strategic results of nearly a quarter of a century of war in Europe when he noted that "there is no mortal to whom Great Britain has greater obligations than this blackguard [Napoleon] for it is the events that he has brought about which have raised England's greatness, security, and wealth so high. They are the lords of the sea and neither in this dominion nor in world trade have they any rivals left to fear." The Prussian field marshal Gebhardt von Blücher was blunter in his appraisal. On a visit to London shortly after Waterloo he commented, "Lord what a city to loot."[145]

PART III

The Fourth Military-Social Revolution: Marriage of the Second and Third Military-Social Revolutions

CHAPTER FIVE

Wars in Europe and America in the Nineteenth Century

And then the war came.

—ABRAHAM LINCOLN, inaugural address, 1864

THE MID-NINETEENTH CENTURY saw five major conflicts, four of which involved European powers: the Crimean War of 1854–1855; the Franco-Austrian War, also called the Second Italian War of Independence (1859); the Austro-Prussian War of 1866; and the Franco-Prussian War of 1870–1871. These European conflicts involved the technological advances of the Industrial Revolution, but except in the Franco-Prussian War, the participants failed to call on the popular mobilization the French Revolution had created.

Across the Atlantic, however, the struggle between the northern and seceding southern states turned into the first truly modern war, one that stretched both sides to the breaking point.[1] That war was the first instance of the fourth great military-social revolution, the direct meshing of the French and Industrial military-social revolutions. It also saw Clausewitz's concept of "total war" reach new levels, particularly in the Confederacy.

The Crimean and Franco-Austrian Wars

The first of the wars among the European powers came because of Russian intervention in the Balkans against the Turks. In 1854, Russian armies invaded Ottoman territory, and both the British and French declared war in response. Here, unlike in the Napoleonic Wars, the Industrial Revolution directly affected the armies' capabilities and the war's course. Steam-powered vessels enabled allied forces to deploy first to the Balkans and then to Crimea with little difficulty, while reporters on the scene telegraphed what was happening to London and Paris.[2] The Russians, however, had no railroads with which to deploy and supply their army in Crimea, which limited its size. The British and French equipped their troops with rifled muskets firing the "minié" bullet, tripling their range with improved accuracy, while Russian rifles were patterned after Napoleonic weapons. Nevertheless, the Crimean War was a nineteenth-century cabinet war that posed little threat to the participants' national survival. Neither side mobilized the popular enthusiasm as in the French Revolutionary and Napoleonic Wars.

Landing on the Crimea in September 1854, French and British armies marched on Sebastopol; on the way they ran into Russian forces on the heights overlooking the Alma River. Given the Anglo-French armies' superior firepower, based on the introduction of the minié bullet, the outcome was never in doubt. That victory allowed them to besiege Sebastopol. Tsarist armies made two attempts to relieve the besieged port; both failed. The first included the charge of the British Army's light brigade, a disastrous bit of military ineptitude that prompted French Marshal Pierre Bosquet's devastatingly accurate comment, "C'est magnifique, mais ce n'est pas la guerre." At the second attempt, the Battle of Inkerman, allied rifled muskets slaughtered massed Russian troops, inflicting twelve thousand casualties while suffering only three thousand.

The campaign settled down to a siege, which lasted through the winter. British staff work was nonexistent; the supply system collapsed, and conditions in hospitals were appalling, in other words, no worse than with other armies in the past. But newspaper reporters sent back dispatches to Britain, and the public outcry dragged the British Army into the modern era. With the garrison in Sebastopol in serious straits, the Russians made a desperate attempt to break through in mid-August 1855; again, the allies repulsed them with heavy casualties. On 8 September, the French stormed the fortress of Malakoff, ending the war.

While the Crimean War gave little indication that the fourth military-social revolution was on the horizon, the steamships and the minié bullet underlined that the Industrial Revolution was already having a substantial impact on the character of war. Without those two products of innovation and change, the war would most likely have had a substantially different outcome. Moreover, the war represented a warning that those who failed to keep up with technological change were going to pay a heavy price on the battlefields of the future.

The Franco-Austrian War deserves no more than a paragraph. Annoyed by the Sardinia-Piedmontese meddling in the Austrian-controlled provinces in northern Italy, the Austrians delivered an ultimatum to its leaders in April 1859. Once fighting began in May, the French rushed significant forces into northern Italy. Until those troops arrived, the Austrians enjoyed an advantage, but their commanders moved with deadening caution. The Battle of Solferino was a French success in that they held the field, but the Austrians pulled back in good order. At that point, Napoleon III, worried that the German states might support the Austrians, terminated French participation. On 11 July 1859, the Austrians and the French agreed to an armistice. In the long run, the conflict put the Italians on the road to unity, but in military terms there were few lessons.

The American Civil War

The election of Abraham Lincoln as president of the United States resulted in the breakup of the democratic experiment that had begun in 1775.[3] To paraphrase Thucydides, the war resulted from the growth of northern power and the fear it occasioned in the South, particularly the fear that Lincoln's election threatened southern whites' "peculiar institution," slavery, on which their economic and political system rested. South Carolina's decision to secede was not unexpected, given the state's political leaders' penchant for demagoguery. The other states of the Deep South— Georgia, Florida, Alabama, Mississippi, Louisiana, Texas, and Arkansas— followed almost immediately. The question was which of the remaining slave states would join. The "Upper South"—North Carolina, Tennessee, and Virginia—remained on the fence but eager to join the Confederacy, while the border states of Kentucky and Missouri were deeply split. On 12 April 1861, the Confederate president, Jefferson Davis began the war by ordering a bombardment of Fort Sumter, in Charleston Harbor. North Carolina, Tennessee, and Virginia immediately joined the Confederacy,

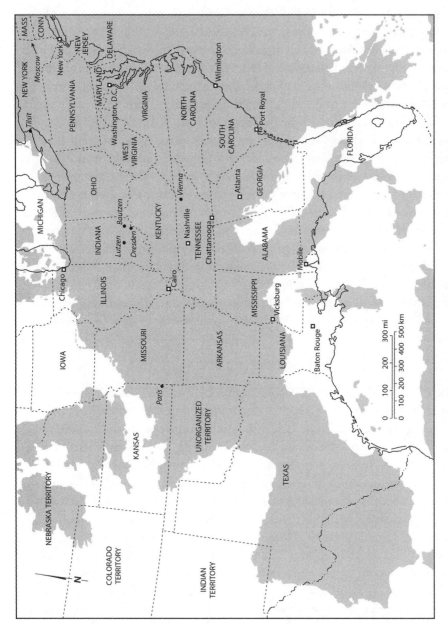

The size of the Confederacy compared to Europe. Cartography by Bill Nelson.

even before Lincoln mobilized the militia. In fact, the states in the Confederacy had begun mobilizing their militia before Sumter's bombardment.

In strategic terms, the political cost of the attack on Sumter was not worth the advantage of pulling the fence sitters of the Upper South into the Confederacy. The attack brought a surge of outrage in the North, which until that point had remained divided on whether to let the southern states go or take action to force their return to the Union. Lincoln responded to Sumter by asking northern states to call up 75,000 militia. Neither side expected the war to last.

Over the forty-five years since the collapse of Napoleon's empire, the Industrial Revolution had spread its tentacles to North America with a profound influence on society and the economy. The railroad, a technological child of the revolution, created bonds across the northern states that would profoundly influence the contest by giving the North the ability to wage a war over continental distances. There would be no decisive victories in this war, but in cold economic terms, the North enjoyed every advantage. Its population was 22.1 million; the Confederacy's was 9 million, of whom nearly 40 percent were enslaved people.

The Industrial Revolution's impact on the North had been enormous. Northern states possessed 110,274 factories in 1860 versus only 18,026—barely 15 percent of the nation's total—in the Confederacy.[4] New York's factories alone produced twice what southern factories produced, and so did Pennsylvania's. Even tiny Massachusetts turned out 60 percent of the Confederacy's manufacturing output. The output per person-year of the North's blast furnaces had increased 120 percent between 1850 and 1860.[5] What makes the North's logistical war even more impressive is that by 1863, factories in Massachusetts had to send their products over a thousand miles just to arrive at supply depots, like Cairo, Illinois, before shipment to front lines deep in Tennessee. The major industries were concentrated almost entirely in the North, which produced 94 percent of the nation's iron, 97 percent of its coal, and 97 percent of its firearms.[6]

Many northern industrial concerns grew impressively during the war, especially those directly linked to the war effort. Iron production by 1864 was 29 percent higher than the total for 1860; coal production increased by 21 percent. Shortages in the workforce and the army's demand for clothing led to the widespread introduction of sewing machines. Overall, the North's manufacturing index was 13 percent higher in 1864 than for the whole country in 1860.[7]

Between 1820 and 1850, the arsenal at Springfield, Massachusetts, and private arms manufacturers in the Connecticut River Valley developed semi-automatic milling machines to cut parts to specific sizes, allowing mass production of interchangeable parts.[8] As a result, American factories produced weapons in unheard-of numbers and at speeds never before possible.[9] Northern industry also played a major role in building and maintaining a powerful navy, as well as the gunboats that quickly controlled the South's river systems in the West. That industrial capacity created the massive expansion of Union forces which enabled them by 1864 to overwhelm Confederate armies. But it would take two years for the North's industrial power to reach the potential required to support the war fully.

The North's railroad and steamship infrastructure underlined the Union's industrial advantage. Steam engines created a transportation revolution in the United States that affected not only industrial production but the agricultural spaces that were being filled by the flow of migrants from the northeastern states and abroad. By 1860, there were thirty thousand miles of American railroads.[10] Northern entrepreneurs had created three major lines that linked the East Coast to Chicago and St. Louis, while trunk lines ran to major and minor cities throughout the North and stretched to Iowa, Wisconsin, and Minnesota. This railroad system tied the midwestern states economically and politically to the Northeast. While northern railroads were an interconnected system, those in the South were not. Southern railroads largely ran from cotton- and tobacco-producing areas to ports where the commodities were loaded onto ships for foreign destinations. Only one line connected the Confederacy from east to west.

Undergirding the northern railroad system in 1860 was an industrial base that produced locomotives, freight cars, and the rails for both North and South. There were no fewer than a dozen independent industrial concerns manufacturing locomotives in the North, while other companies not only repaired locomotives but occasionally built them. On the other hand, not a single southern concern was capable of manufacturing locomotives, and there were few repair facilities.[11] Moreover, when the war began, the weakly financed southern railroads had few of the supplies necessary for major repairs. In 1861, the Virginia Central Railroad, for example, had enough rails on hand to repair just nine miles of track.[12]

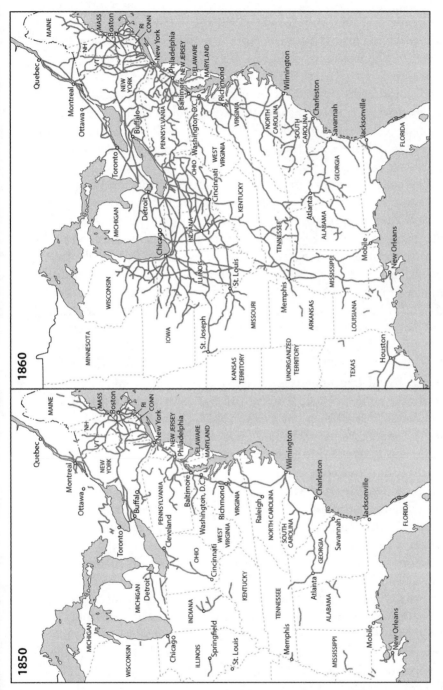

Railroads, 1850 and 1860. Cartography by Bill Nelson.

In 1859, there were 1,096,548 factory workers in the North; in the South, only 128,530.[13] In retrospect, the large number of factory workers provided Union armies a considerable advantage. In the months before the war, southern whites made great fun of the northern "mudsills" (factory workers), who they thought would run away at the first shot. Many of the factory workers in the Union Army manned the repair shops of military railroads and steamships; they fixed broken locomotives, freight cars, and steamships in the field and helped establish depots supplying the armies. William T. Sherman's march on Atlanta would have been impossible without the mudsills.

The concentration of locomotive construction and repair in Union states gave the North a monopoly on mechanics required to maintain and repair engines, brakes, hot boxes, and wheels. The result was that while Confederate railroads steadily collapsed for lack of repair, northern railroads expanded their systems and their passenger and freight trains. Between 1863 and 1864, the Illinois Central increased its number of locomotives from 112 to 148 and the number of freight cars from 2,312 to 3,337.[14] By 1865, northern railroads had increased their railroad trackage by 70 percent over 1860, while the increase in the South was zero.[15]

By the war's end, a new factor had come into the Union's transportation system: the army had built its own railroads to support the logistics of those conducting military operations in occupied Confederate territory. By 1865, the U.S. Military Railroad was the largest rail organization in the world, bigger than any commercial line in the United States or Europe. It controlled 2,600 miles of track over which it ran 433 locomotives and 6,605 cars.[16] In the war's last year, northern military railroads and steamships moved 3,982,438 passengers, 3,376,610 of whom were soldiers, and carried 716,420 animals, including 407,143 horses. They also transported 4.1 million tons of food for the soldiers, 3.7 million tons of quartermaster stores, 1.3 million tons of ammunition and weapons, and over 200,000 tons of other stores, including medical items.[17]

Alongside railroad expansion came the rapid expansion of the telegraph, essential to control of railroad traffic, much of which ran on single-line tracks. The communication revolution that began in the 1840s gave rise to a newspaper-media culture that reached into small towns and farms of both North and South. These newspapers and magazines helped mobilize support for the war on both sides and also provided a barometer of how the population viewed events on the battlefield. They proved crucial to maintaining popular support for the war, especially as casualties mounted.

Mobilization of resources and manpower in both North and South required marrying the French Revolution to the power of the Industrial Revolution, bringing the fourth military-social revolution into being. By 1865, the Confederacy had raised 880,000 troops while the North had put 2.2 million in uniform. Equally impressive was the number of volunteers who swelled the Union armies in 1861 and 1862. In the war's first year, 658,000 enlisted in the North, and in August 1862, when it was clear that the war would not be short, Lincoln's call for volunteers yielded an additional 421,000. Other calls for shorter terms than three years—three months or two years—brought 145,000 more into the field. Perhaps more impressive, in 1864 136,000 Union veterans, their three-year enlistments expiring, volunteered to reenlist.[18]

If the politics of the Civil War failed to reach the extremes of the French Revolution, harsh language came from both sides, particularly from Richmond. Addressing the Confederate Congress in July 1861, Jefferson Davis denounced the Union as acting "with a savage ferocity unknown to modern civilization ... committing arson and rapine, the destruction of private homes and property. ... Mankind will shudder to hear the tales of outrages committed on defenseless females by soldiers of the United States." He invoked the southern white nightmare: Union troops were inciting "a servile insurrection in our midst." In December he denounced "the dirty Yankee invaders" and told his fellow citizens that "you fight against offscourings of the earth ... by showing themselves so utterly disgraced that if the question was proposed to you whether you would combine with hyenas or Yankees, I trust every Virginian would say, give us the hyenas."[19]

Northern rhetoric was nearly as hard. In early 1864, answering Confederate complaints about the Union troops' ruthless behavior toward civilians in northern Alabama, Major General William Tecumseh Sherman replied,

> The Government of the United States has in North Alabama any and all rights which they choose to enforce in war—to take their lives, their homes, their land, their everything—because they cannot deny that war exists there, and war is simply power unrestrained by constitution or compact. If they want eternal warfare, well and good; we accept the issue, and will dispossess them and put our friends in their place. ... To those who submit to the rightful law and authority all gentleness and forbearance; but to the petulant and persistent secessionists, why, death is a mercy.[20]

This impact of the fourth military-social revolution helps explain why the war went on so long. The "decisive" victories Napoleon had won from 1805 to 1809 had disappeared into the dustbin of history. Nevertheless, in the Civil War's first year, both sides tried to fight decisive battles similar to Austerlitz or Jena-Auerstedt. Instead, industrialized war, waged over unprecedented distances and funded by willing populations on both sides, inevitably became a war of attrition. The ability of both sides to maintain political equilibrium in the face of military and economic difficulties and heavy losses kept the conflict going until the Confederacy ran out of manpower and resources.

Adding to the North's strength, the flow of immigrants and internal migration from the less productive states of the Northeast added some 430,000 new farms and 2.7 million acres to the land under production during the war. These farms, on some of the richest agricultural land in the world, were made even more productive by the North's Industrial Revolution. The use of farm machinery and fertilizers considerably increased the yield of individual farms despite many farmhands' having joined the army. During the war, northern factories produced 233,000 reapers.[21]

One should not underestimate the Confederacy's participation in the Industrial Revolution. It too had established considerable industrial resources and had participated in the railroad transportation revolution. But the Confederacy's reliance on northern manufacturing before the war had left it no ability to produce complex machinery like locomotives and steamboats. As the North's blockade bit ever deeper, the Confederacy's only response was blockade runners, which could not carry rails, much less locomotives. Moreover, its leaders made a serious strategic mistake in their attempt to build ironclads. Approximately 25 percent of Confederate iron production went to production of ironclads, but only one such ship, the *Merrimack*, achieved any success. None of the South's iron production went to building new rails. With no new locomotives, and with the rails they rode on steadily deteriorating, it is no surprise that Confederate railroads were in a state of collapse by 1863. By 1864, their condition was so bad that trains could go no faster than fifteen miles per hour.

Given all these advantages, why did it take the North so long to win when, for example, the Prussians needed just months to destroy their Austrian and French opponents? A number of factors contributed to the Civil War's length. The first was distance: the Confederacy covered a vast territory when compared to Europe. Altogether the Confederate states covered some 780,000 square miles—an expanse larger than Britain, France, Spain, Germany, the Low Countries, and Italy combined. Britain today consists of only 80,000 square miles. Making things even more difficult, much of the western Confederacy consisted of wilderness, and even in the relatively settled areas of the East, the road system was appallingly bad. Only railroads and steamboats could provide the logistical capabilities required to supply armies over the distances involved. In effect, the Industrial Revolution allowed the North logistically to support armies deep in the Confederacy.

The second difficulty both sides confronted was the nature of American military forces in 1860. There was no military staff to speak of, none of the lessons-learned mechanisms that beset modern military organizations, and no serious study of military operations. Even Mexican War veterans had minimal experience in leading large bodies of troops. In 1860, the U. S. Army consisted of slightly more than sixteen thousand officers and troops, scattered in small forts along the coast and western frontier. Their duties involved basic tactics, while small frontier companies attempted to keep the peace between settlers and Indians.

For the most part, the officers were not an impressive lot. General Alpheus Williams, a competent volunteer officer during the war, commented about many of his regular army colleagues: "At least fifteen years as a clerk in an army bureau or on duty on a frontier post as a lieutenant to a command of a dozen men, where there were no books, no drill, no military duty, nothing but a vast amount of whiskey drinking, card playing, and terrific profane swearing."[22] Williams was undoubtedly exaggerating, because the officer corps produced a number of excellent combat commanders, while Montgomery Meigs proved a genius in mobilizing and utilizing the North's industrial strength to support its armies logistically.

The expansion of the armies required extraordinary measures. The fact that the Union Army would number nearly a million men with 600,000 in the field by the end of 1863, barely two years after the war's beginning, suggests the extent of the problem. It also underlines the contribution the Industrial Revolution made to the mobilization of a society unprepared for war. Moreover, the projection of Union military power depended on the products of the Industrial Revolution for logistical support for Union armies operating over hundreds of miles. The extent of ammunition, weapons, uniforms, and accoutrements northern industry supplied to Union armies suggests the range of the Industrial

Revolution's contribution to the war effort by the war's second year. In early 1863, the War Department reported that it had procured 1,577 cannons, 1,082,841 muskets, 282,389 carbines and pistols, 48,719,862 pounds of lead, 1,251,995 cannon balls and shells, 259,022,216 cartridges, 5,764,768 pounds of gunpowder, 919,676 sets of accoutrements for soldiers, 96,639 sets of equipment for cavalry horses, and 3,281 sets of artillery harnesses.[23] This was only the first full year of mobilization; the numbers continued to grow over the succeeding years.

In 1861, the War Department consisted of a small number of officers and clerks. Thus, it is not surprising that the mobilization effort in the North and South depended on individual states to organize and field volunteer regiments. This was a messy and at times disorganized process but one that drew on the commitment to the war at a basic, grassroots level. That enthusiasm reflected an upwelling of nationalism much like that seen in France in 1792 and 1793. It would support a continuing and increasingly costly struggle.

The armies that emerged in the crisis possessed different cultures of command. To a considerable extent they reflected the leadership, amateurish though it was, that formed them. For example, the Army of the Potomac's commander from July 1861 through November 1862, George McClellan, appointed its division and brigade commanders. Most of these officers were carbon copies of McClellan himself, seldom willing to take risks or display initiative. The imprint of different commanding officers meant that each of the major Union and Confederate armies—the Union Armies of the Potomac, the Tennessee, and the Cumberland; and the Confederate Armies of Northern Virginia and Tennessee—all had substantially differing command cultures, which distinctly affected their performances in the field.[24]

Raising armies and mobilizing the industrial resources to support them was only a part of the problem. That effort had to be paid for, and here the North had the advantage. Lincoln's appointment of Salmon Chase as secretary of the treasury was a brilliant move because, as a member of the cabinet, he could not publicly disagree with the president. Even though Chase hated the job, he proved a genius in raising the funds the war required. In the first months of Lincoln's presidency, his connection with bankers kept the war effort afloat until Congress met in July 1861 and authorized the government to borrow $250 million. Even with an income tax to raise still more funds, the war was so costly that by early 1862 Lincoln was bemoaning: "The people are impatient. Chase has no money and tells me he can raise no more. . . . The bottom is out of the tub. What Shall I do?"[25]

The answer to the Union's financial difficulties came in the form of a patriotic banker, Jay Cooke. Chase initially authorized Cooke to raise $500 million in bonds to finance the war; his group of agents more than met that target. In 1865, Cooke's propaganda machine raised $830 million to finish the war. In effect, Chase and Cooke created a model that served for how the United States financed the World Wars in the twentieth century—clearly influenced by the British experience in financing the wars against Napoleon. An increased money supply fueled an expansion of the North's economy so that by war's end it had doubled in size. Moreover, the Lincoln administration managed to finance the war while also controlling inflation, something the Confederacy did not do. Instead, the Confederate states printed large amounts of paper currency as a substitute for sensible financial measures. By 1864, inflation had destroyed the southern economy.

At the outset of the war, few on either side had any conception of the casualties or the extent of fighting that was to come. Most northerners believed a small group of fire-breathing radicals had persuaded white southerners, who were at heart pro-Union, to join the rebellion. On the other hand, most southern whites believed northerners were money-grubbing merchants and "mudsills" who had no stomach for battle.

As Lincoln noted in his inaugural address of March 1865, "and then the war came." Both sides were unprepared. The Union Navy had some success in seizing relatively undefended Confederate ports in the war's early months.[26] The Confederates won a victory at the First Battle of Bull Run in July 1861. Both sides showed that, no matter how woeful their preparations, they could face the horrors of Civil War battlefields. Nevertheless, the significant strategic factor in the first year was that the North solidified its hold on the border states of Missouri and Maryland. Then, in September 1861, the Confederates miscalculated by invading Kentucky although it had declared itself neutral; that action pitched most of Kentucky into the Union camp.

As North and South mobilized, the former's industrial power gave it a particular advantage in the West. In July 1861, the Union commander in the West, General John C. Frémont, authorized construction of steamboats and gunboats for a campaign down the Mississippi. Of particular value was the initial production of Pook Turtles, ironclad riverine craft (official termination: City Class). By December 1861, seven would be available, which would allow domination of the river system in the West. Armored, possessing thirteen guns, and with an astonishingly shallow draft, they provided Union amphibious forces with impressive firepower and support for the steamboats carrying soldiers. Their superb design and rapid construction provide a clear example of the North's manufacturing edge. Frémont proved a disaster as a commander; Lincoln relieved him in November 1861 and replaced him with Major General Henry Halleck—but the boats were a brilliant move. The Confederates, meanwhile, were trying to cobble together a single ironclad at Nashville to control the Cumberland River; they failed to complete it before they lost control of the river in early 1862.

Confronted with the spaces in the West, Davis and his advisors spread out the Confederate forces in an attempt to protect everything. Both sides made the mistake of focusing on the Mississippi River, whereas the Tennessee and Cumberland Rivers, which provided access to the heartland of the South on the far side of the Appalachians, held the strategic keys to winning the war in the West. In early 1862, Grant and Admiral Andrew Foote seized on the weak points in southern defenses: Fort Donelson on the Cumberland and Fort Henry on the Tennessee. After gobbling up Henry in February, Union amphibious forces moved against Donelson, where they forced the surrender of a Confederate army of seventeen thousand. These actions opened up the Tennessee River through central Tennessee into northern Mississippi and Alabama all the way to Muscle Shoals, near Chattanooga. They were the most important victories of the war. They broke the Memphis and Charleston Railroad, robbed the Confederacy of its most productive agricultural areas, and closed down one of the South's most important iron-producing areas.

Grant wrote in his memoirs that he thought such a devastating blow would persuade the Confederates to abandon the struggle. But instead of rolling over, the Confederates launched a massive counterattack. Grant's army had concentrated near a small church called Shiloh, where he was awaiting the arrival of Carlos Buell's Army of the Cumberland. The Confederates caught the Army of the Tennessee by surprise. They pushed Union troops toward the Tennessee River; Union divisions barely held the Confederates, who almost pushed Grant's army into the river. At the end of a desperate day, Sherman commented to Grant, "Well, Grant we've had the devil's own day, haven't we." Grant's laconic reply was, "Yes, lick him tomorrow, though."[27] On the next day, with the addition of one of the Army of the Tennessee's divisions and arrival of

Buell's Army of the Cumberland, Union forces drove the Confederates off the field.

The casualty list appalled the North: Union 13,047 (1,754 killed, 8,408 wounded, and 2,885 captured); Confederate 10,694 (1,723 killed, 8,012 wounded, and 959 missing). As the conflict's first great killing battle, Shiloh foretold a war of unprecedented attrition. Grant was one of the few who recognized its significance. He noted that the Confederate armies "not only attempted to hold the line farther south . . . but assumed the offensive and made such a gallant effort to regain what had been lost [that] . . . I gave up all idea of saving the Union except by complete conquest."[28]

The Confederates paid a strategic price for deploying so much of their army to attack the Army of the Tennessee. That massing of troops for Shiloh absorbed most Confederate forces in the West, enabling Union naval forces to seize New Orleans. But the risk-averse Henry Halleck proved to be no better a commander than Frémont. Only his removal to Washington in July 1862 opened matters for further Union advances in the West. Yet given the distances involved, logistical difficulties added to the complexities Union commanders faced in driving farther into the Confederacy.

In the East, that was not the problem; rather, it was a lack of drive. The Union commander, McClellan, moved even more slowly than Halleck. After assuming command, he spent the winter of 1861–1862 training the Army of the Potomac while refusing to engage the Confederates. After pressure from Lincoln, he finally moved in April 1862 but against the York Peninsula and Richmond, not directly on Joe Johnston's army, which had retreated back to the Rappahannock River. The Army of the Potomac's cautious advance eventually reached Richmond, but McClellan refused to attack. Johnston, now defending Richmond, counterattacked. At Seven Pines, in a two-day battle marked by incompetence on both sides, the Confederate commander was wounded.

At that point, Robert E. Lee assumed command of what became the Army of Northern Virginia. After ensuring Richmond's defenses, he struck a series of sharp blows at McClellan, clearly looking for the kind of decisive battles that had marked Napoleon's campaigns. Had Lee's subordinates proved more experienced, the Confederates might have destroyed the Army of the Potomac, but their attacks succeeded only in forcing McClellan to retreat to the James River. Historians have generally counted this series of battles, known as the Seven Days, as a Confederate victory.

But Confederate casualties in their "victories" came to 43,540, against 47,752 for the Union. These were numbers the Confederacy could not afford and an indication that a modern war of attrition depended as much on manpower as on resources.

Lee followed up his peninsula success with a rapid advance to northern Virginia, where he caught and smashed General John Pope's newly formed Army of Virginia at Second Manassas in late August 1862. He then launched his Army of Northern Virginia into Maryland in the belief that Marylanders would rally against the Union and give him the decisive victory that would win the Confederacy its independence. He got neither. The "decisive" battle was Antietam, in which more Americans were killed than on any other day in U.S. military history. Union casualties were 12,410 (14.2% of the Army of the Potomac); Confederate 10,316 (27.1% of Lee's army). McClellan, paralyzed by his fear of Lee, refused to use the full force available to destroy the Army of Northern Virginia despite possessing near perfect intelligence on Confederate plans and dispositions. At best Antietam was a draw, but Lincoln called it a victory and used it to issue the Emancipation Proclamation, freeing the slaves in Confederate states. The proclamation showed that the North was willing to wage economic war on the Confederacy by destroying the basis of its agricultural labor force.

Matters hardly improved for the Army of the Potomac in 1863. At Chancellorsville in early May, now led by "Fighting Joe" Hooker, it achieved an initial success. But then Hooker lost his nerve, and in a series of daring moves Lee outflanked the Army of the Potomac and drove it off the field in disarray. Again, the casualties were heavy. Overall Union losses in the campaign were 17,287 (16.3%); Confederate losses 13,303 (21%). For the Confederacy, Chancellorsville was another Pyrrhic victory.

On 16 May, one of the most important meetings of the war took place. Lee met with Jefferson Davis and the Confederacy's secretary of war, James Seddon, to discuss his army's next move. The two civilians argued for sending James Longstreet's corps west, where matters were taking a dangerous turn. Lee persuaded them instead to let the Army of Northern Virginia invade Maryland and Pennsylvania, where, he argued, his soldiers could achieve a victory that would bring independence to the Confederacy. The result was Gettysburg, which brought defeat for the Army of Northern Virginia and a casualty bill of 22,813 for the Union (22%) and 22,625 (31.2%) for the Confederates.

On the day of Lee's meeting with Davis and Seddon, Grant's Army of the Tennessee was wrecking the Army of Mississippi at the Battle of Champion Hill and driving it into Vicksburg. In that campaign, Grant waged the most imaginative and effective military operation of the war. After crossing the Mississippi River, he cut his supply lines and, after first moving against Mississippi's capital of Jackson, turned back and defeated John C. Pemberton's Army of Mississippi, trapping it in Vicksburg. Ill-prepared to withstand a siege, Pemberton surrendered the town and his army of 29,495 on 4 July. Within the month, with the surrender of Confederate forts downriver, the Mississippi was in the hands of Union gunboats; Grant's success had split the Confederacy from its western states and their agricultural wealth. By this point, the war was indeed becoming a hard war.[29] The governor of Illinois, Richard Yates, addressing Union troops in May, emphasized that the federal government had paid for the Louisiana Purchase and swore that "by heaven we will redeem it or make it one vast burying ground."[30]

Unfortunately for northern strategy, Lincoln and Halleck failed to take Grant's advice to attack Mobile, Alabama, one of the Confederacy's few remaining ports. Instead, Halleck dissipated much of Grant's army to hold positions of little importance. Meanwhile, the Union Army of the Cumberland had chased Braxton Bragg's Army of Tennessee into northern Georgia and captured Chattanooga. In September 1863, alarmed by the deteriorating situation in the West, Davis overruled Lee, who wanted to launch another invasion of the North, and ordered Longstreet west to reinforce Bragg. Longstreet's corps moved over the rickety southern railroads, and its artillery never managed to reach the battlefield of Chickamauga.

But Longstreet's infantry did get there; it smashed through a hole in the Union line that had opened through the incompetence of Major General William Rosecrans and his staff. The result was the only major victory Bragg's Army of Tennessee won in its dismal career. Survivors of the Army of the Cumberland either fled or retreated to Chattanooga. Union forces in the West had received a severe check. Yet casualties again weighed heavily: Confederate, 16,199 (34%); Union, 15,696 (28%). The response from Lincoln and his secretary of war, Edwin Stanton, was immediate and decisive. Here the North's transportation capabilities proved an enormous aid. Three days after the battle, the Union high command ordered two corps under Hooker from the Army of the Potomac, the XI and the XII (not surprisingly, the weakest corps in the army), 20,000 soldiers, and all their impedimenta to eastern Tennessee. Within forty hours the War Department had made the arrangements with the railroads, and the troops were on the move. By 8 October, eleven days later, Hooker's troops were within 26 miles of Chattanooga having completed a deployment of 1,233 miles.

But the most important move Lincoln and Stanton made was to place Grant in overall command in the West. Almost instantaneously, he pulled together the pieces required for a rapid recovery. Reinforcements from the East were welcome, but more important was the speed with which Grant concentrated the western armies and reinforced the Union position at Chattanooga. His strength lay in his ability to make diverse personalities work toward a common goal. By the end of November, he had provided the driving force to break the Confederate blockade of the Army of the Cumberland, restore the logistical lines required to support his armies, and smash Bragg's Army of Tennessee.

Grant's performance made him the obvious candidate to take over military direction of the war from Halleck. But Lincoln hesitated, perhaps worried because so many generals in the Army of the Potomac preferred to play politics. Grant would not take command of the war until March 1864. Before then, he and Sherman prepared for the next campaign in the West, aimed at taking the key industrial center of Atlanta. Their preparations during the winter and spring reveal their sophisticated understanding of logistics. Immediately after their success at Chattanooga, they undertook a complete rehabilitation of the military railroad network in Tennessee and Kentucky. Sherman estimated the distances necessary to support the western armies as 185 miles from Louisville, Kentucky, to Nashville, and 151 miles from there to Chattanooga. The advance on Atlanta would require rebuilding a further 137 miles of railroad.[31] Moreover, many of the supplies for these armies came from factories in the eastern states and would have to move hundreds of miles just to get to Louisville.

Grant put one of his division commanders in charge of the initial work on the railroads, then replaced him in February 1864 with Daniel McCallum, one of the most competent railroad managers in the East. As the roadbed and rails were repaired, McCallum and the army's burgeoning logistical structure created six separate sections with the requisite supply dumps of bridging materials, rails, and ties throughout the system, with soldiers assigned to do the repair work on each of the six divisions. Major bridges received forts and garrisons for protection. Some possessed extensive blockhouses with two layers of logs to withstand bombardment. Between Nashville and Decatur, Alabama, the system had no less than fifty-four major forts protecting the bridges and repair crews.[32] Here, adaptation to new conditions appears to have been at the heart of the northern approach. If you hoped to depend on your logistical system to project military power, you had to protect it.

The supplies supporting Sherman's march moved from the North through to Cairo, Illinois, or Louisville, Kentucky, to Nashville, and then through central Tennessee to Chattanooga on their way to the Georgia battlefront. Reconstructing and rebuilding the rail system went hand in hand with a logistical buildup in Nashville and Chattanooga to provide ammunition and sustenance for the advancing armies as well as fodder for the horses and mules. By April, Meigs, director of Union logistics, reported that his organization had stockpiled enough food in Nashville to feed 200,000 troops in Sherman's armies for the next four months, and enough grain for 50,000 animals.[33]

With the Atlanta campaign, Union engineers followed the same process with the rail system that they had employed in preparing for Sherman's move into Georgia. The result was that over the 150-day campaign to capture Atlanta, Confederate raiders cut the flow of Union rail traffic for a total of just 20 widely dispersed days. Meanwhile, Mc-Callum had Stanton contract with locomotive manufacturers to deliver 140 locomotives to Sherman's armies over the course of a year, as well as an average of 202 new freight cars per month.

In his memoirs, Sherman estimated that his armies required the logistical support of 16 10-car trains per day, with a total weight of 1,600 tons. That effort supported 100,000 men and 35,000 animals from 1 May until 12 November, at which point Sherman cut his supply lines to Chattanooga and began the March to the Sea. He further calculated that using animal power to meet a similar weight of logistical support of forage, ammunition, and food requirements would have taken 38,800 wagons, each with 6 mules, moving at a rate of 20 miles per day, "a simple impossibility in roads such as then existed in that region of the country. Therefore, I reiterate that the Atlanta campaign was an impossibility without these railroads; and only then, because we had the *men and means* to maintain and defend them, in addition to what was necessary to overcome the enemy."[34]

With Grant in charge of military strategy and the president supporting him, 1864 opened with a coherent Union approach to the war—one that should have finished matters. But there were two significant impediments to Grant's strategy. The first was that several key pieces—cleaning out Virginia's Shenandoah Valley; capturing Mobile, Alabama, one of the few remaining ports for blockade runners; and an attack on Richmond from the James River—all failed because these efforts were commanded by incompetent political generals. Yet Grant never complained because he understood that political generals were essential to Lincoln's reelection.[35]

In addition to Grant's other problems, the Army of the Potomac languished under the command culture McClellan had created. Its commanders were loath to display initiative and always prepared to miss an opportunity. The result was a murderous campaign in Virginia. Confederate losses at the Wilderness, Spotsylvania Court House, and Cold Harbor left Lee with a severely depleted army no longer able to launch aggressive attacks and eventually drove the Army of Northern Virginia back to Richmond and Petersburg. Exacerbating the losses, both sides created defensive positions behind dirt and log fortifications, similar to the trenches of World War I, that were almost impervious to breakthrough in a matter of hours. By the time the armies came to a halt at Petersburg, Grant's forces had suffered about 55,000 casualties (44.2%), and the Army of Northern Virginia had lost at least 35,000 (53.8%).

The Army of the Potomac failed to capture Richmond in the 1864 campaign, but it robbed Lee of the initiative that had marked his generalship in the war. In effect, the attrition occurring on the battlefields achieved the same result in 1864 as it did in 1918. In terms of the commitment of Union soldiers, 136,000 (roughly half the army) whose three-year enlistments were up in 1864 reenlisted and agreed to see the conflict through to its bloody conclusion. Astonishingly, 27,000 veterans in the Army of the Potomac, with its grim record of defeats, signed on for the war's remainder.[36]

Much of the weight of success for the Union effort in 1864 fell on the shoulders of Grant's former armies in the West, now commanded by Sherman.[37] The preparation of Grant and Sherman to meet the logistical requirements of the campaign against Atlanta had been impeccable. The constant flow of new locomotives and freight cars from the North kept Sherman's forces fully supplied with ammunition, fodder, and food.

Nevertheless, Sherman was up against a skilled opponent in Joe Johnston. Union forces would take until July to reach Atlanta. At that point Jefferson Davis relieved Johnston and replaced him with John Bell Hood, a competent division commander but a disaster as an army commander. Hood's mind remained fixed on the battles of 1862, with Lee's slashing attacks against Union forces. Hood immediately launched three major attacks during which Union defenders inflicted casualties the Confederacy could not afford. In effect, his losses made Atlanta no longer defensible. The city fell in early September, all but assuring Lincoln's reelection. For the next month, skirmishing occurred in northern Georgia as Hood tried to cut Sherman's logistical lines. Sherman, supported by Grant, then made one of the more imaginative decisions of the war. He sent a portion of the western army back to Nashville to guard against Hood's Army of Tennessee. Then he took sixty thousand of his best soldiers, cut his logistical lines, and launched into central and southern Georgia to destroy its agriculture and manufacturing.

After a Confederate raid up the Shenandoah Valley and then down the Potomac caused panic in Washington, Grant unleashed the ferocious Phil Sheridan not only to destroy Confederate forces in the valley but the valley as well. His instructions were clear: Sheridan was to "eat Virginia clear and clean as far as they go, so that crows flying over it for the balance of the season will have to carry their provender with them."[38] But if Sheridan's destruction of the Shenandoah was a body blow to the Army of Northern Virginia, Sherman's March to the Sea through Georgia's heartland was a stab in the Confederacy's heart. Confederate armies could no longer protect the civilian population from the Union Army's depredations. Sherman estimated that his armies inflicted $100 million worth of damage in Georgia of which only $20 million supported the army in its advance to Savannah. Considering that the entire budget for the Union Army in 1860 was only $20 million, one can sense the magnitude of the destruction.

But Sherman was not through. Instead of resting on his laurels as his army reached Savannah at Christmas 1864, he turned north into South Carolina in early February 1865. Cognizant of that state's role in secession, the troops wrecked it from one end to the other. They finally emerged from the towns they nicknamed "Chimneyvilles"—because that was all that remained of them—and entered North Carolina.

As Sherman's soldiers moved north under winter's appalling conditions of rain, sleet, and overflowing rivers, Grant executed one of the most impressive logistical moves of the war. Worried that Lee might cut the Army of Northern Virginia loose from the siege of Richmond and Petersburg and join up with Confederate forces in the Carolinas to attack Sherman, Grant ordered a corps detached from central Tennessee to meet and reinforce Sherman when he entered North Carolina. In the dead of winter, 21,000 Union troops, their artillery, impedimenta, and horses and mules moved by rail from Tennessee to Annapolis in eleven days and then took steamboats from the Chesapeake to North Carolina—another six days. They moved 1,400 miles in slightly over two weeks.

The denouement came in spring 1865. The collapse of Confederate forces defending Petersburg and Richmond led inevitably to the surrender at Appomattox. Less well known, but symptomatic of the war's ruthlessness, was a major Union drive from central Tennessee aimed at wrecking the largely untouched industry and infrastructure of northern and central Alabama and Mississippi. On 22 March, General James Wilson, one of Grant's protégés, led a force of 13,500 cavalry, equipped with seven-shot Spencers, to complete this bit of unfinished business. Crushing Nathan Bedford Forrest's ill-equipped and undermanned cavalry, Wilson finished the mission by the time Confederate armies surrendered in the East.

An embittered southern woman put the spring of 1865 in perspective: "We never yielded in the struggle until we were bound hand & foot & the heel of the despot was on our throats. Bankrupt in men in money, & in provisions, the wail of the bereaved & the cry of hunger rising all over the land. Our cities burned with fire and our pleasant things laid waste, the best & bravest of our men in captivity, and the entire resources of our country exhausted—what else could we do but give up."[39]

The Wars of German Unification

It has always been a conundrum for military historians that the American Civil War and the German Wars of Unification occurred at virtually the same time but that the latter ended much more quickly. The context within which the European wars took place, and Otto von Bismarck's competence in directing Prussian strategy, had much to do with the outcomes. The way in which the chief of the Prussian general staff, Helmuth von Moltke, conducted military operations also played a role, but without Bismarck's political and strategic framework, it is doubtful the Prussian military would have achieved such stunning successes.

Bismarck became chancellor in 1860 following a power struggle between the king and the Reichstag over Prussia's military budget. Bismarck finessed the crisis by disregarding the constitution and simply collecting the necessary taxes. When the Danish king died without leaving a male heir, the German states refused to recognize Danish claims to the provinces of Schleswig-Holstein. The issue quickly led to a sharp war that began in 1864 but, given the overwhelming power of Austria and Prussia, ended in just nine months.

Most military experts of the time considered Austria the more powerful nation, but there was a crucial, unintended effect of the Congress of Vienna of 1815. When the European powers sorted out the wreckage left by the French, the Russians acquired large portions of what had been the eastern provinces of Prussia, so the latter received parts of the Rhineland in compensation. The strategic aim was to use the Prussians to contain the French should they try to regain their empire. The territory Prussia acquired included the Ruhr River Valley, which by 1860 had become a center of rapid industrialization. Moreover, the development of railroads was transforming the German economy. In 1860, the German Confederation possessed roughly 7,500 miles of railroads, of which 3,500 lay in Prussian territory. Railroad-building in Prussia had a significantly different rationale from that in United States. American railroads ran where capitalistic entrepreneurs hoped to make money. The location of Prussian railroads, meanwhile, partially reflected Moltke's and the general staff's desire to speed up mobilization time for Prussia's reserves, an important concern given that they confronted potential enemies on three sides.

Austria's strategic position and military were weaker than most supposed, and in fact were inferior to Prussia's.[40] On the strategic level, the Russians were thoroughly hostile to Austria, while France hoped to extract territorial concessions from the Prussians but made no preparations for war. The British, sailing on their sea of "splendid isolation," were content to remain observers of Central Europe. Bismarck understood that to realize its aims, Prussia had to win its wars quickly, before other powers could intervene.

Several aspects of the military balance favored Prussia.[41] At the operational level, Prussian railroads allowed a swift deployment and aggressive moves that caught the Austrians and their allies, the German states, by surprise. But perhaps Prussia's most important advantage was the army's general staff. Created in response to the humiliating defeats at Jena-Auerstedt in 1806 and consisting of officers educated at the Kriegsakademie, the German war college, the students of which provided a central command that could react rapidly and effectively to events on the battlefield. At the tactical level, the Prussians possessed the needle gun, the first viable breech-loading rifle equipping a European army, which had a paper cartridge that allowed for rapid firing as well as loading by a soldier in a prone position. That tactical advantage, a product of the Industrial Revolution, proved enormously important.

Enjoying the advantage of faster deployment via railroad, the westernmost Prussian army invaded Hannover and Saxony in mid-June 1864 and overran both states. Meanwhile, Moltke deployed three Prussian armies, totaling 221,000 soldiers, to the borders of Bohemia and proceeded to invade Austria. The Austrian Army slowly muddled through a concentration in central Bohemia. Its commander, Prince Benedek, surprised by the speed of the Prussian advance, retreated to just outside the small town of Königgrätz with an army of 190,000 Austrians and 25,000 Saxons. The size of these armies reflected the growth of Europe's population. At the Battle of Leuthen in 1757, 66,000 Austrians had confronted 29,000 Prussians. A century later, the Austrian population had tripled, and Prussia's had increased sevenfold.[42]

Benedek mistakenly deployed his army with the Elbe River at its rear, which made retreat difficult. Only two of the three Prussian armies confronted the Austrians when the fighting began on 3 July 1866. Benedek, aware of the needle gun's superior firepower, ordered his subordinates to rely on their artillery, which had greater range than that of the Prussians, while holding their infantry in defensive positions. Initially, the Austrian artillery inflicted heavy casualties. But an advance by the Prussian 7th Division seized most of the Swiepwald, a forested area on the right and forward of Prussian positions. Austrian commanders then launched a series of disastrous counterattacks that fell apart under the fire of the needle gun. The Austrians committed over 80 percent of the battalions on their right flank, and out of forty-nine committed to the fight, twenty-eight simply disappeared. The arrival of the Prussian Crown Prince's army, marching to the sound of the guns, ended Austrian hopes. Only desperate cavalry charges and last stands by artillery units prevented their army's destruction. The Austrians lost well over thirty thousand, the Prussians under ten thousand. Moltke and his fellow generals saw the road to Vienna open before them.

But at that moment, Bismarck stepped in and agreed to an armistice.[43] The Iron Chancellor understood there were two fundamental ways that Prussia's triumph could unravel. The first was that continuation of the war might bring the French or Russians into the conflict. More uncertain and threatening was that the Hapsburg monarchy might collapse with unpredictable consequences, none of them to Prussia's advantage. Bismarck offered the Austrians a peace treaty in which they lost no territory and needed only agree to let Prussia absorb the northern German states. The southern principalities would remain independent but closely allied to Prussia, which would control their foreign and military policies.

That settlement, had it lasted, would have kept the Catholics of southern Germany separate from the Protestants in the north. Bismarck might have been satisfied with such a state of affairs, but the French refused and almost immediately began interfering in German affairs in the south. Driving the French was the fact that Napoleon III's so-called empire was in political trouble at home, and the emperor desperately needed a foreign policy success to restore his regime's prestige. By 1870, Franco-Prussian relations had deteriorated almost to the point of war.

Nevertheless, it took Bismarck's careful editing of an account of a meeting between the French ambassador and Prussian king to persuade the French that the king had impugned their honor, and the Prussians that the French ambassador had insulted their king.[44] Bismarck then made a move fraught with danger: he unleashed German nationalism to support the war, in the hope that the southern German states would fall into step with Prussia. But the potential was for a war different from that of 1866 and more like the American Civil War. It might well have united the Industrial and French Revolutions, especially if the French had responded in kind, and it would have brought the fourth military-social revolution to Europe.

By 1870, the balance in weaponry was somewhat different from 1866. The new French rifle, the *chassepot*, was clearly superior to the Prussian needle gun; the French also possessed the *mitrailleuse*, the first machine gun, but had classified it so highly that few generals knew of its existence, much less its capabilities. The Prussians had addressed their weakness in artillery by equipping themselves with steel, breech-loading cannons, clearly superior to what the French possessed. But war is more than just better technology. In the matter of organization and generalship, the French were fighting out of their league. They had no staff to speak of, and their generals were solidly tied to ill-thought-out concepts from the Napoleonic Wars. Georges Clemenceau once described a French general in the late 1870s as possessing the uniform of a marshal but the soul of a second lieutenant. It was an apt description of French generals in 1870. Initial plans involved an invasion of the Rhineland but with no clear purpose or aim.

The French never came close to the Rhineland. Skillfully using Germany's railroads, Moltke and the general staff deployed 380,000 regular and reserve troops on the frontier, while a muddled French mobilization deployed only 224,000. Napoleon III established two armies, but neither possessed the staff or experience to control the corps assigned to it, rendering both armies' logistics and operational movements inept and uncertain. Moltke, as he had done against the Austrians, established three armies, while the general staff used the telegraph to control army movements and the supply systems. From the start, the French *chassepot* dominated the tactical battlefield, but it mattered not a whit. Skillful Prussian movement at the operational level negated whatever tactical advantages the French gained from superior infantry weapons.

On 6 August 1870, the Crown Prince's army defeated the French at Wissembourg, on the Franco-German border; the casualties were nearly the same on both sides, but the Prussians also captured six thousand French soldiers. More importantly, the Prussians turned the flank of Marshal Edme Patrice Maurice de MacMahon's army and forced the French to retreat from Alsace. At nearly the same time, French forces under Marshal François Achille Bazaine failed to support its II Corps and suffered a significant rebuff near Spicheren despite inflicting heavy casualties on the Prussians. But Moltke, controlling the movements of his First and Second Armies, drove a wedge between the two French armies, while the Crown Prince's Third Army, on the Prussian left, outflanked MacMahon's army.

In effect, the Prussians improved their position by working their way around the French flanks. On 16 August, Moltke's armies ran into Bazaine in an encounter at Mars-la-Tour. Casualties on each side were equally matched: seventeen thousand Prussians and sixteen thousand French. The battle may have been a draw in tactical terms, but Bazaine made the mistake of retreating to the north rather than pulling back to the west. His decision made no sense, as it allowed the Prussians to envelop his entire army. Two days later came the decisive battles in the war. Again, the tactical battlefield favored the French, but the operational decisions made by the French high command guaranteed defeat.

The Battle of St. Privat–Gravelotte cost the French any chance of reaching Verdun and preventing the Prussians from surrounding them in the fortress city of Metz. Moltke began the battle by ordering the First and Second Armies to attack French positions. Beginning in the morning, massed Prussian assaults fell on the dug-in French VI Corps. Outnumbered nearly five to one, the French inflicted fearsome casualties on the attackers. Nevertheless, the French generals failed to reinforce the VI Corps. At Gravelotte, the Prussians, supported by superior artillery, gained local successes, but a collapse of command and control led to a stalemate.

By early evening, the French were in a position to gain a significant success and open the way to escape encirclement, but Bazaine refused to launch an attack that might have broken the Prussians. Instead, he pulled back on Metz, guaranteeing that the Prussians would complete their encirclement. Casualties were heavy on both sides, but the Prussians lost more: 20,163 to 12,273. The Prussian Guard Corps lost 8,000 out of 18,000. In his postwar analysis, Moltke recognized the implications of these casualties and noted it was unlikely Prussia could repeat its success in the next war.[45]

Like Grant at Vicksburg, Moltke had maneuvered his enemy into a trap from which there was no escape. The crushing result of this first trial at arms placed Napoleon III's regime in dire political straits; a war the French had started in order to regain the emperor's collapsing prestige now threatened the overthrow of his regime. In response, he ordered MacMahon to gather the remainder of France's regular army, approximately 130,000 men, and relieve Bazaine in Metz. Napoleon III then decided to accompany MacMahon. By maneuvering the relief army along the Franco-Belgian border, MacMahon created an ideal position for the Prussians to outflank his forces, pin his divisions at Sedan against the border, and pound them with artillery fire. On 2 September 1870, the emperor surrendered, along with the remains of MacMahon's army. Having defeated one army at Sedan and trapped the other at Metz, the Prusso-Germans had destroyed the regular French Army in forty-four days.

But the war was not over. While the defeats on the frontier and the surrender of the emperor spelled the end of the Second Empire, new leaders emerged in Paris to declare a republic and a *levée en masse*. Just as in 1792, French nationalist feeling exploded to meet the invader. But unlike in 1792, when many junior officers and NCOs remained to provide experienced leadership for the raw, untrained levees, in 1870 virtually the entire officer and NCO corps was moldering in Prusso-German POW camps. The new French armies were much like the Union and Confederate Armies in 1861. But while those amateur forces had only to confront each other, the French *levées* in the fall and winter of 1870–1871 were up against combat-hardened Prusso-German troops.

Adding to French difficulties, the invasion had put much of the northern, industrialized region of France under German control. Their occupation of this land had little impact, however, because Bismarck ordered German troops not to approach the English Channel for fear of upsetting the British. Instead, the French imported considerable amounts of arms. Nevertheless, they were still in a hopeless operational and strategic position. The Prusso-German armies now marched on Paris, along roads that Phil Sheridan, accompanying Bismarck and the Prussian King Wilhelm, noted were macadamized and hard-surfaced, in stark contrast to the roads in the Confederacy.

On arriving at Paris, Moltke and Bismarck fell into a ferocious quarrel. The latter wanted the army to begin its bombardment of Paris immediately because he feared that the longer the war lasted, the greater the possibility that Russia or Austria might intervene. But Moltke was having considerable difficulty supplying his armies and felt he could not spare the horses and vehicles needed to bring up ammunition for an effective bombardment of Paris. Meanwhile, the Prusso-German staff confronted the fact that French armies, no matter how ill-trained, were forming up to break through and relieve Paris. The French were also waging a sustained guerrilla war, the so-called *francs-tireurs*, who blew up bridges and generally made life miserable for supply columns wending their way through northern France on the way to Paris. In late winter 1871, the French eventually surrendered to the logic of their strategic and operational situation, made worse by the outbreak of a rebellion in Paris that threatened the existence of the new republic.

In the end, the defeat of the French armies ensured that the new republic could not put together an effective military force to challenge the Prusso-German armies. No matter how effective its efforts in calling France's youth to the colors, the republic lacked even a semblance of an NCO or officer corps to organize and train the new recruits. Virtually all of them were in POW camps in Germany. The new armies floundered in the winter mud against the well-trained Germans.

A Century of Peace?

One of the major anomalies of European history lies in the fact that between 1815 and 1914 there were few wars between the major powers. In fact, the nearly one hundred years divides neatly into two periods, 1815 to 1854 and 1871 to 1914. In the case of the first, one suspects that the sheer exhaustion caused by the French Revolutionary and Napoleonic Wars took much of the eagerness for war out of the international system. Moreover, only France had some desire to overthrow the international order, but the fact that it received a relatively easy peace from the victors removed much of the desire for *revanche*. The British sailed unthreatened in a world in which militarily they dominated the world's oceans, and economically the Industrial Revolution provided them with an unassailable position. Finally, in Eastern Europe, the three great powers settled down to attempt to rebuild economies and political systems badly damaged by the wars against the French.

None of those influences were in play after the successful conclusion of the Franco-Prussian War. Nevertheless, there were a number of factors that would keep the peace. For the first two decades of the period, particularly after "the war in sight crisis of 1875," Bismarck understood that the new German state possessed considerable vulnerabilities, given its geographic position in Europe's center. Consequently, he made every effort to maintain the peace, especially given the growing competition of the Russians and Austrians in the Balkans. As he understood, that region of Europe was not worth the bones of a single Pomeranian grenadier. His successors would entirely miss that simple truism.

But perhaps the largest explanation for the European peace before 1914 lay in the mad race of the powers to seize territories across the globe. The weakest proved the easiest targets because they possessed neither the economic powers nor the weaponry to withstand the European outliers. They might win occasional victories, such as the Little Big Horn or Isandlwana, but they lacked the sustained military technology, training, and logistical support to survive against European armies. As Hilaire Belloc commented, "Whatever happens, we have got the Maxim gun and they have not." The colonies the Europeans established all too often resembled the murderous regimes the Spanish had imposed in Mexico and Peru in the sixteenth century, with the Belgians in the Congo and the Germans in southwest Africa as particularly noteworthy. But those conquered by the Europeans in the nineteenth century would have their revenge after World War II.

CHAPTER SIX

The First World War

1914–1916

What made war inevitable was the growth of Athenian power
and the fear which this caused in Sparta.

—THUCYDIDES, *History of the Peloponnesian War*

NINETY-NINE YEARS AFTER the Napoleonic Wars ended, what became
known to contemporaries as the Great War exploded. Between these two
catastrophes, humanity had seen the spread of science, technology, industry,
and engineering to an extent unprecedented in history. It seemed that civilization was heading toward new heights. By the beginning of the twentieth
century, the first period of globalization was well underway. Yet a few bullets fired in Sarajevo in June 1914 plunged Europe and then the world into
a conflict, the length and murderous cost of which few had expected, and
which would destroy many of the sureties on which Western civilization
had comfortably rested. The Great War would come far closer to Clausewitz's concept of "total war" than the Napoleonic Wars or any other war.

This war that seemed to have no end was driven by the fourth military-social revolution, which after its early appearance in the American
Civil War, would again see the French and Industrial Revolutions merge
in a deadly fashion. Industrial developments and economic strength
combined to provide unheard-of wealth as well as political and social

stability, while rabid nationalism provided a willingness to "pay any price, bear any burden." Underlying those revolutions was a growth in population and wealth fueled by advances in science, technology, and agriculture. The extent of improvements in the human condition was to create a battlefield of increasing intensity and complexity that made achieving decisive victory even more an illusion than in the past.

The war would come out of the explosive growth in nationalism that had occurred throughout the Western world over a near half-century of peace since the Franco-Prussian War. The markers are clear to us in the twenty-first century. Winston Churchill expressed that course in his comment that "events got on certain lines, and no one could get them off again. Germany clanked obstinately, recklessly, awkwardly towards the crater and dragged us all with her."[1] The first step had come with Kaiser Wilhelm's death in 1888 and the ending of Bismarck's crucial influence on the Reich's foreign policy. With the Iron Chancellor's removal, Germany lost its compass. The new kaiser, Wilhelm II, was simply incapable of strategic vision. He pandered to a rising nationalism and shared none of Bismarck's caution. Even the military, Wilhelm's one consistent interest, was ruled by chaos rather than coherence. No fewer than forty senior officers possessed the right of direct access to the kaiser.

In 1890, almost immediately after he fired Bismarck, the kaiser terminated the Reinsurance Treaty with Russia, in the mistaken belief that Tsarist Russia would never ally itself with republican France. He and his advisors had badly misjudged the diplomatic realities, and the alliance of Germany and Austria-Hungary soon confronted that of France and Russia. In the first decade of the twentieth century, the incompetence of German diplomacy and strategy steadily drove the British to settle their major differences, first with the French in 1904 and then with the Russians in 1907. Especially egregious was the kaiser's decision to build the High Seas Fleet, derided by Churchill as the "luxury" fleet, a naval force that directly threatened Britain's security. The Germans had no chance of winning a naval race because the Reich required a great army for the Continent.[2]

The crisis began in the early twentieth century with the collapse of the Ottoman Empire, quite accurately known as the "sick man of Europe." Encouraged by the Italian seizure of Libya from the Turks in 1911, Serbia, Bulgaria, Montenegro, and Greece attacked the empire in October 1912. Although they called themselves the Balkan League, they were a collection of small, greedy states with no commitment to unity. They quickly disposed

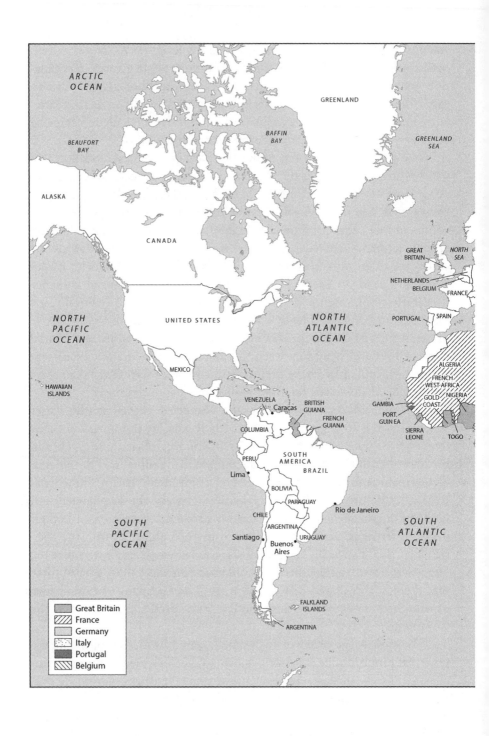

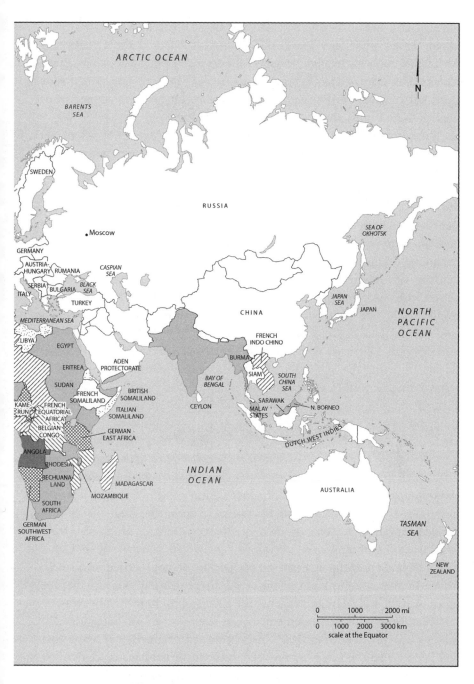

ARCTIC OCEAN

N

BARENTS
SEA

SWEDEN

RUSSIA

• Moscow

SEA OF
OKHOTSK

GERMANY

AUSTRIA-
HUNGARY   RUMANIA

CASPIAN
SEA

SERBIA   BLACK
ITALY   BULGARIA   SEA

TURKEY

CHINA

JAPAN
SEA

JAPAN

NORTH
PACIFIC
OCEAN

MEDITERRANEAN SEA

LIBYA   EGYPT

FRENCH
INDO CHINO

ERITREA

ADEN
PROTECTORATE

SUDAN

FRENCH
SOMALILAND

BURMA

BAY OF
BENGAL

SIAM

SOUTH
CHINA
SEA

BRITISH
SOMALILAND

KAME-
RUN   FRENCH
EQUATORIAL
AFRICA

ITALIAN
SOMALILAND

CEYLON

SARAWAK
MALAY
STATES

N. BORNEO

BELGIAN
CONGO

GERMAN
EAST AFRICA

DUTCH WEST INDIES

ANGOLA

INDIAN
OCEAN

AUSTRALIA

RHODESIA

BECHUANA
LAND

MADAGASCAR

MOZAMBIQUE

TASMAN
SEA

SOUTH
AFRICA

GERMAN
SOUTHWEST
AFRICA

NEW
ZEALAND

0   1000   2000 mi

0   1000   2000   3000 km
scale at the Equator

The world in 1914. Cartography by Bill Nelson.

of the Turks and almost immediately set about quarreling over the spoils. Discontented with their share, the Bulgarians attacked the Greeks and Serbs; the renewed struggle stripped the former of virtually all its gains. The Turks even managed to regain Adrianople. The Serbs made the major gains but remained dissatisfied after the Austro-Hungarians stepped in to prevent them from acquiring a port on the Adriatic.

Bismarck had once commented that the Balkans were not worth the bones of a single Pomeranian grenadier, but that strategic wisdom no longer existed in Berlin. In the crisis over the wars in the Balkans, the Germans stood by the Austrians but hesitated to support military action. Still, the Germans were sufficiently threatening that in 1913 the Russians backed away from war. Matters turned out differently in 1914. The Serbian-sponsored assassination of the Austro-Hungarian Crown Prince, Archduke Franz Ferdinand, offered Austria the opportunity to settle matters with the Serbs. In late July, more than a month after the assassination, the Austrians presented a harsh ultimatum. Even though Serbia refused only one of a number of demands, Austria-Hungary declared war. Russia then began a partial mobilization, which turned into a full mobilization. Germany responded by declaring war on France and Russia and initiating the Schlieffen Plan, which encompassed the invasion of France, Belgium, and Luxembourg.

The Economic Background

The expansion of the modern state's economic and military power in the nineteenth century represents the greatest such advance in history. Even the opening decade of the twenty-first century did not match this era. For one of the few periods in European history, the great powers remained largely quiescent, at least on their continent. Ironically, their focus was on grabbing large portions of the world, particularly in Africa. The result of prolonged peace was a period of unprecedented growth driven by technological and scientific advances that led to a furious pace of innovation and adaptation across the spectrum of human endeavors.

The most important element in the explosion of science and technology was the accelerating feedback between them. Before 1870 that had been far less the case. As one economic historian has noted, the first Industrial Revolution "created a chemical industry with no chemistry, an iron industry without metallurgy, power machinery without thermodynamics. Engineering, medical technology, and agriculture were pragmatic bodies of knowledge in which things were known to work, but rarely was it understood why they worked."[3]

The period after 1850 saw not only technological advances but the combining of innovations with other innovations to create new possibilities. The marriage of the telegraph and the railroad was only the first of these. The invention of the Bessemer process in the 1850s and then the open-hearth method, the latter an invention of two amateurs, made steel relatively cheap. That in turn improved both the locomotives and the rails on which they rode, furthering the transportation revolution. Cheaper steel allowed the introduction of all-metal ships, while the invention of the steam turbine revolutionized their speed and carrying capacity.

The creation of the chemical industry opened a host of new possibilities. The most obvious was Alfred Nobel's invention of nitroglycerine, with its impact on the construction industry. In 1909, two German chemists invented the process of utilizing nitrogen in the atmosphere to produce ammonia, crucial for production of both fertilizer and ammunition. Perhaps the most impressive advance was that of electrical power, which not only turned night into day but revolutionized the design of factories. The appearance of the bicycle and automobile fundamentally altered how humans moved across the landscape. The latter depended on a series of innovations in fields including the ability of the chemical industry to break down crude petroleum into useful fuels. Waiting in the wings was the airplane, which depended on sophisticated improvements in internal combustion engines.

Increases in European industrial output between 1870 and 1913 underlined the extent of growth. During that period, British coal production increased from 112 million metric tons to 292 million (160%). German coal production rose even more, from 26 million tons to 190 million. The increase in pig iron production was similar: for the British, from 6,059,000 metric tons to 10,425,000; for the Germans, from 1,261,000 tons to 16,761,000. The value of German industrial production in 1913 was six times what it had been in 1855.[4] Sustaining the Second Industrial Revolution was an agricultural revolution that altered the methods of production, increased the output of farms by an order of magnitude, allowed the movement of foodstuffs over continental and oceanic distances, and freed up vast amounts of labor for factory and professional work. Crucial to the fourth military-social revolution was the transportation revolution, which allowed movement of foodstuffs over great distances. By the turn of the century, Britain imported nearly 70 percent of its food.[5]

Many factors revolutionized the world's food supply. One was the opening of the great agricultural lands of the United States, Canada, Australia, New Zealand, and Argentina. Adding to the productivity of new as well as old lands was the increasing use of Chilean nitrates. The introduction of fungicides, invented in 1885, reduced the dreaded potato blight to a nuisance. Swift, reliable ocean transport along with refrigeration allowed the shipment of meat products across the oceans. On the surface, the Germans seemed less vulnerable to the loss of agricultural imports, because they imported less food than did the British. But there was a significant discontinuity in the German economy. The Germans were a world-class power in heavy industry, but in other respects, particularly agriculture, their economy was not nearly as impressive. Much of their labor force was employed in low-productivity agriculture. When the war came, the army drafted a large portion of the farm population and their horses, with results that soon became clear.

In the largest sense, the combined influence of the Industrial Revolution and the French Revolution allowed the modern state to mobilize vastly increased populations for war. The fourth military-social revolution put an end to worries about the inability of the modern state to bear the economic costs of a major European war. Improved agriculture provided sufficient food and fodder to sustain both the armies in the field and the workforce at home. The modern state was able to raise unheard-of sums of money and resources to produce enough ammunition and weapons to send endless streams of young men marching off to war.[6]

The problem in 1914 was that military and social leaders could not see, much less understand, the implications of the fourth military-social revolution. They certainly lacked the ability to understand the implications of economic and technological advances. Moreover, financial experts argued that the modern state could not support the burden of a major war, while political analysts, partially influenced by the Russo-Japanese War, suggested that war would quickly bring on a massive social revolution. The result in the prewar period was a search for a decisive victory, whatever the costs, to prevent either revolution or economic collapse.

The Military Implications

It is a truism that stupidity reigned supreme among the military establishments on both sides of World War I. Yet when one examines the period before the war, one is struck by the complexities and difficulties that statesmen as well as generals confronted. At the strategic level, as Germany's official history of the war notes, "All competent authorities ... took the view that in case of war the decision must be sought as quickly as possible ... on economic grounds to achieve a quick victory."[7] The chief of the German general staff at the turn of the century, Graf Alfred von Schlieffen, commented that wars of long duration "are ... impossible at a time when a nation's existence is founded on the uninterrupted continuance of trade and industry; indeed a rapid decision is essential if the machinery that has been brought to a standstill is to be set in motion again."[8]

This view pushed Schlieffen toward the plan for which he became infamous—a massive invasion of the Low Countries. His thinking also reflected an emphasis on what the Germans termed "military necessity," a belief that tactical and operational concerns must always come first. Politics and strategy no longer mattered, especially if they contradicted military necessity. Thus, violating the Low Countries' neutrality did not matter in the face of military necessity.[9]

But even had military organizations recognized the weaknesses in their assumption that a short war represented a mirage, they still could never have foreseen the complexity of tactical problems the war raised. As Paul Kennedy has noted,

> It seems worth claiming that it was at the *tactical* level in this war (much more so than in the 1939–1945 conflict) that the critical problems occurred. The argument, very crudely, would run as follows: because soldiers could not break through a trench system, their generals' plans for campaign successes were stalemated on each side; these operational failures in turn impacted upon the strategic debate at the highest level, and thus upon the strategic options being considered by national policy makers; and these, *pari passu*, affected the consideration of ends versus means at the political level, the changing nature of civil-military relations, and the allocation of national resources.[10]

The fact that the military organizations of 1914 lacked staff organizations to draw significant lessons from what was happening in battlefield tactics and innovations only exacerbated the problem. As Michael Howard has pointed out, "Military organizations invariably get the next war wrong, and [in] these circumstances when everybody starts wrong, the advantage goes to the side which can most quickly adjust itself to the new and unfamiliar environment."[11] In 1914, military organizations found these adaptations extraordinarily difficult. Virtually everything was unexpected, and they had little background against which to analyze what was happening.

Yet they did learn. Ironically, given military leaders' reputation for stupidity in the conflict, their organizations proved adaptive and innovative.[12] David Zabecki notes that the war introduced no less than forty-four technological changes into the conflict, each having a significant impact.[13] Such innovations then had to be worked into tactical concepts, which themselves were changing in response to the enemy's adaptations. One might think of the First World War in biological terms, involving complex, adaptive systems in which the opposing armies found themselves forced to adapt to ever more uncertain realities but with few analytic means to understand the implications of those changes. Another way to consider the extent of the changes is that if one were to take a brigade commander of 1918 to the Gulf War of 1991, he would be able to grasp what was occurring, once he grew accustomed to the increased speed and lethality of the battlespace. But a 1914 brigade commander transported to the battlefield of 1918 would understand nothing.

An End to Illusions: The Battles of 1914

The war began with three great campaigns on land and an attempt by the British to use their control over the oceanic commons to break the German economy. All of these campaigns failed because the armies lacked the tactical and operational means to achieve the ends they sought. The Germans came closest with the Schlieffen Plan, which aimed to outflank the French armies by sweeping through the Low Countries to create a great encirclement battle somewhere east of Paris.[14] The plan's aim was to knock the French out of the war before the Russians could fully mobilize and then turn on them. On the face of it, the Schlieffen Plan looked like a brilliant solution to Germany's need to confront a two-front war in a great-power conflict.

But there were underlying weaknesses. On the strategic level, German violation of the Low Countries would inevitably bring the British into the conflict, with both short- and long-range consequences.[15] On the operational level, the Germans had no plan for handling the problems raised by the French capital. Would the German movement swing

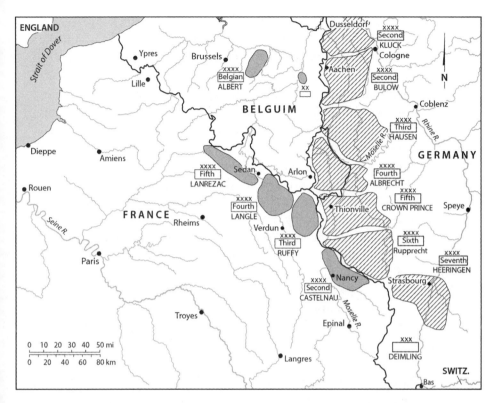

Concentration areas, Northwest Europe, August 1914. Cartography by Bill Nelson.

past Paris or would it storm the city? Moreover, there were major logistical issues, which Belgian demolition of the railroads only exacerbated and for which the Germans did little to prepare.[16]

On 4 August 1914, slightly over 1 million Germans began their offensive against Western Europe. The lead elements, First and Second Armies, deployed through the Liège Gap in Belgium, an opening in the mountainous terrain in northern Belgium approximately twelve miles across with heavy forested hills on both sides. Alexander von Kluck's First Army was to lead the advance and, upon reaching Brussels, pivot ninety degrees to drive into France as the right wing of the German advance. But as Helmuth von Moltke had noted in 1871, "No plan of operations extends with any certainty beyond the first encounter with enemy forces." Or as Mike Tyson noted, "Everyone has a plan until they get punched in the face." And sure enough, the Schlieffen Plan immediately ran into problems. Belgian infantry in the Liège Gap inflicted heavy casualties on attacking German infantry, while major fortresses presented a significant problem. Monstrous Krupp and Skoda mortars eventually destroyed the forts, but the Belgians had already delayed the Germans by several days. Belgian resistance and the destruction of much of the railroad infrastructure further annoyed the Germans. Fury at the resistance led the Germans to murder six thousand Belgian and French civilians through September, most innocent civilians. In addition, they destroyed between fifteen and twenty thousand buildings, including Louvain with its priceless medieval library and manuscripts.[17]

While the Germans drove into the Low Countries, the French launched a series of offensive operations beginning with one near the Swiss border and then moving north. Based on an *offensive à outrance* (offensive to the excess), the attackers suffered 300,000 casualties and one-quarter of their officer corps in the war's first month.[18] Only at the last moment did Joseph Joffre, commander-in-chief, awake to the threat posed by the German right wing. French strategy had rested on the belief the Germans would not use their reserve divisions so that any incursion into Belgium would remain limited to the right bank of the Meuse.

General Charles Lanrezac, commanding the Fifth Army on the French left wing, was the first to awaken to the danger. Worried that he was about to be outflanked, he ordered his army to retreat. The British Expeditionary Force (BEF), which had come up on the Fifth Army's left, also pulled back just as Kluck's First Army was about to swamp it. Had Kluck been allowed to outflank the BEF and Lanrezac's Fifth Army, the Germans might have won the Battle of France, but Kluck had found himself placed under the command of General Karl von Bülow, Second Army commander, who was not about to allow such a move. The result was a rapid Allied retreat to the south as Joffre desperately attempted to transfer forces from his right wing to meet the threat posed by the First and Second German Armies on his left. As the Allies retreated southward, they enjoyed an important advantage. They were falling back on their supply dumps and lines of communication. On the other hand, the Germans were moving steadily away from their supplies of food, fodder, and ammunition. Given that the armies were moving at a rate of twenty miles a day, they were on their last legs by the time they reached the Marne.

To keep contact with the Second Army, Kluck found himself forced to swing to the east of Paris and thereby opened his army to a flank attack by forces Joffre had been building up in the French capital. The counteroffensive in turn forced Kluck to transfer a substantial portion of his forces back to meet the threat coming from his west. In the resulting Battle of the Marne, nearly 2 million soldiers fought for six days between 5 and 10 September.[19] In the end, running out of supplies and with the BEF moving between their First and Second Armies, the Germans began a retreat that took them back to the Aisne River. The gamble had failed.

A number of major errors led to the failure. The most obvious was the fact that there was no overall commander. The younger Moltke found himself babysitting the Kaiser, while Kluck and Bülow argued rather than cooperated. As the Belgian Army pulled back on Antwerp, Moltke detailed two corps off the right wing to cover them, while the advance into France began. Then worried about the battle in East Prussia, he transferred a further two more to East Prussia. Those four corps *might* have made a difference, but in the end the Schlieffen Plan failed because it depended on too many assumptions. The command and control required to deploy and fight massive armies numbering in the hundreds of thousands did not yet exist. Moreover, German logistical preparations were entirely inadequate, as was to be the case in future German campaigns in both World Wars.

Defeat on the Marne did not end the fighting in the west. The Germans made one last effort. General Erich von Falkenhayn had replaced the younger Moltke after defeat on the Marne, and in October he used newly formed divisions, consisting largely of volunteers, to launch a major attack to drive the allies out of the Channel ports. Supposedly singing "Deutschland über alles," half-trained units were slaughtered by the professionals in the BEF. Allied forces almost broke, but they held after severe fighting.[20]

Major fighting was also occurring in the east. Two Russian armies, the First under General Paul von Rennenkampf and the Second under General Alexander Samsonov, struck East Prussia in August well before the Germans expected such an offensive.[21] Rennenkampf's First Army attacked from Vilnius while the Second Army advanced from Warsaw, but the coordinating headquarters provided no guidance. After the First Army moved into East Prussia and gave a German corps a drubbing at Gumbinnen, it halted and provided no support for Samsonov. That gave the Germans the opportunity to defeat the Russians in detail, of which they took full advantage.

At the point of greatest danger in East Prussia, Moltke replaced General Maximilian von Prittwitz with Paul von Hindenburg and Erich

Ludendorff as his chief of staff. By the time they arrived, the Eighth Army's staff had already set in motion the deployments that would take advantage of the Russian mistakes. Alerted by messages sent *en clair*, the Germans concentrated almost the entire Eighth Army against Samsonov while leaving a thin screen of cavalry to cover Rennenkampf. Instead of retreating, the Russians advanced into the sack. By 30 August, the Germans had destroyed Samsonov's army and captured 92,000 soldiers and 400 guns. In succeeding actions, they attempted to destroy Rennenkampf's army but only succeeded in chasing him out of East Prussia.

Meanwhile, to the south, the Austro-Hungarian Army floundered from disaster to disaster. Its commander, Franz Graf Conrad von Hötzendorf, led a badly planned, ramshackle mobilization that began by emphasizing an attack on Serbia but then switched to a deployment aimed at attacking the Russians in southern Poland. Filled with grandiose visions of Napoleonic victories, Conrad sent his armies into Poland where Russian armies overwhelmed them. By fall the Russians had driven the Austrians back on the Carpathians, only to be stopped by the collapse of their own logistical system. Austrian losses were appalling: 100,000 dead, 200,000 wounded, with 100,000 as POWs. Conrad had managed to lose one-third of his army in two months.[22] Heavy fighting in the east continued into the winter with no decisive results.

The casualty bill for 1914 is almost unimaginable. The fate of the BEF is typical: its force of 110,000 suffered 86,237 casualties. German casualties were over 800,000, while the official figure for the Austro-Hungarian Army was 692,195 but was in fact over 1 million, including POWs.[23] Russian casualties matched those suffered by the Germans. The total for all armies was close to 3 million, making the last five months of 1914 the bloodiest period in human history. Modern weapons could kill hundreds of thousands, but they were incapable of achieving anything more than local, transitory successes.

Popular and Industrial Mobilization

Many of Europe's leaders had expected that a declaration of war would be met by riots, strikes, and other signs of rebellion. Nothing of the sort occurred. As Hew Strachan notes, "The picture of widespread enthusiasm for the war does stand in need of modification and amplification. But its fundamental message remains unequivocal. The belligerent peoples of Europe accepted the onset of war; they did not reject it."[24] A new factor had emerged in the last half of the nineteenth century: a mass media, then consisting of daily newspapers, that provided comprehensive and believable accounts of the vicious enemies confronting their various nations. In an age when less information was available about foreign countries and peoples, governments found it easy to portray the war as pitting the civilized against the brutal and uncivilized.

Ironically, the spread of government-sponsored education, which always placed the student's own nation at the heart of civilization, undergirded the period's nationalism. That education also portrayed traditional enemies as existential threats. In Germany, the focus was on the Slavs as the "other." But the press, always flexible, did not hesitate to create new enemies. By 1914, the enemy was the British for many Germans, who were repeatedly told that Britain was robbing Germany of its place in the sun.[25] In the end, it was that deep nationalism, similar in many ways to that the French revolutionaries had raised in 1792, that gave political leaders no choice but to pursue the war to its bitter end. A *status quo antebellum* peace would have led people to ask if their government had unleashed Armageddon only to achieve minimal gains. So, the war continued.

The ongoing and very expensive war focused attention on the contending powers' economic and financial resources. This too echoed the call of the French Revolution: "Henceforth ... the French people are in Permanent requisition [and] married men shall forge arms and transport provisions."[26] The salient difference was that the French Republic's efforts declined over time, while those of the World War I powers tended to increase. The Germans were best prepared to mobilize their population and industry, but in the years leading up to the war they had exerted little effort to create stockpiles of raw materials. In August 1914, the German Interior Ministry questioned the country's five hundred largest firms as to their reserves. On average they reported their stocks would support no more than six months of war.

Two things saved the Germans. The British blockade was not fully effective for another two years, and the Germans established a section in the War Ministry—the Kriegsrohstoffabteilung, under Wichard von Moellendorff and Walther Rathenau—that created the framework for construction of factories to utilize the Haber-Bosch process for nitrogen fixation from the atmosphere. Production of synthetic ammonia allowed the Germans to escape the blockade of Chilean nitrates. Nevertheless, even though German production of gunpowder steadily climbed, it could not keep up with military demand. Little nitrate production was available for fertilizer to help Germany's relatively primitive agriculture. By 1918, Germany faced a condition close to starvation, a contributing factor in that year's collapse.[27]

Germany made impressive gains in the production of artillery and other munitions over the war's first eighteenth months. Between August and December 1914, shell production increased by a factor of seven, reaching over 1.6 million for light and field artillery. One year later that number had doubled. Increases in artillery were equally impressive, from 100 tubes per month in December 1914 to 270 by the following summer and 480 by December 1915. The Germans did suffer considerable damage from the blockade. In 1915, industrial production fell to 81 percent of the 1914 totals and a further 4 percent the following year. Iron and steel production fell to 68 percent of prewar totals.[28]

The Entente powers confronted quite different problems. Over the first month of the campaign, German armies captured much of France's industrial areas. By 1915, France's coal production had fallen to less than half of what it was in 1913, while iron ore was less than 30 percent of prewar levels. The Germans also captured over 57 percent of France's blast furnaces.[29] French industry also faced the problem that the army had called up 63 percent of the nation's workforce. Some eventually returned to the factories, but 184,000 workers from the colonies and a massive influx of women had to make up the difference.

Despite its territorial losses, France survived. A major advantage was that French socialist politicians, who ran industrial mobilization, worked more easily with the industrialists and unions than their German counterparts.[30] Moreover, the British, with their access to raw materials from a vast global empire, provided substantial economic help. Foreign sources, then, helped compensate for the loss of northern France. British coal exports to France rose to 7.9 million tons in 1915. In January 1916, the British exported 115,000 tons of iron to France.[31] In addition, the French significantly expanded their steel furnaces, producing nearly 2 million tons more in 1916 than in 1913.[32]

French production of shells also surged. By the last month of 1914, the country's major munition firms were delivering nearly 24,000 shells a day. But it was in the production of artillery tubes that the French ran into substantial problems. They had lost many artillery pieces in the August retreat, and demands to repair those damaged in combat steadily rose. It was not until the first quarter of 1916 that production of the small cannon known as "light artillery piece 75" hit full stride: French factories turned out as many in that quarter, one thousand, as they had produced in all of 1915.[33] The problem with heavier guns was more serious. The 75, the central weapon in the army's prewar artillery, was not ideal for the medium- to long-range use that the war on the Western Front demanded. Even in 1916, French industry produced only 245 heavy artillery pieces in the first six months and 345 in the second.[34]

The British had the most difficulty in adjusting to the war's industrial demands. They had not prepared for the problems that raising a great army and then maintaining it would create. While the War Office attracted a large number of volunteers at the war's beginning, it was hard-pressed to equip them with uniforms, artillery, rifles, and other impedimenta. By 1917, the office was responsible for well over fifty divisions, up from the six that had trundled onto the Continent in 1914. British financial support for the war suggests its cost. Treasury outlays for the two services (with the creation of the Royal Air Force in 1918 it would be three) were $438 million in 1913, approximately 30 percent of government expenditures. By 1918, they reached $9.388 billion, over 80 percent of government expenditures.[35] From 91 artillery tubes produced in 1914, numbers rose to 8,039 in 1918; machine guns from 300 to 120,900; shells from 500,000 to 67.3 million. Tanks had not existed in 1914; in 1918, British industry produced 1,359.[36]

Until early 1917, when the tsarist regime collapsed, the Russian industrial effort was impressive. Shell production in 1914 was 450,000 per month; by 1916, it had increased by a factor of ten. Production of other armaments improved by 20 percent over prewar levels. Nevertheless, this expanded military production created serious distortions in the economy. The diversion of much of the country's grain production to feed the troops created shortages in the cities, fueling inflation to nearly 400 percent by 1916, with disastrous effects on political stability.

Perhaps the most important revolution in military affairs was the appearance of the airplane as a crucial player on the battlefield. At the war's beginning, aircraft had some utility as a primitive reconnaissance tool. By 1918, air superiority was crucial to success in major ground offensives.[37] Fighters allowed close support of ground troops, interdiction attacks on enemy lines of communication, and reconnaissance of enemy defensive positions among other missions. To support the increasing numbers of sophisticated aircraft the battlespace required, the contending powers had to create massive industrial bases to produce large numbers of planes while innovating and developing improved capabilities to keep pace with the enemy.

The air war was as much a race to build more planes as to develop greater capabilities. By 1914, the nascent aircraft industries were reaching significant levels. In France, 9 separate firms employed 3,000 workers, while the Germans possessed 11 firms with 2,500 workers.[38] By 1916, each side had expanded its aircraft industry enormously to meet demand. In 1914, the Germans manufactured 1,348 aircraft; one year later that number had risen to 4,532. The French made the most impressive advances in air power. In December 1914, France's aircraft industry possessed 12,650 workers; by 1915, the number had grown to 30,960, and a year later to 68,920.[39] The British lagged behind, partly because of bureaucratic indifference. When the undersecretary of war was asked whether British industry could produce three thousand aircraft in six months, he replied that "no good purpose would be served by it, private industry could not deliver them, and the proportion of the air service in the army was adequate." Not surprisingly, the British were still far behind the Germans and French in 1916.[40] Nevertheless, by 1918 the Royal Air Force (RAF) possessed 22,000 aircraft, and its problem was now a lack of trained pilots.

We may think of the first two war years as a race to adapt to two problems. The first was the many difficulties created by the marriage of the Industrial and French Revolutions to form the fourth military-social revolution. The second was a stepchild of the first. The conditions of an entirely unexpected battlefield demanded constant adaptation to new capabilities and tactics. Moreover, as both changed, so did the enemy. New tactics demanded radical changes in training, logistics, technology, production, and weaponry. None of the prewar preparations by Europe's military organizations prepared the generals and their staffs for such an environment.

Blockade and Naval War

When the war began, everyone expected there would be a great naval battle in the North Sea. In July 1914, the Royal Navy possessed twenty modern battleships to the Germans' thirteen, and a four-to-three advantage in battlecruisers with four battlecruisers on detached duty. The leadership of both navies left much to be desired, particularly in organization and culture. The problem was partially the result of how rapidly

technology had developed. But it was also a cultural matter. The Royal
Navy believed it was the heir to Hawke and Nelson, but nincty-ninc
years of peace had drained its admirals of initiative and drive. Andrew
Gordon, the foremost historian of the navy in the war, noted, "Probably
at no other time in history has the [Royal Navy's] officer corps been so
uniformly molded in its cultural self-image as in 1914. They thought
they were good, but in many ways that mattered, they were not. They
thought they were ready for war, but they were not."[41]

Ironically, given that the Germans aimed to challenge the world's
most powerful navy, they were not much better. "It is symptomatic of the
tangled web of German military organization," noted historian Holger
H. Herwig, "that the navy's highest administrative officer, Tirpitz . . .
should have dictated strategy to the fleet. . . . The Admiralty staff, which
was charged with developing strategy at sea, was kept powerless by Tirpitz. There were no less than seven different heads of the organization
between 1899 and 1915."[42]

The Royal Navy's contribution to the Allied victory lay in its conduct of a distant blockade that steadily tightened. Before the war, the Admiralty had a more deadly plan for a war against Germany, centered on
squeezing and then strangling the German economy.[43] Its leaders, however, failed to anticipate that much of the British government would oppose such measures. Among those in opposition were the Foreign Office,
the Colonial Office, and especially the Board of Trade.[44] Whatever the
Admiralty's arguments, the cabinet divided into those urging a harsh
blockade and those favoring a light touch. Prime Minister Henry Asquith followed the avenue of least resistance and appointed two committees, with chairs holding opposing views, to examine blockade issues.[45]
On 14 August 1914, the cabinet released coal from the sanctioned list of
goods and authorized full trade with Denmark, Norway, and Holland.
Andrew Lambert notes, "Thus aggressive implementation of economic
warfare . . . lasted for a grand total of one day . . . or two weeks at most."[46]
The fact that raw materials and foodstuffs in Germany fetched up to
three times the price of such goods in Britain only increased British merchants' willingness to trade with the enemy.[47]

Even with considerable leakage in the blockade, in early 1915 the
Germans declared "unrestricted" submarine warfare in waters around the
British Isles.[48] The decision made little military sense because, at the time,
the navy had only twenty-nine boats. Moreover, construction of battleships was a higher priority; in 1915, German dockyards constructed only

fifteen U-boats.[49] But "unrestricted" submarine warfare provided the British with an excuse to strengthen the blockade. That tightening elicited only mild protests from the neutrals because the U-boats put their shipping at risk as well. By September 1915, American pressure had forced the Germans to abandon unrestricted submarine warfare, at least until 1917.

While the British slowly imposed their blockade, the two great fleets skirmished. In August 1914, Admiral David Beatty launched his battle-cruiser fleet into Heligoland Bight to support a destroyer raid and sank three German cruisers. That November, eight German cruisers crossed the North Sea to bombard the port of Yarmouth. It was the first of three such raids, one of which led to the sinking of the German battlecruiser *Blücher*. By the end of 1914, the British were able to read the German High Seas Fleet's coded message traffic.[50] The High Seas Fleet remained quiescent through most of 1915, but in 1916 it reemerged.

On the morning of 30 May 1916, it prepared to sortie, and within hours the decoded message was in the Admiralty's hands. That night, three hours before the Germans left harbor, the Grand Fleet sortied from Scapa and the battlecruisers left Rosyth. The ensuing Battle of Jutland saw the Germans sink a greater tonnage of British warships, but it mattered not at all. For the remainder of the war German battleships remained bottled up in ports along the German coasts. In the aftermath, as before, the Royal Navy continued to dominate the North Sea as well as the world's oceans.

The Western and Eastern Fronts, 1915

By 1915, the Western Front had settled into a stalemate. Appraising the possibilities, the German chief of staff, Erich von Falkenhayn, decided to target Germany's main effort in the east while German forces in the west would remain on the defensive. He told those defending German positions in the west that they must "hold on to what you have and never surrender a square foot on which you have won."[51] Nevertheless, in April 1915 the Germans could not resist the temptation to try out gas warfare. Driven by their belief in "military necessity," they examined neither its strategic impact nor its tactical implications but instead released chlorine gas in an attack on a French colonial division in April 1915 in Ypres. In the immediate moment, chlorine gas lived up to their expectations, but they had no reserves in place to take advantage of the situation. Strategically, the introduction of gas warfare provided a major propaganda coup for the Allies, and in the long term it gave them two advantages. First, the winds in France most commonly blew from west to east, making it easier for the Allies to use gas on the Germans than vice versa. Second, effective gas masks depended on rubber, which the Germans could not import because of the blockade.

For operations in the east in 1915, serious disagreements erupted between Falkenhayn and the Hindenburg-Ludendorff team (really Ludendorff). The latter argued for striking deep into Russia to destroy not only the Russian Army but Russia itself. Falkenhayn, however, knew that the German Army, with its primitive supply system of horse-drawn wagons, lacked the logistical capabilities to support Ludendorff's megalomania.[52] He hoped only to force Russia out of the war.

The German offensive in the east began on 2 May 1915. Within three days it destroyed two Russian corps while precipitating the collapse of Russian forces facing the Austro-Hungarians along the Carpathians. In effect, the Russian salient formed by Poland disintegrated. Overall, Russian losses reached 420,000.[53] The limited German advance continued through the summer, but while the Germans continued to win tactical victories, they could not knock Russia out of the war. Their limited operations on the empire's borderlands could bleed the Russian Army white but never directly threatened "Mother Russia."

In the west in 1915, Joffre found himself pressured to regain what France had lost. The problem was that the French had not yet developed the tactics to break through the German lines, which were increasingly fortified with dense entanglements of barbed wire and sophisticated trench systems. The French also confronted the problem that their artillery consisted mostly of light 75s and not the heavier pieces trench warfare required. As a result, they launched a number of costly offensives throughout the winter and spring of 1915 that gained little ground.

In March 1915, an attack by the French Fourth Army in Champagne along a narrow front of 1.5 miles gained less than a mile at the cost of 43,000 casualties.[54] In September and early October, the same army launched two major offensives in Champagne and Artois. The losses were appalling: 191,795 casualties, with 30,386 killed in action, 110,725 wounded, and 50,686 missing. The artillery support was massive: 4,369,000 rounds of 75 and 90mm, and 832,100 from their heavies. Yet there were no significant gains.[55]

The British confronted similar problems, made worse by their lack of prewar preparation. They had made major commitments in France as well as the Middle East, leaving their army to train hundreds of thousands of volunteers with little infrastructure. In spite of the heavy losses suffered by the regulars in fall 1914, the army patched together several small attacks with what remained along with units from the Indian Army and the Territorial Army. In March 1915, Lieutenant General Henry Rawlinson's I Corps carried out an attack on Neuve Chapelle. At least here he concentrated sufficient artillery to gain success on the first day. The bombardment destroyed much of the barbed wire and suppressed German defenses so that the British advanced a thousand on a front of three thousand yards. Casualties were 11,562, miniscule compared to those of the French and what was to come. Later, with insufficient artillery, British attacks at Aubers Ridge and Loos in September suffered heavy losses.[56]

1915: The Other Theaters

In late 1914, Winston Churchill noted to Henry Asquith, "I think it quite possible that neither side will have the strength to penetrate the other's line in the Western theatre. The position of both armies is not about to undergo any decisive change—although no doubt several hundred thousand men will be sent to sacrifice the military on that point. . . . Are there not alternatives than sending our armies to chew barbed wire in Flanders."[57] That train of thought led Churchill to move in two different directions, both of which underlined his capacity to see beyond the obvious. The first would eventually lead to the creation of the tank, introduced on the Somme in 1916.

Churchill's second effort to escape the terrible attrition of the Western Front came in the Mediterranean. Turkey's entrance into the conflict on the side of the Central Powers suggested the possibility of an attack on the Dardanelles to knock Turkey out of the war and open a secure route to Russia. The resulting expedition was Churchill's strategic gambit, but others at the political, operational, and tactical levels were responsible for its execution. The earliest discussions among British political and military leaders foreshadow the coming debacle. At the top, Britain lacked a decision-making body capable of addressing the questions such an effort should have raised. The admirals had serious doubts about forcing the Dardanelles, while Lord Kitchener, secretary of state for war, could not make up his mind as to whether sufficient troops would be available for a landing on the shores of the Dardanelles.

Equally important, the two services had made few preparations to coop-erate. And virtually everyone underestimated the Turks.

The initial effort consisted of obsolete British and French battleships bombarding Turkish guns on the Dardanelles to force their way into the Sea of Marmara. In retrospect, it is doubtful a follow-on bombardment of Constantinople would have persuaded the Turks to surrender—they were a ruthless lot, already embarking on genocide in Armenia. The bombardment never happened. The major naval effort on 18 March 1915 was a disaster. The battleships, under fire from both sides of the Dardanelles, ran into recently laid mines, which sank three of them, the French *Bouvet* losing nearly all its crew.

It was now up to the army, which began landings on the Gallipoli Peninsula on 25 April. In command of the effort was Lieutenant General Sir Ian Hamilton, who possessed none of the drive that leadership de-mands. The whole effort was amateurish. No one had a clear idea of what to expect. There were no maps, the intelligence badly underestimated the Turks, while those in charge of the operation had no clear objectives. The British and ANZAC troops immediately ran into fierce Turkish resistance from machine-gun and rifle fire and found their advance inland blocked by barbed wire. They gained just two small lodgments, and by June the battle, like the Western Front, had settled into a stalemate.

In August, Hamilton attempted to break the stalemate by two corps landing at Sulva Bay and a major offensive out of the ANZAC position. British and New Zealand units reached the heights of Chunuk Bair, but Turkish counterattacks drove them back off the summit. Not only the of-fensive but the campaign had failed. How to explain the defeat? Histo-rian Timothy Travers puts it best: "The Allies failed primarily because of their inexperience in modern warfare, especially because the 1915 cam-paign took place early in the war, before the learning curve, greater expe-rience, and vastly improved technical ability provided solutions to trench warfare later in the war. In fact, tactics ate strategy at Gallipoli."[58] More-over, Turkish and German generalship proved far superior to that of the British.

The British would launch three other campaigns against the Otto-mans: one across the Suez Canal into Palestine (modern-day Israel), one into Mesopotamia (modern-day Iraq), and one involving wide-ranging guerrilla warfare across Arabia.[59] The Mesopotamian campaign was ex-traordinarily badly led and featured the surrender of a British army at Kut in April 1916. Eventually all three succeeded, at least for the immediate future, but they resulted in the divisions of the Middle East that haunt to-day's Arab world. In effect, the British were fighting two wars: one against the Germans and one of imperial aggrandizement.

1916: The Most Terrible of Battles

In December 1915, Falkenhayn proposed a major operation that com-bined strategic insight with insanity. He began with the argument that Britain, with its economic resources and control of global commerce, was the glue holding the Allies together. But Germany did not have the means to strike directly at the British. He also argued, far more realisti-cally than the German generals of 1941, that Russia's depths offered no real opportunity: "An advance takes us nowhere."[60] At that point his ar-gument went haywire. If Germany could damage the French military sufficiently, he suggested, it would break the nation's willpower, and "England's best sword [will be] knocked out of her hand." A limited of-fensive could achieve that goal: "Within our reach behind the French sector of the Western Front there are objectives the retention of which the French ... would be compelled to throw in every man they have. If they do so the forces of France will bleed to death."[61] Falkenhayn chose the Crown Prince's army and Verdun for that offensive and began de-ploying an enormous concentration of artillery. Six divisions, supported by over 1,200 guns, would begin the assault. Aiming only to weaken the French, Falkenhayn held the reserves back, thus ensuring that the attack-ers would possess insufficient forces to capture Verdun immediately.

The French had paid minimal attention to Verdun's defenses and woke up only at the last moment. On 21 February the offensive began. German attacks over the first two days achieved considerable success and put the French in serious trouble. In a desperate situation, Joffre ap-pointed General Philippe Pétain to command the battle. At the outbreak of the war, Pétain had been an obscure brigadier about to retire, made ir-relevant by his continued advocacy of artillery and skepticism about ag-gressive prewar infantry tactics. But once the war began, he rose rapidly. Unlike his British and French contemporaries, he favored limited, sharp attacks to impose maximum casualties on the enemy while minimizing his own.[62] By 1916, he was an army commander and now received the ar-my's most important appointment: command of the defenses at Verdun.

Pétain rushed from the arms of his mistress into a desperate situa-tion: Verdun's most modern fort, Fort Douaumont, had fallen. He

quickly recognized that Falkenhayn had made a serious mistake by limiting the German advance to the right bank of the Meuse. That allowed
Pétain to concentrate French artillery on the river's left bank and inflict
heavy losses on the advancing Germans. Moreover, in the mud churned
up by the steady bombardments, German artillery found it difficult to
keep up with the advancing infantry. With mounting losses, the German
advance slowed to a halt. By the end of March, the French had suffered
89,000 casualties, the Germans 81,607. Falkenhayn's effort to bleed out
the French was doing the same to his own army, which was considerably
outnumbered by the total of Allied armies.[63]

In mid-May the Germans made their last major effort to take Verdun. German infantry forced the surrender of Fort Vaux in their drive to
take the city. In taking the fortress the Germans suffered 2,678 casualties,
the French 100. But just as Falkenhayn was on the brink of breaking
through to Verdun, events in the east intervened. Conrad, commander of
the Austro-Hungarian Army, had pulled five of his divisions off the line
to launch an offensive against the Italians. In response to French pleas
for help, the Russians launched a major offensive against the weakened
Austro-Hungarian lines. The forces of General Aleksei Brusilov on the
Southwest Front achieved a stunning success. By the time the front sta-
bilized with considerable German help, the Russians had captured
200,000 Austro-Hungarians and almost reached the Carpathians.

Desperate to save the Austro-Hungarians, Falkenhayn rushed troops
and artillery from Verdun to the Eastern Front. The great battle for Verdun was over. In many ways it epitomized the fourth military-social revolution. The massive casualties and the willingness to bear them were
more than faint echoes of the French Revolution's appeal to nationalism.
Similarly, the very success of the Industrial Revolution ensured the
length and price of the battle. The fighting would continue in the area
until November 1918. A French estimate on casualties at Verdun from
1914 to 1918 for the French and German armies is 420,000 dead and
800,000 gassed or wounded. Alistair Horne estimates the number at
700,000.[64]

The Birth of Modern War

By summer the fourth military-social revolution had come into its
own. There was no end in sight, given the willingness of the opposing
sides to continue the war to the bitter end. The war underlined that

decisive battle was a willow-wisp. With the contenders having already suffered unimaginable losses and their populations worked up, political leaders had little room for maneuver—not that they wanted any. After two years of war, attrition of manpower and resources had yet to exhaust the opponents. Aircraft and submarines had already emerged as revolutions in military affairs, adding to the complexities of the battlespace.

The pressures of the war were spurring development of a whole host of new weapons that were changing the character of war faster than had ever occurred before in history. The inventions and adaptations that technologists and scientists were creating forced armies, navies, and nascent air forces to generate new tactics and intertwine new capabilities in a fashion that would not have been possible before the war. Moreover, the products and innovations of modern science, technology, and industry were outstripping the ability of military organizations to adapt their tactics and operations to the realities of a war that none had foreseen. Everything seemed in flux. There were no simple or obvious answers for either politicians or generals.

CHAPTER SEVEN

Inventing Modern War
July 1916–November 1918

The Hundred Days of 1918 was punctuated by no Waterloo. The First World War ended, as it had mostly been fought, in a succession of dour attritional struggles rather than a thrilling climatic battle. The intensity of the campaign, hard fought almost until the end, shows that the battered and bruised German army, while down, was definitely not yet out. When it finally collapsed in November, it did so more quickly and completely than anyone had expected even a month previously.

—JONATHAN BOFF, *Winning and Losing on the Western Front*

BY 1916, THE FOURTH military-social revolution had reached full bloom. The economic and financial infrastructures of the modern state had proven capable of bearing huge burdens. The problem now was that there existed no obvious tactical solutions to the war of attrition. The battlefronts demanded weapons and ammunition an order of magnitude greater and more numerous than anyone imagined before 1914. That in turn altered the tactical framework of the armies and nascent air forces. Moreover, tactics were under the pressure of constant change because of new and more effective weapons. Constant change, innovation, and attrition were driving the transformation of war into something never before contemplated.

Governments were undergoing similar changes. The demands of the battlefield forced each side into ever more ruthless conscription of the nation's manpower and animals, horses being especially important. National propaganda echoed the French Revolution's slogan that "old men were to go to the town squares to arouse the courage of warriors." Now the old men urged those working in factories and on farms to reach ever greater production.

The Great War had four distinct periods. The armies had begun the conflict believing that rapid mobility would overwhelm the enemy's firepower. The first battles ended that illusion. In the second stage, from 1915 into 1916, the generals aimed at destroying the enemy's trench systems with massive artillery bombardments. The Battle of Verdun inaugurated the third stage, the development of more sophisticated artillery and infantry tactics. Late in the Battle of the Somme, one sees the beginnings of the fourth stage, which emerged full-blown in 1918 as combined-arms tactics restored mobility to the battlefield, at least in a tactical sense.

Above all, the war's last two years saw the marriage of the French Revolution's nationalism with the machine power of the Industrial Revolution. Austria-Hungary and Russia were unable to harness that marriage fully.

The Somme, 1916

The pressure the Germans exerted on the French at Verdun guaranteed the French could not participate in the Somme battle at the level promised in discussions with the British; Verdun also forced the British to begin their offensive on the Somme earlier than planned. In many ways, the battle was a typical World War I battle, with trench lines three deep and extensive entanglements of barbed wire. By June 1916, the Germans had fought on the Somme for nearly two years. Over that period, they had dug into the chalk deposits to construct deep dugouts where their infantry sheltered, as well as utilized villages in the area to serve as strong points. This defensive system was the culmination of two years of tactical, material, and technological adaptations—but it had a weakness. Falkenhayn had issued disastrous tactical instructions: the defenders on the Western Front would hold their positions to the last man, and any territory lost would be immediately regained.[1] With these instructions, the German infantry found themselves forced to deploy within killing range of Allied artillery.

On the opposite side, Rawlinson, the British Fourth Army commander, was responsible for planning and executing the initial portion of the Somme battle. His commander, Douglas Haig, had replaced Sir John French in December 1915. The modern narrative presents Haig as an ignorant, arrogant leader who heartlessly sent his soldiers into the slaughterhouse.[2] But he possessed several strong points: he was a first-class administrator and created an effective logistical system. He also recognized the importance of modern technology and supported the development of the tank and Royal Flying Corps (later the RAF). But Haig surrounded himself with sycophants and had little interest in tactics.[3] He believed a breakthrough of German lines was imminent, which would return maneuver to the battlefield.

The French, from their more extensive experience, recognized the limits of their current capabilities and waged "bite and hold" tactics—grabbing territory after heavy bombardments before attacking and then, after gaining their limited objectives, waiting for the ensuing German counterattacks. The Fourth Army drew up its initial plans for the offensive along similar lines. Rawlinson's conception was to have his infantry conduct a limited advance over an area artillery had thoroughly bombarded. His plan emphasized artillery capabilities that fell within the BEF's level of effectiveness, given the inexperience of staff and troops. Haig, however, demanded a deeper and wider penetration of German lines without adding more guns. This change spread the artillery bombardment over a wider area and inflicted significantly less damage on German positions.

The first of July 1916 represents one of the great catastrophes in military history.[4] Of the 120,000 British soldiers participating in the attack, by evening 57,470 were casualties with 19,240 killed and few objectives in British hands. In comparison, on the southern portion of the attack, the French Sixth Army suffered only 1,590 casualties and captured its objectives. German losses were approximately 11,000. The disaster reflected the failure of British artillery to cut German wire and destroy dugouts in the trenches. Robin Prior and Trevor Wilson, the foremost historians of the battle, note, "As long as most German machine-gunners and artillery men survived the British bombardment, the slaughter of the attacking infantry would occur *whatever* infantry tactics were adapted. . . . In the south, significantly, where the 30th Division seemed to adopt no particularly innovative tactics, success was ensured because British artillery had dealt such severe blows to the German gunners and trench-dwellers. In other words, if the artillery had done its job, it mattered little if the infantry had walked or ran or executed the Highland fling across no man's land."[5]

If the first day on the Somme represented a German victory, on subsequent days they would suffer heavy casualties. Falkenhayn's demand that his troops hold front-line trenches placed the defenders directly in the path of British artillery and forced them to launch costly counterattacks. A German veteran of the Somme recalled, "The terrible losses, out of all proportion to the breadth of the front attacked, were principally due to the old Prussian obstinacy with which the tactics of the line were pursued to their logical conclusion. . . . One battalion after another were crowded into a front already over-manned, and in a few hours pounded to bits."[6]

Nevertheless, Haig refused to recognize the war's character and pursued the mirage of a decisive breakthrough. But the Somme was a battle of attrition and material that increasingly resembled the industrialized society that had spawned it. In late August, a British officer noted, "Observation balloons, ammunition dumps, light railways, camps of prefabricated 'Adrian' barracks; altogether indicative of long preparations, a business mounted deliberately like an industrial effort; nothing improvised, every possibility anticipated; the front seems to work like a large factory, following a plan no one can derail."[7]

On the night of 14–15 July, the Fourth Army launched an impressive assault. With two-thirds the artillery that supported the 1 July attack and less than 5 percent of the trench area, Prior and Wilson write, the BEF achieved "an intensity of fire twice that of Neuve Chapelle [in March 1915] and five times that of the 1 July attack."[8] The result was a significant gain in territory and heavy German casualties. Both sides were learning. By late July, German machine gunners were deploying outside their trenches, which were receiving most of the BEF's fire, leading British gunners to stop firing at specific trenches; instead, they "had to batter down a whole area of ground, using an immense quantity of ammunition" to achieve the desired effects.[9]

From mid-July through mid-September, the total casualties for both sides were nearly 100,000. Falkenhayn's order for front-line commanders to hold the line and counterattack to regain losses substantially increased German casualties.[10] The British extended bombardments beyond the objective to catch German counterattacks in the open. On 15 September, the British introduced the tank, with forty-eight armored fighting vehicles. Only thirty reached the start point, where the attack was to begin.

Haig, who after the war was criticized for not supporting tank development, was in fact so enthusiastic he requested at least a thousand more.[11] The offensive that day was one of the more successful, especially for the 41st Division, which used tanks to chase the Germans out of Flers.

From this point, the battle continued in desultory fashion with heavy losses on both sides. The final British attacks came in mid-November amid worsening weather. The attackers met with relative success, including the capture of the small French village of Beaumont-Hamel, one of the objectives on 1 July. Then, as occurred all too often in 1916 and 1917, the attack continued beyond any reasonable point.[12] Yet at the tactical level the BEF was learning: "The integration of Lewis gun, rifle grenade, and trench mortar fire with the advances carried out by riflemen and bombers, all blended with an increasing confidence on the gunners' ability to lay down creeping barrages, transformed the British battle performance."[13]

Casualties on the Somme failed to match those of Verdun, but they were bad enough. The British suffered 420,000 losses; the French 200,000; and the Germans 465,000. Demands for munitions on the Somme suggest the strain the Allied offensive was placing on the German economy: between 1 July and 11 August, German artillery expended 11 million shells in reply to the Allied offensive, while its units wore out 1,600 light artillery pieces and 760 heavy tubes.[14] The French, with their greater experience, outperformed the BEF. Having committed 44 divisions to the fight, they captured 41,605 Germans and 178 guns. The British, with 52 divisions, captured 31,396 and 125 artillery pieces.[15]

Economic and Military Adaptation

Romania's entrance into the war in August 1916 and political pressure over the war's stalemate led the kaiser to fire Falkenhayn and promote Hindenburg and Ludendorff. One of their first actions was to visit the Western Front. The weakness they saw there horrified them. Ludendorff wrote in his memoirs that "on the Somme the enemy's powerful artillery, assisted by excellent aeroplane observation and fed with enormous supplies of ammunition, had kept down our own fire and destroyed our artillery. The defense of our infantry had become so flabby that the massed attacks of our enemy always succeeded. Without doubt [our infantry] fought too doggedly, clinging too resolutely to . . . the holding of ground, with the result that the losses were heavy."[16]

He concluded that the Germans confronted something new on the Somme—a battle of material (*Materialschlacht*) that called for a radical restructuring of defensive tactics.[17] On 1 December 1916, within two months of Hindenburg and Ludendorff's visit, the German high command (the Oberste Heeresleitung or OHL) had promulgated *The Principles of Command in the Defensive Battle in Position Warfare*. It specified that only a light screen of machine guns would hold forward lines, with stronger positions echeloned in depth. The main reserves would lie in wait out of range of all but the heaviest artillery. As the enemy fought its way through increasingly strong defenses, the Germans would launch heavy counterattacks.[18]

But Ludendorff and Hindenburg had to wrestle with an equally difficult problem: how to address Allied superiority in material resources and production. A simple comparison of spending during the war underlines the imbalance in financial and industrial power. The Allies, including the United States, spent $147 billion on the war; the total for the Central Powers was $61.5 billion.[19] Hindenburg and Ludendorff now demanded a program to double production of munitions and trench mortars, and triple that of machine guns and artillery. The program set in motion by the OHL was put into law, but it immediately ran into difficulties related to problems at the heart of the German economy.[20] The OHL was trying to mobilize the nation, its men, women, and industry to serve the war effort with little or no understanding of the economic and industrial complexities involved.[21]

The program barely increased production.[22] It never had a chance because the planners failed to recognize, much less deal with, insufficiencies in transportation, coal production, and the supply of workers, all of which frustrated the effort to expand production. By early 1916, the Reich's economy had eaten through its fat; stocks of raw materials were depleted, as were those the Germans acquired through conquests or leakages in the blockade. Wear and tear on the transportation infrastructure was becoming a serious problem for the railroads. Deployment of armies deep into France and into the borderlands of Russia, the military demands of transporting and sustaining armies with insatiable demands for ammunition, and the need to support a weak Austro-Hungarian railroad network strained the infrastructure of rails and rolling stock to the breaking point. Added to the strain were the military demands for transporting and sustaining armies with insatiable requests for ammunition, the basis of the *Materialschlacht*.

By January 1917, the German economy had come close to seizing up. A particularly severe winter brought barge traffic to a virtual halt and added to the railroad system's difficulties. From 24 January through 5 February 1917, railroad authorities had to cease additional traffic just to unload the backlog.[23] The rail crisis was only one sign of economic problems. The coal fields, from which the army had conscripted many of the youngest and most productive workers, were also in trouble. Of the 32,000 coal cars arriving in the Ruhr that winter, the miners could fill just 22,000. Steel production in early 1917 underlined the impact of transportation and coal difficulties. February's total was 1,187,000 tons, 225,000 less than the previous August and more than a quarter of a million tons below the target. By simply decreeing goals without considering actual capabilities, the OHL gained nothing and increased industrial difficulties. One senior official noted that "the program was decreed by the military without examining whether or not it could be carried out. Today there are everywhere half finished and finished factories that cannot produce because there is no coal and because there are no workers available. Coal and iron were expended for these constructions, and the result was that munitions production would be greater today if no monster program had been set up."[24]

That winter, a significant food crisis exacerbated German difficulties. Heavy summer rains caused 60 percent of the potato crop to fail, forcing the population to subsist largely on turnips over the winter. That difficulty reflected deeper problems. While the Haber process had saved the army from a shortage of gunpowder after the blockade stopped imports of Chilean nitrates, German factories could not at the same time produce sufficient fertilizer for farmers' needs. Moreover, 40 percent of the male farm population was now in military service, causing a shortage of farm workers that could not be made up with POW labor. Finally, the army had requisitioned approximately 1 million draft horses, which crippled a farm economy. By late summer 1918, meat rations had fallen below 12 percent of prewar standards.[25]

While the Germans were failing even to meet their escalating industrial demands, the Allies were steadily increasing production. They faced fewer supply and raw material problems because they controlled the world's oceans. They only had to pay for imports. By 1916, 40 percent of the British purchases to support their own military, as well as those of their allies, were coming from the United States, a total of $200 million a month. Still, only the German declaration of unrestricted submarine warfare in early 1917 deflected President Woodrow Wilson's annoyance at the blockade. The U.S. entry into the war in April 1917 came none too soon; by then, Britain had sufficient securities to finance just three weeks of purchases.[26]

The British faced the same problem other governments confronted in turning a peacetime economy into a wartime one. Simply put, industrial concerns were not overly eager to invest heavily in constructing new factories to meet a demand that would disappear when the war ended. Nevertheless, with Lloyd George leading, British industry increased shell production to a level that met BEF demands. In the first half of 1915, shell production was 2,278,105; the first half of 1916 saw it rise to 13,995,360 and in six months it reached 35,407,193. Moreover, the British could draw on raw materials, foodstuffs, and industrial production from the Dominions. By 1917, Canada was delivering approximately 30 percent of the BEF's artillery munitions.[27]

Of all the powers, France mobilized the greatest proportion of its population and economy. The loss of much of its industrial areas in the first months of the war created major problems in producing munitions and armaments and forced France to depend on machine tools and manufacturing items imported from the United States.[28] Yet even with their war casualties, the French expanded the workforce engaged in armaments, from 50,000 in 1914 to 1,675,000 in 1918. Many were under military discipline. With a casual disregard for workers' safety, the French achieved astonishing results. Starting from 4,000 shells per day in 1914, they were producing 151,000 by summer 1916; 155mm shell production went from 255 per day to 17,000 a year and a half later; and by 1917, French production of aircraft engines exceeded that of Britain and Germany combined.[29]

On the other hand, the United States failed to come close to the military and economic contributions it would make in the next war. There were two reasons: Wilson ordered the military to make no plans until the United States joined the war—a mistake American leaders would not make in 1939. The second factor was that when the Americans mobilized, they planned for the long haul but the war ended before these efforts bore fruit. Nevertheless, their contribution was significant. American loans kept the Allies in the war. Manufacturing totals in some areas were impressive: 926 million rounds of small arms ammunition, 1.2 million rifles, 31 million artillery shells and explosives—equivalent to fifty months' production of the Hindenburg program.[30]

The war's most impressive technological development was the creation of air forces and the associated industrial concerns. Reconnaissance photographs of the enemy's defensive and artillery positions became more and more valuable as the war progressed. By 1916, the day of the fighter had arrived, since without air superiority, aerial reconnaissance became a losing proposition. Haig noted in December 1916: "I desire to point out that the mastery of the air, which is essential, entails a constant and liberal supply of the most up-to-date machines, without which even the most skillful pilot, cannot succeed."[31] As in World War II, production of first-class combat aircraft in large numbers was essential not only to the conduct of the air war but also for ground forces, which by 1918 depended on air superiority, aerial reconnaissance, close-air support, and interdiction strikes.

By 1916, production totals underlined how seriously the opponents were taking the air war. The Germans outproduced the French with a total of 8,182 aircraft for the year, compared to 7,549. However, the Germans lagged on the logistical side with only 7,823 engines produced, while the French total was 16,875. When added to France's total, British production of 5,716 aircraft and 5,363 engines gave the Allies numerical superiority.[32] When Pétain took over the army after the disaster on the Chemin des Dames in April 1917, he instituted major programs to increase the number of aircraft, tanks, and artillery tubes. Compared to the Germans, the French had better access to raw materials. From 1,420 combat aircraft in January 1917, their fleet grew to 2,100 in June and 2,870 by September.[33] The British also increased their output of aircraft and engines while steadily improving their design. They produced 13,766 airplanes for 1917, nearly doubling production from the first quarter to the fourth and increasing production of aero-engines by nearly two-thirds.[34]

German numbers were worse. Their production totals in 1917 underlined the difficulties encountered by the Hindenburg program. The aim was for approximately a thousand combat aircraft per month, but shortages of raw materials and spiraling costs made that target elusive. The coal and transportation crisis in winter 1917 exacerbated problems, and production plummeted to 400 aircraft in January and 260 in February. Extrapolating from what monthly figures are available, the Germans most likely produced approximately 9,000 aircraft in 1917.[35]

The next year was no better: Germany fell steadily behind. Monthly production of aircraft and engines never came close to the targets of

1,600 and 1,800 respectively. With shortages of raw materials and workers and increasing disaffection at home, average monthly production for aircraft was 1,151 and engines 1,379. British industry, meanwhile, delivered 30,671 aircraft and 1,865 seaplanes, twice the totals of the previous year. Altogether 268,096 workers toiled in the industry, compared to the 5,000 employed in 1915.[36] The French effort was equally impressive in 1918: their factories produced 24,652 aircraft and 44,563 engines with a work force of 185,000.[37]

No other weapons system has had such a transformative impact. At the war's outset, aircraft had only one mission, to scout for the advancing infantry. Four years later, they engaged in air reconnaissance, close air support, air superiority, interdiction strikes, and strategic bombing. The crucial enabler was rapid improvement in aircraft's capabilities, pushed by research and development and unprecedented industrial resources. Moreover, what happened in the air remained symbiotically linked to the ground battle. By 1918, air power and its capabilities represented the war's second major revolution in military affairs, alongside that of combined-arms tactics.

The Darkest Time: 1917

In December 1916, Admiral Henning von Holtzendorff passed along to the Reich's leaders his calculation that resumption of unrestricted submarine warfare would end the war in six months. This represented a serious distortion of reality. At best, unrestricted submarine warfare was a desperate gamble to win before the Americans could bring the Allies a decisive advantage. Again, the basis of the argument was that "military necessity" should trump strategic considerations. On 9 January 1917, supported by leading generals and admirals, the kaiser agreed to resume unrestricted submarine war. Ludendorff commented, "I don't give a damn about America."[38]

Introduction of convoys, though opposed by the Royal Navy (also using faulty statistics), undermined the U-boats' ability to destroy the necessary merchant tonnage.[39] The most obvious German miscalculations were the disregard of neutral shipping, merchant vessels interned in U.S. ports in August 1914, and American industry's productive capacity. By April 1917, America was in the war, and although its military potential showed only in the last months, it had an impact in key areas: the Allies no longer had to worry about paying for imports from North

America. Moreover, with America a participant, the blockade became airtight.[40]

The major problem for Hindenburg and Ludendorff was the manpower shortage. To address this, they first ordered a major withdrawal in France and sited the new defenses, called the Siegfried Line, for defensibility; the defenses in the west would be twenty-five miles shorter, freeing fourteen divisions. But the order for that withdrawal, issued in October 1916, explains why a peace of reconciliation was never possible. "It is necessary," the OHL ordered, "to make extensive preparations for the complete destruction of all rail lines, and further, all streets, bridges, canals, locks, localities, and all equipment and building that we cannot take with us but that could be of any use at all to the enemy."[41] The army was to leave behind nothing but ruin.

In February 1917, the Romanov regime collapsed in Russia. Casualties numbering in the millions, army incompetence, and the tsar's inability to motivate his people brought discontent to a boiling point. The regime dissolved not with a bang but with a whimper, and was replaced by a "liberal" provisional government that aspired to create a democratic regime. Amid political struggles in Saint Petersburg, the new government tried to keep the army in the fight. It was a losing battle.[42] Adding to the chaos, the Germans provided a sealed train for Vladimir Lenin to cross their territory to Sweden while bankrolling the Bolsheviks.[43]

For the Western Allies, the problem was what to do about German defensive strength in the west. In November 1916, Joffre and Haig agreed that the Allies would concentrate between the river Oise (the French) and Arras (the British).[44] By late December, the French had fired Joffre and replaced him with General Robert Nivelle after his major success at Verdun. Using innovative tactics emphasizing rolling barrages, Nivelle had regained most of the territory the French had lost at Verdun in the first half of 1916.

The first Allied blow came in April 1917 near Arras. On the left, four Canadian divisions carried the bulk of the First Army's effort; on the right, General Edmund Allenby's Third Army bore the brunt of the limited offensive. Bombardment in the First Army's area began on 20 March. Overall, the two armies employed 2,817 guns, nearly three times as many as the Germans possessed. Extensive tunneling protected attacking infantry from observation. In addition, the British had the advantage of a shell with a new type of fuse, the 106, which exploded on contact. The Germans, meanwhile, had not yet fully absorbed the new defensive doctrine, which called for a flexible defense in depth. By the battle's end, the Canadians had inflicted twice as many casualties on their opponents.

A comparison of British tactics with those of July 1916 shows the changes in artillery capabilities. The weight of bombardment and the size of the BEF also indicate the degree to which both industry and the population had been mobilized in three years. On 1 July, the preparatory bombardment on the first day of the Somme had been 52,000 tons; for the Arras attack, the total was 88,000 tons over a far smaller area. In the nineteen-day bombardment, the British and Canadian artillery fired off 2,687,000 shells.[45] Haig then ordered the attack to continue into the next week despite mounting casualties and stiffening resistance. At one point, faced with orders to continue attacking, division commanders came close to mutiny.[46]

The focus now reverted to the French. The area that Nivelle chose for his offensive lay along the Chemin des Dames and the railroad system lying immediately to the rear of the enemy's lines, of great importance to German logistics.[47] The French confronted two difficulties. First, unlike the Germans, the French lacked a general staff system with the power to ensure that front-line commanders followed doctrinal innovations. Nivelle's tactical ideas seem not to have filtered through to many of his division commanders, whose preparations were marked by too much enthusiasm and too little retraining. The second difficulty was that the French were attacking a tactical system based on an entirely new approach.

The preparatory bombardment again underlined the extent of the impact of the mobilization of industrial resources. Initial registration and counterbattery fire began on 2 April 1917. On 9 April, the main bombardment began. Between 1 April and 5 May, General Alfred Micheler's army groups fired off 11 million shells, of which 2.5 million were heavy. Overall, 5,350 artillery pieces, including 1,650 heavies, supported the offensive. But the French encountered significant difficulties: the weather was atrocious, and they had lost air superiority.[48] As Nivelle's infantry advanced, they moved ever deeper into defenses that had suffered relatively little from the bombardment. As the premier historian of German defensive tactics noted, "The front-line divisions . . . fought [the battle] in and for the foremost line, and by doing so they . . . succeeded in breaking up and delaying the waves of the assault."[49] The Nivelle offensive was one of the more successful offensives the French launched in terms of casualties.[50] The problem was that Nivelle had raised expectations too high, and a dangerous collapse of morale among many front-line units resulted.

With that, the long-suffering *poilus*, long denied leave, fed atro-
ciously, misused by their generals, and suffering under appalling conditions for three years, mutinied. In some cases, the troops refused to leave
the trenches to attack the Germans.[51] The troubles spread, but the Germans failed to notice their extent. Nivelle's replacement by Pétain saved
the army. With a combination of an iron hand and velvet glove, he restored morale and discipline. On one hand, there were firing squads; of
554 sentenced to death, the French executed 62. On the other hand, Pétain carried out extensive reforms that met the *poilus*'s reasonable demands.[52] As the army restored discipline, Pétain instructed commanders
to execute carefully planned attacks aimed at maximizing German casualties and minimizing French ones. But the French Army was now out of
serious fighting.

That burden shifted to the British. Here, with Lloyd George in a
weak political position, Haig had the decisive vote; he chose to launch a
major offensive in Flanders despite that area's multiple challenges. The
terrain was less than suitable—once a great swamp that had been drained
by medieval peasants. Heavy artillery bombardments were sure to return
the area to its former condition, particularly in the heavy late-summer
rains. A number of senior officers argued for relatively short, sharp attacks, which artillery could support with preliminary bombardments and
then rolling barrages as the troops advanced. But Haig dismissed such
proposals; he still hoped to achieve a decisive Napoleonic victory.[53]

Before the offensive began, on 7 June 1917, the British launched a
"bite and hold" operation against Messines Ridge, led by General Sir
Herbert Plumer and his Second Army. Accompanying an artillery barrage that pumped 3.5 million shells onto German defenses, the British
prepared twenty-one massive mines under German positions.[54] Nineteen
exploded with catastrophic impact, and within six hours the ridge was in
British hands.[55] The first day's operation was impressive, but as usual
Haig ordered the troops to attempt too much. German infantry and artillery reinforcements quickly closed. After the first two days, British
losses rose. While seizure of Messines Ridge was an impressive success, it
could not be exploited beyond the immediate battle areas. The artillery
support for the operation underlined that this was a war not of quick victories but of attrition and production: 1,510 pieces of field artillery, 756
heavy guns, and no less than 144,000 tons of ammunition.[56]

After the Messines operation, Haig paused for nearly two months to
prepare the assault in Flanders. There would be no more bite-and-hold

operations.[57] General Sir Hugh Gough, a cavalryman, would lead the operation. Unlike Plumer at Messines, Gough aimed for deep penetration of German front lines. The Fifth Army assembled 1,422 field guns and 752 heavy pieces of artillery. On its flanks, the French First Army to the north and the BEF's Second Army to the south supported the initial bombardment.

Confronting Gough's Fifth Army was the German Sixth Army, with its chief of staff Colonel Fritz von Lossberg, the German Army's premier defensive expert.[58] Lossberg understood that major artillery bombardments would destroy the area's drainage ditches, causing the trenches to quickly fill with water. He immediately put the Sixth Army to work constructing concrete bunkers that could survive artillery bombardments. These bunker strongpoints would form the heart of the defenses.[59]

The Fifth Army's preparatory bombardment began on 16 July. The offensive opened on 31 July. Worsening weather limited the artillery's effectiveness; nevertheless, it damaged many of the pillboxes on the left and center of the British line. But the rains were rapidly turning the ground into a morass. The Fifth Army suffered 27,000 casualties in the initial fighting, while the Germans lost almost as heavily. In the first four days of August there were sixteen inches of rain, and the total for the month was nineteen—nearly twice the normal August rainfall in Flanders.[60] Egged on by Haig, Gough launched a series of increasingly unsuccessful attacks. Neither man paid much attention to the appalling conditions. After conducting a patrol of the front lines, an Australian officer recorded, "The slope was littered with the dead, both theirs and ours. I got to one pill box to find just a mass of dead, so I passed on carefully to the one ahead. Here I found about fifty men alive, of the Manchesters. Never have I seen men so broken and demoralized. ... The dead and dying lay in piles. The wounded were numerous, unattended and so weak they groaned, some had been there four days already."[61]

Gough's incompetence led Haig to remove the Fifth Army in early September and replace it with Plumer's Second Army. Plumer's first attack, on 20 September, was more successful, but it reflected objectives that were realistic and limited, as well as better weather. Nine divisions and three corps attacked. The artillery bombardment was again impressive: 1,650,000 shells in the preliminary bombardment. The rolling bombardment worked effectively; after the troops reached the objectives, a heavy bombardment saturated their front to break up German counterattacks. Yet the British took heavy casualties: 21,000 to capture 5.5 square miles.[62] In early October heavy rains resumed, turning Flanders into a muddy lake. Nevertheless, Haig persisted. One reason for his obstinacy was that his intelligence chief, Brigadier John Charteris, and his chief of staff, Lieutenant General Lancelot Kiggell, repeatedly assured him that the Germans were on the verge of collapse. In the entire battle, British and Dominion troops suffered some 260,000 casualties (70,000 killed). German casualties were approximately 260,000.[63]

As Passchendaele ground to a stalemate in a morass of mud, two battles, one farther south on the Western Front and one in Italy, pointed toward major tactical and technological innovations. In the first, the BEF launched an offensive that presaged new paths. The attack at Cambrai involved an innovative weapons system, the tank. In the second case, the German offensive at Caporetto, the attackers employed a new system of infantry tactics aimed at exploiting enemy weaknesses by driving deep into rear areas while leaving follow-on forces to mop up strong points.

Planning for Cambrai began when General Julian Byng took over the British Third Army. The author of the attack was Brigadier H. H. Tudor, artillery commander of the 9th Scottish Division. To ensure surprise, Tudor suggested that attacking forces forgo a preliminary bombardment that would warn the Germans. Instead, advanced techniques, involving aerial photography and registering the location of German batteries by sound and flash at night, would allow counterbattery fire to weaken German artillery. Large numbers of tanks would be used to crush heavy wire entanglements. This sector was particularly attractive because only two weak divisions held the line, while the woods behind the British would cover the tank deployment. And the Royal Flying Corps dominated the air.[64]

The attack went in at 6:20 a.m. on 20 November. Compared to Flanders it was a stunning success. Three hundred seventy-eight tanks led five infantry divisions of the III and IV Corps against German lines. The tanks accomplished much, crushing wire entanglements and machine-gun nests. By day's end, the advance had reached a depth of four miles. In one day, with light casualties, the British succeeded in breaking through portions of the Hindenburg Line, capturing four thousand prisoners and one hundred guns. Of the tanks, 178 remained in working order to support the advance the next day, but the crews were exhausted. The Third Army should have halted there, but Haig insisted on continuing despite the arrival of German reinforcements as early as 21 November.[65]

While the British were planning the Cambrai attack, the Germans and Austrians launched a major spoiling attack on the Italians in the

Alps. The Italians had entered the war on the Allies' side in May 1915, shortly after the British landings at Gallipoli, in the belief the war would soon end and they could pick up substantial territorial gains. The Italian commander, Luigi Cadorna, followed the Piedmontese Army's officer corps' tradition of a lack of interest in its profession. "He had . . . simple ideas," notes MacGregor Knox, "none of them susceptible to modification by experience. Frontal attack, not envelopment, was the supreme form of war. 'Extreme measures of coercion and repression' were the essential means of motivating armies largely composed of illiterate *contadini*."[66] The results were the twelve battles of the Isonzo from May 1915 to October 1917, in which Cadorna's incompetence was equaled by that of the Italian officer corps. These offensives contributed over half of Italy's 500,000 combat deaths in the war.

Ludendorff committed seven divisions to the offensive, some participants of the Riga offensive in September, others elite mountain troops. The bombardment began at 2:00 a.m. on 24 October, utilizing the newest techniques of combined arms the Germans were developing. Six hours later, German and Austrian infantry advanced. In the second wave a German lieutenant, Erwin Rommel, led a detachment of three mountain companies and a machine-gun company. By evening his detachment was through the third line, beginning an epic advance that would capture nine thousand prisoners, including a battalion of twelve officers and five hundred soldiers.[67] The combined armies of the Central Powers almost reached Venice and came close to driving Italy out of the war. This astonishing collapse did not reflect on the bravery of the soldiers but on the leadership under which they suffered. Altogether the Italians lost 11,600 killed, 21,900 wounded, and 294,000 prisoners along with 5,000 guns and mortars.[68] Nevertheless, the Caporetto attack represented only a tactical success. It had not forced Italy to drop out of the war.

The End of the War: 1918

Over the course of 1917, Russia, its government, and its military disintegrated.[69] The final blow came with the German offensive in front of Riga on 1 September. After a hurricane bombardment, using gas shells to take out Russian artillery and command posts, the attacking infantry wrecked the last shreds of discipline in a dissolving army.[70] In November the Bolsheviks, supported by German gold, overthrew the provisional republic. Of the Bolshevik leaders only Lenin realized the new regime had to make peace. In effect, the Germans aimed to lop off Poland, Lithuania, Latvia, and parts of Belorussia from Russia, and establish Ukraine as a puppet state. The first negotiations broke down over the demands of the Central Powers. The Germans then began an unhindered advance and forced Lenin and his colleagues to agree to peace. In March 1918, the two sides signed the Treaty of Brest Litovsk, which stripped Russia of most of its western provinces.[71] It underlined German ambitions and makes nonsense of claims Versailles represented a harsh peace.[72] With peace in the east the Germans could transfer forces to the west, but two factors limited the effectiveness of the movement. On one hand, Ludendorff could not resist the urge to seize ever-larger parts of a prostrate Russia. Nevertheless, from November 1917 to March 1918, the OHL withdrew thirty-three divisions from fronts in the east, south, and southeast.[73] The second factor was the army's major morale problems. Of those transferring from east to west, about 10 percent deserted.[74]

The question confronting German leaders was "What next?" Given the state of their economy and exhaustion of manpower, one would think there was a major debate on alternatives. There was none. Ludendorff commented, "We talk too much about operations and too little about tactics."[75] Hindenburg decreed that a great offensive would take place in the west to create a favorable political outcome before American troops could arrive in Europe. On New Year's Day 1918, the OHL issued *Angriff im Stellungskrieg* ("Attack in Position Warfare"). The new doctrine emphasized a new tactical approach based on the defensive doctrine the Germans had applied, with some success, to their battles in 1917. It brought together artillery, infantry, and close air support. Experiences on the Eastern Front had emphasized hurricane bombardments to impair enemy command-and-control centers and artillery, sow disruption, and create breaks in the enemy defensive system. Probing infantry units would bypass strong points and drive deeply into enemy rear areas, which would prevent the enemy from recovering. Once isolated, enemy strong points would collapse.[76]

The Germans had invented what are today called combined-arms tactics. Altogether they prepared fifty-two attack divisions, into which they poured their most experienced officers, NCOs, and soldiers.[77] These divisions received intensive training in the doctrine. But there were difficulties in transport, essential to logistical support. The Germans possessed only 23,000 trucks, equipped with iron rather than rubber tires, as opposed to the Allied total of 100,000. Moreover, the army was so short of horses that even the attack divisions had too few horse-drawn vehicles.[78]

The British were also suffering significant weaknesses that limited their ability to respond. There were serious shortages in manpower. Lloyd George had agreed that the BEF would assume the defense of twenty-plus miles of trenches the French held. He also prevented Haig from continuing offensive operations in the spring by refusing to move replacements to France. Thus, to meet the army's requirement for 615,000, the manpower committee allocated 100,000. Some 120,000 men of the general reserve remained in Britain, supposedly "on the grounds that it would help the British economy if they spent their money at home." But shortages at the front were not just the result of London's machinations.

When the storm broke, the BEF had 88,000 soldiers on leave, even though intelligence estimated a major German offensive was in the offing.[79] If that were not enough, Gough's Fifth Army, which took over some of the French trench lines, was badly prepared. Its troops had little experience with defense. There was some effort to copy German tactics, but the Fifth Army troops were exhausted, the French had not put much work into their trenches, and the concept of defense flew in the face of the army's culture.[80] Its division commanders crammed no fewer than twenty-seven battalions—a third of the available troops—into front-line trenches.[81]

By early January 1918, Ludendorff and OHL staff had settled on the target for the offensive, code-named "Michael." It would encompass an area from Arras in the north to La Fére in the south. There was no clear target; south of the Somme, Amiens, the BEF's crucial logistic center, should have been a major goal, but in both World Wars, the Germans paid little attention to logistics.[82] Moreover, Ludendorff had little interest in operational goals. Shortly before the offensive, Crown Prince Rupprecht, army group commander, asked what Michael's object was; Ludendorff replied, "I object to the word 'operation.' We will punch a hole. ... For the rest we shall see."[83] Overall, the attacking force possessed fifty attack divisions supported by seventeen trench divisions.[84] The weight of the offensive lay with the Seventeenth Army in the north. Its attack sector was twelve miles, while the other armies possessed sectors close to twenty-five.[85]

At 4:40 a.m. on 21 March, German artillery began the bombardment, firing some 3.2 million shells over the first day. One-third were gas shells. So massive was the bombardment that it was heard in London. At 9:40 a.m., the infantry went in. Ernst Jünger, a storm troop company commander in the first wave, recorded the chaos: "At once the hurricane broke loose. A curtain of flame was let down, followed by a sudden impetuous tumult, . . . a raging thunder that swallowed up the reports even of the heaviest guns. . . . We crossed a battered tangle of wire without difficulty and at a jump were over the front line, scarcely recognizable any longer."[86]

Despite the OHL's emphasis on the Seventeenth Army, it made only limited penetrations of the BEF's Third Army. But in the south, Gough's Fifth Army fell apart. The collapse, wrote historian Tim Travers, "was due to a defensive system that was not understood, did not work, and did not properly exist at all."[87] By day two, the Germans had seized the Fifth Army's battle zone, while its corps were retreating back on the Somme. Ludendorff now had to choose whether to reinforce success in the south, despite the lack of major operational targets the Eighteenth Army could reach, or crack the BEF defenses in the north. There was no deliberation.

He gave his subordinates in the south three missions: defeat the British, separate the BEF from the French, and defeat French reserves—missions that were so general they provided little guidance.[88] The critical day came on 26 March. The Germans were threatening to split the BEF from the French—the former falling back on the Channel, the latter retreating to the south. Faced with defeat, the Allies created a combined headquarters with Ferdinand Foch at its head. The French marshal immediately prevented Pétain from pulling away from the British and ordered him to move substantial reinforcements to support Haig.[89] The German side, meanwhile, faced serious logistical problems. The Eighteenth Army was already fifty-six miles beyond its rail heads, and some of its corps had had to cut back on ammunition expenditures.

By 5 April, the Germans had shot their bolt, and the OHL ordered a cessation of major attacks. While they had achieved unheard-of advances in territory captured, they had failed to seize a single objective of importance. Even with the BEF's rail and logistics center at Amiens within range, the Germans failed to bombard the city. Over the fifteen days of Michael, the Germans suffered 239,800 casualties, close to what they had suffered at Passchendaele. On the other side, the Allies suffered 254,739 casualties and 90,000 POWs. But the Germans had won a pyrrhic victory. The Allies could replace their losses, and the Americans were already en route. Nearly 300,000 arrived in France that month.[90]

The Germans turned to other possibilities, but they had already exhausted a significant portion of their attack divisions. The next attack, "Georgette," came in Flanders in mid-April. After an initial success, aided by the collapse of a Portuguese division, the German advance came to a halt. The last major German offensive to achieve any success came at the end of May. This time they targeted the French to the east of Paris. Yet, Operation Blücher did not aim to achieve a major success, only "to . . . create the possibility of renewing the offensive against the British."[91] The target was the Chemin des Dames, an area of little operational or strategic importance. The area to its south was hilly, with ridges and rivers both running east to west, hardly ideal terrain. French general Denis Duchêne paid no attention to Pétain's orders for a defense in depth. Instead, he ordered his divisions to pack the troops in the front line while placing the main defenses with their backs on the Aisne, from which retreat would prove difficult.

The Germans struck on 27 May. They had done outstanding work in preparing the fire plan, and the results were devastating. The bombardment lasted less than three hours but wrecked most of the French artillery. On the first day, the Germans fired nearly 3 million shells, half of them gas. The Allied line collapsed, while the German advance was so rapid that they captured 650 guns that day.[92] By the next day, having achieved their objective, they were supposed to halt and prepare for a decisive offensive against the British. Instead, Ludendorff pushed on. The advance continued to Château-Thierry, but Foch brought reinforcements by rail faster than German troops could advance on foot. Moreover, some eight American divisions would participate in the battle, a clear indication the Doughboys were arriving in numbers. By 5 June, heavy losses and a collapse in the logistical system forced the OHL to call off Blücher. The Germans had gained territory but little else. Allied casualties were 127,337, Germans 105,370.[93]

Ludendorff still intended to launch another offensive against the British but opted first for one more attack on the French, aimed at seizing Reims and its rail center. He hoped for an advance of twelve to eighteen miles on the first day. This time, however, it was the Germans who were surprised. Forewarned, Foch and Pétain concentrated strong reserves in the area, while those in the front lines created a defensive in depth. On 15 July, the initial attack began: "Along a twenty mile front the [German] infantry raced forward. . . . But as the storm troopers pushed deeper . . . into the French positions, machine guns posts were uncovered

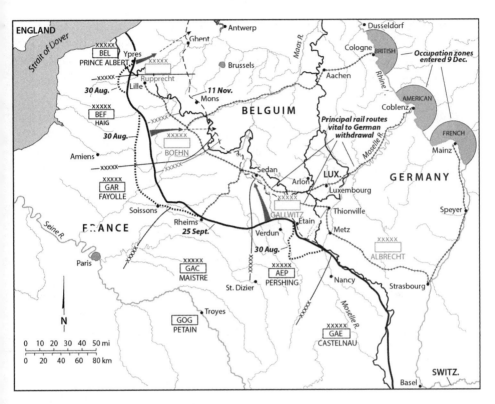

Western Front and final Allied offensives, 25 September–11 November 1918.
Cartography by Bill Nelson.

more often. . . . The Germans pressed onwards . . . until they reached the area of cratered and smoking ground which marked the limit of their own artillery barrage. . . . There, a solid line of French defenses, un-shelled, unbombed, ungassed, riflemen and machine gunners waited."[94]

On 18 July, the French launched a major assault on the far side of the Marne salient. The attack caught the Germans by surprise, as Allied air-craft suppressed German reconnaissance. Two armies, the Sixth and Tenth, with 24 divisions supported by 493 tanks attacked 10 German divisions and immediately threatened the rail junction of Soissons. By evening the Allies had advanced four miles over a twelve-mile front.[95] The Germans had no choice but to retreat. By 3 August, the Germans were back across the Ourcq River and had lost nearly all the territory Blücher had gained.

From 17 March through to mid-July, the Germans had made un-heard-of gains in territory but had captured nothing of operational, much less strategic, significance. The cost had been horrendous. In those four months the Germans suffered 977,555 casualties—a monthly loss greater than any major offensive in the west in 1916 and 1917.[96] Moreover, most combat losses came among the carefully selected officers, NCOs, and troops who made up the attack divisions. The collapse in morale showed not only in increased desertions but in ill-discipline in rear areas.[97] Finally, Ludendorff faced the consequence of the resumption of unrestricted submarine warfare in 1917. The number of American soldiers on the ground had swollen from 284,000 in March 1918 to 1,872,000 by early November.[98]

The Allied Counteroffensives

The increasing Allied superiority was helped by industrial production, which was swinging drastically in their favor. France's effort was extraordinary. In 1918, the French produced 44,563 aircraft engines, more than all of their allies combined.[99] During 1918, the French Army took delivery of 2,653 light tanks. Moreover, the French produced much of the weaponry the American Expeditionary Force (AEF) would use during 1918: two-thirds of the aircraft and virtually all its field guns, tanks, and shells. Across the Channel, the Ministry of Munitions increased output of heavy guns and howitzers by over 4,000, more than enough to make up for the spring's losses. The rise in production of shells was just as impressive: 1917, 38,635 tons; 1918, 65,160 tons.[100]

In early July 1918, British commanders began planning a major offensive against German lines near Amiens. Rawlinson, now the Fourth Army commander, proposed a short, sharp offensive; Haig argued for a longer offensive to reach deeper into German rear areas and doubled the number of artillery pieces to 2,000, along with 534 tanks and a battalion of armored cars.[101] On 8 August, the attack began with a creeping barrage that covered the tanks and infantry. British counterbattery fire blanketed German guns with heavy doses of gas. Here again, the Germans were hoisted on their own petard: without access to rubber because of the blockade, their gas masks were distinctly inferior.[102] Gas shells took German artillery out of the fight. A relatively effective wireless linked the pieces of the combined-arms framework—artillery, aircraft, infantry, engineers, and tanks.[103]

The Fourth Army's attack caught the Germans by surprise. Across the front their defenses collapsed. Some retreating troops cried out to reinforcements moving forward that they were "strike breakers." By day's end, the Australians had advanced eight miles. The tanks suffered heavily, many to mechanical breakdowns, but they gave the Germans serious difficulties.[104] Ludendorff called 8 August "the blackest day of the German Army in the war." On the 9th, the advance slowed. German artillery had severely attrited the tanks, while reinforcements had begun arriving. Over Foch's objections, Haig called the offensive off on the 10th.[105] A comparison of casualties suggests the extent of the victory: Allied, 22,000; German 75,000.[106]

Allied military strategy, articulated by Foch, aimed at launching a concentric series of short, sharp attacks to achieve two objectives: drive the Germans back on their frontiers and wear down their front-line strength. The 8 August success was followed by a series of Allied attacks. Until the armistice, the British would carry the burden of the fighting.[107] On 21 August, the Third Army under General Sir Julian Byng began a series of attacks.[108] The Germans launched a major counterattack on the 23rd, which the British smashed. Byng then resumed the offensive, and the German Seventeenth Army collapsed. The victory was particularly impressive because the Third Army consisted largely of regular divisions that had received a battering from the Germans in the spring and mostly consisted of young conscripts.

Over the first two weeks of September, the British launched a series of smaller attacks to advance closer to the Hindenburg Line. As the British prepared to assault that line, the Americans launched the first major offensive at the Saint-Mihiel salient, which was not heavily fortified and became less so when the Germans began pulling back their artillery. The Americans were so inept at covering their preparations that the Germans concluded they were mounting a deception. After four hours of bombardment, over 500,000 American troops and 100,000 French moved forward. By the time the Germans retreated, they had lost 17,000 men, against American casualties of just 7,000.[109] As soon as U.S. General John J. Pershing closed Saint-Mihiel, Foch persuaded him to move the AEF to attack the Meuse-Argonne sector, a nightmare of bad terrain and well-sited German positions. The attack, beginning on 30 September, initially gained ground but then collapsed in chaos and confusion. The Americans needed two weeks of heavy casualties to reach the main defensive position, the Kriehelde Stellung, with much of that time devoted to reorganization and changes in command. By mid-October the Americans had recovered and resumed their advance to reach Sedan just before the armistice.

While the Americans were mired in the Meuse-Argonne, the British had more success, launching four separate offensives. The most successful, by Byng's Fourth Army on 26 September, broke through the Hindenburg Line.[110] The Australian general Sir John Monash, an engineer in civilian life who now commanded the Australian corps, did most of the planning. A four-day bombardment eliminated most of the German artillery with 62,813 tons of precise, high explosive and gas shells.[111] By 6 October, the Fourth Army had breached the Hindenburg Line and broken onto open ground. In the last three months of the war, the British and their Dominion allies captured 2,840 artillery pieces and 188,700 Germans, while their allies—the French, Americans, and Belgians, with larger forces—captured altogether 196,000 POWs and 3,775 artillery pieces, only slightly more than the BEF.[112] The surrender of close to 400,000 German soldiers in those three months underlined that they were a beaten army.

The events of September 1918 had a cumulative effect on the Central Powers' stability. They caused Ludendorff to suffer a nervous breakdown. Bulgaria capitulated on 29 September, and Allied forces under General Franchet d'Espèrey rolled into the Balkans as the Austro-Hungarian Army dissolved. In the Middle East, Damascus fell on 1 October, and the Turks were out of the war. An Italian attack at Vittorio Veneto on 24 October destroyed what was left of the Hapsburg Army and opened southern Germany to an Allied advance. So desperate was Ludendorff that in early October, he demanded that the new government in Berlin, headed by the liberal Prince Max of Baden, seek an armistice. Staff officers informed the German party leaders, who had never before received a briefing on the military situation, that the war was lost.[113] And the war had been lost. The German Army had taken 1.1 million casualties between March and July 1918 and a further 770,000 between July and November. Another 700,000 had deserted. The Second Army reported in early October that it possessed only 2,683 combat-ready soldiers, with 83 heavy guns and 79 light machine guns, plus reserves of 2,050 soldiers.[114]

The war was lost. At best the German Army could have held the Allies back on the Western Front until January. But it had no way to stop the Italians from crossing the Alps into Bavaria after they crushed the Austro-Hungarian Army in October, or prevent British, French, and Serbian troops from surging into Bohemia and Moravia. Moreover, in October, the Kriegsmarine made its final contribution to the Second Reich's defeat. Without consulting the Reich's new political leaders, the admirals decided to launch a suicide raid for their honor. If the admirals thought this a good idea, the sailors did not. Mutinies immediately broke out on the battleships.

The Lost Generation

The war's terrible cost and length were the result of the fourth military-social revolution: the combination of the Industrial Revolution and the furies unleashed by nationalism, heirs to the French Revolution. The French Revolution had also helped create the administrative and bureaucratic structures that gave the modern state enormous powers to control its citizens, meaning it had both the motivation and means to drive the war. In the end, the Germans, incapable of limiting their megalomania and weighing their conduct only in terms of military necessity, broke their army in the field and their people at home. The German approach to strategy and politics created conditions under which the Reich could not win, even as their tactical expertise lengthened the war and made it hugely costly, while their willingness to break international law and ignore political common sense ensured that a peace of reconciliation was never in the cards.[115]

The First World War's economic and human costs were astronomical. The dead still echo into the twenty-first century: the United Kingdom and its empire, 921,000; France, 1,398,000; Russia, 1,811,000; Italy, 578,000; United States, 114,000; Germany, 2,037,000; Austria-Hungary, 1,100,000; Bulgaria and Turkey, 892,000. The Thiepval Arch in Flanders sums up the extent of the slaughter: it is inscribed with the names of 75,357 British and Commonwealth soldiers who died on the Somme and have no known resting place. What had the war achieved? In the short term, it prevented German hegemony over Europe, but beyond that, its baleful influence extended far into the twentieth century. One could even argue that its political consequences ended only with the fall of the Berlin Wall and the collapse of the Soviet Empire in 1991.

The twenty years of uneasy peace that followed the war's end reflected the failure of Europe's diplomats to create a stable political framework, but that was largely due to the way the war ended and the political chaos that followed. In the east, the Bolsheviks created a regime the ideology of which committed its leaders to a permanent state of hostility with the capitalistic powers. Moreover, the Soviets retained a nostalgic nationalism that never quite accepted the loss of territories the

Tsarist empire had controlled. In Europe's center, Austria-Hungary's collapse created a set of small, quarrelsome states. For the short term they could maintain their independence, but it was not clear that they could do so once the Germans and Russians regained their strength.

To its neighbors, the German problem represented a strategic nightmare. Many historians have denounced the Treaty of Versailles as the major cause of the troubles leading to the Second World War. Supposedly, if the victorious powers had granted the Germans an easier peace, Europe would have avoided the next war. But in the political context of 1919, such a peace was impossible. Germany had played the major role in starting the war, and its conduct of the war itself was atrocious. In the invasion of Belgium and France in 1914, German soldiers had shot some six thousand civilians for the specious reason that they either had been or had abetted *francs-tireurs*. The German Army followed that up by introducing gas war in April 1915. In spring 1917, in executing Operation Alberich, they devastated wide swaths of northwestern France, an action they repeated in their retreat across northern France and western Belgium in 1918. All this was done in the name of "military necessity."[116]

Perhaps the greatest challenge at Versailles was the fact that the war had ended before any Allied troops could set foot on German territory. As the German troops returned home in December 1918, the new Reich's chancellor, Friedrich Ebert, greeted them as "unbeaten." Feeling betrayed by the Allies' supposed failure to follow through on Woodrow Wilson's Fourteen Points and by the dismal conditions following the war's end, many Germans, not just those on the political right, became infatuated with the "stab-in-the-back" legend. They were angered as well by the Versailles Treaty's "War Guilt" clause, which supposedly singled out the Reich for starting the war.[117] Exacerbating such feelings were the actions of the German Foreign Office, which fed these attitudes by distorting the Reich's prewar documents and publishing them in a form one can only describe as "tendentiously edited."[118]

In the end, the Allies failed to enforce Versailles when they had the opportunity. The French, broken by their experiences of the war, drew from their failed occupation of the Ruhr in 1923 the lesson that they could not act without British support. But the British were unwilling to make a commitment to France until spring 1939, by which time it was too late.

CHAPTER EIGHT

Innovation and Preparation for War

1920–1939

When we forge a peace agreement, it is nearly always meant to last. Or at least that is the pretense. We piously presume that peace is the norm and war, an almost unthinkable, highly regrettable exception. Under the influence of Immanuel Kant, many in our number even dream that peace can be made perpetual. We fight wars to end all wars and to make the world safe for democracy. These are the lies we tell ourselves.

—PAUL A. RAHE, *Sparta's First Attic War*

TWO GREAT QUESTIONS CONFRONT historians in examining the history of the Second World War. The first is simply, how did Germany, broken and defeated in the First World War, overthrow the European balance of power within a matter of slightly more than two decades? The second is a corollary to the first: what were the strategic and military factors that explain the catastrophe? The second question is more difficult to answer, because overlying any reasonable answer are the imponderables of history: chance, friction, incompetence, and human foibles.

In November 1918, the sudden collapse of the German Army before the overwhelming military and industrial power of the Allies shocked a population that had believed as late as July of that year that they were winning the war. What followed for Germany were a dismal series of events from the signing of the Versailles Treaty to the massive inflation of 1923, to the Great Depression. Yet by late November 1941, the divisions of the Wehrmacht were at the gates of Moscow with a cowed and beaten continent, outside of Britain and the Soviet Union, lying at its feet. Too many have ascribed the collapse of Europe to the Versailles Treaty. In fact, given the extent of German war crimes, the treaty, if anything, was too lenient. Moreover, two of the major European powers rejected it from the outset. The Soviets rejected Versailles on the basis that the treaty represented the heart of a capitalist conspiracy they intended to overthrow. The Germans for their part refused to come to terms with the reality that the Reich had lost the war. Instead, even before the signing of Versailles, the myth that the army had stood unbroken and unbeaten in the field, only to be stabbed in the back by Jews and Communists, was deeply embedded in the German psyche.

Adolf Hitler's appointment as the Reich's chancellor on 30 January 1933 exacerbated the myopia of too many Germans.[1] Within four days of his appointment, Hitler met with Germany's senior military leaders and issued a blank check to begin a massive program of rearmament. Apart from Hitler's comments, there was no discussion of the strategic possibilities or the economic constraints that might limit rearmament.[2] The result was that the three services went their own separate ways with no effort to develop a coordinated strategy that considered the strategic realities, much less the systemic weaknesses of the German economy.

In fact, the German economy was teetering on the edge of bankruptcy in 1933, as it was to do through much of the 1930s.[3] By September 1939, the economy had produced only 58.6 percent of scheduled and contracted orders for the military due to raw material shortages and lack of industrial capacity.[4] The writing was on the wall as early as 1936. By that point, senior army leaders recognized that massive defense outlays and financial difficulties were making either war or Germany's bankruptcy inevitable.[5] In that year, defense expenditures reached 13 percent of GDP; by 1938, they reached 16.4 percent.[6] The underlying problem the Germans confronted was the fact that the only raw material they possessed in substantial amounts was coal. Even here there were problems, since the mining of coal was manpower-intensive, and manpower, as the Germans had discovered in the last war, was an item in short supply—even for the Reich.

The other factor that was going to impinge on supplies of coal was the fact that the Reich had access to neither petroleum nor rubber, crucial components for an increasingly motorized economy and military operations. The Germans did make substantial efforts to create synthetic fuels and rubber to replace imports of those commodities, but that effort depended on coal as the basic building block of synthetic production. The motorization of the German economy, admittedly far behind that of Britain, much less the United States, increasingly affected both the civilian and military sectors of the economy throughout the 1930s. Demands for diesel fuel grew at an even faster rate than for gasoline: 527,000 tons in 1933 to 1,312,000 in 1937.[7] Access to iron ore was in no better shape. Once war with France broke out, Germany would no longer have access to the Lorraine ore fields, thus making Swedish ore with its 50 percent iron content essential.

In the postwar period an economic historian argued that the Germans had developed what he called a "blitzkrieg strategy" that aimed at overwhelming the Reich's enemies one at a time, before moving onto the next stage.[8] In fact, the German military had no military strategy, much less a grand strategy. Rather they trailed behind their Führer, while Hitler followed his instincts and took advantage of circumstances as they occurred. But he was no opportunist: his larger vision of a Reich triumphant over a world *Judenfrei* lay solidly under all his major decisions.

The great difficulty underlying the Anglo-French response to the rise of Nazism lay in the inability of far too many, especially in Britain, to recognize that Hitler's Germany was a strategic and *moral* danger. The primary culprit in driving appeasement to the disastrous crackup of 1940 was Neville Chamberlain. Simply put, he could not accept the idea that Hitler, or Benito Mussolini for that matter, might not consider war as basic to their policy in the international arena. He once remarked to his foreign minister, Lord Halifax, that the dictators were "men of moods—catch them in the right mood and they will give you anything you ask for."[9] Inherent in the prime minister's approach to questions of national security was a belief that a "modern" statesman could ignore considerations of balance of power, strategic requirements, and military power. British journalist and politician Leo Amery noted acidly about Chamberlain that, "inflexibly dedicated to his self-imposed mission at all costs to avert the risk of a world war, he ignored the warnings of the Foreign Office, dominated his colleagues, over-rode wavering French, brushing aside their moral compunctions as lacking realism, and, to the last moment, refused to acknowledge failure."[10]

Chamberlain was not alone. Not only did he enjoy the enthusiastic support of the majority of the Conservative Party, a support that would

last well into late spring 1940, but the British public remained solidly behind the prime minister and his foreign policy. Moreover, appeasement
ran deep within the intellectual elite as well as the general populace. On
9 February 1933, ten days after Hitler had come to power, the Oxford
Union passed a resolution that "this House will under no circumstances
fight for its King and country." Another major factor in British appeasement was the continued pessimistic strategic assessments produced by
the chiefs of staff. Consistently, they underplayed British and French
military strength while overestimating those of the Germans. One suspects that their dark picture of the international situation was partially
motivated by a desire to push the government into recognizing what
they regarded as the extraordinary military weaknesses of Britain's defense establishment.[11] Their warnings, however, had no effect on a government sure another war was an impossibility.

The record of the French was not much better. Churchill put their
conundrum simply: "Worn down, doubly decimated, but undisputed
masters of the hour, the French nation peered into the future in thankful
wonder and haunting dread. Where then was that SECURITY without
which all that had been gained seemed valueless, and life itself, even amid
the rejoicings of victory, was almost unendurable? The mortal need was
security."[12] Confronting the reality that Germany remained a threat,
French policymakers constructed a series of alliances with the emergent
Eastern European nations, particularly Czechoslovakia and Poland,
while hoping Britain would stand behind them. At the same time,
France's military strategy focused on the creation of the Maginot Line to
prevent the Germans from seizing the industrialized areas in the north.
There was, however, a strategic contradiction. If the Germans moved
first against the east instead of against the west, would France be willing
or able to rescue its allies?

Furthermore, on the military side, struggles for political power in
France interfered with military preparations. The election of a popular
front government in 1936, led by the socialist Léon Blum, did not help.
Domestic reforms slowed the ability of French arms manufacturers to
meet military requirements, while the government siphoned off defense
expenditures for domestic programs. This was the case with the air force,
for example, where first-line fighters failed to arrive in French combat
squadrons until late 1939. Thus, teething problems, affecting all new aircraft, impacted combat capabilities of French air power in the air battles
of May 1940.[13] Still, the French defeat in 1940 had relatively little to do

with a lack of military equipment; rather, it had far more to do with incompetence at the top of the military hierarchy.

If the Western Powers and their strategic approach remained lackadaisical, the American polity withdrew entirely from strategic thinking and preparation for war. Starting with their refusal to ratify the Treaty of Versailles and return to "normalcy," Americans glibly ignored the international scene. Not until 1938 did the navy receive a substantial increase in funding, but the army buildup began only in July 1940. To make matters worse, Congress passed a series of Neutrality Acts in the mid-1930s, forbidding the sale of arms to any nation involved in war. Supposedly this would prevent "the merchants of death" from enticing the United States into another major conflict. Still, whatever the lack of vision among Americans, their president, Franklin D. Roosevelt, would push forward the nation's preparation to the extent political circumstances allowed.

Ironically, the Soviet Union was the only nation besides Germany or Japan to prepare its military forces, particularly the army, for a major war throughout the interwar period. Driven by the paranoia of his ideology, Joseph Stalin began the first of the Soviet Union's Five-Year Plans in 1928 with the explicit aim of increasing Russia's industrial base to support its military forces against an invasion by the capitalists. Along with industrialization came efforts to modernize the Red Army. Through 1937, that effort made it the most innovative of European armies. But in May of that year, Stalin began a devastating series of purges that murdered most of the army's competent officers while derailing efforts to create modern military forces. The disasters of 1941 were very much the result of the murderous purges of the officer corps.

Innovation and Preparation for War

The interwar period saw major improvements in technology and capabilities, but there were few technological surprises, the appearance of radar in the mid-1930s being one of the few exceptions. Nevertheless, the weapons systems of the Great War would undergo significant improvements in battlefield effectiveness, which in turn demanded changes in doctrine and tactical concepts. What was noticeable in the interwar period was that the increasing capabilities of the internal combustion engine carried with them significant implications in terms of operational tempo. Similarly, improvements in radio communications and their derivative radar had a major impact on command and control but also eventually on the tactical employment of weapons. How well military organizations performed in combat was not so much a matter of the number of weapons systems but the larger tactical and operational systems within which they fought. Here the extent and realism within which they tested out their capabilities in exercises and training in peacetime would have a major impact in the campaigns of the early war years.

One of the signal differences between the Axis and the Anglo-Americans lay in how they managed their talent pools. Here, the differences resulted in a major advantage for the Allies. From the onset of rearmament, Germans emphasized pushing talent toward the combat arms, a reflection of national and military culture. On the other hand, Anglo-Americans were willing to protect their young scientists and technologists from the eager grasp of the services. The difference was cultural. The German and Japanese military tended to look down on civilian scientists and technologists. Thus, they minimized the impact and influence of their civilian counterparts, including those who served in design and engineering establishments.[14] There were occasions when the same was true on the Allied side, but for the most part, Anglo-Americans listened to civilian experts. As a corollary, the interest and resources they devoted to code-breaking and intelligence during the war are a case in point. How to explain the advantage? Part of Allied success lay in a willingness to devote greater resources to that effort. But the key lay in a willingness to use human talent in ways that contrasted sharply with that of the Axis Powers.

The Ground Forces

Given that they had been preparing for war seriously since 1921, the Wehrmacht enjoyed a significant advantage over their opponents in the early war years, at least in ground war. Nevertheless, there were systemic weaknesses in the German way of war that would negate those advantages. The most significant revolution in military affairs in the Great War had been the development of combined arms. By 1918, that revolution had incorporated infantry, artillery, engineers, close-air support, intelligence, air superiority, and even tanks into a complex doctrinal framework.[15] With the war's end, the question was how well the lessons of 1918 would find their way into the doctrines and preparations of armies in the postwar period.

Here, the Germans followed the most realistic path, from which the Wehrmacht gained significant dividends in World War II's opening years.[16] The key figure was the second head of the Reichsheer, the name given to the German Army at the time, and first chief of the general staff, General Hans von Seeckt, who took over the reins of the army in March 1920. He confronted two issues: (1) how to downsize the officer corps in accordance with Versailles, and (2) what lessons should the army draw from the war. Seeckt placed the emphasis on retaining general staff officers and ensured they held the command positions. Second, he created a wide-ranging lessons-learned process with fifty-seven different committees to examine changes in tactics and the conduct of operations during the war.[17]

In 1921 and 1923, the general staff produced Army Regulation 487 ("Leadership and Battle with Combined Arms"). It focused on what is today called maneuver war: decentralized execution, responsibility for decision-making left to the officer or NCO on the spot, a requirement that officers and NCOs use judgment in executing orders, and an emphasis on aggressive initiative. The Germans refined the doctrine further with training exercises they conducted as well as debates in the officer corps. Thus, the emphasis in the buildup after 1933 was on combined-arms tactics and not on a revolutionary tank doctrine. German armored development took place within a careful process that examined how tanks could best fit within the combined-arms fight, which would provide a significant advantage in the early war years.

Yet, for all the German success in creating an effective doctrine and system for combined arms, the Wehrmacht, as well as the Luftwaffe and Kriegsmarine, possessed serious weaknesses at the strategic and operational levels. There are three crucial components for success at the operational level: tactical competence on the battlefield, a coherent and relatively accurate understanding of the enemy, and a robust logistical structure. In the latter two areas the Germans failed to provide reasonable support to the sharp end. The weaknesses in intelligence arose partially from the parochialism of German society and the inability or unwillingness of Germans to understand the "other," which Nazi ideology only exacerbated.[18] On the logistical side, Franz Halder, chief of the general staff, summed up German thinking in a postwar comment that "quartermasters [logisticians] must never hamper operational concepts."[19] The Reich's geography encouraged such thinking. At Europe's heart, Germany was at the center of any major war. Thus, German logisticians in both World Wars thought largely in terms of moving supplies to a front within easy reach. However, when operations extended to the distances of the Mediterranean and European Russia, German logisticians found themselves out of their depth.

Moreover, Germany in 1939 was not yet a mechanized society; much of its local transport remained horse- and mule-drawn. A comparison of motor vehicles per thousand in Germany with the Anglo-Saxon countries in 1939 suggests how poorly the Germans were prepared for mechanized war: Germany, 25 motor vehicles; Britain, 51; Canada, 124; New Zealand, 164; and the United States, 227.[20] The lack of an understanding of mechanization in the widest sense resulted in a failure to understand the importance of standardization, of an efficient supply system, and of the fact that quantity had a qualitative impact all of its own.

The French were obviously the first major opponent who stood in Germany's way.[21] The Maginot Line has been the focus of many of the explanations for French defeat in May 1940. In fact, the line served its purpose by preventing the Germans from driving through the Belford Gap. For the French, World War I suggested that offensive operations would inevitably incur heavy casualties. Even when they had employed innovative and adaptive combined-arms tactics, they had suffered prohibitive losses. Part of the problem in the French Army in this period lay in a flawed organization. The general staff, theoretically in charge of the army, had no control over finances, personnel, or administration: "In the final analysis, the French high command lacked a clear chain of authority and responsibility that could provide the army a firm sense of direction for developing its doctrine and designing its weapons. While over-centralization may stifle initiative, the fragmented organization of the French High Command also stifled creative solutions to doctrinal problems."[22] Failures in leadership exacerbated problems. The chief of staff from 1931 to May 1940, General Maurice Gamelin, fulfilled the role of keeping the politicians happy but failed to provide clear direction on innovation or adapting to changes in tactics or technology.

The doctrine and school system reinforced a proclivity that the war's last year had imprinted on French thinking. It emphasized tight control over maneuver. Doctrinal manuals stressed that "firepower [has] given a remarkable strength of resistance to improvised fortifications."[23] The French summed up their thinking in the term "methodical battle," in which commanders and staffs at the top planned and controlled every movement throughout an operation, which allowed little initiative to those at lower ranks. Moreover, Gamelin stamped out debate. In 1935, he demanded that the high command be the sole arbiter of what its officers could publish. One commentator noted, "Everyone got the message and a profound silence reigned until the awakening in 1940."[24]

Across the English Channel, the story was more depressing. As the British were the first to develop the tank, one might have thought they would have continued to innovate with armored fighting vehicles. In addition, in the last months of the Great War, the British Army had proven outstanding practitioners of the combined-arms revolution. However, in the immediate aftermath of the conflict, they simply disregarded the war's tactical lessons. The explicit directions of successive British governments that the army was to prepare only for colonial wars reinforced a lack of interest in the last war. Moreover, the fact that the army failed to establish a committee to study the last war's lessons until 1932 underlines an intellectual laziness.[25] The real problem, which hobbled the army in the next war, lay in its culture.[26] The tribal nature of its regimental organization made combined-arms operations difficult. The regimental system did provide soldiers with a sense of camaraderie and explains how they proved such dogged fighters. But in a broader sense, the regimental system encouraged disparagement of the serious study of war.

On the other side of Europe, the Soviet Union believed it confronted a hostile capitalist world bent on destroying Lenin's and Stalin's experiment. In the first months of the Russian Revolution, the Bolshevik regime eliminated its White opponents and then turned west with the aim of overthrowing the new Polish regime. But in front of Warsaw the Red Army proved incapable of defeating Polish nationalism. Stalin, emerging as the party's leader, settled on creating socialism in one state. There were two tracks the regime and the Red Army followed until the late 1930s.[27] On one hand, beginning in October 1928, Stalin launched his massive Five-Year Plan to build up Russia's heavy industry. Despite the cost, exacerbated by murderous purges and mass starvation, impressive gains occurred in the Soviet industrial base.[28] The eventual success of the Red Army in World War II rested on the industrialization of the late 1920s and 1930s. Not only did the Five-Year Plans allow the Soviets to create an impressive inventory of weapons but they provided the cushion that allowed the regime to survive the onslaught of 1941.[29]

The second track involved the development of strategic and doctrinal thinking within the Red Army.[30] Beginning with the establishment of the general staff in February 1924, two truly innovative leaders emerged:

Mikhail Tukhachevsky and Vladimir Triandafillov. In 1929, in its field regulations, the Red Army's leaders were considering the use of mechanized formations.[31] Triandafillov also enunciated the concept of deep battle that would involve the movement of major mechanized forces into the enemy's rear to destroy its cohesion. Inherent in Soviet military thinking lay an emphasis on material factors. In other words, the Soviets accepted the ramifications of the marriage of ideology and Industrial Revolution. Soviet tactical innovations in the early and mid-1930s included an emphasis on intelligence and logistics. The Soviets had to think in terms of great distances; consequently, logistics played a major role in their planning. In retrospect, they were the real inventors of operational art: the ability to combine combined-arms tactics with logistics and intelligence to execute deep exploitations.

This progress toward developing an effective Red Army collapsed in May 1937. Having purged other potential centers of opposition, Stalin saw the military as the last remaining threat to his power.[32] By the time the military purges ended in late 1939, Stalin had either executed or sent to the Gulag over half of the officer corps (35,000 out of 70,000). By rank Stalin purged 90 percent of the army's generals and 80 percent of its colonels.[33] A few survived to return to the army as the great crisis loomed in 1941, the most significant, the future Marshal K. K. Rokossovsky, who found himself released from the Gulag immediately before the German invasion.

Driven by the unwillingness of the American people to recognize the gathering dangers, the U.S. Army received minimum funding through summer 1940, when France's fall convinced Roosevelt to begin serious rearmament of the ground forces. One of the major problems the army confronted in innovating was the sheer size of the continental United States. With underfunded and undermanned units spread across the nation's expanses, the army was not able to conduct maneuvers to test new concepts. Not until summer 1941 could it conduct major maneuvers. In comparison, the Germans with an army of comparable size from 1920 to 1932 conducted annual exercises, because Germany was so much smaller and it was easy to gather units together for more effective training.

Where the U.S. Army made substantial progress in preparing for war lay in its approach to professional military education. It possessed a robust educational system, the various schools and colleges of which contributed to building a consensus about future war. Admittedly, much of the teaching at the army's staff college at Leavenworth, Kansas, focused on a top-down approach to combat. But students took their studies seriously: Dwight D. Eisenhower graduated as number one in his class, while George Patton was close to the top. If the army failed to hold serious exercises because of its constraints, the students did receive a common education, focusing on combined arms, particularly the interplay between artillery and infantry.

Air and Naval Forces

From our perspective, the lessons of air and naval warfare in the First World War appear obvious. However, as has so often been the case in the past, airmen and naval officers focused during the interwar period on what they thought, believed, or hoped had happened in the past while ignoring the realities of what had actually occurred. Complicating thinking in the air and naval domains was the increasing pace of technological and scientific change, which admittedly made thinking about the future difficult. By 1919, most recognized that the aircraft represented a revolution in military affairs. But what exactly would its impact be? Which of its many missions emerging during the Great War should dominate? Would it still find its justification in support of battles on the ground? How might it change the equation of naval power in the potential clash of great fleets? Or would great air armadas take the war to an enemy's industry or industries? What was clear, however, was that future conflicts involving naval and air forces would increase demands for resources and highly qualified scientists, technologists, and engineers.[34]

For airmen, the nature of their weapon provided considerable latitude for imagination, but they largely ignored the experiences of the last war. The speed of technological change seemed to promise much, but it was difficult to estimate the impact of the various air missions on enemy military forces or civilian populations. Thus, airmen tended to rely on assumptions of what aircraft *might* be able to do. For navies, the problems raised by technology involved those dealing with the increases in range and capability of aircraft. Even more so than with air campaigns, navies confronted the increasing pace of technological change with the impact of aircraft, communications, and electronics. They also faced, somewhat unwillingly, the fact that fleets and merchant commerce would confront threats from submarines. As with air forces, naval capabilities depended on adaptation to new technologies and improvements. The inclusion of these technologies and weapons systems during the interwar period set the stage for naval contests to control the world's oceans. None of the air forces or navies were prepared for the industrial and technological demands war would place on their forces.

The Air Forces

By November 1918, the airplane had proven a versatile and deadly weapon of importance to ground operations. Moreover, aircraft represented an obvious culmination of the Industrial Revolution, while in addition to combined operations their appearance represented the other major revolution in military affairs that had occurred in the First World War. By war's end, aircraft were conducting photo reconnaissance, close air support, air superiority, interdiction, and strategic bombing missions. Above all, air war demanded steady improvements and adaptation in design and capabilities, along with the industrial ability to outproduce the enemy. Thus, the air war became a constant battle of adaptation on the battlefield, in the design processes, and in manufacturing. It demanded more aircraft as well as improved capabilities.[35]

Ironically, theorists of air power, like the Italian Gulio Douhet as well as airmen in both Britain and the United States, imagined air war as a means to escape World War I's costly attrition. Anglo-American airmen, partially because they were protected by bodies of water, placed little emphasis on ground or naval war and considerable emphasis on strategic bombing. The Germans, confronting ground conflict immediately on the outbreak of any war, put less emphasis on strategic bombing. Thus, they proved more realistic in thinking about the aircraft's potential and developed a more holistic view of air power. In their view, aircraft represented the potential to execute a wide variety of missions. It was all very well to think about strategic bombing of Paris or Prague or London, but if the Reich lost the Ruhr or Silesia, Germany would lose the war.

In the period up to Hitler's accession to power, the Germans could only think about the possibility of an air force. Thus, they started at year zero on 30 January 1933. Yet over a period of six years they built up an impressive force, one that focused on the wider aspects of air power employment. The Luftwaffe's basic doctrinal manual, *Die Luftkriegführung*, was more broadly based than thinking in Britain or the United States. It pointed out that "the nature of the enemy, the time of year, the structure of his land [and economy], the character of his people, as well as one's own military capabilities" would have to guide air power's employ-ment. *Die Luftkriegführung* warned that maintenance of air superiority would prove an elusive mission. Success might prove temporary, since changing technical capabilities, continuing production, and replacement of losses could alter the correlation of forces.[36]

The most significant problem the Luftwaffe's leaders confronted was creating a force and industrial base out of whole cloth. In 1933, the Ger-man aircraft industry possessed only 4,000 workers and produced barely 1,000 aircraft per year, mostly training types.[37] By 1938, that industrial base had expanded to 204,100 workers, but aircraft manufacturing re-mained largely on a craft basis rather than mass production.[38] Adding to the problem of creating a new air force was the fact that aircraft design and engineering capabilities improved rapidly in the 1930s, so that initial production runs were obsolete almost immediately. Adding to the Luft-waffe difficulties was the fact that despite resources poured into the in-dustry, production of new aircraft fell steadily behind targets. In 1938, aircraft factories fell 25 percent below target; the following year, output was 30 percent under expectations.[39] The Führer even demanded in late summer 1938 that the Luftwaffe quintuple its force structure—a demand reflecting ignorance of production capabilities.[40]

When Hitler launched the Wehrmacht against Poland in September 1939, the Luftwaffe had a number of deficiencies: its economic and re-source base was inadequate to meet the demands of a sustained, long, drawn-out war. It also lacked access to petroleum, crucial to air war. It was prepared to fight a short war against Poland, but even a war against the west raised almost insoluble economic and strategic problems. Add-ing to the Luftwaffe's long-term weaknesses was Hitler's decision on the outbreak of war to restrict research and development to projects only of immediate use. When the Germans awoke to the consequences in 1942, it was too late.

Alone among the major powers involved in the First World War, the British created an independent air force. That decision had major ramifi-cations in terms of how they prepared for the Second World War. On the side of naval air, creation of an independent air force with its lack of interest in naval matters meant that the Royal Navy entered the next conflict with obsolete carrier aircraft. As for the RAF, it innovated effec-tively in some areas, such as in air defense, but in other areas failed dis-mally, driven by its belief that the "bomber would always get through." In particular, RAF thinking emphasized attacking population centers. No thought was given to the need for escort fighters to protect bombers against enemy fighters. Nor was serious examination devoted to the problems involved in hitting targets accurately in daytime, much less nighttime.

But if preparation for strategic bombing represented flawed innovation, that of air defense represented a different picture. One individual, Air Marshal Hugh Dowding, played the decisive role in developing radar and an effective air defense system.[41] In the early 1930s, as a member of the Air Council responsible for supply and research, he set the specifications of a new generation of fighters, the eventual Hurricane and Spitfire. In July 1936, he assumed command of Fighter Command. Development of an effective air defense system began shortly thereafter when Robert Watson Watt, superintendent of the Radio Research Laboratory, passed along the results of his team's work in using radio waves to detect aircraft.[42]

Dowding immediately understood its significance and implications. He provided initial funding from his limited resources for a series of tests, and his energy never abated. As one historian commented, "Dowding was indisputably the pivotal military figure, providing the pull toward new operational developments and innovation. . . . He also insisted that military personnel be posted right with the 'Boffins,' as the civilian researchers became known. This insured that the RAF personnel actually understood what was happening and that the civilians could be kept aware of military constraints and needs."[43]

One of the advantages Dowding possessed was that Britain already possessed an air defense system based on observation posts scattered along the coast. These were all networked through the post office telephone system to sector stations that controlled the fighter squadrons. It was not terribly effective, but it approached air defense in a systematic fashion, one that radar could easily fit into. By 1937, through a series of experiments run jointly with military personnel, aircraft, and civilians, the RAF had worked out the basic procedures for radar and Fighter Command. By late 1938, a functioning system was in place that Fighter Command further refined so that by September 1939, the RAF had an effective air defense. The key word here is "system." Significantly, the partnership among senior military officers, leading scientists, and engineers worked far better in Britain than in Germany. The British recognized that civilians and military needed to work closely together. That culture represented a critical advantage.

The British scientific intelligence officer R. V. Jones observes in his memoirs:

> German philosophy ran roughly along the lines that there was an equipment [radar] which was marvelous in the sense that it would enable a single station to cover a circle of radius 150 kilometers and detect every aircraft. ... Thus, it could replace a large number of Observer Corps posts on the ground, and so was a magnificent way of economizing on the Observer Corps. [However,] we had realized that in order to make maximum use of radar information the stations had to be backed by a communications network that could handle the information with the necessary speed.[44]

In the early 1920s, a fight broke out over whether the United States should create an independent air force or leave the navy and army air components intact. In 1926, the Morrow Board, appointed in 1925 to study the development and application of airpower to the defense of the United States, settled matters; there would be no separate service. There were unintended consequences. One was the fact that naval air pushed American aviation engine development in a direction quite different from what occurred in Europe. In the early 1920s, the consensus among engineers was that in-line engines offered the best potential in terms of horsepower. What the navy, however, discovered when it began maintaining aircraft on board its first carriers was that in-line engines were more difficult to repair. Any major maintenance work required the engine to be dropped, that is, removed from the aircraft. With a carrier underway this was a difficult process. On the other hand, maintenance personnel could work on a radial engine directly without dropping it.

The long-term result was that American engine development took a different direction from Europe. North American distances placed ease of maintenance at the top of requirements for civil as well as military aircraft. By the early 1930s, American aircraft were largely using radial engines rather than in-line engines. The unintended effect was that in the war, virtually all of the Luftwaffe's and the RAF's first-line bombers and fighters, except for the Fw 190, used in-line engines, while with the exception of the P-51 and P-38, American fighters and bombers utilized radial engines.[45] For the Americans this proved fortuitous, since their air operations took place far from the United States, where ease of maintenance was critical.

The Morrow Board did allow the army's air wing considerable independence as the Army Air Corps. The airmen took advantage of that opportunity.[46] At the U.S. Air Corps Tactical School, they developed a doctrine of air power that profoundly influenced the Army Air Forces in World War II. Like RAF leaders, American airmen believed air power in the form of bombers could attack an enemy nation and bring about its collapse more quickly than traditional ground and naval forces. But unlike the British, the Americans rejected the idea of attacking population centers in favor of key nodes in the enemy's economy. Such attacks would supposedly bring about the collapse of the industrial economy. That approach appealed to the American love of technology; above all it recognized the importance of industrial production.

By the end of the 1930s, air power theorists at the Air Corps Tactical School had evolved a theory of air war that represented a precisely connected body of assumptions. They based those on the belief that a well-led, disciplined bomber formation could fight its way through enemy-controlled air space, unsupported by long-range escort fighters. Once the bombers had made their high-altitude deep penetration, they could, through precision bombing, place sufficient bombs on target to assure destruction. That target would represent a portion of the enemy's economic web, the destruction of which would cause widespread dislocations. The impact would eventually lead to the collapse of the enemy's industrial economy.

Whatever the weakness in airmen's prewar assumptions, the Air Corps Tactical School's thinking provided a theoretical basis on which long-range bombers, such as the B-17 and B-24, could begin a strategic bombing campaign. What the air planners failed to recognize was that a strategic bombing campaign would inevitably turn into a massive battle of attrition. Thus, strategic bombing represented the epitome of the Industrial Revolution; the winner would be the air force that possessed the greatest industrial production and support structure in the face of heavy losses. In the end, it represented an approach to war that fit America's economic strength.

The Navies

As with the air forces, the navies underwent major technological changes during the interwar period. Their problem was that they confronted two new threats: first, the destructive capabilities of aircraft, and second, long-range submarines. The first lay with the increasing capabilities of both land-based and carrier-based aircraft. On the other hand, submarines represented a threat to sea lines of communications (SLOCs) of the three maritime powers, the United States, Britain, and Japan. In addition, radar developed rapidly from a means of detecting enemy aircraft to creation of ship-borne sets that added to the accuracy of naval gunfire and provided more accurate targeting at night.

In retrospect, the submarine, like the aircraft, had appeared to presage a revolution in military affairs. In 1917, the British had come close to having their SLOCs broken by the U-boats, largely through the Admiralty's refusal to use convoys. In 1918, convoys brought merchant losses to tolerable levels. However, the threat had been sufficiently real that the British spent considerable resources in trying to achieve its defeat. By 1918, they had developed a means of detecting the movement of U-boats underwater using sound waves, a technology called ASDIC (the American term is "sonar"). But the war ended too soon to test the new device; nevertheless, the Admiralty assumed it had solved the U-boat problem. In one of the ironies of the interwar period, the other major navies largely accepted the British claim.

The aircraft had also made its appearance in naval operations. While the conduct of the war on land had laid out a number of paths for aircraft to follow, the impact of air power at sea was less clear. Admittedly, the British had developed aircraft carriers, and light bombers from one of them attacked German naval bases in 1918, but there was little evidence on the impact aircraft might have on fleet actions. They would certainly be useful in reconnaissance, but what other roles they might have was open to doubt, given limitations in range and carrying capacity in 1918.

Versailles limited the Weimar Republic to a minuscule navy, which prevented the military from wasting money. Those left in the naval bureaucracy spent their time in dreaming of what should have happened. As with the army, the Kriegsmarine focused on tactics rather than considering changes in technology. Four days after Hitler came to power, he gave the military a blank check.[47] The navy's response to Hitler's promise in February 1933 was to build another great fleet. The shipbuilding program emphasized surface ships, while its leaders displayed little interest in carriers.[48] In every sense, German expenditures on battleships and cruisers represented a waste of resources.

Among its other clauses, Versailles forbade the Germans submarines. They did manage developmental work in Holland and Spain. With the signing of the Anglo-German Naval Treaty in 1935, the navy began construction of a new U-boat fleet. The officer in charge of developing U-boats was Captain Karl Dönitz, whose views of future war were unimaginative at best. He concluded that the way to break the British SLOCs was to sink as much tonnage as possible, regardless of whether merchant ships were sailing fully loaded or empty. His approach to war in the Atlantic picked up exactly where the U-boat battle had left off in 1918 with the Allies using convoys. Dönitz's conception was to concentrate U-boats in wolf packs for sustained attacks on convoys, while a higher headquarters on land controlled the battle, which would occur in areas surrounding the British Isles.

But Dönitz failed to war game his assumptions and focused solely on tactical matters and not on larger operational issues. He neglected to consider the possibility that his enemy would possess options. When confronted with the existential threat U-boats represented, the British adapted, so that by summer 1941 they had created substantially new technologies and tactics that made the environs of the British Isles too dangerous for U-boats.[49] What would happen thereafter, the Germans had not a clue. Moreover, the German side of the contest displayed a distinct disinterest in using technology to aid the U-boats until they had lost the Battle of the Atlantic.[50]

In many respects the Royal Navy was the opposite of the Kriegsmarine. As with the other British services, it found itself starved for funds throughout the interwar period.[51] Even with rearmament, the navy confronted the nightmare of Britain's strategic situation. On the Continent the Germans with their rapid rearmament, which included big-ship construction, represented a long-term threat. In the Mediterranean, Italy's reworking of its older battleships and new construction were a direct threat to British SLOCs. In the Pacific, the Japanese were proving increasingly hostile, while the Americans displayed little interest in cooperating.[52] It is within that context that one must judge the Royal Navy.

With the surface threat of the Axis Powers, the British placed emphasis in their initial rearmament on heavy ships. By 1938, they had laid down or authorized construction of seven battleships, twenty-nine cruisers, and five carriers. Not until 1939 did the navy address the U-boat threat, with construction of sixteen destroyers, twenty fast escort vessels, and three escort vessels.[53] There were some who warned that the limited construction of anti-submarine vessels represented a serious error. Despite the fact that the Royal Navy had developed carriers in World War I, by the late 1930s the British had fallen behind the Americans and Japanese. That the RAF controlled aircraft development and had little interest in carrier aircraft was a major hindrance. Not until 1937 did the Royal Navy regain control of its air element, and by then it was too late to develop aircraft to match the Americans and Japanese. Thus, in 1939 the navy's main aircraft was the Swordfish, a biplane with a speed barely reaching one hundred knots. British carriers did have one advantage: their decks were armored, and in the Pacific that proved to be an important advantage at the end of the war when kamikazes struck their carriers.

Whatever the Royal Navy's weaknesses, its leadership made major efforts to repair the failures in initiative too many of its officers had displayed at Jutland. Thus, in the interwar period it prepared a whole generation of officers to act aggressively in the next war.[54] The navy's fleet exercises in the Mediterranean and Atlantic were realistic and effective in creating officers who would perform at a high level in the next war.[55] Even in anti-submarine war, where the Royal Navy was too optimistic before the war, the British adapted tactically and technologically in the conditions of the Battle of the Atlantic better than the Germans.

With carriers, like the Americans, the Japanese innovated successfully, first with a small eight-thousand-ton carrier and then with an unfinished battle cruiser and battleship, which they either had to scrap or turn into carriers. The result was two large carriers, the *Akagi* and *Kaga*. The development of radial engines to ease maintenance on board carriers followed. In one area the Japanese developed faster than the Americans. Their experiences in China taught them that having carriers operate separately with sections of the fleet minimized the ability to mass naval air power, which clearly would have a major impact on battle at sea.[56]

The design of cruisers underlined Japanese plans to defeat an American fleet crossing the Pacific. The Imperial Japanese Navy's (IJN) heavy cruisers, far heavier than treaty weight mandated, would meet the approaching American fleet east of the mandated islands, the former German colonies, which the Treaty of Versailles had assigned to the Japanese, the American location identified by aircraft flying off cruisers and island bases. The cruisers would then draw the U.S. fleet west into a nighttime engagement, where the ruthless night training of the IJN combined with the deadly long-lance, oxygen-fueled torpedoes, would provide the Japanese an advantage and outweigh whatever numerical superiority the Americans enjoyed. Inherent in the Japanese approach was the hope that better training would prove decisive.[57]

In the end the Japanese possessed only a military strategy with no answer to larger strategic questions. An impressive history of the IJN has noted:

> The most serious strategic failing of the Japanese Navy was to mistake tactics for strategy and strategy for the conduct of war. The navy's overarching concern was for decisive battle. . . . Strategy was not given reasonable consideration, and the navy's early tactical victories were soon undone by disastrous strategic miscalculations. . . . More fundamentally . . . the Japanese navy neither understood nor prepared for *war* at all. Rather it believed in and prepared for *battle*. . . . Superbly armed and trained by 1941 to launch a thunderbolt strike and ready to risk all in furious combat, the Japanese Navy was ill prepared to sustain the effort or injuries of extended war.[58]

In many ways the U.S. Navy proved to be the most innovative and imaginative of the militaries in the interwar period, although it had had little combat experience in the last war.[59] Why that was so rests on the navy's creation of a culture of learning in professional military education and exercises at sea. Exacerbating the difficulties of innovation and developing a coherent theater strategy was the reality of the distances in the Pacific even from America's forward bases on the Hawaiian Islands.[60] One of the strong points of the navy's innovations and preparations lay in the fact that it paid close attention not only to military and operational strategy but to grand strategy as well. The key moment in the navy's preparation came when Admiral William Sims assumed presidency of the Naval War College on his return from Europe in 1920, where he had commanded U.S. naval forces. In a fleet dominated by battleship admirals and which possessed no aircraft carriers, the admiral proved enormously perceptive. He noted at the time, "An airplane carrier of thirty-five knots and carrying one hundred planes . . . is in reality a capital ship of much greater offensive power than a battleship."[61]

Sims's decision to take the war college's presidency heralded a period where naval officers viewed assignment to Newport as career-enhancing. When the navy went to war, eighty-one of its eighty-two admirals had graduated from the war college. During Sims's tenure, he oversaw the creation of two important kinds of war games: strategic games studying the complexities of war in the Pacific and tactical war games examining the interplay of fleets in combat. One insight in early war games was that carrier operations would differ substantially from gunfire engagements; carriers would have to launch pulses of air power.[62] The measure of effectiveness would then be how quickly and how many aircraft a carrier could launch in a single pulse of air power.

The symbiosis between thinking at the war college and fleet experimentation became clear in 1925. Commander of the navy's first carrier, the converted collier the USS *Langley*, was Captain Joseph Reeves, who had served at Newport for two tours, one as a student and one on the faculty for two years as director of tactics.[63] Understanding that the carrier's measure of effectiveness would be the aircraft it could launch, Reeves experimented with a number of innovations: trip wires to halt aircraft, deck parks, and crash barriers. Within a year, the *Langley* was launching an aircraft every fifteen seconds and landing one every ninety seconds. As a result, it went from handling a single squadron of fourteen aircraft to handling four squadrons and forty-eight aircraft.[64] With the arrival of the *Lexington* and *Saratoga* in the late 1920s, the navy could place an aircraft wing of 110 aircraft on each carrier.[65]

Annual fleet exercises and war college's games furthered insights on the impact of aviation on future fleet engagements. An early postwar examination of aviation's role in fleet exercises noted that "the suddenness with which an engagement could be completely reversed by the use of aerial power was brought home to the fleet in no uncertain terms." Fleet exercises provided a particularly useful insight into the willingness of navy leaders to grapple with the evidence, rather than what senior officers hoped. Hot washes in the immediate post-exercise critiques were not limited to a few senior officers but often included a wide selection of officers who had participated in the exercise, including junior officers. The critique of the Fleet Problem IX took place before seven hundred naval officers, while the audience for Fleet Exercise XIV included more than a thousand.[66]

As fleet exercises lengthened in the late 1930s, they underlined the logistical requirements a fleet in heavy action would require during an extended campaign. As early as 1929, exercises suggested that the refueling of ships at sea represented a major problem. Perhaps the most far-reaching insights the navy gained were at the theater strategic level. In the early 1920s, while Guam still represented a waystation en route to the Philippines, the navy could think about deploying its fleet to the western Pacific. But when the Washington treaties of 1921 demilitarized

Guam there was no chance of reaching the Philippines, except in the irresponsible dreams of army generals. The alternative was a drive through the Central Pacific with a concomitant seizure of island bases. That in turn would require amphibious warfare, massive logistical support, sustained operations to bypass Japanese bases, and resupply not only of fuel but ammunition and sustenance.[67] It also meant a sustained war to draw fully on the nation's great industrial base. Naval planners did worry about whether the American people would support a long, sustained, and costly campaign that such a strategy would require. Ironically, the Japanese, with their attack on Pearl Harbor, ensured popular support would be there.

Conclusion

As Michael Howard has suggested, military organizations will always get the next war wrong. Effective combatants are those who can adjust prewar assumptions to actual conditions.[68] Those who gloss over the results of peacetime exercises will, on the other hand, attempt to make reality fit preconceived notions when their organizations find themselves involved in war. Not surprisingly, the performance of military institutions in the next war rests on what they learned or failed to learn in peace.

For the most part, the militaries of the interwar period struggled to find paths to escape the logic of the last war, namely that the French and Industrial Revolutions were inextricably bound together and could not be separated, no matter how effective armies, navies, and air forces might prove. Only the Soviets and the Americans recognized that the next war would prove an extended struggle of attrition resting on industrial power: the Soviets driven by Marxist ideology and a desire to catch up with the industrialized world, the Americans because they had arrived so late in the last war and because the distances to reach future theaters would require time and resources. The Germans foundered in tactical dreams and the hope the Führer's indomitable will would suffice, the British escape came in hopes war was simply unthinkable, and the French that the Maginot Line could prevent another Verdun.

What complicates the problem of military effectiveness is the reality that outstanding performance at one level of war does not guarantee effectiveness on the other. One cannot doubt that the German Army performed in a highly competent fashion at the tactical level in both World Wars. On the other hand, its performance at the strategic level was appalling, while that at the operational level left much to be desired. For those who hope to learn from the past, this represents a particularly vexing problem because the competencies demanded in an officer corps to be tactically proficient may at the same time form stumbling blocks that distort or prevent strategic competency. Yet, in the end, as Allan R. Millett and this author have suggested, "Mistakes in operations and tactics can be corrected, but political and strategic mistakes live forever."[69]

PART IV

The Military-Social Revolutions on a Global Stage

CHAPTER NINE

The European War

1939–1941

When every one of these aids and advantages had been
squandered and thrown away, Great Britain advances, leading
France by the hand, to guarantee the integrity of Poland. . . .
History, which we are told is mainly a record of the crimes,
follies, and miseries of mankind, may be scoured to find a
parallel to this sudden and complete reversal of five or six years'
policy of easy-going placatory appeasement, and its
transformation almost overnight into a readiness to accept an
obviously imminent war on far worse conditions and on the
greatest scale.

—WINSTON CHURCHILL, *The Second World War*

THE CATASTROPHE THAT HAPPENED between September 1939 and December 1941 had many causes. The most obvious was the deep-seated ruthlessness of leaders motivated by ideologies that promised to correct the mistakes of the past, or to march humankind on a revolutionary path foreordained by economic truths embedded in history. Those ideologies placed no worth on human life, because the individual was simply a small participant in the drive to the greater good. For the Germany of Adolf Hitler, biological factors had determined the path to the present, and history,

Leadup to war, 1936–1939. Cartography by Bill Nelson.

thwarted by the malicious actions of Jews, had not been kind to the Aryan race, which had been responsible for the triumphs of civilization.

The most *important* causes of the catastrophe lay in the beliefs and actions of well-meaning individuals in the democracies who simply refused to recognize that Hitler actually meant what he said and wrote. Instead, they dithered, took half-hearted measures toward rearmament, and sacrificed the strategic advantages that they enjoyed from the Treaty of Versailles in the hope that they could avoid a bloody confrontation with the dictators. Winston Churchill aptly described the 1930s as the "locust years." In 1934, he warned, "I marvel at the complacency of ministers in the face of the frightful experiences through which we have so newly passed. I look with wonder upon . . . this unheeding House of Commons, which seems to have no higher function than to cheer a minister; [and all the while across the North Sea] a terrible process is astir. *Germany is arming!*"[1] But Churchill's warnings went unheeded by the politicians and people of Britain, while the American polity buried its collective head ever deeper in the sands of neutrality.

The advantage that the Germans enjoyed in the war's opening two years did not lie in some magic formula—all too often described as Blitzkrieg warfare—but in the meticulous preparation of the Wehrmacht over the previous six years. Possessing sufficient armaments and abetted by the incompetence of military commanders on the other side of the line, the Germans overthrew a European balance of power that had lasted since 1815. In 1939, the Western Powers were more than the equal of the Third Reich in sustained economic and military power because, like Germany, they too possessed access to the powers of the fourth military-social revolution. But they were late to the starting gate, and their people would pay a terrible price for their leaders' errors in delaying serious rearmament to the last moment.

In 1939, Hitler enjoyed a narrow window during which German military power could overthrow the military power of the Western Powers. The war of September 1939 to June 1941 would see the Wehrmacht crash through that window. But with the invasion of the Soviet Union in June 1941, the Germans would confront an opponent with the economic strength, will power, and strategic depth to survive the first shattering blows. Russia too was prepared to utilize the marriage of the French and Industrial Revolutions, and it too had prepared seriously for war.

The War Begins

On 1 September 1939, Hitler launched the Wehrmacht against Poland. As he had just signed the Nazi-Soviet Non-Aggression Pact with Stalin, he did not expect the British and French to intervene despite their having guaranteed Polish independence. He was, however, prepared to face the consequences if they did. In one of his rages over British actions the previous spring, he had announced that he had seen his enemies at Munich, and they were worms.[2] Certainly, the deal with the Soviet Union in mid-August had rendered Poland's position hopeless. Yet given Germany's economic difficulties and the problems in the Wehrmacht's armament programs, war in 1939 still represented a grave risk.

What, then, made Hitler take what even he recognized as a gamble? Inherent in his decision was a conviction that he alone could hold back the dark tides of international Jewry and other inferior races that threatened to overwhelm the Aryan-German nation. It was not the only time that such beliefs would lead him to pursue strategic aims that lay beyond reasonable strategic calculations. What made Nazi ideology so dangerous was not simply that Hitler had fused it with his own identity as the Führer but that he had grafted it onto the tree of German nationalism and the *Weltanschauung* of all too many Germans, including the generals and admirals. After 1941, when the brilliant glow of the Wehrmacht's triumphs dimmed to hopelessness, the generals and populace held on to the bitter end.

The British and French had no intention of coming to Poland's aid. The guarantee to do so, made in March 1939, had been prompted by British political and strategic miscalculations. That month, the Germans had occupied the remainder of Czechoslovakia less than six months after the Munich agreement. Despite the contempt Hitler displayed in occupying the remainder of Czechoslovakia, Neville Chamberlain and his cabinet initially sloughed off German actions with mealy-mouthed explanations in the House of Commons. Yet even the notorious appeaser Nancy Astor asked the prime minister whether he would "lose no time in letting the German Government know with what horror the whole of the country regards Germany's actions."[3]

Confronted with popular outrage and facing a general election within the year, Chamberlain found himself forced to act. The guarantee to Poland was the result.[4] While Britain had seemingly taken a tougher line against the Third Reich, its leaders refused to recognize strategic reality: Hitler was bent on war, and no diplomatic or economic action could deter him. Astonishingly, Chamberlain undertook only half-hearted approaches to the Soviet Union. He appears to have considered the Soviets an unimportant part of the strategic equation. Some historians have argued that the ineptitude of the Western Powers led Stalin to conclude the non-aggression pact with the Nazis. That is nonsense. As a Bolshevik, Stalin regarded both the Western Powers and Nazi Germany with contempt. He cut a deal with the Germans because it allowed him to remain on the sidelines while the capitalists exhausted themselves. It also allowed the Soviets to occupy critical areas, including eastern Poland, the Baltic states, and Finland, while retaining the option to intervene in the larger war at a time of their choosing. But Stalin's strategy rested on one mistaken assumption: he thought the French Army would resist the Germans as effectively as it had in 1914.

Over the summer of 1939, the British began serious rearmament while trying every method, including bribery, to avoid war.[5] The RAF and the Royal Navy pushed ahead in reasonable fashion, but the army lagged, hardly ready for war. Chamberlain had only agreed to prepare the regular army to fight on the Continent in February 1939. Almost immediately, he decided to create a large conscript army for which the government had made no preparations. Little serious thinking or planning went toward supporting a continental commitment, especially since the army was desperately attempting to handle the flood of draftees.

As for helping the Poles, the British and French could do little. The French commander in chief, General Maurice Gamelin, promised his army would begin offensive operations against Germany's *Westwall*, a line of fortifications stretching from the border with the Netherlands to the Swiss frontier, within weeks after the war's outbreak. He lied. The Poles, for their part, overestimated their own capabilities, but in late August they gave the Western Allies a priceless gift: the cryptological work they had done in breaking into the Enigma cyphering system with which the German military transmitted its messages.

Confronting the British guarantee to Poland, the Führer announced he would cook the British a stew on which they would choke.[6] On 3 April 1939, he ordered the Oberkommando der Wehrmacht (OKW, the armed forces high command) to draw up plans for invading Poland.[7] Having resisted Hitler's proposed invasion of Czechoslovakia in the summer of 1938, the generals set about enthusiastically planning Poland's demise. The Wehrmacht's military situation had improved considerably over the past year. The enormous gains from seizing the remainder of Czechoslovakia had left it with a considerable haul of military equipment, raw materials, armaments production, and foreign exchange.[8] Three of the ten panzer divisions invading France in May 1940 were equipped with Czech armored fighting vehicles, while four German reserve divisions as well as the combat divisions of the Waffen SS were armed with Czech weapons.[9]

The Polish Campaign and the Phony War

The Polish Army facing the Germans was not only badly equipped but also not fully mobilized, a result of pressure from the Western Powers, which still hoped to placate Hitler. In addition, the Poles made the operational mistake of trying to defend their whole country instead of retreating behind the Vistula River, the only geographic hindrance to a German advance. The Germans planned two major blows: Army Group South, under Generaloberst Gerd von Rundstedt, would drive northwest from Silesia toward Warsaw, while Army Group North, under Generaloberst Fedor von Bock, would cross the Polish corridor to East Prussia and then swing southeast. No panzer army yet existed. Overall, the Wehrmacht deployed fifty-four divisions against Poland. Six divisions were panzer, four were light mechanized, and four were motorized infantry.[10] The rest were foot infantry, little different from the divisions of 1918. The key to the German victory was a common doctrine emphasizing combined arms, ruthless and aggressive exploitation, and mission-type orders that expected commanders to display initiative, drive, and speed.

The Germans won the campaign in its first days.[11] Army Group South, led by the Tenth Army and possessing the bulk of the mechanized forces (two panzer, three light, and two motorized infantry divisions), advanced fifteen miles on the first day and quickly achieved operational freedom. Five days later, the lead units of the Tenth Army were halfway to Warsaw. In the south, the Fourteenth Army occupied Cracow, while Polish forces north of the Carpathians collapsed. In the air, Polish fighter pilots put up stout resistance; they were very good. But outnumbered and equipped with inferior aircraft, they had no chance. Within days the Luftwaffe had achieved air superiority. By the end of the first week, the Polish government had fled Warsaw. On 17 September, Soviet troops crossed into eastern Poland. Behind the Wehrmacht came the SS.[12]

To understand what followed, one must examine the state of both the German economy and its army in 1939. How those interacted, combined with the failure of Anglo-French strategy, explains how and why the disaster of May 1940 occurred. In August 1939, Hitler assured his generals that the Reich had no economic worries: a British blockade would "be ineffective due to our autarky and because we have economic resources in the East. . . . The east will deliver us grain, cattle, coal, lead, and zinc."[13] In fact, the Soviet Union would not make major deliveries of raw materials to the Third Reich until spring 1940. Hitler was aware of the Reich's economic problems, while armament difficulties had played a major role in his decision for war, given that Germany's military advantages were wasting.[14]

Whatever Hitler's thoughts about war in August 1939, the British and French blockade gave the Germans considerable problems. The most serious was the restriction of fuel supplies. Even though the Germans would execute minimal military operations during the "Phony War," overall petroleum stocks sank by one-third, from 2.4 million tons in September 1939 to 1.6 million by early May 1940. Given that military operations now depended on petroleum far more than in World War I, this drop created a dangerous situation. Gasoline supplies fell from 300,000 tons to 110,000, while diesel fuel fell from 220,000 tons to 73,000, and bunker fuel from 350,000 tons to 255,000.[15]

The story was the same for deliveries of iron ore. In 1938, Germany had imported 22 million tons of iron ore, but with the outbreak of war 9.5 million tons were no longer available.[16] Imports of iron ore from northern Sweden were particularly crucial because of the ore's high iron content. Of the 9 million tons the Germans imported from the Swedes, over half came through the Norwegian port of Narvik. The OKW warned that a major shortfall in the import of Swedish ore could have a serious impact on the German war economy.[17] Other major raw materials were also in short supply, including rubber, chromium, and copper.[18]

The threatening economic situation explains why Hitler demanded an offensive against the West immediately after the collapse of Polish resistance. On 9 October 1939, he issued "Directive No. 6 for the Conduct of the War," in which he made clear his intentions. His strategy, to drive Allied forces out of Holland, Belgium, and northern France, was meant to serve a larger political aim: "The purpose of this offensive will be to defeat as much as possible of the French Army and of the forces of the allies fighting on their side, and at the same time to win as much territory as possible in Holland, Belgium, and Northern France, to serve as a base for the successful prosecution of the air and sea war against England."[19] It appears that Hitler hoped major air and naval operations would drive Britain to agree to peace and out of the war.[20] Given British appeasement over the past several years, this hope was not entirely misplaced.

Franz Halder, chief of the general staff, proceeded to draw up military plans according to the directive. From a tactical point of view, they were not especially imaginative: a direct offensive minimizing the Wehrmacht's mechanized forces. The Germans would have used the plan to attack in fall 1939 if chance had not intervened. During the period from November through January 1940, the Wehrmacht rolled up on the Dutch and Belgian frontiers on several occasions, and each time winter weather forced a stand down.

Meanwhile, a major quarrel broke out between Hitler and the generals. The after-action reports from Poland had revealed deficiencies in the army's tactical performance, leading the army's commander in chief, Walther von Brauchitsch, to complain to the Führer about the state of his forces.[21] He received a furious rebuke. Hitler's demands for an immediate offensive eventually calmed down, given the weather and the Allies' failure to launch any military operations other than the blockade to pressure the Reich's economic weaknesses. The six-month delay over the fall and winter provided the Wehrmacht time to retrain in the light of its campaign in Poland.

Anglo-French strategy rested on using the blockade to starve Germany of raw materials and food. They did not do more because behind the Allied tough talk lay a fear Hitler might launch the Luftwaffe against Paris or London. The Allies thus missed several opportunities to launch significant military operations to force the Germans to begin their offensive in fall 1939, when the Wehrmacht was insufficiently prepared. The most interesting move would have been an effort to drag the Italians into the war. In June 1939, Chamberlain argued that it would be to the Allies' advantage to make an attack in the Mediterranean and force the Germans to expend scarce resources to aid their ally.[22] It was one of the few times his strategic intuition was correct. Nevertheless, his advisors demurred. The Joint Planning Committee asserted, "Italy's intervention against us would add immeasurably to our military anxieties and greatly increase the effectiveness of German attacks on our seaborne trade."[23]

The French added their opposition to a move against Italy.[24] Ironically, any form of diplomatic or economic pressure would have driven Mussolini off the fence and into the war in September 1939. Such a decision would have proven even more disastrous for Italy than the defeats the British and Greeks administered in 1940.[25] Serious reverses to Mussolini's forces would have then forced German intervention, most probably in the form of a premature offensive in the Low Countries and France.

The Allies could also have pressured the Germans in two other areas. The most obvious was on the Western Front, where German defenses, while stronger in 1939 than a year earlier, still had weaknesses. The Wehrmacht deployed thirty-five divisions in the west on 1 September, of which only eleven were regular divisions; the remainder consisted of weak reserve divisions.[26] While the French could not have mounted a major drive against the Rhineland, they could have attacked the Saar, which held significant coal and steel concerns. The Germans were astonished when the French did nothing. Their patrols failed to reach even the *Westwall*'s outposts.

The other possibility was to mine Norwegian territorial waters to block the shipment of Swedish iron ore from Narvik, crucial to the functioning of the German war economy. Churchill, returning to the cabinet as First Lord of the Admiralty that September, suggested that the Allies shut down the ore trade through Norwegian waters.[27] In early October, the minister of economic war seconded Churchill's argument.[28] But Lord Halifax, the foreign secretary, raised serious objections, and Chamberlain was unwilling to decide. The question of whether to mine the Norwegian territorial waters dissipated into fruitless discussions about aiding the Finns or seizing Narvik. The British finally decided to mine Norwegian waters in April 1940, just in time to give Germany an excuse for their decision to invade Norway, which was already underway.[29]

After the Polish campaign, Hitler was in a race against time. Could he launch an offensive quickly enough to defeat the Western Powers before the blockade crippled Germany's war economy? The British and French failure to undertake any military actions allowed the Germans to husband their resources, retrain their troops, and prepare for one throw of the dice in spring 1940. That April, an Allied strategic summary noted that "the Reich appears to have suffered relatively little wear and tear during the first six months of the war, and that mainly the result of the Allied blockade. Meanwhile it has profited from the interval to perfect the degree of equipment of its land and air forces . . . complete the training of its troops and add further divisions to those already in the field."[30]

Scandinavia

The events of spring 1940 constitute one of history's great, avoidable tragedies. A deadly combination of political and military incompetence, chance, and brilliant tactical improvisations by the German Army brought the Allied strategic position crashing down and allowed the Germans for a time to escape their economic weaknesses. In May 1940, the Wehrmacht possessed sufficient fuel supplies for only five months of mobile operations before its tanks and trucks would have run out of fuel.[31] The offensive in the west was a desperate gamble on which the Germans bet their entire strategic position.

The collapse of international order continued in Scandinavia. In November 1939, having grabbed eastern Poland and placed the Baltic states under his control, Stalin decided to gather the remainder of the booty promised him by the Nazi-Soviet pact. He demanded the Finns surrender much of the Karelian Isthmus and allow the Red Army to occupy other strategic points. The Finns attempted to negotiate but refused to surrender their independence. In response, on 30 November 1939 Stalin launched an ill-prepared offensive. The result was a surprise to everyone. The Red Army, fighting in ferocious winter weather, suffered a series of humiliating defeats. Still, the Finns were waging a hopeless battle. By March 1940, the Soviets had gathered sufficient forces to overwhelm Finnish defenses, but they abandoned the demands that compromised Finnish independence.

In early April 1940, Chamberlain announced that "Hitler had missed the bus."[32] The German reply came almost immediately with an amphibious invasion of Norway. Although there had been plenty of advance warning, the German invasion caught the Allies and Norwegians by surprise. The first indication of what was afoot came on 8 April, when the Polish submarine *Orzel* torpedoed and sank the freighter *Rio de Janeiro* with German soldiers, horses, and supplies on board.[33] The rescued soldiers claimed they were on the way to Bergen to save Norway from the British. Despite this clear warning, the Norwegians did nothing while Churchill made the first of his many mistakes.[34] He ordered troops about to sail for Norway to disembark and ordered the navy to move out into the North Atlantic to counter a supposed move by the Kriegsmarine to attack British convoys in the North Atlantic. On 9 April, the Germans seized the major Norwegian ports virtually unopposed.

The Germans were rebuffed in two places. In the early morning hours of 9 April, the new heavy cruiser *Blücher*, with the pocket battleship *Lützow* following, moved up the Oslo fjord. The force ran into a hail of gunfire and torpedoes from the ancient fort guarding the approaches to the capital. With decks crowded with vehicles, gasoline Jerry cans, and bombs, the *Blücher* turned into a blazing wreck.[35] As the *Blücher* capsized in flames, the remainder of the naval force pulled back, and the Germans failed to seize Oslo until paratroopers arrived at 9:00 a.m. By then, having refused to surrender, the government and king had escaped. But the Norwegian cabinet ordered a mobilization with notices sent by mail.[36]

The only other port where the Germans ran into difficulty was at Narvik. Their attack force of ten destroyers, carrying two thousand mountain troops, had little difficulty in crushing Norwegian opposition, but there was only one tanker, the *Jan Wellem*, to refuel the destroyers. With inadequate equipment, the *Jan Wellem* could only fuel two destroyers at a time. Early the next morning, five British destroyers under Commodore Bernard Warburton-Lee entered the Narvik fjord. They caught the Germans by surprise; by the time the battle was over, two British destroyers had been sunk, but the others left in their wake two German destroyers sunk, four more damaged, and five cargo ships sunk. Three days later the Royal Navy returned with the battleship *Warspite* and finished off the German destroyers.[37]

With Churchill having sent the Royal Navy into the North Atlantic, the Germans consolidated their hold on the major Norwegian ports and airfields. The British, with some help from the French, then began inept efforts to reverse the German success. Churchill provided a considerable amount of bad direction, but the unprepared British Army deserves most of the credit for the Allied failure.[38] In early June, the collapse in France forced the British and French to withdraw. The final act came with the sinking of the British carrier *Glorious* off the North Cape by the *Scharnhorst* and *Gneisenau*. In sending the battle cruisers, Admiral Erich Raeder had argued that a major successful operation by them would justify the navy's continued existence after the war.[39] He had deployed them even though Hitler had indicated an invasion of Britain might be necessary. Despite the battlecruisers' success, the *Scharnorst* and *Gneisenau* returned from the North Cape damaged by torpedoes. Both ships remained in dock and under repair throughout 1940, no longer available to support an invasion of the British Isles. Despite their losses in the Norwegian campaign, the Allies gained two major advantages. By June 1940, the Norwegian operation had reduced the Kriegsmarine to one heavy cruiser, two light cruisers, and four operational destroyers. More importantly, the disaster in Norway finally brought Chamberlain down. On 10 May 1940, Winston Churchill became prime minister—ironically, the day the Wehrmacht came west.

The Low Countries and France

In January 1940, because of internal dissent over the initial plans for *Fall Gelb* (Case Yellow, codename for the invasion of the west), which in any case had fallen into the hands of the Allies, the OKH restructured the invasion.[40] The main effort would now move through the Ardennes, with panzer and motorized infantry divisions breaking into the open after crossing the Meuse between Sedan and Dinant. Meanwhile, Army Group A in the north would fix Allied attention on what appeared to be the main German thrust. There was considerable argument among the

German generals as to whether, after transiting the Ardennes, the panzer divisions should wait for the infantry to cross the Meuse or should cross on their own. In the end, Halder decided to allow the panzer divisions to cross, perhaps reasoning that even if they failed to create a breakthrough, they might at least achieve successful bridgeheads on the left bank of the Meuse.[41]

The balance of forces showed little disparity between the two sides, either in numbers or in quality of weapons, on 10 May. In some respects, the Germans were at a surprising disadvantage, an indication that their economy, with its supply problems, could not rearm as fast as their opponents, who had begun later. The German tank force consisted of 1,478 Mark I and Mark II tanks, models already obsolete; 334 Czech tanks, also obsolete; and only 627 modern Mark IIIs and Mark IVs.[42] The French possessed 3,254 tanks, many with superior armor and guns.[43] Interestingly, cooperation between army and Luftwaffe hardly lived up to the narrative of the tank-Stuka team. The 6th Panzer Division's war diary acidly commented that the Luftwaffe was "rather ineffective when it came to hitting the enemy facing the division. But it did a real good job in hitting our own units."[44]

More important than the numbers and quality of each side's tanks was the tactical framework within which they fought, as well as the generalship at the top. The Germans had inculcated their front-line units within a tactical framework of the combined-arms revolution. Their opponents had not. In terms of the command elements, outstanding German leadership would meet appallingly bad French generalship. Through March 1940, the French Seventh Army, with some of France's best-equipped and most mobile divisions (one light mechanized division, two motorized divisions, and four first-wave infantry divisions), deployed near Reims, excellently positioned to counterattack any breakthrough on the Meuse.[45] But that month, General Maurice Gamelin, commander of the French Army, moved the Seventh Army to the far west of the Allied line to link up with the Dutch at Breda. This was a political move that made little military sense. It left the French with no operational reserves to counter a German breakthrough.

The idea that the French did not believe the Germans could cross the Ardennes is wrong. In 1938, they had carried out a map exercise which showed, accurately, that German mechanized forces could cross the Ardennes in approximately sixty hours.[46] To cover the area, the French sent the 5th Light Cavalry Division to reconnoiter. That division's performance was lackluster; its units failed not only to put up resistance but also to report the movement of the panzer divisions. The resistance of a single company of the Belgian Chasseures Ardennais in front of the 1st Panzer Divisions suggests what the French might have achieved. The Chasseures were a light regiment; each company possessed only four machine guns and eight submachine guns. Just two companies defended the village of Bodange against the whole 1st Panzer Division, yet the Belgians held the Germans up for twelve and a half hours before finally receiving orders to pull out.

Along the Meuse, three panzer corps launched the main blow, crossing the Meuse between Dinant and Sedan. The crossing by the panzer divisions occurred almost entirely with infantry and artillery using combined arms. In the north, Major General Hermann Hoth's XV Panzer Corps with the 5th and 7th Panzer Divisions made their crossing immediately southeast of Dinant. In the center, Major General Hans Reinhardt commanded the XXXXI Panzer Corps with the 6th and 8th Panzer Divisions; their objective was to cross at Monthermé. Lieutenant General Heinz Guderian commanded the XIX Panzer Corps with the 1st, 2nd, and 10th Panzer Divisions, which were to cross at Sedan.[47] By the evening of 12 May, the panzer corps had closed on the Meuse and were preparing assault crossings.

The actual crossings underlined how close the breakthrough on the Meuse was. In the north near Dinant, the 5th Panzer Division created a small bridgehead. The real disaster for the French came with the crossing by its neighbor, the 7th Panzer Division under Erwin Rommel. In the prewar period, as an infantryman, Rommel had not supported the panzer concept, but his experience leading Hitler's escort battalion during the Polish campaign made it clear to him that panzer divisions could exploit German combined-arms doctrine.[48] In March 1940, he took command of a light division that was in the process of converting into the 7th Panzer Division. Ironically, many of its tanks were Czech.

Arriving on the banks of the river with the division's crossing in trouble, Rommel kept his infantry moving across the river; once on the other side he helped drive off a French counterattack. That evening, as his engineers desperately attempted to build a bridge so tanks could cross, Rommel jumped in the river to aid the effort.[49] Once his armor was across, the 7th Panzer Division went on a rampage, driving straight through French units. Over the night of 16–17 May, the 7th Panzer Division ran over the bivouacked French 5th Motorized Infantry Division and smashed it to pieces.[50] Meanwhile, Reinhardt's 6th Panzer Division ran into considerable trouble at Monthermé, defended by the French 102nd Fortress Infantry Division. The French might have held out longer, but the Ninth Army Commander, General André-Georges Corap, alarmed by the problems at Sedan and Dinant, ordered those holding Monthermé to retreat. Once in the open, the 102nd as a fortress division with no mobility had no chance.

Guderian's attack ran into serious trouble. All three of his divisions tried to cross with their rifle regiments. West of Sedan, the 2nd Panzer Division's assault barely got into the river. Only one assault boat out of eight made it across. On Guderian's left, the 10th Panzer Division lost forty-eight of fifty assault boats with heavy casualties. In the center, however, the crossing succeeded. The 1st Rifle Regiment hit an inexplicably weak point in French defenses. German infantry, using combined-arms exploitation tactics, quickly broke open the entire position, opening the door for the other two panzer divisions to cross. By early evening of 13 May, soldiers of the 1st Rifle Regiment were on the hills overlooking Sedan.[51]

The battles surrounding the crossing of the Meuse were precisely the ones the French expected to fight. The Germans found themselves fighting a traditional battle of infantry, artillery, and combat engineers under the framework of a common, thoroughly understood combined-arms doctrine. In the early morning hours of 14 May, the French attempted to put together a counterattack from the south to drive the Germans off the heights, but the effort was so laggardly the Germans continued their advance south without pause.

The French had one more chance. On 14 May, the French XXI Corps, consisting of the 3rd Armored and 3rd Motorized Divisions under General J. A. L. R. Flavigny, was available to stem Guderian's advance.[52] Ironically, Flavigny had been one of the French Army's few advocates of armored warfare. But his subordinate division commanders talked him out of launching a counterattack. Instead, he spread his corps out over a defensive line, a tactical decision that epitomized the doctrine of an army that had entirely abandoned offensive operations. Without the pressure of a French counterattack, Guderian turned his three panzer divisions west to join up with Reinhardt and Hoth and advance to the Channel while follow-on infantry covered their rear.

The Battle of France was effectively over. The French collapse continued, while the British scrambled desperately to escape, as the German panzer drive reached Abbeville on 18 May. The BEF would avoid destruction at Dunkirk, a miracle greatly helped by Hitler's stop order, the confusion of two German army groups and at least three or four armies crowding in on Dunkirk, and the skill of the Royal Navy in executing the evacuation.[53] Nevertheless, the Germans had overthrown the European balance of power.

Today, when we examine the German triumph in 1940, we tend to emphasize the Wehrmacht's tactical and operational skill. Yet the ferocious drive the Germans exhibited throughout the campaign underlined that their success also had an ideological component. General Erich Marcks, a senior general staff officer and soon to be one of the foremost planners of Barbarossa, noted after the campaign that "the change in men weighs more heavily than that in technology. The French we met in battle were no longer those of 14/18. The relationship was like that between the revolutionary armies of 1796 and the [First] Coalition—only this time *we* are the revolutionaries and Sans-Culottes."[54]

The Battle of Britain and the Beginning of the Technological War

Drunk with the unexpected success of having crushed the French Army, the Germans now faced the conundrum of what to do with the British. The Führer, glowing in what he saw as *his* triumph, embarked with his cronies on a trip through the World War I battlefields where he had fought, followed by a brief visit to Paris. He left no one in charge of German strategy, no doubt thinking, like most of the Reich's senior leaders, that the British would sue for peace. They were wrong. The war had only begun.

The Battle of Britain represents the beginning of the great battle of attrition between the air and naval forces of the United Kingdom, eventually joined by the United States, and those of the Third Reich. It would be a war of production, which had to be matched up with trained crews for aircraft and ships. But it also increasingly became a technological and intelligence war, in which the opposing sides depended on scientists, technologists, and industrial designers to translate scientific ideas into reality. The intelligence portion depended on highly educated and imaginative individuals, who increasingly worked their way into the minds of the enemy, helped by the mathematics required to break into the enemy's system of cyphers. The combination of scientists with signals and other intelligence gave the Allies an increasingly detailed under-standing of the German military. On the other hand, Allied develop-ments remained almost opaque to the Germans.[55]

This all began with the contest between the RAF and the Luftwaffe in summer 1940. To most of Britain's leaders, particularly in the Conser-vative Party, Britain's situation after the fall of France was hopeless. But Churchill, the new prime minister, understood two larger strategic reali-ties. Unlike the appeasers, he understood that Hitler and the Third Reich represented not only a strategic danger but a moral one as well. As one of the great orators of the twentieth century, he was able to persuade the British people of that danger. The second strategic insight was that the war was not over: in the long term, the United States and the Soviet Union could not allow Nazi Germany to rule all of Europe.

Churchill's first eight weeks in office represent one of history's great turning points. He waged a desperate struggle to keep the French in the war; fended off the many Conservative appeasers; and established firmer relations with the Americans, particularly the president, Franklin Roo-sevelt. At the same time, he prepared Britain to meet a German assault.[56] In early July, he ordered the Royal Navy to attack the French fleet at Mers el Kebir to keep it out of Axis hands. That action sank 2 battleships and killed 1,300 French sailors. It poisoned Anglo-French relations for the rest of the war but achieved the larger strategic purpose of removing the French fleet from the naval balance of power. Most importantly, it signaled to Roosevelt that Britain was in the war to the end.

One of the apparently puzzling aspects of the Battle of Britain was that while the French were out of the picture by mid-June, the Luft-waffe's air offensive against the British Isles did not begin until August. There were reasons for this. In the Battle of France, Anglo-French air resistance had punished the Luftwaffe severely. In a little more than three weeks of heavy aerial combat, the Luftwaffe had lost 30 percent of its Stukas, twin-engine fighters (Bf 110s) and bombers, and 19 percent of its single-engine fighters. In addition, aerial combat damaged between 30 and 40 percent of combat aircraft. The Germans also had to write off 40 percent of their transport aircraft.[57] Thus, right from the start of the Bat-tle of Britain, the Luftwaffe was under considerable strain.

The British had also suffered heavily, but outside of the Hurricanes and Battle bombers sent to support the French, the RAF's losses were less severe. Moreover, the British mounted a massive effort to increase fighter production. In the first half of 1940, German production of Bf

109s averaged 156 per month, while Britain's production of Spitfires and Hurricanes was 247. In the second half of 1940, those numbers diverged radically, with British production reaching 491 per month while the Luftwaffe's rate fell to 146.[58] From July through December, the British aircraft industry produced nearly three thousand single-engine fighters, the Germans under a thousand.

In early July, the German Army began half-hearted preparations for an amphibious landing on the British Isles. It was not in the cards. The invasion of Norway had left virtually no combat-ready ships available to the Kriegsmarine, while the British had stationed thirty-plus destroyers on the southern and northern entrances to the Channel with the Home Fleet's cruisers and destroyers readily available. The head of the OKW, Field Marshal Wilhelm Keitel, summed up the German understanding of amphibious operations by saying that crossing the English Channel would be just like "making a river crossing."[59]

The Germans were no more realistic about British air defenses. When the Luftwaffe's intelligence branch began planning an aerial offensive against Britain, they offered a strikingly inept initial assessment of RAF capabilities. One estimate calculated that it would take four days for the Luftwaffe to achieve air superiority over southern Britain and another four weeks to mop up the RAF. An estimate by General "Beppo" Schmid, the head of Luftwaffe intelligence, was even further off the mark. He posited that the Hurricanes and Spitfires were inferior to even the Bf 110; made no mention of Britain's radar-controlled, systemic approach to air defense systems; and ended with the optimistic note that "the *Luftwaffe*, unlike the RAF, will be in a position in every respect to achieve a decisive effect this year."[60] Crucially, German intelligence officers failed to understand that the British use of radar was entirely different from their own. Instead of using radar to control individual fighters, the British used it in a systemic fashion to control entire squadrons of Spitfires and Hurricanes.

In July and early August, the Luftwaffe launched a series of raids meant to draw the RAF into battle and close the Channel to British convoys. The Germans succeeded in the latter aim but failed in the former. Instead, the raids allowed Fighter Command to work the bugs out of its system. Interpreters of the radar signals learned to discern more accurately the strength and direction of incoming raids. The main German offensive was to begin on "Eagle Day," 13 August, but the raid was botched when many bomber units failed to receive a recall order and flew on to targets in Britain while the fighters returned home. Two days later, Hermann Göring ordered the Luftwaffe to cease bombing radar sites, even though the first attacks had achieved some success. There were two reasons: the attacks were costly, and the Germans failed to recognize that the RAF's radar was part of a *system*. They believed the British were using radar, as the Luftwaffe did, to direct individual aircraft rather than the battle as a whole, and therefore was of relatively minor significance, given the difficulty in destroying the radar towers.

Meanwhile, German bombers, flying from Norway to bomb RAF airfields in northern England, suffered devastating losses, and after Eagle Day they never again attempted another daylight raid from their bases in Norway. With the radar sites off the target list, German raids concentrated on Fighter Command's bases and sector stations in southern England. It quickly became apparent that the twin-engine Bf 110, the long-range escort fighter the Luftwaffe was using to protect its bombers, could not even protect itself. The Bf 109 was the Spitfire's equal, but its short range meant that it could remain over London for barely ten minutes. Any German bomber formations trying to attack beyond London in daylight, or that lacked escort fighters, offered easy targets for British fighters.

Both sides took heavy losses in aerial battles throughout August. In that month the Luftwaffe lost 774 aircraft from all causes, or 18.5 percent of its combat force.[61] On 4 September, furious that British bombers had scattered a few bombs around Berlin, Hitler announced to a packed crowd that "when they declare they will attack our cities in great measure, we will eradicate their cities. . . . The hour will come when one of us will break, and it will not be Nationalist Socialist Germany."[62]

Three days later, the Luftwaffe switched from attacks on Fighter Command's infrastructure to a massed attack on London's docks in the East End. Hugh Dowding and his subordinates were caught by surprise because they expected a continuation of attacks on RAF bases. After the daylight raids ended in mid-September, the Germans continued the bombing at night. London firemen fought nine fires rated at over one hundred pumps, with one on the Surrey Docks requiring three hundred pumps. For the next week, the Germans continued their attacks on London. On the 15th, the Luftwaffe returned with massed bombers. This time the British were ready, and the German bombers cracked, their crews scattering bombs over Kent. Fighter Command's Spitfires and Hurricanes claimed 185 aircraft destroyed; in fact, the Germans lost only 60, while the RAF lost 30.[63] By that point, Fighter Command was under a heavy strain from aircraft and pilot losses, but the Luftwaffe was suffering more. The number of fully operational crews in the Bf 109 squadrons had declined to 67 percent; in Bf 110 squadrons the number was 46 percent, and for the bomber squadrons it was 59 percent.[64]

As in World War I, the air war in World War II turned out to be a war of attrition much like that in the trenches, except that it took place in the skies and involved expensive equipment. Losses in aircraft and crews were already high and would only rise. On 10 May 1940, when the Wehrmacht began military operations against the west, the Luftwaffe had numbered 5,349 combat aircraft; over the next five months it lost 3,064, or 57 percent of its combat force.[65] In August, the Luftwaffe lost 22.4 percent of its Bf 109s; in September, 26.5 percent; bomber losses were 19.6 and 18.9 percent.[66]

When the night bomber offensive began in September, German bombers had already suffered serious losses from five months of daylight raids against targets in France, the Low Countries, and Britain. In 1940, the Luftwaffe possessed the only true strategic bombing capability, with both a pathfinder force and navigational aids for blind bombing, code-named *Knickebein* (Crooked Leg). But through imaginative scientific and detective work by a young scientist, R. V. Jones, and despite opposition from the RAF bureaucracy, the British discovered the existence of the navigational beams and were able to jam them.[67]

Even without the beams, London was such a large and easily identifiable target that Luftwaffe bombers could hardly miss it. Moreover, on clear, moonlit nights, German bomber pilots and navigators had no difficulty picking out targets, as was to happen at Coventry in November. The Germans focused their nighttime bombing offensive, the Blitz, on three areas, each of which reflected different conceptions. The heavy bombing of London represented a belief that such raids could break British morale, based on the ideas of Italian air power theorist Giulio Douhet. The second target set was the manufacturing cities in the Midlands: Manchester, Coventry, Sheffield, and Nottingham. In these raids the Luftwaffe inflicted heavy damage, but British countermeasures distorted the blind-bombing beams and mitigated bomber accuracy. The third target set involved raids on British ports, particularly Liverpool and Glasgow, the major ports for trans-Atlantic shipping, but also Bristol, Portsmouth, Southampton, Belfast, and Plymouth.[68] Given that a major focus in German strategy aimed at cutting off British imports, an emphasis on the third target set would have made the most strategic sense.

British efforts to distort the beams increasingly affected German pilots and navigators. The Germans eventually introduced a new variant, *X-Gerät*, but the British soon solved that too. A German raid on 8 May 1941 shows how effective British countermeasures had become: Luftwaffe bombers, supposed to attack Derby, instead bombed Nottingham, while other crews assigned to bomb Nottingham dropped their loads onto open countryside.[69] In May 1941, the Luftwaffe transferred most of its bomber squadrons to the east in preparation for Barbarossa. But the Blitz would have ended soon anyway, because in April the British had begun fielding night fighters equipped with airborne radar in substantial numbers. In the first three months of 1941, the Germans had lost only ninety bombers to British air defenses. In April alone they lost seventy-five.

In all respects, the Germans had lost not only the production side of the Blitz but the technological and scientific sides. The gap would grow. The Luftwaffe would invade the Soviet Union at the end of June 1941 with two hundred *fewer* bombers in its inventory than it had possessed on 10 May 1940, an indication of how severely attrition had affected a force the production base of which had remained static.[70] The Germans were so focused on operational and tactical issues that they failed to see the long-term threat. In effect, they were gambling they could beat their opponents before the Wehrmacht ran out of people, aircraft, U-boats, and other armaments.

At the same time that the British appeared under the existential threat of the Luftwaffe's strategic bombing, they also confronted a more dangerous threat from Admiral Karl Dönitz's U-boat offensive against their sea lines of communications (SLOCs). The German success against Norway and France had significantly enhanced the U-boats' geographic position. U-boat bases in Brittany were closer to the North Atlantic SLOCs than the Royal Navy's main bases. However, as with their surface fleet, the Germans had already lost much of their submarine fleet, so that Karl Dönitz could barely keep seventeen U-boats on station in the summer and fall of 1940. Nevertheless, the Germans enjoyed considerable success. The fact that the Royal Navy had deployed much of its destroyer force to the English Channel coast to meet the threat of an invasion weakened British efforts in the Atlantic. With little protection, inbound and outbound convoys were an easy target. However, as in World War I, ships sailing without escort suffered the most heavily. Between July and November 1940, the British lost 144 unescorted merchant vessels, while the number lost in convoys was 73.[71]

The U-boat threat pushed the British into a search for tactical and technological responses. Churchill, not surprisingly, fully supported both. Technologically, the British set in motion innovations that included improving ASDIC (sonar); developing ship-borne radar and providing it ever more widely to the escort force; equipping Coastal Command's aircraft with radar and Leigh lights (high-powered searchlights); increasing the killing power of depth charges; developing a new anti-submarine weapon, the "hedgehog"; and providing short-range radios so that escorts could communicate without their transmissions being picked up by German direction-finding stations. Here scientists would play a key role not only in specific technological areas but in inventing the wholly new discipline of operational research.

The most important advantage the British gained was their ability to read substantial portions of German U-boat Enigma transmissions. The first break into German U-boat codes came in April 1941. When they learned that German weather ships stationed off Iceland were using the same Enigma codes as the U-boats, the British Admiralty immediately mounted a cutting-out operation, with a vice admiral commanding three cruisers and four destroyers. The expedition trapped the German weather ship *München* along with its Enigma settings. Shortly thereafter, British escorts captured U-110, captained by Fritz-Julius Lemp, with additional settings. In late June, the Royal Navy mounted another cutting-out operation to capture a second weather ship off Iceland, which the Germans had foolishly sent to replace the first and which still used the U-boat Enigma codes. The Admiralty report called the captured material of "inestimable value."[72]

The British code breakers' ability to read many of the messages between the U-boats and Dönitz's headquarters in France, which maintained top-down control of submarine movements, gave the Allies a key advantage. Over the last half of 1941, based on this intelligence, code-named Ultra, the British routed many convoys away from U-boat patrol lines. The authors of the German history of the war have estimated that on the basis of convoy movements, the number of U-boats at sea, and the numbers and capabilities of Allied escort forces, Ultra intelligence during these six months saved the British roughly 1.5 million tons of shipping.[73]

In many ways, March 1941 represented the first step toward winning the Battle of the Atlantic. During that month, the British captured Otto Kretschmer, one of the most formidable U-boat aces, with his crew, while Günther Prien's U-47 and Joachim Schepke's U-100 went to watery graves. Their losses showed that the waters around the British Isles had become too dangerous even for experienced U-boat skippers. The battle then moved into the central Atlantic, where intelligence was crucial and where the Type VII U-boats were at an increasing disadvantage, given their shorter range, fewer torpedoes, less time on station, and a distinct disadvantage in crew comfort compared to Type IXs.[74] Yet Dönitz, like Hitler, was enthralled with numbers and persisted in continuing Type VII production to war's end, largely because the shipyards could produce more of them than Type IXs.

At the strategic and operational levels, German military leaders never grasped the challenges confronting them. In some areas, like intelligence, the failures should have suggested the need for a fundamental reevaluation. That this never happened is a reflection not only of the nature of the Führer but of the cultural arrogance of many Germans. Ironically, given their scientific and technological skills, their greatest failing lay in an inability to recognize the wider possibilities that new systems and technologies offered not only to them but to their opponents.

This showed clearly in the war in the Atlantic.[75] Perhaps the greatest weakness was that Dönitz was not interested in adding technology to his boats. It is instructive to compare the improvements in German U-boats after two years of war with those in U.S. fleet boats after a similar period in the Pacific. By late 1943, the American boats possessed radar to pick up ships and aircraft, short-range radios to communicate with other fleet boats, direction-finding gear to help locate convoys, and sophisticated sonar. German U-boats possessed few of those improvements; apparently Dönitz was afraid that adding them would take boats out of service and slow production and training of new boats. He also probably feared he might lose some of the tight control he exercised over the U-boats and the campaign.

The British displayed far more willingness to innovate. By late 1941, reforms and technological innovations had created the basis on which they and their Canadian and American allies would win the Battle of the Atlantic. Still, it would take a year and two months, beginning in January 1942, for British and American industry and navies to produce and train enough ships and crews in the new technologies to break the back of the U-boat force.

Distractions

In early July 1940, Halder and Brauchitsch began initial planning for an invasion of the Soviet Union. At the end of the month, they held an extended discussion with Hitler in which the Führer made clear he believed the only reason Britain was remaining in the war was that it hoped the Soviet Union and United States would join. Therefore, Hitler continued, the obvious solution was to eliminate the Soviet Union and then take care of the Anglo-Saxons.[76] Over the next ten months, various German leaders proposed alternatives to an invasion, while the Wehrmacht found itself involved in subsidiary operations. But Hitler had made up his mind and would not waver. At first, he suggested launching the invasion in late summer 1940, but Brauchitsch and Halder talked him out of that idea, given the realities of Russia's distances and weather. Still, Hitler's intentions were clear in the ways the Third Reich spent its resources. The initial months after the fall of France saw the demobilization of a number of divisions, with the soldiers returned to the armament industries. But by early fall the high command had reversed that decision; instead of a major buildup of the Luftwaffe and Kriegsmarine, the army would receive the bulk of human and material resources.

In addition to the problem posed by the British, troubles in the Balkans and Mediterranean drew German attention to theaters in which they had no desire to involve themselves. Immediately after the fall of France, Francisco Franco and his fascist regime in Spain suggested that for a price, his country would join the war against Britain in exchange for virtually all of French North Africa. The Germans at first displayed little interest, but in October 1940, after their defeat in the Battle of Britain, they changed their minds. Hitler even met with Franco, saying afterward that he would rather have his teeth pulled than endure another such discussion. By then, however, Franco was also having second thoughts. Germany's failure in the Battle of Britain showed that the British were not yet finished, while Churchill's negotiators had made clear that should Spain enter the war, it would face a blockade that would reduce its people to starvation.

Germany's problems with the Spanish were nothing compared with the complexities of Italy's entrance into the war. In a move Roosevelt described as stabbing his neighbor in the back, Mussolini had declared war on France and Britain on 10 June 1940. The declaration could not have come at a worse time: France was virtually prostrate. But the Italians were almost totally unprepared for war.[77] The Italian naval ministry had not even sent out orders in May for Italian merchant shipping to return to Italy, leaving millions of tons of shipping to fall into Allied hands. Mussolini and his generals decided that Italy would fight a "parallel war" in the Mediterranean that would have little connection with the Germans.

After innumerable arguments about Italy's strategy, Il Duce finally ordered the Italian commander in Libya, Marshal Rodolfo Graziani, to advance, an order the latter made every effort to delay executing. Meanwhile, troubles between Hungary and Romania almost erupted into war. Without reference to the Soviets, the Germans stepped in to settle matters. Hitler, without informing Mussolini, authorized a military mission to Romania to secure control of its oil. The large size of the German mission—the 13th Motorized Infantry Division (reinforced), the 16th Panzer Division, two fighter squadrons, one reconnaissance squadron, and two Flak regiments—suggests that the Reich had little concern for the sensibilities of its allies.[78]

The Italians were even more upset than the Soviets. Furious at what he regarded as German impudence, Mussolini ordered his military to invade Greece from Albania. The army began planning for the invasion immediately, but at the same time, the War Ministry decided to demobilize 400,000 of the 1.1 million troops in Italy. Moreover, the personnel system did so by age group, so that every division lost approximately 40 percent of its end strength, leaving no division combat ready. Worse, Italian forces in Albania barely matched Greek strength, while the tonnage capacity of Albanian ports was sufficient only to allow transshipment of food, ammunition, and supplies to support the fighting, not to bring substantial reinforcements.

The result was a disaster. Within days, Greek troops had driven the Italians back into Albania in disarray, while Mussolini's army commander in the theater, General Ubaldo Soddu, spent his evenings composing film scores.[79] The Italian defeat in Albania forced the Germans to intervene in the Balkans just as they were ramping up preparations to invade the Soviet Union. The Greek disaster was only the first piece of bad news for the Italians. In November, the British launched a nighttime air attack on the Italian fleet in the southern Italian port of Taranto. By the time the torpedo planes returned to their carrier, three Italian battleships were resting in the mud, one irreparably damaged. That same night, British cruisers sank four merchant vessels in the Straits of Otranto and temporarily cut the SLOCs between Italy and Albania.[80]

Meanwhile, the advance from Libya into Egypt's western desert had gone forward in September. The offensive was a shambles. One commander, who had neglected to take along either a map or his Arab

guides, got his brigade lost on the Italian side of the border and almost
ran out of water.[81] The advance eventually halted at Sidi el Barrani, far
from the intended target of Alexandria. On the night of 8–9 December, a
massive artillery bombardment caught the Italians by surprise. The British intended their offensive to remain limited, but the British 7th Armored Division and the 4th Indian Division, moving through gaps in
Italian defensive positions—none of which were mutually supporting—
destroyed the Italian forces. By January 1941, British forces had moved
into Cyrenaica and the entire Italian position in the western half of
Libya had collapsed.

The Germans now had to bail out their allies in North Africa *and*
the Balkans. The solution to the former problem was to send General
Erwin Rommel, who had performed spectacularly in France, to Libya
with a corps-sized force. He received orders to remain on the defensive,
but to Halder's horror, Rommel immediately attacked badly deployed
and inexperienced British units. Within weeks, Axis forces were back on
the Libyan-Egyptian frontier, although the British did hold onto the
port of Tobruk. Still, despite Rommel's successes, North Africa remained
a sideshow to the Germans.

Over the winter of 1940–1941, Germany deployed the forces and logistical support through Hungary and Romania for an offensive from
Bulgaria into Greece. On 25 March 1941, the Germans forced the Yugoslavs to join the Axis, but no sooner had their government signed than
pro-British officers overthrew it. Hitler was furious. He immediately ordered the OKW to expand the offensive against Greece to include Yugoslavia. Within a week, the Germans had deployed the forces necessary to
smash the Yugoslavs as well as the Greeks. In addition, the Führer ordered the "destruction of Belgrade through a great air attack." The code
name was *Gericht*—the modern German word for "punishment" but also
possessing the older meaning of "execution."[82] Two days of bombing lev-
eled the city and left seventeen thousand dead.

The ensuing offensive against Yugoslavia and Greece was a walkover.
While it did not force the Germans to postpone Barbarossa, it caused
considerable wear and tear on mechanized forces that participated in the
campaign and that would form most of Army Group South's mechanized
forces in the upcoming invasion of the Soviet Union. The campaign
closed with an airborne assault on Crete, which the Germans feared the
British would use to attack Romania's oilfields.[83] The British should have
held. However, despite intelligence on the plans for an airborne assault

on the Maleme airfield, acquired from a shot-down Bf 110, General Bernard Freyberg chose instead to defend the beaches of northern Crete. The Royal Navy sank all but one of the landing craft attempting to cross the Aegean. But the German airborne assault came close to defeat. The paratroopers barely captured the Maleme airfield, but once they were established there, the British had to withdraw. Casualties among the paratroopers were so heavy, 25 percent, that Hitler refused to authorize another major airborne operation.[84]

The conquest of Greece and Yugoslavia took little more than a month. As soon as it was done, the panzer and mechanized troops that had completed the conquest pulled out to participate in the invasion of the Soviet Union. The third-rate German and Italian troops left behind almost immediately confronted major uprisings in the countryside. By winter 1941–1942, partisan warfare had exploded throughout the mountains of Greece and Yugoslavia—a bitter, merciless war where atrocities were the order of the day.

Return to the Past

Despite British intransigence and the Italian military collapse in the Mediterranean, the Germans pressed ahead with plans to invade the Soviet Union.[85] Victory in the West had provided an enormous booty in goods and raw materials. The Germans had seized 81,000 tons of copper, enough to meet their needs for the next eight months, and enough nickel and tin to meet industry's requirements for a full year. Especially helpful were the 4,260 locomotives and 140,000 freight cars stolen from France and the Low Countries, which were a godsend since the Reichsbahn, the German national railway, had received little investment in the 1930s.[86] Yet these spoils were hardly enough to cover the demands of Barbarossa, once the war in the east was in full swing. By October 1941, the Reichsbahn was short by an average of 98,000 cars per day.[87]

The petroleum captured in the western campaign returned German stocks to where they had been at the outbreak of the war. But the British blockade meant that this booty was an irreplaceable asset.[88] Soviet deliveries of raw materials proved helpful before the invasion, but Soviet deliveries were the last thing on which Hitler wanted to rely. Moreover, even the captured petroleum stocks could not alleviate Germany's fuel shortages. With too few drivers to handle the increased numbers of trucks required by mechanized forces, the army training program provided licenses to drive heavy trucks to new drivers after less than ten miles of road experience.[89]

Moreover, there was a downside to the captured industrial resources. The railroad equipment the Germans had seized, for example, was still needed to support French, Belgian, and Dutch industry. Steel production in the occupied areas of France and Belgium collapsed because of a lack of coal.[90] And the workforce in the newly captured areas had to be fed. The agricultural areas occupied by the Germans required vast amounts of fertilizer, which could no longer be imported, while the production of ammunition was sucking up the available nitrates in the Reich and Western Europe. The workforce also presented intractable problems. The decision to invade the Soviet Union halted demobilization of soldiers, further straining an already tight manpower pool.[91] In July 1941, because of a shortage of workers for the coal mines, production of iron and steel dropped by 350,000 tons from the previous month.[92] Here Nazi ideology provided a stumbling block to the expansion of the war economy, since Hitler refused to allow full mobilization of women for the workforce.

The sudden reversals in emphasis, first to the Luftwaffe and Kriegsmarine in July 1940 and then back to the army in late summer, meant that Germany was taking the pressure off the British SLOCs at precisely the moment when the British were most vulnerable. It was all well to talk about the great U-boat program Germany would set in motion after the conquest of Russia, but between June 1940 and March 1941, German dockyards barely turned out seven submarines a month, many of which had to be diverted into building up the training force. Once Barbarossa started, the Luftwaffe could bring little pressure on Britain. The constant shifting of priorities and production targets, not only by Hitler but by the system, "called into question the equilibrium between requirements and resources." Adding to the difficulties was that Hitler's order for the army to receive priority in armaments production put the OKW and the Luftwaffe at cross purposes.[93]

As for the ground forces, historian Adam Tooze notes that "fundamentally, the Wehrmacht was a 'poor army.' "[94] Nothing underlined that statement more than the army's desperate efforts to cobble together sufficient divisions to undertake Barbarossa. To equip the divisions for the invasion, the army drew not only on its own stocks and production but a wide variety of weapons captured in 1939 and 1940 from Czechoslovakia, Poland, the Netherlands, Belgium, Norway, and France. German infantry divisions invaded Russia with Norwegian and French artillery and antitank guns, as well as civilian trucks from every area the Germans had captured.

For the Army Group Center's logisticians, this created a nightmarish situation, with some two thousand different vehicles requiring over a million different types of spare parts, which had to move over a transportation system that often passed through combat zones.[95] Of 152 divisions scheduled for Barbarossa, 75 were equipped with captured vehicles, while 71 depended wholly or largely on horse-drawn transport.[96] Overall, the army required between 650,000 and 750,000 horses to transport supplies and artillery for the infantry divisions.[97] In effect, the German Army was a World War I ground force with a small add-on of mechanized formations.

For the panzer and motorized infantry divisions, the situation was just as bleak. Three of the motorized infantry divisions and one of the panzer divisions were equipped with foreign vehicles. Like the Luftwaffe in 1940, the army went into Barbarossa with its armored and mechanized forces not significantly improved over the previous year. Although the Germans had doubled the number of panzer divisions, from ten in May 1940 to twenty in 1941, they had done so by reducing the number of tank regiments per division from two to one. Thus, the number of tanks available was only 3,648, up from the 2,580 that had invaded France. Like the infantry divisions, the tank force was a patchwork quilt: 1,832 were Mark Is, Mark IIs, and Czech tanks, all obsolete, with only 1,816 of the relatively modern Mark IIIs and Mark IVs. Astonishingly, the German factories had increased their production of Mark IIs.

Even more than the weaponry, the supporting logistical force was an ad hoc mix of German, captured, and civilian trucks, assigned to the mechanized divisions seemingly at random. The 18th Panzer Division possessed no fewer than 96 different types of personnel carriers and 111 different types of trucks.[98] Moreover, efforts to standardize production on single models foundered on the preference for short runs, which allowed engineers to tinker with each model but created further headaches for those who had to manage spare parts.[99] The implications of German weaknesses in supply and maintenance were frustratingly clear to the logisticians, who warned that their capabilities could support an advance of only 300 miles into Russia before logistical difficulties arose.[100]

While much of the army had enjoyed a rest from the fall of France to Barbarossa, the Luftwaffe had not. The long campaign against the British Isles, as well as commitments to the Mediterranean and Balkans, had had a steady, cumulative impact on force structure. Its numerical strength was no greater than at the start of the French campaign on 10 May 1940. In June 1941, the Luftwaffe possessed 200 fewer bombers, 84 more Bf 109s, 10 more Stukas, and 166 fewer Bf 110s than the previous year.[101] Overall, in 1941, the German aircraft industry produced only 950 more aircraft than in 1940.[102] The Germans' failure to increase the immediate production of weapons for the army significantly reflected not only Hitler's but the military's belief that Barbarossa would present no more difficulties than the French campaign.

Such attitudes explain why there was no serious angst over difficulties in equipping the combat forces to the extent that a war against the Soviet Union with its resources and spaces might have suggested. The army high command accepted that a substantial portion of its divisions would not possesses up-to-date weapons and that any effort to ensure production of an adequate replacement of weapons and supporting equipment was not necessary.[103] The warnings of the general staff's own geographic section, that much of Russia's heavy industries had shifted to the east of Moscow as far as the Urals, or of German industrialists, who were shown some of the more impressive Soviet industrial concerns in spring 1941, were simply ignored.[104]

From the beginning, Hitler made clear the war against the Soviet Union would be an ideological conflict. In March 1941, Halder noted the following about an address Hitler gave to the generals about the nature of the coming war: *"Clash of two ideologies:* crushing denunciation of Bolshevism. . . . Communism is an enormous danger for our future. . . . This is a war of extermination . . . extermination of Bolshevist Commissars and of the communist intelligentsia."[105] It was not just Hitler who defined Barbarossa as a racial war against Jews and subhuman Slavs: so too did most army leaders. The commander of Panzer Group 4, Colonel General Erich Hoepner, gave the following order to his troops on 12 May 1941 that they were fighting against Slavdom and especially against the Jewish-Bolshevik regime. They were to wage it, he said, with "unprecedented hardness with the aim being the total annihilation of the enemy [*völligen Vernichtung des Feindes*]."[106] That ideological framework reached deep into the mental fabric of German soldiers at the front and would be met with equal ruthlessness by the other side.[107] The result was a war of unmatched brutality.

By late July 1940, Halder had developed his own ideas for the campaign: a drive on Moscow to force a Soviet "concentration in the

Ukraine and on the Black Sea to accept battle on an inverted front."[108] On 5 August, General Erich Marcks, commissioned by Halder to draw up initial plans, presented his conception. Marcks argued that the main drive should take place north of the Pripyet Marshes, with subsidiary drives targeting the Baltic states and Ukraine. Both Halder and Marcks assumed the Wehrmacht would defeat the Soviets before winter. They believed the German Army could destroy the Red Army in the border areas and thus gain an unimpeded advance into Russia's depths. Marcks allowed seventeen weeks to accomplish the conquest of European Russia. Over fall and winter of 1940–1941, the views of Hitler and his army leaders diverged; Hitler placed his emphasis on capturing Ukraine and Leningrad, while the generals focused on Moscow. Halder finessed the fundamental disagreement by limiting planning to the first stage, in which the Wehrmacht would presumably destroy the Red Army.

The Germans, however, were not the only ones that spring making astonishingly flawed strategic assessments. Stalin, with equal ineptitude, believed until the opening hours of the German invasion that Hitler did not intend to attack him. Certainly, the purges of the Soviet military, which had begun in May 1937 and continued into 1940, do not suggest he feared a military confrontation with the Third Reich, at least in the immediate future. After the fall of France, Stalin's ideology suggested that the Germans had no reason to invade. Wasn't Hitler merely the puppet of the German industrialists? Why would they want to invade the Soviet Union when they controlled the industries of Western Europe? Despite the accurate intelligence Soviet spies had winkled out about German intentions and deployments, Stalin obdurately refused to believe the warnings.

Moreover, fearing the political reliability of his own people, especially in the newly acquired border areas, Stalin deployed much of the Red Army's regular force forward. He had no intention of trading space for time. While deployed forward, Soviet first-line forces were also undergoing a major shift to large, mechanized units just as many were re-equipping with new weapons. Yet whatever its weaknesses, the Red Army was also motivated by strong ideological and nationalist feelings. Once Stalin recognized the extent of the German threat to the Soviet Union, he would call on the deep well of Russian nationalism, which even communism had not destroyed.

Some 3 million German soldiers began the invasion; they found themselves divided into three army groups: Army Group North under

Ritter von Leeb with Panzer Group 4 under Hoepner; Army Group Center under Bock with Panzer Group 3 under Hoth and Panzer Group 2 under Guderian; and Army Group South under Field Marshal Gerd von Rundstedt with Panzer Group 1 under Ewald von Kleist. In the pre-dawn hour, the Germans struck. Minutes before the artillery bombardment began the last goods train from the Soviet Union trundled onto German territory. The surprise was complete. A German radio unit intercepted the following Soviet radio transmission: "Front line unit: 'We are being fired upon. What shall we do?' Army headquarters: 'You must be insane and why is your signal not in code.' "[109]

Stalin's foreign minister, V. Molotov, caught the sorry results of Stalin's strategic policy, when he replied to the German declaration of war with the question, "What have we done to deserve this?"[110] Soviet forces floundered under the fury of the German offensive. Luftwaffe bombers and fighters had a field day, catching much of the Soviet air force on the ground. Field Marshal Erhard Milch, the Luftwaffe's chief logistic officer, reported the destruction of 1,800 Soviet aircraft on the first day, 800 more on 23 June, 557 on the 24th, and 351 on the 25th.[111]

The ground war proved even more disastrous for the Soviets. Nevertheless, in the north, because Halder had refused to indicate his intentions beyond the opening movements to prevent Hitler's interference, Leeb and Hoepner faced difficulty in figuring out whether their mission was to cover the left flank of the advance on Moscow or drive north on Leningrad.[112] Still, there was considerable success, as Leeb's forces drove through the Baltic states. Erich von Manstein's LXVI Panzer Corps seized bridges over the Dvina, two hundred miles from their starting point, within four days. By late July, Army Group North was three-quarters of the way to Leningrad but at the end of its logistics tether.

The victories of Army Group Center were even more impressive. The Soviet commander in the region, General D. G. Pavlov, one of the sycophants Stalin had raised above their level of competence, botched the battle. His reward for loyalty to Stalin was the firing squad. Within three days, Panzer Groups 2 and 3 had closed a first encirclement around Minsk and headed off to Smolensk. They left behind a pocket formed by the Soviet Tenth and Third Armies. When follow-on infantry divisions finished cleaning up the encirclement, the Germans counted 330,000 prisoners, over 3,000 artillery pieces, and 3,332 tanks. In early July, Halder trumpeted in his diary: "One can already say that the task of destroying the Red Army in front of the Dvina and Dnepr has been fulfilled. . . .

It is therefore not claiming too much when I assert that the campaign against Russia has been won in fourteen days."[113]

The outcome in the Smolensk cauldron was almost an exact repetition of the Minsk disaster. The German haul was huge: 300,000 prisoners, 3,205 tanks, and 3,000 artillery pieces.[114] But substantial problems were already arising. By 7 July, the foot-slogging German infantry was more than a hundred miles behind the mechanized divisions, and large numbers of Soviet units remained in the gaps, causing trouble for the supply trucks trying to get fuel and ammunition to the panzers.[115]

How to explain the huge numbers of prisoners the Germans captured in the first months of the campaign? There were a number of factors. Disaffection with the regime undoubtedly played a role.[116] Stalin's constant demand that Soviet armies hold their positions despite steadily worsening situations as the Germans drove deep into Soviet rear areas was also a factor. Particularly important was the general breakdown of command and control, not only at the highest levels but throughout the system, down to platoon levels. Unit cohesion was extremely low because units had received large numbers of ill-trained recruits shortly before the invasion.

The Germans were also encountering difficulties. Dusty or muddy tracks played havoc with vehicles designed to operate on the paved roads of Western and Central Europe, rather than what the Soviets called roads. German armored units had already suffered severe attrition. On 7 July, the tank forces of the 18th and 3rd Panzer Divisions were just 35 percent combat ready, while the 4th and 17th were at 60 percent readiness.[117] The 4th Panzer Division, which had had 169 tanks on 22 June, was down to only 40 by 16 July; on 21 July, the 7th Panzer Division, which had begun the war with 300 armored fighting vehicles, had written off 77 as total losses by 21 July, while another 120 were in various stages of disrepair. On the same day, Panzer Group 3 reported that only 42 percent of its strength was combat ready; it had already lost 27 percent of its tanks.[118] Casualties in the mechanized units were heavy and mounting: the 20th Panzer Division had lost 35 percent of its officers, 19 percent of its NCOs, and 11 percent of its men by 26 July.[119]

It was at this point, at the end of July, that Soviet reserve armies began to attack the German mechanized units, which could receive little support from the infantry divisions because most of them were still over a hundred miles behind the front. Marshal Semyon Timoshenko, in command of Soviet forces in the center, received the first wave of reserve armies. In the desperate battle that followed, German panzer and motor-ized infantry divisions teetered on the brink of defeat, forced to use whatever ammunition and fuel wended its way through rear areas where Soviet units were still attempting to escape. The so-called August pause, during which Hitler and the generals argued about whether to continue the advance on Moscow or support drives on Leningrad and Ukraine, happened because the Germans had disastrously miscalculated the Red Army's strength and the impact of their inadequate logistical system.

On 11 August, Halder admitted in his diary, "The whole situation shows more and more clearly that we have underestimated the colossus of Russia. ... This conclusion is shown both on the organizational and economic levels, in the transportation, and above all in infantry divisions. We have already identified 360. These divisions are admittedly not armed and equipped in our sense, and tactically they are badly led. But there they are; and when we destroy a dozen, the Russians simply estab-lish another dozen."[120] By mid-August there was some improvement in the supply situation. Yet Soviet counterattacks, particularly around Yel-nya in Army Group Center, wrecked five infantry divisions and severely reduced German front-line strength. These attacks had also, however, weakened the Soviet ability to resist German thrusts when they came at the end of the month. Significantly, the Germans, who had launched three great thrusts at the beginning of Barbarossa, could now conduct only one major offensive at a time, such were their logistical limits after their forces had expanded into the funnel-shaped theater.

Panzer Group 2 swung south from south of Smolensk, and by 26 Au-gust the 3rd Panzer Division had created a bridgehead over the Desna and broken through the Soviet southwestern and Bryansk fronts. Mean-while, Kleist's Panzer Group 1 crossed the Dnieper and was driving north. The Soviets failed to respond as Stalin, ignoring advice from his generals, demanded that the Red Army stand fast in Ukraine. It was a di-sastrous mistake. On 15 September, the two panzer groups met near Lokhvytsya, one hundred miles east of Kyiv, and created a vast encircle-ment of the Soviets' Fifth, Twenty-First, Twenty-Sixth, and Thirty-Sev-enth Armies. By the time mopping-up operations had ended, the Germans claimed an additional 665,000 prisoners, 884 tanks, 3,719 artil-lery pieces, and 418 antitank guns.[121]

Even as they were finishing up Ukraine—and slaughtering Jews at Babi Yar, just outside Kyiv, with extensive cooperation between the army and SS executioners—the Germans' attention was already shifting. At the beginning of September, Hitler ordered Leeb to complete the encirclement of Leningrad, starve the population out, and destroy the city with air and artillery bombardment. The Führer also decided to unleash Army Group Center against Moscow, the fall of which he believed would collapse Stalin's regime. The generals were in full accord. On 6 September, the OKW issued a new directive ordering that Moscow be the main focus, with the goal of capturing it before winter.

There were, however, warning signs that Soviet distances were fracturing the German logistical system. The Fourteenth Army reported to Berlin that "for the moment [the supply system meets] current consumption only. The transportation [has] not so far allow[ed] the establishment of depots sufficiently large to enable the troops to receive what they need in accordance with the tactical situation. . . . The army lives from hand to mouth, especially in regards the fuel situation."[122] The difficulty of building supply stocks showed that the strain of constant operations was biting ever deeper into the logistical structure. One of Guderian's units, XXXXVII Panzer Corps, recorded in its war diary on 18 September, "The status report submitted . . . showed that because of the heavy demands over the last weeks on outrageously bad roads the state of trucks has worsened. Owing to the failure to deliver spare parts innumerable instances of damage, often only minor, cannot be repaired. This in part, therefore, explains the high percentage of conditional and non-serviceable trucks."[123]

Nevertheless, with units cobbled together with stocks from the bottom of the barrel, the Germans kept moving forward. Hoth's Panzer Group 3 returned from the north to Army Group Center while Guderian began his advance from Ukraine in the general direction of the Soviet capital. The Soviets had made inadequate efforts to prepare defenses against a potential German offensive in the center, with Stalin's attention focusing on the northern and Ukrainian fronts. Coming directly from its operations in Ukraine, Guderian's Panzer Group 2 moved northeast and within two days had cut the Bryansk-Orel Road. On 1 October, its lead units captured Sevsk after an advance of eighty-five miles. Two days later, the 4th Panzer Division reached Orel and caught the Soviets so much by surprise that the trams were still running. On 2 October, the other two panzer groups began their advance, breaking out into the open almost immediately.

The Soviet command-and-control system collapsed so completely that Moscow did not know the extent of the disaster. The only warning signal was that communications with virtually all the units on the central front had ceased. On 5 October, Moscow sent out reconnaissance aircraft to check on what was happening. They reported on landing that a German armored column, some twenty-five miles long, was advancing along the Smolensk to Moscow's major highway behind Russian lines. The Soviet secret police, the NKVD, tried to arrest the pilots "for spreading panic," but wiser heads prevailed.[124]

In effect, the Germans had ripped an enormous gap across the entire central front, leaving the road to Moscow open. The panzers encircled three Soviet armies in the north near Vyazma; to the south, German spearheads surrounded three more Soviet armies around Bryansk. On 15 October, Bock's Army Group Center calculated it had captured 558,825 prisoners while destroying or capturing 1,076 tanks and 3,735 artillery pieces.[125] Nevertheless, despite the massive victory over Soviet forces in the Bryansk-Vyazma pocket, Operation Typhoon exhausted the German mechanized forces. Out of 3,580 tanks at the start of Barbarossa, the panzer divisions had only 601 on 10 November. The situation with logistics was worse. Of the roughly 500,000 trucks German divisions had possessed on 22 June, only 75,000 were still usable on 10 November.[126]

As the Germans policed up the wreckage of the Bryansk-Vyazma pocket, the road to Moscow appeared open. It was not. In mid-October, the Russian *rasputitsa* arrived, the period when heavy rains turned roads into quagmires.[127] Both the spearhead units and logistical system bogged down in a sea of mud. Astonishingly, with winter around the corner, the OKH thought the cold would freeze up the mud and permit the continued advance on Moscow. In mid-November, Halder told the assembled chiefs of staffs of the army groups and armies that over the next six weeks, where the cold would freeze the ground for farther advances, there would be minimal snowfall. One of the generals acidly replied that "we are not in the spring, nor are we in France."[128] On 22 November, the OKH's intelligence section added to its abysmal record by reporting that the Soviets most likely had no more reserve troops available to bring into the fight.[129]

But the hard reality had been clear even before Operation Typhoon. The question now was whether to continue the advance on Moscow or halt and bring up stockpiles of winter clothing, winter-weight fuels, rations, and ammunition to handle the Russian winter. Field Marshal Günther von Kluge, Fourth Army commander, noted in the army's war diary that operations in Russia had reached a critical point, "since the troops on one hand with no winter clothing and on the other facing impossible and tenacious opponents defending the roads [are finding] the advance extraordinarily difficult."[130] One of Hoth's corps commanders, General Heinrich Freiherr von Vietinghoff, noted on 1 November that "after careful evaluation of all experiences of the past weeks I am forced to conclude ... that no benefits are to be expected from the deployment of the panzer corps under present and expected weather and road conditions. The wear on the troops, equipment, and fuel bears no relationship to the possible success."[131]

Despite these warnings, it was clear which path the German generals would take. As Bock noted, the October victories "made it possible for [the army] to take risks."[132] With temperatures dropping and snow arriving, Army Group Center struggled toward Moscow. By 4 December, the temperature was –25 degrees Fahrenheit and the last efforts to advance flickered out. The next day, General Georgy Zhukov, who had persuaded Stalin to husband reinforcements until the Germans exhausted themselves, began his counteroffensive. Over the following months, Soviet troops, equipped for winter, came close to destroying large portions of Army Group Center. Halder's diary recounts German troops' struggle to survive: "20 December: Still very tense ... 29 December: *A very bad day!* ... 30 December: *Again a hard day!* ... Very serious crisis in Ninth Army ... 31 December: *Again an arduous day* ... 2 January: A day of wild fighting."[133]

The Battle of Moscow, which continued until March 1942, exploded the myth of the Wehrmacht's invincibility. It might have achieved far more operationally and tactically if Stalin's baleful influence had not continued to hobble the Red Army. By 13 December, Army Group Center was on the brink of collapse. Zhukov planned to batter the Germans back to Smolensk, but Stalin took the four reserve armies, which were available to the Stavka (Soviet high command), and instead of giving them to his best general, allocated them to new attacks on the flanks. The dispersion of the Soviet effort brought no significant operational success other than pushing the Germans back from Moscow.[134] Zhukov commented in a draft of his memoirs (removed before publication): "The history of the Great Fatherland War still comes to a generally positive conclusion about the [first] winter offensive of our forces despite the lack of success. I do not agree with this evaluation. ... If you consider our losses and what results were achieved, it will be clear it was a Pyrrhic victory."[135]

On the tactical level the Soviet loss of junior officers and NCOs created an inability to launch anything more than suicidal attacks into enemy firepower in the hope of overwhelming the Germans. As one German soldier noted early in the winter, "The Russian is a very good, hard soldier. None of us thought the Russian would be as good as he is. He is as strong as us in weaponry, only the leadership is missing."[136] Soviet losses from December through March more than bear out Zhukov's comment about Pyrrhic victory: December 1941, 552,000 casualties; January 1942, 558,000; and February, 520,000, for a total of 1,638,000. Over a similar period, 26 November to 28 February, German casualties were 262,524.[137]

How Close?

The outbreak of another great war meant that the efforts of the 1920s and 1930s to escape the First World War's military and social lessons had gone for naught. The combination of the French and Industrial Revolutions had again seized the combatants in its grasp. For a brief period, the Wehrmacht's success over the French and Western Europeans suggested the conduct of war had moved in a new direction. But Barbarossa provided proof of the old saying, "The more things change the more they stay the same." Moreover, by their nature, Nazism and Soviet communism brought an unparalleled ferocity into the struggle, even as both powers' massive, industrialized economies ensured that no technological or military development would provide a silver bullet to let the combatants escape the iron laws of attrition.

What about the impact of revolutions in military affairs? Clearly, the German Army's willingness to absorb the lessons of the combined-arms revolution of 1914–1918 was crucial to its ability to destroy the armies it faced early in the war. But in 1941, the Germans ran into the Red Army. The expanses of Russia created logistical and intelligence problems the Wehrmacht was not prepared to address. The Soviets staggered but did not collapse. Although the Red Army suffered appalling casualties in the winter of 1941–1942, waiting in the wings, as the experience of the war educated the Soviets on its realities, was the concept of operational maneuver, based on logistics, industrial power, and sophisticated intelligence.

CHAPTER TEN

World War II

Ideology, Economics, Intelligence, and Science

When whole communities go to war—whole peoples, and especially *civilized* peoples—the reason always lies in some political situation, and the occasion is always due to some political object.

—CARL VON CLAUSEWITZ, *On War*

THE FOUR DAYS FROM 7 to 11 December 1941 are when Japan and Germany lost the war—Japan by attacking Pearl Harbor, Germany by declaring war on the United States. The Japanese strike ensured the United States entered the conflict with unity of purpose. Hitler's declaration persuaded Americans they confronted a unified Axis alliance. Yet the length of the war was not a given. Above all, the conflict required an intelligent allocation of resources, manpower, military forces, and technology. A major factor would be how the contestants mobilized their economies and manpower, especially those whose brains and imagination could contribute in a way unimaginable before 1939.

World War II represented qualitative changes in the ways the French and Industrial Revolutions influenced war. The mass mobilization im-

248

posed on the French in 1793 by the *levée en masse* was never equaled in the nineteenth century. But by the time of World War II, the contending states could impose an increasing mobilization of resources and man-power that placed unheard-of demands on civilians, the military, and thei... Th... would be no slackening until collapse or victory.

For... quired public sup-
po... listances, as well as
m... to the raw materi-
als... ower depended. It
w... that the Germans
ar... the economic and
st... et even more than
t... ideologies and the
I...

... ectiveness

...braced by Hitler's
...e enemy in terms
...s of barbarity.[1] Sta-
...the more radical as-
...logical targets were the
...their "subhuman" ene-
...er groups. The British
...ideals bordering on the

...storians argued that Hit-
...little more than a skilled
...istorians demolished that
..."message was comp... in its own right," as Mac-
...s. "The widespread assumption that National Social-
...oherence or content is only sustainable by ignoring
...r's speeches and writings. ... Hitler's synthesis was
...and consistent: an all-embracing all-explanatory
...at civilizations, Hitler argued, had resulted from
...axis of world history was the cosmic Darwinian-
...een the Aryans—the one 'race' qualified as 'bear-
...ure—and the Jewish 'world-pestilence.' "[5] This

was the French Revolution with racial overtones: Germany had to eliminate all Jewish influence from its body politic.

Equally important to Hitler was his belief that the German people
were too constrained within their small space. To realize its destiny, the
Reich needed to expand, not merely by regaining the land Versailles had
stolen but by expanding radically the territory the German race inhabited. Germany's future lay in Ukraine's agricultural spaces, which the
Reich could take only by conquest. Those Slavs who survived would become like the Spartan helots. The preparation and execution of Barbarossa in 1941 underlined the generals' acceptance of Hitler's
Weltanschauung.[6] Orders of the day issued by senior generals suggest how
deeply Nazi ideology reached. One 1941 missive from Colonel General
Erich von Manstein, for instance, stated, "The Jewish-Bolshevist system
must be eradicated once and for all. It must never be allowed to intrude
on our European sphere again. . . . Soldiers must show understanding for
the necessity of harsh measures against Jews."[7]

The military displayed its support for Nazi ideology in more than
words. In May 1941, the OKW's legal department defined all Jews as
partisans under military law and thus eligible to be shot. An exhibit in
the 1990s that traveled throughout Germany entitled "The German
Army and Genocide" described this approach as "partisan struggle without partisans."[8] But the worst crime in which the Wehrmacht involved itself lay in the treatment of Soviet prisoners of war. By the Wehrmacht's
own count, 3.4 million soldiers of the Red Army surrendered to it in
1941. When the war ended, only 100,000 had survived. The rest had
been shot, starved, beaten to death, or allowed to die of disease.[9]

Ideology's influence on Soviet soldiers in "defense of the motherland" possessed similarities to the German situation. The massive surrenders of 1941 reflected the breakdown of Soviet command and control
and cohesion, not a fundamental disaffection with the regime. Although
some of that was present, the war brought an upswelling of volunteers,
mostly from cities, to defend the motherland. As one woman noted, "My
motherland, Russia, is the same to all of us. But every one of us has a
small corner of this vast motherland, our own motherland, where we
were born, raised, went to school, and set off on life's path."[10]

The surrenders in 1941 and 1942 forced the regime to take extraor-
dinary steps, which even included rehabilitation of the Orthodox
Church. Typifying the approach were Order No. 270 in August 1941 and
Order No. 227 in July 1942. The latter demanded no unit retreat and

posed on the French in 1793 by the *levée en masse* was never equaled in the nineteenth century. But by the time of World War II, the contending states could impose an increasing mobilization of resources and manpower that placed unheard-of demands on civilians, the military, and their societies. There would be no slackening until collapse or victory. For the Allies, particularly the Americans, the war required public support for the projection of military power over great distances, as well as mobilization of massive industrial strength and access to the raw materials on which mechanized forces and air and naval power depended. It was a war the Japanese were unsuited to conduct and that the Germans and Soviets had difficulty in waging but that suited the economic and strategic strengths of the Anglo-American alliance. Yet even more than the Great War, the conflict turned into an embrace of ideologies and the Industrial Revolution.

Ideology, Nationalism, and Combat Effectiveness

With the coming of World War II, the ideology embraced by Hitler's Third Reich and Stalin's Soviet Union identified the enemy in terms of race, nationality, and class, driving war to new levels of barbarity.[1] Stalin's brand of Bolshevik communism was the child of the more radical aspects of the French Revolution. Its foremost ideological targets were the enemies of the working class. The Nazis found their "subhuman" enemies among not only Jews but Slavs and other groups. The British and Americans also identified their cause with ideals bordering on the ideological.

In the decades after World War II, some historians argued that Hitler had not possessed a real ideology and was little more than a skilled political manipulator.[2] In the 1970s, other historians demolished that view.[3] The Führer's "message was compelling in its own right," as MacGregor Knox argues. "The widespread assumption that National Socialist ideology lacked coherence or content is only sustainable by ignoring its basic texts—Hitler's speeches and writings. ... Hitler's synthesis was uniquely compelling and consistent: an all-embracing all-explanatory system of belief."[4] Great civilizations, Hitler argued, had resulted from the Aryan races: "The axis of world history was the cosmic Darwinian-biological struggle between the Aryans—the one 'race' qualified as 'bearers' and 'founders' of culture—and the Jewish 'world-pestilence.' "[5] This was the French Revolution with racial overtones: Germany had to eliminate all Jewish influence from its body politic.

Equally important to Hitler was his belief that the German people were too constrained within their small space. To realize its destiny, the Reich needed to expand, not merely by regaining the land Versailles had stolen but by expanding radically the territory the German race inhabited. Germany's future lay in Ukraine's agricultural spaces, which the Reich could take only by conquest. Those Slavs who survived would become like the Spartan helots. The preparation and execution of Barbarossa in 1941 underlined the generals' acceptance of Hitler's *Weltanschauung.*[6] Orders of the day issued by senior generals suggest how deeply Nazi ideology reached. One 1941 missive from Colonel General Erich von Manstein, for instance, stated, "The Jewish-Bolshevist system must be eradicated once and for all. It must never be allowed to intrude on our European sphere again. . . . Soldiers must show understanding for the necessity of harsh measures against Jews."[7]

The military displayed its support for Nazi ideology in more than words. In May 1941, the OKW's legal department defined all Jews as partisans under military law and thus eligible to be shot. An exhibit in the 1990s that traveled throughout Germany entitled "The German Army and Genocide" described this approach as "partisan struggle without partisans."[8] But the worst crime in which the Wehrmacht involved itself lay in the treatment of Soviet prisoners of war. By the Wehrmacht's own count, 3.4 million soldiers of the Red Army surrendered to it in 1941. When the war ended, only 100,000 had survived. The rest had been shot, starved, beaten to death, or allowed to die of disease.[9]

Ideology's influence on Soviet soldiers in "defense of the motherland" possessed similarities to the German situation. The massive surrenders of 1941 reflected the breakdown of Soviet command and control and cohesion, not a fundamental disaffection with the regime. Although some of that was present, the war brought an upswelling of volunteers, mostly from cities, to defend the motherland. As one woman noted, "My motherland, Russia, is the same to all of us. But every one of us has a small corner of this vast motherland, our own motherland, where we were born, raised, went to school, and set off on life's path."[10]

The surrenders in 1941 and 1942 forced the regime to take extraordinary steps, which even included rehabilitation of the Orthodox Church. Typifying the approach were Order No. 270 in August 1941 and Order No. 227 in July 1942. The latter demanded no unit retreat and spelled out draconian punishments for malingerers and deserters. The NKVD made sure that punishment for units and individuals who failed in their duty was swift and merciless.[11] Also, by late summer 1941, much of the Soviet population were aware the Germans had come as conquerors. As the Red Army advanced westward after Stalingrad, the extent of Nazi atrocities became increasingly clear. Knowledge of the Wehrmacht's crimes became both a combat motivator and an encouragement for the mass rapes and murders that occurred in 1945 as Soviet troops moved onto German territory.

The Japanese were obviously not heirs to the French Revolution, yet educational reforms, modeled on Germany's, imbued a new sense of Japanese nationalism. Nationalism had provided the glue for the economic explosion during the Meiji Restoration; it was equally impressive in the discipline of military forces during World War II. Moreover, that discipline provided support for an economy that performed more impressively than prewar observers believed possible. Those responsible for the Meiji Restoration had learned well from their European mentors in building an impressive military. At its heart lay *bushido*, a concept of nationalism that made the Japanese soldier a fanatical and obedient fighter. Yet once Japan involved itself in war with the United States, there was nothing economic or military performance could do to avert defeat. The only question was how terribly damaged Japan would be before the military acknowledged the hopelessness of its position.

Max Hastings has argued that apart from certain elite formations, British and American soldiers never attained the same combat effectiveness as their German opponents.[12] He has a point, but he misses the political and strategic framework within which British and American ground forces fought. Perhaps the most important factor was the quality of manpower the two nations put into their armies. Unlike their opponents, they syphoned off those with the highest intelligence into the air forces and navies, precisely those apt to possess a deep commitment.

The casualty rate among those who flew in the Anglo-American air forces, particularly in bombers, underlines that commitment. They were not dragooned into flying. Only volunteers became pilots, engineers, navigators, bombardiers, or gunners. All one had to do to cease flying was to indicate that one no longer wished to fly. Yet in 1942, 1943, and 1944, the casualties in Bomber Command were appalling. The statistics speak for themselves. Of approximately 125,000 aircrew who served in that command, over half were killed or wounded on operations.[13] For the

Eighth Air Force from May 1943 through April 1944, crew losses most months averaged over 30 percent.[14]

The Economics of the Warring Nations

The marriage of the French and Industrial Revolutions took an even nastier turn in World War II than in the Great War. The modern state provided the structure and discipline to marshal required manpower and material, while ideology supplied popular support and modern economic systems dispensed the means to wage war on a scale never before seen. War economies provided almost endless impedimenta for the military organizations they supported.

In the winter of 1941–1942, Germany found itself engaged in a two-front war with its Wehrmacht and economy in disarray. The worst troubles were on the Eastern Front, where the sudden and unexpected Soviet counteroffensives had brought the army to the brink of collapse. The Germans held, but their army suffered irreparable harm. On 25 March 1942, Halder recorded German losses in the east as 32,485 officers and 1,040,581 NCOs and enlisted, from a force numbering 3,200,200 at Barbarossa's start.[15] This did not include those reporting sick or frostbite victims. Considering that the initial figure included support troops, combat casualties were close to 50 percent.

Equipment losses were unprecedented.[16] Tank losses had reached 3,486, from a force numbering 3,350 at the start. Over the period, the Eastern Front received only 873 new armored fighting vehicles. In December 1941, the panzer divisions in the east reported only 140 tanks available.[17] Losses in support vehicles, such as trucks, motorcycles, and personnel carriers, were even worse: the army lost 74,000 between October 1941 and March 1942, of which industry replaced one-tenth.[18] Merely reequipping the army on the Eastern Front was a major challenge, given that the output of armaments had increased only slightly from 1939. Both the culture of the Wehrmacht and that of industry affected production. Unlike the Soviets and Americans, who emphasized mass production, the Germans focused on small production runs, allowing fine-tuning of each series but minimizing numbers.

Less obvious but equally dangerous was the Luftwaffe's near collapse. Its difficulties had begun to emerge in June 1941 after nearly two years of major commitments. Göring, furious at the disparity between planned and actual production, reinserted Field Marshal Erhard Milch, one of the few Germans who understood production and maintenance, to oversee aircraft production. The Reichsmarshall gave Milch the authority to close or seize factories, confiscate raw materials, transfer or dismiss designers, and reorganize production. Göring's orders to the state secretary were simple: he was to quadruple production.[19]

The Germans had already fallen seriously behind the production of Anglo-American factories. In fighters alone in the last quarter of 1941, they were being outproduced by nearly 400 percent. The British built an average of 471 single-engine fighters per month in the first half of 1941 and 553 in the second half, while German factories averaged 243 single-engine fighters per month in the first half of the year and just 231 over the last six months.[20] In 1942–1943, German production increased from 15,556 aircraft to 25,527, but Anglo-American production went from 97,000 to 147,000. Moreover, the German air units suffered heavy attrition. From a front-line strength of between 5,300 and 5,600 aircraft in 1942, the Luftwaffe wrote off 13,000—meaning they were replacing the entire fleet every few months. Aircrew losses were also increasing while hours devoted to crew training were dropping because of fuel shortages.[21]

In November 1941, Milch visited the Eastern Front to gain a sense of the Luftwaffe's difficulties. What he saw was eye-opening: forward airfields contained hundreds of inoperable aircraft. They had either broken down or been damaged in combat and were idle for lack of spare parts failing to flow through the system. In-commission rates for combat aircraft told a depressing story. By December 1941, the rate for fighters was 52 percent and bombers 32 percent.[22] Simply put, the Luftwaffe's logistical system had broken down. Such was the state that crew training could not keep up with losses. In January 1942, the lack of pilots forced front-line squadrons to rob operational training units of pilots before completion of their syllabus. It was the start of a vicious cycle in which mounting losses caused cutbacks in training hours, which led to more losses. In short, the production system created a planning nightmare. By February 1942, the Luftwaffe's quartermaster general no longer knew how many aircraft German factories would produce.[23]

The Luftwaffe's difficulty in meeting the demands of the ever-expanding war reflected the economy's larger problems. Despite efforts to increase production in 1941, the Germans were behind the power curve in virtually every index of armament manufacturing. Part of the problem lay in "victory disease," as well as the confusion characteristic of the Führer state. The economy was hampered by competing authorities; a lack of focused direction at the top, particularly from Hitler; and a nonexistent strategic framework to connect ends and means. Overall, production remained stationary between 1940 and 1941.[24]

While German armaments production was stagnating in 1941, American production doubled while that of the United Kingdom increased by approximately 70 percent. The following year, the increases were 45 percent for the Reich, approximately 70 percent for Britain, and a whopping 327 percent for the United States. In 1943, the percentages were 60 percent for Germany, 20 for Britain, and nearly 100 for the United States.[25] Dollar totals are even more graphic. While German expenditures remained static in 1940–1941 at approximately $6 billion, American tripled from $1.5 to $4.5 billion, while Britain's almost doubled, from $3.5 billion to $6.5 billion.[26]

In January 1942, when the Germans became aware of how far they were falling behind, their answer was not an economic miracle but a series of measures resembling efforts already in place in Britain and the United States. Moreover, much of what was later called the "Speer miracle" reflected steps tentatively put in place between the fall of France and late 1941. There were three constraints on the war economy affecting military operations as well that inhibited the economy's growth: the lack of access to petroleum, manpower shortages in the workforce, and insufficient coal. The lack of oil had haunted both the economy and military operations since 1939. Even with substantial Soviet help, petroleum stockpiles fell throughout 1941, a decline that accelerated once Barbarossa stopped oil deliveries from Russia.[27] The fuel situation in late 1941 was so serious that an OKW memorandum warned of "the complete paralysis of the army."[28] Fuel shortages reached the point in summer 1942 that the Kriegsmarine halted combat training for heavy ships in Norway. All that remained in fuel depots were emergency stocks in case of a British invasion.[29]

The most serious difficulties occurred in the Luftwaffe, where beginning in summer 1942, fuel shortages shut down several training schools. By late 1942, training hours for pilots dropped by over 10 percent, while training in front-line aircraft declined by close to 50 percent. Thus, of 1,671 fighter pilots in front-line squadrons in early 1943, only 916 were fully combat ready.[30] Increases in the Luftwaffe's size demanded an equivalent increase in fuel supplies, not just because of operational demands but for an increased training establishment. Moreover, occupied areas of Western Europe all required imports of oil, which the Germans

had to supply, if they were to wring production out of conquered territories. Synthetic production helped with an increase from 4 million tons in
1940 to 6.5 million in 1943, while supplies from Romania reached close
to 2 million tons. Yet, comparison of the availability of oil to the British
alone suggests a great deal about the German situation. In 1942, despite
serious losses in tankers, Britain imported 10.2 million tons of petroleum. That total reached 20 million tons in 1944.[31]

The petroleum shortage explains the strategy behind Operation Blue
in summer 1942. As the German history of the war notes, "The predom-
inant factor in the plans for the war in the east during the first half of
1942 was not, therefore, the acquisition of settlement space or the crushing of Bolshevism, not even, indeed, the annihilation of the Red Army—
although hopes for all of these continued to be the driving force behind
further efforts—but the conquest of a raw material basis which would be
sufficient in the medium and long term, especially in the area of [petro-
leum], where a dramatic shortage had been beginning to take shape ever
since late summer 1941."[32]

The manpower problem was equally pressing.[33] Losses in the last six
months of 1941 on the Eastern Front were nothing short of catastrophic.
First the fighting and then the arctic cold killed or maimed a substantial
portion of nineteen- to thirty-year-old Germans, the strongest and best
workers. The workforce shortages were made worse by cultural factors,
including the regime's refusal to employ women, the one-shift schedule
in armament factories, and a commitment to short factory runs that did
not utilize mass production to the fullest.[34]

With the failure of Barbarossa and entrance of the United States
into the fighting, the Germans confronted a global war. Such a conflict
demanded major increases in production that only an expanding workforce could meet. Were the prisoners the Wehrmacht had captured in
the first months of Barbarossa available? Most were dead by February
1942.[35] Thus began one of the Third Reich's great crimes: the enslave-
ment of millions of laborers from across Europe. In March 1942, on Hitler's authority, Fritz Sauckel began a merciless program of "recruiting"
foreign workers. By June 1943, he had added 2.8 million workers to the
2.5 million, including POWs, who were guests of the Reich. By fall 1944,
that total reached nearly 8 million. Miserably housed, badly fed, refused
shelter during Allied air raids, they made up in numbers, if not quality,
the draining of German workers to meet the Wehrmacht's insatiable demand for soldiers.[36]

In January 1942, Hitler's armaments minister, Fritz Todt, died when his He 111 crashed on takeoff. Hitler appointed Albert Speer, his architect and close companion, as Todt's replacement. Recent historians have done an admirable job of deconstructing the myth that Speer was largely responsible for the rise in German production. The way had already been opened by investments in armament factories after the fall of France. Speer did contribute to the war effort by tying it to a propaganda blitz that emphasized the importance of war workers, supposedly only Germans, to armament production. Speer's friend, the malicious Dr. Joseph Goebbels, contributed his talents. As a propaganda ministry slogan announced, "The best weapons bring victory." But the upsurge continued only until spring 1943. Until then numbers were impressive: Speer announced in May 1943 that monthly production of tanks was twelve-and-a-half times greater than in 1941.[37] The problem was that no matter how successful he was, German output remained well behind the Soviets. "The Speer miracle," notes Adam Tooze, "was not unconstrained. The German war economy after 1942 was limited by the same fundamental trade-offs that had restricted it since the first years of the war. By summer 1943, these constraints, combined with the first systematic attack against German industry by Allied bombers, brought Speer's miracle to a halt."[38]

The first shock the Combined Bomber Offensive (CBO) inflicted on the German economy came in spring 1943 in the Battle of the Ruhr, in which the RAF savaged cities and factories.[39] Lancaster bombers carrying specially designed bombs blew out the Eder and Möhne dams, the latter creating a path of destruction in the valleys below. The Wehrmacht's Armament's Inspectorate for the Ruhr described the damage to industrial concerns as a "catastrophe." From April to June, it reported a decline in coal production of 813,278 tons: 416,464 tons from bomb damage to infrastructure, 272,870 tons caused by the Möhne flood, and 153,944 tons from damage to workers' houses in the Ruhr.[40] Speer immediately mounted an effort to rebuild the dams, whose water supply was essential for Ruhr industry. To his surprise, the dams were rebuilt by fall without interference from Allied bombers.[41]

Because coal was essential to the war economy, affecting steel production, synthetic fuel and rubber, electricity, and numerous other industries, the Ruhr offensive played a significant role in halting the surge in armament production. The drop in coal, and thus coke, production had a direct impact on steel output. For the first quarter of 1943, German planners had aimed to produce 8.4 million tons; what they got was a shortfall of 400,000 tons. The drop in steel and coal production cascaded into other areas. Disruptions resulted in a crisis in availability of parts, castings, and forgings.[42]

In summer 1943, a new contestant appeared over the Reich: the American Eighth Air Force began daylight operations. While it suffered heavy losses, it also added to the pressure on the war economy.[43] The CBO also halted the rise in German aircraft production, particularly in the manufacture of fighters. In July 1943, total output of new and reconditioned fighters reached a high of 1,263 Bf 109s and Fw 190s. From that point there was a steady drop, to 985 in November and 687 in December.[44] Worse, there was a considerable gap between what the factories produced and what reached front-line squadrons. The raid on the Marienburg factory producing Fw 190s destroyed approximately a hundred new fighters awaiting delivery.[45] Despite taking heavy losses, B-17s raiding Schweinfurt and Regensburg on 17 August severely damaged the ball-bearing plants. One estimate of the damage to the Regensburg factory noted that it destroyed more fighters "than an entire month's losses on either the Mediterranean or Eastern Front."[46]

The final nail in the war economy's coffin came in spring 1944, when the Americans turned on the oil industry. In April, the Fifteenth Air Force's B-17s and B-24s began attacking Romania's oil refineries. Raids on synthetic oil factories followed in May. By August, German fuel production was below 50 percent of capacity. In November, it struggled to reach 60 percent, and thereafter it continued to fall. The situation with aviation gas was even worse. By September, American attacks had driven production down to 30 percent of its levels in April 1944.

British production stands in contrast to that of the Germans. Of all the combatants, the British mobilized their economic strength to the greatest extent—obviously with help from American resources. The allocation of Britain's available labor shows the extent of mobilization. By 1943, nearly 23 percent of the labor force was in the armed forces or civil defense, with another 23 percent in armaments production.[47] The British devoted over 50 percent of their national income to the war.[48] A civil service report of 1944 describes the extent of the effort: "In five years of drastic labor mobilization, nearly every man and every woman under fifty without children has been subject to direction to work, often far from home. The hours of work average fifty-three for men and fifty overall; when work is done, every citizen who is not excused for reasons of family circumstances, work, etc., has had to do forty-eight hours in the

Home Guard or Civil Defense. Supplies of all kind have been progressively limited by shipping and manpower shortage; the queue part of life."[49]

Whatever their economic weaknesses, the British punched above their weight. They carried the bulk of the effort in the Battle of the Atlantic; waged a major air, naval, and ground war in the Mediterranean; carried out a major campaign against the Japanese in Burma; and bore the weight of strategic bombing against Germany through late 1943. British production numbers were quite extraordinary. Their aircraft factories outproduced the Germans from 1940 through 1943.[50] The cost of Bomber Command's efforts in the Battle of the Ruhr reveals the extent of the attrition in the air war over Germany: 872 bombers shot down and 2,162 others damaged. Yet the number of bombers available to Bomber Command continued to rise. In February 1943, fully crewed aircraft stood at 593; six months later it was 787.[51]

Outside of armored fighting vehicles, British military equipment was of reasonably high quality. "Not everything the British made in the air and sea war was the best or even close to it," historian Phillips Payson O'Brien writes, "but the fact that they were able to make what they did across such a wide range of technologically advanced weaponry was one of the remarkable achievements of World War II."[52] The British led in several areas of aircraft design. The Spitfire was not only one of the best fighters at the war's outset but remained among the best at the end through upgrades. The Lancaster was the best heavy bomber in Europe, and its special weaponry, from the barrel bombs that took out so many of Germany's dams to the grand slam bombs that sank the *Tirpitz* and destroyed the Bielefeld and Arnsberg viaducts, was unmatched. The Mosquito twin-engine bomber was, in this author's view, the best strategic bomber of the war in both cost and survivability.

The story was the same with the Royal Navy, whose weapons and radio and radar aids were crucial in winning the Battle of the Atlantic. Only in radar were the Americans more advanced, but their radar depended on the 1939 invention of the cavity magnetron, accomplished by British scientists. The British were also particularly good in adapting technology and science to the U-boat war. Finally, one must note the extraordinary support that Bletchley Park, its mathematicians, and its scientists provided Allied forces with their decrypts and analysis of high-level German message traffic.[53]

America's industrial mobilization began in 1938 with an emphasis on building up the navy and army air forces. Ground forces received little attention until 1940 when the collapse of France brought home to the Americans that they required a bigger army. After they entered the war, the size of that force became a major issue. The army, overestimating German strength, argued for a number of divisions and their equipment that would have absorbed far too much of the nation's productive capacity.[54] The decisive arguments took place in late summer and fall 1942. On one side were two economists, Stacy May and Simon Kuznets, who had played a role in Roosevelt's New Deal. Utilizing new economic tools, they created a picture of what was feasible to prevent bottlenecks from delaying production. They calculated that even in the best case, the United States would not possess sufficient weapons and material to invade Europe until spring 1944. Lieutenant General Brehon Somervell, head of army service forces, demanded a greatly enlarged army program. In the end, after a bitter fight, Somervell and the army conceded. Thus was born the eighty-nine-division army.[55]

The mobilization of military and economic power astonished even the Americans. So impressive was the output that the economy could tolerate strikes in the coal fields that resulted in a production loss of 20 million tons of coal, delaying the output of 100,000 tons of steel.[56] Out of unimproved fields, the Americans constructed factories, dock yards, and petroleum installations along with the supporting infrastructure. In March 1941, Ford began construction of a factory to produce B-24s. The plant, at Willow Run, was to be 3,200 feet long with a total of 3.5 million square feet. In December 1942, it produced only 56 aircraft; by early 1944, it was building 500 a month.[57] Willow Run was not exceptional. Having produced 153 four-engine bombers per month in the first half of 1942, the U.S. aircraft industry raised its total to 1,024 per month in the last half of 1943.[58] The increase in bombers had a direct impact on combat theaters, especially in the CBO against the Germans. Despite losing 30 percent of its aircraft and crew in the last six months of 1943, the Eighth Air Force saw its front-line bombers rise from 589 in July 1943 to 1,067 by December. The number of fully operational crews rose from 315 in July to 949 in December.[59]

But mass production of aircraft, such as B-24s, was only a part of the American success. In March 1941, Henry Kaiser's corporation began work in constructing new shipyards in Richmond, California, to build Liberty ships. These vessels were approximately 10,000 tons, powered by an engine that Kaiser chose not for its modern design but because several firms could construct it. After clearing 2.5 million cubic feet of mud to create a launch basin, they constructed a dozen shipways with the necessary gantries, wiring, and assorted equipment. They set a target of 105 days for constructing and outfitting a Liberty ship, and launched the first one at the end of 1941. By spring 1942, the Richmond shipyards had cut the production time to eighty days. One ship finished in July, the *Thomas Bailey Aldrich*, took just 43 days. Between 1941 and 1945, eighteen American yards constructed and outfitted 2,708 Liberty ships.[60] Even in the grim year of 1942, the Allies saw a net loss of tonnage only in the first seven months. From August 1942, apart from November, they showed a gain every month.[61] Starting in May 1943, the gain never fell below 1 million tons a month.[62]

The story of combat-ship construction was similar. By 1945, the U.S. Navy had accepted 17 fleet carriers, 10 fast battleships, 2 battle cruisers, 13 heavy cruisers, 33 light cruisers, 9 light carriers, 77 escort carriers, and 349 destroyers.[63] In addition to carriers, the navy trained up the fighter, torpedo, and dive bomber squadrons, plus all of the personnel required to maintain them.[64] Fuel demands for the Mariana Campaign in June 1944 suggest the extent of the American effort. By the end of its one-month operation, forty-six tankers had disgorged "4,496,156 barrels of standard oil, 8,000,000 gallons of aviation fuel, and 275,000 barrels of diesel." The fuel used in that one campaign was equivalent to the German military's total monthly usage in the first half of 1944.[65]

Finally, through the Lend-Lease program, the Americans played a major role in keeping their allies in the war. Britain and the Soviet Union were the main beneficiaries, the former receiving $31,387,100,000 in value, the latter $10,082,100,000. By June 1944, the U.S. government had shipped 11,000 aircraft, 6,000 armored fighting vehicles, and 300,000 trucks and jeeps to the Soviets. To support Soviet railroads, Lend-Lease included 350 locomotives, 1,640 flat cars, and half a million tons of rails, axles, and wheels. In his memoirs, Nikita Khrushchev recorded a comment Stalin had made after the war that "if the United States had not helped us, we would not have won the war. If we had had to fight Nazi Germany one on one, we could not have stood up against Germany's pressure."[66]

Lend-Lease involved more than just weapons. The German seizure of Narvik in April 1940 cut the British off from Swedish iron ore, a major factor in Britain's steel production. Lend-Lease supplies of finished steel products then saved considerable shipping space as well as labor, allowing the British to maximize armament production.[67] Food shipments to the British and Soviets were crucial to both countries. For the latter, the 3 million tons of food the Americans provided prevented mass starvation after the Germans seized much of the wheat-growing areas of Ukraine and the northern Caucasus.[68]

Moreover, it was not just in the big-ticket items where the American economy provided essential aid. Shipments of electrical equipment, radars, and the Bombes (the devices necessary to help decipher Enigma transmissions) that supported Bletchley Park reached unheard-of levels once America's electrical concerns had ramped up. Before the war, U.S. factories were manufacturing 600,000 valves for radios and other electrical components per day. By 1944, Sylvania's twenty-three plants alone were fabricating 400,000 per day, while General Electric and Westinghouse were turning out similar numbers.[69]

In retrospect, given the loss of some of its most valuable industrial regions, the Soviet economic performance was extraordinary.[70] In the first months of Barbarossa, the Soviet government uprooted workers and machinery from the path of the invasion and transferred whole factories to the newly industrialized regions along and behind the Urals. Altogether they evacuated 1,523 factories, including 1,360 armament plants, to areas east of Moscow, along the Volga, in the Urals, and even deeper in Siberia. They often did this at the last possible moment. The evacuation of Leningrad's factories, for instance, did not begin until 3 October 1941, with the result that few escaped before the Germans isolated the city.[71] Once in their new locations, the workers rushed to reassemble the factories and restart production. One factory, evacuated from Kharkov on 8 October, was back in operation by early December.[72]

The service time of Soviet weapons suggests the extent to which the war in the east was a battle of attrition. "A Soviet gun," the historian Fred Kagan noted, "would last eighteen weeks in the field. The average life of a Soviet combat aircraft was three months, and that of a Soviet tank barely longer. In the winter of 1941–2, the Soviet front-line forces would lose one-sixth of their aircraft, one-seventh of their guns and mortars and one tenth of their armoured equipment *every week*."[73] Even with the shock of the initial industrial losses, Soviet industry produced impressive numbers of weapons over the winter and spring of 1942: 4,500 tanks, 3,000 aircraft, 14,000 artillery pieces, and over 50,000 mortars.[74] By late 1942, the Soviets had outproduced the Germans by four to one in tanks and three to one in artillery over the year.[75] That alone explains how they launched two major offensives in late 1942, one of which, at Stalingrad, destroyed the German Sixth Army.

The Japanese had scant ability to stand up against their main opponent once the Americans had mobilized. Even more than Germany, Japan lacked raw materials in its Home Islands, and its industrial base was the smallest of the major powers. The Japanese recognized this reality but hoped that initial defeats would lead the Americans to seek a compromise that would leave Imperial Japan in control of Southeast Asia. Pearl Harbor put paid to that idea before the last Japanese aircraft exited Hawaii. Nevertheless, Japanese industrial performance proved impressive. In December 1941, it possessed the best fighter aircraft of any nation, the longest-range and deadliest torpedo, a highly trained naval force that excelled at night fighting, and an understanding that carriers should be grouped together to maximize their potential.

Until summer 1943, Japanese shipping suffered insignificant losses, while their economy chugged along. In 1942 and 1943, it outproduced or nearly equaled the Soviets in the production of steel ingots, coal, iron ore, and aluminum ingots.[76] British shipyards fabricated only 14 percent more tonnage than Japanese yards.[77] The problem came in the summer of 1943, when the American submarine force reached a level of effectiveness that allowed it to devastate the Japanese merchant marine. The Imperial Navy had done nothing to prepare to defend these ships, and as they sank, the Japanese economy had no ability to withstand the resulting shortages.

It was in the production of aircraft that Japanese industry proved most impressive. In 1942 and 1943, it outproduced the Soviets in number of aircraft by a wide margin. Japanese numbers only began to fall in 1944, after American submarines destroyed their supply chains. Significantly, the Imperial Navy's fighter, the Frank, produced at war's end, had better range, speed, and maneuverability than anything the Soviets put in the air.[78]

Intelligence and Imagination

Intelligence involves the dull business of collecting innumerable pieces of minutiae and placing them into a larger whole. Ninety-eight percent of it is bean-counting. But the other two percent involves the flash of genius that recognizes what is not obvious—or sometimes what is obvious but against the conventional wisdom. In that two percent, the Allies proved superior to their Axis opponents. This was partially because interpretation of raw intelligence rests on analysts' talent rather than their rank in the hierarchy. More often than not, the hierarchal nature of Axis intelligence thwarted imaginative input. Moreover, their contempt for civilians stands in contrast to the Allies' extensive use of them.

The greatest triumph of British intelligence, the breaking of the Enigma codes, remained the untold story of World War II until the 1970s.[79] Then, for a time, Ultra intelligence became the factor that explained how and why the Allies won the war. In fact, while important, Ultra itself was rarely decisive—and it was more important in some areas than others. Above all, breaking the Enigma codes depended on German arrogance and incompetence. The German assumption that their codes could not be broken proved a disastrous miscalculation. As one of the Allied code breakers commented after the war, "We were very lucky."[80] The signals failure lay in the carelessness with which the Germans used the Enigma machine. They unwittingly provided Bletchley Park with cribs that allowed easier entrance into settings for a particular day.[81] Along with the cribs were egregious mistakes, such as that the Kriegsmarine's U-boats and its weather ships off Iceland both used the same Enigma settings. That allowed the British to use cutting-out operations not once but twice, each time yielding a treasure trove of Enigma settings for the U-boats.

The unsung heroes of the British intelligence effort worked in the establishment that supported not only Ultra but other intelligence activities, such as the so-called Y Service.[82] That service involved a massive effort to intercept German radio transmissions numbering in the tens of thousands each day. The intercepts, meaningless to those doing the intercepting, had to be letter-perfect or they would have defeated all efforts to decipher them. Once the code breakers had produced intelligible messages, it was the job of analysts to provide usable intelligence that could be passed to field and combat commanders.

Each of the Anglo-American services had quite different experiences with intelligence and Ultra.[83] For the navies in the Battle of the Atlantic, intelligence was far more crucial at the operational level than on the tactical level. From July through December 1941, Ultra helped guide convoys around U-boat patrol lines. The subsequent year brought serious losses because the Germans introduced a fourth rotor to Enigma, and it was not until late 1942 that Bletchley Park again broke the U-boat codes. Nevertheless, during periods when Ultra was not available, other British capabilities, such as direction-finding and U-boat signal traffic, allowed the Admiralty's tracking room to build a picture of Dönitz's intentions. In the Allied victory over the U-boats in spring 1943, Ultra played a role, but the major factor was coverage of convoy routes by Allied anti-submarine aircraft, as well as increasingly sophisticated radar, weapons, and direction-finding equipment.

For the British and American armies, Ultra was useful at the tactical level. It could provide a depiction of German intentions, but it could be misleading. In Normandy, for instance, it provided warning about the Mortain counteroffensive of August 1944. Intelligence was least useful for the generals and air marshals who commanded the CBO. The most important information they required was the impact their raids were having on German production, but such information usually traveled by land lines and was not available for interception. Similarly, photographic intelligence could only show that bombs had hit a factory, not the extent of damage to the machinery lying underneath the wreckage.[84] The one area where Ultra information did play a significant role in the CBO came in 1944, with messages to and from air and ground combat units, as well as reports indicating raids were causing widespread shortages of petroleum, affecting everything from flying hours to ground operations.

Both the Germans and the Japanese were hampered by a deeply held belief in their racial superiority over their opponents, a handicap that was made worse by both militaries' practice of underestimating the importance of intelligence. Unlike the Germans, the Soviets, with a paranoid heritage embedded in their Bolshevik culture, had built a first-class intelligence organization before the war. Tragically, Stalin refused to listen to its warnings before June 1941—but once the fighting began, he gave the intelligence services free rein.[85] By fall 1942, the Soviets had gained a clear picture not only of their opponents' troop movements but, equally important, their intentions. That intelligence, combined with brilliant camouflage efforts by the Red Army, allowed the Soviets to deceive the Germans about nearly every major offensive from Stalingrad to the end of the war.[86]

British recruitment of intelligence personnel stands in stark contrast to the German practice. The British used the civilian sector widely, and they looked particularly to the academic world for mathematicians, scientists, and those with liberal arts backgrounds. The fruits of that effort led to the recruitment of some extraordinary minds: Solly Zuckerman, outstanding biologist; Alan Turing, who founded the science of artificial intelligence; Harry Hinsley, a major historian after the war; and Rodger Winn, one of Britain's leading barristers. Most important was that senior Allied commanders such as Lord Louis Mountbatten, Dwight Eisenhower, and Air Marshal Arthur Tedder placed great trust in civilian intelligence experts and analysts.

Beyond the Ultra success, the Allies cast a wide net over the actions of their opponents. British counterintelligence broke the network of spies whom the Germans had put in place before the war.[87] A few they hanged but most they turned and used to send spurious information to their masters. The few spies the Germans attempted to infiltrate during the war suffered the same fate. That network of spies-turned-double-agents provided the "information" for Operation Fortitude, which from June through August 1944 persuaded the Germans that the main Allied landing would occur along the beaches of Pas de Calais, not Normandy.[88]

Three examples demonstrate the importance of the Allied political and military leaders' willingness to employ talented analysts whatever their background. The first involved a young physicist, R. V. Jones, twenty-eight years old in 1939 and a scientific officer attached to Air Ministry intelligence. On the basis of scanty evidence, Jones divined in May 1940 that the Germans were using radio beams to guide their bombers to targets in bad weather and at night. On 21 June 1940, called before some of members of the cabinet, the RAF, several leading scientists, and Churchill to explain his theory of *Knickebein* (Crooked Leg), Jones ran into skepticism.

In his memoirs, the prime minister commented that "when Dr. Jones had finished there was a general air of incredulity." But Churchill understood the significance of Jones's insight. Even if there were only a 5 percent chance he was right, the hypothesis had to be tested. That night an RAF aircraft identified the beams.[89] On that basis, the British jammed the Luftwaffe's beams throughout the Blitz of 1940–1941—the only defense Britain had against German night bombing until April 1941, when workable radar became available to the night fighters.

Equally impressive was the contribution of F. H. Hinsley. Although still a Cambridge undergraduate in 1939—majoring in history—he was recruited by Bletchley Park for his language skills and put to work at uncovering the call signs of major German war ships. Having identified these call signs, Hinsley was then assigned to track them. In early April 1940, he suggested to his superiors that traffic in the Baltic indicated a major German operation was about to occur in Scandinavia. They paid no attention. Shortly thereafter, the Nazi invasion of Norway began. In early June, he reported that significant German fleet units were operating off the North Cape; again, his superiors disbelieved him. Almost immediately, the *Scharnhorst* and the *Gneisenau* sank the aircraft carrier *Glorious*.[90]

At this point, those in command started taking Hinsley seriously. In March 1941, he recognized that German surface weather ships operating off northern Iceland were using the same code as the U-boats. The implications were clear: the British would gain entry to U-boat cyphers if they could capture a weather ship and its code books with Enigma settings. The response was immediate. The cutting-out operation involved assignment of three cruisers and four destroyers under command of a vice admiral, based on the analysis of a twenty-year-old Cambridge undergraduate. The result was the first capture of the settings, the first step to breaking the U-boat codes.[91]

The third individual is Rodger Winn, who had had been crippled by polio as a child. He could stand only with difficulty and considerable pain. After studying law at Cambridge, he began an immensely successful law career. Thirty-six years old at the war's outbreak, he volunteered and was accepted for work in intelligence. Assigned to the U-boat tracking room in the Admiralty's Operational Intelligence Center, by 1941 he had become that organization's head due to his uncanny ability to sense Dönitz's intentions. Since it was a bit much for the Admiralty to place a civilian in charge of one of its most important intelligence organizations, he received the rank of commander in the Royal Naval Reserve. Winn was undoubtedly the most important figure in the Battle of the Atlantic.

The incident in which Churchill stepped in over his ministers and senior military to support R. V. Jones was not atypical: other Allied leaders went out on limbs to follow their analysts against military preferences. When the analysts at Bletchley Park complained to the prime minister in October 1941 that they were short on analysts and tradesmen for making the Bombes, his response was direct and immediate: *support Bletchley Park to the degree its analysts feel necessary*. In under a month, the bureaucracy had met those demands.[92] One cannot imagine anything similar occurring in the Third Reich.

Science

Given the position of scientists and technologists in their culture, the Germans should have had a considerable advantage. The traditional explanation for why they did not is that anti-Semitic policies had driven many of the brightest scientific minds out of Germany. That may have been true of physicists, but plenty of first-rate scientists remained behind and were delighted to help develop sophisticated weapons for the Fatherland. Their relative lack of success was due to the same weaknesses that marked the Reich's intelligence. The foremost contributor to the difficulties faced by German science lay in the society's culture and its members' belief in their innate superiority. German scientists were as prone to such attitudes as the military. Since they believed they led in most technological and scientific areas in 1939, they found it easy to think those advantages would persist. In the aftermath of the Battle of Britain and the night Blitz, the Germans seem to have made no serious effort to examine what had gone right and wrong with their technology.

This failure marks a significant contrast between the Germans and British—and eventually the Americans. The British, believing they were behind in the scientific and technological race, paid careful attention to their opponents in an effort to bring their technological capabilities up to the level they thought the enemy possessed. Moreover, the Western Allies were thus more willing to bet on a variety of possibilities, some of which paid off.

Another significant problem with the German approach to science was that its system encouraged bureaucratic infighting and made cooperation among the services almost nonexistent. The historians Monika Renneberg and Mark Walker noted that German science resembled a "cartel of overlapping, competing and contradictory power blocks [that] effectively hindered and sometimes prevented the systematic and thorough development and implementation of specific technologies and policies."[93] In the Führer's state, egos ran wild. It explains the failure of German physicists to create a chain reaction.[94]

The divide between civilian scientists and the military only made things worse. Most German officers regarded scientists as technocrats hired to do their bidding.[95] They seldom saw the scientists as partners who might provide insights into the problems front-line forces were facing. There was none of the collaboration so essential to development of new capabilities and in some cases even tactics. On the Allied side, the case of anti-submarine warfare provides an obvious point of comparison. The physicist P. M. S. Blackett, using simple arithmetic, persuaded the British Admiralty that the perimeter of a convoy was the crucial element in deciding how many escorts were necessary to defend it; consequently, increasing the size of convoys would only marginally increase the number of escorts required.[96] The Admiralty almost immediately followed his advice.

One of the few times the German military called on civilian scientific help occurred the day before Dönitz pulled the U-boats out of the North Atlantic on 23 May 1943. He brought together a large group of scientists and asked them to develop countermeasures to the use of radar by Allied anti-submarine forces. Werner Gerlach, a leading German physicist, later noted that "this was the first and last time that the services and the scientists ever got together."[97] Unlike the Admiralty, which had a keen interest in developing a group of research scientists to advise it during the war, the Germans had no such group. To a considerable extent that was because Dönitz and his senior admirals focused almost exclusively on tactics and not on the technological changes taking place in the North Atlantic. The British and Americans, on the other hand, created an atmosphere of consistent and enthusiastic cooperation between scientists and military commands throughout the war. Scientists and technicians gained a clear understanding of what the military needed, and the military gained an understanding of what was possible. That symbiosis was a major factor in Allied success.

Germany also faced a severe shortage of industrial scientists and electrical engineers. Between 1932 and 1939, the number of students of electrical engineering in Germany dropped by half, a reflection perhaps of the emphasis on service in the Wehrmacht. By 1943, the economy was short fifty thousand electrical engineers.[98] Adding to the problem was Hitler's decision at the beginning of the war that the military and industry should support only research and development that would have an immediate impact on tactics and operations. By 1942, as a result, the Germans were behind not only in the number of weapons but in quality, particularly in the air and naval domains. The Luftwaffe and Kriegsmarine began a desperate effort to catch up, but they wasted too many resources trying to do too much, with no analysis of the costs and benefits of producing new weapons systems. The V-2 rocket is the prime example of a cost-ineffective weapons system that involved massive outlays of manpower and resources with no significant military payback.[99]

Nothing epitomizes the contribution of science more than the invention of the cavity magnetron early in the war, by the British physicists John Randall and Harry Boot. The initial push came from the British Admiralty and Air Ministry, both of which had expressed interest in the development of a radar system that worked on the 10-cm wavelength. In summer 1939, scientists at the University of Birmingham attempted to find a powerful generator for microwave radar. Neither of the two possibilities, the klystron and the magnetron, proved capable of producing sufficient power. In February 1940, two physicists, Randall and Boot, then combined the two into a workable system. The cavity magnetron allowed far more accurate depictions of aircraft flying at low levels and small targets at sea, such as surfaced U-boats, and allowed the development of smaller antennas suitable for airborne radars.

Engineers from General Electric refined the initial prototype of the cavity magnetron, and by the end of the year Fighter Command possessed a flyable radar. In November 1940, a British night fighter used airborne radar to shoot down a German bomber, but there were teething problems, and it was not until spring 1941 that night fighters achieved significant success. By April 1941, the boffins had ironed the wrinkles out of the system, and Fighter Command's night fighters began shooting down large numbers of German bombers. Between January and March 1941, radar-equipped night fighters engaged only twenty-seven bombers. In April the number increased to fifty, and in May it reached seventy-four.[100] At that point the Luftwaffe transferred its bombers to the east for Barbarossa, but the increasing effect of Fighter Command would have soon halted German night attacks anyway.

In August 1940, Churchill directed a group of eminent scientists, including Henry Tizard, to journey to the United States to exchange their newest scientific developments with the Americans. Initially, they ran into some suspicion from American scientists, until Tizard showed them the cavity magnetron. The Americans were also working on radar but were having difficulty generating sufficient power, and the cavity magnetron clearly was the answer. As the official historian of America's wartime research organization noted, it was probably "the most valuable cargo ever brought to our shores."[101] Within two months Bell Laboratories had developed a cavity magnetron that increased the output by a factor of a thousand.[102] The result in radar and other electronic weapons systems gave the Western Allies a significant advantage over the Germans.

Both scientists and RAF leaders worried that using the cavity magnetron over German-held territory would enable the Luftwaffe's scientists to unravel its secret. But when the Germans discovered one and their scientists reported its existence, they dismissed it as being of no significance in comparison to their own technology.[103] It later came as a great shock, as Guy Hartcup notes, "that the British were using microwaves. Until then the German scientific orthodoxy was skeptical of their value and no priority had been given to the production of the transmitting valves necessary for microwaves. In contrast to Allied teams of scientists who were free to handle their own affairs, the German technical staffs were frightened of being proved wrong and being exposed to ridicule. . . . There was 'no place where the *Führerprinzip* was less applicable than in the research library.'"[104]

The difference between the Germans and their opponents lay in how their political and military leaders regarded science as an asset to support the air and naval wars. Göring offered a prime example of the Nazi mindset. He once commented to his staff in discussing German radar sets, "I have frequently taken a look within such sets. It does not look all that imposing—just some wires and other bits and pieces—and the whole apparatus is remarkably primitive even then."[105] While Churchill and Roosevelt probably would not have understood much more if they disassembled a radar set, both held scientists in enormous respect, and so did most of their military leaders.

This failure to imagine what the British and eventually the Americans were achieving through scientific and technological advances was the Germans' greatest weakness. As the *Bismarck* and the *Prinz Eugen* transited the Denmark Straits in late May 1941, they ran into two British cruisers, HMS *Suffolk* and HMS *Norfolk*, the former equipped with the most up-to-date radar. Despite rain, fog, and miserable visibility, the *Suffolk* had little difficulty in maintaining a constant safe distance from the *Bismarck*'s 15-inch guns. It was clear to the German officers that the British possessed a highly effective radar, a fact they radioed to Berlin. Back came the reply that they should pay no attention to such a capability: "In the ice-cold waters of the Denmark Strait, normal hydrophones could pick up the noise from the task force's propellers."[106]

The Underpinnings of Success

One could, of course, argue that massive industrial and resource superiority, by itself, won the Second World War. But that would miss the salient fact that the war might have lasted longer, and the Germans might have had a far more severe impact in certain campaigns, like the Battle of the Atlantic, had Allied decision-making, buoyed by an imaginative use of personnel beyond the cloistered *Weltanschauung* of the military, not tipped the playing field. It was the wide use of Anglo-American resources and manpower that led to German defeat in May 1945. Soviet economic strength created a nightmarish war of attrition on the Eastern Front that kept the Germans focused in two different directions with very different challenges in each.

That the war took so long to end reflected the enormous lead in military capabilities and strength the Germans and Japanese had built up before the outbreak of the conflict. It took crushing defeats administered to the Allies to awaken the slumbering giants of the Western Powers. But the spaces and territories Germany and Japan seized in the early years of the war made the task of retrieving victory much more difficult. The fanaticism of German and Japanese nationalism made the road long and hard.

The last half of the war revealed not only the marriage of the French and Industrial Revolutions but the first stages of what would become the fifth military-social revolution. That was certainly not clear to those at the time, but by 1943 the utilization of the imponderables of imagination, intelligence, and science, combined with inherent economic strength, allowed the Allies to overwhelm the Axis Powers. Moreover, the emergence of new capabilities would alter the character of war. By the 1980s, the extent of those changes had begun to affect society and military forces in fundamental ways. The most obvious of these developments was the appearance of the atomic bomb, but the intensive work at Bletchley Park in creating analytic machines would lead to the computer and its descendants, which have had such an enormous impact on our world.

CHAPTER ELEVEN

The Air and Sea Campaigns

1942–1945

Everything in war is simple, but the simplest thing is difficult.
The difficulties accumulate and end by producing a kind of
friction that is incomprehensible unless one has experienced war.

—CARL VON CLAUSEWITZ, *On War*

IN 1942, GERMANY CONTROLLED the resources and populations of most of
Western and Central Europe and much of European Russia. The ability
to mobilize its own population and conscript those of the conquered and
neutral nations (such as Switzerland and Sweden) into the war effort explains how they held off the Allies for three and a half more years. Yet in
the end they lost, largely because the Anglo-Americans gained control of
the world's oceans and the air over Europe. How that came about is a
product of the two sides' strategic approaches.

In the largest sense, the problem with the Reich's military strategy
was the lack of overall joint-service coordination.[1] Nor was there an effort to connect means with ends, or any attempt to coordinate strategy
with the Reich's allies, which the Germans either treated as puppets
(Italy and assorted European allies) or urged to pursue operations that
made little sense (the Finns and Japanese).[2] The German history of the
war describes the Reich's strategy in the following terms: "In 1942 the

war at sea and the war on land remained without a common [strategic] conception in which goals and realizable potential would have provided the direction for the employment and *Schwehrpunkt* [focused-emphasis] of military forces."[3] Thus, the services waged independent wars. The only coordinating authority was Hitler's addled mind.

The wars at sea and in the air involved not only production and mobilization but increasing technological sophistication, which depended on the imaginative and creative use of science. As designers and factories introduced new capabilities, they found themselves in competition in a world dominated by constant improvements in weapons systems. The Industrial Revolution had become a matter of innovation and adaptation as well as production. Over its last three and a half years, World War II separated into three theaters: the air and naval struggle between the Western Powers and Germany; the Eastern Front, with its murderous war of attrition between the Wehrmacht and the Red Army; and the Pacific, with the struggle between the navies of the United States and Japan. All three of these struggles involved the ideological commitment of the combatants, but in the end the outcome was decided by industrial and economic power.

In the west, Allied navies struggled to hold open the SLOCs across the Atlantic to Britain and the Mediterranean while the CBO attempted to break the will and industrial might of Nazi Germany. The contest was one in which science, technology, adaptation, and intelligence dominated and in the long term changed the nature of human society. The Eastern Front, on the other hand, was much like the First World War except that the opposing forces possessed far greater mechanized mobility. Its battles featured massed firepower and an enormous attrition of men and material.

The war in the Pacific escaped the massive attrition battles on land that marked the fighting between the Germans and the Soviets but only because the Pacific islands limited the size of both Japanese garrisons and American amphibious assaults. Nevertheless, by 1942 the Pacific war was already one of material attrition. As it spiraled toward conclusion, the battles and casualties increased, Okinawa providing a nightmarish foretaste of what an invasion of the Japanese Home Islands would have entailed.

With the opening of the Red Army archives after the Soviet Union's collapse, the war's narrative has increasingly emphasized the Eastern Front as the war's decisive battleground. Moreover, historians have shown increasing distaste for the CBO, which the current narrative depicts as a murderous assault on Germany's civilian population—which it was. Yet to judge by their allocation of resources, the Germans saw the CBO as a greater threat than the war in the east. A recent study shows that in the last two years of the war, "The *Luftwaffe* received more than half of German production. When one adds to this the enormous German effort in anti-aircraft construction from 1943 onwards, the vast majority of which was for the air war over Germany, approximately 60 percent of the German [economy went to production of] aircraft and anti-aircraft weaponry when munitions output reached its peak."[4] If we add the Kriegsmarine's expenditure of resources in the Battle of the Atlantic, the German focus on the war in the west reached well over 60 percent.

The first and most important campaign the Anglo-American Allies had to win was the Battle of the Atlantic. Without victory in that arena, the CBO could not have received the fuel, munitions, raw materials, and supplies on which it depended, and the Americans and British could not have built up the ground forces and supplies for their campaigns in North Africa, Sicily, Italy, and eventually northwest Europe. Following victory in the Atlantic, the CBO proved vital in capping expansion of the German war economy. Moreover, the defeat of the Luftwaffe enabled the Allies to gain air superiority over northern France and Belgium. In effect, the CBO forced the Germans to expend much of their war economy's effort on defending the homeland, measures that contributed little to damage the strategic approach of the Anglo-Americans.

The Battle of the Atlantic

The Battle of the Atlantic, the longest campaign of the Second World War, began on 3 September 1939 and ended on 7 May 1945. It was to prove the great enabler of Anglo-American military operation. Success in the war to control the SLOCs across the Atlantic kept Britain in the war, enabled the flow of Lend-Lease to the Soviet Union, supported the CBO, and provided the logistical base on which the campaign in northwest Europe rested.

Britain's survival depended on America's ability to project economic and military power across the Atlantic.[5] The year 1941 had been unsatisfactory for U-boats. After a period of rising success in the first six months, the Germans ran into a period during which the convoys had disappeared. After a supposedly thorough examination of signals security, the Germans dismissed the possibility the British had broken the Enigma, which in fact they had. Also starting in spring 1941, anti-submarine defenses surrounding the British Isles, particularly RAF Coastal Command's aircraft, had caused increasing losses of U-boats. Karl Dönitz found it necessary to send his boats farther into the Atlantic, where Ultra allowed the British to maneuver convoys away from where the U-boats were concentrated.

The battle that occurred around convoy HG 76 in December 1941 gave a clear warning that the tactical and technological framework of the struggle in the North Atlantic was also beginning to swing against the U-boats. Convoys sailing from Gibraltar to Britain were always vulnerable, as the Spanish informed the Germans of all shipping arriving and leaving the Rock. The British Admiralty therefore provided an especially strong escort of two sloops and seven corvettes with three destroyers on attachment to the convoy. In charge was Commander F. J. Walker, the greatest killer of U-boats in the war. The Admiralty also provided its first escort carrier, HMS *Audacity*, which was not under Walker's command.[6]

On 14 December, the convoy sortied. Two days out, the destroyer *Nestor* caught *U 127* and sank it. The next day, one of the *Audacity*'s aircraft sighted another U-boat and attacked it; the Germans shot the aircraft down. But escorts arrived almost immediately and sank *U 131*. On the 18th, HMS *Stanley*, using its ASDIC, caught *U 434* and forced it to the surface, where its crew scuttled it. Early the next morning U-boats torpedoed and sank the *Stanley*, exacting a measure of revenge. But Walker then counterattacked, and after driving the *U 574* to the surface, rammed and sank it. On the night of the 21st, the escort carrier pulled out of the convoy despite Walker's warnings that the ship would be better protected within it. *U 751* caught the *Audacity* and sank it, and two and a half hours later Walker's escorts destroyed *U 567*. With the loss of a fifth U-boat, Dönitz gave up and pulled his boats off. Altogether the convoy had lost one merchant vessel, one destroyer, and one escort carrier, the last due to the captain's ignorance.[7]

Over the summer of 1941, Raeder and Dönitz, displaying how little they had learned from the last war, attempted to persuade Hitler to declare war on the United States so U-boats could attack North America's East Coast. Astonishingly, despite their eagerness to take on the United States, the Kriegsmarine had done little to prepare for such a campaign. Even amid worsening relations with the Americans, Hitler had directed the OKW to force Dönitz to deploy twenty-three boats to the Mediterranean and sixteen to Norway. Since the Germans had only ninety-three operational U-boats at the time, these efforts, which achieved little, represented a significant drain on forces.[8]

Nevertheless, after Hitler's declaration of war on the United States, Dönitz immediately launched Operation "Drumbeat" with five type IX boats to attack America's East Coast, while Type VIIs with limited range would operate off Newfoundland and Halifax. The results were spectacular: within two weeks, the five Type IXs had sunk 15 ships of 97,242 gross register tonnage (GRT). In February 1942, a second group of long-range boats began operating in the Caribbean to strike tanker traffic. By March these boats had sunk 23 ships of 64,492 GRT. In May, eighteen U-boats were operating off the East Coast and eight more in the Caribbean. The result was a disaster for Allied shipping. Between January and July, U-boats sank 3,040,089 GRT of shipping while losing only 23 boats.[9] German submariners titled the period the second "happy time." Beyond American incompetence, the Germans enjoyed an advantage with the addition of a fourth rotor to Enigma at the beginning of 1942, which prevented the British from breaking into U-boat transmissions for the rest of the year.

How to explain this disaster? There were exculpating factors. The desperate situation in the Pacific left the U.S. Navy with few resources for the U-boat war. Moreover, the navy had to escort two major troop transports across the Atlantic, one to Iceland and one to Northern Ireland. But the Americans also made little effort to utilize British intelligence and failed to organize convoys in the belief that without sufficient escorts, convoys would be of little use. British experience counseled the opposite. Of ships not in convoys, 20 percent went to the bottom. Of those lucky enough to find themselves in a convoy, the U-boats sank only 4 percent.[10] Not surprisingly, the British were furious about the losses. In spring 1942, they sent Rodger Winn, head of the Admiralty's U-boat tracking center, to Washington to force the Americans to pay attention to the U-boat menace. Historian Patrick Beesley notes that when Chief of Naval Operations Ernest J. King's chief of staff, Rear Admiral Richard Edwards, told Winn that "the Americans wished to learn their own lessons," Winn caustically replied, "The trouble is, admiral, it's not only your bloody ships you're losing: a lot of them are ours."[11]

Adding to Allied troubles, in February 1942 the Germans reconstructed much of the Allied Cypher No. 3, used for routing convoys in the North Atlantic. They could thus read 80 percent of that message traffic over 1942. That intelligence success came just as Bletchley Park lost its ability to read U-boat message traffic. For once, the U-boats had significant intelligence as to the movement of Allied convoys. Under pressure from Army Chief of Staff George Marshall—and probably the president as well—King finally turned to the Atlantic in April.[12] Establishment of an intelligence center, like the British one at Bletchley Park, represented a first step. The creation of convoys on the East Coast and in the Caribbean as well as provision of additional aircraft also had a significant impact. Moreover, in April, the Americans began a crash program to build sixty escort vessels in sixty days. But simply providing more escort vessels and aircraft was not enough; the solution to the U-boat threat lay in integrating new technological aids such as improved sonar and depth charges, sophisticated radars that could identify U-boats on the surface, and other anti-submarine weapons—and training the escorts to use them effectively.

By July, better Allied defenses along the East Coast and Caribbean caused sinkings to drop by a third, while Dönitz lost ten boats that month versus only four in May.[13] By this point, American defenses as well as the travel required to reach U.S. waters were making North America less attractive for U-boats, and Dönitz moved the U-boat focus back to the mid-Atlantic. By then the number of U-boats had risen to 330, but only 138 were on operations, the remainder either working up or sidetracked for training. Given that at any time at least a third of available boats were undergoing refit and a third were transiting to and from operating areas, Dönitz had fewer than fifty boats at the sharp end.

Moreover, the growing number of long-range aircraft available to anti-submarine forces was shrinking the areas where convoys had no air cover. That patrol aircraft possessed more sophisticated radar made them more deadly. The battle thus returned to the North Atlantic, but by October the U-boats could not sink more ships there than on North America's coasts. Even Dönitz saw the writing on the wall. He noted that Allied aircraft, which now reached far into the North Atlantic, would soon threaten the whole U-boat campaign.[14]

By fall, the number of U-boats had increased as the training logjam eased, while the intelligence effort to break German codes proceeded. In late 1942, recognizing that the Germans had compromised the codes, the British radically improved their cyphers for convoys. At the same time, Bletchley Park broke back into U-boat cyphers. By early 1943, Dönitz was so worried by British knowledge of the location of U-boats that he asked that the security of U-boat cyphers be reexamined. A committee led by the head of German signals examined the problem and reported that "the enemy is not decrypting, not even partially decrypting" U-boat traffic. It argued that since German code breakers had difficulty breaking into British codes, it was inconceivable that their opponents, given their technological inferiority, could have any greater success.[15]

August 1942 saw the Germans refocus on the North Atlantic's air gap. That month, 18 U-boats attacked convoy SC 94 and sank a third of the 34 ships, for a total tonnage of 53,421. But the price was steep. The Germans lost two boats, and the escorts seriously damaged four more.[16] Moreover, they were still struggling to find convoys. Between August and December, even with intelligence gleaned from their code breakers, U-boats sighted only 34 percent of the convoys crossing the North Atlantic and were able to attack only 14 percent; bad weather, the convoys' locations, and increasing effectiveness of escort forces protected the rest.[17]

But if the Germans had difficulties in the North Atlantic, Dönitz's boats achieved tactical successes in the convoy routes rounding the Cape of Good Hope to supply British forces in the Middle East. In October 1942, U-boats sank 156,235 tons of Allied shipping in that area, and in November and December they added 25 ships and 134,780 tons. Significantly, there was no cooperation with the Japanese, who might have played a major role in attacking the SLOCs circumnavigating southern Africa. Moreover, the Germans only turned to southern Africa late in the game. Thus, those sinkings came too late to affect resupply of the British Eighth Army and preparations for the Battle of El Alamein, which took place in late October. That failure reflected the German services' inability to see the larger war in joint operational terms.[18] They never considered how operations in one area might improve the operational possibilities of a fellow service in another area.

By January 1943, Dönitz had at his disposal 212 front-line boats, of which 164 were assigned to the North Atlantic. Only 50 or so were ready to conduct operations at any given time. Winter of 1942–1943 brought exceptionally harsh weather to the North Atlantic, making it difficult to conduct U-boat attacks.[19] Even so, March 1943 proved the darkest period for the Allies. Between 6 and 11 March, U-boats caught two eastbound convoys and sank 16 ships with a tonnage of 79,836 GRT. A week later, they caught two more convoys, one fast and one slow, proceeding to Britain in the gap where no air cover existed, and sank 21 ships with a tonnage of 140,842 GRT, while the escorts sank only a single submarine.[20] Over the course of that month the Allies lost 70 ships, 60 in convoy, for a loss of 646,937 tons.[21] Given the heavy losses, some in the Admiralty even suggested the need to abandon the convoy system.

Yet two months later, the U-boat force suffered a catastrophe that pushed Dönitz to admit defeat and pull his boats out of the battle. Even in February and March, losses were reaching unsustainable levels, with thirty-six U-boats sunk. On 4 May, the westbound convoy ONS 5, protected by seven escort vessels, found itself under attack by forty U-boats. In two days, the Germans sank 11 ships of 55,760 tons. But fog descended on the night of the 5th. The escorts' radar allowed them to pick out the U-boats while the Germans, without radar, were blind. By morning the Germans had lost five boats.[22] It was the beginning of a disastrous month in which they lost forty-one boats, twenty-nine in the North Atlantic. Between May and October 1943, Allied escort vessels and aircraft sank 135 U-boats. In the three and a quarter years before then they had sunk only 153.[23]

What had happened? On the technological side, escort forces had received the aids the Allies had been developing since 1940—an indication of the importance of long-term research and development. Direction-finding equipment was now available on board escort vessels, so that anti-submarine forces could locate U-boat transmissions in their area, while the new 271M radar allowed escorts to see through fog and the night. But the greatest boon was the presence of air cover, either from escort carriers or from long-range aircraft flying out of Iceland, Gander, or Newfoundland. Here, increasing American production had reached the tipping point.[24]

Other factors also favored the Allies. Operations research had come into its own. Analysis by researchers under Patrick Blackett, assigned to Coastal Command, refined the tactics and weaponry its aircraft used in attacking U-boats. Notably, leaders in Central Command and the Royal Navy's Western Approaches Command listened to him. By persuading the command to switch weapons from 100-pound bombs to 450-pound depth charges, Blackett's team increased lethality of air attacks. By shortening spacing between depth charges and setting them to explode at a twenty-five-foot depth, they increased the effectiveness of attacks on the surface by a factor of *ten*.[25] Through to the war's end, operational research teams consisting of scientists, mathematicians, and even actuaries provided substantial help in making escort forces more effective. There was no equivalent on the German side.

Equally important, production of merchant shipping in the United States was hitting high gear. Between 1941 and 1945, 18 American yards constructed and outfitted 2,708 Liberty ships, a number that overwhelmed the German U-boat offensive.[26] Despite the hopeless situation, Dönitz persisted in sending obsolete Type VIIs and IXs out into the Atlantic to be slaughtered by Allied escort forces. In 1944, the Germans sank 31 ships but lost 111 U-boats. The figure for the five months of 1945 was even more dismal: 19 Allied ships sunk at a cost of 71 boats.

The Combined Bomber Offensive

The war in the air represented one of the Industrial Revolution's most important contributions to military operations in World War II. It demanded the mobilization of population and industrial resources on a scale that dwarfed those of the last war. The result was not decisive victories but a long, slogging match reminiscent of the attrition battles of Verdun, the Somme, and Passchendaele but more costly in material and resources. Casualties were less, but they involved volunteers, men of high intelligence and commitment. Moreover, the CBO targeted not only the Reich's factories and industrial infrastructure but the German population as well.

In June 1941, Churchill asked the chief of the air staff, Sir Charles Portal, about the possibility of creating long-range escort fighters. Portal answered that such a fighter could never hold its own against short-range fighters. Churchill's reply was that such a view closed many doors.[27] In fact, the RAF already possessed a fighter, the Spitfire, capable of becoming a long-range fighter. In 1941, photo-reconnaissance versions of the Spitfire were already flying missions deep into Germany.[28] In late 1943, General Henry "Hap" Arnold, commander of the U.S. Army Air Forces, found himself worried about the survival of American bombers against Germany.[29] On 22 March 1944, at his request, two new Spitfires arrived at Wright Field for modification by American engineers. Within forty-seven days they had sufficiently extended the aircraft's range that they qualified as long-range escort fighters. In early July, those two Spitfires flew across the Atlantic and landed at Boscombe Downs. The Americans had proven that "essentially, it had always been possible to significantly extend the range of the Spitfire despite the claims of the RAF otherwise." Astonishingly, RAF leaders still refused to believe the Spitfire possessed long-range possibilities.[30]

Throughout the war, that lack of imagination relegated the RAF Bomber Command to bombing almost exclusively at night, making it extraordinarily difficult to identify targets. Not until the Butt report of summer 1941 indicated that only one in three crews could hit within an area of seventy-five square miles did RAF leaders take serious interest in technological aides to bombing.[31] Bomber Command's culture as well as capabilities began to change in January 1942, when Air Marshal Arthur Harris assumed command. Crucial to improved capabilities were the appearance of Lancaster bombers and navigational aids, such as Gee, to find targets.

When Harris assumed his position, Bomber Command had limited numbers and types of aircraft. Yet it inflicted substantial damage in spring 1942 on Lubeck and Rostock, both of which were easily identified by their coastal locations and had central areas filled with medieval wooden buildings that were very flammable. In May 1942, Harris launched his bombers, augmented by planes from Coastal Command and RAF training squadrons, in a thousand-aircraft raid on Cologne. The large fleet of bombers swamped German defenses and wrecked much of the city while suffering minimal casualties. Photo reconnaissance showed that the raid had destroyed 600 acres, 300 of them at the city's center, with the dead numbering close to 1,000.[32]

Hitler was furious, especially after the Luftwaffe underestimated the attacking force and termed the battle a victory. Berating the Luftwaffe's chief of staff, Hans Jeschonnek, the Führer ridiculed the defensive effort and quite accurately opined that the raid indicated the British were planning to open a second front. But he then added that the only answer to such raids would have to be terror raids, a strategic approach he forced on the Luftwaffe and which severely limited its ability to defend the Reich.[33] Despite the successes of the attacks on Lubeck, Rostock, and Cologne, however, Bomber Command's efforts were simply not effective over the remainder of 1942. Hitler lost his focus on the threat. However, by fall 1942, the waging of a war on three major fronts was taking a heavy toll on the Luftwaffe. From January to October, it had lost 5,793 aircraft, equivalent to 91.5 percent of its force strength at year's outset. Combat operations damaged a further 4,248 aircraft.[34]

In November, the encirclement of Stalingrad and the Anglo-American invasion of North Africa exacerbated the pressures on the Luftwaffe. On the Eastern Front, the Germans lost 961 aircraft in November and December, while losses in other theaters—mainly the Mediterranean—

reached 682 aircraft.[35] Göring's commitment of the Luftwaffe to supply the Stalingrad pocket only increased the losses. But just as serious was the deployment of major air units to North Africa to meet Allied forces attacking Tunisia from the west. The German aircraft industry could barely replace what the combat squadrons were losing, while the size of the air forces opposing them steadily grew. In January 1943, Luftwaffe front-line fighter squadrons possessed 80.3 percent of authorized strength and the bomber squadrons 71.3 percent. By late August those percentages had dropped to 71 and 56 percent, respectively. German aircraft losses in the Mediterranean that month reached 1,032 aircraft and on the Eastern Front 998. At that point, American daylight strategic bombing swung into gear, creating a steadily growing air threat that left the Germans able to do little more than defend the Reich.[36] For the remainder of the war, Wehrmacht ground forces rarely saw German aircraft.

Through 1942, the RAF's Bomber Command was steadily increasing its capabilities. Its raids had not achieved notable successes over the year, but in the late winter and spring of 1943 it made a series of major attacks on the Ruhr. Harris's aim was to "dehouse" the German population. Hitler's response was twofold. He demanded that the Luftwaffe pay the British back in kind, meaning that German bomber production continued at current rates, at the expense of any increase in fighter production. And he demanded increases in Flak production despite objections that anti-aircraft artillery was cost ineffective against high-altitude bombers, especially in comparison to night fighters.[37]

The expansion of the heavy Flak forces, driven by the Führer's wishes, represented a significant economic and military drain throughout the war.[38] The number of heavy batteries rose from 791 in 1940 to 1,148 in 1942, and 2,655 in early 1944. With four artillery pieces in each battery, the number of heavy guns (88mm, 105mm, and 120mm) rose from 4,292 to 10,620. In addition, there were 1,612 light Flak batteries, most also assigned to defending the Reich. The damage that Flak caused to Allied bombers was not insignificant, yet unlike the underfunded fighters, the barrage of the anti-aircraft fire never threatened to defeat the CBO. Slightly more than 20 percent of the Eighth Air Force's returning aircraft suffered Flak damage, but most were repairable.[39]

The effort to man the Flak forces represents one of the major unintended effects of the bombing. By 1944, over 1 million Germans were participating in or supporting the Flak effort. About half were civilians, but without the bomber offensive, Germany certainly could have utilized them more profitably. The cost of the anti-aircraft effort in equipment and ammunition had an equally large negative impact. In 1944 alone, between 25 and 27 percent of resources went to production of anti-aircraft weapons. About 18.5 percent of monthly German ammunition production went to the Flak forces.[40]

As the weight of bombing increased, the Germans turned to the world's first cruise and ballistic missiles, the V-1 and V-2, the *Vergeltungswaffen* (Revenge Weapons). Those efforts sucked up substantial production capacity that could have gone to manufacturing day and night fighters, and to building precision electronics crucial for electronic systems. In retrospect, the V-1 forced the Allies to make a major effort in attacking the launching sites the Germans were constructing, but V-2 had difficulty even in hitting cities.

The damage inflicted by Bomber Command in the Battle of the Ruhr in spring 1943 was on a scale not previously seen in the air war.[41] But the British paid a heavy price: in forty-three major attacks, the RAF lost 872 bombers with a further 2,126 damaged.[42] In June, satisfied he had done sufficient damage to the Ruhr, Harris turned against Hamburg. Given the heavy losses in the Battle of the Ruhr, he decided to employ what the British called "Window"—thin strips of aluminum cut to a certain length that when picked up by German radar gave the same return as a bomber.

The second raid on Hamburg turned out to be the equivalent of a perfect storm: Window blinded the defenses, the weather was warm and dry, and the first markers dropped by pathfinders landed in the middle of the largest lumber yard in Germany.[43] The ensuing fires made a precise target for follow-on bombers. The result was a firestorm in which temperatures reached 1,500 degrees Fahrenheit with winds of 250 miles per hour. The bombing and firestorm killed some 40,000 Germans and inflicted damage on an extraordinary scale: out of 122,000 apartments, 40,000 were damaged or destroyed; out of 450,000 houses, 250,000. The raid knocked out 75 percent of the electric works, 60 percent of the water system, and 90 percent of the gas system. Factory production fell by 40 percent for large firms and 80 percent for medium and small firms. Albert Speer informed Hitler that six more attacks like that would bring German armaments to a halt. But the conditions were never again as perfect for Bomber Command until Dresden in February 1945.[44]

In late fall 1943, Harris determined to launch a massive assault on Berlin. That November he penned a note to Churchill underlining his

rationale. He listed nineteen German cities as almost completely destroyed, nineteen others seriously damaged, and a further nine partially
damaged. He concluded that "we can wreck Berlin from end to end if the
USAAF [U.S. Army Air Force, i.e., the Eighth Air Force] will come in on
it. It will cost us between 400–500 aircraft. It will cost Germany the
war."[45]

But Harris was wrong; he could not have selected a more difficult target. Berlin lay deep inside Germany, and it contained a great metropolitan
area. Moreover, German defenses had improved considerably. From December 1943 through early March 1944, Bomber Command waged a piti-
less effort to destroy the German capital. It damaged Berlin but suffered
appalling losses. Four months of the battle cost the command no less than
966 bombers. The head of the pathfinder force, Air Marshal D. C. T. Bennett, noted after the war that the Battle of Berlin was "the worst thing that
could have happened to the command."[46] By March, Harris was forced to
call off the offensive against Berlin.

The U.S. Eighth Air Force had begun arriving in force in spring
1943. Its commander, Lieutenant General Ira Eaker, was not enthusiastic
about using long-range escort fighters to support deep raids into the
Reich. Unlike their British cousins, however, the Americans intended to
bomb during the daytime in the belief that heavily armed B-17s and
B-24s could fight off German fighters while suffering, in the euphemism
of the day, "acceptable losses." American doctrine aimed at attacking key
sectors of the German war economy, such as ball-bearing plants, synthetic oil and rubber factories, the transportation network, and the electric grid, the destruction of any one of which would reverberate through
the Nazi economy.[47]

In late spring and early summer of 1943, the Eighth's efforts reached
into the western portions of the Reich. Operations in June and July
tested German defenses, and American bombers suffered heavy losses.
On 22 June, the Eighth struck the I. G. Farben synthetic rubber plant at
Hüls and lost twenty bombers (6.7% of the attacking force). That attack
was one of the most successful of the war: it shut down the plant for a
month and left the German military with a one-and-a-half-month supply
of rubber. Unfortunately, as in the raid on the Ruhr's dams, the bombers
did not return, and the Germans repaired the damage. In March 1944,
after desperate efforts, Hüls reached its peak production.[48]

By August 1943, the Eighth reached a level where Eaker believed it
possessed sufficient B-17s to attempt raids deep in Germany. The first

such raid involved half the force attacking the ball-bearing factories at Schweinfurt before returning to England, while the lead formation flew on to Regensburg to attack a Messerschmitt factory that was producing Bf 109s.[49] Losses were heavy. The Regensburg force, led by Curtis LeMay, lost 24 B-17s out of 146 dispatched (a loss rate of 16.4%).[50] The second force lost 36 out of 230 (15.7%). In total, the raid cost the Eighth 10.3 percent of its bombers, an unacceptable loss rate by any standard.

The damage inflicted on the Schweinfurt factories appeared impressive. However, the Americans were only using five-hundred-pound bombs, which knocked most buildings down. Nevertheless, the bombs only partially damaged machine tools lying underneath. The raid did decrease ball-bearing production significantly. What the Americans had not calculated on were several factors that helped the Germans avoid a crisis: most factories possessed an emergency supply of ball bearings; roller bearings in some cases could substitute for ball bearings; and the Swedes, always helpful to the Nazi regime, stepped in to help meet German needs.[51] The Regensburg raid was more successful: it inflicted heavy damage on the Messerschmitt factory so that the production loss was approximately three hundred Bf 109s for the month.[52]

However, the Schweinfurt-Regensburg raid proved so costly that the Eighth did not again venture deep into Germany until October. The Luftwaffe had two months to repair the damage and disperse the ball-bearing industry before the Eighth returned. Major deep-penetration raids began again on 8 October with attacks on Bremen and Vegesack. On 10 October, the Eighth attacked Münster. Relays of German fighters attacked the lead formations on the way into and out from the target. Not one of the 100th Bombardment Group's twelve B-17s, the lead formation, returned. Out of 119 bombers in the first wave the Germans shot down 29 (24.4%).[53] For the next three days, the command stood down.

On the 14th, the Eighth returned to Schweinfurt. German fighters savaged the B-17s on the way in and out. By the time the survivors escaped, the Eighth had had 60 bombers shot down, 17 irreparably damaged on return, with 121 aircraft damaged but reparable. The loss rate was 20.7 percent and damage rate was 47.4 percent. For the week, the Eighth had lost 148 bombers in deep-penetration raids.[54] In the face of what appears to have been a crew mutiny, Eaker shut down deep-penetration raids until February 1944. Yet the American raids had achieved significant successes. An attack on the Folke Wolfe plant at Marienburg destroyed approximately one hundred new Fw 190s on the ground.[55]

The second raid on Schweinfurt was more effective than the first. It knocked out 67 percent of Schweinfurt's production capacity and caused serious reverberations throughout the war economy. Speer was forced to initiate another crash program, in this case to disperse the bearings industry and find substitutes.[56] Moreover, German losses in fighter aircraft and crews were also substantial. By April 1943, the Luftwaffe was losing 16 percent of its operational fighter pilots in front-line squadrons each month, and it continued to do so through November, when American deep-penetration raids finally let up.[57] The losses in Bf 109s and Fw 190s were even higher than pilot losses, reaching 41.9 percent in October.[58]

The attrition rate for the Eighth Air Force over the last half of 1943 was heavy. Losses of B-17s beginning in May 1943 ran at over 20 percent per month with the exception of September and November, as losses in August forced Eaker to cease deep-penetration raids and loss rates dropped to 15.6 percent in September and 18.9 percent in November. But it was crew losses that underlined the cost of the air war: May, 37.6 percent crew loss; June, 38.3 percent; July, 34.7 percent; August, 31.3 percent; September, 20.3 percent; October, 37.4 percent.[59] Nevertheless, despite high losses, the American factories and training bases continued turning out so many new aircraft and crews that their output more than offset these horrific numbers. In May 1943, there were 340 B-17s available in front-line squadrons. Seven months later that number had risen to 1,057. The number of operational crews rose from 140 in May 1943 to 949 in December.[60]

The Americans returned to deep-penetration raids in February 1944 with the arrival of the long-range escort fighter, the P-51, the finest piston engine fighter of the war.[61] In a Christmas message to the Eighth, Arnold stated the mission for 1944: "Destroy the enemy air force wherever you find them, in the air, on the ground, and in the factories."[62] Arnold also shipped Eaker off to command Allied Air Forces in the Mediterranean and replaced him with Lieutenant General Jimmy Doolittle. General Carl "Tooey" Spaatz assumed command of all American strategic bombers in Europe.

The weather cleared at the end of the third week of February 1944, allowing the Eighth to begin a week of intensive operations. With 329 P-51Bs, it could provide fighter coverage deep into the Reich. On 20 February, the Americans launched a multitarget series of raids on the Luftwaffe's aircraft industry. Over 1,000 B-17s and B-24s sortied, covered by a force of 835 escort fighters while over German-held territory.

The week that followed saw a series of massed raids, nearly all targeting the aircraft industry. The Luftwaffe came up with everything it had to protect its manufacturing base. Thus began a massive, three-month battle of attrition.

Bombing attacks on the German aircraft industry retarded production while the fighter force suffered unsustainable losses. A deciphered message reported, "The extraordinary difficult situation in the air defense of the homeland requires with all emphasis: (1) The speedy salvage of all fighters and heavy fighters [Bf 110s] and their immediate return for repair. (2) The unrestricted employment of salvage personnel for salvage tasks. . . . (3) That spare parts be acquired by repair and salvage units by removal from aircraft worth salvaging only in case of absolute necessity. (4) That repair of aircraft in your area be energetically speeded up."[63] The number of bombers lost by the Eighth underlined the impact of America's productivity: 211 in January, 299 in February, 349 in March, and 409 in April (1,268 altogether).[64]

In effect, the bombers were the bait that pulled the Luftwaffe's fighters up to fight. Its losses swelled each month: from 30.3 percent of fighters in January to 56.4 percent in March, and 43 percent in April.[65] But what broke the Luftwaffe's fighter force was the impact of pilot losses. Most of the pilots killed or wounded were from among the least experienced, but the fighting inevitably took its toll on the more experienced. From January 1944, with the loss of 12.1 percent of fighter pilots in front-line squadrons, losses rose to 17.9 percent in February, 21.7 percent in March, 20.1 percent in April, and 25 percent in May. Over that five-month period, the Luftwaffe's fighter force averaged 2,383 pilots on duty each month; during that period, it lost 2,262 killed, wounded, or missing.[66] An eighteen-year-old German in 1942 stood a better chance of surviving by joining the Waffen SS and fighting in the east than by becoming a fighter pilot.

In May 1944, the Luftwaffe's fighter defenses broke, and the Allies gained air superiority over Western Europe and Germany. American bomber losses dropped. While bombing the Reich was never a cakewalk, the threat to bombers was now more from Flak than from fighters. Ironically, the Germans increased the number of single-engine fighters produced, but that was only because they stopped manufacturing other types of aircraft; thus, the weight of production increased by only 20 percent, an insignificant amount.[67] Moreover, two other factors made the increase in fighter production a nonfactor. The first was that these aircraft were so badly made as to be a danger to those who flew them. Second, those coming out of the flying schools had received so few hours of training in combat aircraft that they could only serve as fodder for Allied fighter pilots.

British and American commanders of the strategic bombers turned to two new focuses in the bombing campaign: an offensive against the German oil industry and another against the transportation network in northern France. Eisenhower's chief deputy, Air Marshal Arthur Tedder, devised a plan with his chief scientist Solly Zuckerman to use air power to destroy railroads and major bridges in the Low Countries and northern France to prevent the Wehrmacht from reinforcing the beachhead in Normandy faster than the Allies.[68] Bomber leaders were reluctant to embark on such a campaign, largely because of their fixation, almost ideological, on bombing German cities and industry. Spaatz opposed it because it would divert the Eighth's bombers from the mission of attacking German industry. Harris argued that Bomber Command was so inaccurate its attacks would kill tens of thousands of civilians.

Churchill, not surprisingly, worried about how the killing of French civilians might affect Britain's postwar relations with France. But Charles de Gaulle ended that argument by saying he cared not how many French the bombing killed if it contributed to freeing France. In the end, Eisenhower went to his political masters, who made it clear that Overlord took precedence over all other missions. Ironically, Bomber Command, using its technologies and tactics, proved better able to destroy precise targets in France and Belgium than did American daylight bombing.

On 1 April 1944, the Allied air campaign began its campaign against the road and rail network in the Low Countries and northern France. It was a major success. By early June the bombing had shut down nearly the whole rail system west of Paris. On 3 June, the German military authorities reported that "as a result [of the bombing] it is only by exerting the greatest efforts that purely military traffic and goods essential to the war effort . . . can be kept moving. . . . The [enemy's purpose is to] completely wreck [the rail network]. Local and through traffic is to be made impossible, and all efforts to restore the services are to be prevented."[69] The destruction that Allied air power inflicted on the transportation network made movement of Nazi reserves to Normandy extraordinarily difficult.[70] For example, the 2nd SS Panzer Division, "Das Reich," took two weeks to arrive there from Limoges, when it should have taken a few days.[71] Along the way it murdered hundreds of French civilians, including the massacre of 643 at Oradour sur Glane.

The Eighth directed its other major attacks against the synthetic oil industry. The Fifteenth Air Force, based in southern Italy, supplemented with raids on Romanian oilfields. On 12 May 1944, Spaatz launched 935 B-17s and B-24s against seven major synthetic fuel producing plants. Follow-on attacks occurred on 28 May, and in June he launched a series of major raids on the German oil industry. Through to the war's end Enigma intercepts kept the Americans informed of attempts to repair the damage. An intelligence officer, handling Ultra at the Eighth, noted that intercepts indicating fuel shortages were general and not local convinced "all concerned that the air offensive had uncovered a weak spot in the German economy and led to the exploitation of this weakness to the fullest extent."[72] By mid-June German production of aviation fuel had dropped by 90 percent; by the end of July the Americans had knocked out 98 percent of production.[73] Matters were not better with the production of other fuels. From August through October, production ran well under 50 percent.[74]

Militarily, the raids deep into German territory continued the destruction of the Luftwaffe and prevented a reconstitution of German air power. The pressure also kept the Me 262 jet fighter from becoming anything more than a nuisance.[75] Once the Allies had won air superiority by May 1944, the Germans had no options except to dig in and die. The losses suffered by opposing sides in the air war over Germany and France explain how Professor Phillips O'Brien came up with his estimate that the Germans devoted over 60 percent of their resources to the air war in the west against the Anglo-American powers.[76] Each aircraft the opposing sides built and then lost required a greater input in terms of worker skills, technological sophistication, tolerances in terms of engine design and performance, and expenses involved in production than the most sophisticated armored fighting vehicles. When added to the cost of training programs in aircraft and fuel expended, one realizes the cost of the air war.

One also needs to add the peripheral effects of having in excess of ten thousand high-velocity artillery pieces firing at the aircraft flying over Germany.[77] The construction of anti-aircraft weapons alone took up 28 percent of the German weapons budget.[78] Finally, the CBO motivated the Germans to pursue the enormously costly V-1 and V-2 programs. The U.S. Strategic Bombing Survey estimated that their expenditures in raw materials and instrumentation for these rockets could have bought them 24,000 fighters.[79]

In the end, the CBO was a costly and messy effort, but it was crucial in Nazi Germany's defeat. It had a symbiotic relationship with the fighting on the Eastern Front. On one hand, the bombing campaigns forced the Germans to expend immense resources to defend their homeland from destruction. The number of soldiers tied up in the anti-aircraft forces and their weapons suggests the contribution the CBO made to the Red Army's operations. On the other hand, the ferocity of the fighting on the Eastern Front limited the effort the Germans could devote to the Reich's defense. The CBO "was not elegant, it was not humane, but it was effective."[80]

War of Attrition

The naval and air wars in the Mediterranean, in the Atlantic, and over Europe determined the war's outcome. Two critical aspects of Allied superiority provided the support that won the wars in the air and at sea: first, using a combination of science and technology to improve capabilities, and second, the productive capabilities of sophisticated economic systems. In addition, the creation of operational research to systematically address the U-boat menace in the Battle of the Atlantic and to use submarines against the Japanese gave the Allies an enormous advantage.[81] On one hand, the war in the west between the Germans and Anglo-American powers was a war of the future, where science and technology dominated. On the other, the war in the east resembled the First World War but with the greater firepower and maneuverability.

The Anglophone nations' control of the world's oceans gave them the immense advantage of access to raw materials. From the German point of view, the effort to expand the Luftwaffe occurred as the roof was falling in. By placing so much hope in the idea that will, tactical effectiveness, efficiency, and innovation could triumph over superior numbers, Germany demanded of itself that it fight three kinds of war against three of the world's great industrial powers. But it failed on the ground, at sea, and in the air. Part of the reason was that its superiority in certain areas was illusory: its supposed efficiency was hampered by politics, vindictiveness, and adherence to tradition, and its supposed advantage in innovation rested on false ideas of hierarchy and racial supremacy that in fact undermined its ability to innovate.

Perhaps the greatest irony of the war was that victory ultimately boiled down to the attrition of men and machinery on both sides. It also involved massive assaults on the economies of the opposing sides. The German U-boats waged a flawed effort to strangle the British economy and people. On the other side, the Anglo-American war against the Reich's economy and population came at an extraordinarily high cost for victors as well as the losers. Over 60 percent of Bomber Command's crews had died on active operations by the war's end.

CHAPTER TWELVE

The War on the Ground

1942–1945: Maneuver and Industrial Attrition

A war launched by Germany would immediately cause other countries to intervene in support of the attacked country. In a war against a world coalition, Germany would be defeated and then be at the mercy of vengeful victors.

—COLONEL GENERAL LUDWIG BECK

BECAUSE OF STRATEGIC DECISIONS made in 1941, the Third Reich confronted a global coalition with greater economic resources. Barbarossa's failure, which revealed the limitations of Germany's military power, should also have made clear its economic weaknesses. Yet not only Hitler but his senior military advisors as well continued to underestimate their enemy's industrial and military capacities while overestimating their own. Hitler's declaration of war on the United States was not an aberration on the Führer's part. Walter Warlimont, a senior staff officer in the OKW, noted that his fellow officers greeted the declaration with "an ecstasy of rejoicing."[1]

The Campaign in the East, 1942–1943

The spring mud season of 1942 brought German operations in the east to a halt after a calamitous winter.[2] As planning for a summer offensive began in March, an overview of the army's combat effectiveness suggests how badly the Wehrmacht was debilitated by nine months of fighting in the east. Of 162 divisions, only 8 were judged capable of offensive operations, 10 were conditionally ready, while 102 were fit only for the defensive.[3] Finally, in an army still dependent on horses, the supply services could replace only 20,000 of the 180,000 horses lost over the winter.[4]

Why then did the Germans consider a summer offensive in 1942? There were three reasons: first, as in 1918, Operation Blau, code name for the summer offensive, represented an attempt to eliminate the near enemy before the far enemy (in both cases the United States) could enter the war. Second, if the Wehrmacht could seize the Caucasus oilfields, it would supposedly ease the Reich's petroleum shortage. Third was a continued underestimation of Soviet industrial potential. Foreign Armies East estimated Soviet aircraft production for 1942 as 6,600 planes (the actual number was 21,684); for tanks, 6,000 (actual 24,446); for artillery, 7,800 (actual 33,111).[5]

In the strategic sense, Blau represented an effort to square the circle. With Barbarossa's failure, Germany confronted a drawn-out war of industrial attrition, exacerbated by Hitler's declaration of war on the United States. The war economy confronted shortages of raw materials, of which petroleum was the most serious. Losses in the east and an economy incapable of producing replacement weapons and equipment in sufficient numbers led to the perception that the Reich needed to seize a larger raw material base for the medium and long term. The 1942 campaign was thus an effort to bridge present weaknesses to meet the larger demands of the future. The campaign's purpose was to seize raw materials rather than military objectives. Ironically, when intelligence estimates became more pessimistic, they then formed further justification for the Wehrmacht's path.[6]

The forces available limited the OKW to one major front, Army Group South. With the oil-rich Caucasus as the primary target, the Germans selected Stalingrad as their secondary target because if they seized it, they would cut off transportation of petroleum up the Volga. In the planning for Blau, the inadequacy of the army's logistical capabilities to support such divergent thrusts was never discussed. Moreover, given the destruction the Soviets had carried out in 1941, there was little prospect that oil-bearing areas that came under Nazi control could produce oil in less than a year. Finally, the Germans were so short of manpower that they had to rely on Italian, Romanian, and Hungarian divisions to protect the flanks of the advance.

The 1942 campaign on the Southern Front began with German operations in Crimea, followed by a failed Soviet attack on Kharkov. In June, the Eleventh Army captured Sevastopol and destroyed what remained of Soviet forces in Crimea. Blau began on 28 June. Initially, the Germans were successful, but as the advance continued, it encountered increasing logistical difficulties. There were also serious troubles in the German high command. Hitler, convinced he was a military genius, fired Field Marshal Fedor von Bock and assumed personal command of Blau. The drive now diverged on two axes: the Sixth Army moved toward Stalingrad while the Fourth Panzer Army drove into the Caucasus. After capturing Rostov, the latter captured the Maikop oilfields, which the Soviets had thoroughly wrecked. The pursuit of oil in the Caucasus was always a pipe dream. The Germans never possessed the means to repair the damage the Soviets inflicted on captured oilfields or any way to transport oil to the Reich.

By 23 July, Hitler had turned his attention to Stalingrad.[7] On 23 August, German spearheads reached the Volga and the city's northern suburbs. The Luftwaffe opened the fighting with a massive air raid, ironically causing damage that made the city easier to defend. As the German advance continued, divisions from the Reich's allies deployed to cover the Sixth Army's northwestern flank. From late August through the end of October the Germans advanced through Stalingrad block by block. Throughout September and October, the Stavka fed in just enough reinforcements to continue the battle.[8] *Maskirovka* (deception measures) covered Soviet movements so effectively that German intelligence uncovered no indication of enemy armies deploying north and south of Stalingrad.[9]

In late September, Stalin gathered his senior generals to decide the Red Army's operational plans. Given Soviet industrial production, which the Germans had done little to weaken, the Stavka decided to launch two offensives: one against Stalingrad, Operation Uranus, and another, Operation Mars, against the Rzhev salient in the center. Zhukov would command Mars; Colonel General Aleksandr Vasilevsky, Uranus. The Stavka scheduled the offensives to open almost simultaneously, with the aim of destroying German forces in the south and opening a gigantic hole in Army Group Center. On 19 November, the storm broke with the launching of Uranus on Stalingrad's northern flank.[10] The next day the southern arm of the Soviet encirclement struck. Romanian troops, ill-equipped and ill-trained, collapsed. There were virtually no German reserves behind. On 23 November, the pincers met, and the Sixth Army found itself trapped.

Its commander, Friedrich Paulus, received guidance from neither the OKW nor the OKH.[11] As soon as it was clear the Sixth Army was in trouble, Hitler hustled back from Bavaria to Rastenburg, his headquarters in East Prussia, after having celebrated the 1923 putsch with the party faithful. He was in transit during the critical period when the Sixth Army might have escaped. Those in the OKH were not about to make decisions on their own. After Hitler's return, Göring stepped in to argue that the Luftwaffe could meet the Sixth Army's logistical needs. Hitler, having promised his beer hall cronies in Munich that the German Army would stay on the Volga, had already made his decision.[12]

Without orders, Paulus displayed no initiative. From the start the Germans had little hope of breaking out; the Sixth Army was largely an infantry army, and it lacked the mobility and fuel to support a retreat. Even a successful breakout, which would involve a mobile battle, carried much danger. With winter coming, the Luftwaffe had little chance of supplying the 350 tons per day of food and ammunition Göring had promised (the Sixth Army had warned it would need 600 tons). Over the next two months, the air bridge flew in 300 tons on only three days, while most of the time its efforts barely reached 100 tons. On days with bad weather, no transports at all reached Stalingrad.[13] Even before the encirclement, the Sixth Army had been living hand to mouth because of logistics problems. Thus, it could barely last more than a few months before running out of fuel, ammunition, and sustenance.

Hitler cobbled together a patchwork force, led by Erich von Manstein, to relieve the Sixth Army. It had little chance of breaking through, and even had it succeeded, most likely few could have escaped, given shortages of fuel and vehicles. Hanging like a sword of Damocles over the Germans was their dependence on Romanian, Italian, and Hungarian troops to protect their northern flank on the Don. As Manstein's divisions fought toward Stalingrad, the Soviet Sixth Army struck the Third Romanian and Eighth Italian Armies, destroying the Italians and forcing the Romanians into a wild retreat. By 24 December, Soviet mechanized forces had overrun the Luftwaffe advance base at Tatsinskaya.[14] The collapse on the Don ended Manstein's efforts. By early January 1943 the Germans had lost their main airfield at Morozovskaya,[15] a loss that sealed Stalingrad's fate. In early February the Sixth Army surrendered; some 147,000 Germans and Romanians died in the cauldron with 97,000 becoming POWs of whom only 5,000 survived. Soviet casualties were 154,870 dead and 330,865 wounded.[16] The Red Army's expenditure of ammunition underlined the ferocity of the fighting: 911,000 artillery shells, 900,000 mortar shells, and 24 million rifle and machine gun rounds.[17]

While Stalingrad was undergoing its initial siege, on 25 November 1942, Zhukov launched Operation Mars. Army Group Center had one important advantage compared to the Sixth Army. The Ninth Army possessed substantial reserves of relatively fresh divisions: three panzer and two motorized infantry. Moreover, the army group had three panzer divisions in reserve.[18] Zhukov's forces made several tactical breakthroughs, but German counterattacks prevented serious damage. By mid-December the Soviet offensive had burned itself out with heavy losses: 100,000 dead, 250,000 wounded, 1,847 tanks and 279 field pieces destroyed.[19] The defeat disappeared into the archives, overshadowed by the success in Stalingrad.

In the south, the collapse of the Hungarians and Italians made it questionable whether the Germans could save Army Group South. Manstein, now its commander, faced a battle on two fronts: the first was to persuade Hitler to accept a degree of realism; on the other, Soviet offensive operations were driving deep into Ukraine, threatening all of Army Group South. While they had opened a yawning gap in German lines, the Soviets faced the task of completing destruction of the Stalingrad pocket while exploiting the collapse along the Don. They overreached.[20]

With divisions retreating from the Caucasus as well as reinforcements from the Reich, Manstein concentrated a substantial force on the southern flank of the Soviet army advancing into Ukraine. By mid-February 1943, Kharkov had fallen, but the Red Army's advance units were at the end of their logistical tether. On 17 February, Hitler arrived at Manstein's headquarters intending to relieve the field marshal but relented because the latter was about to launch a major counterattack. With three well-equipped Waffen SS divisions and seven under-strength but veteran panzer divisions, Manstein commanded a powerful force. Moreover, the Luftwaffe had refitted its units in the south with 950 reinforcing aircraft.[21] Beginning on 20 February, the Fourth and First Panzer

Armies crushed Group Popov and came close to encircling the Soviet Sixth and First Guards Armies. By 5 March, the Germans had retaken Kharkov and fighting subsided.[22]

Immediately after Stalingrad, Joseph Goebbels called down the gods of the French Revolution in an appeal for "total war" to meet the enemies of the Reich. But no appeal could counteract the disparity in numbers. Exacerbating Germany's strategic situation was the fact that in addition to the Eastern Front the Reich confronted threats that were increasingly interrelated. The seriousness of those threats explains why Hitler launched Operation Citadel, the attempt to take out the Kursk salient and Soviet forces defending it. At best, Citadel represented an effort to maintain the initiative. Its initiator was Manstein, who proposed attacking Soviet forces holding the salient in early spring 1943, although he really preferred abandonment of the Donets coal region to draw the Soviets into a massive trap. But what that proposal ignored was the coal in the basin, which Speer pointed out to Hitler was essential to a continuing buildup of German armaments production.[23]

Distracting the Führer was the fact that the Allies were about to launch a major strategic offensive in the Mediterranean, given their success in destroying Axis forces in Tunisia. Citadel represented the largest land battle of the Second World War, but it was in no sense a turning point.[24] Unlike the previous two years, when they thought they would rout the Red Army, Hitler and his advisors now hoped only to damage it enough to prevent a major offensive operation over the summer. That would allow the Germans to withdraw reserves to handle the looming threat in the west. That the Soviets deployed not only a front (the equivalent of a German army) to cover each flank but possessed a front in reserve suggests the extent of Soviet strength as well as continued German underestimation of their capabilities.[25] Altogether, to defend Kursk, the Red Army deployed 1,426,352 soldiers, 4,938 armored fighting vehicles, and 31,415 artillery tubes; on the other side, the Germans deployed 518,000 men, 2,365 armored fighting vehicles, and only 7,417 artillery tubes.

Citadel began on 5 July 1943 and almost immediately ran into difficulties. By 9 July, the Ninth Army in the north had run out of steam. Three days later the Soviets struck the northern flank of the Orel salient and immediately broke through. Virtually all of the Ninth Army's armor had to redeploy north; its participation in Citadel was over.[26] The pincer in the south had more success, but it was making a direct attack against a well-prepared opponent. By 12 July, the Germans had reached Prokhorovka, where one of the most misunderstood tank battles in history occurred. It was not, as some have suggested, the death knell of the panzers with "over three hundred German tanks destroyed on the 12th alone."[27] In fact, Soviet tank losses were high—one corps lost 172 out of 195 tanks—while German tank losses were minimal.[28] But while the effort of German armor at Prokhorovka was a tactical success, it did nothing to halt a series of major operations launched by the Red Army over the coming months.

On 10 July, the Allies landed in Sicily. Hitler confronted the potential collapse of Mussolini's fascist regime, with implications not only for Italy but the Balkans, where Italian troops occupied much of Yugoslavia and Greece. Hitler's decision on 16 July to halt Citadel and pull the Waffen SS Corps out of the battle to reinforce Italy thus made strategic sense. Manstein argued against terminating Citadel, but one suspects he did so largely because he was afraid Hitler would transfer divisions to the west. He later nonsensically claimed that Hitler "had thrown away the victory" by failing to continue Citadel.[29] The operation cost the Germans 54,182 casualties, including 9,063 dead, while achieving a few local successes.[30]

With the attack on the northern flank of the Orel Bulge on 12 July, the Soviets began a series of offensives that ground down the German forces in the east while pushing the front lines steadily westward. The Soviet series of offensives kept the Germans off-balance and never allowed them time to recover. To meet each new attack, the Germans had to rush reinforcements from some other portion of the front, which was thus weakened by the move. With the conclusion of Kursk, the Soviets launched no less than six major operations in the last five months of 1943.[31] There were no stunning successes, but Soviet superiority in manpower and weapons allowed them to drive deep into Ukraine while imposing casualties the Wehrmacht could not afford. From early July through late August, Army Group South lost 7 division commanders, 38 regimental commanders, and, in a catastrophic loss of midlevel leadership, 252 battalion commanders.[32]

Finally allowed to retreat, the Germans reached the major crossing points on the Dnieper at the end of August, but the Soviets bounced the river at other points and within days were able to expand the small bridgeheads between Kremenchug and Dnepropetrovsk.[33] Once the Soviets achieved bridgeheads on the Dnieper, Army Group South had no chance to hold the line. By early November, Soviet spearheads had arrived on the Black Sea, trapping the German Seventeenth Army in

Crimea. The increasing speed of logistically supported forces enabled the Red Army to drive the Germans out of virtually the whole of Ukraine by winter. Throughout this time, German mechanized formations achieved several tactical victories, but none came close to stemming the Soviet tide. Moreover, these tactical successes came at a heavy price to the elite mechanized forces. The army was forced to continue demotorizing its divisions and rely increasingly on horse-drawn wagons and artillery pieces, along with the feet of its soldiers.

The War in the Mediterranean and West, 1942–1943

Before the Anglo-American forces were able to establish themselves in northern France, the ground war against the Germans on Europe's periphery was barely equivalent to a single battle in the east. Nevertheless, for logistical and strategic reasons, the Mediterranean war had considerable significance. The most important reason for moving against the Italians was that opening the Mediterranean would take much of the pressure off Allied shipping. By one estimate, the opening saved 3–4 million tons of shipping from U-boat attacks in the Atlantic.

In late May 1942, Field Marshal Erwin Rommel moved against the British Eighth Army in Libya with a lightening move; astonishingly, the British expected him to attack against the center of their line, but he outflanked them and drove deep into the heart of their defensive positions, where he found himself and the Afrika Korps trapped.[34] After defeating a series of uncoordinated counterattacks, Rommel opened a line to his supply bases. On 5 June, his antitank screen crushed an attack by British armor and destroyed 240 tanks. The British still enjoyed an advantage in armor but lost it through further uncoordinated attacks. A general collapse followed. The Afrika Korps then moved on to seize Tobruk, and the catalogue of British disasters appeared to open Egypt to German conquest.

But the iron law of logistics caught up with Rommel while the British gathered to defend at El Alamein. That line had the advantage that the Qattara Depression, a deep salt sea, impassable for heavy vehicles, lay immediately to the south. Thus, a flanking move into the desert was not possible. Rommel initially tried to break through British positions in early July, but he possessed neither the forces nor the fuel. He concentrated on building up his forces for another try, but British air and naval forces, alerted by Ultra, took a heavy toll on Axis shipping.[35]

In July 1942, the Anglo-American leadership made two crucial decisions. In Cairo, Churchill replaced his commanders in the Middle East and named General Harold Alexander to command the theater and General Bernard Law Montgomery to command the Eighth Army. Meanwhile, in Washington, Roosevelt was having a contentious debate with his chief military advisors, George Marshall and Ernest King. Marshall had been pushing hard for a cross-Channel invasion, if not in 1942 then certainly 1943. By July it was clear the British were not willing to cooperate; they demanded a landing in North Africa that fall. At this point, Marshall and King pushed hard against this strategic approach and argued for transfer of the American effort to the Pacific. For one of the few times in the war, Roosevelt overruled his military chiefs, telling them that the Allies would launch a major operation against Morocco and Algeria in the fall, code-named Torch, since the British refused to consider an invasion of France in 1942.[36]

As he took over the Eighth Army, Montgomery understood that he had first to restore its morale and then retrain it in combined arms. The first he accomplished in short order, but he lacked the time to alter the army's culture. With so many officers unwilling to display initiative and with no realistic doctrine, Montgomery found himself forced to fight a conservative battle that relied on having greater numbers. By late October he had built up overwhelming superiority: three to one in tanks (1,500 to 500), nearly four to one in troop strength (230,000 to 80,000), and nearly four to one in aircraft (1,200 to 350).[37]

The Eighth Army struck on 23 October. Rommel was home on sick leave and did not return for forty-eight hours, by which time his subordinates had already put the Afrika Korps in desperate straits. Nevertheless, it was hard going for the British. Despite claiming after the war that everything had worked according to plan, Montgomery adapted. The Eighth Army engaged in a battle of attrition that steadily ground Axis forces down. On 3 November, with only thirty tanks left, Rommel ordered a withdrawal.

As the Afrika Korps retreated across western Egypt into Libya, the strategic situation in North Africa altered. On 8 November, Anglo-American forces landed in Morocco and Algeria. Vichy French military forces put up some initial resistance, but that soon collapsed. Everything west of Tunisia quickly fell into Allied hands.[38] The German response was swift but lacking in strategic analysis. Hitler was in Munich when news of the landings arrived, and without consulting the OKW, which was in East Prussia, he ordered paratroopers to Tunisia with follow-on reinforcements of armor and infantry.

The OKW staff argued the Axis should abandon North Africa, but as one of its members commented, their estimate "passed unnoticed in the general jumble of vague political and strategic ideas based primarily on considerations of prestige."[39] Rommel, returning from North Africa at the end of November and displaying greater strategic wisdom and moral courage than his colleagues, urged Hitler to abandon North Africa, which resulted in a furious explosion.[40] In retrospect, Hitler's decision to counter the invasion of French North Africa was an egregious strategic error. It placed an Axis army in as desperate a situation as the one trapped at Stalingrad. Moreover, the campaign provided the Americans a salient warning about how far they had to go before their ground forces could match the Germans. Rommel's attack on American troops at Kasserine Pass in winter 1943 was a thoroughly humiliating experience. It did not mislead Rommel, who noted that the Americans were quick learners.

By late March 1943, Allied navies had shut off resupply to Tunisia, so the Germans had to rely on aerial resupply, which worked no better in North Africa than at Stalingrad.[41] Aerial battles over Tunisia and Sicily between November 1942 and May 1943 helped grind down German air power. In that period, the Luftwaffe lost 2,422 aircraft, or 40.5 percent of its force structure as of November 1942.[42] When the Tunisian pocket surrendered in early May 1943, the Axis losses approached those in Stalingrad: 267,000 with some 40,000 soldiers killed or wounded and the rest captured.[43] Nearly all of fascist Italy's best troops went into Allied POW camps.

In January 1943, Churchill and Roosevelt, along with their senior military advisors, met in Casablanca, Morocco, to hammer out an Anglo-American strategy for 1943 and 1944. For much of the last seven decades, the historical narrative has had Marshall and his staff arguing for a landing on the northwest French coast in 1943. In fact, by the time the Americans left for North Africa, the army chief of staff had been fully briefed on the arguments between Brehon Somervell and the economists, which had clarified a number of issues. First, the army would not be ready for a major campaign in northwest Europe in 1943: the United States could not train enough soldiers or build enough equipment for such a venture until 1944. Until then, the Anglo-American ground effort would have to remain confined to the Mediterranean.[44] Nevertheless, despite the Americans' recognition that a landing in France was not possible in 1943, considerable disagreements flared up about Anglo-American strategy for the year.

In the end, the Allies agreed that after clearing up Axis forces in North Africa, they would proceed against Sicily. That conquest would open the Mediterranean to Allied SLOCs, saving some 3 to 4 million tons of shipping.[45] The Americans also agreed to a landing in Italy, which would allow the Allies to build airfields on the plains of Calabria, from which they could strike at German industrial sites in Austria, southern Germany, and Eastern Europe. The Americans further extracted an agreement for landings in spring 1944 on France's northwest and southern coasts. The British reluctantly accepted the American proposals. Still traumatized by the memory of their losses in France in World War I, they clung to the bizarre idea that a drive through the Alps into southern Germany represented a more effective approach.

In retrospect, it is surprising that the Allies took two months after the fall of Tunisia to launch Operation Husky, the invasion of Sicily.[46] British deception efforts went a long way to persuading the Germans that Sardinia, southern France, Greece, and the Balkans offered other options for an Allied landing.[47] During June and July the OKW sent one panzer, one mountain, and three infantry divisions to Greece to guard against that possibility.[48] The German forces sent to bolster the Italians were too small to hold Sicily but strong enough to cause problems for the Allies. American and British forces raced to get to Messina first, but it was irrelevant because Allied air and naval commanders allowed most of the German ground forces to escape across the Straits of Messina. Perhaps the worst incident for the Allies came when George Patton, always on the brink of madness, accused several enlisted men who were suffering from battle fatigue of cowardice and slapped them. The incident almost ended his career and ensured he would not become the American commander of ground forces in the landing in France. That assignment went to the less-competent Omar Bradley.[49]

The successful Allied landing in Sicily in July finally toppled Mussolini. His successors, all culpable in fascist crimes, tried to bail out of the Axis alliance but, as with everything these politicians and generals had inflicted on the Italian people over two decades, they did it badly. While they dawdled, the Germans infiltrated forces in preparation for the day the Italians abandoned the alliance. On 8 September, the Allies landed on the mainland. The king and his generals decamped to join the Allies and left no orders to their military forces. The German response was swift and ruthless; virtually the whole Italian Army, lacking orders, surrendered without firing their weapons. Only on the Greek island of Cephalonia did Italian troops resist. For their troubles, the Germans executed 155 officers and 4,750 soldiers.

On 9 September, the Eighth Army took the easy route of landing at the tip of the Italian boot while a combined Anglo-American army, landing at Salerno, ran into heavy German opposition. By the end of the day there remained a seven-mile gap between the two forces, which was quickly filled with German reinforcements. Only the intervention of naval gunfire prevented them from driving the Allies into the sea.[50] Not until 13 September, after their own reinforcements arrived, did the Allies stabilize the beachhead. The Germans' success in defending Salerno led Hitler to take Albert Kesselring's advice that they could defend Italy with modest forces. The Allied advance up the spine of the Apennines turned into a crawl. By early November 1943, the Germans, ensconced in the Gustav position south of Rome, had brought the advance to a halt. At least the Allies had gained Naples, and the U.S. Army Air Forces' control of the airfields around Foggia would allow American bombers to attack southern Germany and Romania's oilfields.

It was not until May 1944 that the Allies, led by French Moroccan goumiers (indigenous Moroccan soldiers), succeeded in breaking through German positions with the opportunity to put the German Tenth Army in the bag. But in a vainglorious pursuit of publicity, the overall commander, U.S. General Mark Clark, ordered American troops to liberate Rome instead of entrapping the beaten Germans.[51] Rome fell to U.S. troops on 4 June, and Clark had one day of glory before Overlord seized the headlines, leaving the Italian theater largely ignored for the remainder of the war.

The Germans carried out a careful retreat up the Apennines until they reached the Gothic Line south of the Po River in late August. By then the Allies had withdrawn three veteran divisions, one special forces division, and all six French divisions to participate in Operation Dragoon, landings in southern France in August, leaving them in no position to drive beyond the Po. After the war, several British commentators argued that by siphoning troops for Dragoon, the Allies had missed the opportunity to drive through the Alps. Such arguments miss two points: not only do the Alps provide wonderful defensive positions but Dragoon opened the Rhone River to supply the Western Front through December 1944 with 40 percent of the logistical support it required.[52]

The War in Northwest Europe, 1944

Operation Overlord, the invasion of France, represented a triumph of Anglo-American industrial power and mobilization.[53] It required defeating the U-boats and gaining air superiority over Europe. Until late 1943, planning for the invasion was the responsibility of a special British staff. The planners settled on Normandy because swampy terrain to the east and the Cotentin Peninsula to the west would cover the invaders' flanks. The alternative, the area around Pas de Calais, was open to attack from the east, west, and south. Initial plans called for a three-division landing supported by one airborne division. But when they arrived from the Mediterranean in January 1944, Dwight Eisenhower, the overall commander, and Bernard Montgomery, the commander of land forces, demanded a five-division landing with three airborne divisions. Under Montgomery were Omar Bradley, commander of the U.S. First Army, and General Miles Dempsey, commander of the British Second Army.

On the other side, only Rommel understood the danger that Anglo-Saxon numbers, logistics, and air superiority represented. But as commander of Army Group B, he was only in charge of coastal defenses from Brittany to Denmark. In command of the defense of France was the ancient field marshal Gerd von Rundstedt. The two field marshals disagreed fundamentally on defensive strategy. Rommel argued that the Germans needed to defeat the landings on the first day to prevent an Allied buildup. He warned that a successful landing would quickly turn into a massive contest to see which side could deploy their ground forces fastest, a contest the Allies would inevitably win. Rundstedt argued the Wehrmacht should conduct a mobile defense, using its superior tactics. In the end, Hitler stepped in and allowed Rommel to build up defenses on the coast but held most of the armor in reserve.

With his usual enthusiasm, Rommel pushed the effort to reinforce defenses along the Pas de Calais and the Cotentin Peninsula. However, he had neither the time nor the resources to cover the Seventh Army's front in Normandy. Caught between the demands of the Eastern Front and Italy, the attempt to build up an armored reserve for the German defenders in the west fell short. Altogether, there were eleven mechanized and motorized divisions available in the west in early June 1944. Of those, six had substantial shortages, and none possessed even a hundred tanks. At least Rommel ordered the divisions under his command to deploy close to the beaches.

On the Allied side, there was considerable experience with amphibious operations. Montgomery, having commanded landings on Sicily, did
the best job of preparing to break through the defensive crust along the
beaches. The one Canadian and two British divisions, landing on Sword,
Juno, and Gold, respectively, received a solid dose of naval gunfire support. The American landing on Omaha Beach was another story. Warned
that experience in the Pacific suggested the naval gunfire support was inadequate, Bradley replied, "What do we have to learn from a bush league
theater?"[54] Three hundred amtracs, semi-protected amphibious vehicles
with caterpillar tracks to carry troops over the beaches, had arrived in
Britain but remained unused until the Canadians employed them to clear
the Scheldt in October. The forces assembled testified to the effort the
Allies put into the landing.[55] There were 138 warships, 221 escort vessels,
and 287 minesweepers to shepherd invasion forces across the English
Channel. Including landing craft, the number of naval vessels was over
4,000—and this invasion occurred as U.S. naval forces were also striking
at the Marianas in the Pacific. Over 11,500 Allied bombers and fighters
supported the invasion, while 1,400 troop transports flew in three airborne divisions.[56]

Overlord began on 6 June 1944. In the hour before D-Day began,
the pathfinders marked the drop zones. Weather over the British areas
was clearer so the 6th Airborne on the invasion's east end was not as dispersed as the U.S. 82nd and 101st drops. But the dispersal of the American airborne drops confused the Germans and broke the back of
defenses. British landings succeeded with relatively few casualties, although Montgomery failed in his goal of capturing Caen on the first day.
American efforts at Utah were the most successful, aided by weak defenses where the landing took place. The only landing that ran into trouble was at Omaha, and here Bradley's lack of interest in learning from
the Pacific cost the Americans. The bombardment was too short; the air
attack found the target enshrouded in clouds and dropped well inland.
Despite heavy losses, survivors of the 29th and 1st Infantry Divisions
clawed their way up the cliffs and achieved a toehold by afternoon. At
the end of the first day, the Allies had landed 155,000 troops—72,215
across the British beaches, 57,500 across Utah and Omaha, and 23,000
airborne by parachute and glider. Within twenty-four hours, eight divisions and three armored brigades were ashore. By early July the flow of
reinforcements had brought more than 1 million men ashore along with
190,000 vehicles.[57]

Rommel had been right. Once the Allies were ashore, the Germans had no chance. Allied air superiority combined with the damage inflicted on the French transportation system slowed the flow of German reinforcements.[58] The Wehrmacht held on through the tenacious tactical competence of its infantry and tankers, aided by the nature of the terrain with its thick hedgerows. The British ran into fierce resistance on their way toward Caen.[59]

German tactical finesse went only so far: the weight of Allied superiority ground the best of the Wehrmacht into dust. Because a British breakthrough seemed the most threatening, Dempsey's forces pulled the bulk of German panzer divisions to the eastern edge of a growing Allied pocket. Two factors slowed the American advance: the bocage country with its thick hedges and Bradley's practice of launching his divisions in individual assaults. Not until 25 July with Operation Cobra, supported by heavy bombers, did the American VII Corps break through German lines. By 30 July, their spearheads had reached Avranches, which sits on high bluffs with roads leading west into Brittany and south and east deep into Normandy.

Even though the Breton ports would be of little use, Bradley persisted in ordering the initial divisions passing through Avranches to advance into Brittany, as the original plan had ordered, ironically away from the main battlefront. That was the first mistake in the breakout. Hitler then ordered his panzer divisions to move west to close off the corridor. Alerted by Ultra, the Americans put up a spirited defense at Mortain. A single battalion of the 120th Infantry Regiment held Hill 317 against ferocious attacks while calling in massive artillery fire on its tormentors. Less than half of the battalion's soldiers walked off the hill. All four company commanders received the Distinguished Service Cross.[60] The Allies were now able to encircle German forces defending Normandy, but Bradley refused to recognize the opportunity, and the British, advancing from the north, found it difficult to work through German defenses. Only Patton, leading the Third Army, grasped the possibilities. At first he urged Bradley to launch a deep drive across the Seine to destroy forces defending Pas de Calais but then suggested at least a push to close the Falaise Gap. But Bradley limited the advance, and a significant number of Germans escaped.

As the German front in western France was dissolving, Operation Dragoon, the landings in southern France, began on 15 August. German resistance quickly collapsed, and the drive up the Rhone River Valley linked up with the American force advancing from Normandy. Dragoon cleared southern France and opened the undamaged port of Marseilles and the railroad system that ran up the Rhone River Valley to northern France. These railroads provided crucial logistical support to the Western Front because British forces failed to open the Scheldt, the pathway to Antwerp, until late November 1944 due to Montgomery's lack of interest. By spring 1945, Antwerp would be the busiest port in the world.

Once it appeared that the Third Reich was on the brink of defeat, a furious argument broke out between Montgomery and Eisenhower as to the best operational strategy. Montgomery argued that he should receive most of the Allied logistical support to mount a drive across the Rhine and onto the north German plain. Eisenhower, attuned to the nuances of the Anglo-American alliance, recognized that a broad front was necessary for political reasons. Given the strength of national feeling in Britain and the United States, he could not appear to favor either nation's military.

Nevertheless, Eisenhower did provide substantial support to Montgomery with the understanding he would clear the Scheldt. This was a mistake. First, Montgomery failed to emphasize opening the Scheldt. Without Dragoon, the Allies would have had difficulty logistically supporting a front line on the German frontier in the fall. Instead, Montgomery put his eggs in Operation Market Garden, in which three Allied airborne divisions tried to capture the bridges leading through Holland to the north German plain.

The operation never had much chance of success: the drops were badly placed, and the failure to open the Scheldt had allowed the German Fifteenth Army, with approximately eighty thousand troops, to escape and help block Market Garden. The idea of driving armored divisions up a single road, open to attack by heavy enemy forces from both sides, was nonsensical, and the British could not have logistically supported a major battle on the far side of the Rhine.[61] Market Garden represented a combination of arrogance, incompetence, and British military culture.

The Allied forces' failure to drive deep into Germany in fact reflected logistical realities. Having made a desert of the French rail and road networks so that the Wehrmacht could not defend Normandy, the Allies could not use those networks to bring supplies to the German frontier. A series of campaigns floundered on mud and insufficient resources. The Americans suffered a dismal defeat in their First Army's efforts to break through the Hürtgen Forest.[62] These attacks, including an effort to force American troops through the Kall River Gorge, resulted in a bloodbath.

The Battle of the Bulge was the Wehrmacht's swan song. On 16 December, the Germans struck through the Ardennes where they had attacked in 1940. Although surprised by the initial thrusts, for the most part the Americans reacted well.[63] Two regiments of the new 106th Division surrendered, largely because of the division commander's incompetence. In the north, Sepp Dietrich's Sixth SS Army, though the strongest, had the least success. While Bradley panicked, Patton did not, and with superlative skill he turned much of the Third Army around to drive into the southern flank of the German salient. On 26 December 1944, his army's relief column reached the 101st Airborne Division, besieged at Bastogne. The German offensive was on the brink of defeat.

The War in the East, 1944

By January 1944, the Red Army possessed 6.4 million soldiers against 2.5 million Germans and 700,000 other Axis troops on the Eastern Front. The Soviets had an even greater advantage in numbers of armored fighting vehicles: 5,800 tanks to Germany's 2,300, with the Soviets supported by masses of American-built trucks and jeeps. As historians Karl-Heinz Frieser and colleagues put it, "On the German side [this phase of the war] largely consisted . . . in inglorious withdrawal battles, and on the Soviet side in inglorious victories achieved at far too great a cost."[64] By this point, the CBO was severely stressing German defenses: in January 1944 the Luftwaffe deployed two thousand more artillery tubes in the Reich than the Wehrmacht had in the east.[65]

German defeats in the north were only a foretaste of the attacks the Soviets launched in the south. Over the first four months of 1944, a series of Soviet offensives drove the Germans out of Ukraine and Crimea. Twice they came close to encircling large bodies of German troops; Soviet command and control was steadily improving, while Hitler refused to pull the Wehrmacht's armies back as Soviet mechanized formations broke through. The most serious threat to Army Group South came in early March, when Georgy Zhukov launched a major offensive in the area between the First and Fourth Panzer Armies. The Soviet offensive not only split the two armies apart and pushed them in separate directions; it created a situation that threatened to surround the First Panzer Army. Only after a furious row with Hitler did Erich von

Manstein gain permission on the evening of 25 March for the army to break out.[66]

Besides allowing the First Panzer Army to escape, Manstein's move also destroyed substantial portions of Soviet supplies for the pincer's western arm. But success came too late; Hitler had already fired him, and he would not hold another position. The German history puts Manstein's success in an unambiguous framework: "It had long since ceased to be a matter of 'lost victories,' ... but only of 'victoriously' prevented disasters."[67] Nevertheless, the Soviet offensives of early 1944 to retake Ukraine came at a price. Of 2,230,000 soldiers participating, 1,192,900—over half—became casualties.[68]

With the coming invasion of northwest Europe, Hitler's focus switched to the west, hoping that a quick victory in northern France would allow transfer of forces back to the east. As for the Soviets, the OKW thought they would either launch an offensive to reach into the Balkans or one to capture the Baltic states. Soviet *maskirovka* reinforced both misconceptions. But those on the spot picked up warnings that the Soviets would launch a major offensive in the center.[69]

The commander of Army Group Center, Field Marshal Ernst Busch, had no intention of disputing Hitler's insistence that German troops hold every piece of ground. The balance weighed against Busch's forces. For the first phase of Bagration, code name for the offensive, the Soviets deployed 1,254,300 soldiers, 4,060 armored fighting vehicles, 24,383 artillery pieces, and 6,334 aircraft. The second phase consisted of 416,000 soldiers, 1,748 tanks, and 8,335 artillery tubes. Altogether Army Group Center (the Second, Fourth, and Ninth Armies and Third Panzer Army) possessed 486,493 soldiers. Moreover, the group had been particularly affected by demotorization. The Third Panzer Army did not possess a single tank but it did have 60,000 horses.[70]

Bagration began on 22 June 1944, three years after Barbarossa. The Soviets might have begun earlier, but Stalin waited to see how the Normandy invasion went. Once it was clear the Allies were succeeding, the dictator unleashed his armies. The first to feel the hammer was the Third Panzer Army, which had received orders from Hitler to hold the town of Vitebsk, which lay at the end of a narrow salient. That order allowed the Soviets to trap five divisions holding a worthless piece of real estate. Meanwhile, on the 23rd, the Second and Third Belorussian Fronts rapidly broke though the Fourth Army, thereby threatening both Mogilev and Orsha. The last German army the Soviets struck was the Ninth, on the 24th.

Army Group Center dissolved into pockets attempting to claw their way back to German lines. The largest pockets were around Bobruisk and Minsk.[71] In a sign of how weak the German panzer forces had become, the breakthrough to the trapped Ninth Army consisted only of the 12th Panzer Division, possessing forty Mark III and Mark IV tanks. It succeeded, but only because the Soviets were moving so rapidly to the west: "Soviet tank commanders were now avoiding engaging with German panzer units, which brought them little apart from high losses, and instead pressed forward in depth as fast as possible to fulfil their operational mission, just as German armor had [once] done."[72]

On 3 July, Minsk fell to mechanized forces, while follow-on forces cleaned up pockets in the rear. The Germans believed the rush of Soviet forces would come to a halt shortly after they reached Minsk, but the logistical support rendered by Lend-Lease trucks and jeeps soon disabused them of that notion. By the 8th the Soviets had reached Vilnius. The increasing sophistication of their command and control allowed their units to take advantage of the splintering of German forces.[73] Within twelve days, the Soviets had destroyed Army Group Center's twenty-five divisions. Between 22 June and 10 July, the German losses reached 250,000 soldiers. By 31 August, those losses had reached 399,102, with 262,929 of that total missing and many POWs.[74] But the Soviet losses were heavy, reaching 770,888 soldiers and 2,957 tanks.[75]

Adding to German difficulties, the Stavka then unleashed a series of follow-on operations. On 13 July, Marshal Ivan Konev's forces attacked Army Group North Ukraine, and after initial resistance the defenders collapsed. Within five days Konev's armor had encircled the XIII Corps east of Lvov, while his mechanized forces continued their drive into eastern Poland. By the end of July, the Red Army's lead mechanized units were near Warsaw. At this point the Soviet drive ran out of logistical support. But it had regained Belorussia, driven the Germans out of most of the Baltic states, and reached East Prussia. "The Soviet potential," write Frieser and colleagues, "had grown so much that it was no longer a matter of quantitative increase. What had happened was a qualitative increase to a new manner of operational warfare."[76]

The End in Europe

On 1 January 1945, the Wehrmacht still controlled virtually all of the Reich's territory as of 1939, as well as much that it had conquered since then. Yet Germany's position was weaker than it looked. Anglo-American air forces had achieved general air superiority. The CBO, augmented by tactical air power, was systematically destroying the Reich's transportation system and consequently its war economy, as well as its production of synthetic petroleum. Moreover, the Ardennes attack was destroying the Wehrmacht's mobile reserves. In the east, the Wehrmacht found itself robbed of its reserves, while its remaining panzer divisions possessed hardly any petroleum to support operations.

The Soviets bided their time, building up their forces along the Vistula to ensure that they could achieve their goals in the Balkans. In August 1944, after Bagration was finished, rather than continue west their forces headed south to Romania. The Romanian regime crumbled in the face of the massive Soviet offensive.[77] With the Romanians now incorporated into their own forces, the Soviets destroyed the German Sixth Army for a second time and then quickly overtook Bulgaria. As German occupiers scrambled to escape Greece, the Red Army moved into southern Yugoslavia to link up with Marshal Josip Tito's partisans. By November the Soviets had "liberated" Belgrade while spreading a reign of looting and rapine over the territory of their supposed allies. But as Stalin commented to his Yugoslav comrades, there was nothing wrong with his soldiers "having some fun with a woman."[78] The Red Army's treatment of its allies offered a foretaste of the unbridled terror about to fall on eastern Germany.

The German population reaped the whirlwind it had so enthusiastically sown in the war's early years. With four months to prepare their forces along the Vistula, the Soviets possessed a juggernaut to destroy what was left of the Wehrmacht in the east. Four massive fronts—the First Ukrainian under Konev, First Belorussian under Zhukov, Second Belorussian under Rokossovsky, and Third Belorussian under Ivan Chernyakhovsky, possessing nearly 4 million soldiers, over 40,000 artillery pieces, and 9,800 tanks—conducted the offensive. Its main weight came in southern and central Poland with the aim of taking out Silesia, the last functioning center of Germany's war economy. At the same time, Rokossovsky's front was to destroy German forces in East Prussia and Pomerania. Heinz Guderian, now the chief of the general staff, attempted to persuade the Führer to release what was left of the Wehrmacht to support the forces defending the Eastern Front. But Hitler, living in a world ever farther from reality, dismissed all estimates of the looming threat.

On 12 January 1945, the First Ukrainian Front opened the Soviet offensive in the south. Within hours its armor had destroyed two panzer divisions in a one-day advance of twenty miles. The other three fronts followed, and everywhere, despite desperate resistance, the Wehrmacht collapsed. While they went about the business of killing German soldiers, the Soviet soldiers looted, destroyed, murdered, and raped. As many as 3 million Germans may have died as a result of Soviet atrocities. As the Grand Alliance met at Yalta, Soviet forces conquered virtually all of Silesia, East Prussia, and Pomerania and rolled up on the Oder River.

The Americans and British were still fighting their way toward the Rhine as the Soviets pulled up on the Oder.[79] But as February moved into March, the Anglo-American drives picked up speed. Having obeyed Hitler's demand that the Wehrmacht defend the western side of the Rhine, the Germans were incapable of making a serious stand on the river's eastern bank. Moreover, the Americans ran into an enormous piece of luck. On 9 March, German combat engineers failed to destroy the Remagen bridge, allowing the American 9th Armored Division to achieve a lodgment on the east bank of the Rhine. Within a day, the Americans had nine thousand men across. Lacking all mobility with the destruction of the Reich's oil industry, the Wehrmacht's battered units had no chance of holding back the Allied tide that swept into the heartland. Yet despite the blue lines that surged across central Germany, much of the German Army still fought on. The number of Americans killed in April's fighting was almost as high as those killed in June 1944, and more than those killed in February 1945.

One final dispute marred relations between the British and the Americans. Churchill desperately wanted the Western Allies to capture Berlin; Eisenhower and Marshall demurred, since Berlin was to lie within the Soviet zone of occupation. The Red Army was thus left to conquer the German capital. Having refitted their troops along the Oder River a mere thirty-seven miles from Berlin, the Soviets opened their offensive on 16 April. Within four days, Zhukov's First Belorussian Front and Konev's First Ukrainian Front began shelling the capital. By early May the city was in their hands, although some pockets of resistance continued fighting until the final surrender. The cost was heavy. The Soviets lost 81,116 killed in action and 286,251 wounded, along with 1,997 armored fighting vehicles.

An End to War in Europe?

In the end, the Allied victory in Europe was a matter not only of possessing bigger battalions but of overwhelming industrial strength that won the Battle of the Atlantic, tore the roof off the Reich, and provided superiority on the ground. Both sides mobilized their populations ruthlessly, and the desire to finish off the opponent raised the deepest feelings of nationalism, while the Industrial Revolution provided the means to fight the war to the bitter end. But unlike in 1918, at the end of the war the Allied forces directly occupied the smashed ruins of what its leaders had proclaimed a "thousand-year Reich."

In the largest sense the war on the ground was a reflection of the war in the oceans and in the air. There were no decisive battles. The calculus of victory and defeat reflected the ability to sustain great numbers of casualties and losses of equipment. Attrition ruled the outcome. For the Germans, motivation was very much a matter of ideology, reinforced by knowledge of the crimes the Wehrmacht's soldiers had perpetrated in their travels across Europe. A macabre comment popular in the Reich in the last months of the conflict was "enjoy the war, because the peace will be hell."

Yet for all its similarities to war in the other domains, the war on the ground was affected far less by science and technology than the wars in the air and at sea. Change and adaptation in weapons systems were incremental. The tanks of 1944 worked in much the same fashion as those of 1940. They were faster, bigger, and more heavily armed, but they worked on the same principles. The fifth military-social revolution would not emerge from the war on the ground.

CHAPTER THIRTEEN

The War in the Pacific

Kind-hearted people might come to think there was some
ingenious way to disarm or defeat an enemy without too much
bloodshed and might imagine that this is the true goal of the art of
war. Pleasant as it sounds it is a fallacy. . . . War is such a dangerous
business that the mistakes which come from kindness are the worst.

—CARL VON CLAUSEWITZ, *On War*

IN DECEMBER 1940, JAPAN sent a delegation of senior officers under
Lieutenant General Tomoyuki Yamashita to Germany to study the Wehrmacht's stunning successes of the previous spring.[1] Yamashita reported to
his superiors that Japan was behind the Germans technologically and in
much of its military equipment, a gap that would steadily expand as the war
continued.[2] Japan, he warned, lacked the resources and scientific talent to
match the Germans, much less the British and Americans. As the bringer of
bad news, Yamashita found himself immediately shipped off to Manchuria.

The Japanese embarked on war in the belief that a few decisive victories would persuade the soft Americans to accept the peace that Japan
dictated. Underlying those assumptions was a belief that the will of their
soldiers would overcome any obstacle.[3] Over the next three-plus years,
those soldiers proved their commitment to emperor and country. Of
2,571 naval infantry defending Tarawa in November 1943, the Americans
captured 8. At Kwajalein, 98.4 percent of the Japanese garrison died; at

314

The Far East and Pacific, 1941. Cartography by Bill Nelson.

Saipan in 1944, 97 percent; Japanese losses on Iwo Jima and Okinawa in 1945 were as great.[4] John Masters, a British regular officer who depicted his army before and during the war, noted, "In our armies, any of them, nearly every Japanese would have had a Congressional Medal [of Honor] or Victoria Cross. It is the fashion to dismiss their courage as fanaticism. . . . They believed in something, and they were willing to die for it, for any smallest detail that would help to achieve it. What else is bravery?"[5]

In retrospect, the Japanese stood no chance. Nevertheless, in the context of early 1942, with the collapse of Allied military forces in

Asia, America's political and military leaders believed they confronted a desperate situation in the Pacific.[6] Before 7 December 1941, they minimized Japan's potential. The "Germany first" strategy rested on a belief it would be relatively easy to hold the Japanese while Allied forces destroyed German military power. However, the collapse in Malaya, the Philippines, and the Dutch East Indies created a different set of perceptions.[7] At the time, it was a political necessity to halt the Japanese tide.

Japan's successes were not a fluke. In early 1942, they possessed first-class naval and air forces that were far superior to those of their opponents. Japanese naval vessels were first class, the Zero was the finest first-line fighter in the world, naval pilots had received a training regimen that made them the best in the world, their oxygen-powered torpedoes were the most lethal in the world, and the Imperial Japanese Navy's (IJN) night-fighting ability was superior to any other navy. Finally, in combining the carriers into a united striking force, known as the Kidō Butai, the Japanese had created a unique operational capability.

At the war's outset, Japanese military strategy aimed at dealing a series of sharp defeats to the U.S. Navy.[8] Yet after the Kidō Butai succeeded in sinking much of the obsolete U.S. battlefleet, the Japanese turned to Southeast Asia while ignoring the Americans. They attacked northern Australia and even made a raid deep into the Indian Ocean against the subcontinent and the island of Ceylon. In Malaya, despite being outnumbered, Yamashita's troops overwhelmed the British, Australian, and Indian units to conquer Singapore and Malaya. In the Battle of the Java Sea on 27 February 1942, Japanese cruisers wiped out an Allied naval force of two heavy cruisers, three light cruisers, and nine destroyers. Amphibious forces defeated the Dutch defenders of the East Indies.

The defense of the Philippines lasted longer because the invasion force was small and American resistance tough. But General Douglas MacArthur, commander of U.S. Army Forces in the Far East, had altered defense plans. Instead of retreating to the Bataan Peninsula, he ordered the defense of all of Luzon and also ordered supply dumps to be spread across the island.[9] He and his staff found themselves caught by surprise even though the Japanese air attacks came nine hours after Pearl Harbor. Landings on 21 December 1941 disabused MacArthur of the idea that he could hold Luzon, and he ordered a withdrawal to Bataan. In the hasty retreat, American and Filipino troops abandoned most of their supplies. Once on the peninsula the Americans would hold out until April 1942, but on starvation rations. Their condition contributed substantially to their losses on the Bataan "death march."[10] Ronald Spector in his account of the Battle of Bataan noted that MacArthur's "presence in the Philippines gave rise to ... exaggerated hopes, the ridiculous overestimate of the Philippine army's capabilities ... and muddled planning. The troops in Luzon would have been defeated in any case, but without MacArthur they might have been defeated without being racked by disease and tortured by slow starvation."[11]

Meanwhile, U.S. carriers, untouched on 7 December 1941, launched a series of raids against Japanese islands in the Central Pacific. None of these alarmed the Japanese, who were overrunning the British and Dutch colonies in Southeast Asia, but they inflicted considerable damage on air bases in the Marshall Islands while providing American taskforce commanders and aviators with combat experience.[12] What caught Japanese attention was a strike of B-25B twin-engine Mitchell bombers, launched from the carrier *Hornet*, against the Home Islands on 18 April 1942. The raid was the brain-child of a member of Ernest King's staff, who suggested in early January that twin-engine army bombers could fly off a carrier, bomb Japan, and then reach China. The operation was put together in two and a half months; its leader was Lieutenant Colonel Jimmy Doolittle, who later commanded the Eighth Air Force against Nazi Germany. Bomb damage was minimal, and all the planes were lost. But as a propaganda ploy, it was a stroke of genius.

The strategic effect of bombing the Home Islands was felt immediately. The commander of the Japanese fleet, Admiral Isoroku Yamamoto, set in motion plans to attack and seize the American island base of Midway, intending to draw out the U.S. fleet and destroy it. Before that operation could begin, the Japanese had to complete seizure of Port Moresby in New Guinea. Carrier taskforces of the two navies ran into each other in the Coral Sea in early May 1942. It was the first major naval engagement in history in which the opposing forces were out of each other's sight. The battle ended in a tactical victory for the Japanese, who sank the carrier *Lexington* and damaged the carrier *Yorktown*.[13] Nevertheless, it was a strategic victory for the Americans because the battle took two of Japan's fleet carriers out of operations against Midway and forced them to cancel the amphibious operation against Port Moresby.

Japanese preparations for Midway indicate their leaders suffered a severe case of "victory disease." War-gaming for the assault was superficial if not dishonest. When the officers playing the Americans managed to sink several Japanese carriers, the referee discounted the results. Moreover, the plan was overly complex, involving three separate taskforces for the move against Midway plus an entirely independent operation attacking Dutch Harbor in Alaska and seizing several islands in the Aleutian chain.[14]

While the Japanese were preparing to move against Midway, U.S. code breakers uncovered intelligence about their intentions, allowing Admiral Chester Nimitz, commander in chief of the Pacific Fleet, to concentrate his forces there.[15] The Americans fought the battle only with carriers. Two carriers were already in Hawaii. The third, the *Yorktown*, damaged at Coral Sea, arrived on 27 May in the repair basin in Pearl Harbor needing an estimated three months of repair. A horde of 1,400 shipyard workers were waiting. At 9:00 a.m. on 30 May, slightly less than seventy-two hours later, the *Yorktown* put to sea with twenty-five Wildcats, thirty-seven dive bombers, and fourteen torpedo bombers, ready to join the *Enterprise* and *Hornet* northeast of Midway.[16]

On 3 June, an American PBY, a reconnaissance aircraft, picked up the Japanese invaders approaching from the south with transports and heavy cruisers. B-17s launched from Midway three hours later. None of their bombs hit anything. In early dawn on 4 June, Japanese cruisers flew off scout aircraft to check areas to the east and northeast of Midway. The cruiser *Tone*'s reconnaissance aircraft, assigned to search the area where U.S. carriers were located, left half an hour late because of engine troubles; its pilot failed to report the presence of carriers.[17] As they launched their scouts, the Japanese flew off the first strike package to attack Midway and prepare the way for the invading force. They succeeded in damaging the facilities on Midway, but the American base clearly needed another strike.

At this point Admiral Chūichi Nagumo, commander of the carriers, received word of an American force, of unknown composition, to the northeast. Then a scout aircraft reported at least one American carrier. The Japanese began first recovering their aircraft from Midway and then changing aircraft armament scheduled for the next strike to armor-piercing bombs and torpedoes to attack the American carrier. At 9:00 a.m., the Japanese fleet came under attack from U.S. torpedo aircraft. Zeros on combat air patrol splashed all attacking aircraft, but that effort pulled them down to a low altitude. Having survived, the Japanese began to bring the attack wave of dive and torpedo bombers from the hanger deck for launching at precisely the moment American dive bombers arrived overhead.[18] SBD-3 Dauntless dive bombers planted their cargo on the decks of the *Sōryū*, *Akagi*, and *Kaga*. The aircraft and ordnance still in the hanger decks turned the carriers into funeral pyres.

The American attack began at 10:22 a.m.; by 10:30, the naval balance in the Pacific was drastically altered. Later in the day, the Japanese also lost the carrier *Hiryū*, while the *Yorktown* received damage that eventually spelled its doom. Yamashita's warnings to his fellow generals and admirals came back to haunt them. The American carriers possessed radar, while the Japanese did not. Thus, the Americans could guide their fighters into intercepting Japanese aircraft well beyond the fleet. Meanwhile, the Japanese had no warning when enemy aircraft were approaching. Midway was a shattering defeat, but instead of examining its lessons, the admirals in charge hid what had happened from the Japanese people, the army, and even the rest of the navy.

While the Japanese were licking their wounds, the Americans struck at the Solomon Islands. Their opponents had deposited a detachment of engineers and third-rate troops to build an airfield on the island of Guadalcanal.[19] Given the island's strategic importance—it represented a direct threat to the SLOCs between the United States and Australia—the force's composition made no sense. But it reflected Japanese contempt for the Americans, as well as the fact that their army was so overcommitted in China that it had little left for Pacific operations. King, the driving force for the Pacific war in Washington, took the risk of sending an unprepared 1st Marine Division to capture the island before the Japanese could utilize the partially completed air base. Assured they would not be committed for very long, the marines were not ready to launch a serious amphibious assault on Guadalcanal. For once in the Pacific, they were lucky. The Japanese were no more ready to defend it.[20]

On 7 August 1942, the invasion force, covered by a carrier taskforce under Vice Admiral Frank Jack Fletcher, invaded Guadalcanal and the smaller island of Tulagi. Fletcher, who had already lost two carriers, left the area after the first day, taking the carriers' aircraft with him. The marines encountered heavy opposition from the Japanese garrison on Tulagi but minimal resistance on Guadalcanal, where the Japanese engineers fled into the jungle, abandoning their supplies, including engineering equipment in undamaged condition. The marines set to work using that equipment to make the airfield workable, which they completed by 12 August.[21] In effect, King had gambled that the Japanese would not react with the full force of their battlefleet—and the Japanese, engaged at the time in New Guinea, confronted the dilemma of whether to concentrate there or on Guadalcanal. They tried to do both.

Meanwhile, the U.S. Navy suffered the worst defeat in its history.[22] As Fletcher's carriers withdrew, a formidable Japanese taskforce of five heavy cruisers sortied from Rabaul and New Ireland in the Bismarck

Archipelago. Weighing anchor at 4:30 p.m. on 7 August, Admiral Gunichi Mikawa and his force sped through the Solomons in what became known as the "slot." Allied reconnaissance aircraft picked up the task-force during daylight on the 8th but misreported what they saw. Over the night of 8–9 August, Mikawa's cruisers sailed past the picket destroyers, which possessed radar; engaged the Allied cruisers deployed south of Savo Island; blew the bow off USS *Chicago;* and turned HMAS *Canberra* into a blazing wreck. The *Chicago* sailed off into the darkness and failed to warn the heavy cruisers deployed north of Savo. Those cruisers could not have missed the flashes of heavy gunfire to the south, but they did nothing. The Japanese cruisers rounded Savo, found the *Vincennes, Quincy,* and *Astoria* with their guns trained fore and aft, and turned those ships too into blazing wrecks. Mikawa then exited the area without attacking the merchant shipping that had not finished unloading supplies. The Battle of Savo Island killed over a thousand Allied sailors, sank four heavy cruisers, and damaged one. The Japanese had one heavy cruiser slightly damaged and thirty-five sailors killed. Admiral Kelly Turner commented that the surface navy was "obsessed with a strong feeling of technical and mental superiority. . . . Despite ample evidence as to enemy capabilities, most of our officers and men despised the enemy."[23]

Each side was still underestimating the other's military effectiveness. After the Battle of Savo, the Japanese sent a regimental-sized force to Guadalcanal. Its commander, Colonel Kiyonao Ichiki, as a company commander had been an instigator of the Marco Polo Bridge Incident in July 1937, which had led to war with China. Even though the evidence was available that a sizeable force of marines was on Guadalcanal, Ichiki and his superiors thought a single regiment, attacking at night, would suffice to clean up the soft marines.

A detachment of 917 soldiers landed by destroyer over the night of 18–19 August and headed straight for the marine positions without any reconnaissance. With no security, the lead platoon wandered into a marine patrol. It died in an hour while providing its enemies with a host of intelligence. Ichiki paid not the slightest attention to the destruction of his lead platoon and marched his soldiers straight into marine defenses on Alligator Creek. Launching its attack in the early morning of 21 August, the Ichiki detachment was nearly all dead by morning.[24]

While the Japanese cruisers headed to Savo, the Japanese launched a series of heavy air raids from bases on Bougainville in the northern Solomons. The raiders ran into Fletcher's Wildcats still covering the marines from carriers south of Guadalcanal. Out of the attacking force, the Japanese lost twenty-eight aircraft while the Americans lost twenty-one fighters.[25] This was the first foretaste of what would prove to be the disastrous maiming of Japanese air power, army as well as navy. Moreover, maintenance personnel, lost in the murderous, disease-ridden climate, proved difficult to replace, given how few Japanese possessed a background in internal combustion engines and radio technology.[26]

On the afternoon of 20 August, flying off the escort carrier *Long Island*, the first F4F Wildcats and SBD Dauntless dive bombers arrived on Henderson Field, completed by the marines with the equipment abandoned by the Japanese. The markers were down. With a limited number of aircraft, supplied with fuel and armament by destroyer transport, the Americans ruled the air and waters surrounding Guadalcanal by day while at night Japanese destroyers ferried in troops and supplies. Both sides fed reinforcements intermittently, the Japanese by choice because they could have launched their main battlefleet from Rabaul. Instead, they fought a battle of attrition, one in which they funneled enough troops and supplies into Guadalcanal to become an increasing threat but never enough to retake the airfield.

The initial night naval battles found the Americans at a disadvantage, largely because of the obtuse unwillingness of taskforce commanders to rely on radar rather than their own eyeballs. But they learned, and with the technological advantage of radar they were going to win. By September 1942, attrition had reduced the Americans to one carrier and one modern battleship in the Pacific. But a steady flow of new aircraft and crews kept Henderson Field operating and dominating Japanese efforts to reinforce their forces. Moreover, attempts to bring transports with substantial reinforcements and supplies invariably failed, while destroyers could not carry enough supplies to give Japanese troops on Guadalcanal a fighting chance.

The Japanese made three attempts to drive the marines off the air base. The largest came on 26 October in division strength. The marines, reinforced by the army's 164th Infantry Regiment, held off the attackers. The soldiers flowed seamlessly into the marine positions; they were particularly welcome because their semi-automatic M-1 rifles provided greater firepower than the marine's Springfields. The attacks were fierce but sporadic, partly because it proved impossible to coordinate large movements in the jungles. In January 1943, the Japanese recognized a hopeless situation, cut their losses, and withdrew.[27]

In terms of naval battles won and lost, the Japanese had a slight advantage at Guadalcanal, but in terms of the larger strategic framework, the battle was a disaster for them. The army and navy could make up the approximately 25,000 soldiers and naval personnel lost in the fighting on the island.[28] But the exchange ratio in ships favored the Americans, because their shipyards were making up for their losses with new production. The warships the opposing navies brought online during this period showed the disparity between the wartime economies: the United States introduced one heavy carrier, one light carrier, one battleship, four light cruisers, sixty-two destroyers, and eighteen submarines; the Japanese, one light cruiser, seven destroyers, and fourteen submarines.[29]

Japan's air losses were a disaster from which its naval air force never recovered. From 1 August through 15 November, 1942, the Japanese lost 507 aircraft, the Americans 480. But Japanese losses included a substantial number of their most skilled naval pilots. By forcing their pilots to make long over-water flights from Rabaul to attack Henderson, leaders ensured there would be no rescue for those shot down. Aircraft production in 1942 reveals how serious the losses were for the Japanese: American, 49,445 aircraft; Japanese, 8,861. But the cumulative pilot losses from May 1942 through January 1943 hurt the Japanese the most. In December 1942, a Japanese admiral commented that the naval pilots arriving in the theater were only one-third as capable as those lost so far in the war.[30]

After Guadalcanal, the Japanese husbanded their resources and attempted to rebuild their naval pilot force. Moreover, the U.S. Army was contributing significant reinforcements to the Pacific. To the west, MacArthur, with Australian help, began moving up the north coast of New Guinea; by September his troops had landed on New Britain. Meanwhile, to the east, U.S. forces closed in on Rabaul. In effect, the Americans isolated the Japanese base at Rabaul and bypassed it, leaving its garrison of 100,000 soldiers to wither on the vine.[31]

The United States would now mount two drives in the South Pacific, one up the coast of New Guinea, the other through the Central Pacific. That division of labor reflected Roosevelt's desire to keep the politically ambitious MacArthur as far away from North America as possible, as well as the cleft between the navy and army. King and the navy had no intention of placing the great fleet cascading into the Pacific from American industry under MacArthur's command. Thus, the Americans, outraged at having to mount two major drives in Europe—in the Mediterranean and northwestern Europe—were guilty of the same strategic sin in the Pacific but for more ignoble reasons.

By August 1943, the Japanese had fallen back to the treaty islands in the mid-Pacific. To that point, U.S. submarines had played a minor role because their torpedoes rarely worked.[32] But in the last months of 1943, with better torpedoes, radar to identify enemy aircraft and ships, short-range radio gear that let them combine in wolf packs, active and passive sonar, and intelligence on Japanese movements, U.S. submarines became a more dangerous force than Dönitz's U-boats. American wolf packs were not controlled from their headquarters but by those on the spot. Unprepared to wage anti-submarine warfare, the Japanese watched as the American wolves destroyed their merchant marine.[33] Ironically, the IJN's introduction of a convoy system in summer 1944 may have increased losses by making it easier for American wolf packs to find targets. Without enough escorts and with primitive technology, Japanese convoys had no chance, while the convoys made it easier for U.S. subs to find and destroy Japanese shipping.[34] By late 1944, Japanese merchant shipping had declined from 5 million tons to 2.5 million, while the American underwater offensive had cut the Home Islands off from the raw materials of Southeast Asia.[35]

In summer 1943, the U.S. Navy began receiving the bounty of the Roosevelt administration's ship-building program. From that July and nearly every month thereafter, a new *Essex*-class carrier, with a fully trained crew and air group, arrived in Pearl Harbor. Six light carriers also arrived over the next twelve months.[36] The balance had now shifted entirely in favor of the Americans. The first great strike in the Central Pacific drive came in the Gilbert Islands against the islands of Tarawa and Makin, defended by first-rate Japanese naval infantry prepared to fight to the last man. The landings, particularly on Tarawa by the 2nd Marine Division, proved the Americans still had much to learn about amphibious warfare. The naval bombardment was too brief, and the Japanese were deeply dug in. Estimates of the tidal reef surrounding the main atoll, Betio, miscalculated the depth of the water; it turned out to be too shallow. The initial wave had to wade through chest-deep water to reach a seawall six hundred to a thousand yards away. The wounded, dragged down by equipment, drowned. By the time it had ended, the 2nd Marine Division had suffered 1,000 dead and 2,300 wounded.

Nimitz now took a major gamble. Instead of moving against the southern Marshalls, he ordered Admiral Raymond Spruance with his taskforce to attack Kwajalein in the north, while the carriers raided air bases throughout the island chain. On 31 January 1944, two divisions spearheaded the landing force, the new 4th Marine Division and the veteran army 7th Division. The former possessed 370 and the latter 174 amtracs to aid the marines and soldiers in crossing beach defenses. The move against Kwajalein caught the Japanese by surprise, since they believed the Americans would attack the southern islands rather than the chain's northern end, and had not completed their defenses. The garrison's destruction came at a cost of two thousand casualties in four days. Less than two weeks later, Spruance struck Eniwetok with an amphibious force of marines and soldiers.

The American moves in the Central Pacific, which eliminated Truk as a strategic base and positioned the Allies 1,300 miles closer to the Home Islands, came as a shock in Tokyo. Hideki Tojo took over as minister of war in addition to duties as prime minister. His response was typical of Japanese military leaders: attack. The Japanese strategy contained three elements: an offensive in China to capture U.S. air bases on the mainland, an offensive in Burma to drive the British into India, and a joint army-navy effort to defeat the U.S. fleet in the Central Pacific. The Japanese offensive in China achieved its aim, chasing Chinese armies into the mainland's endless distances. Air bases, which the Americans had expended time and resources to build to attack the Home Islands, fell like ripe tomatoes. The collapse of Nationalist armies underlined that supporting Chiang Kai-shek's Nationalist regime was not worth the effort.

In Burma, the most outstanding British general of the war, William "Bill" Slim, had taken command of an army the Japanese had chased out of the region in 1942.[37] Starting as a corps commander and working up to command the Fourteenth Army, Slim led a force of British, Indians, Gurkas, and Africans, a force that truly reflected the British Empire.[38] He trained his front-line soldiers as well as his subordinates, and even his staff, so that they could more than handle Japanese tactics in jungle fighting.[39] In March 1944, the Japanese struck first.

The swiftness with which they moved as well as their audacity caught the Fourteenth Army's commander by surprise. Nevertheless, the IV Corps fell back onto fortified positions on the Imphal plain. In fierce fighting around Kohima, the British-Indian 5th Division held. By April, the Japanese lack of attention to logistical support brought the attacks to a halt. A fierce battle for the Chin ridges then ensued in appalling monsoon conditions. Both sides suffered heavy losses, but the Japanese were on the verge of starvation while the Fourteenth Army had superior logistics, medical support, artillery, and numbers. It also possessed air superiority *and* air transport superiority, with the Americans supplying numbers of C-46s and C-47s.

The end in Burma came in January 1945. The well-supplied Fourteenth Army threw the Japanese out of Burma and recaptured Rangoon. The advance represented a textbook case of operational art. After faking a crossing at Meiktila, the Fourteenth Army crossed the Irrawaddy River south of the town. Having pushed the Japanese out of Meiktila and then battered them out of Mandalay, Slim never allowed them to regain their balance. His army raced south, reaching Rangoon just after the monsoons began, having smashed the Burma Area Army and killed over fifty thousand Japanese. Even more impressive was the bond Slim established with his soldiers. As a lance corporal in his army noted after the war, "When it was over and he spoke of what his army had done, it was always 'you,' not even 'we,' and never 'I.' "⁴⁰

In 1944, the war in the Central Pacific turned harshly against the Japanese. Despite initial worries about attacking the Marianas, Nimitz and Spruance decided to seize Saipan, Guam, and Tinian to provide air bases the army air forces required for their B-29 offensive. The Japanese also knew that American possession of the Marianas would bring long-range bombers within range of the Home Islands, and they brought their First Mobile Fleet out of Southeast Asia to defend them. The fleet consisted of six battleships, nine carriers with approximately five hundred aircraft, thirteen cruisers, and twenty-eight destroyers. The Japanese also deployed a thousand Zeros and torpedo aircraft in islands surrounding the Philippine Sea. Spruance's Fifth Fleet possessed 7 fast battleships, 15 carriers with 891 aircraft, and 21 cruisers. The campaign to take the Mariana Islands began in June 1943.

Turner's Fifth Amphibious Force also provided direct support with four hundred ships, including older battleships sunk on 7 December 1941 that had been pulled out of the mud and refurbished.⁴¹ With new aircraft possessing longer range, the Japanese attacked. Their weakness, however, was that most of their pilots had little solo experience, while American pilots had received a superior training syllabus. The latter also possessed the Grumman Hellcat, a better fighter than the Wildcat or Zero. Spruance's aircraft began operations with attacks throughout the Marshalls; they destroyed most of the Japanese aircraft on the islands. Amphibious forces then landed on Saipan; in response, the Japanese Combined Fleet weighed anchor.

Spruance delayed the landings on Guam and turned to face the Japanese. The ensuing battle has the official name of the Battle of the Philippine Sea, but the aviators called it the "Marianas Turkey Shoot." The Americans shot down 378 Japanese aircraft while losing only 50 Hellcats. U.S. subs also sank two Japanese carriers. But with the bulk of Japanese carriers keeping out of range, Spruance turned his fleet westward for the night. His mission was to protect landings on Saipan, not to sink carriers. The action the next day was disappointing. The Americans sank one light carrier and damaged six other ships. The remainder of the Japanese carriers escaped, although with no pilots left they were useless.

Fighting was fierce on both Saipan and Guam, but the Japanese had no chance given American numbers and firepower. But what took place at the end horrified even toughened marines and soldiers. Hundreds of Japanese civilians jumped to their deaths from the cliffs at Saipan—some pushed by Japanese soldiers, many of their own volition.[42] The Americans moved on. Admiral William "Bull" Halsey with his Third Fleet staff took over the Pacific fleet from Spruance and his Fifth Fleet staff, which returned to Pearl Harbor to plan the next operation, but the carrier taskforces remained at sea. In late July 1944, the Americans landed on Tinian, just north of Saipan, and built a great air base there.

While the Central Pacific drive was occurring, MacArthur was launching his own assault on the Japanese Empire in the west. Beginning with the defeat of Japanese forces at Milne Bay in September 1942, the general began his return to the Philippines with an assault on Buna-Gona by the American 32nd Infantry Division and the Australian 7th Division. The Americans were a poorly trained lot and badly led. It is the latter that explains their dismal performance: the marines on Guadalcanal were no better prepared but had exceptional leadership. From the conquest of Buna, MacArthur's conduct of the campaign displayed considerable imagination and operational adaptation.

For the Battle of the Bismarck Sea, which took place from 1 to 3 March 1943, MacArthur's air deputy, Major General George Kenney, had retrained his B-25s to skip bomb their ordnance into Japanese ships and reequipped them with eight 50-caliber machine guns in the nose. Attacking a Japanese transport force, U.S. aircraft sank all 8 transports and 4 destroyers, and in the process killed approximately 4,200 Japanese troops. Having bypassed the isolated Japanese troops on Rabaul at the end of 1943, MacArthur drove up the northern coast of New Guinea in a leap-frogging advance that continually caught the Japanese by surprise.

The landings at Hollandia on 22 April 1944 represented a leap forward of six hundred miles, beyond Allied air coverage. But MacArthur surmounted that difficulty with air coverage off carriers and the rapid seizure of airfields.

The division of the American effort in the Pacific came with considerable risk because the Japanese might have focused their remaining air and naval power on one of the drives. Yet they failed to do so largely because the U.S. moves consistently caught them off-guard. The Philippines were next, but first, for reasons that made little sense, the decision was made to attack the island of Peleliu.[43] By now, the Navy carriers were able to suppress any land-based aircraft the Japanese hoped to use against landings in the Philippines. Thus, the airfield on Peleliu no longer represented a threat. It would have been far better for American amphibious forces to have struck at Iwo Jima, where the Japanese had just begun constructing a formidable island fortress. Peleliu's defenders were ten thousand first-class troops whose commanders had abandoned Banzai charges and instead had their soldiers fight from dugouts and caves to minimize American firepower. It took the 1st Marine and the army's 81st Divisions a month and ten thousand casualties to eliminate the garrison.

Halsey and his Third Fleet were so successful in attacking Japanese air and naval bases on Yap, Mindanao, the Palaus, and Formosa that he persuaded Nimitiz and MacArthur to abandon landings on Mindinao in favor of Leyte. In September the joint chiefs approved with landings scheduled the following month. The Japanese admirals' plan for responding to the threat was too clever—and then, on the verge of success, they abandoned it. From the north, Admiral Ozawa led a decoy force of carriers, no longer useful since the Marianas Turkey Shoot. A center force, commanded by Admiral Takeo Kurita, consisting of modern battleships and cruisers, sortied through the San Bernardino Straits. Two separate taskforces of older and slower ships would move through the Surigao Straits to attack Luzon from the south.

There were two major American naval forces. Halsey's Third Fleet commanded Task Force 38, with the fast carriers, and Task Force 34, with the fast battleships. Admiral Thomas Kinkaid commanded the slower, prewar battleships and support forces for the Luzon landings. To muddy the waters, Nimitz ordered Halsey to seek a decisive fleet engagement while also protecting the landings, leaving it unclear who was to coordinate naval forces to protect the landings.[44] Halsey's carrier aircraft had no difficulty in ravaging Kurita's force as it moved through the

Sibuyan Sea on 24 October. American aircraft hit the super battleship *Musashi* with seventeen bombs and nineteen torpedoes before it turned turtle and sank. Three other battleships, including the *Yamato*, received some damage but not enough to injure their combat effectiveness.[45]

Distracted, Kurita ordered his ships to retreat to the west. As his aircraft returned, Halsey received a sighting of Ozawa's decoy carriers north of the Philippines. Buoyed by reports that Kurita was fleeing to the west, he ordered the Third Fleet north to destroy the carriers, leaving nothing to guard the San Bernadino Straits. Meanwhile, Kurita had received a blast from Tokyo, demanding he turn back and fight to the finish. As Halsey headed north, he received intelligence Kurita had turned around and was moving through the straits. Halsey paid no attention.

Early on 25 October, astonished American escort carriers and destroyers protecting MacArthur's shipping discerned Kurita's force, with their unmistakable pagoda-like superstructures, sailing straight at them.[46] The transport fleet, which had at least unloaded much of its cargo and soldiers, was vulnerable to the Japanese fleet. Taffy 3, consisting of six escort carriers and seven destroyers and destroyer-escorts, fought the Japanese off; its aircraft could only drop general-purpose, high-explosive bombs and machine gun the decks of Japanese ships. The fight lasted four hours. Then, inexplicably, Kurita turned back to retreat through the San Bernadino Straits. At this point, with their fleet largely sunk, the Japanese played one more card. On 25 October, the Special Attack Force, the first kamikazes, tried to crash their aircraft into American ships. They sank one escort carrier and damaged four other ships.

The liberation of the Philippines proceeded apace. General Yamashita was in charge of the defense of Luzon. Unlike MacArthur in 1941, he did not defend all of the island but divided his forces with the emphasis on the eastern mountains. Meanwhile, an independent command under Rear Admiral Sanji Iwabuchi, consisting of naval infantry and rear area personnel, were to destroy Manila's military facilities and retreat into the mountains. Sanji disobeyed orders and stayed to defend the Philippine capital. On 9 January 1945, four U.S. Army divisions under the Sixth Army landed on Luzon and the battle began.[47]

It took nearly all of February for the Americans to retake Manila.[48] MacArthur forbade utilization of air power to support his troops in the street fighting for fear of causing civilian casualties, but that made little difference because both sides used artillery liberally. By the end, nearly 100,000 civilians had died.[49] While the fighting in Manila was ongoing, the Americans found themselves in a struggle with Yamashita's main forces. MacArthur's forces never succeeded in eliminating Japanese forces in the mountains. All in all, Yamashita's performance underlined that he was one of the more competent generals of the war.

The biggest project the American war economy undertook during the war was the building of the B-29. The developmental and production costs were between $3 and $3.7 billion.[50] In comparison, the Manhattan Project cost only slightly more than $2 billion. In conception and design, the B-29 represented a leap forward in technology, with a pressurized cabin, huge range, and massive carrying capacity.[51] Its development proved a nightmare. In July 1944, the first B-29s deployed to air bases in China. The first long-distance flight came against targets in Bangkok; the second attack, against the Imperial Iron and Steel Works in Yahata, Japan, hardly inflicted any damage but used up nearly all the fuel that transports had carried over the Himalayas. The whole effort to bomb Japan from China was a waste, and the Marianas became the focus for the strategic bombing of Japan. Army engineers constructed two airfields on Tinian, two on Guam, and one on Saipan. Each could hold approximately 180 B-29s.

The bombing effort from the Marianas began in November 1944, with little more success than the bombing from China. The problem was twofold. Unlike that of the United States or Europe, Japanese industry had few industrial nodes. Production was spread across small family concerns. The second problem was weather. Directly over the Home Islands, a jet stream of upwards of 130 mph roared over Tokyo, making high-altitude, accurate bombing impossible.[52] Major General Haywood Hansell Jr. commanded the initial raid; at the end of November the first raiding force lifted off—its target the Nakajima Musashino aircraft engine factory on Tokyo's north side. Neither that mission nor subsequent ones achieved much.

For the leaders of the army air forces, who were counting on the B-29 to justify their push to create an independent service after the war, this was not good news. Hap Arnold sacked Hansell and replaced him with the army air forces' most outstanding combat leader, Curtis LeMay. The message to LeMay from Arnold was clear: "You go ahead and get results with the B-29. If you don't get results, you'll be fired."[53] In March 1945, LeMay turned XXI Bomber Command in a new direction, at odds with the doctrine of precision bombing. The B-29s would fly much lower; they would not fly during daytime, but at night; their defensive armament would be removed; they would carry incendiaries rather than high explosive bombs.

The first target was Tokyo. LeMay ordered a maximum effort.[54] On 10 March, 346 B-29s sortied from the Marianas loaded with a new incendiary, napalm.[55] Each aircraft carried a greater bomb weight than any of the Eighth Air Force's thousand bomber raids against Germany in 1944. The result was a "success" for the Americans and a catastrophe for the Japanese. Air raid sirens sounded at 10:30 p.m. With minimal shelters, antiquated fire services, and structures almost entirely built of wood, Tokyo was a fire trap. Fires exploded, whipped by the winds, from the moment the incendiaries hit. The firestorm dwarfed Hamburg and Dresden, reaching such intensity tail gunners on return flights could see its glow 150 miles away.[56] The raid brought the horror of war to a Japanese people who had so enthusiastically supported the murderous war in China and against the United States.[57] By the time the bombers completed their mission, 83,793 Japanese had died and over a million were homeless. Twenty-nine hours after the return of the last aircraft, LeMay launched the next attack, on Nagoya. Yet despite continuous B-29 raids, the war did not end. The military were resolutely unwilling to explore any terms of peace.

While the bombing continued, two major island campaigns proceeded. The first was the February American landing on Iwo Jima. In charge of the defense was Lieutenant General Kuribayashi Tadamichi, who unlike most Japanese generals knew a great deal about the Americans, since he had served in Washington as an assistant military attaché and traveled extensively across the country. He assumed command in fall 1944 and proceeded to turn the island into a fortress. There would be no Banzai charges. With a division's worth of soldiers and sailors, Kuribayashi created a nightmarish defensive scheme.

American intelligence picked up little of this. The general estimate was that the marines would conquer the island in five or six days. The Japanese allowed the marines to land and then began a furious deluge of artillery. Interlocking fire from bunkers inflicted a terrible toll. Three marine divisions took almost a full month to secure the island. American casualties, including the other services, were close to 30,000, with more than 6,000 killed in action. Virtually the entire Japanese garrison of 21,000 died. Of the twenty-four marine infantry battalion commanders, only seven remained in command.[58]

If Iwo Jima was terrifying, the battle for Okinawa represented a nightmare. These two battles show that an invasion of the Home Islands would have been a catastrophe for both sides. For the first time, the Americans ran into a full Japanese army, the Thirty-Second under Lieutenant General Mitsuru Ushijima. It was not at full strength, since the imperial high command had shipped some of its best units to reinforce Formosa. In total, the defenders had 76,000 regulars and 24,000 conscripts. They did not try to defend everything but instead focused on Okinawa's south, abandoning even the airfields. The invading force, the Tenth Army, consisted of four army and two marine divisions.

The landings began on 1 April with a massive bombardment.[59] To the Americans' astonishment there was little opposition. The marines turned north to find only a few Japanese defending that portion of the island. It was another matter in the south. The XXIV Army Corps, with the 7th and 96th Divisions leading the way, ran into skillfully dug in, fanatical resistance. Adding to the horror of a murderous battle of attrition was the arrival of the yearly monsoon, which turned everything into a quagmire. The fighting continued to the end of June, when there were no more Japanese for the Americans to kill. As the fighting continued, the Fifth Fleet had to remain off Okinawa to provide air support and protect against a sally by the remains of the enemy fleet.[60] The Japanese launched over 1,500 suicide aircraft, which sank 15 destroyers and 15 amphibious ships, and damaged 386 others, including the carriers *Bunker Hill, Franklin, Wasp, Yorktown,* and *Enterprise,* all of which had to be withdrawn. Some 110,000 Japanese soldiers died. The Tenth Army lost 7,613 dead and missing with 32,000 wounded, while the navy suffered 5,000 dead and more than 7,000 wounded—heavier losses than all the others over the previous two years. Another 26,000 Americans died or were injured by accidents and disease, a casualty bill close to 80,000. Civilian casualties ranged from 30,000 to 100,000.[61]

With the closing of the Okinawa campaign at the end of June, fighting settled down to continued bombardment of Japan by LeMay's B-29s and fighter bomber sweeps off American carriers. The Japanese sullenly took the blows American air power inflicted on the islands without responding.[62] They were saving their aircraft for a massive kamikaze attack on the expected invasion fleet. Meanwhile, the Americans began preparations for Operation Olympic, code name for the invasion of Kyushu, southernmost of the Home Islands. Planning began in late May. The navy agreed to the operation grudgingly, King particularly having worries about the prospect of heavy casualties. He believed, as did Nimitz, that blockade and air bombardment would bring the Japanese to their knees. But the army, particularly MacArthur, pressed for invasion. Rather than start a major interservice fight, King agreed to Olympic with the understanding the Joint Chiefs of Staff would revisit the decision. In early August, King and Nimitz considered raising objections as the number of Japanese troops deployed to Kyushu swelled. Only the dropping of the atomic bombs prevented the navy's leaders from starting a furious quarrel with the army.

With the tentative service agreement, planning for Olympic went ahead. The navy would supply direct air support with sixteen fleet and four light carriers, while the Royal Navy would add six fleet and four light carriers. The armada would possess 1,914 aircraft. In addition, 1,315 amphibious ships would support the invasion. Landing forces under the Sixth Army would consist of four corps with a total of twelve divisions (three marine). Altogether, the Sixth Army would consist of 766,700 men and 134,000 vehicles.[63] B-29s and long-range escort fighters would support the invasion from Guam, Tinian, and Saipan.

What would they be up against? American intelligence estimates, supported by Ultra decrypts of Japanese message traffic, placed the number of Japanese troops on Kyushu in May 1945 at approximately 100,000, with three divisions defending the island's north and three covering the southern beaches.[64] Whatever their weaknesses at the strategic level, it did not take the Japanese long to figure out that Kyushu would be Olympic's first target. As a Japanese staff officer noted, it "made strategic common sense."[65] By early August, the Japanese had packed the island with an additional eight divisions and eleven brigades. Moreover, the defenders had received 40 percent of all the ammunition available in the Home Islands. Accompanying the deployment of regulars was a program to turn the civilians of Kyushu into fighters to resist the invaders. Their participation in the fighting would have led to innumerable atrocities, as soldiers and marines became increasingly angered by civilians attacking them.

Even the appearance of carriers off the Home Islands, with hundreds of fighter bombers adding to the damage already inflicted by B-29s, hardly drew a response. Instead, the Japanese built up the stable of kamikaze aircraft and small vessels with which they planned to savage the invasion fleet.[66] Unlike what had happened at Okinawa, this time kamikaze pilots would surprise the Americans by targeting transports, hospital ships, destroyers, and destroyer escorts.

There were, of course, Japanese leaders who understood the insanity of continuing. Unbeknownst to the military, the foreign office had tried to use its embassy in Moscow to see whether the Soviets might intercede to achieve peace. The ambassador there, thoroughly sensible, understood how unrealistic such efforts were. On 15 July, he cabled, "In the long run ... [Japan] has no choice but to accept unconditional surrender or terms closely equivalent thereto."[67] The problem was the military was in control, and its leaders had no interest in escaping the disastrous situation into which they had dragged their country. Captain Rikibei Inoguchi, commander of the Tenth Fleet's training for kamikazes, noted, "In as much as the *Kamikazi* attacks were the last means of any favorable chance for breaking down American resistance a little, we did not care how many planes we lost. Poor planes and poor pilots were used, and there was no ceiling on the number of either available for use."[68]

The decision to drop the atomic bomb was inherent from its inception. There was some discussion before the weapon was used that a demonstration drop might spare Japanese lives, but the issue was framed around the belief the Japanese should be informed ahead of time so its leaders could see what they confronted. The suggestion was then rejected because of the possibility the weapon might not work and lose its impact. Thus, at 2:45 a.m. on 6 August, the *Enola Gay* began its takeoff roll; five and a half hours later "Little Boy" detonated, and the atomic age had begun. For Hiroshima's survivors, the horror of innumerable burns and injuries would be followed by radiation sickness lasting years into the future.[69] The initial response in Tokyo was muted because so little information was available. The second response was one of denial, namely the military argued the Americans could only possess one such weapon.[70]

But Hiroshima was only the first of the disasters to strike the Japanese in August. Three days later, Soviet spearheads from Outer Mongolia struck at the debilitated Kwantung Army. While the military in Tokyo received both the Soviet declaration of war and the news of military operations in Manchuria, its leaders had no idea of the extent of the Red Army's drives. On one hand, the Kwantung Army underestimated the Soviet drive into eastern Manchuria, but even worse, its intelligence sources missed entirely the sledgehammer blow rolling over western Manchuria.[71]

Then, on 11 August, the Americans dropped a second bomb, on Nagasaki, putting paid to the arguments that it was doubtful the Americans possessed more such weapons. Now it appeared they might have many. Crucially, the atomic bombs gave military leaders the excuse they needed to accept the emperor's decision for peace. As the emperor's advisor Lord Keeper of the Privy Seal Marquis Koici Kido noted, "If military leaders could convince themselves that they were defeated by the power of science but not by lack of spiritual power or strategic errors, they could save face to some extent."[72] For those Japanese who recognized that further struggle would only lead to the slaughter of millions of their fellow countrymen, the dropping of the atomic bombs offered the opportunity to open serious discussions about the need for peace, even if it involved "unconditional surrender."

But efforts at peace were a close-run thing that at several points threatened to collapse. The decisive cabinet meeting occurred at 6:00 p.m. on 9 August. With the military demanding continued resistance, Prime Minister Admiral Kantaro Suzuki informed the emperor that his ministers could not reach agreement. Shortly before midnight, Emperor Hirohito met with the cabinet, each of whom presented his position. When the statements were concluded, Suzuki asked the emperor for *his* decision. In clear words, Hirihito decided for peace.[73]

This was followed by a desperate effort to maintain control of the military, especially the army. An attempted coup by junior officers failed but only after fierce intercession by one of the army's most senior generals. "Only on August 9," Richard Frank notes, "after withstanding months of blockade and bombardment, obvious preparations for invasion, two atomic bombs, and Soviet intervention, did the Big Six [cabinet ministers] formulate terms for ending the war. Even then Minister Anami and Chiefs of Staff Umezu and Toyoda insist[ed] on maintaining the old order—a position completely unacceptable to the allies."[74] But with the threat of future atomic bombs hanging over them, military leaders grudgingly agreed to impose the emperor's wishes on their subordinates.

There is one important postscript that none of those who criticize the dropping of the bomb have been willing to address. The decision for peace could not have been timelier. In August 1945, LeMay's XX Bomber Command was almost out of Japanese cities to bomb, while American airmen were receiving the first tentative conclusions of the Strategic Bombing Survey of the bombing of Germany. One conclusion was that the bombing of rail and transportation networks had played a major role in the Normandy campaign and the collapse of the German war economy. As a result, the B-29s were about to begin a campaign to destroy the Japanese rail network. Had such a campaign been launched, it would have brought mass starvation to Japan's population because there would have been no way to transport food throughout the Home Islands. Even with that network still in place at the end of the war, the Japanese came close to starvation over the winter of 1945–1946.[75]

The End to the Other War

The same factors that destroyed Nazi Germany drove Japan to defeat. No matter how fanatically the Japanese military and people devoted themselves to the war, they could not overcome America's economic power. The Japanese had begun the war believing that a few sharp, decisive defeats would lead a divided American people to accept a peace that would leave the empire in control of the vast resources of Southeast Asia. But the success of that first strike unified Americans and placed the immense resources of the American economy behind a military effort that was beyond what most Japanese leaders could have imagined. The result was catastrophic defeat.

PART V

The Emergence of the Fifth Military-Social Revolution

CHAPTER FOURTEEN

The War That Never Was

What was it all about? It bothers me that we didn't learn a lot. If we had, we wouldn't have invaded Iraq.

—GENERAL WALT BOOMER on the Vietnam War

THE PERIOD FROM 1945 to the present, seventy-five-plus years, has seen the emergence of what we might best term the fifth military-social revolution. Its origins lie in the last years of the Second World War, but its initial progress after 1945 was slow. For the first three decades, assorted technologies, particularly computers and their scientific support structure, gained in useful capabilities, but the road forward remained ambiguous. In the 1980s, the revolution picked up speed, with a major impact on the military and civilian worlds. Gordon Moore's 1965 observation that the number of transistors in an integrated circuit would double every two years represents an apt expression of the increasing pace of the fifth military-social revolution.

The end of World War II did not bring an end to war or maintain the "grand alliance." John Lewis Gaddis notes that the Allies achieved victory over Nazi Germany "by the pursuit of compatible objectives by incompatible systems."[1] The resulting peace carried the possibility of a Third World War waged by ideologically opposed antagonists with weapons that would have ended the human experiment with an eruption of violence spectacular for its brevity. But that war never occurred (or at least has not yet) because the potential opponents were deterred by the power of the weapons at their disposal. On a few occasions, notably the Cuban Missile Crisis, the United States and Soviet Union trembled on the brink but at the last moment drew back.

That is not to say there were no wars. Human nature, the wreckage of World War II, and the collapse of colonial regimes made fighting inevitable. Occasionally the superpowers found themselves embroiled in colonial conflicts, but rarely did these threaten a great-power war. What is important is how those conflicts influenced the evolution of military capabilities. The significance of these technological developments lay not just in the correlation of forces but in their influence on the civilian world.

The irony of the atomic bomb was that while it promised decisive destruction of the enemy, such a victory would also bring about the destruction of one's own polity. The bomb's impact since the late 1940s has been to splinter the character of war into four specific forms.[2] The first is the reality that those possessing nuclear weapons would use them only in desperate circumstances. But even though they have not been used, superpower competition required development of ever more sophisticated nuclear weapons and delivery systems, which demanded enormous investments in technology and science, as well as innovation and adaptation.

At the same time, these powers also built conventional forces—in the case of the West, primarily to deter the Soviet Union from invading Europe. This second form of conflict, best characterized as conventional warfare, possessed the characteristics of combat in World War II. The impact of technological developments occurring with new conventional weapons has been considerable.

Inevitably, the Americans and Soviets allowed themselves to become involved in proxy wars in the developing world—the Americans in Korea and Vietnam, the Soviets in Afghanistan. In these wars, conventional forces proved incapable of winning decisive victories against irregular guerilla forces. In Vietnam, the United States might have defeated the North Vietnamese by unlimited firepower but at a moral cost American society was not willing to tolerate. Vietnam and Afghanistan are examples of the third form that conflict took, in which weaker opponents attempted to exhaust their opponents by draining their political will to continue. Irregular war has reversed the impact of attrition on the conduct of war. Whereas for five hundred years attrition in the Western way of war favored the side with the biggest battalions and greatest resources, since World War II it has become a strategy of the weak, who use irregular war to destroy the morale and will of the great-power opponent.

Not surprisingly, conventional and irregular conflicts have involved not only the superpowers but other nations as well. Alongside the proxy wars of the superpowers, there have occurred a number of conventional and irregular wars around the globe. Initially, these have involved efforts by colonial peoples to throw off the rule of their colonial masters, the war between the French and the Viet Minh over control of French Indochina being the most obvious.[3] There have also been conventional wars between Arab states and Israel, which because of the latter's technological developments influenced the thinking of the Soviet military in the 1980s. Finally, we might note non-state terrorism as a fourth form of war that has begun to affect not only the use of military forces by the developed world but also the societies they protect.

All four of these forms of post–World War II warfare were subject to the accelerating pace of innovation in military technologies and were affected as well by the changes in civil societies that come from technological change. The dropping of the atomic bombs on Japan was a harbinger of things to come. Yet it reflected just one of many advances emerging from World War II. No matter how primitive those devices may seem today, they were the first steps in unleashing the fifth military-social revolution, which has rested on precision weapons, sophisticated communication technologies, the influence of space-based systems, and the arrival of miniaturized computers—all of which grew out of developments that occurred during the Second World War.

The results of this fifth military-social revolution have swamped military and civilian worlds over the past four decades and will almost certainly continue to do so. The revolution emerged fully in the early 1980s and has only accelerated since then. While it got its start from military research and development during the Cold War, the civilian world has now become the primary driver, though there remains much feedback among military and civilian innovators, scientists, and experimenters. Even though it involved no direct combat between the superpowers, the Cold War brought investment not only in immediate military equipment but in research and development to improve weapons systems. For the Soviets, expenditure on weapons was almost wholly negative in that it imposed demands on an economic system that was too dysfunctional to adapt military innovations for civilian use. For Americans and a number of nations within their alliances, military developments in science and technology brought numerous benefits to the civilian world as well as to their armed forces.

In many respects the Cold War resembled World War II but without a clash of arms between the superpowers. Until almost the end, with the fall of the Berlin Wall, there were no decisive political or military victories. From its onset, the Cold War was a war of attrition in which economic power was more important than military forces. New capabilities, more expensive than those they replaced, appeared decade after decade and eventually joined the discarded piles of the obsolete, destroyed not by combat but by the introduction of ever more sophisticated weapons. In the end, like Nazi Germany and Imperial Japan, the Soviet Union collapsed into the wastebin of history—in this case because its economy failed to bear the cost of even a peaceful contest.

The Outbreak of the Cold War

Three great powers fought World War II: Britain, the United States, and the Soviet Union. Although Winston Churchill termed it the "grand alliance," in reality it was a Faustian bargain. While the British and Americans cooperated to an unprecedented extent to defeat the Axis Powers, the Soviets remained secretive, suspicious, and uncooperative. What held the alliance together was the homicidal Nazi regime. Even Stalin saw the implications of trying to make another deal with Hitler despite the failure of the British and Americans to launch a second front in 1942 or 1943. Given differing aspirations and ideologies, it was not a matter of whether the alliance was going to terminate but when. Only the West's illusions of Soviet tractability kept the alliance from dissolving immediately after the war.

With the coming of peace, Britain's position as a great power collapsed. The sacrifices made in waging the war against the Axis Powers deeply harmed its economic strength. In addition, the Labour government's efforts to create a more equitable society complicated efforts to play the role of a great power. The nation's leaders and people had neither the ruthlessness nor the financial strength to hold the empire together. The granting of independence to India in 1948 was the first step in dissolution of the largest empire in history. While the British made efforts to maintain their military, the war's damage made it impossible to maintain even a facade of power.

The United States faced no such difficulties: it emerged from the war in 1945 as the world's only superpower, an economic giant in every category. Alone among the victorious powers, it remained untouched by the physical ravages of war, and it had expanded industrial production by nearly 100 percent. Economists feared the country would confront a recession at the war's end, as it had after World War I, but that did not occur. The pent-up demand of wartime savings unleashed a wave of consumer spending that continued the economic expansion the war had begun.

Right after the war, the Americans set about tearing apart their military machine. They would rely on sole possession of the atomic bomb to protect the nation's security. By 1947, the U.S. military had shrunk to less than a quarter of its size in August 1945, and its overseas commitments were limited to occupation forces in western Germany and Japan. Even these burdens seemed too heavy for the isolationists deeply embedded in American politics. Despite the worsening international situation, the Americans failed to begin major rearmament until the outbreak of war in Korea.

The Soviets, unlike the British, possessed the ruthlessness not only to hold their empire but to expand it as well to control satellite states in Eastern Europe.[4] On the basis of the Nazi-Soviet Non-Aggression Pact of August 1939, the Soviets regained Lithuania, Latvia, and Estonia as well as substantial portions of eastern Poland and Romania, territories that Russia had held under the tsars. Finland was also meant to be a part of the booty gained from Stalin's enthusiastic cooperation with Hitler, but the Finns had proven too tough for incorporation into the "workers and peasants paradise." In the postwar period, strategic concerns most probably led the Soviets to refrain from incorporating Finland. Doing so might have led the Swedes to join the North Atlantic Treaty Organization (NATO), placing American air power in the Baltic. In addition, Stalin had no compunction in establishing puppet regimes in those Eastern European countries the Red Army had rolled over in 1944. Poland, Romania, and Bulgaria found themselves in the world of Stalinist communism so wonderfully depicted by George Orwell's *Animal Farm*. A 1948 coup d'état incorporated Czechoslovakia into the new empire.

Unlike the Americans, the Soviets kept much of their population under arms. Their military forces had totaled 11,365,000 at war's end but shrunk to 2,874,000.[5] Much of that strength aimed at ensuring those the Red Army had "liberated" remained in the Soviet orbit, but it was also a product of Stalin's paranoid inability to trust either the British or the

Americans.[6] In every respect the Soviet dictator matched Hitler and Mao in bloody-mindedness, but he was no Hitler. He was not about to embark on war with the United States when the correlation of economic forces was so unfavorable, particularly given the damage Russia had absorbed in the war. The atomic bomb in American hands was an imbalance he set his minions to rectify immediately because, as he observed, "brains—and the military technology they could produce—now counted for just as much as the divisions with which the Red Army had occupied Eastern Europe."[7]

Yet Stalin was willing to undertake aggressive diplomatic and political moves where he felt weakness, and given the war's devastation, Western Europe appeared a prime target. Germany, now divided into American, British, French, and Soviet occupation zones, was certainly in his sights. From the first, the Soviets made every effort to undermine the Western Powers' control over their zones in order to prevent the emergence of a unified non-Communist Germany. In their own zone, they stripped the landscape of everything they might use to rebuild the wreckage left by the Germans. But the behavior of their troops in eastern Germany hardly made the Soviets attractive to those living in the other zones.

The Cold War's chill settled in immediately after the war. Despite fears the United States would return to isolation, the Americans inevitably found themselves intertwined in the affairs of Europe and Asia. Their positions as an occupying power in Germany and the only one occupying Japan both carried important responsibilities. In fall 1945, faced with the collapse of Japan's food stocks, Douglas MacArthur persuaded Washington to provide enough food to prevent mass starvation—perhaps his most sagacious political move.

A few in the West saw the danger Stalin represented. Churchill publicly warned, in a speech at Westminster College in Missouri in March 1946, that "from Stettin in the Baltic to Trieste on the Adriatic, an iron curtain has descended across the continent" of Europe. Thirteen days earlier, George Kennan, a U.S. diplomat in Moscow, had dispatched a lengthy cable—later known as the "Long Telegram"—in which he both warned of Soviet ambitions and laid out a strategy for dealing with them. An anonymous version, published the next year in *Foreign Affairs*, summed up his approach: the United States needed to follow a "long-term, patient but firm and vigilant *containment* of Russian expansive tendencies."[8]

In the end, Stalin's policies proved that the Soviets represented a political and military threat to the West. Had he not followed such aggressive tactics so soon after the war, he might have achieved more, particularly given economic difficulties in Western Europe and the strength of Communist parties in France and Italy. Stalin pushed first in the Middle East. The British and Soviets had occupied Iran in summer 1941, both to provide military aid to the Russians and protect Middle Eastern oil. The British withdrew at the end of the war, but the Soviets continued to occupy northern portions of the country. But in early 1946, the British and Americans took the continued presence of Soviet forces in Iran to the United Nations, and Stalin withdrew his military forces and overt political operatives.

Even more important was Anglo-American support for Turkey's rejection of Soviet demands for joint control over the Dardanelles and bases on its territory. A year later, in 1948, the Americans stepped in and assumed British programs of support for Turkey as well as Greece, which was confronting an insurgency waged by Communists supported by Yugoslavia.[9] The most important American step to contain the Soviets came with George Marshall's announcement in June 1947 of the European Recovery Act, which aimed at rebuilding war-ravaged Europe.[10] In announcing America's desire to participate in Europe's recovery, the State Department skillfully included not only Western European nations but the Soviet Union and its satellites.

Stalin initially sent a delegation to the startup conference for the European Recovery Act in France but almost immediately withdrew it. The last thing he wanted was American access to Soviet territories. The USSR's withdrawal, along with that of its puppet regimes, gave the Americans a major propaganda coup. The Marshall Plan succeeded in boosting Western Europe's economies well beyond American expectations. The annual growth rate of European per capita income between 1948 and 1962 suggests the extent of recovery: Britain, 2.4 percent; France, 3.4; Italy, 5.6; and West Germany, 6.8.[11] Between 1948 and 1952, the West German economy increased industrial production by 110 percent and GNP by 67 percent.[12]

Stalin continued to draw a hard line between the Soviet Union and its former allies. In February 1948, the Communists in Czechoslovakia overthrew the democratic regime and tossed the Czech foreign minister, Jan Masaryk, son of the founder of the republic, from the window of his apartment. The Prague coup persuaded Congress to stop dragging its feet and pass the European Recovery Act. If the Czech coup were not sufficient, Stalin blockaded Berlin in June 1948. Several factors lay behind his decision, the most important being the city was a magnet drawing East Germans. Eleven months later, after an airlift had successfully supplied a city of over 2 million with coal and sustenance, Stalin abandoned the blockade. By then the Western Powers had created NATO, and the Western sectors of Germany were on the way to creation of an economic miracle.

As the Cold War deepened, momentous events were occurring in Asia. In 1949, Mao Zedong completed the Communist regime's takeover of China. Initially, Washington hoped it could work with the new regime, but Mao was in Stalin's camp from the moment his troops drove Chiang Kai-shek and the Nationalists off the mainland.[13] Nevertheless, the Americans took no substantive moves against the new regime. They even refused to protect the island bases to which Chiang had retreated. Hainan Island fell to the People's Liberation Army (PLA) in March 1949, while Mao and his military prepared to invade Taiwan.

At the end of World War II, the Soviets had moved into northern Korea while American soldiers occupied the south, the two powers agreeing on a demarcation line on the 38th parallel. Each side established a client government that had no intention of cooperating with efforts at reunification. In the north, the Soviets established a murderous regime under Kim Il-sung; in the south, the Americans backed Syngman Rhee, an autocrat cut from the same cloth as Chiang. Having supported Rhee and provided him with a minimal army focused on counter-guerrilla operations, the Americans withdrew in 1949. The following year, the American secretary of state, Dean Acheson, announced that neither Taiwan nor South Korea lay within America's Asian defense perimeter.[14]

For over a year after Mao's takeover of China, Kim Il-sung had urged both Mao and Stalin to allow him to unleash his army against South Korea.[15] Pushing him in that direction was the fact that guerrilla efforts, supported by infiltration of North Koreans, had failed by early 1950. Their efforts had led the United States to withdraw its troops. That factor influenced Stalin, along with Acheson's delineation of America's sphere of interest, to give permission for the North Koreans to launch their invasion. Kim seems to have believed his North Korean invaders would spark a nationwide uprising against Rhee.

The North Koreans enjoyed overwhelming military superiority, including a full complement of armored fighting vehicles and two hundred Soviet aircraft. The South Koreans possessed no tanks, and their artillery was outmatched.[16] The invasion, which began on Sunday, 25 June 1950, almost immediately caused both sides' assumptions to collapse. Stalin's approval of Kim's invasion proved one of his worst strategic mistakes. The United States did intervene, and because the Soviets were boycotting the UN's Security Council over its refusal to seat the Chinese Communists, the Americans were able to cover their intervention under a UN cloak.

On a strategic level, the invasion's most important result was that it forced the Americans to bring their military means into balance with their foreign policy. In March 1950, under the leadership of Paul Nitze, a study group formed by the State and Defense Departments had produced a report known as NSC 68, which called for a major U.S. program of rearmament. It recommended service force structures that would have tripled the 1951 defense budget: an increase in aircraft carriers from four to twelve, a growth in the army from ten under-strength divisions to eighteen combat-ready divisions and seventeen regimental combat teams, and an increase in the air force to ninety-four wings.[17] Without the Korean War, NSC 68 would have been dead on delivery. The North Korean invasion validated Nitze's strategic assumptions and formed the basis for American rearmament.

The unintended consequences of the invasion were equally important for the Communists. From the Chinese point of view, they were strategically disastrous. Within four days, President Harry Truman had ordered the Seventh Fleet to blockade the straits of Formosa so that the PLA could not overthrow Nationalist China's last stronghold. In Southeast Asia, the Americans reversed their policy of refusing to help the French, whose efforts to crush the Viet Minh uprising in Vietnam were on the brink of collapse, the first in a long series of ill-considered decisions that would lead to the catastrophe of America's involvement in the Vietnam War.

The Communists fared little better on the tactical and operational levels. The assumption that North Korean forces would reach Seoul and end the war within four days proved wrong. The South Koreans performed better than expected; some of their troops ran away but others fought well, while the military leadership was equally spotty.[18] Yet the South Korean Army remained a force blocking the way south. As the North Koreans advanced, they committed atrocities against class and ideological enemies, targeting Christians in particular.

Despite their best efforts to build Kim's army, the Soviets paid insufficient attention to logistics, and the push south ran into increasing supply difficulties. It also suffered heavy attacks by American aircraft, first based in Japan and then off carriers and temporary fields in South Korea. The first American troops arrived in mid-July and fared no better than the South Koreans. The U.S. divisions in Japan were little more than garrison troops, undermanned, inadequately trained, and poorly equipped.[19] The result was not pretty. Even when they fought well, the Americans found themselves outclassed by North Korean tanks and artillery. Not until August, when reinforcements arrived from the United States, were those deficiencies fixed.

As more and more American troops arrived from Japan and the United States, and as Allied aircraft attacked their opponents' supply lines, attrition took its toll. The North Korean advance ground to a halt in front of the port of Pusan, the only harbor able to accept the flood of U.S. equipment and reinforcements deluging the peninsula. As the Americans and South Koreans held tightly to their perimeter, MacArthur prepared his last great operational stroke. He had to persevere against opposition from most in Washington and many in the Far East, who considered an amphibious landing at Inchon too dangerous.[20] Marines, soldiers, and sailors made the landing work. Recapture of Seoul soon followed, while operations after the landings cut supply lines to North Koreans surrounding Pusan. In just days, what had been a desperate attempt by UN forces and South Koreans to hold onto the port became a rout of the North Koreans.

The question now was whether UN forces should cross the 38th parallel and liberate North Korea. MacArthur, not surprisingly, was a firm advocate, and he assured Truman there was little chance of Chinese intervention. In fact, from the start of discussions about a North Korean invasion, Mao had made it clear the PLA might have to intervene. In early August, he remarked that "we should not fail to assist the Koreans. We must lend them our hands in the form of sending our military volunteers there."[21] As UN forces rolled north in September, the Chinese had already deployed substantial forces in Manchuria. In October they crossed the Yalu River, catching the UN forces overextended, outnumbered, and unprepared. Arrival of winter from Siberia ended their advance.

In late November 1950, the western wing of UN forces ran into attacks that destroyed two forward deployed South Korean divisions. The Chinese followed with attacks that wrecked much of the U.S. 2nd Infantry Division, with only the 23rd Regimental Combat Team escaping. In the east, the PLA destroyed a U.S. Army regiment at Chosin Reservoir and surrounded the 1st Marine Division. But the marines were better deployed and fought their way out to the coast by "attacking in a different direction." They brought out their wounded and most of their dead, and withdrew from Wonsan to help form a defensive line close to the 38th parallel.[22]

The intervention by the Chinese ended whatever hopes Truman had of limiting defense spending. The administration faced many demands: meeting the Soviet military threat, supporting Europe's economic recovery, providing military aid to NATO, and the war in Korea. On 14 December 1950, Truman adopted much of NSC 68. The war in Asia alone was going to cost between $13 and $15 billion, more than the entire prewar defense budget. The overall defense budget for FY 1951 reached $56.2 billion and would rise to $70 billion for the following year.[23] Beyond its deterrent value, the buildup of forces laid the groundwork for research and development efforts that contributed greatly to the fifth military-social revolution.

Major tax increases to pay for these outlays followed. Mobilization of the economy went hand in hand with a call-up of young Americans. In the Korean War's first year, the administration drafted 585,000 and called 806,000 reservists and National Guardsmen to active duty.[24] Total defense spending quadrupled between 1951 and 1952.[25] The mobilization of American manpower and economic resources begun in 1950 would last, with ups and downs, until the end of the Cold War. It also removed the last prop from the isolationist wing of the Republican Party.[26] At their 1952 national convention, the Republicans would choose Dwight Eisenhower, leader of the Allied invasion of Europe during World War II and later the first supreme commander of NATO, as their presidential nominee over Robert Taft, the last prominent isolationist in American politics.

Since they were largely motorized, the UN forces were able to retreat from North Korea well ahead of the massed Chinese forces, which could only follow on foot. Mao's armies suffered continued attention from American air power on their march south, affecting both their advance and their logistical sustainment. On 29 December 1950, after the death of General Walton Walker, Lieutenant General Matthew Ridgway assumed command of the Eighth Army. Ridgway, undoubtedly the most outstanding tactical commander in the U.S. Army, inherited a serious situation: the full weight of Communist armies drove UN forces over the 38th parallel and again captured Seoul.

Ridgway more than justified his reputation. His divisions were undermanned but possessed overwhelming firepower. By late January 1951, with the Chinese troops exhausted by losses and air strikes on their supply lines, Ridgway launched a reconnaissance in force that turned into a counteroffensive that bloodied the Communists. By this point he had restored the UN troops' confidence. The Chinese resumed the offensive on 11 February but admitted defeat after seven days of ferocious fighting. Manpower against firepower was an equation they could not master. UN forces began a series of drives in mid-February with Operation Killer, followed by Operation Ripper, which recaptured Seoul at the end of March.[27]

While these battles were playing out in Korea, MacArthur stepped over the line into the political sphere. He urged expanding the war into Manchuria. Chair of the Joint Chiefs of Staff Omar Bradley put the strategic issue succinctly: an invasion of Manchuria represented "the wrong war, at the wrong place, at the wrong time, and with the wrong enemy."[28] By April, Truman had had enough: he fired MacArthur.

The UN offensives continued into June, by which point they had reached well beyond the 38th parallel and given the Communists a severe mauling. Exacerbating Chinese problems was the continued battering of their logistics system by American air power. In retrospect, had offensive operations continued, it is likely the Communists would have had to agree to an immediate armistice. But the UN high command halted offensive operations in the belief that the Communists, on the brink of further defeats, would begin serious negotiations. They did not, and the Korean War continued for two more years in a stalemate resembling World War I. It continued because Stalin found it useful to keep the Americans engaged in Asia. His death in March 1953 opened the way for an armistice. Peace, however, failed to provide hope for a unified Korea but instead set the stage for an economic and political competition in which South Korea, slowly at first but then more rapidly, built an economic powerhouse and eventually a democracy while the North sank into a merciless dictatorship incapable of feeding its people.

Korea was a major turning point in the Cold War. It showed that while nuclear weapons had changed the strategic framework in the ideological struggle between the superpowers, they had not lessened the importance of conventional war. The threat of nuclear war would continue to play a role in the contest, but it was conventional conflict among states that would ravage the human landscape. It seemed imperative that

American and NATO forces remain strong enough to deter the Soviets from risks that might escalate into war. But one of the conundrums of the Cold War was that neither the American people nor the Europeans were enthusiastic about building up conventional forces to match those of the Soviets.

The war in Korea did not introduce any new weapons, but it played a role in the long run: as the historian Walter A. McDougall noted, "It had locked into the American system the techniques of large-scale R & D, integration of science, industry and government, and economic controls."[29] Eisenhower, in his farewell address in 1961, would label this "the military-industrial complex." It was not entirely a bad thing: defense budgets would include commitments in research and development, investments that widened the gap between American and Soviet technologies. The advantages were not immediate but emerged over decades. The American R&D effort created the foundations on which much of the fifth military-social revolution would rest.

The Economic Competition, 1945–1990

Had Joseph Stalin lived for another five years, he might have embarked on a course leading to World War III. But his successors, though Marxist ideologues at least in rhetoric, had no intention of unleashing a nuclear war if they could avoid it. The struggle between the Soviet Union and the United States turned into a long political and economic contest in which development of new weapons, supported by technology, formed the backdrop. Yet as in World War II, the outcome was determined by the opposing sides' ability to develop the economic and financial strength to support their military organizations and research and development.

The Soviets embarked on this contest of economic systems in 1945 with an infrastructure devastated by war. Their first task was thus to rebuild. Several major factors burdened their efforts, the most obvious of which was the nature of the Soviet economic system.[30] While the centrally planned economy proved capable of rebuilding heavy industry to support the armed forces, it lacked the flexibility to match the West's scientific and technological developments after 1970. It also could not adapt to major unexpected innovations that provided new paths for economic development.

One problem for the Western Powers was the difficulty of calculating the Soviet economy's size, and thus the percentage of GNP devoted to military expenditures. The CIA's assessments in the early 1970s came under so much fire that the agency finally raised its estimates to 11 to 13 percent. But even these higher estimates, consistent with those of the academic world, underestimated reality. The problem was the denominator. Both the CIA and academics calculated that the Soviet economy was approximately half as large as that of the United States. In retrospect, it was at best one-third the size, especially when factoring in issues such as the system's waste.[31] In the post–Cold War period, the Pentagon's Office of Net Assessment estimated that in the 1970s and 1980s, the Soviet GDP was never more than 25 percent of America's.[32] Others estimated in the last decades of the Cold War that the Soviets were spending between 25 and 40 percent of GDP on defense.[33]

American expenditures on defense were much smaller as a percentage of GDP, but the U.S. economy was approximately three times larger. In 1960, American defense expenditures were 8.62 percent of GDP. The high point during the last three decades of the Cold War was 9.02 percent in 1967, during the Vietnam War.[34] Even at the low point during this period, 1979, defense expenditures were 4.77 percent of GDP. In 1982, during the Reagan buildup, they would reach 6.57 percent. Because Soviet GDP was one-third that of the United States, the Soviets would have had to raise defense spending by over 7 percent of their GDP to match American increases from 1979 to 1982.[35]

As one historian has noted, "Western economies were embedded in a vast economic system, in which technology transfer was relatively easy and the level of competition—and thus the spur to innovation—was relatively high."[36] That was simply not true of the Soviet system. Beginning in the 1970s, as the industrial age in the West gave way to the information age, innovation in computers and electronics grew increasingly important in supporting economic growth. Moreover, the Soviet agricultural system paid no attention to human nature, resulting in one disastrous harvest after another.

Adding to Soviet economic burdens was the fact that in 1945 Stalin initiated three major defense programs in addition to major commitments to conventional ground and air forces.[37] The first was the effort to build an atomic bomb, the second was a program to expand on the German V-2 ballistic program to deliver nuclear weapons over intercontinental distances, and the third was to develop an integrated air defense system. Stalin's stress on the last effort grew out of the Soviet experience in World War II: the impact of the Luftwaffe's raids in 1941 and their destructive attacks on Soviet industry, the wreckage created by the Allied CBO, and finally the devastation left by the atomic bombs. The emphasis on air defense was meant to ensure that the Americans would not repeat the CBO on the Soviet Union.

Building an air defense system required investments in radar and communications technology; radar-guided anti-aircraft artillery; sophisticated, radar-equipped fighter aircraft; and eventually surface-to-air missiles (SAMs)—none of which had received emphasis during the war. Moreover, the Soviet air defense system had to protect vast expanses of territory, covering eleven time zones as well as the puppet regimes in Eastern Europe. One commentator has noted that this system was equal in sophistication to the Soviet nuclear program.[38] None of the programs involved in air defense had been major factors in the Soviet forces in World War II; moreover, they overlapped with other bureaucratic interests that exacerbated difficulties in creating the system.[39] Yet while the Americans stopped investing in air defense in the late 1960s, the Soviets persisted in supporting theirs. By the 1980s, they had ten thousand SAMs and over three thousand interceptors deployed around the Soviet Union's immense periphery.

The Nuclear Technological Standoff

The costs of the buildup during Korea led Eisenhower, as president, to recast defense policy with the "New Look." He aimed to reduce defense spending by making American strategy dependent on deterrence through the threat of massive retaliation by nuclear weapons. The means of deterrence would be the Strategic Air Command (SAC).[40] The Soviet explosion of an atomic bomb in 1949 set off a race for superiority in nuclear weapons and delivery systems between the two superpowers that would have long-term consequences.

In 1946, the United States possessed only nine atomic bombs and twenty-nine B-29s capable of dropping them.[41] The bombs remained under the control of the Atomic Energy Commission, while the B-29s, with their primitive navigational systems, would have had difficulty finding targets in the Soviet Union in anything other than clear weather. In October 1948, Lieutenant General Curtis LeMay took over command of SAC. "Old iron pants," as his crews not so affectionately called him, soon had SAC and eventually the entire air force following his no-nonsense, by-the-book approach. LeMay's thinking about how his command would operate in a war with the Soviets tells us much about American strategy at the time. His initial briefing for the proposed SAC attack on the Soviet Union carried the Strangelovian title "To Kill a Nation." It proposed throwing all of America's nuclear weapons against the Soviets in one massive strike, some 133 atomic bombs on 70 cities. This, in the planners' words, represented "an opportunity to put warfare on an economical, sensible, reasonable basis."[42]

The aircraft had thus emerged as the premier weapon of war, permitting military forces to strike their enemies at increasing distances and with increasing lethality. This strategy placed a premium on research and development. The difficulty, however, would soon become apparent: air power could not hold ground or destroy ideas. And in the Cold War political arena of limited wars, that reality would impose serious limitations on its effectiveness.

The U.S. emphasis on nuclear forces required improvements in aircraft speed, range, and carrying capacity. By 1948, the B-29 was already obsolete for carrying out strategic nuclear attacks on the Soviet Union. The first replacement was the B-36, a massive bomber with six radial engines.[43] After building the first 84, the manufacturer added two jet engines in pods on each wing with 176 of this variant built. The B-36 came into service in 1948 and would be phased out of inventory in 1959.[44] It was the first true intercontinental bomber with a range of ten thousand miles, but given the Soviet Mig-15 jet fighter, the air force recognized B-36s were too vulnerable, as well as too expensive, to maintain.

The first American all-jet bomber, the B-47, followed the B-36 in 1951 and provided the bulk of the deterrence mission through to the early 1960s. Altogether, Boeing built 1,741 combat versions and a further 287 reconnaissance aircraft. Nevertheless, the B-47 was not a true intercontinental bomber because of its limited range. To fill the gap, the air force purchased 811 KC-97s, a derivative of the B-29, as tankers to refuel bombers on their way to bomb targets in the Soviet Union. By 1957, Boeing had completed work on the jet-powered tanker KC-135, which it developed with its 707, the latter soon dominating civil aviation. This spinoff of a military aircraft into the civilian world had an enormous impact on travel. Altogether the air force bought 811 of the tanker variants.[45]

The B-52 entered service in 1955. Boeing would produce 742 of this extraordinary aircraft, of which 76 of the H models were still in service in 2020. The last rolled off the assembly lines in 1963. The B-52 was the first true intercontinental bomber, especially when its range was expanded through refueling by KC-135s. Production runs of bomber and tanker aircraft suggest the strength of American technology and industry. The only heavy bomber the Soviets produced in the 1950s was the Mya-sishchev M-4. It was incapable of round-trip missions from the Soviet Union to North America and was so unsatisfactory that the Soviets turned most into long-range tankers.[46]

The 1950s also saw major programs derived from the V-2 ballistic missile technology the Nazis had developed during World War II. The Soviet launch of the first successful satellite, *Sputnik*, in 1956 led to a speeding up of U.S. ballistic missile programs.[47] After considerable interservice squabbling, the air force took the lead. The first two it deployed, the Atlas and Titan, were liquid fueled and difficult to maintain. The introduction of the solid fueled Minuteman in 1965 made America's nuclear deterrent far more responsive. By the 1970s, the air force had deployed a thousand intercontinental ballistic missiles (ICBMs).[48] The navy also joined the nuclear business. Driven by the chief of naval operations, Admiral Arleigh Burke, it produced the first SSBN (ship, submersible, ballistic missile), the *George Washington*, in December 1959. Five months later it launched the first Polaris missile from underwater, and by the mid-1960s the navy had forty-one SSBNs. The nuclear triad of bombers, land-based missiles, and sea-based missiles—the three main delivery systems—was now complete.

By the mid-1960s, the services, apart from the marine corps, had moved enthusiastically down the nuclear road. Conventional capabilities atrophied. But it was the air force that fell most heavily under the nuclear spell. As soon as the Korean War was over, its leaders concluded that the past was irrelevant. This myopia partly came from the political constraints Truman and Eisenhower placed on air operations in Korea, and partly from the emphasis on building up nuclear forces to deter the Soviet Union. Robert F. Futrell, an air force historian, argues that this approach placed "the emphasis . . . in making war fit a weapon—nuclear air power—rather than [in] making the weapon fit the war. It was a weapons strategy wherein the weapons determined the strategy rather than the strategy determining the weapons."[49]

In fall 1962, the American military came close to fighting the nuclear war it had so assiduously prepared for. When Nikita Khrushchev, the Soviet leader, recognized that his nation lagged behind the United States in the arms race, he took an enormous gamble: he compensated for American advantages by deploying intermediate missiles to Cuba. The Soviets also brought their most up-to-date SAM, the SA-2, to Cuba. For a week the world found itself on the brink of nuclear catastrophe, until Khrushchev, aware of Soviet weaknesses, backed down. He fell from power soon after, and his successors, determined that the Soviet Union would never again confront the Americans from a position of weakness, initiated major rearmament programs in both conventional and nuclear realms. Given their economic vulnerabilities, that was a dangerous strategic choice.

The U.S. military that entered the Vietnam War was undoubtedly the best prepared peacetime military in the nation's history. Major increases in the defense budget by the Kennedy administration had built up conventional capabilities. But they were fighting a guerrilla conflict against a politically and militarily sophisticated opponent. Most American leaders, military as well as civilian, were ignorant of their opponents' ideological toughness and entirely ignored the French experience of eight years earlier that had ended ignominiously in the Battle of Dien Bien Phu in 1954. North Vietnamese leaders, many educated at the French lycée Quoc Hoc, had inherited the French Revolution in its most virulent form. They proved an intractable enemy who refused to surrender, however much pressure the Americans applied. To confront the war in the south, Military Assistance Command Vietnam (MACV) responded with firepower that killed large numbers of civilians as well as the enemy.[50] The American approach employed conventional military power against an enemy that, for the most part, relied on irregular warfare and a willingness to endure hardship and loss.

The conflict in the north was an air war, driven by a belief that precisely targeted air strikes would bring the North Vietnamese to the peace table. Eventually, the air force and navy were forced to recognize that there were problems in their approach to air power. The first was that pilots were not sufficiently trained for air-to-air combat. The second was that the precisely targeted bombings were actually not that precise. Those weaknesses led to important innovations in weaponry and tactics. By 1972, the air force had acquired laser guided bombs, 28,000 of which it expended in that year's Linebacker bombings.

With its withdrawal completed by 1975, quickly followed by the collapse of South Vietnam, the United States confronted the wreckage left by a bitter conflict that had divided American society and nearly wrecked the nation's military organizations. Moreover, procurement, apart from weapons applicable to the conflict, had atrophied. The strategic impact of defeat in Vietnam proved less than one might have expected. Ironi-

cally, the "Vietnam syndrome" and the condition of their military prevented Americans from launching another Vietnam in the 1980s.

On the other hand, the Soviets viewed the United States' relatively
weak position as an opportunity to expand their influence. The support
tendered to Egypt in the mid-1950s and to Fidel Castro in the early
1960s represented the opening wedges. Both efforts were expensive, and
the Egyptians proved incompetent as well. Despite these difficulties, the
Soviets made considerable efforts in the 1970s to pull other states in the
developing world within their orbit: Somalia, Ethiopia, Eritrea, and Afghanistan all moved in the Soviet direction. Yet all became major drains
on a Soviet economy increasingly unable to support them.

The Soviet intervention in Afghanistan turned into a military and
political disaster. A coup in 1973 had overthrown the Afghan monarchy
with Soviet acquiescence. But events soon spiraled out of control, and in
December 1979 the Soviets, somewhat unwillingly, found it necessary to
take matters into their own hands and sent in their army. The Americans
enthusiastically threw themselves into supplying the Mujahideen with
weapons and other support that made Afghanistan a nightmare for the
occupying forces. The Afghan War was a major contributing factor to
the collapse of the Soviet Union. It also had a disastrous blowback effect
in the 1990s after the Soviet withdrawal, with the creation of a sanctuary
for radicalized Arabs.

The Recovery of the American Military

After the Vietnam experience nearly destroyed military discipline, the
Americans first had to restore order in their own house. They also had to
address the increasingly rapid technological changes in weaponry, which
were making weapons more expensive. The most obvious improvements
came in training regimens of ground and air forces. Throughout the
1970s, the navy's "Top Gun" and the air force's "Red Flag" improved the
ability of the air crews to simulate air-to-air combat situations while also
improving evaluation of the participants' performance. By the early
1980s, the army had created a National Training Center and Joint Maneuver Training Center, which provided a similar high-tech training environment for ground forces.

In retrospect, the late 1970s and 1980s were a time of extraordinary
innovation and adaptation for the U.S. military. Research on cruise missiles and stealth aircraft, which would reap dividends in the 1980s, received

support from the Carter administration. The weaknesses revealed by the Vietnam War formed the basis for expansion of military capabilities in the 1980s and the beginning of a revolution in military affairs that would increase aircraft capabilities and weapon accuracy by an order of magnitude. Jimmy Carter entered the presidency in January 1977 with the belief that the United States could cut defense spending and reach an accommodation with the Soviets. Some at the time argued that since the Soviets had reached nuclear parity with the United States, they would therefore stop building missiles. They did not.

Perhaps the most important change that occurred in the American military in the 1970s was the Nixon administration's decision in the summer of 1970 to end the draft. The rationale was political: to remove the psychological pressure that had radicalized America's draft-age youth during Vietnam. The path toward an all-volunteer military began with a draft lottery in 1972. After much difficulty in creating the necessary framework, the system for an all-volunteer military was in place by the mid-1970s, a change that would have crucial and unintended consequences. By requiring volunteers to serve for four years, the military gained personnel who had the time and interest to achieve higher standards than the draftees who served after World War II. It allowed the services to spend less time on new recruits while focusing on more sophisticated and complex training regimens. This proved a major advantage in a military with increasingly sophisticated weapons systems. That training would play a decisive role in the performance improvements that emerged in the 1980s.[51]

The 1970s also saw the steady, impressive development of computing capabilities. It is difficult for those living in the third decade of the twenty-first century to imagine how primitive computers were in the 1960s and 1970s. The size of the computer in Stanley Kubrick's 1969 movie *2001* suggests the extreme miniaturizing of computers that has occurred since then.[52] Among the innovations that drove the emerging revolution, two of the most important came from military needs.

The first of these resulted from intelligence agencies' efforts to break into Soviet codes after World War II. The Western Powers expected to enjoy the same success against the Soviets that they had had against the Axis Powers, and for a short period they did. But it did not last because the Soviets became aware of their weaknesses. In November 1948, they began making upgrades to their enciphering systems that made their message traffic unreadable. Desperate to find keys to access

Soviet cyphers, the National Security Agency (NSA) threw increasing manpower at the problem, then the first digital computers, and then more computing power. Much of this was in partnership with the private sector. This cooperation led some major companies, particularly IBM, to develop increasingly sophisticated computers.[53] While these efforts failed to break Soviet cyphers, IBM and other computer manufacturers applied what they learned in cryptoanalysis to their work for other governmental agencies and eventually the civilian world.

In 1956, NSA launched what it called "Recommendations for a Full-Scale Attack on the Russian High-Level Systems." At the time, IBM was pushing a proposal to increase the speed of its main computer, the IBM 705, by a factor of one hundred. It had developed the 705 for NSA but was also selling it to Los Alamos, the Weather Service, and army ordnance labs. IBM had a policy of ensuring that the machines it fabricated for NSA had other uses. By the late 1950s, there was a love affair between NSA and IBM. The firm was supplying half the computers used by the agency and raking in over $4 million each year in the fees attached to its products.

These fees accelerated as the firm's efforts yielded ever bigger computers. By 1962, the IBM 7950 was ready for delivery at a cost of $19 million, to which the company added $1 million for supplies, $4.2 million for software development and training those who were to operate the system, and nearly $200,000 for installation. There was also a rental fee of $765,000 for every year NSA used the computer. In the 1950s and early 1960s, NSA spent over $100 million for computers from various manufacturers. But the result, as a history of the agency admitted, was that NSA acquired only "rather low-level information."[54] A government panel concluded in 1958 that to break into the most sophisticated Soviet cypher machines would "involve testing about 10^{16} possibilities, [and] would cost $2,000,000,000,000,000,000,000,000,000 per message for the electricity required to power any known or projected computing device."[55] Thirty years later, a machine costing only $250,000 solved that level of problem in two days.[56] One can see why there was such pressure from NSA's perspective to develop more capable machines. Nevertheless, while its computers had little success against Soviet cyphers, they found major uses in other spheres.

The second push in the development of computer technology came from the space race. Both sides owed much to the German V-2, which had been only a waste of resources for the Third Reich.[57] The Soviets, largely at Stalin's direction, pushed their missile program harder than the Americans. By the mid-1950s, both sides had substantial missile programs. For a variety of reasons, Soviet rockets were substantially larger: partially because of weaknesses in their manufacturing capabilities, they built more redundancies into rockets, hence the need for size. In fact, Walter McDougall notes, "Giganticism in Soviet rocketry was a sign of primitivism, and the very . . . system that made the Soviets appear to be ahead in the 1950s inhibited their efforts to keep up in the 1960s."[58] Moreover, the rockets' size led the Soviets to place less emphasis on the miniaturizing of guidance and electronic components.

The Soviets achieved the first major success in the space race with their successful launching of the first satellite, *Sputnik*. That kicked off a furor in the United States that profoundly influenced science education. The Americans were not actually behind the Soviets, but the Eisenhower administration failed to anticipate the propaganda fallout that would result from the Soviets' launching a satellite first. The first American attempt to put a satellite in space, the TV-3, using a four-stage Vanguard rocket, ended in humiliating failure: "The rocket rose about four feet before falling back to the launch pad and exploding."[59] The Soviets also launched the first man into space, Yuri Gagarin, on 12 April 1961. Nevertheless, by 1960, the Americans were ahead in most areas of space technology, including guidance systems, warhead design, and solid-fuel manufacture. The guidance systems of the U.S. missiles were a particularly important sign of the Americans' ever-widening advantage. The miniaturization of computer technology and microprocessors eventually bled over into the civilian world in the 1980s. But in the early 1960s, none of this was apparent.

The Military-Social Revolution Emerges

The proxy wars between the Arabs and Israelis gave both the United States and the USSR opportunities to test new weapons systems. The overwhelming Israeli victory in the Six-Day War brought the Soviets into play directly. Fighting along the Suez Canal in 1968 led them to introduce their most up-to-date SAMs, as Israeli fighter bombers reached deeper into Egyptian territory. On 30 July 1970, Israeli F-4s and Mirages engaged twelve MiG-21s and shot down four. But that advantage did not last.

Entranced by the Six-Day War and successes in the War of Attrition, the Israelis rested on their laurels.[60] The Yom Kippur War of October

1973 came as a nasty shock, not only to the Israelis but to the Americans. The first attempts to use air attacks to turn the tide on the ground were a disaster, as SAMs devastated Israel's fighter bombers. In some 1,220 sorties flown to support the fighting in the first three days, the Israelis lost 50 aircraft.[61] Nevertheless, they repaired their air capabilities with help from the Americans, who rushed over their latest electronic countermeasures (ECM) gear. But aircraft losses remained heavy.

The following decade saw Israeli air force leaders absorb American inputs while expending financial and intellectual resources on developing and coordinating the complex emerging pieces of technology. They had no intention of repeating the experience of 1973. The chief science advisor to the Ministry of Defense suggested that advances in microprocessors and PGMs (Precision-Guided Munitions) offered the possibility of enabling "on-time assessments of threats, real-time battlefield intelligence, swift target acquisition, efficient command and control, and precision fire strike."[62] Yet Israeli military leaders never had the sense that they were embarking on a revolution in military affairs. They made improvements and changes on an ad-hoc basis with the aim of improving particular capabilities.

The denouement came in summer 1982. The Syrians had established a dense line of SAMs in the Bekaa Valley with the most modern Soviet missiles, and in 1982 they reinforced it. The Israelis responded on 8 June. Having scouted the location of SAM sites with remotely piloted vehicles (RPVs), they monitored Syrian electronic transmissions while their fighter bombers attacked the sites. Jammers harried missile sites. RPVs led SAM sites to turn on their radars, which F-4s then destroyed with anti-radiation missiles. Israeli command and control managed the battle space as if controlling an orchestra. As Dima Adamsky describes it, "The real-time battlefield picture was produced by the data fusion from the airborne surveillance radar, remotely piloted and unmanned flying vehicles, which monitored the area uninterruptedly."[63]

As the Syrians watched their missile umbrella literally go up in smoke, they sent their fighters up to halt the wreckage. But their MiG-21s and MiG-23s found themselves in a hopeless position. With their communications jammed by the Israelis, they had no clear picture of threats. During the first thirty minutes, the Israelis shot down twenty-seven MiGs. Within two hours, they had destroyed nineteen SAM sites and shot down eighty-seven Syrian fighters. Meanwhile, the Israelis had lost not a single F-4, F-15, or F-16. With destruction of the SAM sites and removal of the air threat, the Israelis then used laser-guided munitions to savage Syrian armor moving into Lebanon with laser-guided munitions.[64]

While the Israelis were developing and integrating sophisticated technologies, the Americans, in their efforts to rebuild their military, had initiated several weapons programs. In 1976, Andrew Marshall, director of net assessment, and Jim Roche, his assistant, produced a seminal paper, "Strategy for Competing with the Soviets in the Military Sector of the Continuing Political Military Competition," in which they argued the Defense Department should seek to compete in areas where the Soviets were weak, especially the electronic and computer fields and areas such as stealth technology.[65] They favored building the B-1 bomber, which would force the Soviets to continue heavy investments in air defense. But Carter canceled the program.

Donald Rumsfeld left the Defense Department the next year to be replaced by Harold Brown, who had earned a doctorate in physics from Columbia at the age of twenty-one. Brown was as impressed by the Marshall-Roche paper as Rumsfeld had been, and over his four-year tenure, he poured resources into an organization Eisenhower had created in 1958, the Defense Advanced Research Projects Agency (DARPA).[66] In 1978, DARPA began a project titled "Assault Breaker," which included a host of projects that would emerge in the 1980s. Among them were the Joint Surveillance Target Attack Radar System (JSTARS), stealth aircraft, electrical optical sensors, micro-electronic data processors, highly accurate cruise missiles, high-energy laser technology, and defense-related computer technology.[67] These programs provided the basis for the Reagan defense buildup. That rearmament presented the Soviets with unpalatable choices.

The Soviet arms buildup and the invasion of Afghanistan had prompted some increases in defense spending during Carter's last years. But the real expansion came under Ronald Reagan. The new secretary of defense, Casper Weinberger, was not in the same mold as his predecessors, James Schlesinger, Rumsfeld, and Brown; he had little interest in strategy. Given that Weinberger and Reagan believed the United States was behind the Soviets in all categories of military power, their solution was to increase spending at every level, including military bands. But no strategy emerged until the end of their tenure. At that point, because of external criticism and with the help of the Office of Net Assessment, the strategy of "competitive strategies" emerged. The United States would confront the Soviets with unpalatable defense choices that would add to their defense burdens.[68]

The Reagan buildup paid substantial dividends. Early in his presidency, he reinstated the B-1, this time as a subsonic bomber, which decreased its price but also its capabilities for a nuclear war. Nevertheless, it forced the Soviets to focus on air defense, which added nothing to their offensive capabilities. The decision to limit the B-1 to subsonic speed reflected the imminent arrival of stealth technology. National Security Decision Directive 12, which announced the reemergence of the B-1, also noted that the Defense Department would proceed with the B-2, the stealth bomber, which began production at the end of the decade.

The appearance of ground-launched cruise missiles and the Pershing, a mobile, intermediate-range missile, removed the possibility that the Soviets might destroy U.S. tactical nuclear capabilities in Europe with a first strike.[69] The high point from Reagan's point of view was the announcement of the Strategic Defense Initiative (SDI), or as it soon became known, "Star Wars." In retrospect, SDI's critics were correct: the means did not yet exist to enable widespread interception of incoming missiles, much less multiple independently targeted vehicles. What mattered, however, was not the system's potential but how the Soviets perceived it. To them, SDI represented one more indication of America's lead in technology, a capability they could not match.[70] According to Secretary of Defense Robert Gates, SDI became "the single most important object of Soviet diplomacy and covert action."[71] What mattered was not what the Americans could do but what the Soviets thought they could do.

In the 1980s, the United States and NATO began to develop a coherent effort to attack weak spots in the Soviet approach to a war in Europe. The most impressive concepts emerged out of the army and air force, buttressed by the technologies and capabilities that had emerged in the 1970s. Follow on Forces Attack (FOFA) was a response to the fact that while NATO might hold off Soviet forces stationed in the frontier districts between NATO and the Warsaw Pact, Soviet forces deploying from the western provinces of Russia would overwhelm NATO forces exhausted in the initial battles. FOFA thus aimed at using air attacks, cruise missiles, and other stand-off weapons to strike deeply at Soviet logistic and transportation grids, moving the second and third echelons through Poland and East Germany to the front. The ancestor of FOFA and its necessary weapons was the "Assault Breaker" concept developed by DARPA.

The army put forward the second major concept with input from the air force. Titled "Air-Land-Battle," the concept aimed at taking on the Soviet second-echelon forces by using aggressive tactics and deep fires. Developing out of work by General Don Starry and his successors, Air-Land-Battle emphasized using maneuvers and guided munitions to disrupt and degrade Soviet second-echelon forces while holding the first-echelon forces through aggressive counterattacks with new systems. Yet however forward-thinking these and other efforts were, few analysts in the West recognized that a major shift in capabilities was creating new possibilities for military operations.

While the Americans and Israelis worked on tactical and operational capabilities, the Soviets had been examining a larger picture. Unlike Anglo-Americans, who have had little interest in war at the theoretical level, the Soviets have been theorizing about war since the 1920s. In the early 1960s, they concluded that the twentieth century had seen two major military-technical revolutions. The first was the mechanization of air and ground war that allowed for "deep operations."[72] They had developed the theory of such operations and applied it in the great offensives against the Wehrmacht in 1944 and 1945.[73] Similarly, they argued that the Anglo-Americans had realized deep air operations in the CBO against the Reich, which had destroyed the Reich's economic and transportation systems.

The Soviet thinkers identified the appearance of nuclear weapons and missile technology in the 1950s as the second military-technical revolution. These developments had altered the character of war.[74] Then, in the 1970s, watching the Americans work on new capabilities, Soviet military thinkers believed they were seeing a third military-technical revolution emerging. The increases in American bombing accuracy as well as electronic countermeasure gear and anti-radiation missiles gave them reason for thought. While American strategists and economists overestimated the size of the Soviet economy, the Soviets were overestimating the ability of the Americans to develop weapons systems at the edge of technological possibilities.

The openness of U.S. society to developments in defense led the Soviets, in their paranoiac world view, to estimate that the Americans were far ahead of what public discourse suggested. "Assault Breaker," to the Soviets, was more than a concept: it was an emerging capability the Warsaw Pact would face as it attempted to move second-echelon forces forward. By the mid-1970s, Dima Adamsky notes, Soviet defense experts were discussing the implications of "military applications of microelectronics, laser, kinetic energy, radio frequencies, electro-optic, electro-magnetic pulse, remote control, and particle beam technologies."[75] The Reagan buildup intensified the nightmare because much of American spending was occurring on precisely those capabilities, such as stealth, guided munitions, and eventually SDI, which the Soviets were character-izing as the third military-technical revolution. The accuracy of Ameri-can precision weapons particularly worried Soviet military thinkers as they grappled with improvements in U.S. and NATO capabilities.

In 1984, Marshal Nikolai V. Ogarkov, chief of the Soviet general staff, characterized advances in non-nuclear technology, including "auto-mated reconnaissance-and-strike complexes (the 'Assault Breaker')," in terms of long-range and precision guided munitions and electronic con-trol systems. Such emerging capabilities, he wrote, "make it possible to sharply increase (by at least an order of magnitude) the destructive po-tential of conventional weapons, bringing them closer . . . to weapons of mass destruction in terms of their effectiveness."[76] Ogarkov was admit-ting, in effect, that the new American weapons could take out Soviet command-and-control systems and much of the second echelon without use of nuclear weapons. This was a challenge to which the Soviets had no effective response. Moreover, they were steadily falling behind in creat-ing such technologies.

Ogarkov's solution called not only for reforms in the Soviet defense establishment but for major increases in defense spending. But in the mid-1980s, as the leadership grappled with the Soviet system's economic difficulties, his recipe was as unpopular with civilian leaders as with the conservative military leadership. The financial resources and economic sophistication were not there for increases in defense spending, and much of the Soviet officer corps had little interest in changing how it did business. Ogarkov was removed from his position and transferred to a command in the Warsaw Pact.

The significance of what the Soviets saw as a third military-technical revolution appears to have passed by the Americans, who hammered away at creating new capabilities without considering how the pieces might fit together in a larger whole. While in retrospect the American military was on the brink of creating a revolution in military affairs, that was not apparent to them. It would take a major success after the Cold War to wake them up to the extraordinary advances they had created.

The efforts of Mikhail Gorbachev and his reformers came too late to save a system that had been slowly collapsing from within. As one worker said of the utterly dysfunctional Soviet economy, "We pretend to work, and they pretend to pay us." The end came suddenly and was surprisingly quiet. Like Britain's leaders in the immediate aftermath of World War II, those of the Soviet Union in 1989 were no longer willing to use bullets to hold their empire together. Not only did the regimes in Eastern Europe collapse—a reality signaled by the fall of the Berlin Wall—but the Soviets lost control of their internal empire with the Baltic states, Ukraine, and Central Asian republics declaring independence. The collapse reflected a broken economic and political system that could not support a military burden that throughout the Cold War had gobbled up between one-fifth and one-quarter of the nation's GDP. The impact of such spending was twofold. It narrowed research and development efforts solely to the military, and it prevented investment in other sectors that might have contributed to growth.

At the Cold War's onset, the Soviet Union's economic weaknesses were not so clear, at least in traditional economic calculations. Up to 1960, the Soviets rebuilt their economy with the emphasis on coal and steel. If the military products, especially aircraft, were not up to Western standards, the numbers of divisions more than made up for whatever qualitative advantages Western forces enjoyed.[77] But beginning in the early 1970s, technological advances put the Soviets at an increasing disadvantage. The collapse of 1989 was not inevitable; it reflected Gorbachev's unwillingness to employ the same ruthlessness of his predecessors. Had Yuri Andropov not died when he did, the Soviet Union would have stumbled on for a few more years. But the Soviet economy could no longer sustain its monstrous defense establishment.

After the Cold War

Even before the Cold War ended, major technological developments were beginning to seep from the military into civilian society. In the 1980s, Reagan released GPS (global positioning satellites). While initially its possibilities remained somewhat opaque (the air force almost killed the program early in its development), by the 1990s it had exploded. The release of the internet into the civilian world by President George H. W. Bush in the late 1980s had a similar impact. Historians a century from now—if they still exist—will mark the period beginning in 1990 as one of the most revolutionary in history. What refocused the U.S. military's attention on the larger possibilities was a crisis in the Persian Gulf that threatened America's supply of Middle Eastern oil. That the Soviet Union was collapsing freed the United States and its allies to use their military's emerging capabilities.

The crisis began in July 1990 when Saddam Hussein, Iraq's dictator, found himself in a perilous financial situation. Iraq had just finished a long and costly war with Iran that began in September 1980.[78] Iraq's victory over Iran in 1988 was hardly a cause for celebration in Baghdad. The war had been so costly that Iraq was on the brink of bankruptcy; to support it, Saddam had borrowed billions of dollars from the Gulf States to pay for arms purchases. Now he had to pay off those loans. His solution was to seize the oil-rich sheikdom of Kuwait, a military operation his army accomplished in a matter of hours.

The Americans responded with a major military buildup to force Saddam to disgorge Kuwait. The F-15s arriving in Saudi Arabia in August 1990 would have had little difficulty gaining air superiority, but as Lieutenant General Chuck Horner, the air component commander and acting theater commander, commented, the initial brigade of the 82nd Airborne Division represented little more than a "speed bump" should the Iraqi Army attack Saudi Arabia. By October the Americans and their allies, which included British and French divisions, had built up sufficient ground forces that even Saddam at his most irrational would not have dared to invade Saudi Arabia. But it was another problem to force the Iraqis out of Kuwait, especially given that the American military overestimated Iraqi military capabilities. Some pundits described the Iraqi Army as equivalent to the battle-hardened soldiers of the Waffen SS. In fact, its military organizations were a shambles.

At least in terms of the coalition air threat, Saddam had reason for confidence. During the Iran-Iraq War the Iraqis had bought state-of-the-art systems from the Soviets and French for their air defenses. KARI, the Iraqi air defense system, represented an order-of-magnitude increase in complexity, extent, and numbers over what the Israelis had faced in the Bekaa Valley in the early 1980s. Overall, Iraqi air defenses consisted of some five hundred radars located in over one hundred sites, and eight thousand anti-aircraft weapons. To defend Baghdad, the Iraqis deployed four thousand fixed and mobile artillery pieces and SAMs.[79]

The coalition had assembled a huge aerial armada. The Americans alone brought over a thousand combat aircraft. But only a few of these were precision-capable aircraft that could drop laser-guided munitions. The two most important in that category were F-117 stealth fighters (thirty-six available) and F-111Fs (sixty-four available). The new F-15Es, which were night capable with precision capabilities, possessed only four targeting pods when deployed in January. For high-value targets that needed to be hit precisely, the F-117s carried the load; altogether they hit 78 percent of precision targets on the first night.[80]

Led by Lieutenant Colonel Dave Deptula, Horner's planners calculated that one bomb each, instead of the four required for total destruction, would render the air defense centers unusable, given the Iraqis' unwillingness to tempt fate and return to a site once hit. At 2:51 a.m. on 17 January 1991, an F-117 dropped the first laser-guided bomb on the Nukhayb Intercept Operations Center, the central headquarters for air defense. The planners were right; the central headquarters and all four sector sites remained silent for the remainder of the war after each was hit with a single bomb. A series of F-117 attacks throughout Iraq followed the first strikes. These hit all of the sector stations and the communication center in Baghdad.

The attacks on Baghdad took place while the F-117s were flying over the capital, unseen by the massive air defenses. Meanwhile, the navy fired off fifty-two Tactical Land Attack Missile-Tomahawks against leadership, chemical, and electrical power targets around Baghdad; all hit their targets between 3:06 and 3:11 a.m. These initial stealth and cruise missile attacks paralyzed the Iraqi air defenses. A series of conventional attacks wrecked most of the SAM sites and anti-aircraft positions with HARM (high-speed anti-radiation missile) anti-radiation missiles. When the night was over, the KARI system was dead. The coalition had estimated the attack would cost it twenty-five aircraft; it lost a single navy F/A-18.[81]

The remainder of the air war was a foregone conclusion. Nevertheless, in one major respect the coalition leaders were lucky. As the air war pounded the Iraqis, Saddam had the option to withdraw from Kuwait before the ground war began. Had he done so, he could have argued that Iraq had stood up against the Americans, who had proven too cowardly to attack him on the ground. This was not true, but such a claim would have proved effective propaganda. Fortunately, he was stubborn. He stood his ground until coalition divisions were ready. They then gave his army as severe a drubbing as his air forces had received at the conflict's beginning.

Not surprisingly, the victory in the Gulf War—astonishing at least to military pundits—led to a hallelujah moment in which many saw the bright light of an entirely new way of war. The Office of Net Assessment initially used Soviet terminology in describing what had happened as a "military-technical revolution." In 1992, one of its assessments proposed that "a Military-Technical Revolution occurs when the application of new technologies into military systems combines with innovative operational concepts and organizational adaptations to alter fundamentally the character and conduct of military operations. ... Such adaptations are characterized by: Technological Change; Military Systems Evolution; Operational Innovation; Organizational Adaptation."[82] Those in the Office of Net Assessment understood that it was the concepts and organizational adaptations that mattered, not just the technology. But in their enthusiasm, the office's analysts failed to dampen down much of the overwrought response that misunderstood the extent and implications of the revolution. Many in the Pentagon's leadership accepted the terminology but identified a revolution in military affairs as a purely technological change—the more rapid the better.[83]

History had no role in their conceptions. The claims of what the revolution might bring were extraordinary. Leading generals and admirals emphasized that technological changes made Clausewitz's warnings about the prevalence of friction in war irrelevant. The vice chair of the Joint Chiefs of Staff went so far as to argue "that technology could enable US military forces in the future to 'lift the fog of war.' ... The emerging system of systems promises the capacity to use military force without the same risks as before."[84]

The air force was no less enthusiastic, at least among its leadership. In that service's *New World Vistas*, a pamphlet on the future, the authors argued that "the power of the new information systems will lie in their ability to correlate data automatically and rapidly from many sources to form a complete picture of the operational area, whether it will be of the battlefield, or the site of a mobility operation."[85] By the late 1990s, some enthusiasts were arguing that new and emerging capabilities were such that "rapid decisive operations" were now possible. Once again, the mirage of decisive victory shimmered in the distance. Such thinking contributed to the belief that what mattered in the 2003 offensive against Saddam Hussein's bedraggled army was the destruction of his military forces.

How far removed such thinking was from reality became clear in America's first two campaigns of the twenty-first century. In just a few weeks in 2001, the United States projected its air and ground power across continental and oceanic distances to overthrow the Taliban in Afghanistan. Two years later it achieved similar success in destroying Saddam Hussein's army, causing his regime to fall. But the conventional victories of 2001 and 2003, which seemed so impressive, mutated into political and guerrilla wars for which the American military had little preparation and to which it proved astonishingly slow to adapt. In its conduct of those wars, the United States repeated every mistake it had made in Vietnam. Twenty years on, the Taliban again control Afghanistan. In Iraq, a dispirited and incompetent regime appears to be under Iranian control. The American effort in those two wars has brought it no political or strategic success—the reason one supposedly fights wars.

On 24 February 2022, Vladimir Putin launched Russia's military forces in what was supposed to be a Blitzkrieg that would overwhelm Ukraine's corrupt and incompetent regime. However, his military proved, in the best traditions of Russian history, to be a "Potemkin village." Moreover, Russian troops have also lived up to the performance of their ancestors who ravaged and raped their way through Eastern Europe in 1944 and 1945. In the spring, the Russian spearheads that had approached Kyiv at the war's outset ignominiously retreated back to the Russian-Belorussian frontier. Meanwhile, the Ukrainians managed to retake Snake Island and sink the cruiser *Moskva*, ending Russian pretensions of possessing control of the Black Sea. This was followed by massive artillery bombardments by the Russians and attacks in the Donetsk and Luhansk provinces, which gained little ground at huge cost. And then in September, the Ukrainians struck, capturing several thousand square miles to the east of Kyiv. Now, as this is being written, they have retaken Kherson.

How will it end? There are three possibilities: The first is an outright Russian victory, which given the performance of their military thus far seems unlikely. The second is that exhaustion will force both sides to agree to an armistice that fails to meet their expectations. At present that is unlikely from the Ukrainian perspective, given the extent of Russian atrocities. The third possibility is an outright Ukrainian victory, but that depends on two factors: the collapse of the Russian Army and the continued support of NATO. Either is uncertain and dependent on factors that remain unpredictable. What is certain is that whatever occurs on the battlefield, the Russians will remain a power, hostile to the international order, much as with the Weimar Republic, where Germans enthusiastically supported myths about being stabbed in the back and greeted the arrival of the Third Reich with enthusiasm.

The war in Ukraine has thus far resembled everything from World War I's massed artillery duels to cyberattacks. Ironically, given prewar predictions, the Ukrainians displayed an extraordinary popular response that led amateurs to rush to defend their country. It was a similar response to what occurred in the first years of the French Revolution. As for the impact of the Industrial Revolution, NATO and others appear to be in the process of creating a modern military with their shipment of weapons to the Ukrainians.

The shambles of the Russian mobilization suggests how badly prepared to handle a conflict lasting more than a couple of months they are. In the long run the Russian underestimation of the impact of sanctions on their ability to import chips may prove to be even more disastrous than their ill-thought-out and executed invasion. Those chips are crucial to the successful production not only of industrial goods but of virtually all weapons systems. As long as the Russians no longer have access to them, they will not be able to produce modern weapons in the numbers an extended war would require. That undoubtedly explains their desperate purchases of Iranian drones in large numbers.

The new and the old have coexisted on the Ukrainian battlefield. Unmanned aerial vehicles provide unheard-of intelligence about what is on the other side of the hill even to squads and platoons. They clearly are critical for precise artillery firing. Western artillery, such as the American HIMARS (High Mobility Artillery Rocket System), allow Ukrainians to hit precise targets and then move even before the rockets hit the ground. While the devastating losses of tanks and armored personnel carriers in the opening days of the war have led some to argue that the day of the tank is over, placed in combined arms units, the day of armor is not yet over. In the end, it will be the soldiers on the sharp end who will determine the outcome.

The Emergence of the Next Military-Social Revolution

The decades since 1945 have seen an extraordinary explosion of knowledge. The implications of the fifth military-social revolution for the wider human condition are for others to examine. But while it has given military organizations extraordinary new capabilities and fundamentally changed the character of war, it has not altered the nature of that grim endeavor, which human beings have pursued with such enthusiasm over the past five centuries. The tragic end to America's wars in Iraq and

Afghanistan should burn those harsh experiences into the hearts of every future military and political leader of the United States. But that is unlikely to happen, any more than it happened after the Vietnam War, of which Iraq and Afghanistan were mere dismal replays. Unwilling to learn from their own history, Americans will stumble into the future fully capable of repeating their errors. Maybe the Ukrainians will teach us something.

CHAPTER FIFTEEN

The Dark Future

But dreadful is the mysterious power of fate: there is no deliverance from it by wealth or by war, by fenced city, or dark, sea-beaten ships.

—SOPHOCLES, *Antigone*

THE MURDEROUS HISTORY OF the past five hundred years suggests all too much about the coming century.[1] Geoffrey Parker, commenting on the rise of the West, recently noted that "the history of the West, both at home and overseas, has centered on a ferocious competition for mastery among uncompromisingly ambitious powers, in which the ruthless, the innovative, and the decisive, displaced the complacent, the imitative, and the irresolute."[2] The problem now confronting the inheritors of that tradition is that others from outside the West have joined the competition, both at the high end of technology and by reversing the paradigm of attrition that had allowed practitioners of the Western way of war to crush their opponents through superior economic and military strength.

There is an ironic disconnect between the ever more impressive and destructive weapons being designed, produced, and deployed and their likely irrelevance to most of this century's wars. While they can kill, destroy, and maim at an impressive rate, they seem largely counterproductive to the political and strategic purposes such wars are supposed to serve. Most of these weapons were designed for fighting opponents at the high end of a great-power war. One can only hope that they serve as deterrence rather than in actual combat, for great-power war, even with conventional weapons, has become so lethal that it might well threaten the survival of humanity.

As it was in the 1980s, Afghanistan has once again been the venue for a fundamental shift in the character of war. The vast resources of modern-day great powers, their expensively trained high-tech militaries, constant innovation, and economic power no longer seem able to prevail against lateral thinking, a willingness to adapt, and the commitment to see the struggle through to the end no matter the cost. The wars of the great against the small no longer hinge on the attrition of manpower and resources by the greater power; instead, they are decided by the attrition of will. At least in democratic states, where popular opinion has a significant say, the willingness to stay the course is no longer a certainty in wars where there is no discernable end state.

That was the lesson the American polity should have learned from Vietnam. The casualties American firepower could impose on the Viet Cong and North Vietnamese were irrelevant because they failed to weaken the will of the leaders in Hanoi. There was, of course, Curtis Le-May's solution, which was to "bomb the North Vietnamese into the stone age." But the American people would not accept such a course because the threat did not justify such a merciless use of their military power. Iraq and Afghanistan repeated that warning. Only where the existence of the American polity is at stake will U.S. military leaders be allowed to employ the full panoply of their sophisticated weapons, including nuclear weapons, against an enemy.

The wars the United States is likely to fight in the twenty-first century, however, will not be wars of national survival. The Western way of war for the past one hundred years has relied on increasingly sophisticated logistical support and effective and adaptive systems of training, deployment, and employment. But the experiences of the past seventy-five years, from the viewpoint of smaller powers, suggest that a willingness to stay the course and the ability to wait out the great powers, while they fritter away billions and lose their morale and will to continue, is a costly but ultimately winning strategy.

Does this new reality represent a fundamental overthrow of the Western dominance of the conduct of war? MacGregor Knox has written of the difficulties of using history as a guide to the future that "the owl of history is an evening bird. The past as a whole is unknowable;

only at the end of the day do some of its outlines dimly emerge. The future cannot be known at all, and the past suggests that change is often radical and unforeseeable rather than incremental and predictable. Yet despite its many ambiguities, historical experience remains the only available guide both to the present and to the range of possibilities in the future."[3]

The collapse of the Soviet Union in 1991 only increased America's economic and military dominance. Nevertheless, one might characterize the thirty years that followed with the phrase Churchill used to describe the 1930s: the "locust years." These recent years saw the United States not only pursue decisive victory in Iraq and Afghanistan but embrace the delusion that it could remake those societies.

How to explain the extraordinary missteps of American strategy in that era? Perhaps it is useful to contrast the worldviews of the presidents and those who advised them on strategic issues in the forty years before 1992 with those that have come since. Franklin Roosevelt, Harry Truman, Dwight Eisenhower, John Kennedy, Richard Nixon, and Ronald Reagan were all to some extent students of history, and many of those who advised them also possessed a deep sense of the past. They included George Marshall, George Kennan, Henry Kissinger, George Shultz, and James Schlesinger. The presidents since 1992 have been remarkable for their lack of interest in history. Bill Clinton's hunt for the mantra of globalization had a disastrous impact not only on the economic future of the United States but on the nation's politics and ironically even his political party. Barack Obama may have been one of the most intelligent American presidents, but one can sum up his lack of understanding of the world outside Columbia and Harvard by his disastrous policies toward the drawdown of U.S. forces in Iraq, the war in Afghanistan, and the "line in the sand" in Syria. Then, of course, there is Donald Trump, who has rarely, if ever, opened a book, much less a history book.

It became popular among certain academics to suggest that the world is entering a period of relative peace after the bloody twentieth century. One of the foremost exponents of this view, the Harvard psychologist Steven Pinker, argues that states are increasingly finding war of less utility.[4] But Pinker bases his argument on a misreading of trends and a general ignorance of history. He seems not to understand that history (to borrow a term from evolutionary theory) is a punctuated equilibrium: at some moments a placid ocean, at others a massive tidal wave that swamps whole societies and leaves the landscape permanently changed.

Perhaps nothing epitomizes this reality more than the Russian invasion of Ukraine, which in many ways resembles Hitler's invasion of Poland in 1939 and Stalin's attack on Finland the same year. Before 24 February 2022, the world of ordered, law-abiding states that comfortably inhabited the European Union, parts of Asia, and North America found it inconceivable that Russia would embark on a murderous invasion of Ukraine. What has happened since is a destructive misuse of military force that still appears unbelievable. But there we are. In the real world, dictators like Vladimir Putin will continue to exist. The world is not going to become a more peaceful place, whatever middle-class Americans and Europeans may think.

In the light of the past five centuries, the challenges of the future appear daunting. There are many. The most obvious is the coronavirus, which has proven insidious in its ability to spread and adapt but even more frightening is the fact that it may be a harbinger of the future. Perhaps the greatest danger of the virus comes from its political impact, and not just in the United States, where irresponsible politicians and media worsened its impact. Moreover, it represents a significant warning on how the human race might react should a more dangerous disease appear.

Equally worrisome has been the decline of the global order established by the Americans after World War II. The explosive military-social revolution that emerged in the 1980s has accelerated that decline. Another contributing factor is the appalling ignorance of an American polity about the world it lives in, exacerbated by a general contempt for history among both leaders and citizens. It only adds to the complexity of international politics that over the past two decades the great-power arena has changed significantly. The economic and political rise of the People's Republic of China has given the United States one of the greatest long-term challenges in its history.

In the end the greatest dangers are those we cannot or do not want to see. Those living in the present have always been riding on a world awash in uncertainty. Their actions have often resulted in second- and third-order effects they can barely sense. Radical and unforeseen change, the black swans of history, is so fundamental to the world in which we live that attempts to forecast the future will always founder in the unexpected.

Bismarck once wrote that "in politics you cannot focus on a long-range plan and proceed blindly with it. All you can do is draw the broad outlines of the direction that you wish to follow."[5] One can argue that

Western nations have lacked a strategic framework since the end of the Soviet threat. If that lack of direction were not a dark enough threat, it comes at a time when the fifth military-social revolution is altering not only the character of war but of human society.

The Fifth Military-Social Revolution

The Cold War saw accelerated scientific and technological developments that not only created military possibilities but ultimately altered the entire fabric of societies around the world. Previous military-social revolutions occurred in the West and were brought from there to other countries and continents largely by conquest. The fifth military-social revolution is global, and it directly affects not only nation-states but non-state actors as well. It may take different paths in different places, but it is occurring simultaneously and affects all to one degree or another.

At its onset in the 1960s, few in the military, and few scientists for that matter, foresaw the effects the transfer of technologies and innovations would have beyond their own narrow worlds. At a meeting of computer scientists at MIT in the late 1970s, participants wondered what possible use computers might have in people's day-to-day lives. For the most part, they were thinking of innovations in the classic pattern of improving current capabilities. The synergies inherent in new technologies are always much harder to imagine. No one at that meeting, for instance, could have predicted that a handheld computer merging the functions of a camera, a telephone, and a radio would someday be used to transmit images of social unrest instantly around the world.

The internet emerged out of research done by the Advanced Research Products Agency (the forerunner of DARPA) in the 1960s. By the 1970s, that research had morphed into a nascent communications system used by military research organizations to coordinate with collaborators in university research centers. But few of those developing the internet—or DARPAnet, as it was then known—had any sense of what would happen when it exploded in the 1990s. As we saw in the last chapter, the intercontinental missile and its accompanying weapons forced Americans to create smaller and smaller microprocessors, which, when they became cheap enough to be available to the civilian market, created the computer revolution—an unforeseen and unintended effect.

Until the end of the Cold War, research and development for the military largely drove technological improvements and innovations.

Since the end of the Cold War, the opposite has been occurring. The great grandchildren of the Bombes, which unraveled the mysteries of the German Enigma machines for Bletchley Park, have now given humanity the ability to build weapons of an accuracy, sophistication, and magnitude previous generations would not have thought possible. They have also led to advances in civilian capabilities—personal computers, communications satellites, mobile phones, GPS, the internet, and so on, all of which have altered the character of societies. The explosion of technological, computer-driven change in the civilian world has had a direct impact on the military. Much of the continuing computer revolution is being driven by those outside the military. The Ukrainian soldiers using handheld drones and encrypted cell phones are an example. The implications are difficult to grasp, but they will continue to influence the course of events.

There is a dichotomy here. On one hand, the ever-faster rate of technological change and adaptation has created unheard-of possibilities for improving everyday life. On the other hand, it has given us impressive military capabilities: hypersonic missiles, stealth aircraft, and ever more complex weapons for air, naval, or ground war. The irony is that the two sets of capabilities overlap, blurring and ultimately erasing the distinction between war and peace. And these technologies are so widespread that for those under forty, the world's digital natives, no nation has a real advantage.

The complexities of the civilian world, with its dependence on computers and microprocessors, have also created a world of unimagined vulnerabilities. A few small atomic bombs of the size of the ones that destroyed Hiroshima and Nagasaki, exploded a hundred miles above the East Coast of the United States, would be enough to turn virtually *everything* off from Maine to Florida and New York to Ohio. It would not be the explosive effect of those weapons but rather the electromagnetic pulse (EMP) that would fry every chip not shielded by lead. It would not be surprising to discover that the R&D labs of major powers are working on how to unleash EMP effects without having to use nuclear weapons.

The implications of the fifth military-social revolution are such as to suggest that only the most reasoned and intelligent statesmanship can prevent Armageddon. It will require a deep knowledge of history and the "other"—resources that have been in short supply over the past three decades, particularly in the United States. Moreover, one confronts the harsh reality that we live in a world of the Taliban, Al Qaeda, and ISIS, and they are not going to disappear. The current strategic environment requires not only a military of immense technological capabilities to deter the use of nuclear weapons but an officer corps familiar with history, literature, and the other, who may sometimes think in terms of the seventh century. There is another irony here: the complexities of modern societies have created vulnerabilities that technologically savvy members of the terrorist world can use to their advantage.

Perhaps the larger challenge confronting the developed world is that the West's approach to war has spread well beyond Europe and North America. The most recent edition of the *Cambridge History of War* posits the following five characteristics in explaining the military superiority of the West since the Ancient Greeks: "This emphasis on *finance, technology, eclecticism, discipline, and an aggressive military tradition* conferred a unique resilience and lethality upon Western Warfare."[6] Those characteristics are now available to major powers everywhere.

The sorry history of the past five centuries suggests that Western states have never been able to control their aggressive instincts and avoid war. The history of the past fifty years intimates that the world is in for more of the same. Our present abundance of high-tech weaponry reminds us that even if we avoid using nuclear weapons, future conflicts are likely to be more lethal than those of the past. The wreckage of Syria and Ukraine suggests the carnage and destruction that modern conventional warfare can inflict on the landscape.

The Future?

We stand now amid another military-social revolution, which is altering the character of both war and the civilian world. It is having a greater impact than any earlier military-social revolution—and only partly because the communication and computer revolutions of the past thirty years make it a worldwide phenomenon. The societal changes caused by the vicious children of the internet such as Twitter and Facebook are now beginning to emerge, with divisive effects of which the American population's reaction to the coronavirus pandemic provides only a foretaste. Given the adaptability of smaller actors to technological change, there is the danger that the developed world (no longer just the West) will not be able to anticipate how to utilize the fifth military-social revolution. We have no way of knowing who will combine the unexpected and the unpredictable to their advantage, and to what effect. We have seen already that technological and communication changes have not all been for the better.

The computer revolution has changed everything from automobiles to how we do our shopping, but there is no indication that these massive technological and social changes have ended the possibility of war. What it does suggest is that military organizations, struggling with these technological changes in their own spheres of interest, will confront even larger issues than those raised by the great military-social revolutions of the past.

Perhaps the most important point about history is that it offers a path to understanding not only the other but ourselves as well. Colin S. Gray's brilliant book *Another Bloody Century* best sums up the likely prospects for what we might now term the global way of war. War is no less likely in the coming decades of the twenty-first century than it was in the course of its predecessors. Human nature has not and will not change. Putin's invasion of Ukraine should have been no more surprising than Hitler's invasion of Poland in 1939. There is, of course, the hope that things will turn out better in the future. But as the Athenians commented to the Melian negotiators in 416 BC, "Hope, that great comforter in danger! . . . [It] is by nature an expensive commodity, and those who are risking their all on one cast find out what it means only when they are already ruined."[7]

Acknowledgments

THERE ARE INNUMERABLE INDIVIDUALS who have contributed to the journey that has resulted in this book. I cannot name them all, given the space allowed, so I can only suggest a few of the deserving. My intellectual journey began at Yale with Hajo Holborn during my undergraduate years and was followed by Hans Gatzke and Donald Kagan in my graduate studies, who formed and at times dragooned an unformed lump of clay into a reasonable scholar. Professor Kagan continued to exercise that influence on me until his death. My travels throughout the academic and intellectual worlds have led an extraordinary group of professors and officers to form and continue my education. During the twenty years that I spent as a colleague at Ohio State, Allan Millet provided me with guidance and wisdom in beginning to understand the complexities of military organizations. During that period, John Lynn became both a friend and mentor, a relationship that has continued to the present day. In the last two decades, Jim Lacey, Richard Sinnreich, Frank Hoffman, and Peter Mansoor have proven particularly valuable in expanding my knowledge of not only military history but the military organizations that seem so resistant to change. I should also mention the contribution that Jim Mattis has made to my thinking about the real world of strategy. In addition, my doctors (Marc Wish, Mariano Chutuape, Joann Pfundstein, and Eunice Yang) have kept me alive so that I could complete this manuscript. The Andrew W. Marshall Foundation provided a wonderfully useful grant that helped me focus my time on this work. In terms of the editing of this book, I owe a deep set of gratitude to Bill Frucht, my Yale University Press editor, who showed me what thorough editing and rewriting should involve. Finally, I owe a deep debt of gratitude to my Oxford-trained historian wife, Lesley Mary Smith, who has tolerated my explosive and boisterous behavior while guiding this manuscript through to completion with wonderfully sharp and incisive commentary.

Notes

Chapter One. The Dark Path of War in the Western World

Epigraph: Michael Howard, *The Causes of War and Other Essays* (London, 1984), p. 214.

1. What is particularly interesting about the Roman Empire is the absence of major warfare impacting the empire's heart for sustained periods. For nearly 250 years, outside of frontier wars, the empire saw few major conflicts that directly impacted the homeland. These were the War of the Three Emperors (69–71 AD), the Roman Jewish War (67–71 AD), the Bar Kobar War (135–136 AD), the German invasion of Italy (172–175 AD), and the civil war following the death of Emperor Commodus (190–193 AD).

2. For a brilliant examination of the factors that contributed to the Roman Empire's demise, see Kyle Harper, *The Fate of Rome: Climate, Disease and the End of Empire* (Princeton, NJ, 2019).

3. For the cultural and political mechanisms that allowed the Greeks to control the impact of their wars, see Victor Davis Hanson, *The Western Way of War: Infantry Battle in Classical Greece* (New York, 1989).

4. Far and away the most impressive historian of the rise of the West has been William H. McNeill. See his *The Rise of the West: A History of the Human Community* (Chicago, 1963). For his examination of the role that war and technology played in the rise of the West, see *The Pursuit of Power: Technology, Armed Force, and Society Since A.D. 1000* (Chicago, 1982), and *The Age of Gunpowder Empires, 1450–1800* (Washington, DC, 1989).

5. Paul Kennedy, *The Rise and Fall of the Great Powers: Economic Change and Military Conflict from 1500 to 2000* (New York, 1987), p. 4.

6. McNeill, *The Rise of the West*, pp. 569–570.

7. Among a host of other works, see particularly Russell F. Weigley, *The Age of Battles: The Quest for Decisive Warfare from Breitenfeld to Waterloo* (Bloomington, IN, 1991). For the emphasis on technology, see McNeill, *The Pursuit of Power.*

8. For the importance of culture in the effectiveness of military organizations, see Peter R. Mansoor and Williamson Murray, eds., *The Culture of Military Organizations* (Cambridge, UK, 2019).

9. For a persuasive and interesting argument that decisive victory has largely existed in the minds of historians, see Cathal Nolan, *The Allure of Battle: A History of How Wars Have Been Won and Lost* (Oxford, 2017).

10. For Marlborough as a general and statesman, see Winston S. Churchill, *Marlborough: His Life and Times*, 4 vols. (London, 1933–1938), and David Chandler, *The Art of Warfare in the Age of Marlborough*, rev. edition (New York, 1995).

11. Napoleon's army of 1813 had far fewer veterans than the Grand Army of 1805 since it consisted of so many conscripts. Moreover, it was also weaker in artillery and cavalry.

12. For a military history of the Civil War, see Williamson Murray and Wayne Wei-Siang Hsieh, *A Savage War: A Military History of the Civil War* (Princeton, NJ, 2016).

13. For the Battle of Chancellorsville, see Stephen W. Sears, *Chancellorsville* (New York, 1996).

14. For Antietam, see Stephen W. Sears, *Landscape Turned Red: The Battle of Antietam* (New York, 1983), and for Gettysburg, see Sears, *Gettysburg* (New York, 2003).

15. Holger H. Herwig, *The Battle of the Marne: The Opening of World War I and the Battle That Changed the World* (New York, 2009).

16. For the German effort to win the war, see David T. Zabecki, *The German 1918 Offensives: A Case Study in the Operational Level of War* (London, 2006).

17. There were of course battles such as Tannenberg and Caparetto where the victor destroyed much of the opposing army but failed to change the strategic outcome.

18. The German historian Klaus Reinhardt argued that by Operation Typhoon in October 1941, the Wehrmacht had lost the campaign. See Reinhardt, *Die Wende vor Moskau: Das Scheitern der Strategie Hitlers im Winter 1941/1942* (Stuttgart, 1972). A more recent study by the Australian historian David Stahel argues that Barbarossa had failed as early as July. See Stahel, *Operation Barbarossa and Germany's Defeat in the East* (Cambridge, UK, 2009).

19. For the performance of the American military in their efforts to adapt to the Iraqi insurgency after the victory of 2003, see among others Rajiv Chandrasekaran, *Imperial Life in the Emerald City: Inside Iraq's Green Zone* (New York, 2006); Thomas E. Ricks, *Fiasco: The American Military Adventure in Iraq* (New York, 2006); Charles H. Ferguson, *No End in Sight: Iraq's Descent into Chaos* (New York, 2008); and Michael R. Gordon and Bernard E. Trainor, *Cobra II: The Inside Story of the Invasion and Occupation of Iraq* (New York, 2006).

20. Carl von Clausewitz, *On War*, ed. and trans. Michael Howard and Peter Paret (Princeton, NJ, 1976), p. 579.

21. For a discussion of Bismarck's political and strategic approach to the reunification of Germany, see Marcus Jones, "Strategy as Character: Bismarck and the Prusso-German Question, 1862–1878," in *The Shaping of Grand Strategy: Policy, Diplomacy, and War*, ed. Williamson Murray, Richard Hart Sinnreich, and James Lacey (Cambridge, UK, 2011), pp. 79–110.

22. See particularly Geoffrey Parker, *The Military Revolution: Military Innovation and the Rise of the West, 1500–1800*, 2nd edition (Cambridge, UK, 1996).

23. For Philip's strategic emphasis on religious factors, see Geoffrey Parker, "The Making of Strategy in Hapsburg Spain: Philip II's 'Bid for Mastery,' 1556–1598," in *The Making of Strategy: Rulers, States, and War*, ed. Williamson Murray, MacGregor Knox, and Alvin Bernstein (Cambridge, UK, 1994).

24. See particularly Geoffrey Parker, *The Army of Flanders and the Spanish Road, 1567–1659: The Logistics of Spanish Victory and Defeat in the Low Countries' Wars* (Cambridge, UK, 1972).

25. In the case of the Thirty Years' War, the participants were on the brink of financial and economic collapse when they signed the Peace of Westphalia.

26. The Office of Net Assessment altered the terminology to a "revolution in military affairs" in an attempt to underline that what was occurring was much more than a change in technology. It succeeded in changing the terminology but failed to alter the rush to believe that technology was the center of all military developments.

27. Admiral William Owens quoted in Thomas Duffy, "Breakthrough Could Give Forces Total Command of a Future Battlefield," *Inside the Navy*, 23 January 1995.

28. Admiral William Owens, "System of Systems," *Joint Force Quarterly* (January 1996).

29. USMC, FMFM 1, "Warfighting," chap. 1.

30. For Thucydides as a theorist of war, see Williamson Murray, "Thucydides, Theorist of War," *Naval War College Review* 66, no. 4 (Autumn 2013): art. 5, https://digital-commons.usnwc.edu/nwc-review/vol66/iss4/5.

31. For military innovation, see Williamson Murray and Allan R. Millett, eds., *Military Innovation in the Interwar Period* (Cambridge, UK, 1996). For adaptation in war, see Williamson Murray, *Military Adaptation in War: With Fear of Change* (Cambridge, UK, 2011).

32. My arguments rest on the work of giants. The initiator of the great discussions and debates over military revolutions was Michael Roberts's groundbreaking lecture given at Belfast in January 1955, "The Military Revolution, 1560–1660," Queen's University of Belfast (Belfast, 1956). Almost immediately historians took to debating Roberts and each other. The most important work on the military revolution was that of Parker, *The Military Revolution*. Parker's work extended and spread understanding of the complexity of the military revolution as no other historian has done. It remains the premier work on the military revolution and the period 1500–1800.

Well worth also consulting is Clifford J. Rogers, ed., *The Military Revolution Debate: Readings on the Military Transformation of Early Modern Europe* (Boulder, CO, 1995). For a dissenting view, see Jeremy Black, *A Military Revolution? Military Change and European Society, 1550–1800* (London, 1991).

33. Clifford J. Rogers, in Rogers, ed., *The Military Revolution Debate*, pp. 6, 76.

34. I am indebted to Professor Holger Herwig of the University of Calgary for this point.

35. Mentioned in a treatise by Roger Bacon in 1267.

36. For sixteenth-century naval war in the Mediterranean, see John Francis Guilmartin Jr., *Gunpowder and Galleys: Changing Technology and Mediterranean Warfare at Sea in the 16th Century*, rev. edition (1974; London, 2003).

37. Thucydides, *History of the Peloponnesian War*, trans. Rex Warner (London, 1954), pp. 404–405.

38. For the British system of financing wars by taxes and borrowing, see among others John Brewer, *The Sinews of Power: War, Money, and the English State, 1688–1783* (New York, 1989).

39. For British support of finances and weapons during this period, see John M. Sherwig, *Guineas and Gunpowder: British Foreign Aid in the Wars with France, 1793–1815* (Cambridge, MA, 1969).

40. Quoted in Jeremy D. Popkin, *A New World Begins: The History of the French Revolution* (New York, 2019), p. 390.

41. See Murray and Hsieh, *A Savage War*, for further discussion of the larger issues involved in the conduct of the Civil War.

42. One of the major factors that led to a four-year struggle to destroy the Confederacy lay in the fact that the distances involved were an order of magnitude greater than those in Europe. See the map with an overlay of Europe on the Confederacy in ibid., p. 42.

43. Ulysses S. Grant, *Personal Memoirs of U. S. Grant*, ed. (New York, 1999), p. 198.

44. The Cowboy Museum in Oklahoma displays no less than ten thousand different forms of barbed wire.

45. Michael Howard, "Men Against Fire: The Doctrine of the Offensive in 1914," in *The Makers of Modern Strategy from Machiavelli to the Nuclear Age*, ed. Peter Paret with Gordon A. Craig and Felix Gilbert (Princeton, NJ, 1986), pp. 510–526.

46. For an impressive rethinking on how the British military performed in the two World Wars, see Brian Bond, *Britain's Two World Wars Against Germany: Myth, Memory and the Distortions of Hindsight* (Cambridge, UK, 2014).

47. For an examination of the miscalculation British leaders made, see among others Williamson Murray, *The Change in the European Balance of Power, 1938–1939: The Path to Ruin* (Princeton, NJ, 1984), chap. 1.

48. See ibid., chap. 2. This was widely believed not merely by the radical right but by most of the population.

49. For an examination of the German lessons-learned processes, see James S. Corum, *The Roots of Blitzkrieg: Hans von Seeckt and German Military Reform* (Lawrence, KS, 1992). See also Williamson Murray, "Armored Warfare: The British, French, and German Experiences," in *Military Innovation in the Interwar Period*, ed. Murray and Millett, pp. 6–49.

50. Approximately 50 percent of the crews who flew in Bomber Command were killed on operations.

51. For the impact of the strategic bombing offensive on the German war economy, see particularly Adam Tooze, *The Wages of Destruction: The Making and Breaking of the Nazi Economy* (London, 2006), pp. 597–600.

52. And one should not underestimate the gross military incompetence of the French high command in ensuring that the French armies confronted defeat almost immediately as the German offensive began. For the most recent examination of the military factors involved in the defeat of Allied armies, see Karl-Heinz Frieser with John T. Greenwood, *The Blitzkrieg Legend: The 1940 Campaign in the West* (Annapolis, MD, 2005).

53. Among a host of books on this subject, the following are among the best: R. V. Jones, *The Wizard War: British Scientific Intelligence, 1939–1945* (New York, 1978); Solly Zuckerman, *From Apes to Warlords: The Autobiography (1904–1946) of Solly Zuckerman* (London, 1978); Patrick Beesley, *Very Special Intelligence: The Story of the Admiralty's Operational Intelligence Centre, 1939–1945* (London, 1977); and Michael I. Handel, ed., *Leaders and Intelligence* (London, 1989). The British official history is quite useful: F. H. Hinsley et al., *British Intelligence in the Second World War*, 5 vols. (London, 1979–1990).

Chapter Two. The Rise of the Modern State and Its Military Institutions

Epigraph: Victor Davis Hanson, *The Western Way of War: Infantry Battle in Classical Greece* (Berkeley, CA, 1984), p. 224.

1. In this regard, see William H. McNeill, *The Rise of the West: A History of the Human Community* (Chicago, 1963).

2. As early as October 1559, Philip II of Spain had begun the process of closing his country off from the intellectual ferment in the rest of Europe as he swore to support the Inquisitor General's efforts to stamp out heresy throughout Spain. Geoffrey Parker, *Imprudent King: A New Life of Philip II* (New Haven, CT, 2014), p. 132.

3. The impact of global cooling took a considerable period of time to work its baleful influence on the medieval world. The bubonic plague, however, clearly did impact the thinking of those who survived as well as their progeny. One of the patterns of history appears to be the breakdown of traditional beliefs after outbreaks of plagues. That which decimated the Roman Empire in the 160s AD was followed by the collapse of the ancient

Greco-Roman religion a century and a half later. Similarly, the plague of Justinian's time saw the collapse of the Christian religion before the onslaught of Islam in the Middle East and much of the Mediterranean world. Likewise, the emergence of the Reformation in the early sixteenth century—heralded by the appearance of Jan Hus and John Wycliffe in the fifteenth century—would further fracture the religious sureties of Europeans and add to their competitiveness.

4. Clifford J. Rogers, "The Military Revolutions of the Hundred Years War," in *The Military Revolution Debate: Readings on the Military Transformation of Europe*, ed. Clifford J. Rogers (Boulder, CO, 1995), p. 58.

5. For the effectiveness of the longbow as a weapon, see Clifford J. Rogers, "The Efficacy of the English Longbow: A Reply to Kelly DeVries," *War in History* 5, no. 2 (April 1998): 233–242, and "The Development of the Longbow in the Late Medieval England and 'Technological Determinism,'" *Journal of Medieval History* 37, no. 3 (September 2011): 321–341.

6. Clifford J. Rogers, "The Battle of Agincourt," in *The Hundred Years War*, vol. 2, *Different Vistas*, ed. L. J. Andrew Villalon and Donald J. Kagay (Leiden, 2008), p. 44.

7. Before the discovery and recovery of Henry VIII's flagship, the *Mary Rose*, in the 1970s and 1980s, historians had argued about the longbow's lethality. One longbow had been recovered from the ditch of an English castle, which indicated a draw pull of over one hundred pounds, but most historians dismissed that possibility. Archeologists examining the wreckage of the *Mary Rose*, however, discovered 138 longbows, with the average draw pulls of over 100 pounds, with some ranging up to 180 pounds. Rogers, "The Military Revolutions of the Hundred Years War," p. 82, n38.

8. For a clear exposition of gunpowder weapons by the Europeans from inception through the Renaissance, see Thomas Arnold, *The Renaissance at War* (London, 2000), pp. 24–35. For the development of gunpowder in China and its impact on the West, see Tonio Andrade, *The Gunpowder Age: China, Military Innovation, and the Rise of the West in World History* (Princeton, NJ, 2016).

9. Arnold, *The Renaissance at War*, p. 24.

10. See William H. McNeill, *The Age of Gunpowder Empires, 1450–1800* (Washington, DC, 1989), pp. 3–5. How to explain that effort when the catapults already available were for the most part superior in their impact? Here the human psyche undoubtedly came into play. It was not the effectiveness of early cannons that attracted the attention of the commanders of the armies, it was the sound of the explosion and the smoke and fire that accompanied the firing of the early primitive artillery pieces.

11. William H. McNeill, *The Pursuit of Power: Technology, Armed Force, and Society Since A.D. 1000* (Chicago, 1982), pp. 83, 86.

12. Quoted in Geoffrey Parker, *The Military Revolution: Military Innovation and the Rise of the West, 1500–1800*, 2nd edition (Cambridge, UK, 1996), p. 10.

13. I am indebted to John Lynn for this point.

14. See Clifford J. Rogers, "Gunpowder Artillery in Europe, 1326–1500: Innovation and Impact," in *Technology, Violence, and War: Essays in Honor of Dr. John F. Guilmartin, Jr.*, ed. Robert S. Ehlers Jr., Sarah K. Douglas, and Daniel P. M. Curzon (Boston, 2019), p. 40.

15. Josephus, *The Jewish War*, trans. G. A. Williamson (London, 1959), pp. 194–195.

16. For a discussion of military revolutions during this period, see David Parrott, *The Business of War: Military Enterprise and Military Revolution in Early Modern Europe* (Cambridge, UK, 2012).

17. For a description of the development of the new systems of fortification, see Arnold, *The Renaissance at War*, pp. 35–47.

18. Parker's *The Military Revolution* is particularly good on this.

19. Geoffrey Parker, *Emperor: A New Life of Charles V* (New Haven, CT, 2019), p. 509.

20. Ibid., p. 509.

21. Geoffrey Parker, *The Army of Flanders and the Spanish Road, 1567–1659: The Logistics of Spanish Victory and Defeat in the Low Countries' Wars* (Cambridge, UK, 1972), p. 6.

22. Parker, *Emperor*, p. 171.

23. Parker, *The Army of Flanders and the Spanish Road*, p. 185.

24. Geoffrey Parker, *The Dutch Revolt* (Ithaca, NY, 1977), pp. 178–179.

25. Parker, *The Military Revolution*, pp. 11–13.

26. J. R. McNeill and William H. McNeill, *The Human Web: A Bird's-Eye View of World History* (New York, 2003), pp. 163–164.

27. Herodotus reported that the Phoenicians claimed they had managed to sail around Africa but disbelieved their story because they reported that as they sailed from west to east, the sun was on their left; in fact, that indicates they had indeed managed to achieve what they claimed.

28. For the significance of the Portuguese efforts, see John Francis Guilmartin Jr., *Gunpowder and Galleys: Changing Technology and Mediterranean Warfare at Sea in the 16th Century*, rev. edition (1974; London, 2003), pp. 23–29.

29. For the Spanish conquest of the Indian empires in the Americas, see Hugh Thomas, *Conquest: Montezuma, Cortés, and the Fall of Old Mexico* (New York, 1993), and John Hemming, *The Conquest of the Incas* (New York, 1970).

30. This is brilliantly discussed in Guilmartin, *Gunpowder and Galleys*.

31. See the discussion in McNeill and McNeill, *The Human Web*, pp. 163–164.

32. For the most thorough study of Charles V's reign, see Parker, *Emperor*.

33. For an excellent summation of warfare during the period of the Renaissance, see Arnold, *The Renaissance at War*.

34. Guilmartin, *Gunpowder and Galleys*, pp. 230–231.

35. Ibid., p. 281.

36. Ibid., p. 287.
37. For the best biography of Philip II, see Parker, *Imprudent King*.
38. See particularly Geoffrey Parker, *The Grand Strategy of Philip II* (New Haven, CT, 1998). See also Geoffrey Parker, "The Making of Strategy in Hapsburg Spain: Philip II's 'Bid for Mastery,' 1556–1598," in *The Making of Strategy: Rulers, States, and War*, ed. Williamson Murray, MacGregor Knox, and Alvin Bernstein (Cambridge, UK, 1994).
39. For an excellent account of the Dutch revolt, see Parker, *The Dutch Revolt*.
40. Ibid., p. 104.
41. Geoffrey Parker, "Dynastic War, 1494–1660," in *The Cambridge History of Warfare* (Cambridge, UK, 2005), p. 154.
42. Parker, *The Dutch Revolt*, p. 172.
43. Ibid., p. 178.
44. Ibid., pp. 123–125.
45. For the fate of the Spanish Armada, see Colin Martin and Geoffrey Parker, *The Spanish Armada* (London, 1988).
46. Hans Delbrück, *The Dawn of Modern Warfare*, trans. Walter J. Renfroe Jr. (Lincoln, NE, 1990), p. 157.
47. Ibid., pp. 157–159.
48. In this regard, see the enormously imaginative study William H. McNeill, *Keeping Together in Time: Dance and Drill in Human History* (Cambridge, MA, 1995).
49. Parker, "Dynastic War," p. 155.
50. Delbrück, *The Dawn of Modern Warfare*, p. 161.
51. Parker, "Dynastic War," p. 156.
52. Geoffrey Parker, *Global Crisis: War, Climate Change, and Catastrophe in the Seventeenth Century* (New Haven, CT, 2013), p. 26. For an earlier, multiauthored examination of the period, see also Geoffrey Parker and Lesley M. Smith, eds., *The General Crisis of the Seventeenth Century* (London, 1978).
53. Parker, *Global Crisis*, p. 32.
54. John A. Lynn, *The Wars of Louis XIV, 1667–1714* (Harlow, Essex, UK, 1999), pp. 47–48.
55. The Czechs and Slovaks would not recover as a nation until the nineteenth century.
56. See Parrott, *The Business of War*, p. 116–117.
57. For the impact of the war and climate change in the seventeenth century, see the brilliant work by Parker, *Global Crisis*.
58. *The Thirty Years' War*, ed. Geoffrey Parker, pp. 90–91.
59. Ibid., p. 101.
60. See Parrott, *The Business of War*, p. 119.
61. The great biography on Gustavus Adolphus is Michael Roberts, *Gustavus Adolphus: A History of Sweden, 1611–1632*, 2 vols. (London, 1953, 1958).
62. For the military reforms that Gustavus instituted, see among others Michael Roberts, *Gustavus Adolphus and the Rise of Sweden* (London, 1973),

pp. 99–114, and Williamson Murray, "Breitenfeld: The Creation of Modern War (1631)," in *Moment of Battle: The Twenty Clashes That Changed the World*, ed. James Lacey and Williamson Murray (New York, 2013).

63. The following account of the Battle of Breitenfeld is drawn from Murray, "Breitenfeld."

64. Delbrück, *The Dawn of Modern Warfare*, p. 209.

65. Parker, ed., *The Thirty Years' War*, p. 125.

66. Parrott, *The Business of War*, pp. 127–128.

67. Parker, ed., *The Thirty Years' War*, p. 146.

68. The most impressive works on the French Army in the seventeenth and early eighteenth centuries are by John A. Lynn: *Giant of the Grand Siècle: The French Army, 1610–1715* (Cambridge, UK, 1997), and *The French Wars, 1667–1714* (Harlow, Essex, UK, 1999).

69. John A. Lynn, "States in Conflict, 1661–1763," in Parker, ed., *The Cambridge History of Warfare*, p. 167.

70. Lynn, *The Wars of Louis XIV*, p. 53.

71. Lynn, "States in Conflict," p. 168.

72. For the weaknesses of the French fiscal system, see Paul Kennedy, *The Rise and Fall of the Great Powers: Economic Change and Military Conflict from 1500 to 2000* (New York, 1987), pp. 82–84.

73. Lynn, "States in Conflict," p. 169.

74. Lynn, *Giant of the Grand Siècle*, pp. 104–105, 486.

75. Kennedy, *The Rise and Fall of the Great Powers*, p. 75.

76. David Chandler, *The Art of Warfare in the Age of Marlborough* (New York, 1976), p. 241.

77. Lynn, "States in Conflict," p. 169.

78. Peter Paret, *Yorck and the Era of Prussian Reform, 1807–1815* (Princeton, NJ, 1966), p. 271.

79. Parrott, *The Business of War*, p. 284.

80. Lynn, "States in Conflict," p. 173.

Chapter Three. The Arrival of the Modern State

Epigraph: Thucydides, *History of the Peloponnesian War*, trans. Rex Warner (London, 1954), pp. 404–405.

1. For a general history of this period, see J. S. Bromley, ed., *The New Cambridge Modern History*, vol. 6, *The Rise of Great Britain and Russia, 1688–1725* (Cambridge, UK, 1970).

2. For a discussion of the factors that have influenced the making of strategy, see Williamson Murray and Mark Grimsley, "Introduction: On Strategy," in *The Making of Strategy: Rulers, States, and War*, ed. Williamson Murray, MacGregor Knox, and Alvin Bernstein (Cambridge, 1994), pp. 1–23.

3. For Spanish strategy, see Geoffrey Parker, "The Making of Strategy in Hapsburg Spain: Philip II's 'Bid for Mastery,' 1556–1598," in Murray, Knox, and Bernstein, eds., *The Making of Strategy.*

4. For a critique of B. H. Liddell Hart's argument that the British had waged a "blue water" strategy in the eighteenth century, see Williamson Murray, "Grand Strategy, Alliances, and the Anglo-American Way of War," in *Grand Strategy and Military Alliances,* ed. Peter R. Mansoor and Williamson Murray (Cambridge, UK, 2016), 19–46.

5. N. A. M. Rodger, *The Command of the Ocean: A Naval History of Britain, 1649–1815* (London, 2004), p. 142.

6. Rodger, *The Command of the Ocean,* pp. 189.

7. For William III, see Stephen B. Baxter, *William III and the Defense of European Liberty, 1650–1702* (New York, 1966).

8. Rodger, *The Command of the Ocean,* p. 137.

9. For a discussion of the strategic and political ramifications of the Glorious Revolution, see Brendan Simms, *Three Victories and a Defeat: The Rise and Fall of the First British Empire* (New York, 2007).

10. For an account of how the English and then the British financed their wars, see John Brewer, *The Sinews of Power: War, Money, and the English State, 1688–1783* (New York, 1989). For the financing of the English effort in the War of the Spanish Succession, see D. W. Jones, *War and Economy in the Age of William III and Marlborough* (New York, 1988).

11. Simms, *Three Victories and a Defeat,* pp. 38–39.

12. Andrew Lambert, *War at Sea in the Age of Sail, 1650–1850* (London, 2000), p. 87.

13. Brewer, *The Sinews of Power,* p. 31.

14. Rodger, *The Command of the Ocean,* p. 291.

15. John A. Lynn, *The Wars of Louis XIV, 1667–1714* (Harlow, Essex, UK, 1999), pp. 244–245.

16. Ibid., pp. 99–100.

17. Paul Kennedy, *The Rise and Fall of British Naval Mastery* (London, 1976), p. 79.

18. For English strategy in the War of the Spanish Succession, see among others John Hattendorf, *England in the War of Spanish Succession: A Study of the English View and the Conduct of Grand Strategy, 1701–1713* (New York, 1987); Jamel Ostwald, "Creating the British Way of War: English Strategy in the War of the Spanish Succession," in *Successful Strategies: Triumphing in War and Peace from Antiquity to the Present,* ed. Williamson Murray and Richard Hart Sinnreich (Cambridge, UK, 2014), pp. 100–129; and William Maltby, "The Origins of a Global Strategy: England from 1558 to 1713," in Murray, Knox, and Bernstein, eds., *The Making of Strategy.*

19. For the War of the Spanish Succession, see David G. Chandler, *Marlborough as Military Commander* (New York, 1973), for the English side. For the French, see Lynn, *The Wars of Louis XIV.*

20. Among the innumerable works on the Duke of Marlborough, Winston S. Churchill's *Marlborough: His Life and Times*, 4 vols. (London, 1933–1938) remains the most outstanding both for its literary qualities and for Churchill's understanding of the interplay among statesmen, diplomats, and military leaders. For insight into Churchill's work as a historian, see Maurice Ashley's *Churchill as Historian* (New York, 1968).

21. Lynn, *The Wars of Louis XIV*, p. 271.

22. For the Battle of Blenheim, see Charles Spencer, *Blenheim: Battle for Europe* (London, 2004).

23. Chandler, *Marlborough as Military Commander*, pp. 148–149.

24. Text on the Column of Victory in the grounds of Blenheim Palace, Woodstock, Oxfordshire, England.

25. Chandler, *Marlborough as Military Commander*, pp. 256–266; Lynn, *The Wars of Louis XIV*, pp. 332–336.

26. Ernst Jünger, noted war hero and author, fought in a Hanoverian regiment in the First World War that possessed a depiction of Gibraltar on its cap badge.

27. The act of union between Scotland and England was agreed to in July 1706 and passed by the two parliaments in January and February 1707.

28. Lynn, *The Wars of Louis XIV*, p. 362.

29. Ibid., p. 359.

30. For a biography of Charles XII, see R. M. Hatton, *Charles XII of Sweden* (New York, 1968).

31. Charles would be killed by a stray bullet in 1718.

32. Among others, see Gerhard Ritter, *Frederick the Great: A Historical Profile*, trans. Peter Paret (Berkeley, CA, 1968), and Christopher Duffy, *Frederick the Great: A Military Life* (New York, 1985).

33. For that incident, the rising tension between the French and British (particularly the colonists), and the role of the Indian tribes, see the brilliant study by Fred Anderson, *Crucible of War: The Seven Years' War and the Fate of Empire in British North America, 1754–1766* (New York, 2000), pp. 73–76.

34. Wayne E. Lee et al., *The Other Face of Battle: America's Forgotten Wars and the Experience of Combat* (New York, 2021).

35. Quoted in Rodger, *The Command of the Ocean*, p. 261.

36. For the great war between the British and French for global supremacy, see particularly Daniel Baugh, *The Global Seven Years War, 1754–1763: Britain and France in a Great Power Contest* (London, 2011). For French thinking about the threat the colonies posed and why Canada should form an essential part of French strategy, see ibid., pp. 5–8.

37. For the German penchant to strike first that Frederick epitomized, see Robert M. Citino, *The German Way of War: From the Thirty Years' War to the Third Reich* (Lawrence, KS, 2005).

38. Daniel Baugh makes an excellent case that Byng deserved his fate. Baugh, *The Global Seven Years War*, pp. 229–235.

39. Ibid., p. 267.
40. Anderson, *Crucible of War*, pp. 211–212.
41. Baugh, *The Global Seven Years War*, p. 242.
42. Anderson, *Crucible of War*, pp. 225–229.
43. Up to this point, any subaltern in the British Army outranked the highest colonial officer. Now, colonial officers were outranked only by officers of the same rank or higher.
44. Duffy, *Frederick the Great*, pp. 143–144, 150–153.
45. For a description of the siege, see particularly Anderson, *Crucible of War*, pp. 250–255. See also Rodger, *The Command of the Ocean*, pp. 268, 276.
46. Yet in many respects the Indian approach to war was less destructive.
47. For the Indian approach to war, see Lee et al., *The Other Face of Battle*.
48. For the successful and incredibly lucky taking of Quebec, see Anderson, *Crucible of War*, pp. 349–365; Beckles Wilson, *The Life and Letters of James Wolfe* (London, 1909), p. 339.
49. For the terms the British gave the French, see Anderson, *Crucible of War*, p. 365.
50. For an excellent description of the battle, see ibid., pp. 381–383.
51. Ibid., p. 383.
52. Rodger, *The Command of the Ocean*, p. 294.
53. Ibid., p. 301.
54. Ibid., p. 305.
55. Simms, *Three Victories and a Defeat*, p. 462.
56. The last chapters of Anderson's *Crucible of War*, set in London the faulty decision-making that played such a crucial part in the outbreak of the revolution.
57. Quoted in Rick Atkinson, *The British Are Coming: The War for America, Lexington to Princeton, 1775–1777* (New York, 2019), p. 25.
58. Michael Stephenson, *Patriot Battles: How the War of Independence Was Fought* (New York, 2007), pp. 116–117.
59. For a discussion of the major impact that the French and Indian War had in creating a cadre of experienced soldiers, see Fred Anderson, *A People's Army: Massachusetts Soldiers and Society in the Seven Years' War* (Chapel Hill, NC, 1984).
60. Quoted in George F. Sheer and Hugh F. Rankin, *Rebels and Redcoats: The American Revolution Through the Eyes of Those Who Fought and Lived It*, reprint (1957; New York, 1987), p. 43.
61. For a discussion of the historical antecedents of hybrid warfare, see Williamson Murray and Peter R. Mansoor, eds., *Hybrid Warfare: Fighting Complex Opponents from the Ancient World to the Present* (Cambridge, UK, 2012). For the importance of the militia in the war, see Marl V. Kwasny, *Washington's Partisan War, 1775–1783* (Kent, OH, 1996).

Chapter Four. The French Revolution and the Industrial Revolution

Epigraph: Victor Davis Hanson, *The Western Way of War: Infantry Battle in Classical Greece* (Berkeley, CA, 2009), p. 225.

1. For a general history of France during this period, see Colin Jones, *The Great Nation: France from Louis XV to Napoleon* (New York, 2003).

2. See particularly R. R. Palmer, *The Age of the Democratic Revolution: A Political History of Europe and America, 1760–1800* (Princeton, NJ, 1964).

3. The most outstanding military history of Napoleon's campaigns remains David G. Chandler, *The Campaigns of Napoleon* (New York, 1966). For a recent examination of the Napoleonic Wars in their global context, see Alexander Mikaberidze, *The Napoleonic Wars: A Global History* (Oxford, 2020).

4. For the origins of the French Revolutionary Wars, see T. C. W. Blanning, *The Origins of the French Revolutionary Wars* (London, 1986).

5. William H. McNeill, *The Pursuit of Power: Technology, Armed Force, and Society Since A.D. 1000* (Chicago, 1982), p. 185. McNeill attributes the growth of population across Europe in the eighteenth century to the lessening incidence of "lethal infection." In this regard, see particularly McNeill, *Plagues and Peoples* (Garden City, NY, 1976), pp. 240–246.

6. For the origins and course of the French Revolution, see among others MacGregor Knox, "Mass Politics and Nationalism as Military Revolution: The French Revolution and After," in *The Dynamics of Military Revolution, 1300–2050,* ed. MacGregor Knox and Williamson Murray (Cambridge, UK, 2001); Christopher Hibbert, *The Days of the French Revolution* (New York, 1980); R. R. Palmer, *Twelve Who Ruled: The Year of the Terror in the French Revolution* (Princeton, NJ, 1941), and *The World of the French Revolution* (London, 1971); and Georges Lefebvre, *The Coming of the French Revolution,* trans. R. R. Palmer (Princeton, NJ, 1947). For the most recent examination of the revolution, see Jeremy D. Popkin, *A New World Begins: The History of the French Revolution* (New York, 2019).

7. Mikaberidze, *The Napoleonic Wars,* pp. 6–7.

8. See in particular Samuel F. Scott, *The Response of the Royal Army to the French Revolution, 1787–93* (New York, 1978). See also Elizabeth Andrews Bond, *The Writing Public: Participatory Knowledge Production in Enlightenment and Revolutionary France* (Ithaca, NY, 2021).

9. David Hackett Fischer, *The Great Wave: Price Revolutions and the Rhythm of History* (Oxford, 1996), p. 147.

10. Popkin, *A New World Begins,* pp. 139–141.

11. For that effort and its impact on the ability of the major powers to deal with the French Revolution, see particularly Paul W. Schroeder, *The Transformation of European Politics, 1763–1848* (Oxford, 1994), pp. 11–19, 136–150.

12. Carl von Clausewitz, *On War,* ed. and trans. Michael Howard and Peter Paret (Princeton, NJ, 1976), p. 591.

13. Quoted in Williamson Murray, *America and the Future of War: The Past as Prologue* (Stanford, CA, 2017), p. 7.

14. Quoted in Mikaberidze, *The Napoleonic Wars,* p. 48.

15. Quoted in Knox, "Mass Politics and Nationalism as Military Revolution," p. 64.

16. Wolfgang Kruse, "Revolutionary France and the Meaning of Levée en Masse," in *War in an Age of Revolution, 1775–1815,* ed. Roger Chickering and Stig Förster (Cambridge, UK, 2010), p. 302.

17. Quoted in Knox, "Mass Politics and Nationalism as Military Revolution," p. 63.

18. John A. Lynn, *The Bayonets of the Republic: Motivation and Tactics in the Army of Revolutionary France, 1791–1794* (Urbana, IL, 1984), p. 4.

19. Ibid., p. 7.

20. Hibbert, *The Days of the French Revolution,* pp. 170–177.

21. Ibid., p. 7–9.

22. Quoted in ibid., p. 179.

23. Quoted from Thucydides on the revolutionary situation in Corcyra, 427 BC: Thucydides, *History of the Peloponnesian War,* trans. Rex Warner (London, 1954), p. 242.

24. I am indebted to John Lynn for pointing this quote out to me.

25. Tournachon-Molin, Ville Affranchie, n.d. [1793], trans. Mitchell Abidor, 2015, Marxists.org, https://www.marxists.org/history/frane/revolution/1793/lyon.htm.

26. Hibbert, *The Days of the French Revolution,* p. 194.

27. Knox, "Mass Politics and Nationalism as Military Revolution," p. 65.

28. Quoted in Stanley Chodorow and Joseph R. Stayer, *The Mainstream of Civilization,* 5th edition (1969; New York, 1989), p. 659.

29. Quoted in Kruse, "Revolutionary France and the Meaning of Levée en Masse," p. 397.

30. Quoted in Chandler, *The Campaigns of Napoleon,* p. 143.

31. Quoted in Lynn, *The Bayonets of the Republic,* p. 56.

32. Kruse, "Revolutionary France and the Meaning of Levée en Masse," p. 311.

33. Knox, "Mass Politics and Nationalism as Military Revolution," p. 65.

34. Quoted in Wikipedia.org, s.v., "Conscription."

35. Quoted in John A. Lynn, *Battle: A History of Combat and Culture from Ancient Greece to Modern America* (New York, 2003), p. 187.

36. J. P. Bertaud, *The Army of the French Revolution: From Citizen Soldier to Instrument of Power,* trans. R. R. Palmer (Princeton, NJ, 1988). See also John A. Lynn, "Nations in Arms, 1763–1815," in *The Cambridge History of Warfare,* ed. Geoffrey Parker (Cambridge, UK, 2005), p. 196.

37. Lynn, *The Bayonets of the Republic,* p. 75.

38. McNeill, *The Pursuit of Power,* p. 195.

39. Lynn, *The Bayonets of the Republic*, p. 207.
40. Quoted in Theodore Ropp, *War in the Modern World*, rev. edition (1959; Baltimore, 2000), p. 111.
41. Clausewitz, *On War*, pp. 591–592.
42. For a thorough examination of the restructuring and organization of the new French Army, see Lynn, *The Bayonets of the Republic*, pp. 43–96.
43. Popkin, *A New World Begins*, p. 364.
44. Chandler, *The Campaigns of Napoleon*, p. 24.
45. Mikaberidze, *The Napoleonic Wars*, p. 51.
46. That softening up process was essential. As Napoleon remarked after a disastrous series of column attacks that were not supported at the Battle of Bussaco in Portugal in September 1810: "Why the devil did Massena thrust himself into that muddle at Bussaco? Even in a plain country, columns do not break through lines unless they are supported by a superior artillery fire." Quoted in David Gates, *The Spanish Ulcer: A History of the Peninsular War* (New York, 1986), p. 232.
47. Chandler, *The Campaigns of Napoleon*, p. 138n.
48. Lynn, "Nation in Arms," p. 201.
49. Ibid., p. 199.
50. The diplomatic and strategic history of the period is admirably covered by Schroeder, *The Transformation of European Politics*.
51. Popkin, *A New World Begins*, p. 406; Jean Matrat, *Robespierre; or, The Tyranny of the Majority* (New York, 1971), p. 271.
52. For an excellent discussion of the botched coup that finally succeeded in spite of itself, see Hibbert, *The Days of the French Revolution*, pp. 260–268.
53. For a concise description of the coup that overthrew Robespierre and his associates, see Crane Brinton, *A Decade of Revolution, 1789–1799* (New York, 1934), pp. 190–194.
54. Popkin, *A New World Begins*, p. 454.
55. Chandler, *The Campaigns of Napoleon*, p. xxxv.
56. For Napoleon's campaign in Italy, see ibid., pp. 53–132.
57. Using the traditional British subsidies, Pitt had created the First Coalition in 1793 in response to the French declaration of war on Britain. The members were Britain, Austria, Prussia, Holland, and Spain. By 1797, the French had conquered the Dutch, while the Prussians had withdrawn from the coalition in 1795, leaving the Austrians alone with the British. The Treaty of Campo Formio ended the coalition.
58. N. A. M. Rodger, *The Command of the Ocean: A Naval History of Britain, 1649–1815* (London, 2004), p. 400.
59. Chandler, *The Campaigns of Napoleon*, p. 256.
60. Mikaberidze, *The Napoleonic Wars*, p. 81.
61. Nevertheless, the British were to confront enormous difficulties in making their strategy first against the power of a resurgent revolutionary France and then against Napoleon. For the difficulties that led to the collapse of

the Second Coalition, see particularly Piers Mackesy, *War Without Victory: The Downfall of Pitt, 1799–1802* (Oxford, 1984).

62. John M. Sherwig, *Guineas and Gunpowder: British Foreign Aid in the Wars with France, 1793–1815* (Cambridge, MA, 1969), p. 345.

63. Ibid., p. 289.

64. Ibid., pp. 287–288.

65. Chandler, *The Campaigns of Napoleon*, p. 873.

66. Jeremy Black, *European Warfare, 1660–1815* (London, 1994), p. 57. The number of small arms produced may well have been an underestimate.

67. Interestingly, economic historians have displayed little interest in the impact of the French Revolutionary and Napoleonic Wars on the growth of the Industrial Revolution. Nevertheless, the economic statistics that they present underline the contribution the wars made to the growth of the British economy.

68. J. Steven Watson, *The Reign of George III, 1769–1815* (Oxford, 1960), pp. 375–376.

69. *The Cambridge Economic History of Europe*, vol. 6, *The Industrial Revolutions and After: Incomes, Population and Technological Change*, ed. H. J. Habakkuk and M. Postan (Cambridge, UK, 1965), p. 274.

70. R. M. Hartwell, "Economic Change in England and Europe," in *The New Cambridge Modern History of Europe*, vol. 9; *War and Peace in an Age of Upheaval, 1793–1830*, ed. C. W. Crawley (Cambridge, UK, 1965), pp. 43–44.

71. Based on table 1, "Indices of English Population and Trade in the Eighteenth Century," in Habakkuk and Postan, eds., *The Cambridge Economic History of Europe*, vol. 6, p. 8.

72. Ibid., 6: (I), p. 296. For the importance of the financial system the British had developed over the eighteenth century, see also Felix Markham, "The Napoleonic Adventure," in Crawley, ed., *The New Cambridge Modern History*, 9:329.

73. *The Fontana Economic History of Europe: The Emergence of Industrial Societies*, part 1, ed. Carlo M. Cipolla (Glasgow, 1973), p. 167.

74. R. M. Hartwell, "Economic Change in England and Europe," in Crawley, ed., *The New Cambridge Modern History*, vol. 9, pp. 34, 44.

75. For a discussion of the steady improvement of the European infrastructure from 1700 on, see Stephen Broadberry and Kevin H. O'Rourke, eds., *The Cambridge Economic History of Modern Europe*, vol. 1, *1700–1870* (Cambridge, UK, 2010).

76. Habakkuk and Postan, eds., *The Cambridge Economic History of Europe*, vol. 6: pp. 277–278.

77. R. M. Hartwell, "Economic Change in England and Europe," in Crawley, ed., *The New Cambridge Modern History*, vol. 9, p. 40.

78. And, of course, the size of the British population had grown enormously over that period. Habakkuk and Postan, eds., *The Cambridge Economic History of Europe*, vol. 6, pp. 293–295.

79. R. M. Hartwell, "Economic Change in England and Europe," in Crawley, ed., *The New Cambridge Modern History*, 9:44.

80. Habakkuk and Postan, eds., *The Cambridge Economic History of Europe*, 6: (I), p.325.

81. Ibid., 6: (I), p. 318.

82. James Boswell, *The Life of Samuel Johnson, LL.D., Including a Journal of a Tour to the Hebrides* (Boston, 1832), p. 42.

83. Joel Mokyr, *The Levers of Riches: Technological Creativity and Economic Progress* (Oxford, 1990), pp. 87–88.

84. Ibid., p. 104.

85. The importance of the steam engines to pumping water out of mines is suggested by the fact that in Warwickshire no fewer than five hundred horses were engaged in that activity, "bucket by bucket." Habakkuk and Postan, eds., *The Cambridge Economic History of Europe*, 6:326.

86. Mokyr, *The Levers of Riches*, p. 98.

87. Ibid., pp. 98–99.

88. Ibid., p. 111.

89. Habakkuk and Postan, eds., *The Cambridge Economic History of Europe*, 6: (I), pp. 274–275.

90. Watson, *The Reign of George III*, pp. 467–470. See also Kevin H. O'Rourke, Leandro Prados de la Escosura, and Guillaume Daudin, "Trade and Empire," in Broadberry and O'Rourke, eds., *The Cambridge Economic History of Modern Europe*, vol. 1, p. 117, figure 4.4.

91. Quoted in Felix Markham, "The Napoleonic Wars," in Crawley, ed., *The New Cambridge Modern History*, vol. 9, p.330.

92. Broadberry and O'Rourke, eds., *The Cambridge Economic History of Modern Europe*, vol. 1, p. 99.

93. John Brewer, *The Sinews of Power: War, Money, and the English State, 1688–1783* (New York, 1989), pp. 194–195.

94. Adam Nicolson, *Seize the Fire: Heroism, Duty, and the Battle of Trafalgar* (New York, 2005), p. 42.

95. Paul Kennedy, *The Rise and Fall of British Naval Mastery* (London, 1976), pp. 130–133.

96. Rodger, *The Command of the Ocean*, pp. 484–485.

97. Piers Mackesy, *The War for America, 1775–1783*, p. 178.

98. McNeill, *The Pursuit of Power*, p. 212.

99. Kennedy, *The Rise and Fall of British Naval Mastery*, p. 141.

100. McNeill quotes one economic historian arguing the Revolutionary and Napoleonic Wars do "not seem to have caused more than superficial fluctuations in the pace and content of the British Industrial Revolution." McNeill, *The Pursuit of Power*, p. 210: n48.

101. See particularly the discussion in ibid., pp. 209–212.

102. For the Napoleonic Wars in general, see David A. Bell, *The First Total War: Napoleon's Europe and the Birth of War As We Know It* (Boston, 2007). See

also Gunther E. Rothenberg, *The Art of Warfare in the Age of Napoleon* (Bloomington, IN, 1978).

103. Felix Markham, "The Napoleonic Adventure," in Crawley, ed., *The New Cambridge Modern History*, 9:312.

104. For Napoleon's Grand Army, see among others Rory Muir, *Tactics and the Experience of Battle in the Age of Napoleon* (New Haven, CT, 1998); Charles J. Esdaile, *The Wars of Napoleon* (London, 1995); and Michael J. Hughes, *Forging Napoleon's Grand Armée: Motivation, Military Culture, and Masculinity in the French Army, 1800–1808* (New York, 2012).

105. Mikaberidze, *The Napoleonic Wars*, p. 185.

106. At least in the sense that the French Navy never again attempted to engage the Royal Navy in another major battle.

107. Mikaberidze, *The Napoleonic Wars*, p. 200.

108. Ibid., p. 292.

109. On the Austrian Army, see Gunther E. Rothenberg, *Napoleon's Great Adversary: Archduke Charles and the Austrian Army, 1792–1814* (Bloomington, IN, 1982).

110. Sherwig, *Guineas and Gunpowder*, p. 149.

111. For an outstanding discussion of Napoleon's contributions to the creation of the Third Coalition, see Schroeder, *The Transformation of European Politics*, pp. 264–268.

112. D. Leonard, *Nineteenth Century Premiers: Pitt to Roseberry* (London, 2008), p. 25.

113. Chandler, *The Campaigns of Napoleon*, p. 438.

114. Ibid., p. 502.

115. For the reformation of the Prussian Army, see among others Charles Edward White, *The Enlightened Soldier: Scharnhorst and the Militärische Geselschaft in Berlin, 1801–1805* (New York, 1988), and Peter Paret, *Yorck and the Era of Prussian Reform, 1807–1815* (Princeton, NJ, 1966).

116. For an examination of the problems involved in the culture of military organizations since the American Civil War, see Peter R. Mansoor and Williamson Murray, eds., *The Culture of Military Organizations* (Cambridge, UK, 2019).

117. Quoted in Gordon A. Craig, *The Politics of the Prussian Army, 1640–1945* (Oxford, 1955), p. 43.

118. Chandler, *The Campaigns of Napoleon*, p. 594.

119. Quoted in ibid., p. 608.

120. For a discussion of the modern term in examining the war in Spain against the French, see Richard Hart Sinnreich, "That Accursed Spanish War: The Peninsular War, 1807–1814," in *Hybrid Warfare: Fighting Complex Opponents from the Ancient World to the Present*, ed. Williamson Murray and Peter Mansoor (Cambridge, UK, 2012), pp. 104–150.

121. For the background to Wellington's army, see Kevin Linch, *Britain and Wellington's Army: Recruitment, Society, and Tradition, 1807–15* (New York, 2011).

122. Sherwig, *Guineas and Gunpowder*, pp. 255–258.

123. Gates, *The Spanish Ulcer*, pp. 230–239.

124. Mikaberidze, *The Napoleonic Wars*, p. 546.

125. Quoted in Arthur Bryant, *The Great Duke; or, The Invincible General* (New York, 1972), p. 224.

126. Gates, *The Spanish Ulcer*, p. 215.

127. Quoted in Harold Nicolson, *The Congress of Vienna: A Study in Allied Unity, 1812–1822* (New York, 1946), p. 41.

128. For Napoleon's logistical problems, see Martin van Creveld, *Supplying War: Logistics from Wallenstein to Patton* (Cambridge, UK, 1977). For another study of logistics with an excellent bibliography, see John A. Lynn, ed., *Feeding Mars: Logistics in Western Warfare from the Middle Ages to the Present* (London, 1993).

129. In 1810, Napoleon sent a message to Marshal Louis-Gabriel Suchet that he should levy "a contribution of many millions from Lerida in order to get the means with which to feed, pay, and dress his army off the country. . . . War should nourish war." Creveld, *Supplying War*, p. 257n64.

130. The French engineer Charles Joseph Minard's map of the attrition of the Grand Army on the way to and back from Moscow presents a graphic picture of the impact of attrition. Online version of map can be viewed at https://bigthink.com/strange-maps/229-vital-statistics-of-a-deadly-campaign-the-minard-map/.

131. The decline was not entirely due to casualties. Various detachments had dropped off on the march to Vitebsk.

132. The numbers are based on Minard's map.

133. Armand de Caulaincourt, *With Napoleon in Russia: The Memoirs of General de Caulaincourt, Duke of Vicenza* (New York, 1935), p. 103.

134. Chandler, *The Campaigns of Napoleon*, p. 807.

135. For the strategic importance of the convention, see Peter Paret, *Yorck and the Era of Prussian Reform, 1807–1815* (Princeton, NJ, 1966), p. 195.

136. Chandler, *The Campaigns of Napoleon*, p. 873.

137. The most recent study of the 1813 campaign is Michael V. Leggiere's *Napoleon and the Struggle for Germany: The Franco-Prussian War of 1813*, vol. 1, *The War of Liberation, Spring 1813*, and vol. 2, *The Defeat of Napoleon* (Cambridge, UK, 2015).

138. Quoted in Chandler, *The Campaigns of Napoleon*, p. 867.

139. Ibid., p. 887.

140. Ibid., pp. 935–936.

141. McNeill, *The Pursuit of Power*, p. 213.

142. Ibid., p. 213.

143. For an analysis of the pursuit of decisive victory in the eighteenth century and into the Napoleonic era, see particularly Russell F. Weigley, *The Age of Battles: The Quest for Decisive Warfare from Breitenfeld to Waterloo* (Bloomington, IN, 1991).

144. The casualty figure estimates are from Charles Tilly, *Coercion, Capital, and European States, AD 990–1992* (London, 1990), pp. 165–166. Another historian gives the following figures for French killed in the Revolutionary and Napoleonic Wars: military dead at least 3 million and civilian dead at 1–4 million total. Esdaile, *The Wars of Napoleon*, p. 300.
145. Gneisenau quoted in Rodger, *The Command of the Ocean*, p. 574; Blücher quoted in Bernard Cornwell, *Waterloo: The History of Four Days, Three Armies, and Three Battles* (New York, 2016), p. 341.

Chapter Five. Wars in Europe and America in the Nineteenth Century

Epigraph: Quoted in Williamson Murray and Wayne Wei-Siang Hsieh, *A Savage War: A Military History of the Civil War* (Princeton, NJ, 2016), p. 65.

1. The greatest work on the Civil War remains James M. McPherson, *Battle Cry of Freedom: The Civil War Era* (Oxford, 1988), which destroyed the Confederate narrative that had dominated much of the writing about the Civil War for nearly a century. For an analysis of the military side, see Murray and Hsieh, *A Savage War*.
2. For the Crimean War, among others see Christopher Hibbert, *The Destruction of Lord Raglan: A Tragedy of the Crimean War, 1854–1855* (London, 1961), and Orlando Figes, *The Crimean War: A History*, 2nd edition (London, 2012).
3. Much of the discussion in this portion of the chapter on the Civil War and the impact of the fourth great military-social revolution is drawn from Murray and Hsieh, *A Savage War*.
4. Ibid., pp. 47, 132–133.
5. *The Cambridge Economic History of Europe*, vol. 6; *The Industrial Revolutions and After: Incomes, Population and Technological Change*, ed. H. J. Habakkuk and M. Postan (Cambridge, UK, 1966), p. 703.
6. Mark Grimsley, "The U.S. Civil War," in *The Dynamics of Military Revolution, 1300–2050*, ed. MacGregor Knox and Williamson Murray (Cambridge, UK, 2001).
7. Patricia L. Faust, *The Historical Times Illustrated Encyclopedia of the Civil War* (New York, 1986).
8. William H. McNeill, *The Pursuit of Power: Technology, Armed Force, and Society Since A.D. 1000* (Chicago, 1982), p. 233.
9. Ibid., pp. 232–233.
10. Gregor Edgar Turner, *Victory Rode the Rails: The Strategic Place of the Railroads in the Civil War* (Lincoln, NE, 1953), p. 32.
11. Ibid., p. 42.
12. Ibid., p. 105.
13. Habakkuk and Postan, eds., *The Cambridge Economic History of Europe*, vol. 6, p. 697.
14. Turner, *Victory Rode the Rails*, p. 43.

15. Faust, *The Historical Times Illustrated Encyclopedia of the Civil War.*

16. Earl J. Hess, *Civil War Logistics: A Study of Military Transportation* (Baton Rouge, LA, 2017), p. 95.

17. Ibid., p. 261.

18. Grimsley, "The U.S. Civil War."

19. Quoted in James M. McPherson, *Embattled Rebel: Jefferson Davis as Commander in Chief* (New York, 2014), pp. 119–120.

20. U.S. War Department, *The War of the Rebellion: A Compilation of the Official Records of the Union and Confederate Armies,* 128 vols. (Washington, DC, 1880–1901), series 1, vol. 32, pt. 2, pp. 280–281 (hereafter *Official Records*).

21. Murray and Hsieh, *A Savage War,* p. 47.

22. Milo M. Quaife, ed., *From the Cannon's Mouth: The Civil War Letters of General Alpheus S. Williams* (Detroit, MI, 1959), pp. 40–41.

23. Murray and Hsieh, *A Savage War,* p. 50.

24. For a discussion of this factor, see ibid., pp. 54, 544–547.

25. Quoted in "General M. C. Meigs on the Conduct of the Civil War," *American Historical Review* 26, no. 2 (1921): p. 292.

26. For the war at sea, see particularly James M. McPherson, *War on the Waters: The Union and Confederate Navies, 1861–1865* (Chapel Hill, NC, 2012).

27. Quoted in Murray and Hsieh, *A Savage War,* p. 156.

28. U. S. Grant, *Personal Memoirs of U. S. Grant* (New York, 1999), vol. 1, p. 368.

29. For a discussion of this phenomenon, see Mark Grimsley, *The Hard Hand of War: Union Military Policy Toward Southern Civilians, 1861–1865* (Cambridge, UK, 1995).

30. Quoted in Murray and Hsieh, *A Savage War,* p. 327.

31. The distance over which the Prusso-German Army moved to besiege Paris was only 250 miles with the additional support of macadamized roads. There were no significantly modernized roads in Georgia in 1870.

32. Hess, *Civil War Logistics,* p. 240.

33. Turner, *Victory Rode the Rails,* p. 326.

34. William T. Sherman, *Memoirs of General William T. Sherman, by Himself,* (New York, 1875), vol. 2, p. 399; emphasis added.

35. Lincoln's reelection in 1864 turned out to be a closer affair than the election of 1860.

36. Grimsley, "The U.S. Civil War."

37. These armies were Buell's Army of the Cumberland under Major General George "Pap" Thomas; the Army of the Tennessee, Grant's old army, under Major General James McPherson; and the newly created Army of the Ohio under Major General John Schofield.

38. *Official Records,* series 1, vol. 37, pt. 2, p. 366.

39. Quoted in Murray and Hsieh, *A Savage War,* p. 468.

40. For the war between Austria and Prussia, see particularly Geoffrey Wawro, *The Austro-Prussian War: Austria's War with Prussia and Italy in 1866* (Cambridge, UK, 1996).

41. For an examination of how the Prussian military developed into a formidable instrument, see Dennis E. Showalter, *Railroads and Rifles: Soldiers, Technology, and the Unification of Germany* (Hamden, CT, 1986).

42. Gerhard P. Gross, *The Myth and Reality of German Warfare: Operational Thinking from Moltke the Elder to Heusinger* (Lexington, KY, 2016), p. 24.

43. One might argue that Königgrätz was a decisive battle, but that was so only because Bismarck offered the Austrians a deal they could not refuse: namely, they would lose no territory.

44. For the Franco-Prussian War, see particularly Michael Howard, *The Franco-Prussian War: The German Invasion of France, 1870–1871*, 2nd edition (1961; London, 2001), and Geoffrey Wawro, *The Franco-Prussian-War: The German Conquest of France in 1870–1871* (Cambridge, UK, 2003).

45. Gross, *The Myth and Reality of German Warfare*, p. 41.

Chapter Six. The First World War: 1914–1916

Epigraph: Thucydides, *History of the Peloponnesian War*, trans. Rex Warner (London, 1954), p. 49.

1. Winston S. Churchill, *The World Crisis*, 6 vols. (Toronto, 1923–1931), 6. For recent examinations of the causes of the war, see Christopher Clark, *The Sleepwalkers: How Europe Went to War in 1914* (New York, 2012), and Margaret MacMillan, *The War That Ended Peace: The Road to 1914* (New York, 2013).

2. For the German Navy, see Holger H. Herwig, *"Luxury" Fleet: The Imperial German Navy, 1888–1918* (London, 1980).

3. Joel Mokyr, "The Second Industrial Revolution, 1870–1914," (August 1998): 1.

4. Hew Strachan, *The First World War*, vol. 1, *To Arms* (Oxford, 2001), p. 5.

5. Avner Offer, *The First World War: An Agrarian Interpretation* (Oxford, 1989), p. 83.

6. Strachan, *The First World War*, 1:chap. 10.

7. Quoted in Offer, *The First World War*, p. 350.

8. Quoted in Gerd Hardach, *The First World War, 1914–1918* (Berkeley, CA, 1977), p. 55.

9. On this, see particularly Isabel V. Hull, *Absolute Destruction: Military Culture and the Practices of War in Imperial Germany* (Ithaca, NY, 2005).

10. Paul Kennedy, "Military Effectiveness in the First World War," in *Military Effectiveness*, vol. 1, *The First World War*, ed. Allan R. Millett and Williamson Murray (London, 1988), p. 330.

11. Michael Howard, "Military Science in an Age of Peace," *Journal of the Royal United Services Institute* March 1974.

12. For an excellent short discussion of the firepower revolution of 1914, see Gary Sheffield, *Forgotten Victory: The First World War: Myths and Realities* (London, 2001). See also Shelford Bidwell and Dominick Graham, *Fire-*

Power: The British Army Weapons and Theories of War, 1904–1945 (London, 1982).

13. Among the technological innovations he cites are airships (Zeppelins), observation balloons, observation and liaison aircraft, bombers, fighters, ground attack aircraft, aerial photography and stereoscopic photo analysis, motor vehicles, massive fuel requirements, tanks, artillery-delivered weaponized gas, gas masks, specialized artillery shells, and so on. David T. Zabecki, *The Generals' War: Operational Level Command on the Western Front in 1918* (Bloomington, IN, 2018), pp. 13–14.

14. At the turn of the century, Terence Zuber, *Inventing the Schlieffen Plan: German War Planning, 1871–1914* (Oxford, 2002), argued that there never was a "Schlieffen Plan." More recent scholarship from the German archives has demolished his argument.

15. The British Army would play an important role in both the Battle of the Marne and the fighting in Flanders. For the long term, the blockade would severely impede the German war effort.

16. For the German logistical failures in 1914 and their impact on German operations, see Martin van Creveld, *Supplying War: Logistics from Wallenstein to Patton* (Cambridge, UK, 1977), chap. 4.

17. Moltke quoted in *Moltke on the Art of War: Selected Writings*, ed. Daniel J. Hughes and Harry Bell (Novato, CA, 1993), p. 92; John Horne and Alan Kramer, *German Atrocities, 1914: A History of Denial* (New Haven, CT, 2001), pp. 74–75.

18. Alistair Horne, *The Price of Glory: Verdun, 1916* (New York, 1962), p. 18.

19. For an outstanding account of the Marne campaign, see Holger H. Herwig, *The Battle of the Marne: The Opening of World War I and the Battle That Changed the World* (New York, 2009).

20. For the BEF's contribution, see Anthony Farrar-Hockley, *Death of an Army* (New York, 1968).

21. For the campaign in East Prussia in 1914, see Dennis E. Showalter, *Tannenberg: Clash of Empires, 1914* (Washington, DC, 2004).

22. For the extraordinary incompetence of Austro-Hungarian military leadership, see Geoffrey Wawro, *A Mad Catastrophe: The Outbreak of World War I and the Collapse of the Habsburg Empire* (New York, 2014).

23. Holger H. Herwig, *The First World War: Germany and Austria-Hungary, 1914–1918* (London, 1996), pp. 119–120.

24. Strachan, *The First World War*, 1: p. 110.

25. For the growing Anglo-German antagonism, see Paul Kennedy, *The Rise of the Anglo-German Antagonism, 1860–1914* (London, 1980).

26. John Hall Stewart, "French Military," in *A Documentary Survey of the French Revolution*, 8th edition (New York, 1951), pp. 472–474.

27. Gerald D. Feldman, *Army, Industry, and Labor in Germany, 1914–1918* (New York, 1992), p. 45.

28. Strachan, *The First World War,* 1: pp. 1036, 1037. Strachan's brilliant work on the war's first year provides much of the statistics for this section.
29. Ibid., 1:1049. William H. McNeill gives the losses of French industry due to German occupation as "64 percent of pig iron, 26 percent of steel capacity, and 85 out of 170 blast furnaces." McNeill, *The Pursuit of Power: Technology, Armed Force, and Society Since A.D. 1000* (Chicago, 1982), p. 318.
30. Douglas Porch, "The French Army in the First World War," in Millett and Murray, eds., *Military Effectiveness,* 1: pp. 197–199.
31. Strachan, *The First World War,* 1: p. 1065.
32. Ibid., 1: p. 1051.
33. Ibid., 1: pp. 1055–1058.
34. Ibid., 1: p. 1059.
35. Paul Kennedy, "Britain in the First World War," in Millett and Murray, eds., *Military Effectiveness,* 1: p. 33.
36. From the table in Hardach, *The First World War,* pp. 326–327.
37. See Williamson Murray, *War in the Air, 1914–1945* (Washington, DC, 1999).
38. William H. Morrow Jr., *The Great War in the Air: Military Aviation from 1909 to 1921* (Tuscaloosa, AL, 1993), p. 55.
39. Ibid., pp. 55, 102, 112, 146.
40. Ibid., pp. 121, 123, 185.
41. Andrew Gordon, *The Rules of the Game: Jutland and British Naval Command* (London, 1996), p. 594.
42. Holger H. Herwig, "The Dynamics of Necessity: German Military Policy in the Great War," in Millett and Murray, eds., *Military Effectiveness,* 1:119–120.
43. Nicholas A. Lambert, *Planning Armageddon: British Economic Warfare and the First World War* (Cambridge, MA, 2012), p. 137.
44. Ibid., p. 162.
45. Ibid., p. 231.
46. Ibid., p. 223.
47. Ibid., pp. 272–275.
48. The following figures indicate the extent of the blockade's leakage: In March 1915, German exports to the United States reached 60 percent of prewar levels; lubricating oil exported from the United States to Holland and Scandinavia had risen from 6,448 gallons in April and May 1914 to 419,485 gallons one year later. Over the first half of 1915, exports of cotton from the United States to Central Europe had increased by 2.2 million bales over the previous year. Ibid., pp. 436–438.
49. Herwig, *"Luxury" Fleet,* pp. 163–164.
50. See particularly Patrick Beesly, *Room 40: British Naval Intelligence, 1914–1918* (London, 1982). See also David Boyle, *Before Enigma: The Room 40 Codebreakers of the First World War* (London, 2016).
51. Quoted in Herwig, *The First World War,* pp. 116–117.

52. Gerhard P. Gross, *The Myth and Reality of German Warfare: Operational Thinking from Moltke the Elder to Heusinger* (Lexington, KY, 2016). The distances Ludendorff was suggesting would prove beyond the capabilities of the Wehrmacht's mechanized units twenty-six years later.

53. For Russian incompetence that contributed to the defeat, see Norman Stone, *The Eastern Front, 1914–1917* (London, 1975), pp. 129–130.

54. Robert A. Doughty, *Pyrrhic Victory: French Strategy and Operations in the Great War* (Cambridge, MA, 2005), p. 142.

55. Ibid., p. 201.

56. Robin Prior and Trevor Wilson, *Command on the Western Front: The Military Career of Sir Henry Rawlinson, 1914–18* (Oxford, 1992), p. 68.

57. Quoted in Andrew Roberts, *Churchill: Walking with Destiny* (New York, 2018), p. 196.

58. Tim Travers, *Gallipoli 1915* (Bloomington, IN, 2001), p. 228.

59. The political results of these campaigns are brilliantly examined in David Fromkin, *A Peace to End All Peace: The Fall of the Ottoman Empire and the Creation of the Modern Middle East* (New York, 1989).

60. Quoted in Horne, *The Price of Glory*, p. 35.

61. Ibid., p. 36.

62. Doughty, *Pyrrhic Victory*, p. 287.

63. Horne, *The Price of Glory*, p. 61.

64. Ibid., pp. 327–328.

Chapter Seven. Inventing Modern War

Epigraph: Jonathan Boff, *Winning and Losing on the Western Front: The British Third Army and the Defeat of Germany in 1918* (Cambridge, UK, 2012), p. 243.

1. Robin Prior and Trevor Wilson, *The Somme* (New Haven, CT, 2005), p. 128.

2. For an outstanding biography of Haig, see J. P. Harris, *Douglas Haig and the First World War* (Cambridge, UK, 2008).

3. His diary, for example, possesses virtually no references to tactical issues. National Library of Scotland, https://www.nls.uk/collections/manuscripts/collections/military-naval/haig-diary/.

4. For the first day on the Somme and its terrible results, see John Keegan, chapter 4, in *The Face of Battle* (London, 1976), and Martin Middlebrook, *The First Day on the Somme* (London, 1975).

5. Prior and Wilson, *The Somme*, p. 115.

6. Ernst Jünger, *Storm of Steel*, pp. 108, 110.

7. Quoted in William Philpott, *Three Armies on the Somme: The First Battle of the Twentieth Century* (New York, 2010), pp. 261–264.

8. Robin Prior and Trevor Wilson, *Command on the Western Front: The Military Career of Sir Henry Rawlinson, 1914–18* (Oxford, 1992), p. 191.

9. G. C. Wynne, *If Germany Attacks: The Battle in Depth in the West* (London, 1940), p. 123.

10. Holger H. Herwig, *The First World War: Germany and Austria-Hungary, 1914–1918* (London, 1996), p. 202.

11. J. P. Harris, *Men, Ideas and Tanks: British Military Thought and Armoured Forces, 1903–1939* (Manchester, UK, 1995), pp. 64–69.

12. Prior and Wilson, *The Somme*, pp. 294–299.

13. John Lee, "Some Lessons from the Somme: The British Infantry in 1917," in *Look to Your Front: Studies in the First World War*, ed. British Commission for Military History (London, 1999), p. 80.

14. Herwig, *The First World War*, pp. 203–204.

15. Philpott, *Three Armies on the Somme*, p. 408.

16. Erich von Ludendorff, *Ludendorff's Own Story, August 1914–November 1918* (New York, 1919), pp. 313, 316, 321.

17. The most thorough examination of the development of German tactics, unfortunately published at the beginning of the Second World War when no one was interested in what had happened in the last war, is Wynne, *If Germany Attacks*.

18. For a more extended discussion of the new defensive tactics, see Williamson Murray, *Military Adaptation in War: With Fear of Change* (Cambridge, 2011), pp. 98–103.

19. Based on the chart in David Stevenson, *Cataclysm: The First World War as Political Tragedy* (New York, 2004), p. 181.

20. For Germany's difficulties in terms of its lack of access to raw materials, see the discussion about the situation in the period before World War II in Williamson Murray, *The Change in the European Balance of Power, 1938–1939: The Path to Ruin* (Princeton, NJ, 1984), chap. 1.

21. For what Ludendorff and his chief staff officers were attempting to do, see particularly Michael Geyer, *Deutsche Rüstungspolitik, 1860–1980* (Frankfurt, 1984).

22. Herwig, *The First World War*, pp. 262–265.

23. Gerald D. Feldman, *Army, Industry, and Labor in Germany, 1914–1918* (New York, 1992), p. 259.

24. Quoted in ibid., 273. For a less critical examination of the Hindenburg program, see Gerd Hardach, *The First World War, 1914–1918* (Berkeley, CA, 1977), pp. 63ff.

25. MacGregor Knox, *To the Threshold of Power, 1922/33: Origins and Dynamics of the Fascist and National Socialist Dictatorships* (Cambridge, UK, 2007), 1:184.

26. Stevenson, *Cataclysm*, p. 186.

27. Ibid., p. 190. The price of transporting that ammunition from Canada to Britain was quite high. In December 1917, a collision between two ships in the harbor of Halifax set one of them, a freighter carrying ammunition, afire. The resulting explosion killed approximately two thousand and injured nine thousand.

28. David Stevenson gives the percentage losses of major industrial capacity as 58 percent of steel production, 83 percent of iron ore, and 49 percent of coal output. Ibid., p. 187.

29. Ibid., p. 189.

30. Hardach, *The First World War*, pp. 98–99.

31. Quoted in William H. Morrow Jr., *The Great War in the Air: Military Aviation from 1909 to 1921* (Tuscaloosa, AL, 1993), p. 197.

32. Ibid., p. 96.

33. Robert A. Doughty, *Pyrrhic Victory: French Strategy and Operations in the Great War* (Cambridge, MA, 2005), p. 367.

34. Morrow, *The Great War in the Air*, table 4, p. 251.

35. Ibid., pp. 226–227.

36. Ibid., pp. 122, 329.

37. Ibid., p. 294.

38. Quoted in Holger H. Herwig, *"Luxury" Fleet: The Imperial German Navy, 1888–1918* (London, 1980), p. 310.

39. Ironically, the Royal Navy's leaders refused to consider convoys as a means to counter the U-boat threat, first with the argument that there were too many ships to convoy (there weren't), and second that civilian sailing ship-masters lacked the discipline to stay on station (even though in the eighteenth century, sailing ships had stayed on station in convoys).

40. In addition to bringing the United States into the war, the unrestricted submarine war, with the Germans targeting all shipping, caused a significant drop in the number of neutral vessels carrying cargoes to Holland and the Scandinavian countries. A comparison of ships arriving in the ports of those countries during the first three months of 1915 to those arriving in 1917 saw a drop from 1,070 to 313. Hardach, *The First World War*, p. 28.

41. David T. Zabecki, *The Generals' War: Operational Level Command on the Western Front in 1918* (Bloomington, IN, 2018), p. 40; Isabel V. Hull, *Absolute Destruction: Military Culture and the Practices of War in Imperial Germany*, (Ithaca, NY, 2005).

42. For the collapse in the army's discipline, see Allan K. Wildman, *The End of the Russian Imperial Army*, vol. 1, *The Old Army and the Soldiers' Revolt (March–April, 1917)* (Princeton, NJ, 1980).

43. The British and Canadian authorities were equally helpful. The Canadians had pulled Leon Trotsky, who was attempting to return to Russia from Brooklyn, off a steamer in Halifax and confined him at a prison camp in Amherst. After just one month the Canadians acceded to a British order and released Trotsky to return to Russia at the provisional government's request.

44. For the extensive discussions among Anglo-French politicians and generals, see Harris, *Douglas Haig and the First World War*, pp. 279–286.

45. For an analysis of the battle and its course, see ibid., pp. 300–313. See also Gary Sheffield, *Forgotten Victory: The First World War: Myths and Realities* (London, 2001), pp. 90–199.

46. Harris, *Douglas Haig and the First World War*, p. 317.

47. For the most thorough examination of the Nivelle offensive, see Doughty, *Pyrrhic Victory*, pp. 320–352.

48. Morrow, *The Great War in the Air*, p. 199.

49. Wynne, *If Germany Attacks*, p. 302.

50. Doughty, *Pyrrhic Victory*, p. 356.

51. For the extent of the French mutinies and the methods by which they were suppressed, see Richard M. Watt, *Dare Call It Treason* (New York, 1963).

52. Doughty, *Pyrrhic Victory*, p. 363.

53. For a brilliant rethinking of the planning and course of the Flanders offensive, known popularly as Passchendaele, see Robin Prior and Trevor Wilson, *Passchendaele: The Untold Story* (New Haven, CT, 1996).

54. Brian Bond, *Britain's Two World Wars Against Germany: Myth, Memory and the Distortions of Hindsight* (Cambridge, UK, 2014), p. 134.

55. Prior and Wilson, *Passchendaele*, p. 61.

56. Ibid., p. 59.

57. For the planning and training of the troops for the operation, see ibid., pp. 70–77.

58. For Lossberg's orders, see Fritz von Lossberg, *Lossberg's War: The World War I Memoirs of a German Chief of Staff*, ed. and trans. David T. Zabecki and Dieter J. Biedekarken (Lexington, KY, 2017), pp. 289–299.

59. For a short description of the German system, see Prior and Wilson, *Passchendaele*, pp. 71–72.

60. Ibid., pp. 93–95.

61. Quoted in Leon Wolff, *In Flanders Fields: The 1917 Campaign* (New York, 1958), p. 361.

62. Prior and Wilson, *Passchendaele*, p. 115.

63. Sheffield, *Forgotten Victory*, p. 262.

64. This analysis is largely drawn from the discussions about the development of the plan and the forces involved in Harris, *Douglas Haig and the First World War*, pp. 388–398.

65. Ibid., pp. 398–403.

66. Knox, *To the Threshold of Power*, 1:165.

67. For Rommel's performance, which won him the coveted *pour le mérit*, see David Fraser, *Knight's Cross: A Life of Field Marshal Erwin Rommel* (New York, 1993), pp. 63–73.

68. Knox, *To the Threshold of Power*, 1:216.

69. For the army's death throes, see Allan K. Wildman, *The End of the Russian Imperial Army*, vol. 2, *The Road to Soviet Power and Peace* (Princeton, NJ, 1987).

70. For Georg Bruchmüller's career and contribution to the development of German artillery tactics, see David T. Zabecki, *Steel Wind: Colonel Georg Bruchmüller and the Birth of Modern Artillery* (Westport, CT, 1994). See also Stevenson, *Cataclysm*, p. 307.

71. For the negotiations that resulted in the Treaty of Brest Litovsk, see John W. Wheeler-Bennett, *The Forgotten Peace: Brest-Litovsk, March 1918* (New York, 1939).

72. For a rethinking of Versailles, see Williamson Murray, "Versailles: The Peace Without a Chance," in *The Making of Peace: Rulers, States, and the Aftermath of War*, ed. Williamson Murray and Jim Lacey (Cambridge, UK, 2009), pp. 209–239.

73. Wilhelm Deist, "The Military Collapse of the German Empire: The Reality Behind the Stab-in-the-Back Myth," trans. E. J. Feuchtwanger, *War in History* 3, no. 2 (April 1996): 190.

74. Ibid., p. 195.

75. Quoted in Zabecki, *The Generals' War*, p. 93.

76. Timothy T. Lupfer, *The Dynamics of Doctrine: The Changes in German Tactical Doctrine During the First World War*, Leavenworth Papers no. 4 (Fort Leavenworth, KS, 1981), p. 41.

77. David T. Zabecki, *The German 1918 Offensives: A Case Study in the Operational Level of War* (London, 2006), p. 132.

78. Deist, "The Military Collapse of the German Empire," p. 191.

79. Harris, *Douglas Haig and the First World War*, pp. 433–434.

80. For the difficulties the British had in adjusting to the new defensive tactics, see Tim Travers, *How the War Was Won: Command and Technology in the British Army on the Western Front, 1917–1918* (London, 1982), p. 22.

81. Sheffield, *Forgotten Victory*, pp. 271, 280.

82. For the foremost critique of German planning for the 1918 offensives, see particularly ibid.

83. Crown Prince Rupprecht, *Mein Kriegstagebuch*, vol. 2, ed. Eugen von Frauenholz (Munich, 1929), p. 372n. Ludendorff is also recorded as having commented, "In Russia we always merely set an intermediate objective, and then discovered where to go next." Quoted in Zabecki, *The German 1918 Offensives*, p. 109.

84. Interestingly the official history (only published in 1956) indicates that the number of divisions fully worked up and characterized as attack divisions was over thirty. Reichsarchiv, *Der Weltkrieg: 1914–1918*, vol. 14, *Die Kriegführung an der Westfront im Jahre 1918* (Berlin, 1944), pp. 41–42.

85. The trench divisions were second-class divisions, far less well equipped than the attack divisions.

86. Jünger, *Storm of Steel*, pp. 250–255.

87. Travers, *How the War Was Won*, p. 65.

88. Zabecki, *The German 1918 Offensives*, p. 145.

89. For the BEF's conduct of the fight, see among others Harris, *Douglas Haig and the First World War*, pp. 450–467.

90. Zabecki, *The Generals' War*, p. 125.

91. Zabecki, *The German 1918 Offensives*, p. 210.

92. Ibid., pp. 216–218.

93. Ibid., p. 226.
94. Rudolf Binding, a German writer who served primarily on the Western Front, quoted in Barrie Pitt, *1918: The Last Act* (London, 1962), pp. 179–181.
95. Zabecki, *The German 1918 Offensives*, pp. 265–267.
96. Watson, *The People's War*, p. 524.
97. Ibid., pp. 525–526.
98. Stevenson, *Cataclysm*, p. 342.
99. Morrow, *The Great War in the Air*, p. 294.
100. Stevenson, *Cataclysm*, p. 369.
101. Harris, *Douglas Haig and the First World War*, p. 489.
102. For the importance of gas to the BEF's success in 1918, see Albert Palazzo, *Seeking Victory on the Western Front: The British Army and Chemical Warfare in World War I* (Lincoln, NE, 2000).
103. Bond, *Britain's Two World Wars Against Germany*, p. 141.
104. For the success of the armored cars and the overall offensive, see Pitt, *1918*, pp. 195–205.
105. Harris, *Douglas Haig and the First World War*, pp. 492–494.
106. R. Asprey, *The German High Command at War: Hindenburg and Ludendorff and the First World War* (New York, 1991). Harris gives a figure of 22,000 Allied casualties and only 30,000 German prisoners but no wounded or dead. Whatever the numbers, the Germans who surrendered represented an indication of the breakdown in morale.
107. For British accounts of the British offensives, see J. P. Harris with Niall Barr, *Amiens to the Armistice: The BEF in the Hundred Days' Campaign, 8 August–11 November 1918* (London, 1998), and Sheffield, *Forgotten Victory*.
108. For an excellent study of the Third Army during this period, see Boff, *Winning and Losing on the Western Front*.
109. Edward M. Coffman, *The War to End All Wars: The American Military Experience in World War I* (Lexington, KY, 1998).
110. Stevenson, *Cataclysm*, p. 351.
111. Gary Sheffield, *Command and Morale: The British Army on the Western Front, 1914–1918* (Barnsley, UK, 2014), p. 15.
112. Bond, *Britain's Two World Wars Against Germany*, p. 143.
113. For the discussions between army leaders and the politicians, see Herwig, *The First World War*, pp. 425–427.
114. Deist, "The Military Collapse of the German Empire," pp. 202–203.
115. For the German disregard of international law and norms in their emphasis on "military necessity," see Isabel V. Hull, *A Scrap of Paper: Breaking and Making International Law During the Great War* (Ithaca, NY, 2014).
116. For the German military culture that excused all actions, no matter what their impact on civilians, see Isabel V. Hull, *Absolute Destruction: Military Culture and the Practices of War in Imperial Germany* (Ithaca, NY, 2005).

117. While the Germans had not ignited World War I with the same malice aforethought that characterized Hitler's regime in September 1939, their actions in encouraging Austria-Hungary's irresponsible actions in July 1914 indict them as the main culprits in the outbreak of the war.

118. Stevenson, *Cataclysm*, p. 434. For a thorough examination of this story, see Holger H. Herwig, "Clio Deceived: Patriotic Self-Censorship in Germany after the Great War," *International Security* 12, no. 2 (Fall 1987): 5–44.

Chapter Eight. Innovation and Preparation for War

Epigraph: Paul A. Rahe, *Sparta's First Attic War: The Grand Strategy of Classical Sparta, 478–446 B.C.* (New Haven, CT, 2019), p. 230.

1. For the sordid story of the Nazi seizure of power, see MacGregor Knox, *To the Threshold of Power, 1922/33: Origins and Dynamics of the Fascist and National Socialist Dictatorships* (Cambridge, UK, 2007), vol. 1.

2. The major economic and resource constraints on German rearmament are discussed in Williamson Murray, *The Change in the European Balance of Power, 1938–1939: The Path to Ruin* (Princeton, NJ, 1984), chap. 1.

3. For the financial and economic difficulties the Germans confronted during rearmament before the war, see Adam Tooze, *The Wages of Destruction: The Making and Breaking of the Nazi Economy* (London, 2006).

4. Gerhard Förster, *Totaler Krieg und Blitzkrieg: Die Theorie des totalen Krieges und des Blitzkrieges am der Militardoktrin des faschistischen Deutschlands am Vorabend des Zweiten Weltkrieges* (Berlin, 1967), p. 101.

5. For the 1936 discussions among the army's senior generals about the implications of the rapidly expanding rearmament programs by the end of the 1930s, see Wilhelm Deist, *The Wehrmacht and German Rearmament* (New York, 1981), pp. 46–51.

6. Murray, *The Change in the European Balance of Power*, table I-5, pp. 20–21.

7. Reichskredit Gesellschaft, April 1938, Treibstoffwirtschaft in der Welt und in Deutschland, pp. 34–38, T-84/51/1332658, National Archives and Records Service, Kew, UK (hereafter NARS).

8. Alan S. Milward, *The German Economy at War* (London, 1965).

9. Neville Chamberlain to Lord Halifax, PREM 1/276, NARS.

10. L. S. Amery, *My Political Life*, vol. 3, *The Unforgiving Years, 1929–1940* (London, 1955), p. 292.

11. Eden A. Smith, "King and Country—'That Abject, Squalid, Shameless Avowal,'" Notable Debates, The Oxford Union, https://oxford-union.org/pages/notable-debates; Murray, *The Change in the European Balance of Power*.

12. Winston S. Churchill, *The Second World War*, vol. 1, *The Gathering Storm* (Boston, 1948), p. 6.

13. For a discussion of French capabilities and their aircraft industry, see Murray, *The Change in the European Balance of Power*, pp. 107–108.

14. As the historian Alan Beyerchen noted, "From 1938 onward, civilian scientists were brought in under military contract to investigate specific problems but did not set the agenda for research." Beyerchen, "From Radio to Radar: Interwar Military Adaptation to Technological Change in Germany, the United Kingdom, and the United States," in *Military Innovation in the Interwar Period*, ed. Williamson Murray and Allan R. Millett (Cambridge, UK, 1996), pp. 265–299.

15. For the German failure to think beyond the tactical level, see David T. Zabecki, *The German 1918 Offensives: A Case Study in the Operational Level of War* (London, 2006), pp. 311–328.

16. The best overall study of German rearmament in the interwar period remains Wilhelm Deist, "Die Aufrüstung der Wehrmacht," in Wilhelm Deist et al., *Das Deutsche Reich und der Zweite Weltkrieg*, vol. 1, *Ursachen und Voraussetzungen der Deutschen Kriegspolitik* (Stuttgart, 1979).

17. Ibid., p. 37.

18. For an examination of the weaknesses of German intelligence, see Williamson Murray, "Net Assessment in Nazi Germany in the 1930s," in *Calculations: Net Assessment and the Coming of World War II*, ed. Williamson Murray and Allan R. Millett (New York, 1992).

19. Quoted in Dennis Showalter, *Instrument of War: The German Army, 1914–18* (London, 2016), p. 188.

20. Bernard R. Kroener, Rolf-Dieter Müller, and Hans Umbreit, *Das Deutsche Reich und der Zweite Weltkrieg*, vol. 5, part 1, *Kriegsverwaltung, Wirtschaft, und Personelle Ressourcen* (Stuttgart, 1988), p. 651.

21. For the French military in the interwar period, see Robert A. Doughty, "The French Armed Forces, 1918–40," in *Military Effectiveness*, vol. 2, *The Interwar Period*, ed. Allan R. Millett and Williamson Murray (London, 1988).

22. Robert A. Doughty, *The Seeds of Disaster: The Development of French Army Doctrine, 1919–39* (Mechanicsburg, PA, 1985), p. 72.

23. Paul Marie de la Gorce, *The French Army: A Military-Political History*, trans. Kenneth Douglas (New York, 1963), p. 271.

24. André Beaufre, *1940: The Fall of France*, trans. Desmond Flower (New York, 1968), p. 47.

25. One should also note that the official histories were not completed until the late 1940s, and the last volumes dealt with the critical battles of 1918.

26. For a larger examination of British Army culture, see Williamson Murray, "The Culture of the British Army, 1914–1945," in *The Culture of Military Organizations*, ed. Peter R. Mansoor and Williamson Murray (Cambridge, UK, 2019).

27. The best general account of the rise of the Red Army to eventual victory in the Second World War remains David M. Glantz and Jonathan M. House, *When Titans Clashed: How the Red Army Stopped Hitler* (Lawrence, KS, 2015).

28. At the onset of German military planning for Barbarossa, the General Staff's geographic section warned that the Five-Year Plans had placed much of the Soviet Union's new industrial plant in the Urals and to the east of that mountain range. Williamson Murray and Allan R. Millett, *A War to Be Won: Fighting the Second World War* (Cambridge, MA, 2000), pp. 115–116.

29. John Erickson, *The Soviet High Command, 1918–1941* (London, 1962), p. 585.

30. For a theoretical examination of Soviet doctrinal thinking, see Shimon Naveh, *In Pursuit of Military Excellence: The Evolution of Operational Theory* (London, 1997).

31. Glantz and House, *When Titans Clashed*, pp. 6–12. See also Naveh, *In Pursuit of Military Excellence*.

32. On Stalin's purges in general, see the masterful work by Robert Conquest, *The Great Terror: Stalin's Purge of the Thirties* (London, 1968).

33. For the impact of the purges on the military and the general unpreparedness of the Red Army to meet the German invasion, see David M. Glantz, *Stumbling Colossus: The Red Army on the Eve of World War* (Lawrence, KS, 1998).

34. In this regard the simplest example was the intuitive discovery by the scientist P. J. Blackett that the larger the convoy, the fewer anti-submarine escorts required per ship to protect it. For Blackett's contribution, see Stephen Budiansky, *Blackett's War: The Men Who Defeated the Nazi U-Boats and Brought Science to the Art of War* (New York, 2013).

35. For the issues involved in military adaptation during wartime, see Williamson Murray, *Military Adaptation in War: With Fear of Change* (Cambridge, UK, 2011).

36. *Die Luftkriegführung* (Berlin, 1935).

37. For a full discussion of the Luftwaffe's buildup, see Edward Homze, *Arming the Luftwaffe: The Reich Air Ministry and the German Aircraft Industry, 1919–39* (Lincoln, NE, 1976).

38. Deist et al., *Das Deutsche Reich und der Zweite Weltkrieg*, 1:480–481.

39. Richard J. Overy, "German Aircraft Production, 1939–1942: A Study in the German War Economy" (Ph.D. dissertation, Cambridge University, 1977), p. 2.

40. Such a demand also ignored that such an increase would require an aviation gas production equivalent to three-quarters of the world's in 1938.

41. For Dowding's performance in the first year of World War II, see Murray, *Military Adaptation in War,* chap. 4.

42. The comparative development of radar in Germany, Britain, and the United States is brilliantly set out by Alan Beyerchen in "From Radio to Radar," pp. 269–299.

43. Ibid., p. 282.

44. R. V. Jones, *The Wizard War: British Scientific Intelligence, 1939–1945* (New York, 1978), p. 199.

45. The P-51 was a combined Anglo-American development. For its developmental history, see Paul Kennedy, *Engineers of Victory: The Problem Solvers Who Turned the Tide in the Second World War* (New York, 2013).

46. The Army Air Corps name was changed in June 1941 to the Army Air Forces to give greater prominence to what American political and military leaders believed would be its heightened significance in the coming war.

47. For the German Navy during the era of the Third Reich, see Michael Salewski, *Die deutsche Seekriegsleitung* (Frankfurt am Main, 1970).

48. Ibid., p. 29.

49. For a discussion, see Williamson Murray, "The Battle of the British Isles: June 1940–May 1941," in Murray, *Military Adaptation in War*.

50. The best way to gain some sense of the German failure to innovate with new technologies is to compare pictures of the Type VII or XII U-boats on one hand and the new American fleet boats at the beginning of the war and then after three years in combat. In the German case the boats look virtually the same. The American fleet boats, on the other hand, in 1943 look entirely different with radars and communication gear cramming the center island structure.

51. The semi-official history of the Royal Navy in the interwar period by Stephen Roskill remains the best history of the period. Roskill, *Naval Policy Between the Wars*, vol. 1, *The Period of Anglo-American Antagonism, 1919–1929*, and vol. 2, *The Period of Reluctant Rearmament, 1930–1939* (London, 1966). Also worth reading for its criticism of the Royal Navy is Correlli Barnett, *Engage the Enemy More Closely: The Royal Navy in the Second World War* (New York, 1991). For a more positive view of the Royal Navy, see Corbin Williamson, "The Royal Navy, 1900–1945: Learning from Disappointment," in Mansoor and Murray, eds., *The Culture of Military Organizations*.

52. On Britain's overall strategic position, see particularly Murray, *The Change in the European Balance in Power*, chap. 2.

53. F. H. Hinsley, *Command of the Sea: The Naval Side of British History from 1918 to the End of the Second World War* (London, 1950), pp. 32–33.

54. See Andrew Gordon, *The Rules of the Game: Jutland and British Naval Command* (London, 1996).

55. In this regard, see particularly Williamson, "The Royal Navy, 1900–1945."

56. David C. Evans and Mark R. Peattie, *Kaigun: Strategy, Tactics, and Technology in the Imperial Japanese Navy, 1887–1941* (Annapolis, MD, 2012), pp. 347–349.

57. Ibid., p. 210.

58. Ibid., pp. 515–516.

59. This section on the U.S. Navy is largely developed from Williamson Murray, "US Naval Strategy and Japan," in *Successful Strategies: Triumphing in War and Peace from Antiquity to the Present*, ed. Williamson Murray and Richard Hart Sinnreich (Cambridge, UK, 2014), pp. 280–313. Recent historical studies have overturned the postwar narrative that "big-gun" battle-

ship admirals dominated the navy in the interwar period. Among the more important works are Alfred F. Nofi, *To Train the Fleet for War: The U.S. Navy Fleet Problems* (Newport, RI, 2010); Craig C. Felker, *Testing American Sea Power: U.S. Navy Strategic Exercises, 1923–1940* (College Station, TX, 2007); Thomas C. Hone, Norman Friedman, and Mark D. Mandeles, *American and British Aircraft Carrier Development, 1919–1941* (Annapolis, MD, 1999); John T. Kuehn, *Agents of Innovation: The General Board and the Design of the Fleet That Defeated the Japanese Navy* (Annapolis, MD, 2008); and Edward S. Miller, *War Plan Orange: The U.S. Strategy to Defeat Japan, 1897–1945* (Annapolis, MD, 1991).

60. The distances in the Pacific run from San Diego to Oahu, 2,612 miles; from Honolulu to Tokyo, 3,862 miles; and from Pearl Harbor to Australia, 5,388 miles.

61. Quoted in John H. Maurer, "The Giants of the Naval War College," *Naval War College Review* 37, no. 5 (September–October 1984).

62. For the most thorough examination of the U.S. Navy's carrier development and a comparison with that of the Royal Navy, see Hone, Friedman, and Mandeles, *American and British Aircraft Carrier Development.*

63. Reeves became an admiral and eventually commander in chief of the U.S. fleet.

64. For Reeves's experimentation with the *Langley,* see particularly Hone, Friedman, and Mandeles, *American and British Aircraft Carrier Development,* pp. 40–47.

65. Barry Watts and Williamson Murray, "Military Innovation in Peacetime," in *Military Innovation in the Interwar Period,* ed. Murray and Millett, p. 402.

66. James M. Grimes, "Aviation in Fleet Exercises, 1911–1939," in *U.S. Naval Administrative Histories of World War II* (Washington, DC, n.d.), 16:62, 40.

67. As early as 1937, naval planners were considering the possibility of bypassing Japanese garrisons that were too strongly held. Miller, *War Plan Orange,* p. 351.

68. Michael Howard, "The Uses and Abuses of History," in *The Causes of War and Other Essays* (Cambridge, MA, 1978), pp. 188–197. Thus, the requirement to adapt to the ever-changing character of war, a subject that is addressed in Murray, *Military Adaptation in War.*

69. Allan R. Millett and Williamson Murray, "Lessons of War," *The National Interest* no. 14 (1988): pp. 83–95.

Chapter Nine. The European War

Epigraph: Winston Churchill, *The Second World War,* vol. 1, *The Gathering Storm* (Boston, 1948), p. 347.

1. Quoted in *Military Effectiveness,* vol. 2, *The Interwar Period,* ed. Allan R. Millett and Williamson Murray (London, 1988), p. 99.

2. For German foreign and strategic policy leading up to the outbreak of the war, see Gerhard L. Weinberg, *The Foreign Policy of Hitler's Germany*, vol. 2, *Starting World War II, 1937–1939* (Chicago, 1980), and Wilhelm Deist et al., *Das Deutsche Reich und der Zweite Weltkrieg*, vol. 1, *Ursachen und Voraussetzungen der Deutschen Kriegspolitik* (Stuttgart, 1979).

3. *Hansard's Parliamentary Debates*, 5th series, vol. 345, House of Commons, (London, 1939), cols. 437–440.

4. For an examination of the political and diplomatic events as well as their military consequences, see Williamson Murray, *The Change in the European Balance of Power, 1938–1939: The Path to Ruin* (Princeton, NJ, 1984), pp. 283–294.

5. For British efforts to bribe the Germans to avoid war, see ibid., pp. 305–307.

6. Alan Bullock, *Hitler: A Study in Tyranny* (London, 1964), p. 445.

7. "Weisung des Chefs des Oberkommandos der Wehrmacht," 3 April 1939, in *Akten zur deutschen auswärtigen Politik*, series D, vol. 6, doc. 149.

8. For the extent that the Germans had improved their military situation, see Murray, *The Change in the European Balance of Power*, chap. 7.

9. Ibid., p. 292.

10. Williamson Murray and Allan R. Millett, *A War to Be Won: Fighting the Second World War* (Cambridge, MA, 2000), p. 46.

11. For the campaign, see Robert M. Kennedy, *The German Campaign in Poland (1939)* (Washington, DC, 1956), and Klaus A. Maier et al., *Das Deutsche Reich und der Zweite Weltkrieg*, vol. 2, *Die Errichtung der Hegemonie auf dem Eurpäischen Kontinent* (Stuttgart, 1979), p. 3.

12. For the remainder of the war, army generals would actively participate in major atrocities.

13. International Military Tribunal, *Trial of Major War Criminals*, vol. 26, doc. 798 PS, pp. 342–343.

14. Adam Tooze, *The Wages of Destruction: The Making and Breaking of the Nazi Economy* (London, 2006), pp. 315–318.

15. Maier et al., *Das Deutsche Reich und der Zweite Weltkrieg*, 2:267.

16. General Thomas, speech to Members of the Foreign Office, in International Military Tribunal, *Trial of Major War Criminals*, vol. 36, doc. 028EC, p. 123.

17. Maier et al., *Das Deutsche Reich und der Zweite Weltkrieg*, 2:195.

18. For further discussion, see Murray, *The Change in the European Balance of Power*, pp. 326–332.

19. "Directive No. 6 for the Conduct of the War," 9 October 1939, in *Blitzkrieg to Defeat: Hitler's War Directives, 1939–1945*, ed. H. R. Trevor Roper (New York, 1965), p. 13.

20. Historians have paid no attention to the directive because the British survived the Luftwaffe assault in summer 1940, didn't they? What that misses is that Churchill was not yet in power, and Hitler was fundamentally con-

temptuous of Chamberlain. Like everyone else in 1939, Hitler overrated the capabilities of the German Air Force.

21. For a discussion of these deficiencies and the steps the army took to correct them, see Williamson Murray, "The German Response to Victory in Poland: A Case Study in Professionalism," *Armed Forces and Society* 7, no. 2 (Winter 1981): 285–298.

22. CID Minutes of the 360th Meeting, 22 June 1939, 2/8/252, National Archives and Records Service, Kew, UK (hereafter NARS).

23. CID, Joint Planning Sub-Committee, "Military Implications of an Anglo-French Guarantee to Poland and Rumania," 28 March 1939, JP 388, 55/15/12, NARS.

24. Murray, *The Change in the European Balance of Power*, p. 319.

25. For an examination of how close Mussolini came to joining the Germans in September 1939, see MacGregor Knox, *Mussolini Unleashed, 1939–1941: Politics and Strategy in Fascist Italy's Last War* (Cambridge, UK, 1986).

26. Murray, *The Change in the European Balance of Power*, p. 348.

27. CAB 65/1 WM (39), War Cabinet 20 (39), 19 September 1939, NARS.

28. CAB 65/1 WM (39), War Cabinet 37 (39), 4 October 1939, NARS.

29. For British decision-making about Scandinavia, see Murray, *The Change in the European Balance of Power*, pp. 341–347, and John Kiszely, *Anatomy of a Campaign: The British Fiasco in Norway, 1940* (Cambridge, UK, 2017).

30. Allied Military Committee, "The Main Strategy of the War, Note by the French Delegation," 11 April 1940, CAB 85/16, M.R. (J)(40)(s) 2, NARS.

31. Tooze, *The Wages of Destruction*, p. 378.

32. Quoted in Alistair Horne, *To Lose a Battle: France, 1940* (Boston, 1969), p. 170.

33. Telford Taylor, *The March of Conquest: The German Victories in Western Europe, 1940* (New York, 1958), p. 111. For the campaign, see also Earl F. Ziemke, *The German Northern Theater of Operations, 1940–1945* (Washington, DC, 1959), and Geirr H. Haarr, *The German Invasion of Norway, April 1940* (Annapolis, MD, 2009).

34. For the disastrous British effort, see particularly Kiszely, *Anatomy of a Campaign*.

35. Taylor, *The March of Conquest*, p. 116.

36. Ibid., p. 117.

37. For the naval battle of Narvik, see Stephen Roskill, *The War at Sea, 1939–1945*, vol. 1, *The Defensive* (London, 1956), chap. 10.

38. For the wretched effort on the ground, see Kiszely's outstanding study *Anatomy of a Campaign*.

39. Raeder's decision came despite the fact that he had had a conversation with Hitler on 20 May in which the Führer had indicated that he believed an invasion of Britain might be necessary. Thus, Raeder risked the few heavy ships the Kriegsmarine possessed to influence the navy's postwar political prestige. Maier et al., *Das Deutsche Reich und der Zweite Wetkrieg*, 2:221.

40. There are innumerable books about the German offensive against the west and the fall of France. The best among them are Taylor, *The March of Conquest*; Karl-Heinz Frieser, *Blitzkrieg Legende: Der Westfeldzug, 1940*, 2nd edition (Munich, 1996) (English translation: *The Blitzkrieg Legend: The 1940 Campaign in the West* [Annapolis, MD, 2005]); Robert A. Doughty, *The Breaking Point: Sedan and the Fall of France, 1940* (Mechanicsburg, PA, 1990); and Horne, *To Lose a Battle*.

41. For a discussion of this, see Williamson Murray, "Contingency and Fragility in the German RMA," in *The Dynamics of Military Revolution, 1300–2050*, ed. MacGregor Knox and Williamson Murray (Cambridge, UK, 2001).

42. The Mark IVs of the time possessed only a low-velocity gun.

43. Frieser, *The Blitzkrieg Legend*, p. 37.

44. Ibid., p. 219.

45. Doughty, *The Breaking Point*, p. 17.

46. Ibid., pp. 77–78.

47. Hoth's panzer corps was assigned directly to the Fourth Army, while the other two panzer corps were under Lieutenant General Ewald von Kleist as a panzer group—less than an army but more than a corps.

48. Virtually all of the panzer commanders were not tank men but were infantry in their background, but they had all been educated in the army's combined-arms doctrine.

49. For Rommel's own account, see Erwin Rommel, *The Rommel Papers*, ed. B. H. Liddell Hart (New York, 1953), pp. 8–11. Frieser in *Blitzkrieg Legende*, p. 289, suggests that Rommel's performance outshined even Guderian's.

50. Frieser, *The Blitzkrieg Legend*, pp. 268–269.

51. This account relies largely on ibid., pp. 150–260, and Doughty, *The Breaking Point*, pp. 131–265.

52. See particularly the maps indicating the times when French units in the area received the warning order to move, when they moved, and when they actually arrived on the battlefield in Frieser, *Blitzkrieg Legende*.

53. For the escape from Dunkirk, see among others Walter Lord, *The Miracle of Dunkirk* (New York, 1982), and more recently David Boyle, *Dunkirk: A Miracle of Deliverance* (London 2017).

54. General Erich Marcks, 19 June 1940, quoted in Murray, "Contingency and Fragility of the German RMA," p. 156.

55. See particularly R. V. Jones, *The Wizard War: British Scientific Intelligence, 1939–1945* (New York, 1978).

56. For the tangled relations between Britain and France during those dark days, see P. M. H. Bell, *A Certain Eventuality: Britain and the Fall of France* (London, 1974).

57. Williamson Murray, *Luftwaffe* (Annapolis, MD, 1985), tables 3 and 4. These two tables are drawn from "Front-Flugzeug-Verluste," 1940, gen. Qu. 6. Abt. (III A), Bundesarchiv/Militärarchiv (BA/MA), RL2 III/1025.

58. The figures are based on Sir Charles Webster and Noble Frankland, *The Strategic Air Offensive Against Germany*, vol 4, *Annexes and Appendices* (London, 1961), appendix 34, p. 497.

59. Murray and Millett, *A War to Be Won*, p. 84.

60. Murray, *Luftwaffe*, p. 49.

61. Air Historical Branch (AHB), Translation No. VII/107, "Luftwaffe Strength and Serviceability Tables, August 1938–April 1945," and AHB Translation No. VII/83, "German Aircraft Losses, September 1939–December 1940."

62. Quoted in Maier et al., *Das Deutsche Reich und der Zweite Weltkrieg*, 2:386.

63. Francis K. Mason, *Battle over Britain* (London, 1969), pp. 363, 391–392.

64. Based on the quartermaster returns, 14, 21 September 1940, in BA/MA, RL gf2 III/709.

65. Murray, *Luftwaffe*, table 10.

66. Ibid., tables 5, 6.

67. Perhaps the most important moment in the conduct of operations in 1940 came when Jones persuaded Churchill over the opposition of ministers and senior RAF officers that the RAF needed to conduct a test to see whether the beams existed. The tests were conducted and confirmed that the beams existed. For Churchill's side of the incident, see Churchill, *The Second World War*, vol. 2, *Their Finest Hour* (Boston, 1949), p. 384. See also Jones, *The Wizard War*, pp. 102–105.

68. Basil Collier, *The Defence of the United Kingdom* (London, 1957), pp. 278–279. See also map 26, "The German Night Offensive, September 1940–May 1941," which provides a clear representation of German efforts.

69. Ibid., p. 280.

70. Murray, *Luftwaffe*, table 12.

71. Roskill, *The War at Sea*, 1:349.

72. Patrick Beesly, *Very Special Intelligence: The Story of the Admiralty's Operational Intelligence Centre, 1939–1945* (London, 1977), p. 74.

73. Horst Boog et al., *Das Deutsche Reich und der Zweite Weltkrieg*, vol. 6, *Der globale Krieg* (Stuttgart, 1990), table on p. 337. For the explanation of how the authors came to this estimate, see the discussion on p. 336.

74. Ibid., 6: p. 332.

75. For the war in the Atlantic, among others see John Terraine, *The U-Boat Wars, 1916–1945* (New York, 1989), and Correlli Barnett, *Engage the Enemy More Closely: The Royal Navy in the Second World War* (New York, 1991).

76. Halder Diaries. https://cgsc.contentdm.oclc.org/digital/collection/p4013coll8/id/2003/.

77. Much of the following discussion of fascist Italy's abysmal performance in the war rests on Knox, *Mussolini Unleashed*.

78. Murray and Millett, *A War to Be Won*, p. 96.

79. Knox, *Mussolini Unleashed*, p. 257.

80. Murray and Millett, *A War to Be Won*, p. 97.

81. Knox, *Mussolini Unleashed*, p. 164.

82. "Befehl für die Luftkriegführung Jugoslavien," 31 March 1941, Luftwaffen-kommando 4, Führungsabteilung Ia op Nr 1000/41, Wein, BA/MA, RL7/657.

83. For an excellent, short history of the battle for Crete, see Antony Beevor, *Crete 1941: The Battle and the Resistance* (London, 2014).

84. Hans-Otto Mühleisen, *Kreta 1941: Das Unternehmen "Mekur"* (Freiburg, 1968), p. 102.

85. The literature on the German invasion of the Soviet Union is vast and steadily growing. Among those that I have used extensively are Horst Boog et al., *Das Deutsche Reich und der Zweite Weltkrieg*, vol. 4, *Der Angriff auf die Sowjetunion* (Stuttgart, 1987); Gerhard L. Weinberg, *A World at Arms: A Global History of World War II* (Cambridge, UK, 1994); Klaus Reinhardt, *Die Wende vor Moskau: Das Scheitern der Strategie Hitlers im Winter 1941/1942* (Stuttgart, 1972); David Stahel, *Operation Barbarossa and Germany's Defeat in the East* (Cambridge, UK, 2009); and David M. Glantz and Jonathan M. House, *When Titans Clashed: How the Red Army Stopped Hitler* (Lawrence, KS, 2015).

86. Tooze, *The Wages of Destruction*, p. 385.

87. Reinhardt, *Die Wende vor Moskau*, p. 113.

88. "Bericht des Herrn Dr. C. Krauch über die Lage auf dem Arbeitsgebiet der Chemie in der Sitzung des Generalrates am 24.6.41," T-84/217/1,586,749, NARS.

89. Tooze, *The Wages of Destruction*, p. 412.

90. Ibid., p. 415.

91. For an excellent discussion of German manpower difficulties, see ibid., pp. 436–437.

92. Reinhardt, *Die Wende vor Moskau*, p. 30.

93. Ibid., pp. 177–178.

94. Tooze, *The Wages of Destruction*, p. 454.

95. Stahel, *Operation Barbarossa and Germany's Defeat in the East*, p. 129.

96. For the equipment the army possessed for Barbarossa, see Boog et al., *Das Deutsche Reich und der Zweite Weltkrieg*, 4:183–188, and especially the accompanying tables.

97. For the army's dependence on horse-drawn transport, see R. L. DiNardo, *Mechanized Juggernaut or Military Anachronism? Horses and the German Army of World War II* (New York, 1991), pp. 35–42.

98. Stahel, *Operation Barbarossa and Germany's Defeat in the East*, p. 131.

99. All of this is clearly discussed in Boog et al., *Das Deutsche Reich und der Zweite Weltkrieg*, 4:180–183.

100. Stahel, *Operation Barbarossa and Germany's Defeat in the East*, p. 132.

101. Murray, *Luftwaffe*, table 12.

102. Ibid., table 20.

103. Bernhard R. Kroener, Rolf-Dieter Müller, and Hans Umbreit, *Das Deutsche Reich und der Zweite Weltkrieg*, vol. 5, *Organisation und Mobilisierung des Deutschen Machtbereichs* (Stuttgart, 1988), p. 513.

104. Boog et al., *Das Deutsche Reich und der Zweite Weltkrieg*, 4:150–151.

105. Franz Halder, *The Halder War Diary, 1939–1942*, ed. Charles Burdick and Hans-Adolf Jacobsen (Novato, CA, 1988), p. 346.

106. Boog et al., *Das Deutsche Reich und der Zweite Weltkrieg*, 4:446.

107. For the Nazi ideological framework's impact on the cohesion of the army on the Eastern Front, see Omer Bartov, *Hitler's Army: Soldiers, Nazis, and War in the Third Reich* (Oxford, 1991).

108. Halder, *The Halder War Diary*, p. 233.

109. Quoted in John Erickson, *The Soviet High Command, 1918–1941* (London, 1962), p. 587.

110. Quoted in Adam Ulam, *Expansion and Coexistence: Soviet Foreign Policy, 1917–73* (New York, 1974), p. 284.

111. David Irving, *The Rise and Fall of the Luftwaffe: The Life of Field Marshal Erhard Milch* (Boston, 1973), p. 123.

112. Murray and Millett, *A War to Be Won*, p. 121.

113. Halder, *The Halder War Diary*, pp. 446–447.

114. Murray and Millett, *A War to Be Won*, p. 124.

115. See the maps in David M. Glantz, *Barbarossa Derailed: The Battle for Smolensk, 10 July – 10 September 1941*, vol. 4, *Atlas* (London, 2015).

116. The following argument is largely drawn from the careful and deeply researched work of Roger R. Reese in *Why Stalin's Soldiers Fought: The Red Army's Military Effectiveness in World War II* (Lawrence, KS, 2011).

117. Stahel, *Operation Barbarossa and Germany's Defeat in the East*, p. 215.

118. Ibid., p. 282.

119. Murray and Millett, *A War to Be Won*, p. 125.

120. Halder, *The Halder War Diary*, p. 506.

121. For the terrible fate that awaited the Russian prisoners of war at the hands of their German Army captors, see particularly Christian Streit, *Keine Kameraden: Die Wehrmacht und die sowjetischen Kriegsgefangenen, 1941–1945* (Stuttgart, 1978).

122. Quoted in Martin van Creveld, *Supplying War: Logistics from Wallenstein to Patton* (Cambridge, UK, 1977), p. 171.

123. David Stahel, *Kiev 1941: Hitler's Battle for Supremacy in the East* (Cambridge, UK, 2012), pp. 250–251.

124. Reinhardt, *Die Wende vor Moskau*, p. 69.

125. David Stahel, *Operation Typhoon: Hitler's March on Moscow, October 1941* (Cambridge, UK, 2013), p. 151.

126. Ibid., p. 115.

127. After the war, a number of German generals claimed that the *rasputitsa* of fall 1941 had been particularly heavy. In fact, the period was relatively mild in Russia. Reinhardt, *Die Wende vor Moskau*, pp. 78–79.

128. Ibid., pp. 139–140.

129. David Stahel, *Retreat from Moscow: A New History of Germany's Winter Campaign, 1941–1942* (New York, 2019), p. 18.

130. Reinhardt, *Die Wende vor Moskau*, p. 77.
131. David Stahel, *The Battle for Moscow* (Cambridge, UK, 2015), p. 69.
132. Reinhardt, *Die Wende vor Moskau*, p. 71.
133. Halder, *The Halder War Diary*, pp. 596–600.
134. Stahel *Retreat from Moscow*, p. 141.
135. Ibid., pp. 13–14.
136. Quoted in ibid., p. 91.
137. Ibid., pp. 9–10.

Chapter Ten. World War II

Epigraph: Carl von Clausewitz, *On War*, ed. and trans. Michael Howard and Peter Paret (Princeton, NJ, 1976), p. 86.

1. For an examination of the role of ideology in the conduct of the war by the Wehrmacht on the Eastern Front, see Gerhard L. Weinberg, *A World at Arms: A Global History of World War II* (Cambridge, UK, 1994), pp. 190–193.
2. The leading proponent of this view was the British historian A. J. P. Taylor in *The Origins of the Second World War* (London, 1961).
3. See particularly Eberhard Jäckel's *Hitler's Weltanschauung: A Blueprint for Power* (London, 1972).
4. MacGregor Knox, *To the Threshold of Power, 1922/33: Origins and Dynamics of the Fascist and National Socialist Dictatorships* (Cambridge, UK, 2007), 1:340.
5. Ibid., 1:346.
6. For the overall picture of the military cooperation in the crimes of the Third Reich during the invasion of Russia, see Jügen Förster, "Das Unternehmen 'Barbarossa' als Eroberungs-und Vernichtungskrieg," in Horst Boog et al., *Das Deutsche Reich und der Zweite Weltkrieg*, vol. 4, *Der Angriff auf die Sowjetunion* (Stuttgart, 1987), pp. 413–450.
7. Quoted in Wolfram Wette, *The Wehrmacht: History, Myth, Reality*, trans. Deborah Lucas Schneider (Cambridge, MA, 2006), p. 96.
8. Ibid., p. 128.
9. For the full extent of this crime see Christian Streit, *Keine Kameraden: Die Wehrmacht und die sowjetischen Kriegsgefangenen, 1941–1945* (Stuttgart, 1978).
10. Quoted in Roger R. Reese, *Why Stalin's Soldiers Fought: The Red Army's Military Effectiveness in World War II* (Lawrence, KS, 2011), p. 23.
11. For a discussion of what kept Soviet soldiers fighting and the role of the NKVD in keeping them at the front, see ibid., pp. 151–175.
12. Richard J. Evans, "World War II, from the Ground Up," *New York Times*, 20 November 2011, https://www.nytimes.com/2011/11/20/books/review/inferno-the-world-at-war-1939-1945-by-max-hastings-book-review.html. There are those who take quite a different view. See Michael D. Doubler, *Closing with the Enemy: How GIs Fought the War in Europe, 1944–1945* (Law-

rence, KS, 1994), and Peter R. Mansoor, *The GI Offensive in Europe: The Triumph of American Infantry Divisions, 1943–1945* (Lawrence, KS, 1999).

13. Andrew Roberts, "High Courage on the Axe Edge of War," *The Times* (London), March 2007.

14. For crew losses in the Eighth Air Force in 1943, see Williamson Murray, *Luftwaffe* (Annapolis, MD, 1985), table 30.

15. Halder, *Kriegstagebuch*, vol. 3, entry for 22 February 1942, p. 540.

16. Burkhart Müller-Hillebrand, *Das Heer, 1933–1945*, vol. 3, *Der Zweifronten Krieg* (Frankfurt am Main, 1969), table 2, "Verluste Panzerkampfwagen."

17. Klaus Reinhardt, *Die Wende vor Moskau: Das Scheitern der Strategie Hitlers im Winter 1941/1942* (Stuttgart, 1972), p. 258.

18. Horst Boog et al., *Das Deutsche Reich und der Zweite Weltkrieg*, vol. 6, *Der Globale Krieg* (Stuttgart, 1990), p. 871.

19. Hermann Göring to Erhard Milch, June 1941, Milch Documents, vol. 57, p. 3213, Imperial War Museum, London. See also Richard Suchenwirth, *Command and Leadership in the German Air Force* (Alabama, 1969), pp. 99–101.

20. Murray, *Luftwaffe*, table 22, p. 104.

21. Boog et al., *Das Deutsche Reich und der Zweite Weltkrieg*, 6: pp. 563–564.

22. Murray, *Luftwaffe*, table 18.

23. "Übersicht über Soll, Istbestand, Verluste, und Reserven der fliegende Verbände," Gen. Qu. 6. Abt. (1), Bundesarchiv/Militärarchiv (BA/MA), RL 2 III/717.

24. Adam Tooze points out that while there was general stagnation in German production from 1940 to 1941, the Germans did make major investments in factories that would produce weapons in the later years. Tooze, *The Wages of Destruction: The Making and Breaking of the Nazi Economy* (London, 2006), pp. 448–449.

25. The percentages are in Bernhard R. Kroener, Rolf-Dieter Müller, and Hans Umbreit, *Das Deutsche Reich und der Zweite Weltkrieg*, vol. 5, *Organisation und Mobilisierung des Deutschen Machtbereichs* (Stuttgart, 1988), p. 523.

26. Ibid., based on the table on p. 526.

27. Ibid., based on the table on p. 584.

28. Quoted in Tooze, *The Wages of Destruction*, p. 493.

29. Ibid., pp. 411–412.

30. Boog et al., *Das Deutsche Reich und der Zweite Weltkrieg*, 6:548.

31. Tooze, *The Wages of Destruction*, pp. 411–412.

32. Boog et al., *Das Deutsche Reich und der Zweite Weltkrieg*, 6:1207.

33. For an exhaustive examination of the German manpower situation and the problems confronting the Wehrmacht and the war economy, see Boog et al., *Das Deutsche Reich und der Zweite Weltkrieg*, 4:part 3.

34. The war diary for the Ruhr district's armament inspectorate for the period 1 April to 30 June 1943 reported the appearance of women for the first time in its workforce. BA/MA, RW20/6/9.

35. Streit, *Keine Kameraden*, p. 9.
36. Tooze, *The Wages of Destruction*, p. 517. How much of the quality of German weapons declined over the course of the war is suggested by the experience of the Swiss, who bought fifty Bf 109s in 1942. Those aircraft remained in service through the 1960s. In 1944, they bought another fifty Bf 109s. The Swiss junked them in the late 1940s because they were so badly made.
37. Ibid., pp. 553–555.
38. Ibid., p. 557.
39. Ibid., p. 597.
40. The estimate on tonnage lost due to the damage done to workers' houses reflected absenteeism, as well as loss of life and injuries sustained in the bombing. Kriegstagebuch der Rüstungsinspektion VI, 1 April–30 June1943, BA/MA, RW 20/6/9.
41. See Max Hastings, *Bomber Command* (New York, 1979), p. 208.
42. Tooze, *The Wages of Destruction*, p. 598.
43. For its difficulties see the next chapter.
44. Murray, *Luftwaffe*, table 45, "Production of New and Reconditioned Fighter Aircraft—June–December 1943." As part of the effort to impress Hitler with the number of aircraft produced each month, aircraft shipped back to the factories with 30 percent or less damage were repaired and then counted as new aircraft.
45. Phillips Payson O'Brien, *How the War Was Won: Air-Sea Power and Allied Victory in World War II* (Cambridge, UK, 2015), p. 297.
46. Ibid.
47. W. K. Hancock and M. M. Gowing, *British War Economy* (London, 1949), p. 352.
48. Ibid., p. 347.
49. Ibid., p. 519.
50. That disparity reflected the fact that the British were producing bombers and the Germans fighters.
51. Sir Charles Webster and Noble Frankland, *The Strategic Air Offensive Against Germany*, vol. 2, *Endeavor* (London, 1961), pp. 110–111.
52. O'Brien, *How the War Was Won*, p. 35.
53. The official history of intelligence in the Second World War is of considerable use in understanding the workings and impact of Ultra and other intelligence sources. F. H. Hinsley et al., *British Intelligence in the Second World War* (London, 1979), vol. 1. On the naval side of Ultra, see Patrick Beesley, *Very Special Intelligence: The Story of the Admiralty's Operational Intelligence Centre, 1939–1945* (London, 1977). For air intelligence, see R. V. Jones, *The Wizard War: British Scientific Intelligence, 1939–1945* (New York, 1978). And for the war on the ground, see Ralph Bennett, *Ultra in the West: The Normandy Campaign, 1944–45* (London, 1980), and *Ultra and Mediterranean Strategy, 1941–1945* (London, 1989).

54. For portions of the so-called Wedemeyer Plan, which in fact had little influence over debates on the army's planning efforts in 1942, see Jim Lacey, *Keep from All Thoughtful Men: How U.S. Economists Won World War II* (Annapolis, MD, 2011), appendix 3.

55. For the crucial portions of the debate, see ibid., pp. 96–116.

56. James Lacey, *The Washington War: FDR's Inner Circle and the Politics of Power That Won World War II* (New York, 2019), p. 367.

57. Arthur Herman, *Freedom's Forge: How American Business Produced Victory in World War II* (New York, 2012), pp. 240–241. The advantage that the Americans enjoyed, as did the Soviets once they had moved their production centers to the east of Moscow, was that the great mass production factories lay beyond the range of air attacks.

58. Murray, *Luftwaffe*, table 24, "Average Monthly Production by Half Years: Four-Engine Aircraft."

59. Ibid., table 33, "Aircraft Written Off: Eighth Air Force 1943 (Heavy Bombers)," and table 34, "Crew Losses Eighth Air Force 1943 (Heavy Bombers)."

60. David Fairbank White, *Bitter Ocean: The Battle of the Atlantic, 1939–1945* (New York, 2006), p. 201.

61. For the swelling upsurge of new production of merchant shipping and tankers by the Allied powers from 1941 to the end of the war, see M. M. Postan, *British War Production* (London, 1952), p. 415.

62. "Der Tonnage Wettlauf, Der Kampf um die Seetransportkapazität 1939–1943," in Boog et al., *Das Deutsche Reich und der Zweite Weltkrieg*, 6:308.

63. Based on the numbers in O'Brien, *How the War Was Won*, p. 56.

64. Clark G. Reynolds, *The Fast Carriers: The Forging of an Air Navy* (New York, 1968), p. 411.

65. O'Brien, *How the War Was Won*, p. 121.

66. Nikita Khrushchev, *Memoirs of Nikita Khrushchev*, vol. 1, *Commissar, 1918–1945* (College Park, PA, 2005), pp. 675–676.

67. Hancock and Gowing, *British War Economy*, p. 239.

68. The American Historical Association, "How Much of What Goods Have We Sent to Which Allies?" in Horace Taylor, *How Shall Lend-Lease Accounts Be Settled?* (Washington, DC, 1945), https://www.historians.org/about-aha-and-membership/aha-history-and-archives/gi-roundtable-series/pamphlets/em-13-how-shall-lend-lease-accounts-be-settled-(1945).

69. Guy Hartcup, *The Effect of Science on the Second World War* (New York, 2000), p. 43.

70. Adam Tooze estimates the economic loss as being 25 percent of GDP. Tooze, *The Wages of Destruction*, p. 588.

71. David M. Glantz and Jonathan M. House, *When Titans Clashed: How the Red Army Stopped Hitler* (Lawrence, KS, 2015), pp. 71–72.

72. Frederick Kagan, "The Evacuation of Soviet Industry in the Wake of 'Barbarossa': A Key to Soviet Victory," *Journal of Slavic Military Studies* 8, no. 2 (June 1995): 387–414.

73. Ibid.
74. Glantz and House, *When Titans Clashed*, p. 101.
75. Tooze, *The Wages of Destruction*, p. 588.
76. O'Brien, *How the War Was Won*, table 15.
77. Ibid., pp. 63–64.
78. Ibid., p. 68.
79. From 1942 on, the Americans were integrated into Bletchley Park and the utilization of Ultra intelligence based on the breaking of the Enigma codes.
80. Gordon Welchman, *The Hut Six Story: Breaking the Enigma Codes* (London, 1997), p. 169.
81. Cribs were incidents where, for example, the same station came up at the same time each day, or where a particular sender used the same address heading on each one of its messages.
82. For one woman's experiences working in the Y Service, see Aileen Clayton, *The Enemy Is Listening* (New York, 1980).
83. For the clearest discussion of the breaking of the U-boat codes, see David Kahn, *Seizing the Enigma: The Race to Break the German U-Boat Codes, 1939–1945* (Garden City, NY, 1991).
84. For a discussion of the difficulties that air intelligence confronted, see Ralph Bennett, *Behind the Battle: Intelligence in the War with Germany, 1939–45* (London, 1994), pp. 133–167.
85. Stalin's disastrous refusal to believe the evidence was largely the result of his disbelief that Hitler was serious in the Nazi desire to seize control of the agricultural areas of the Soviet Union.
86. Among others, see the groundbreaking work by David Glantz, *Soviet Military Deception in the Second World War* (London, 1989).
87. For the account of the British intelligence deception efforts, see J. C. Masterman, *The Double-Cross System in the War of 1939 to 1945* (New Haven, CT, 1972).
88. For British deception efforts during the war, see Hinsley et al., *British Intelligence in the Second World War*, vol. 5.
89. Jones, *The Wizard War*, pp. 103–104.
90. The sinking was the result of the egregiously incompetent performance of the ship's captain, who was proceeding at a slow speed, neglected to mount an effective watch, and had no aircraft prepared to respond. His incompetence resulted in not only the loss of the *Glorious* but also the loss of a whole squadron of Hurricane fighters and their pilots, with only the squadron commander surviving.
91. For an analysis of what this success meant, see the last chapter.
92. Andrew Hodges, *Alan Turing: The Enigma* (London, 1983), pp. 219–221.
93. Monika Renneberg and Mark Walker, eds., *Science, Technology, and National Socialism* (Cambridge, UK, 1994), p. 6.
94. For the best work on German physicists during the war, see Alan D. Beyerchen, *Scientists Under Hitler: Politics and the Physics Community in the Third Reich* (New Haven, CT, 1977).

95. The one exception was the V-2 rocket program, but in this case the whole program was started within the army and the civilian scientists were firmly placed within the army's bureaucracy.

96. Stephen Budiansky, *Blackett's War: The Men Who Defeated the Nazi U-Boats and Brought Science to the Art of War* (New York, 2013).

97. Quoted in Hartcup, *The Effect of Science on the Second World War,* p. 15.

98. Ibid.

99. In the end the most thorough study of the V-2 estimated that the program cost the equivalent of one-third the cost of the Manhattan Project. For a weapon that had a CEP of approximately six miles, this represented an allocation of resources that the Reich could not afford. See Michael J. Neufeld, *The Rocket and the Reich: Peenemünde and the Coming of the Ballistic Missile Era* (Washington, DC, 1995).

100. See particularly Basil Collier, *The Defence of the United Kingdom* (London, 1957), pp. 275–281, and appendix 34, p. 510.

101. Quoted in Budiansky, *Blackett's War,* p. 127.

102. Hartcup, *The Effect of Science on the Second World War,* pp. 25–26.

103. James Goodrich suggests that they did so on the instructions of those above—"perhaps Hitler." It is far more likely that it was simply German arrogance that dismissed the cavity magnetron. The Digital Collections of the WWII Museum (https://www.ww2online.org/search-page?keyword=goodrich%2C%20james).

104. Hartcup, *The Effect of Science on the Second World War,* p. 38.

105. Quoted in David Irving, *The Rise and Fall of the Luftwaffe: The Life of Field Marshal Erhard Milch* (Boston, 1973), p. 210.

106. David J. Bercuson and Holger H. Herwig, *Bismarck: The Story Behind the Destruction of the Pride of Hitler's Navy* (London, 2002), p. 134.

Chapter Eleven. The Air and Sea Campaigns

Epigraph: Carl von Clausewitz, *On War,* ed. and trans. Michael Howard and Peter Paret (Princeton, NJ, 1976), p. 119.

1. It is hard to use the term "strategic aims," as all three services were focused on tactical aims throughout the war.

2. For the Axis alliance in the Second World War, see Williamson Murray, "The Axis," in *Grand Strategy and Military Alliances,* ed. Peter R. Mansoor and Williamson Murray (Cambridge, UK, 2016), pp. 313–342.

3. Horst Boog et al., *Das Deutsche Reich und der Zweite Weltkieg,* vol. 6, *Der globale Krieg* (Stuttgart, 1990), p. 302.

4. Phillips Payson O'Brien, *How the War Was Won: Air-Sea Power and Allied Victory in World War II* (Cambridge, UK, 2015), p. 484.

5. For the war against the U-boats, see among others John Terraine, *The U-Boat Wars, 1916–1945* (New York, 1989); for the German side see the excellent discussion in Boog et al., *Das Deutsche Reich und der Zweite Weltrkrieg,*

6:275–404. For the contribution of Ultra to the Allied victory in the Battle of the Atlantic, see among others Patrick Beesley, *Very Special Intelligence: The Story of the Admiralty's Operational Intelligence Centre, 1939–1945* (London, 1977), and David Kahn, *Seizing the Enigma: The Race to Break the German U-Boat Codes, 1939–1945* (Garden City, NY, 1991). For what the Battle of the Atlantic was like to its participants on the Allied side, see Nicholas Monsarrat, *The Cruel Sea* (London, 1951). The official intelligence of British intelligence is also well worth reading, even given its length: F. H. Hinsley et al., *British Intelligence in the Second World War*, 5 vols. (London, 1979–1990).

6. Walker and his team of escorts would eventually be responsible for sinking twenty U-boats before he died of a stroke in 1944 while at sea. Correlli Barnett, *Engage the Enemy More Closely: The Royal Navy in the Second World War* (New York, 1991), p. 802.

7. The account of the battle over convoy HG 76 is in ibid., pp. 396–399.

8. Williamson Murray and Allan R. Millett, *A War to Be Won: Fighting the Second World War*, (Cambridge, MA, 2000), p. 249.

9. Boog et al., *Das Deutsche Reich und der Zweite Weltkrieg*, 6:339–345. In addition, Italian submarines operating in the Atlantic sank 177,057 tons of Allied shipping.

10. Montgomery C. Meigs, *Slide Rules and Submarines: American Scientists and Subsurface Warfare in World War II* (Washington, DC, 1990), p. 53.

11. Beesley, *Very Special Intelligence*, pp. 114–115.

12. Marshall wrote King directly that the German U-boat attacks were significantly crippling the overall Allied strategic situation and America's ability to bring its economic power to bear. Terry Hughes and John Costello, *The Battle of the Atlantic* (New York, 1977), p. 203.

13. Williamson Murray and Allan R. Millett, *A War to Be Won: Fighting the Second World War* (Cambridge, MA, 2000), p. 252.

14. Boog et. al, *Das Deutsche Reich und der Zweite Weltkrieg*, 6: pp, 348–349.

15. Ibid., 6: p. 357.

16. Ibid., 6: p. 348.

17. Ibid., 6: p. 356.

18. Ibid., 6: p. 352.

19. Ibid., 6: p. 356.

20. Martin Middlebrook's *Convoy* (New York, 1976) represents a clear account of the battle between the U-boats and Convoys HX 229 and SC 122.

21. Boog et al., *Das Deutsche Reich und der Zweite Weltkrieg*, 6: pp. 359–360.

22. Ibid., 6: p. 365.

23. Murray and Millett, *A War to Be Won*, p. 256.

24. Ibid., pp. 177–191.

25. Stephen Budiansky, *Blackett's War: The Men Who Defeated the Nazi U-Boats and Brought Science to the Art of War* (New York, 2013), pp. 142–143. One of the additional insights was to persuade Coastal Command to paint its air-

craft white instead of black, which made them 20 percent more difficult for the lookout on U-boats to see.

26. David Fairbank White, *Bitter Ocean: The Battle of the Atlantic, 1939–1945* (New York, 2006), p. 201.

27. Sir Charles Webster and Noble Frankland, *The Strategic Air Offensive Against Germany*, vol. 1, *Preparation* (London, 1961), p. 177.

28. The cameras on the reconnaissance version of the Spitfire weighed approximately the same amount as the guns those aircraft carried in the fighter version.

29. The Luftwaffe's Research and Development Branch assured its leadership that a long-range escort fighter was "a technological impossibility" just a few months before the P-51 arrived to wreck the German fighter force in the winter-spring of 1944. Anthony Verrier, *The Bomber Offensive* (New York, 1969), p. 310.

30. The astonishing story is told in depressing detail in David Stubbs, "A Blind Spot? The Royal Air Force (RAF) and Long-Range Fighters, 1936–1944," *Journal of Military History* 78, no. 2 (April 2014): 673–702.

31. For the full Butt report, see Sir Charles Webster and Noble Frankland, *The Strategic Air Offensive Against Germany*, vol. 4, *Annexes and Appendices* (London, 1961), appendix 13.

32. Webster and Frankland, *The Strategic Air Offensive Against Germany*, 1:406–411.

33. *Kriegstage Buch Oberkommado der Wehrmacht*, vol. 2, entry for 3 June 1942, p. 400. See also Nicolaus von Below, *Als Hitlers Adjutant, 1937–45* (Mainz, 1980), pp. 311–312.

34. Williamson Murray, *Luftwaffe* (Annapolis, MD, 1984), table 29, "German Losses—January to October 1942."

35. Ibid., table 25, "German Losses Jun–Dec 1942 by Theater."

36. Ibid., table 30, "German Losses by Theater Jan–Nov 1943."

37. Below, *Als Hitlers Adjutant*, pp. 335–336.

38. The heavy Flak batteries consisted of 88mm, 105mm, and 128mm high-velocity guns.

39. Edward B. Westermann, *Flak: German Anti-Aircraft Defenses, 1914–1945* (Lawrence, KS, 2001), pp. 272, 273, 287.

40. Ibid., p. 273.

41. See the previous chapter for a discussion of the extent of the impact of the bombing on coal and steel production.

42. Sir Charles Webster and Noble Frankland, *The Strategic Air Offensive Against Germany*, vol. 2, *Endeavor* (London, 1961), pp. 110–111.

43. The best account of the Hamburg raid is Martin Middlebrook, *The Battle of Hamburg: Allied Bomber Forces Against a German City in 1943* (London, 1980). The lumber yard was responsible for trans-shipping the lumber that arrived in Germany from the Baltic.

44. OKW Wehrwirtschaftsstab, "Erfahrubgen bei Luftangriffen," von Oberst Luth, Wwi O/WK Kdo X, 15 January 1944, T-79/81/000641, National Archives and Records Service, Kew, UK (hereafter NARS); Murray and Millett, *A War to Be Won*, p. 311.

45. Arthur Harris to Winston Churchill, 3 November 1943, PREM 3/14/1, NARS.

46. Interview with D. C. T. Bennett, Royal Air Force Archives, https://www.nationalarchives.gov.uk/help-with-your-research/research-guides/royal-air-force-personnel.

47. For a discussion of the development of American air doctrine, see Murray, *Luftwaffe*, appendix 1. See also Allen Fabyanic, "A Critique of United States Air War Planning, 1941–1944" (Ph.D. dissertation, St. Louis University, 1973).

48. Wesley F. Craven and James L. Cate, *The Army Air Forces in World War II*, 7 vols. (Chicago, 1948–1958), 2: pp. 670–672.

49. For a thorough look at the raid from the German side, see Friedhelm Golücke, *Schweinfurt und der strategische Luftkrieg, 1943* (Paderborn, Germany, 1980).

50. In fact, the loss rate was higher than that, because LeMay's group left twenty B-17s in North Africa written off because of battle damage.

51. Webster and Frankland, *The Strategic Air Offensive Against Germany*, 2: 274.

52. O'Brien, *How the War Was Won*, p. 297.

53. Craven and Cate, *The Army Air Forces in World War II*, 2:698–699.

54. "Statistical Summary of Eighth Air Force Operations, European Theater, 17 August 1942–8 May 1945," Air Force Archives, Maxwell Air Force Base.

55. O'Brien, *How the War Was Won*, p. 297.

56. Albert Speer, *Inside the Third Reich: Memoirs* (London, 1970), p. 286; Golücke, *Schweinfurt und der strategische Luftkrieg*, pp. 351–380.

57. For the losses in single-engine fighter pilots, see Murray, *Luftwaffe*, tables 38 and 46. The tables are based on the figures on fighter pilot strength and losses in "Übersicht über Soll, Istbestand, Einsatzbereitschaft, Verluste und Reserven der fliegenden Verbänden," Genst. Gen. Qu.6. Abt. (I), Bundesarchiv/Militärarchiv RL 2 III/722, 723, 724, 725.

58. Murray, *Luftwaffe*, table 37.

59. Crew percentages were higher than aircraft because there were fewer crews. Ibid., tables 33 and 34.

60. Ibid.

61. Paul Kennedy, *Engineers of Victory: The Problem Solvers Who Turned the Tide in the Second World War* (New York, 2013).

62. Robert Frank Futrell, *Ideas, Concepts, Doctrine: Basic Thinking in the United States Air Force, 1907–1960* (Montgomery, AL, 1989), p. 139.

63. Quoted in Williamson Murray, *Strategy for Defeat of the Luftwaffe: 1933–1945*, "Ultra: History of US Strategic Air Forces Europe vs German Air Forces," p. 155. https://www.ibiblio.org/hyperwar/AAF/AAF-Luftwaffe/AAF-Luftwaffe-6.html#fn149.

64. Murray, *Luftwaffe*, table 50.
65. Ibid., table 52.
66. Ibid.
67. I am indebted to Dr. Horst Boog of the Militärgeschictliche Forschungs-amt for that point.
68. For Zuckerman's fascinating memoirs as a zoologist and then as a scientific advisor to Air Marshal Tedder, see Solly Zuckerman, *From Apes to Warlords: The Autobiography (1904–1946) of Solly Zuckerman* (London, 1978).
69. Air Historical Branch, "Air Attacks Against German Rail Systems During 1944," Luftwaffe Operations Staff/Intelligence, no. 2512/44; "Air Operations Against the German Rail Transport System During March, April, and May 1944," 3 June 1944.
70. Ironically, the success Allied air power enjoyed in making a transportation desert in western France and Belgium would come back to haunt the Allies. After their successful advance to the German frontier in August and September, they found that transportation desert to their rear.
71. Max Hastings, *Das Reich: The March of the 2nd SS Panzer Division Through France, June 1944* (London, 1981).
72. Major Ansel E. M. Talbert, "The Handling of Ultra Information at Headquarters Eighth Air Force," 31/20/16, NARS.
73. Speer's memorandum to Hitler on the fuel situation, 29 July 1944, Speer Collection, FD 2690/45 GS, vol. 3, Imperial War Museum, London.
74. Murray, *Luftwaffe*, table 58, p. 275.
75. The Me 262 has been surrounded by myths, mostly perpetrated by the Luftwaffe's leaders in the postwar period. In fact, the delay in having the Me 262 operational had nothing to do with Hitler's demand that it be made into a fighter bomber. The delay in its serial production had to do with providing engines that would last for more than a few hours of running time. Until German technologists had solved that problem, the aircraft was a death trap.
76. Phillips Payson O'Brien estimates that "the construction of airframes, air engines, and the weapons and machinery needed to power and arm aircraft made up at least 50 percent of German production every year of the war, and at certain times it reached up to 55 percent." O'Brien, *How the War Was Won*, p. 3.
77. In spring 1944, the Luftwaffe had 6,387 heavy Flak guns, 9,333 light Flak guns, and 5,360 searchlights operating on German territory in defense of the Reich. The total number of personnel involved in the anti-aircraft effort was 1,110,900, of whom 528,000 were Luftwaffe soldiers, the remainder women, members of the Hitler Youth, and Soviet POWs. Westermann, *Flak*, pp. 247, 272. Phillips O'Brien gives the following figures for the German Flak forces deployed over the whole of occupied Europe in November 1943: 13,500 heavy guns, 37,500 light guns, and 1,365,585 personnel, civilian as well as military, serving in the Flak forces. O'Brien, *How the War Was Won*, p. 305.

78. O'Brien, *How the War Was Won*, p. 305. Westermann's estimate is between 25 and 27 percent. See chapter 11, note 46, above.
79. U.S. Strategic Bombing Survey, "V-Weapons (Crossbow) Campaign," Military Analysis Division, report no. 60, January 1947.
80. Murray and Millett, *A War to Be Won*, p. 335.
81. In this regard, see particularly Meigs, *Slide Rules and Submarines*.

Chapter Twelve. The War on the Ground

Epigraph: Quoted in Gerhard P. Gross, *The Myth and Reality of German Warfare: Operational Thinking from Moltke the Elder to Heusinger* (Lexington, KY, 2016), p. 189.

1. Walter Warlimont, *Inside Hitler's Headquarters, 1939–1945* (New York, 1964), p. 208. Warlimont should have known better because he was married to an American and had spent considerable time in the United States.
2. For an excellent operational history of the war on the Eastern Front after Stalingrad from the German point of view, see Earl F. Ziemke, *Stalingrad to Berlin: The German Defeat in the East* (Washington, DC, 1968).
3. Based on table VI.1.2 in Horst Boog et al., *Das Deutsche Reich und der Zweite Weltkrieg*, vol. 6, *Der globale Krieg* (Stuttgart, 1990), p. 792.
4. Ibid., 6:786–788. For the enormous importance of horses to a Wehrmacht where less than 20 percent of its force structure was mechanized, see R. L. DiNardo, *Mechanized Juggernaut or Military Anachronism? Horses and the German Army of World War II* (New York, 1991). In fact, outside of its weaponry, the German Army of 1942–1945 was closer to World War I than its opponents.
5. Based on table VI.1.6 in Boog et al., *Das Deutsche Reich und der Zweite Weltkrieg*, 6: p. 806.
6. Ibid., 6: p. 947. See also insightful thinking in ibid., 6:1206–1210.
7. David M. Glantz and Jonathan M. House, *When Titans Clashed: How the Red Army Stopped Hitler* (Lawrence, KS, 2015), p. 120.
8. For the German efforts to fight their way into and through the city, see particularly Boog et al., *Das Deutsche Reich und der Zweite Weltkrieg*, 6: pp. 976–997.
9. For the groundbreaking study on the Soviet development and use of deception to cover their major offensives during the war on the Eastern Front, see David Glantz, *Soviet Military Deception in the Second World War* (London, 1989).
10. For the strength of the opposing forces at the onset of the Soviet counteroffensive, see Boog et al., *Das Deutsche Reich und der Zweite Weltkrieg*, 6: pp. 1000–1007.
11. Ziemke, *Stalingrad to Berlin*, p. 55.
12. Boog et al., *Das Deutsche Reich und der Zweite Weltkrieg*, 6: p. 1031–1033.
13. Williamson Murray, *Luftwaffe* (Annapolis, MD, 1985), p. 148.

14. Glantz and House, *When Titans Clashed*, p. 140.

15. Ibid., p. 148.

16. Ibid., p. 142.

17. Williamson Murray and Allan R. Millett, *A War to Be Won: Fighting the Second World War* (Cambridge, MA, 2000), p. 291.

18. Ibid., p. 285.

19. David M. Glantz, *Zhukov's Greatest Defeat: The Red Army's Epic Disaster in Operation Mars, 1942* (Lawrence, KS, 1999), p. 106.

20. The Soviets planned no less than three major operations aimed at Army Group Center in the last half of February. Glantz and House, *When Titans Clashed*, p. 145.

21. Murray and Millett, *A War to Be Won*, pp. 292–293.

22. For the factors behind Manstein's success, see Boog et al., *Das Deutsche Reich und der Zweite Weltkrieg*, 6:1081.

23. When General Günther Blumentrill was asked after the war about the economic basis for Blau, he commented that "he did not know about that, as he was not acquainted with the economic side of the war." B. H. Liddell Hart, *The Other Side of the Hill: Germany's Generals, Their Rise and Fall, with Their Own Account of Military Events, 1939–1945* (London, 1948), p. 297.

24. For works on the Battle of Kursk that strip away many of the myths that have surrounded it until recently, see among others Karl-Heinz Frieser et al., *Germany and the Second World War*; David M. Glantz and Jonathan M. House, *The Battle of Kursk* (Lawrence, KS, 1999); and William S. Dunn Jr., *Kursk: Hitler's Gamble, 1943* (Westport, CT, 1997). For an excellent examination of the literature on the battle, see Robert M. Citino, *The Wehrmacht Retreats: Fighting a Lost War, 1943* (Lawrence, KS, 2012), pp. 317–320. See also Dennis E. Showalter, *Armor and Blood: The Battle of Kursk, the Turning Point of World War II* (New York, 2013).

25. Citino, *The Wehrmacht Retreats*, p. 119.

26. Ibid., pp. 109–111.

27. Richard Overy, *Why the Allies Won* (London, 1995), p. 96.

28. Frieser et al., *Germany and the Second World War*, 8: pp. 128–138.

29. Erich von Manstein, *Verlorene Siege* (Bonn, 1955), p. 502.

30. Frieser et al., *Germany and the Second World War*, 8: p. 152.

31. David M. Glantz, "Soviet Military Strategy During the Second Period of the War, November 1942–December 1943: A Reappraisal," *Journal of Military History* 60 (January 1996): 115–150.

32. Citino, *The Wehrmacht Retreats*, p. 225.

33. Murray and Millett, *A War to Be Won*, p. 393.

34. For the war in North Africa, see particularly Major General I. S. O. Playfair, *The War in the Mediterranean and Middle East*, vols. 2–4 (London, 1956, 1960, 1966).

35. For the impact of Ultra on the war in the Mediterranean, see particularly Ralph Bennett, *Ultra and Mediterranean Strategy, 1941–1945* (London, 1989).

36. Murray and Millett, *A War to Be Won*, p. 273.

37. Ibid., p. 271.
38. For the transformation of the U.S. Army out of its prewar doldrums, see Rick Atkinson, *An Army at Dawn: The War in North Africa, 1942–1943* (New York, 2002).
39. Warlimont, *Inside Hitler's Headquarters*, p. 272.
40. Boog et al., *Das Deutsche Reich und der Zweite Weltkrieg*, 6:730–731.
41. RAF Historical Branch, "The Luftwaffe in the Battle for Tunis: A Strategical Survey," a study prepared by the Luftwaffe's 8th Abteilung, 17 October 1944, Translation no. VII/v.
42. Murray, *Luftwaffe*, p. 158.
43. Frieser et al., *Germany and the Second World War*, 8:1109.
44. For what occurred at Casablanca, see Jim Lacey, *Keep from All Thoughtful Men: How U.S. Economists Won World War II* (Annapolis, MD, 2011), pp. 117–129.
45. Murray and Millett, *A War to Be Won*, p. 303.
46. For how the Americans handled the Sicilian and Italian campaigns, see Rick Atkinson, *The Day of Battle: The War in Sicily and Italy, 1943–1944* (New York, 2007). For the Sicilian campaign, see Carlo D'Este, *Bitter Victory: The Battle for Sicily, 1943* (New York, 2008).
47. For British deception efforts in the Mediterranean in 1943, see Michael Howard, *Strategic Deception in the Second World War* (London, 1996), pp. 71–103.
48. Murray and Millett, *A War to Be Won*, p. 302.
49. The most outstanding biography of Patton is Carlo D'Este, *Patton: A Genius for War* (New York, 1995).
50. Murray and Millett, *A War to Be Won*, p. 380. An American Brooklyn-class cruiser, for example, could throw 1,500 5-inch shells onto German positions in a 10-minute period.
51. Ibid., p. 385.
52. It is clear that without that logistical support, the Americans would not have been able to support their forces on the German frontier but that the battlefront would have been well to the west in fall 1944.
53. The most thorough account of the Normandy campaign remains Carlo D'Este, *Decision in Normandy* (London, 1983). For the overall campaign in the West in 1944 and 1945, see Rick Atkinson, *The Guns at Last Light: The War in Western Europe, 1944–1945* (New York, 2014). See also Charles B. MacDonald, *The Mighty Endeavor: American Armed Forces in the European Theater of Operations in World War II* (Oxford, 1969).
54. The difference in the gunfire support provided the Kwajalein landings (three divisions) and the landings on the Normandy coast was considerable. For the Marianas landing: seven battleships, three heavy cruisers, and eighteen destroyers, the bombardment lasting for approximately two days. For Omaha and Utah: two battleships, four light cruisers, and eighteen destroyers.

55. For the naval side of the invasion, see Craig L. Symonds, *Operation Neptune: The D-Day Landings and the Allied Invasion of Europe* (Oxford, 2016).

56. Murray and Millett, *A War to Be Won*, pp. 420–421.

57. Ibid., pp. 422–425.

58. The 2nd SS Panzer Division, which was supposed to take two days to arrive in Normandy from southern France, in fact took two weeks during which it was responsible for a number of horrific massacres. See Max Hastings, *Das Reich: The March of the 2nd SS Panzer Division Through France, June 1944* (London, 1981).

59. For a positive view of the British Army in the northern European campaign, see John Buckley, *Monty's Men: The British Army and the Liberation of Europe, 1944–5* (New Haven, CT, 2013).

60. Murray and Millett, *A War to Be Won*, p. 431. See also Mark J. Reardon, *Victory at Mortain: Stopping Hitler's Panzer Counteroffensive* (Lawrence, KS, 2002).

61. For the most recent study of the Arnhem campaign, see Antony Beevor, *The Battle of Arnhem: The Deadliest Airborne Operation of World War II* (London, 2018). Still worth reading is Cornelius Ryan's *A Bridge Too Far* (New York, 1974). For the difficult campaign to open the Scheldt, see R. W. Thompson, *The 85 Days* (New York, 1957).

62. For the Hürtgen Forest, see particularly Charles B. MacDonald, *The Battle of the Huertgen Forest* (Washington, DC, 1963).

63. For the Battle of the Bulge, see among others Charles B. MacDonald, *A Time of Trumpets: The Untold Story of the Battle of the Bulge* (New York, 1985), and, more recently, Antony Beevor, *Ardennes 1944: Battle of the Bulge* (New York, 2015).

64. Frieser et al., *Germany and the Second World War*, 8: p. 275.

65. Murray and Millett, *A War to Be Won*, p. 395.

66. Ibid., p. 400.

67. Frieser et al., *Germany and the Second World War*, 8: p. 445.

68. Ibid., pp. 435–441.

69. For the Soviet planning for Bagration, see Glantz and House, *When Titans Clashed*, pp. 196–201.

70. Frieser et al., *Germany and the Second World War*, 8: p. 526–527.

71. Glantz and House, *When Titans Clashed*, pp. 204–207.

72. Frieser et al., *Germany and the Second World War*, 8: p. 554.

73. Glantz and House, *When Titans Clashed*, p. 180.

74. In July 1944, Stalin would order sixty thousand German POWs, including generals, to march through Moscow. Films of the march through Moscow are available on YouTube.

75. Frieser et al., *Germany and the Second World War*, 8: p. 591.

76. Ibid., 8: p, 592.

77. Murray and Millett, *A War to Be Won*, p. 452.

78. Milovan Djilas, *Wartime* (New York, 1977), p. 429.

79. Given the context of February 1945, the Yalta agreement looked like a good deal for the Western Powers; the fact that the American advance in April 1945 on the east bank of the Rhine would reach deep into what would become the Soviet Zone and East Germany would lead to denunciations by the Republicans in the postwar period, who entirely ignored the reality on the ground in February 1945.

Chapter Thirteen. The War in the Pacific

Epigraph: Carl von Clausewitz, *On War*, ed. and trans. Michael Howard and Peter Paret (Princeton, NJ, 1976), p. 75.

1. For a general history of the Japanese Empire during this period, see John Toland, *The Rising Sun: The Decline and Fall of the Japanese Empire, 1936–1945* (New York, 1970). For the period 1937 to May 1942, see Richard B. Frank, *Tower of Skulls: A History of the Asia-Pacific War, July 1937–May 1942* (New York, 2020).

2. The Japanese got access to the Luftwaffe's top-secret research station at Reclin, which their allies in Berlin had refused to show them, by simply showing up and acting as if they were there by invitation. I am indebted to Tomiuko Ishuzu of the National Institute of Defense Studies in Tokyo for this point.

3. One must not underestimate the role of Japanese education in fostering and encouraging that deep sense of nationalism. Since the Germans provided much of the advice in establishing the Japanese educational system, one should not underestimate the impression the Germans made on the Japanese system.

4. Richard B. Frank, *Downfall: The End of the Imperial Japanese Empire* (New York, 1999), pp. 28–29.

5. Quoted in ibid., p. 28.

6. For the best single-volume history of the war in the Pacific, see Ronald H. Spector, *Eagle Against the Sun* (New York, 1985); the most thorough, although somewhat dated, remains Samuel Eliot Morison's magisterial *History of United States Naval Operations in World War II*, 15 vols. (New York, 2001); see also his *The Two-Ocean War: A Short History of the United States Navy in the Second World War* (New York, 1963).

7. For the most thorough examination of the early period of the war in the Pacific, see H. P. Willmott, *Empires in the Balance: Japanese and Allied Pacific Strategies to April 1942* (Annapolis, MD, 1982), and *The War with Japan: The Period of Balance, May 1942–October 1943* (Wilmington, DE, 2002).

8. For the Imperial Japanese Navy in the war, see Paul S. Dull, *A Battle History of the Imperial Japanese Navy (1941–1945)* (Annapolis, MD, 1978).

9. MacArthur's approach probably rested on a belief that the defensive forces could hold out long enough for the U.S. Navy to fight its way across the Pacific with relief forces. It was a totally unrealistic assessment. For MacAr-

thur's role in the defense of the Philippines, see Spector, *Eagle Against the Sun*, pp. 106–119, 135–138.

10. For the campaign in the Philippines, see Louis Morton, *United States Army in World War II: The War in the Pacific: The Fall of the Philippines* (Washington, DC, 1984).

11. Spector, *Eagle Against the Sun*, p. 138.

12. For U.S. naval operations during the first six months of the war, see John B. Lundstrom, *The First South Pacific Campaign: Pacific Fleet Strategy, December 1941–June 1942* (Annapolis, MD, 1976), and *The First Team: Pacific Naval Air Combat from Pearl Harbor to Midway* (Annapolis, MD, 1984). For the raid on the Marshalls, see Ian W. Toll, *Pacific Crucible: War at Sea in the Pacific, 1941–1942* (New York, 2012), pp. 202–230.

13. For the Battle of the Coral Sea, see Samuel Eliot Morrison, *Coral Sea, Midway and Submarine Actions, May 1942–August 1942* (Boston, 1980), and Spector, *Eagle Against the Sun*, pp. 158–162.

14. By far and away the most careful examination of the flawed Japanese strategy to the Battle of Midway is Jonathan B. Parshall and Anthony P. Tully, *Shattered Sword: The Untold Story of the Battle of Midway* (Washington, DC, 2005). Also worth consulting is Craig L. Symonds, *The Battle of Midway* (Oxford, 2011).

15. For the code breaking by American intelligence, see particularly W. J. Holmes, *Double-Edged Secrets: U. S. Naval Intelligence in the Pacific During World War II* (Annapolis, MD, 1979); Edward J. Drea, *MacArthur's ULTRA: Codebreaking and the War Against Japan, 1942–1945* (Lawrence, KS, 1992); Ronald Lewin, *The American Magic: Codes, Ciphers, and the Defeat of Japan* (New York, 1982); and John Prados, *Combined Fleet Decoded: The Secret History of American Intelligence and the Japanese Navy in World War II* (New York, 1993).

16. Parshall and Tully, *Shattered Sword*, p. 94.

17. Ibid., pp. 146–161.

18. Parshall and Tully in their account of the battle make it clear that the Japanese attack force was not positioned on the flight deck ready to take off but was still in the hangar decks where the armoring and fueling was just being completed. The Japanese rearmed and refueled their aircraft in the carrier hanger decks, which, unlike American carriers, were not open to the sea so that they had no ventilation. Thus, when the American bombs exploded among the aircraft, the explosions were magnified and focused inward into the heart of the ships. Ibid., p. 231.

19. The best overall study from the joint perspective is Richard B. Frank, *Guadalcanal: The Definitive Account of the Landmark Battle* (New York, 1990). For the naval side of the struggle, see James D. Hornfischer, *Neptune's Inferno: The U.S. Navy at Guadalcanal* (New York, 2011).

20. Frank, *Guadalcanal*, p. 126.

21. Ibid., p. 127.

22. The most thorough account of the disaster in the waters surrounding Savo Island is Bruce Loxton with Chris Coulthard-Clark, *The Shame of Savo: Anatomy of a Naval Disaster* (Annapolis, MD, 1994).
23. Quoted in Hornfischer, *Neptune's Inferno*, pp. 95–96.
24. Frank, *Guadalcanal*, pp. 142–157.
25. Williamson Murray and Allan R. Millett, *A War to Be Won: Fighting the Second World War* (Cambridge, MA, 2000), p. 211.
26. Parshall and Tully, *Shattered Sword*, p. 417.
27. Frank, *Guadalcanal*, pp. 351–356, 361–365.
28. Figures are based on the discussion in ibid., pp. 607–616.
29. Ibid., p. 615.
30. Ibid.
31. Murray and Millett, *A War to Be Won*, p. 217.
32. For the U.S. submarine war in the Pacific, see Clay Blair Jr., *Silent Victory: The U.S. Submarine War Against Japan* (Annapolis, MD, 2001). For outstanding personal accounts, see Richard H. O'Kane, *Clear the Bridge: The War Patrols of the U.S.S.* Tang (Navato, CA, 1996), and Charles A. Lockwood, *Sink 'em All: Submarine Warfare in the Pacific* (New York, 1951).
33. Mark P. Parillo in *The Japanese Merchant Marine in World War II* (Annapolis, MD, 1993) recounts the whole sorry story of Japanese incompetence.
34. Willmott, *The War with Japan*, p. 167.
35. Murray and Millett, *A War to Be Won*, p. 352.
36. For the history of the fast carriers see Clark G. Reynolds, *The Fast Carriers: The Forging of an Air Navy* (New York, 1968).
37. Slim's memoirs represent one of the few honest, deeply thoughtful memoirs by a first-rate general. It ranks with those of Ulysses S. Grant as a must-read for those who are serious about thinking about leadership and generalship. Field Marshal William Slim, *Defeat into Victory: Battling Japan in Burma and India, 1942–1945* (London, 1956). For a history of the war in Burma, see Louis Allen, *Burma: The Longest War, 1941–1945* (London, 1984).
38. The most outstanding memoir by a common soldier fighting in the Second World War is George MacDonald Fraser, *Quartered Safe Out Here: A Harrowing Tale of World War II* (London, 2000).
39. Lord Mountbatten was by no means a military genius, but he possessed a first-class sense of talent, which he supported. After all, he had discovered and supported the scientist Solly Zuckerman. With a real *noblesse oblige*, Mountbatten possessed none of the arrogance and snobbishness that marks so many of the British upper class.
40. Fraser, *Quartered Safe Out Here*.
41. Murray and Millett, *A War to Be Won*, pp. 356–357.
42. The wonderful PBS film *Victory in the Pacific* begins with film footage taken by marine and navy cameramen of Japanese civilians committing suicide by jumping off the cliffs.

43. The brutality between the Americans and Japanese in the last stages of the war is caught by the brilliant wartime memoir of a marine private: E. B. Sledge, *With the Old Breed: At Peleliu and Okinawa* (New York, 1981).

44. Samuel Eliot Morison, *History of United States Naval Operations in World War II*, vol. 12, *Leyte, June 1944–January 1945* (Boston, 1956).

45. Ibid., pp. 430–431.

46. For a first-class account of the desperate struggle to fight off the Japanese battle fleet, see James D. Hornfisher, *The Last Stand of the Tin Can Sailors: The Extraordinary World War II Story of the U.S. Navy's Finest Hour* (New York, 2005).

47. Murray and Millett, *A War to Be Won*, p. 497.

48. For the Battle of Manila, see Richard Connaughton, John Pimlott, and Duncan Anderson, *The Battle for Manila* (London, 1995).

49. Spector, *Eagle Against the Sun*, p. 524.

50. Kenneth P. Werrell, *Blankets of Fire: U.S. Bombers over Japan During World War II* (Washington, DC, 1996), p. 82.

51. That research and development would play a major role in the explosion of American civil aviation after the war.

52. Frank, *Downfall*, p. 33.

53. Quoted in ibid., p. 64.

54. Wesley F. Craven and James L. Cate, *The Army Air Forces in World War II*, 7 vols. (Chicago, 1948–1958), 5:614.

55. Up to this point, the main incendiary devices had been made out of magnesium, but napalm consisted of jellified gasoline that burned both hotter and flowed once heated so that it was much more difficult to extinguish.

56. Craven and Cate, *The Army Air Forces in World War II*, 5:615.

57. For a depressing account of what the firestorm inflicted on the people of Tokyo, see Frank, *Downfall*, pp. 8–19.

58. Murray and Millett, *A War to Be Won*, p. 513.

59. For the Battle of Okinawa, see George Feifer, *Tennozan: The Battle of Okinawa and the Atomic Bomb* (New York, 1992).

60. The *Yamato* did come out on 7 April and was promptly sunk by American dive bombers and torpedo planes.

61. Murray and Millett, *A War to Be Won*, pp. 515–516.

62. D. M. Giangreco, *Hell to Pay: Operation Downfall and the Invasion of Japan, 1945–1947* (Annapolis, MD, 2009), pp. 80–81.

63. Ibid., p. 118.

64. For an excellent summary of the role of intelligence in providing American political and military leaders with the overall position of the Japanese military, see Edward J. Drea, "Previews of Hell: Intelligence, the Bomb, and the Invasion of Japan," *Military History Quarterly* 16, no. 1 (Spring 1995): 51–57.

65. Quoted in Giangreco, *Hell to Pay*, p. 47.

66. For an excellent discussion of Japanese efforts to prepare a massive suicide force of aircraft, swift small boats, and torpedoes guided by sailors, see ibid., pp. 61–91.
67. Quoted in Frank, *Downfall*, p. 226.
68. Quoted in Giangreco, *Hell to Pay*, p. 78.
69. For the horror of the Hiroshima bombing, see particularly Max Hastings, *Retribution: The Battle for Japan, 1944–45* (London, 2009), pp. 458–482.
70. Ibid., pp. 444–457.
71. David M. Glantz, *August Storm: Soviet Tactical and Operational Combat in Manchuria, 1945* (Leavenworth, KS, 1983), p. 33. Interestingly, in his discussions both in the last moments of the war and in the postwar period, the emperor cited the Soviet intervention only once as a factor. Frank, *Downfall*, pp. 345–346.
72. Quoted in Frank, *Downfall*, p. 347.
73. No transcript of the emperor's words was taken. Robert J. C. Butow has reconstructed the emperor's remarks in his *Japan's Decision to Surrender* (Stanford, CA, 1954), pp. 175–176.
74. Frank, *Downfall*, p. 345.
75. Ibid.

Chapter Fourteen. The War That Never Was

Epigraph: Quoted in Max Hastings, *Vietnam: An Epic Tragedy, 1945–1975* (London, 2018), p. 752.
1. John Lewis Gaddis, *The Cold War: A New History* (London, 2007), p. 7.
2. I am indebted to my good friend John Lynn for this important point.
3. The war between Argentina and Britain in 1982 is often referred to as the last of the colonial wars. This is nonsense because there has never been a significant Argentinian population living on the Falklands.
4. The colonial empire, which tsarist Russia accumulated in the eighteenth and nineteenth centuries in the Caucasus and Central Asia and which its Soviet successors perpetuated, finally collapsed along with the Soviet Union in 1990.
5. Adam Ulam, *Expansion and Coexistence: Soviet Foreign Policy, 1917–73* (New York, 1974), pp. 403–404.
6. For the nature of Stalin's rule, see among others Adam B. Ulam, *Stalin: The Man and His Era* (Boston, 1973); Simon Sebag Montefiore, *Stalin: The Court of the Red Tsar* (New York, 2003); Robert Conquest, *The Great Terror: A Reassessment* (Oxford, 1990); Timothy Snyder, *Bloodlands: Europe Between Hitler and Stalin* (New York, 2010); and Karl Schlögel, *Moscow, 1937* (Chicago, 2005). How much Stalin allowed his ideological views to get in the way of a realistic assessment of the global picture is suggested by the fact that for a short period at the end of the war he considered the possibility that the

United States and Great Britain might actually turn on each other in their competition for markets.

7. Quoted in Gaddis, *The Cold War*, pp. 25–26.
8. "X," "The Sources of Soviet Conduct," *Foreign Affairs*, July 1947.
9. American military and economic aid would prove of considerable importance, but the split between Stalin and Tito, which removed the bases supporting the Greek Communists, was equally important.
10. Truman had the Recovery Act renamed the Marshall Plan. Whatever his faults, Harry Truman was a generous man.
11. Paul Kennedy, *The Rise and Fall of the Great Powers: Economic Change and Military Conflict from 1500 to 2000* (New York, 1987), p. 433.
12. Ibid., p. 426.
13. For Mao's decision to ally himself tightly with the Soviets and Stalin in spite of the less-than-enthusiastic reception he received from the Soviets, see Sergei N. Goncharov, John W. Lewis, and Xue Litai, *Uncertain Partners: Stalin, Mao, and the Korean War* (Stanford, CA, 1993).
14. Gaddis, *The Cold War*, p. 41.
15. The most up-to-date and thorough account of the origins of the Korean War is Allan Millett's three-volume study of the war, of which the first two have been published: Allan R. Millett, *The War for Korea, 1945–1950*, vol. 1, *A House Burning* (Lawrence, KS, 2005), and *The War for Korea, 1950–1951*, vol. 2, *They Came from the North* (Lawrence, KS, 2010).
16. For a comparison of the initial military forces, see Millett, *They Came from the North*, pp. 29–37.
17. Ibid., pp. 64–65. For an analysis of NSC 68, see Paul Y. Hammond, "NSC-68: Prelude to Rearmament," in *Politics and Defense Budgets*, ed. Warner Schilling, Paul Y. Hammond, and Glen Snyder (New York, 1962).
18. For the initial response of the South Korean Army, see Millett, *They Came from the North*, pp. 87–106.
19. For the condition of American troops in Japan at the start of the Korean conflict, see ibid., pp. 75–84.
20. For the arguments about whether to land at Inchon or farther to the south, see ibid., pp. 208–213.
21. Quoted in Gaddis, *The Cold War*, p. 45.
22. Millett, *They Came from the North*, pp. 334–355.
23. Ibid., p. 368.
24. Williamson A. Murray, "The Post-War World, 1945–1991," in *The Cambridge History of Warfare*, 2nd edition, ed. Geoffrey Parker (2005; Cambridge, UK, 2020), p. 389.
25. Andrew Krepinevich and Barry Watts, *The Last Warrior: Andrew Marshall and the Shaping of Modern American Defense Strategy* (New York, 2015), p. 18.
26. Millett, *They Came from the North*, pp. 366–367.
27. These operations are covered in excellent fashion in ibid., pp. 383–415.

28. Testimony of General Omar Bradley before the Senate Committees on Armed Services and Foreign Relations, May 15, 1951. *Military Situation in the Far East*, hearings, 82d Congress, 1st session, part 2, p. 732 (1951).

29. Walter A. McDougall, . . . *The Heavens and the Earth: A Political History of the Space Age* (Baltimore, MD, 1985).

30. The work of Frederick Hayek made this clear as early as 1944: See F. A. Hayek, *The Road to Serfdom: Text and Documents—The Definitive Edition* (1944; Chicago, 2007).

31. One Soviet economist estimated in 1990 that of the 90 million tons of potatoes harvested by the Soviet Union, only 21 million managed to reach consumers. Andrew W. Marshall and Abraham N. Shulsky, "Assessing Sustainability of Command Economies and Totalitarian Regimes: The Soviet Case," *Orbis*, February 2018.

32. Krepinevich and Watts, *The Last Warrior*, p. 150.

33. Robert M. Gates, *From the Shadows: The Ultimate Insider's Stories of Five Presidents and How They Won the Cold War* (New York, 1996), p. 319.

34. Also, the high point of the Vietnam War.

35. Figures based on World Bank reports.

36. Mark Tractenberg, "Assessing Soviet Economic Performance in the Cold War: An Intelligence Failure?" *Texas National Security Review* 1, no. 2 (March 2018).

37. See particularly Dimitri (Dima) Adamsky, "The Art of Net Assessment and Uncovering Foreign Military Innovations: Learning from Andrew W. Marshall's Legacy," *Journal of Strategic Studies* 43 (July 2020): 5.

38. Ibid.

39. Krepinevich and Watts, *The Last Warrior*, 131. How successful that effort was is open to question. One of its fighters, a SU-15 fighter interceptor, was responsible for shooting down Korean Airlines flight 007 on 1 September 1983.

40. For SAC's early years, see Melvin G. Devile, *Always at War: Organizational Culture in Strategic Air Command, 1946–62* (Annapolis, MD, 2018).

41. David A. Rosenberg, "American Atomic Strategy and the Hydrogen Bomb Decision," *Journal of American History* (June 1979). See also his "The Origins of Overkill: Nuclear Weapons and American Strategy, 1945–1960," in *Strategy and Nuclear Deterrence*, ed. Steven E. Miller (Princeton, NJ, 1984).

42. Stephen Budiansky, *Code Warriors: NSA's Codebreakers and the Secret Intelligence War Against the Soviet Union* (New York, 2016), p. 123.

43. The fact that the first H-bomb in the U.S. inventory, the MK-17, weighed 41,000 pounds suggests why the air force needed such heavy bombers as the B-36 and B-52. Krepinevich and Watts, *The Last Warrior*, p. 32.

44. Meyers K. Jacobsen, *Convair B-36: A Comprehensive History of America's "Big Stick"* (Atglen, PA, 1997).

45. Robert S. Hopkins, *Boeing KC-135 Stratotanker: More Than Just a Tanker* (Leicester, UK, 1997).

46. Krepinevich and Watts, *The Last Warrior*, p. 48.

47. For Eisenhower's approach to the development of missiles and the contest with the Soviets over space, see Nicholas Michael Sambaluk, *The Other Space Race: Eisenhower and the Quest for Aerospace Security* (Annapolis, MD, 2015).

48. See Norman Polmar and Robert S. Norris, *The U.S. Nuclear Arsenal: A History of Weapons and Delivery Systems Since 1945* (Annapolis, MD, 2009).

49. Robert F. Futrell, "The Influence of the Air Power Concept on Air Force Planning, 1945–1962," paper presented at the Eleventh Air Power History Symposium, U.S. Air Force Academy, Colorado Springs, CO, 1984, p. 19.

50. For the American air war in Vietnam, see particularly Wayne Thompson, *To Hanoi and Back: The U.S.A.F. and North Vietnam* (Washington, DC, 2000), and Marshall L. Michel III, *Clashes: Air Combat over North Vietnam* (New York, 2007). See also Hastings, *Vietnam*, chap. 4.

51. I am indebted to Major General William Mullen, USMC, ret., for this point.

52. Another way to look at the advancing world driven by computer chip technology is to look at the phones in use in the TV comedy *Seinfeld* in the 1990s and those in use today.

53. Budiansky, *Code Warriors*, pp. 110–112.

54. Ibid., pp. 214–216.

55. Ibid., p. 216.

56. Ibid., p. 213.

57. The Americans probably owed more because they got the cream of the V-2 scientists. The Russians, moreover, had been tinkering with long-range rockets before the Second World War.

58. McDougall, . . . *The Heavens and the Earth*, p. 250.

59. Ibid., p. 154.

60. For the egregious mistakes the Israelis made at the outset of the Yom Kippur War, especially at the tactical and operational levels and then their recovery under the enormous pressures of a war that appeared lost, see Williamson Murray, *Military Adaptation in War: With Fear of Change* (Cambridge, 2011).

61. Rebecca Grant, "The Bekaa Valley War," *Air Force Magazine*, June 2002.

62. Dima Adamsky, *The Culture of Military Innovation: The Impact of Cultural Factors on the Revolution in Military Affairs in Russia, the US, and Israel* (Stanford, CA, 2010), p. 94.

63. Grant, "The Bekaa Valley War"; Adamsky, *Culture of Military Innovation*.

64. The equivalent in ground war would be the destruction of an Iraqi armored brigade by an American cavalry troop at 73 Easting during the 1991 Gulf War.

65. Krepinevich and Watts, *The Last Warrior*, p. 129.

66. At its start, the agency had the title of Advanced Research Projects Agency.
67. JSTARS was a command-and-control aircraft with the ability to stand-off from the air and ground battle, and by using its systems to control the air battle while also monitoring the movement of vehicles on the ground.
68. Krepinevich and Watts, *The Last Warrior,* p. 155.
69. The appearance of these weapons in NATO were the occasion of massed demonstrations in both Britain and on the Continent, demonstrations largely organized by the KGB and their fellow travelers throughout Europe.
70. Krepinevich and Watts, *The Last Warrior,* pp. 169–170.
71. Gates, *From the Shadows,* p. 539.
72. The following argument draws considerably from the excellent discussion in Adamsky, *The Culture of Military Innovation,* chap. 2.
73. The fact that "deep battle" failed to emerge until late in the war on the Eastern Front was a reflection of two factors. First, Stalin's purge of the Red Army's officer corps removed most of the competent and imaginative officers at the highest levels and replaced them with sycophants. It took two terrible years before the war had worked them out of the system. The second factor was the fact that it was not until 1944 that the Red Army possessed the logistical infrastructure in jeeps and American trucks to support deep battle.
74. Adamsky, *The Culture of Military Innovation,* p. 27.
75. Ibid., p. 27.
76. Quoted in Barry Watts and Williamson Murray, "Military Innovation in Peacetime," in *Military Innovation in the Interwar Period,* ed. Williamson Murray and Allan R. Millett (Cambridge, UK, 1996), pp. 376–377.
77. It is well worth remembering that the AK-47 was the finest small arms weapon of the twentieth century.
78. For the Iran-Iraq War, see particularly Williamson Murray and Kevin M. Woods, *The Iran-Iraq War: A Military and Strategic History* (Cambridge, UK, 2014).
79. Williamson Murray with Wayne Thompson, *Air War in the Persian Gulf* (Baltimore, MD, 1996), pp. 67, 102.
80. Government Accounting Office, "Operation Desert Storm, Evaluation of the Air Campaign," pp. 62, 67–70.
81. For an account of the first night attack, see Murray, *Air War in the Persian Gulf,* pp. 101–124.
82. Quoted in Krepinevich and Watts, *The Last Warrior,* p. 205.
83. History did play a significant role in the thinking in the Office of Net Assessment, which sponsored a number of studies of innovation and adaptation in the past, such as Murray and Millett, eds., *Military Innovation in the Interwar Period,* and Murray, *Military Adaptation in War.*
84. Quoted in Williamson Murray, *America and the Future of War: The Past as Prologue* (Stanford, CA, 2017), pp. 30–31.
85. U.S. Air Force, *New World Vistas: Air and Space Power in the 21st Century* (Washington, DC, 1995).

Chapter Fifteen. The Dark Future

Epigraph: Sophocles, *Antigone*, in *Great Books of the Western World*, ed. Robert Maynard Hutchins (Chicago, 1952), p. 139.

1. The late political scientist Colin S. Gray has suggested much about the nature of the coming century in the title of his book: *Another Bloody Century: Future Warfare* (London, 2005).
2. Geoffrey Parker and Leif A. Torkelson, "Epilogue: The Future of Western Warfare," in *The Cambridge History of Warfare*, 2nd edition, ed. Geoffrey Parker (2005; Cambridge, UK, 2020), p. 465.
3. MacGregor Knox, "What History Can Tell Us About the 'New Strategic Environment,'" in *Brassey's Mershon American Defense Annual, 1995–1996*, ed. Williamson Murray (Washington, DC, 1996).
4. Steven Pinker, *The Better Angels of Our Nature: Why Violence Has Declined* (New York, 2011).
5. Quoted in Marcus Jones, "Strategy as Character: Bismarck and the Prusso-German Question, 1862–1878," in *The Shaping of Grand Strategy: Policy, Diplomacy, and War*, ed. Williamson Murray, Richard Hart Sinnreich, and James Lacey (Cambridge, UK, 2011), p. 86.
6. Peter Mansoor and Geoffrey Parker, "The New World Disorder, 1991–2019," in Parker, ed., *The Cambridge History of Warfare*, p. 451.
7. Thucydides, *History of the Peloponnesian War*, trans. Rex Warner (London, 1954), p. 404.

Index

Aboukir Bay, Battle of, 81

Acheson, Dean, 346

adaptation, 2, 8, 10–11, 15, 357, 378; American Civil War, 123; French Revolution, 76–77; interwar period, 192, 195–96, 202–3; military organizations, 19, 142; military-social revolutions, 17; military-technical revolutions, 369; modern state, 43, 138; nuclear weapons, 340; revolutions in military affairs, 18; World War I, 15, 150, 158, 160–61; World War II, 258, 273, 313

Adolphus, Gustavus, 3, 37–40, 43

Afghanistan, 340, 357, 362, 370, 372, 374–75

Africa, 133, 278, 324. *See also* North Africa

Agincourt, Battle of, 21

air power, 343, 349–50, 354–56; interwar period, 16, 188, 196–97, 200–201, 203, 205; World War I, 150, 168; World War II, 229, 288–89, 301, 311, 321, 328, 331, 433n70

Aisne, Battle of the, 178

Akagi, IJN aircraft carrier, 203, 318

Alba, Duke of, 30–31

Albania, 234

Alberich, Operation, 184

Albuquerque, Afonso de, 2

Aleutian Islands, 318

Alexander I of Russia, 91, 96, 100

Alexander, Harold, 300

Algeria, 300

Allenby, Edmund, 169

Allied Powers (WWI), 164–69, 174–75, 177–79, 184–85, 202; counteroffensives, 180–82; Somme, Battle of the, 160, 163

Allies (WWII), 221, 226, 373–74, 279, 302–3, 307, 309, 339; air superiority, 289, 306, 311; anti-submarine aircraft, 264, 268, 275; Combined Bomber Offensive, 283, 287; Cypher No. 3, 276; Enigma 215, 231; intelligence, 262–66, 271; Lend-Lease, 260–61; Normandy invasion, 265, 288, 304–6; operations research, 231, 279, 290; Pacific theater of war, 316, 320, 324, 327, 334; Phony War period, 218–19; projection of power, 249; science and technology, 267–71, 290; shipping, 260, 276–80; strategy of, 216, 218

Almeida, Francisco de, 2

Al Qaeda, 378

American Civil War, 4, 10, 13, 68, 100, 105, 126; armies (*see* Confederate

Axis Powers (WWII), 226, 248, 271, 308, 342; intelligence, 262–63, 299; inter-war period, 190, 202, 230; North Africa, 235, 297, 300–302
Aztec Empire, 26

Bagration, Operation, 309–10
Balkans, 27, 29, 106, 133; World War I, 138, 182; World War II, 233–35, 238, 298, 302, 311
Baltic states, 27, 39, 52–53, 135, 343–44; World War II, 214, 219, 240–41, 265, 309–10
Bannockburn, Battle of, 20
Barbarossa, Operation, 230, 232–33, 236–46, 255, 261, 292, 308–12; Blau, Operation, 293–94; Kharkov, Battle of, 296–97; Kursk, Battle of, 297–98; Stalingrad, Battle of, 294–96
Barras, Paul, 79–80
Bataan, Battle of, 316–17
Bautzen, Battle of, 3, 97
Bavaria, 36–37, 42, 50
Bazaine, François Achille, 130–31
Beatty, David, 152
Belgium, 138, 143–45, 182, 184; World War II, 217, 223, 237, 274, 288
Bell Laboratories, 269
Belorussia, 175, 309–12, 370
Benedek, Ludwig von, 128
Bennett, Donald C. T., 284
Bennington, Battle of, 62
Berlin Wall, 183, 342, 366
Bismarck, German battleship, 270
Bismarck, Otto von, 128–29, 132–33, 135, 138, 376, 404n43; strategy of, 4, 6, 56, 126–27
Bismarck Sea, Battle of the, 326
Blackett, Patrick M. S., 267, 279
Blau, Operation, 255, 293–94, 359–61, 435n23
Blenheim, Battle of, 50
Bletchley Park, 258, 261, 263, 265–66, 277, 378, 428n79

Blücher, Gebhard von, 101, 178–79
Blücher, German battle cruiser, 152, 220
Blum, Léon, 188
Bock, Fedor von, 216, 241, 245–46, 294
Boeing Company, 354
Bohemia, 36, 57, 91, 128, 182
Bolsheviks, 169, 174, 183, 193, 214, 239, 249, 264
Bonaparte, Napoleon. See Napoleon
Boomer, Walt, 339
Boot, Harry, 17, 268–69
Borodino, Battle of 96, 100
Bosquet, Pierre, 106
Boulton, Matthew, 86–87
Bouvet, French battleship, 155
Braddock, Edward, 55
Bradley, Omar, 302, 304–6, 308, 350
Bragg, Braxton, 121–22
Brauchitsch, Walther von, 218, 232–33
Breitenfeld, Battle of, 3, 38–39, 43
Brest Litovsk, Treaty of, 175
Britain, 7, 12–14, 43, 45–47, 127; Admiralty, 151, 201, 231, 263, 266–68, 275; aid to allies, 83, 86, 89, 97–100; aircraft industry, 167–68, 226–27; air defenses of, 16, 198–99, 227–28, 230; air power, 196–98; economy of, 83–85, 88–89, 176, 257–58; financial system of, 46–47, 85; French Revolution, 68, 71, 78; French Revolutionary Wars, 81; German appeasement, 187–88, 211–14, 217; industrial production of, 86–87, 139, 148–50, 166, 254, 257; Industrial Revolution in, 68, 82–90, 98, 100, 133; intelligence operations, 225, 231, 258, 263–66, 276–78, 289; interwar period, 187–88, 192–99, 201–3, 206, 214–15; Lend-Lease aid, 260–61, 274; Marshall Plan, 345; mil-itary-social revolution, 83; mobiliza-tion, 257; Napoleonic Wars, 90–91; Nine Years' War, 48; post-WWII period, 342–45; radar development,